QUAKER FAITH & PRACTICE

QUAKER
FAITH & PRACTICE

The book of
Christian discipline
of the Yearly Meeting of the
Religious Society of Friends
(Quakers) in Britain

Quaker faith and practice: the book of
Christian discipline of the Yearly Meeting
of the Religious Society of Friends
(Quakers) in Britain
was approved by Yearly Meeting 1994.
Second edition, with revisions approved 1995-1998.

The book is printed on Kingsbury Script 70gm^2 manufactured by
Nordland Papier AG, Germany. The paper is made with pulp from
sustainable, responsibly managed forests in Finland.

The typeface is *Sabon*, designed by Jan Tschichold in
1966 and derived from the types used by Garamond in
Paris in the sixteenth century.

ISBN 0 85245 306 X (paperback)
ISBN 0 85245 307 8 (hardback)

Published by The Yearly Meeting of the
Religious Society of Friends (Quakers) in Britain
173 Euston Road, London NW1 2BJ

Printed by Warwick Printing Company Limited,
Theatre Street, Warwick CV34 4DR

Quaker faith and practice

Introduction

This book of faith and practice constitutes the Christian discipline of the Yearly Meeting of the Religious Society of Friends (Quakers) in Britain. Discipline is not now a popular word. It has overtones of enforcement and correction but its roots lie in ideas of learning and discipleship. Discipline in our yearly meeting consists for the most part of advice and counsel, the encouragement of self-questioning, of hearing each other in humility and love.

Words must not become barriers between us, for no one of us can ever adequately understand or express the truth about God. Yet words are our tools and we must not be afraid to express the truth we know in the best words we can. It is this conviction which has prompted the selection of a wide variety of extracts for inclusion in this book, confirming our testimony that truth cannot be confined within a creed. We must trust that faith is robust, compassionate and 'not quick to take offence', and that the Spirit which gives the words is communicated through them.

Our book of discipline was first issued – in manuscript form – in 1738. There had been requests for a compilation to be made of the minutes of advice and counsel which had been sent out from time to time in earlier years to quarterly and monthly meetings. The first printed collection appeared in 1783 with many deletions and additions. Every generation has felt the need for revision; the present is the tenth edition. Pressure for revision has always come from the generality of Friends, but each revision has met with resistance from some who had lived with the old words and had found them entirely satisfying. Nevertheless, it has been the experience of Britain Yearly Meeting that necessary change has, despite occasions of great tension, been effected in love and unity.

From 1861, the book of discipline was divided into separate chapters – later, parts – *Christian doctrine*, *Christian practice*, and *Church government*. In 1921, *Christian doctrine* became *Christian life, faith and thought*, substantially a new work attempting, as was said in the preface, 'to state truth, not by formulating it, but by expressing it through the vital personal and corporate experience of Friends'. Thus began the use of extracts which has subsequently been developed as an acceptable method of expressing the breadth of our theology.

The 1959 revision brought together *Christian life, faith and thought* and *Christian practice* into one volume, *Christian faith and practice*, which, with the 1967 revision of *Church government* (including the 1964 revision of *Advices and queries*) comprised the book of discipline at the time of the present revision.

Again, in 1985, London Yearly Meeting responded to proposals for revision that had arisen 'not from the centre but from local meetings and individual Friends, as well as committees', and asked Meeting for Sufferings to appoint a Revision Committee. The previous thirty years had seen changes in language, in religious thought and social attitudes and in the nature of British society itself. Lives of ordinary people had been affected by advances in communication. Images of famine, war and disaster, wherever they occur in the world, are now brought into our own homes. The immediacy of our knowledge oppresses us with the feeling that the distress and violence of our time are greater than ever before. In Britain, however, it has been the good fortune of this generation to be free from war and conscription and, though poverty, homelessness and unemployment are widespread, many live with expectation of comfort, care and length of life.

There is no yardstick by which the experience of one generation can be judged against that of another, but we do know that whatever the circumstances, we are called to rediscover the Quaker way and to find appropriate words to express it. We are not without consolation. Signals come to us from all over the world that there is in the human spirit a prompting towards a better way that is persistent and will not be put down. This enduring hope confirms the truth asserted in John's gospel that the light shines in darkness.

The arrangement of the text within this book is intended to show the interdependence of our faith and our practice. Therefore matters of church government no longer stand alone, but are integrated with other material in order to encourage deeper understanding of the nature of our organisation as an expression of community, of the right ordering of our affairs and of the religious foundations on which our structures are built. The revised advices and queries – which may prompt the ministry that enriches and deepens our meetings for worship – form the opening chapter of the book. They are an essential part of it but they are also printed separately.

Worship is at the heart of Quaker experience. For God is met in the gathered meeting and through the Spirit leads us into ways of life and understandings of truth which we recognise as Quaker. As we follow these leadings in our community and in the wider world we are enabled to reflect on their meaning, testing our vision within our discipline and tradition. This book follows this sequence. It begins with worship and the gathering and ordering of our worshipping community; then it shows the ways of life, both individual and corporate, which have sprung from our faith, and the testimonies into which we have been guided. The book includes accounts of the lives of individual Friends whose commitment is an example to us. Towards the close of the book come statements and descriptions of our faith that spring from our experience. These in turn lead on to the final chapter which indicates some of the ways in which the Holy Spirit is still known among us and challenges us to create anew a Society in which human lives are changed.

Special attention has been given to the inclusion of a wider range of contributions from women, from earlier days as well as more recent times.

Friends are enjoined in *Advices and queries* to 'avoid hurtful criticism and provocative language', but sensitivity to gender-exclusive language and the hurt it causes has only now become recognised amongst us. Effort has been made to avoid such modes of expression, accepting that quotations from earlier times must remain in the language of their age, but exercising discretion when there has been a choice of extracts. The aim has been to be truthful to the testimony of the past as well as the present. Similarly, we recognise the likelihood that in other areas the language used now may in the future seem insensitive.

Britain Yearly Meeting is becoming increasingly aware that it is part of a world-wide Quaker family. It is privileged to be geographically where George Fox was called to undertake his mission and where Margaret Fell nourished the publishers of truth, but there are now over sixty yearly meetings together with other groupings of Friends in six continents. Friends World Committee for Consultation performs an essential role in supporting this international community and Britain Yearly Meeting is committed to this work.

Many other yearly meetings publish their own books of discipline and we are finding, increasingly, that we are learning from and valuing a shared understanding. Writings by Friends in other countries which reflect our shared experience find a place in our book.

The extension of Quakerism world-wide has added diversity of theological outlook, varieties of worship and forms of organisation. When three hundred Young Friends from thirty-four countries met in North Carolina in 1985, they were 'challenged, shaken up, at times even enraged by these differences in each other'. After much travail, they came through this experience and were able to say, in a final epistle:

> We have wondered whether there is anything Quakers today can say as one. After much struggle we have discovered that we can proclaim this: there is a living God at the centre of all, who is available to each of us as a present teacher at the very heart of our lives. We seek as people of God to be worthy vessels to deliver the Lord's transforming word, to be prophets of joy who know from experience and can testify to the world, as George Fox did, 'that the Lord is at work in this thick night'.

The final chapter to this book, *Leadings*, which looks for signs of how the Spirit is continuing to lead us, contains this epistle in full.

There is also diversity among us in Britain Yearly Meeting. It is reflected in part in the number of informal groups established in recent years. Some welcome this development as an indication of vigorous life, while others view it anxiously as a threat to the corporate commitment of Friends. However, we continue to know the experience of unity. Week by week, in Britain, more than four hundred meetings of Quakers assemble in expectant worship. They know the seventeenth-century experience of Robert Barclay: 'When I came into the silent assemblies of God's people, I felt a secret power among them, which touched my heart...'

Friends find unity in the depth of the silence, when the worshippers are truly gathered and deeply centred on the things of the spirit. We struggle with differences in our meetings for church affairs and here, too, as we consider what action we are called to take over issues that confront us, we know the experience of unity in conviction and purpose. It is a unity which is not to be found in optional attitudes but in discovering the place in which we can stand together.

It is hoped that readers of this book will pick up some responsive echoes from its pages, a resonance which touches their own lives, for, as London Yearly Meeting asserted in 1978:

> We have great riches to share in; riches from the words used by Friends down the last three centuries who have put their experience of God down on paper and have searched out new ways to describe the infinite variety of God... There are great riches too in other branches of the Christian Church and in other faiths, for each one who seeks the truth may see a different part of it.

We are seekers but we are also the holders of a precious heritage of discoveries. We, like every generation, must find the Light and Life again for ourselves. Only what we have valued and truly made our own, not by assertion but by lives of faithful commitment, can we hand on to the future. Even then, we must humbly acknowledge that our vision of the truth will, again and again, be amended.

In the Religious Society of Friends we commit ourselves not to words but to a way.

Chapter 1

Advices and queries

INTRODUCTION

1.01   As Friends we commit ourselves to a way of worship which allows God to teach and transform us. We have found corporately that the Spirit, if rightly followed, will lead us into truth, unity and love: all our testimonies grow from this leading.

Although the corporate use of advices and queries is governed by more flexible regulations (1.05-1.07) than in the past, they should continue to be a challenge and inspiration to Friends in their personal lives and in their life as a religious community which knows the guidance of the universal spirit of Christ, witnessed to in the life and teachings of Jesus of Nazareth.

Advices and queries are not a call to increased activity by each individual Friend but a reminder of the insights of the Society. Within the community there is a diversity of gifts. We are all therefore asked to consider how far the advices and queries affect us personally and where our own service lies. There will also be diversity of experience, of belief and of language. Friends maintain that expressions of faith must be related to personal experience. Some find traditional Christian language full of meaning; some do not. Our understanding of our own religious tradition may sometimes be enhanced by insights of other faiths. The deeper realities of our faith are beyond precise verbal formulation and our way of worship based on silent waiting testifies to this.

Our diversity invites us both to speak what we know to be true in our lives and to learn from others. Friends are encouraged to listen to each other in humility and understanding, trusting in the Spirit that goes beyond our human effort and comprehension. So it is for the comfort and discomfort of Friends that these advices and queries are offered, with the hope that we may all be more faithful and find deeper joy in God's service.

Dearly beloved Friends, these things we do not lay upon you as a rule or form to walk by, but that all, with the measure of light which is pure and holy, may be guided; and so in the light walking and abiding, these may be fulfilled in the Spirit, not from the letter, for the letter killeth, but the Spirit giveth life.

Postscript to an epistle to 'the brethren in the north' issued by a meeting of elders at Balby, 1656

ADVICES AND QUERIES

1.02 1. Take heed, dear Friends, to the promptings of love and truth in your hearts. Trust them as the leadings of God whose Light shows us our darkness and brings us to new life.

2. Bring the whole of your life under the ordering of the spirit of Christ. Are you open to the healing power of God's love? Cherish that of God within you, so that this love may grow in you and guide you. Let your worship and your daily life enrich each other. Treasure your experience of God, however it comes to you. Remember that Christianity is not a notion but a way.

3. Do you try to set aside times of quiet for openness to the Holy Spirit? All of us need to find a way into silence which allows us to deepen our awareness of the divine and to find the inward source of our strength. Seek to know an inward stillness, even amid the activities of daily life. Do you encourage in yourself and in others a habit of dependence on God's guidance for each day? Hold yourself and others in the Light, knowing that all are cherished by God.

4. The Religious Society of Friends is rooted in Christianity and has always found inspiration in the life and teachings of Jesus. How do you interpret your faith in the light of this heritage? How does Jesus speak to you today? Are you following Jesus' example of love in action? Are you learning from his life the reality and cost of obedience to God? How does his relationship with God challenge and inspire you?

1.02   5. Take time to learn about other people's experiences of the Light. Remember the importance of the Bible, the writings of Friends and all writings which reveal the ways of God. As you learn from others, can you in turn give freely from what you have gained? While respecting the experiences and opinions of others, do not be afraid to say what you have found and what you value. Appreciate that doubt and questioning can also lead to spiritual growth and to a greater awareness of the Light that is in us all.

6. Do you work gladly with other religious groups in the pursuit of common goals? While remaining faithful to Quaker insights, try to enter imaginatively into the life and witness of other communities of faith, creating together the bonds of friendship.

7. Be aware of the spirit of God at work in the ordinary activities and experience of your daily life. Spiritual learning continues throughout life, and often in unexpected ways. There is inspiration to be found all around us, in the natural world, in the sciences and arts, in our work and friendships, in our sorrows as well as in our joys. Are you open to new light, from whatever source it may come? Do you approach new ideas with discernment?

———

8. Worship is our response to an awareness of God. We can worship alone, but when we join with others in expectant waiting we may discover a deeper sense of God's presence. We seek a gathered stillness in our meetings for worship so that all may feel the power of God's love drawing us together and leading us.

9. In worship we enter with reverence into communion with God and respond to the promptings of the Holy Spirit. Come to meeting for worship with heart and mind prepared. Yield yourself and all your outward concerns to God's guidance so that you may find 'the evil weakening in you and the good raised up'.

10. Come regularly to meeting for worship even when you are angry, depressed, tired or spiritually cold. In the silence ask for and accept the prayerful support of others joined with you in worship. Try to find a spiritual wholeness which encompasses suffering as well as thankfulness and joy. Prayer, springing from a deep place in the

1.02   heart, may bring healing and unity as nothing else can. Let meeting for worship nourish your whole life.

11. Be honest with yourself. What unpalatable truths might you be evading? When you recognise your shortcomings, do not let that discourage you. In worship together we can find the assurance of God's love and the strength to go on with renewed courage.

12. When you are preoccupied and distracted in meeting let wayward and disturbing thoughts give way quietly to your awareness of God's presence among us and in the world. Receive the vocal ministry of others in a tender and creative spirit. Reach for the meaning deep within it, recognising that even if it is not God's word for you, it may be so for others. Remember that we all share responsibility for the meeting for worship whether our ministry is in silence or through the spoken word.

13. Do not assume that vocal ministry is never to be your part. Faithfulness and sincerity in speaking, even very briefly, may open the way to fuller ministry from others. When prompted to speak, wait patiently to know that the leading and the time are right, but do not let a sense of your own unworthiness hold you back. Pray that your ministry may arise from deep experience, and trust that words will be given to you. Try to speak audibly and distinctly, and with sensitivity to the needs of others. Beware of speaking predictably or too often, and of making additions towards the end of a meeting when it was well left before.

14. Are your meetings for church affairs held in a spirit of worship and in dependence on the guidance of God? Remember that we do not seek a majority decision nor even consensus. As we wait patiently for divine guidance our experience is that the right way will open and we shall be led into unity.

15. Do you take part as often as you can in meetings for church affairs? Are you familiar enough with our church government to contribute to its disciplined processes? Do you consider difficult questions with an informed mind as well as a generous and loving spirit? Are you prepared to let your insights and personal wishes take their place alongside those of others or be set aside as the meeting seeks the right way forward? If you cannot attend, uphold the meeting prayerfully.

1.02   16. Do you welcome the diversity of culture, language and expressions of faith in our yearly meeting and in the world community of Friends? Seek to increase your understanding and to gain from this rich heritage and wide range of spiritual insights. Uphold your own and other yearly meetings in your prayers.

———

17. Do you respect that of God in everyone though it may be expressed in unfamiliar ways or be difficult to discern? Each of us has a particular experience of God and each must find the way to be true to it. When words are strange or disturbing to you, try to sense where they come from and what has nourished the lives of others. Listen patiently and seek the truth which other people's opinions may contain for you. Avoid hurtful criticism and provocative language. Do not allow the strength of your convictions to betray you into making statements or allegations that are unfair or untrue. Think it possible that you may be mistaken.

18. How can we make the meeting a community in which each person is accepted and nurtured, and strangers are welcome? Seek to know one another in the things which are eternal, bear the burden of each other's failings and pray for one another. As we enter with tender sympathy into the joys and sorrows of each other's lives, ready to give help and to receive it, our meeting can be a channel for God's love and forgiveness.

19. Rejoice in the presence of children and young people in your meeting and recognise the gifts they bring. Remember that the meeting as a whole shares a responsibility for every child in its care. Seek for them as for yourself a full development of God's gifts and the abundant life Jesus tells us can be ours. How do you share your deepest beliefs with them, while leaving them free to develop as the spirit of God may lead them? Do you invite them to share their insights with you? Are you ready both to learn from them and to accept your responsibilities towards them?

20. Do you give sufficient time to sharing with others in the meeting, both newcomers and long-time members, your understanding of worship, of service, and of commitment to the Society's witness? Do you give a right proportion of your money to support Quaker work?

1.02   21. Do you cherish your friendships, so that they grow in depth and understanding and mutual respect? In close relationships we may risk pain as well as finding joy. When experiencing great happiness or great hurt we may be more open to the working of the Spirit.

22. Respect the wide diversity among us in our lives and relationships. Refrain from making prejudiced judgments about the life journeys of others. Do you foster the spirit of mutual understanding and forgiveness which our discipleship asks of us? Remember that each one of us is unique, precious, a child of God.

23. Marriage has always been regarded by Friends as a religious commitment rather than a merely civil contract. Both partners should offer with God's help an intention to cherish one another for life. Remember that happiness depends on an understanding and steadfast love on both sides. In times of difficulty remind yourself of the value of prayer, of perseverance and of a sense of humour.

24. Children and young people need love and stability. Are we doing all we can to uphold and sustain parents and others who carry the responsibility for providing this care?

25. A long-term relationship brings tensions as well as fulfilment. If your relationship with your partner is under strain, seek help in understanding the other's point of view and in exploring your own feelings, which may be powerful and destructive. Consider the wishes and feelings of any children involved, and remember their enduring need for love and security. Seek God's guidance. If you undergo the distress of separation or divorce, try to maintain some compassionate communication so that arrangements can be made with the minimum of bitterness.

26. Do you recognise the needs and gifts of each member of your family and household, not forgetting your own? Try to make your home a place of loving friendship and enjoyment, where all who live or visit may find the peace and refreshment of God's presence.

27. Live adventurously. When choices arise, do you take the way that offers the fullest opportunity for the use of your gifts in the service of God and the community? Let your life speak. When decisions have to be made, are you ready to join with others in seeking clearness, asking for God's guidance and offering counsel to one another?

1.02   28. Every stage of our lives offers fresh opportunities. Responding to divine guidance, try to discern the right time to undertake or relinquish responsibilities without undue pride or guilt. Attend to what love requires of you, which may not be great busyness.

29. Approach old age with courage and hope. As far as possible, make arrangements for your care in good time, so that an undue burden does not fall on others. Although old age may bring increasing disability and loneliness, it can also bring serenity, detachment and wisdom. Pray that in your final years you may be enabled to find new ways of receiving and reflecting God's love.

30. Are you able to contemplate your death and the death of those closest to you? Accepting the fact of death, we are freed to live more fully. In bereavement, give yourself time to grieve. When others mourn, let your love embrace them.

———

31. We are called to live 'in the virtue of that life and power that takes away the occasion of all wars'. Do you faithfully maintain our testimony that war and the preparation for war are inconsistent with the spirit of Christ? Search out whatever in your own way of life may contain the seeds of war. Stand firm in our testimony, even when others commit or prepare to commit acts of violence, yet always remember that they too are children of God.

32. Bring into God's light those emotions, attitudes and prejudices in yourself which lie at the root of destructive conflict, acknowledging your need for forgiveness and grace. In what ways are you involved in the work of reconciliation between individuals, groups and nations?

33. Are you alert to practices here and throughout the world which discriminate against people on the basis of who or what they are or because of their beliefs? Bear witness to the humanity of all people, including those who break society's conventions or its laws. Try to discern new growing points in social and economic life. Seek to understand the causes of injustice, social unrest and fear. Are you working to bring about a just and compassionate society which allows everyone to develop their capacities and fosters the desire to serve?

1.02   34. Remember your responsibilities as a citizen for the conduct of local, national, and international affairs. Do not shrink from the time and effort your involvement may demand.

35. Respect the laws of the state but let your first loyalty be to God's purposes. If you feel impelled by strong conviction to break the law, search your conscience deeply. Ask your meeting for the prayerful support which will give you strength as a right way becomes clear.

36. Do you uphold those who are acting under concern, even if their way is not yours? Can you lay aside your own wishes and prejudices while seeking with others to find God's will for them?

37. Are you honest and truthful in all you say and do? Do you maintain strict integrity in business transactions and in your dealings with individuals and organisations? Do you use money and information entrusted to you with discretion and responsibility? Taking oaths implies a double standard of truth; in choosing to affirm instead, be aware of the claim to integrity that you are making.

38. If pressure is brought upon you to lower your standard of integrity, are you prepared to resist it? Our responsibilities to God and our neighbour may involve us in taking unpopular stands. Do not let the desire to be sociable, or the fear of seeming peculiar, determine your decisions.

39. Consider which of the ways to happiness offered by society are truly fulfilling and which are potentially corrupting and destructive. Be discriminating when choosing means of entertainment and information. Resist the desire to acquire possessions or income through unethical investment, speculation or games of chance.

40. In view of the harm done by the use of alcohol, tobacco and other habit-forming drugs, consider whether you should limit your use of them or refrain from using them altogether. Remember that any use of alcohol or drugs may impair judgment and put both the user and others in danger.

41. Try to live simply. A simple lifestyle freely chosen is a source of strength. Do not be persuaded into buying what you do not need or cannot afford. Do you keep yourself informed about the effects your style of living is having on the global economy and environment?

1.02 42. We do not own the world, and its riches are not ours to dispose of at will. Show a loving consideration for all creatures, and seek to maintain the beauty and variety of the world. Work to ensure that our increasing power over nature is used responsibly, with reverence for life. Rejoice in the splendour of God's continuing creation.

Be patterns, be examples in all countries, places, islands, nations, wherever you come, that your carriage and life may preach among all sorts of people, and to them; then you will come to walk cheerfully over the world, answering that of God in every one.

George Fox, 1656

CYNGHORION A HOLIADAU

1.03 1. Ystyriwch, Gyfeillion annwyl, gymhellion cariad a gwirionedd yn eich calonnau. Ymddiriedwch ynddynt fel arweiniad Duw, Goleuni yr hwn sy'n dangos i ni ein tywyllwch gan ein dwyn i fywyd newydd.

2. Dygwch eich holl fywyd dan reolaeth Ysbryd Crist. A ydych yn agored i allu iachusol cariad Duw? Coleddwch yr hyn sydd o Dduw ynoch, fel y bo i'r cariad hwn dyfu ynoch a'ch arwain. Boed i'ch addoliad a'ch bywyd beunyddiol gyfoethogi ei gilydd. Trysorwch eich profiad o Dduw, pa fodd bynnag y daw i'ch rhan. Cofiwch nad damcaniaeth yw Cristnogaeth, eithr ffordd.

3. A ydych yn ceisio neilltuo adegau o dawelwch i fod yn agored i'r Ysbryd Glân? Y mae ar bob un ohonom angen canfod ffordd i mewn i ddistawrwydd sy'n ein galluogi i ddyfnhau'n hymwybyddiaeth o'r dwyfol ac i ganfod tarddle mewnol ein nerth. Ceisiwch lonyddwch mewnol, hyd yn oed ynghanol gweithgareddau bywyd beunyddiol. A ydych yn meithrin ynoch eich hun ac mewn eraill yr arfer o ddibynnu ar arweiniad dyddiol Duw? Daliwch eich hunain ac eraill yn y Goleuni, gan wybod fod Duw yn coleddu pawb oll.

1.03   4. Gwreiddiwyd Cymdeithas Grefyddol y Cyfeillion mewn Cristnogaeth a chafodd ysbrydoliaeth yn wastad o fywyd a dysgeidiaeth Iesu. Pa fodd y dehonglwch eich ffydd yng ngoleuni'r dreftadaeth hon? Pa fodd y llefara Iesu wrthych heddiw? A ydych yn dilyn esiampl Iesu o gariad ar waith? A ydych yn dysgu o'i fywyd realiti a chost ufudd-dod i Dduw? Pa fodd y mae ei berthynas â Duw yn eich herio a'ch ysbrydoli?

5. Cymerwch amser i ddysgu am brofiadau pobl eraill o'r Goleuni. Cofiwch bwysigrwydd y Beibl, ysgrifeniadau Cyfeillion a phob llyfr sy'n datguddio ffyrdd Duw. A chwithau'n cael eich dysgu gan eraill, a fedrwch yn eich tro gyfrannu'n rhydd o'r hyn a dderbyniasoch? Tra'n parchu profiadau ac opiniynau pobl eraill, nac ofnwch fynegi yr hyn a gawsoch a'r hyn yr ydych yn ei gyfrif yn werthfawr. Cofiwch y gall amheuaeth a chwestiynu arwain hefyd at dwf ysbrydol ac at ymwybyddiaeth ehangach o'r Goleuni sydd ynom oll.

6. A ydych yn cydweithio'n llawen gyda grwpiau crefyddol eraill tuag at amcanion cyffredin? Gan fod yn ffyddlon i'r weledigaeth Grynwrol, ceisiwch gyda dychymyg ran ym mywyd a thystiolaeth aelwydydd eraill o ffydd, gan greu ynghyd rwymau cyfeillgarwch.

7. Ymglywch ag ysbryd Duw ar waith yng ngweithgareddau cyffredin a phrofiad eich byw beunyddiol. Pery addysg ysbrydol gydol bywyd, yn aml mewn ffyrdd annisgwyl. Ceir ysbrydoliaeth o'n hamgylch ym mhobman, ym myd natur, yn y gwyddorau a'r celfyddydau, yn ein gwaith a'n cyfeillgarwch, yn ein gofidiau fel yn ein llawenydd. A ydych yn agored i oleuni newydd, o ba ffynhonnell bynnag y dêl? A ydych yn ddetholgar wrth ystyried syniadau newydd?

---

8. Addoliad yw ein hymateb i ymglywed â Duw. Gallwn addoli ar ein pennau'n hunain, ond pan ymunwn ag eraill mewn aros disgwylgar, gallwn ddarganfod ymwybyddiaeth ddyfnach o bresenoldeb Duw. Yn ein cyrddau addoli ceisiwn ymgynnull mewn llonyddwch fel y cawn oll deimlo nerth cariad Duw yn ein tynnu ynghyd ac yn ein tywys.

1.03
9. Yn yr addoliad, fe awn gyda pharch i gymundeb â Duw, gan ymateb i anogaethau'r Ysbryd Glân. Deuwch i'r cyfarfod addoli wedi ymbaratoi yn eich calon a'ch meddwl. Ildiwch eich hunain a'ch holl ofalon allanol i arweiniad Duw, fel y caffoch 'y drwg yn gwanhau ynoch a'r da yn ymddyrchafu'.

10. Deuwch yn gyson i'r cwrdd addoli, hyd yn oed pan fyddoch ddig, neu'n isel-ysbryd, neu'n flinedig, neu'n oer yn ysbrydol. Yn y distawrwydd, ceisiwch a derbyniwch gefnogaeth weddigar eich cyd-addolwyr. Ceisiwch ganfod cyfanrwydd ysbrydol sy'n cwmpasu dioddefaint yn ogystal â diolchgarwch a llawenydd. Yn anad unpeth arall fe all gweddi sy'n tarddu o ddwfn y galon ddwyn gwellhad ac undod. Gadewch i'r cwrdd addoli faethu eich holl fywyd.

11. Byddwch onest â chwi'ch hunan. Pa wirioneddau diflas y dichon eich bod yn eu hosgoi? O adnabod eich ffaeleddau, na foed i hynny eich digalonni. Mewn cydaddoli, gallwn ganfod y sicrwydd o gariad Duw a chanfod o'r newydd y dewrder i ddal ati.

12. Pan fyddoch synfyfyriol neu ddryslyd yn y cwrdd addoli, gadewch i feddyliau cyndyn neu anesmwyth ymollwng yn dawel i'r ymwybod o bresenoldeb Duw yn ein mysg ac yn y byd. Derbyniwch weinidogaeth lafar eraill mewn ysbryd addfwyn a chreadigol. Estynnwch am yr ystyr sy'n ddwfn ymhlyg ynddo. Hyd yn oed os nad yw'n air Duw i chwi, gall fod felly i eraill. Cofier ein bod oll yn rhannu cyfrifoldeb am y cwrdd addoli, pa un bynnag ai mewn distawrwydd neu ynteu trwy'r gair llafar y bo'n gweinidogaeth.

13. Na thybiwch na fydd eich rhan chwi byth yn weinidogaeth lafar. Fe ddichon cywirdeb a didwylledd wrth siarad, hyd yn oed yn fyr, agor y ffordd i weinidogaeth lawnach gan eraill. Pan ysgogir chwi i lefaru, arhoswch yn amyneddgar i wybod fod yr arweiniad a'r adeg yn briodol, ond na foed ymdeimlo â'ch annheilyngdod eich hun yn rhwystr. Gweddïwch am i'ch gweinidogaeth godi o ddyfnder profiad, ac ymddiriedwch y rhoir geiriau i chwi. Ceisiwch siarad yn glywadwy a chroyw, gan feddwl am anghenion pobl eraill. Gochelwch rhag siarad yn ystrydebol neu'n rhy aml. Gochelwch rhag ymhelaethu tua diwedd cwrdd pan fyddid eisoes wedi'i iawn derfynu.

1.03   14. A gynhelir eich cyrddau ynglŷn â materion eglwysig mewn ysbryd addolgar gan ddibynnu ar gyfarwyddyd Duw? Cofiwch nad ydym yn ceisio penderfyniad trwy fwyafrif na hyd yn oed trwy gonsensws. Tra'n aros yn amyneddgar am arweiniad dwyfol, ein profiad yw y bydd y llwybr iawn yn ymagor ac y cawn ein tywys i undod.

15. A ydych yn cymryd rhan mor fynych ag y galloch mewn cyrddau ynglŷn â materion eglwysig? A ydych yn ddigon cyfarwydd â'n llywodraeth eglwysig i gyfrannu i'w phrosesau disgybledig? A ydych yn ystyried cwestiynau anodd gyda meddwl gwybodus yn ogystal ag mewn ysbryd haelfrydig a chariadus? A ydych yn fodlon i'ch dirnadaeth a'ch dymuniadau personol gymryd eu lle ochr yn ochr â'r eiddo eraill, neu gael eu gosod o'r neilltu, wrth i'r cwrdd chwilio am y llwybr cywir ymlaen? Oni ellwch fod yn bresennol, cynhaliwch y cwrdd yn weddigar.

16. A ydych yn croesawu'r amrywiaeth mewn diwylliant ac iaith a mynegiant ffydd sydd o fewn ein cyfarfod blynyddol ac yn y gymuned fyd-eang o Gyfeillion? Ceisiwch gynyddu eich amgyffred gan elwa o'r dreftadaeth gyfoethog hon a'r ystod eang o ddirnadaeth ysbrydol. Cynhaliwch yn eich gweddïau eich cyfarfod blynyddol a hefyd gyfarfodydd blynyddol eraill.

---

17. A ydych yn parchu'r hyn sydd o Dduw ym mhawb, er y gall fod wedi ei fynegi mewn ffyrdd anghyfarwydd neu ynteu'n anodd ei ddirnad? Y mae i bob un ohonom brofiad neillduol o Dduw a rhaid i bob un ohonom ganfod sut i fod yn ffyddlon i'r profiad hwnnw. Pan fo geiriau'n ddieithr i chwi neu'n tarfu arnoch, ceisiwch synhwyro o ba le y daethant, gan ystyried yr hyn a fu'n maethu bywydau pobl eraill. Gwrandewch yn amyneddgar, a cheisiwch y gwirionedd fo i chwi yn naliadau pobl eraill. Gochelwch rhag beirniadaeth sy'n clwyfo ac iaith sy'n cythruddo. Peidiwch â gadael i gryfder eich argyhoeddiadau beri ichwi wneud gosodiadau neu honiadau annheg neu anwir. Ystyriwch y gellwch fod yn camsynied.

18. Pa fodd y gallwn wneud y cwrdd yn gymuned lle caiff pob person ei dderbyn a'i faethu, a lle caiff dieithriaid groeso? Ceisiwch

1.03   adnabod eich gilydd yn y pethau tragwyddol; dygwch faich methiannau'ch gilydd a gweddïwch bawb dros eich gilydd. Wrth i ni gyfranogi mewn tynerwch o lawenydd a thrallod bywyd beunyddiol ein gilydd, yn barod i roddi help ac i'w dderbyn, gall ein cwrdd fod yn gyfrwng i gariad a maddeuant Duw.

19. Llawenhewch ym mhresenoldeb plant a phobl ifanc yn eich cwrdd, gan gydnabod y doniau sydd ganddynt. Cofiwch fod y cwrdd oll yn rhannu cyfrifoldeb am bob plentyn yn ei ofal. Ceisiwch iddynt hwy, fel i chwi'ch hunain, ddatblygiad llawn o ddoniau Duw a'r bywyd helaeth y dywedodd Iesu y gallem ei feddiannu. Pa fodd yr ydych yn cydrannu'ch daliadau dyfnaf â hwy, gan adael rhyddid iddynt ddatblygu yn y modd yr arweinio ysbryd Duw hwynt? A ydych yn eu gwahodd i rannu gyda chwi eu dirnadaeth? A ydych yn barod i ddysgu ganddynt ac, ar yr un pryd, i dderbyn eich cyfrifoldebau tuag atynt?

20. A roddwch ddigon o amser i rannu gydag eraill, yn newydd-ddyfodiaid ac yn rhai a fu'n aelodau ers tro, eich dealltwriaeth o addoli ac o wasanaeth ac o ymrwymiad i dystiolaeth y Gymdeithas? A roddwch gyfran briodol o'ch arian i gynnal gwaith Crynwrol?

21. A ydych yn anwylo pob cyfeillgarwch, fel y byddont yn dyfnhau ac yn cynyddu mewn dealltwriaeth a pharch o'r ddeutu? Ym mhob perthynas glòs efallai y bydd raid mentro poen yn ogystal â chanfod llawenydd. Wrth brofi hapusrwydd mawr neu loes fawr, efallai ein bod yn fwy agored i waith yr Ysbryd.

22. Perchwch yr amrywiaeth eang sydd yn ein mysg yn ein bywydau a'n cysylltiadau. Gochelwch rhag ffurfio barn ragfarnllyd am deithiau bywyd pobl eraill. A ydych yn meithrin yr ysbryd o gyd-ddyheu ac o faddeuant a fynnir gennym, a ninnau'n ddisgyblion? Cofiwch fod pob un ohonom yn unigryw, yn werthfawr, yn blentyn i Dduw.

23. Ystyriodd Cyfeillion erioed fod priodas yn ymrwymiad crefyddol yn hytrach na chytundeb sifil yn unig. Dylai'r ddeuddyn gynnig gyda chymorth Duw fwriad i goledd y naill a'r llall gydol eu hoes. Cofiwch fod hapusrwydd yn dibynnu ar ddealltwriaeth a serch diysgog o'r ddeutu. Pan ddaw amseroedd anodd, cofiwch werth gweddi a dyfalbarhad a synnwyr digrifwch.

1.03   24. Y mae ar blant a phobl ifanc angen cariad a sefydlogrwydd. A ydym yn gwneud a allom i gynnal rhieni ac eraill sy'n dwyn y cyfrifoldeb o ddarparu'r gofal hwn?

25. Y mae perthynas tymor-hir yn dwyn tyndra yn ogystal â boddhad. Os yw eich perthynas â'ch partner dan straen, ceisiwch gymorth i ddeall safbwynt y llall ac i archwilio'ch teimladau eich hunan, teimladau a all fod yn bŵerus a dinistriol. Ystyriwch ddymuniadau a theimladau unrhyw blant sydd ynghlwm wrthych, gan gofio eu hangen parhaol am gariad a sicrwydd. Ceisiwch arweiniad Duw. Os wynebwch y trallod o ymwahanu neu o ysgaru, ceisiwch gadw rhyw gyswllt tosturiol fel y galloch wneud trefniadau heb fwy o chwerwder nag sydd raid.

26. A ydych yn adnabod anghenion a doniau pob aelod o'ch tŷ a'ch tylwyth, heb anghofio'r eiddoch chwi'ch hunan? Ceisiwch wneud eich cartref yn drigfa cyfeillgarwch cariadus a mwynhad, lle y gall pawb sy'n byw neu'n ymweld ddod o hyd i dangnefedd ac adfywiad presenoldeb Duw.

27. Byddwch byw yn anturus. Pan fo modd dewis, a ddewiswch y llwybr a rydd ichwi fwyaf o gyfle i ddefnyddio'ch doniau yng ngwasanaeth Duw a'r gymuned? Boed i'ch bywyd lefaru. Pan fo'n rhaid penderfynu, a ydych yn barod i ymuno ag eraill wrth chwilio am lwybr eglur, gan ofyn am arweiniad Duw a chan gynnig cyngor y naill i'r llall?

28. Ym mhob gris yn ein bywyd y mae cyfleusterau newydd o hyd. Gan ymateb i arweiniad dwyfol, ceisiwch ymglywed â'r adeg briodol i ysgwyddo neu i drosglwyddo cyfrifoldebau heb falchder nac euogrwydd amhriodol. Gofalwch am yr hyn a ofyn cariad oddi arnoch; efallai nad prysurdeb mawr mo hynny.

29. Wynebwch henaint yn ddewr a gobeithiol. Hyd y gellir, gwnewch mewn da bryd drefniadau am eich gofal, fel na bo baich afresymol yn disgyn ar bobl eraill. Er y dichon henaint ddwyn anabledd ac unigrwydd cynyddol, gall hefyd ddod â llonyddwch ac arwahanrwydd a doethineb. Gweddïwch am gael eich galluogi yn eich blynyddoedd olaf i ganfod ffyrdd newydd o dderbyn ac adlewyrchu cariad Duw.

1.03   30. A ydych yn abl i ystyried eich marwolaeth a marwolaeth eich anwyliaid? O dderbyn marwolaeth fel ffaith, fe'n rhyddheir i fyw yn llawnach. Mewn profedigaeth, caniatewch i chwi'ch hunan amser i alaru. Pan fo eraill yn galaru, gadewch i'ch cariad eu cofleidio.

———

31. Gelwir arnom i fyw 'yn rhinwedd y bywyd a'r gallu sy'n symud achos rhyfeloedd'. A ydych yn cynnal yn ffyddlon ein tystiolaeth fod rhyfel, a pharatoi am ryfel, yn anghyson ag ysbryd Crist? Chwiliwch yn eich ffordd o fyw am unrhyw arwydd o hadau rhyfel. Sefwch yn gadarn yn ein tystiolaeth, hyd yn oed pan fo eraill yn cyflawni neu'n paratoi i gyflawni gweithredoedd o drais; ond cofiwch eu bod hwythau hefyd yn blant i Dduw.

32. Dygwch i oleuni Duw yr emosiynau, yr agweddau, y rhagfarnau hynny ynoch eich hunan sydd wrth wraidd gwrthdaro dinistriol, gan gydnabod fod arnoch angen maddeuant a gras. Ym mha ffyrdd yr ydych yn llafurio i gymodi rhwng unigolion a grwpiau a chenhedloedd?

33. A ydych yn effro i arferion, yma a thrwy'r byd, sy'n gwahaniaethu yn erbyn pobl ar sail pwy neu beth ydynt neu oherwydd yr hyn a gredant? Dygwch dystiolaeth i ddynoliaeth pob un, gan gynnwys y rhai sy'n tramgwyddo confensiynau neu ddeddfau cymdeithas. Ceisiwch ddirnad y mannau lle ceir tyfiant newydd mewn bywyd cymdeithasol ac economaidd. Ceisiwch ddeall yr achosion am anghyfiawnder ac aflonyddwch cymdeithasol ac ofn. A ydych yn gweithio i greu cymdeithas gyfiawn a thosturiol a rydd gyfle i bawb ddatblygu eu galluoedd ac a feithrin eu hawydd i wasanaethu?

34. Cofiwch eich cyfrifoldeb fel dinesydd am reolaeth materion lleol, cenedlaethol a rhyng-genedlaethol. Peidiwch ag arbed yr amser a'r ymdrech y gall eich ymrwymiad ei hawlio.

35. Perchwch ddeddfau'r wladwriaeth ond boed eich teyrngarwch pennaf i fwriadau Duw. Os cymhellir chwi gan argyhoeddiad cryf i dorri'r ddeddf, chwiliwch eich cydwybod i'w ddyfnderau. Gofynnwch i'ch cwrdd am y gefnogaeth weddigar a'ch nertha wrth i'r llwybr cywir agor o'ch blaen.

1.03   36. A ydych yn cynnal y rhai hynny sydd yn gweithredu dan gonsyrn, hyd yn oed os nad yw eu ffordd yr un â'r eiddoch chwi? Tra'n chwilio gydag eraill am ewyllys Duw ar eu cyfer, a ellwch osod o'r neilltu eich dymuniadau a'ch rhagfarnau eich hunan?

37. A ydych yn onest a didwyll ym mhob peth a ddywedwch ac a wnewch? A ydych yn gwbl onest mewn trafodion masnachol ac yn eich ymwneud ag unigolion a sefydliadau? A ydych yn trin arian a gwybodaeth a ymddiriedir i chwi mewn modd doeth a chyfrifol? Y mae tyngu llwon yn awgrymu safon ddeublyg o wirionedd: wrth ddewis yn hytrach gadarnhau, cofiwch eich bod yn haeru onestrwydd.

38. Os pwysir arnoch i ostwng eich safon o gywirdeb, a ydych yn barod i wrthsefyll hynny? Gall ein cyfrifoldebau i Dduw ac i'n cymydog olygu gwneud safiad amhoblogaidd. Na foed i'r awydd am fod yn gymdeithasol, neu ofn ymddangos yn od, gyflyru eich penderfyniad.

39. Ystyriwch pa ffyrdd i hapusrwydd a gynigir gan gymdeithas sy'n rhoi gwir fodlonrwydd a pha rai sy'n dwyn hadau llygredd a dinistr. Byddwch yn ofalus wrth ddewis cyfryngau difyrrwch a gwybodaeth. Gwrthwynebwch yr awydd i ennill meddiannau neu incwm trwy fuddsoddi'n anfoesol, neu trwy fentro arian yn anfoesol, neu trwy hap-chwarae.

40. Yn wyneb y niwed a achosir trwy'r defnydd o alcohol a thybaco a chyffuriau eraill sy'n creu dibyniant, ystyriwch a ddylech gyfyngu eich defnydd ohonynt neu ymwrthod yn gyfan-gwbl â hwynt. Cofiwch y gall unrhyw ddefnydd o alcohol neu gyffuriau amharu ar eich gallu i farnu, gan roi'r defnyddiwr ac eraill mewn perygl.

41. Ceisiwch fyw yn syml. Y mae dewis dull syml o fyw yn ffynhonnell cryfder. Peidiwch â chael eich perswadio i brynu dim nad oes arnoch mo'i angen neu na ellwch ei fforddio. A ydych yn gofalu cael gwybod am effeithiau eich dull chwi o fyw ar yr economi a'r amgylchedd byd-eang?

42. Nid ni piau'r byd, ac nid eiddom ni mo'i oludoedd i'w gwaredu fel y mynnom. Dangoswch ofal cariadus am bob creadur, a cheisiwch warchod prydferthwch ac amrywiaeth y byd.

Ymdrechwch i sicrhau fod ein goruchafiaeth gynyddol ar natur yn cael ei defnyddio'n gyfrifol, gyda pharch at fywyd. Llawenhewch yn ysblander creadigaeth barhaol Duw.

Byddwch yn batrymau, yn esiamplau yn y gwledydd, lleoedd, ynysoedd a'r cenhedloedd oll, i ba le bynnag y deloch; fel y byddo eich ymarweddiad a'ch bywyd yn bregeth ymhlith pobl o bob math, ac yn llefaru wrthynt. Felly y derfydd i chwi deithio drwy'r byd yn siriol, gan ymateb i'r hyn sydd o Dduw ym mhob dyn.

George Fox, 1656

HISTORY

1.04 When Yearly Meeting in 1682 decided to ask the representatives from each quarterly meeting to reply to three questions orally, Yearly Meeting itself had only been meeting consecutively for the previous few years and the systematic organisation of quarterly and monthly meetings had been recently completed. These questions were intended to produce factual information from Friends with local knowledge, so that the progress of the Society throughout the country could be seen and help given in the areas where it was most needed.

What Friends in the ministry, in their respective counties, departed this life since the last yearly meeting?

What Friends imprisoned for their testimony have died in prison since the last yearly meeting?

How the Truth has prospered amongst them since the last yearly meeting, and how Friends are in peace and unity?

These three questions were expanded into six in 1694 and further amended in the early 1700s but their purpose was still mainly to elicit factual information. The practice of requiring oral replies to the questions soon became too cumbersome and was replaced, following Yearly Meeting decisions in 1700 and 1706, by written replies from the quarterly meetings. The system of replying to the questions took root in the Society and the term 'query' was increasingly used, in Yearly Meeting minutes from 1723 onwards, instead of 'question'.

As the practice of replying to the queries became more formal their purpose also began to change. In the early eighteenth century Friends generally ceased to believe that the whole nation would accept the truth that they had been preaching and became more concerned in preserving the Society as 'a precious remnant' devoted to the truth. The queries were increasingly used to ensure consistency of conduct among Friends and to obtain information as to the state of the Society. In 1721, for example, a query was added as to the receipt and payment of tithes, and in 1723 as to defrauding the king of his customs and excise, and many other subjects were included in additional queries.

The Society declined in numbers in the eighteenth century. Yearly Meeting in 1760, troubled that standards in the Society were falling, set up a committee 'for the promotion and revival of wholesome discipline', which visited meetings all over the country. One of its principal instruments was to insist on a more systematic reading and answering of the queries by monthly and quarterly meetings. The purpose of the queries after 1760 became principally disciplinary, and monthly and quarterly meetings and their elders and overseers regarded the queries as a touchstone on which they could rely in administering the discipline.

There were periodic revisions of the queries during the next hundred years, although the number of substantial changes was few. When the queries were revised in 1791 Yearly Meeting adopted the first 'general advices' for consideration by monthly and quarterly meetings. They were short, and mainly concerned with the domestic life of the Society and its members. They were regarded as being of subsidiary importance to the queries, and were treated as an additional aid to the discipline. During the early nineteenth century Friends were much influenced by the evangelical movement and this was illustrated in the revision of the general advices in 1833. They were completely re-written and much expanded. They became of much greater importance than before, and their purpose was no longer mainly disciplinary but instead they were used to emphasise the importance of evangelical principles and to encourage Friends to consider whether they should not adopt them personally.

As Friends in the early nineteenth century entered more into the public and social life of the times, many of them began to question traditional practices of the Society including the very large amount of time spent at business meetings in reading and drawing up answers to the queries, which were often formal in nature. The value of the queries for self-examination had been commended by Yearly Meeting from 1787 onwards; increasingly Friends came to regard this aspect as more important than their disciplinary use and this change in emphasis resulted in the revision of the queries in 1860 and 1875. The requirement of preparing written answers was virtually abolished, and while the regulations continued to provide for a corporate consideration of the queries by monthly and preparative meetings, this in turn became in many places a formality. The general advices were revised over the same period. They were lengthened and extended in scope, and provision was made for them to be read at the close of meeting for worship.

No major revision of the general advices and queries took place until 1928. By this time many Friends considered that they were too negative in approach, had become uneasy at the evangelical language then in use, and wished for greater emphasis on the social responsibilities of Quakerism. These views were reflected in the revised general advices and queries; the general advices were again increased in length, and divided for convenience into three parts, while the queries, covering much of the same ground as the general advices, were also increased in number. The requirement of corporate deliberation on the queries by Friends' business meetings remained but this became of much less significance. The use of the queries became increasingly devotional – 'a collection of exhortations on the right management of one's own affairs both inward and outward, and a collection of questions, or groups of questions, in pondering which a whole meeting can achieve a corporate examination of conscience'. The practice was established in many meetings of reading the queries in meetings for worship in addition to the general advices, which under the regulations adopted in 1931 were required to be read there.

In 1928 the advices on ministry were for the first time brought before members of the yearly meeting as a whole. Twenty years later, in response to a plea that they should be rewritten in modern language and should encourage those who had not yet taken part in vocal ministry, additional advice on ministry was adopted in 1949.

A revision of *Advices and queries*, adopted in 1964, contained a number of alterations to the previous edition and included references to social problems not apparent in 1928. The principal change was that the advices on ministry and additional advice were no longer separate documents, although much of the material in them was again included.

By 1984 some monthly meetings were expressing unease with the 1964 edition of *Advices and queries*. Hesitations had been aroused by the use of masculine nouns and pronouns no longer seen as justifiable, by some of the theological language used, by the difficulty of reading aloud some of the longer paragraphs and by the absence of reference to some more recently evolved concerns. In 1986 Meeting for Sufferings appointed a Book of Discipline Revision Committee, and among the earliest tasks which this committee took up was a revision of the advices and queries.

As part of a major programme of consultation with the yearly meeting, the committee drafted a provisional document with the title *Questions and counsel*. Meeting for Sufferings agreed to publish the draft in 1988 and invited meetings to use it for two or three years and to join in the process of revision by telling of their experience. In the light of these responses and after several more years of work on the revision of the whole book, the committee submitted a text to Yearly Meeting 1994, which, after making a number of changes and additions, approved a final text.

DUTY OF READING

1.05   The advices and queries are intended for use in our meetings, for private devotion and reflection, as a challenge and inspiration to us as Friends in our personal lives and in our life as a religious community, and as a concise expression of our faith and practice readily available to enquirers and to the wider world.

Their use will vary in different meetings according to the needs of the members. Generally it will be helpful to arrange for the reading of the advices and queries in meetings for worship over a specified period, while taking care that such reading should not be carried out within too limited a time. Friends may wish to consider during the year one or more of the sections in their meetings for church affairs or to hold special meetings and discussion groups for their consideration. The only duties laid down are as follows:

Monthly meetings

1.06 Monthly meetings should consider regularly the use made of *Advices and queries* in their constituent meetings. This consideration should be undertaken annually or triennially as each monthly meeting determines. Preparative meetings should be asked to report on the use made of this document so that monthly meetings may be fully informed. It is hoped that out of such sharing of experience monthly meetings may be enabled to give advice and encouragement where necessary in order to ensure that this document is used to the best advantage.

Monthly meetings should also consider whether it would be helpful to arrange for the reading of sections of *Advices and queries* during their own periods of worship, and to make suitable arrangements for such reading. Some monthly meetings may also wish to arrange periodically for the discussion of appropriate sections.

Preparative meetings

1.07 Preparative meetings should give periodic consideration to the ways in which advices and queries can be used and they are to report to their respective monthly meetings annually or triennially, as directed, on the use made of them.

Chapter 2

Approaches to God – worship and prayer

EXPERIENCE AND NATURE OF WORSHIP

2.01 Worship is the response of the human spirit to the presence of the divine and eternal, to the God who first seeks us. The sense of wonder and awe of the finite before the infinite leads naturally to thanksgiving and adoration.

Silent worship and the spoken word are both parts of Quaker ministry. The ministry of silence demands the faithful activity of every member in the meeting. As, together, we enter the depths of a living silence, the stillness of God, we find one another in 'the things that are eternal', upholding and strengthening one another.

1967; 1994

2.02 On one never-to-be-forgotten Sunday morning, I found myself one of a small company of silent worshippers who were content to sit down together without words, that each one might feel after and draw near to the Divine Presence, unhindered at least, if not helped, by any human utterance. Utterance I knew was free, should the words be given; and, before the meeting was over, a sentence or two were uttered in great simplicity by an old and apparently untaught man, rising in his place amongst the rest of us. I did not pay much attention to the words he spoke, and I have no recollection of their purport. My whole soul was filled with the unutterable peace of the undisturbed opportunity for communion with God, with the sense that at last I had found a place where I might, without the faintest suspicion of insincerity, join with others in simply seeking His presence. To sit down in silence could at the least pledge me to nothing; it might open to me (as it did that morning) the very gate of heaven. And, since that day, now more than seventeen years ago, Friends' meetings have indeed been to me the greatest of outward helps to a fuller and fuller entrance into the spirit from which they have sprung; the place of the most soul-subduing, faith-restoring, strengthening, and peaceful communion, in feeding upon the bread of life, that I have ever known.

Caroline E Stephen, 1890

2.03 Some Friends are able to recall with clarity the first occasion on which they attended a Quaker meeting. While I cannot remember when or where I did so, I do have a vivid recollection of the meeting which I began to attend regularly.

It was held in a rather hideous building: the meeting room was dingy. We sat on rickety chairs that creaked at the slightest movement. The whole place gave little hope that those who worshipped there might catch a glimpse of the vision of God. It was in stark contrast to the splendour of the Anglican churches to which I had been accustomed, where through dignified ritual the beauty of holiness was vividly portrayed.

However, it was in this unlikely setting that I came to know what I can only describe as the amazing fact of Quaker worship. It was in that uncomfortable room that I discovered the way to the interior side of my life, at the deep centre of which I knew that I was not alone, but was held by a love that passes all understanding. This love was mediated to me, in the first place, by those with whom I worshipped. For my journey was not solitary, but one undertaken with my friends as we moved towards each other and together travelled inwards. Yet I knew that the love that held me could not be limited to the mutual love and care we had for each other. It was a signal of transcendence that pointed beyond itself to the source of all life and love.

George Gorman, 1973

2.04 *Daniel Wheeler (1771-1840) went to St Petersburg as agricultural adviser to tsar Alexander I and helped with the draining of marshes; he later spent four years sailing the South Seas as a missionary.*

Last First Day, in our little meeting, the Master was pleased to preside, and it was indeed a 'feast of fat things'; and the language which arose in my heart was, 'Take, eat, this is my body'. I never remember being under such a covering, and my desire is, that I may never forget it; and oh! that the fear of the Lord may so prevail amongst us, as to entitle us to His Love, which can alone enable us to 'run through a troop, or leap over a wall': and which at this time enableth me to call every country my country, and every man my brother.

Daniel Wheeler, written in Ochta near Petersburg, 1818

2.05 A'r pryd y gwelo Duw yn dda roddi gair yng ngenau neb ohonynt, mae hwnnw i ddywedyd y peth y byddo yr Arglwydd wedi ei ddatguddio a'i ddysgu iddo. Felly mae ef i roddi allan yn eglurhad yr ysbryd a'i nerth, ac yn y rhinwedd a'r bywyd, fel y byddo er adeiladaeth yn yr eglwys; canys mae dyfnder yn galw ar ddyfnder, a bywyd yn cyrraedd at fywyd, a'r gynulleidfa yn cyd fyned i'r dyfroedd i yfed yn rhad. Yna os datguddir dim i'r un a fyddo yn eistedd ger llaw, mae y cyntaf i ddistewi, oblegid mae y ffrwd honno o ddawn ysbrydol yn cael ei throi ar olwyn y dyn arall; canys mae y rhyddid ysbrydol hwnnw, yn y wir eglwys, i bob un, i lefaru megis ag y cynhyrfer hwynt, gan yr Ysbryd Glân.

Ellis Pugh, c1700

An English translation 'from the British tongue' was published in 1732:

And when God sees meet to put a Word into the mouth of any one of them, he is to speak what the Lord hath revealed and taught him (I Cor 2:4). So is he to give it forth in demonstration and power, and in the virtue and life of the Spirit, that it may be to edification in the church; for deep calleth unto deep, and life reacheth unto life, and the congregation go together to the waters to drink freely (Ps 42:7). And if anything be revealed to one that sits by, when the first is silent, that stream of the spiritual gift is turned to the other, because that spiritual liberty is in the true church, for every one to speak as they are moved by the Holy Spirit.

2.06 The treasure I had found [in meeting for worship] seemed startlingly simple, and I held this treasure quietly to myself, exploring its significance, feeling it almost too good to be true. Part of its simplicity was that I and others were to start just where we were at the moment and proceed at our own pace from there. How blessed that there were no restraints of belief. The promptings of love and truth were the starting places and we could move at our own pace to recognise them as the leadings of God – the beyond which drew me and others on from our limitations and despairs and smallnesses.

Ruth Fawell, 1987

2.07 Worship is essentially an act of adoration, adoration of the one true God in whom we live and move and have our being. Forgetting our little selves, our petty ambitions, our puny triumphs, our foolish cares and fretful anxieties, we reach out towards the beauty and majesty of God. The religious life is not a dull, grim drive towards moral virtues, but a response to a vision of greatness.

Thomas F Green, 1952

2.08 To me, worship is recognising and communing with the divine, whether it is within myself, in others, or in the world. The precondition of worship is my belief in worth-ship, my own and that of other people.

A member of the Quaker Women's Group, 1986

2.09 All true worship is inspired by God. The place of worship is the place of dependence, the place of wonder and of power, the place of fellowship and of communion... Worship links us to God and implies faith in a God who is in some sense personal. Personality is the highest category we know and we cannot worship a Being who is less than the highest of which we conceive... Thus the act of worship presupposes on our part a sense of dependence on God and the acknowledgment of our need of him, and this means that the element of adoration and thanksgiving should always be present in worship. Worship in Christian experience is our response to the God of Love.

Robert Davis, 1933

2.10 *Thomas Kelly (1893-1941) was a scientist from Ohio who taught philosophy at Earlham and Haverford colleges. Towards the end of his life he had vivid experiences of the love of God, of which he spoke and wrote, in his* Testament of devotion.

In this humanistic age we suppose man is the initiator and God is the responder. But the living Christ within us is the initiator and we are the responders. God the Lover, the accuser, the revealer of light and darkness presses within us. 'Behold, I stand at the door and knock.' And all our apparent initiative is already a response, a testimonial to His secret presence and working within us. The basic response of the soul to the Light is internal adoration and joy, thanksgiving and worship, self-surrender and listening.

Thomas R Kelly, 1941

2.11　True worship may be experienced at any time; in any place – alone on the hills or in the busy daily life – we may find God, in whom we live and move and have our being. But this individual experience is not sufficient, and in a meeting held in the Spirit there is a giving and receiving between its members, one helping another with or without words. So there may come a wider vision and a deeper experience.

1925; 1994

SILENT WAITING

2.12　In silence which is active, the Inner Light begins to glow – a tiny spark. For the flame to be kindled and to grow, subtle argument and the clamour of our emotions must be stilled. It is by an attention full of love that we enable the Inner Light to blaze and illuminate our dwelling and to make of our whole being a source from which this Light may shine out.

Words must be purified in a redemptive silence if they are to bear the message of peace. The right to speak is a call to the duty of listening. Speech has no meaning unless there are attentive minds and silent hearts. Silence is the welcoming acceptance of the other. The word born of silence must be received in silence.

Pierre Lacout, 1969

2.13　True silence ... is to the spirit what sleep is to the body, nourishment and refreshment.

William Penn, 1699

2.14 We highly prize silent waiting upon the Lord in humble dependence upon him. We esteem it to be a precious part of spiritual worship, and trust that no vocal offering will ever exclude it from its true place in our religious meetings. Let not the silence ... be spent in indolent or vacant musing but in patient waiting in humble prayerful expectancy before the Lord.

Yearly Meeting in London, 1884; 1886

2.15 I know of no other way, in these deeper depths, of trusting in the name of the Lord, and staying upon God, than sinking into silence and nothingness before Him... So long as the enemy can keep us reasoning he can buffet us to and fro; but into the true solemn silence of the soul before God he cannot follow us.

John Bellows, 1895

2.16 [The early Friends] made the discovery that silence is one of the best preparations for communion [with God] and for the reception of inspiration and guidance. Silence itself, of course, has no magic. It may be just sheer emptiness, absence of words or noise or music. It may be an occasion for slumber, or it may be a dead form. But it may be an intensified pause, a vitalised hush, a creative quiet, an actual moment of mutual and reciprocal correspondence with God.

Rufus Jones, 1937

2.17 Meeting is the chance to escape from the trivial thoughts of everyday living, and to find answers from yourself or from God. Some people are scared of the silence. Without the noise that serves to reassure us, that blocks out thoughts we'd rather not have, we're vulnerable and find it's time to face ourselves. We can never hide from God, but it's easy to minimise the effect he has on our lives – except in the silence where he can be heard. Don't feel restricted by the silence, it is there to set you free from the pressures of life. No-one is judging your movements, your thoughts... Freedom of expression is the freedom to worship God on your own terms. Value the opportunity to think unguided by the world. Learn what you feel you need to know, let other information pass. No moment of silence is a waste of time.

Rachel Needham, 1987

PRAYER

2.18 Be still and cool in thy own mind and spirit from thy own thoughts, and then thou wilt feel the principle of God to turn thy mind to the Lord God, whereby thou wilt receive his strength and power from whence life comes, to allay all tempests, against blusterings and storms. That is it which moulds up into patience, into innocency, into soberness, into stillness, into stayedness, into quietness, up to God, with his power.

George Fox, 1658

2.19 *William Leddra of Barbados on the day before he was martyred in 1661 wrote:*

As the flowing of the ocean doth fill every creek and branch thereof, and then retires again towards its own being and fulness, and leaves a savour behind it; so doth the life and virtue of God flow into every one of your hearts, whom he hath made partakers of his divine nature; and when it withdraws but a little, it leaves a sweet savour behind it; that many can say they are made clean through the word that he hath spoken to them. In which innocent condition you may see what you are in the presence of God, and what you are without him... Stand still, and cease from thine own working, and in due time thou shalt enter into the rest, and thy eyes shall behold his salvation, whose testimonies are sure, and righteous altogether.

2.20 Do you make a place in your daily life for reading, meditation, and waiting upon God in prayer, that you may know more of the presence and guidance of the Holy Spirit? Do you remember the need to pray for others, holding them in the presence of God?

Queries, 1964

2.21 I read that I was supposed to make 'a place for inward retirement and waiting upon God' in my daily life, as the *Queries* in those days expressed it... At last I began to realise, first that I needed some kind of inner peace, or inward retirement, or whatever name it might be called by; and then that these apparently stuffy old Friends were really talking sense. If I studied what they were trying to tell me, I might possibly find that the 'place of inward retirement' was not a place I had to go to, it was there all the time. I could know the 'place of inward retirement' wherever I was, or whatever I was doing, and find the spiritual refreshment for which, knowingly or unknowingly, I was longing, and hear the voice of God in my heart. Thus I began to realise that prayer was not a formality, or an obligation, it was a *place* which was there all the time and always available.

Elfrida Vipont Foulds, 1983

2.22   How, then, shall we lay hold of that Life and Power, and live the life of prayer without ceasing? By quiet, persistent practice in turning all our being, day and night, in prayer and inward worship and surrender, towards Him who calls in the deeps of our souls. Mental habits of inward orientation must be established. An inner, secret turning to God can be made fairly steady, after weeks and months and years of practice and lapses and failures and returns. It is as simple an art as Brother Lawrence found it, but it may be long before we achieve any steadiness in the process. Begin now, as you read these words, as you sit in your chair, to offer your whole selves, utterly and in joyful abandon, in quiet, glad surrender to Him who is within. In secret ejaculations of praise, turn in humble wonder to the Light, faint though it may be. Keep contact with the outer world of sense and meanings. Here is no discipline in absent-mindedness. Walk and talk and work and laugh with your friends. But behind the scenes keep up the life of simple prayer and inward worship. Keep it up throughout the day. Let inward prayer be your last act before you fall asleep and the first act when you awake. And in time you will find, as did Brother Lawrence, that 'those who have the gale of the Holy Spirit go forward even in sleep'.

Thomas R Kelly, 1941

2.23   Prayer is experienced as deeper than words or busy thoughts. 'Be still and cool in thy own mind and spirit from thy own thoughts', said Fox. It is marked by a kind of relaxed readiness, a 'letting-go' of the problems and perplexities with which the mind is occupied, and a waiting in 'love and truth': the truth about oneself, the truth about the world, deeper than the half-truths we see when we are busy in it about our own planning and scheming, the love in which we are held when we think of others more deeply than our ordinary relations with them, the love that at root holds us to the world. Prayer is not words or acts, but reaching down to love: holding our fellows in love, offering ourselves in love; and being held by, being caught up in love. It is communion, an opening of the door, an entry from the beyond. This is the point where secular language fails, for this cannot be spoken about at all: it can only be known.

Harold Loukes, 1967

2.24   Consider now the prayer-life of Jesus. It comes out most clearly in the record of St Luke, who leaves us with the impression that prayer was the most vital element in our Lord's life. He rises a great while before day that he may have some hours alone with His Father. He continues all night in prayer to God. Incident after incident is introduced by the statement that Jesus was praying. Are we so much nearer God that we can afford to dispense with that which to Him was of such vital moment? But apart from this, it seems to me that this prayer-habit of Jesus throws light upon the *purpose* of prayer.

I think of those long hours alone with God. Quite obviously *petition* can have had a very small place in our Lord's thoughts. We cannot suppose that He whose chief desire was that God's will should be done in all things could have been incessantly asking, asking. There must have been a sacred interchange far deeper than this. Especially are we sure that He was not praying for material blessings to be enjoyed by Himself alone. On the only occasion recorded in which He asked (in perfect submission) something for Himself, at Gethsemane, His request was not granted.

My own belief is that outward circumstances are not often (I will not say *never*) directly altered as a result of prayer. That is to say, God is not always interfering with the working of the natural order. But indirectly by the working of mind upon mind great changes may be wrought. We live and move and have our being in God; we are bound up in the bundle of life in Him, and it is reasonable to believe that prayer may often find its answer, even in outward things, by the reaction of mind upon mind. Prayer is not given us to make life easy for us, or to coddle us, but to make us strong ... to make us masters of circumstance and not its slaves. We pray, not to change God's will, but to bring our wills into correspondence with His.

William Littleboy, 1937

2.25 Prayer is not an occasional nod
Given in passing to God.
It's more like marriage – a closeness of living,
A constant receiving and giving.

Louie Horne, 1987

2.26 Prayer, we learn gradually, has far more to do with listening than with talking. In emotional stress the thoughts are so obsessive that they leave one no opportunity to listen. So, when we know someone is in trouble, we can and must listen (pray) for them. A Friend who had missed meeting for several weeks told us that she knew we had been praying for her before we said so; she had felt it and been sustained by it. She had thought there was no point in prayer or belief in God, but she had been helped by the knowledge that we still prayed and believed. It seems that one can do no less than this. We are seldom given guarantees that it is effective, just hints along the way; but they are hints we cannot ignore. We cannot prove the effectiveness of prayer, but nor can we cast scorn on examples of the kind I have given.

A friend tells me that when she prays for someone she does not so much pray *to* God for them as *for* God for them. This seems to me a vital clue about prayer. It is God that the troubled person needs, not our advice and instructions. As we learn more about worship we learn to listen more deeply so that we can be channels through which God's love reaches the other person. It is God at work, not we ourselves; we are simply used.

Diana Lampen, 1979

2.27 Prayer is an act of sharing with God, the Spirit, and not an attempt to prompt God to action. It is a promise that I will do my best, even if what I am able to do seems too insignificant to be worthwhile. When I pray for peace, and that the hearts of those in authority may be changed, it is a promise that I shall do such things as write to those in power, share in vigils, and above all lead my own life, as far as possible, in such a manner as to take away the occasion for strife between individuals and between peoples. When I pray for others who are in need, it is a promise to make my own contribution, perhaps by writing, by visiting, by a gift, by telling someone whom I know could help. When I pray for forgiveness, for strength and courage, I try to open my heart, making it possible for me humbly to receive.

'Anna', 1984

2.28 There is little point in praying to be enabled to overcome some temptation, and then putting oneself in the very position in which the temptation can exert all its fascination. There is little point in praying that the sorrowing may be comforted and the lonely cheered, unless we ourselves set out to bring comfort and cheer to the sad and neglected in our own surroundings. There is little point in praying for our home and for our loved ones, and in going on being as selfish and inconsiderate as we have been. Prayer would be an evil rather than a blessing if it were only a way of getting God to do what we ourselves will not make the effort to do. God does not do things for us – he enables us to do them for ourselves.

Elisabeth Holmgaard, 1984

2.29 The sick and those caring for them have need of our prayers. But let us not imagine ... that a few sentimental good wishes from a distance are all that is needed. Whenever we intercede in prayer we must be prepared for an answer which places a practical obligation upon us. A prayer is always a commitment.

Thomas F Green, 1952

2.30 A silent pause before meals is the Friends' equivalent for 'saying grace' – a practice which I own I think has much to recommend it. Here again there is, of course, the opportunity for words, should words spontaneously arise to the lips of any of those present.

Caroline E Stephen, 1890

2.31 Do not let us be discouraged because we find the path of silent prayer difficult or because we do not experience that joy of conscious communion which is given to some. The sunlight shines through the cloud; even when the cloud is so thick that we cannot see the sun at all, its rays carry on their healing work, and it does us good to go out into the open, even on a grey day. The experience of many of the greatest saints points to the traversing of a dark night of the soul before the light of full communion dawns, and to times of dryness of spirit coming at intervals to test the faith and perseverance of the seeker.

T Edmund Harvey, 1929

2.32 There is no use trying to conceal how difficult it is to find time for private prayer in the congested schedules under which most modern people live. But at the bottom it is not a question of finding time ... [but] of the depth of the sense of need and of the desire. Busy lovers find time to write letters to one another, often ... long letters; although what really matters is not the length of the letter any more than it is the length of the prayer. In this life we find the time for what we believe to be important.

Douglas Steere, 1938

2.33 Prayer is not just a matter of the feelings, but of the will. When we least feel like praying and when prayer seems pointless because there appears to be no-one to accept it – when God indeed seems absent, then is the time to call our will into action and refuse to give up. There will be occasions when our desert will seem only dry and barren. But refreshment is not far away, and we must persevere, holding on to the promise that the parched ground shall become a pool and the thirsty land springs of water.

Jack Dobbs, 1984

2.34 Prayer, then, is *communion*, whether it takes the form of petition, intercession, thanksgiving, or whether it be just the quiet unveiling of the heart to a trusted friend, the outpouring of the soul to the one who is nearest of all.

William Littleboy, 1937

See also 20.01-20.14

MEETING FOR WORSHIP

2.35 Friends, meet together and know one another in that which is eternal, which was before the world was.

George Fox, 1657

2.36 In worship we have our neighbours to right and left, before and behind, yet the Eternal Presence is over all and beneath all. Worship does not consist in achieving a mental state of concentrated isolation from one's fellows. But in the depth of common worship it is as if we found our separate lives were all one life, within whom we live and move and have our being.

Thomas R Kelly, 1938

2.37 Friends have never regarded [worship] as an individual activity. People who regard Friends' meetings as opportunities for meditation have failed to appreciate this corporate aspect. The waiting and listening are activities in which everybody is engaged and produce spoken ministry which helps to articulate the common guidance which the Holy Spirit is believed to give the group as a whole. So the waiting and listening is corporate also. This is why Friends emphasise the 'ministry of silence' and the importance of coming to meeting regularly and with heart and mind prepared.

John Punshon, 1987

2.38 In a gathered meeting there may be few spoken words, but there is rich ministry. An hour passes quickly. Other meetings are lifeless. They may be full of words, but there is little ministry, little that is of service. Time drags and people feel the need to fill the silence.

A gathered meeting has the strength to absorb the differences and support the needs of those who attend it; this is easier when the meeting is a community of people who know and trust each other, who are not afraid to share their experience of worship and to learn from one another.

Conference: *Exploring the fundamental elements of Quakerism*, 1986

2.39   A Friends' meeting, however silent, is at the very lowest a witness that worship is something other and deeper than words, and that it is to the unseen and eternal things that we desire to give the first place in our lives. And when the meeting, whether silent or not, is awake, and looking upwards, there is much more in it than this. In the united stillness of a truly 'gathered' meeting there is a power known only by experience, and mysterious even when most familiar. There are perhaps few things which more readily flow 'from vessel to vessel' than quietness. The presence of fellow-worshippers in some gently penetrating manner reveals to the spirit something of the nearness of the Divine Presence. 'Where two or three are gathered together in His name' have we not again and again felt that the promise was fulfilled and that the Master Himself was indeed 'in the midst of us'? And it is out of the depths of this stillness that there do arise at times spoken words which, springing from the very source of prayer, have something of the power of prayer – something of its quickening and melting and purifying effect. Such words as these have at least as much power as silence to gather into stillness.

Caroline E Stephen, 1908

2.40   What is the ground and foundation of the gathered meeting? In the last analysis, it is, I am convinced, the Real Presence of God.

Thomas R Kelly, 1940

The individual in meeting

2.41   The first that enters into the place of your meeting ... turn in thy mind to the light, and wait upon God singly, as if none were present but the Lord; and here thou art strong. Then the next that comes in, let them in simplicity of heart sit down and turn in to the same light, and wait in the spirit; and so all the rest coming in, in the fear of the Lord, sit down in pure stillness and silence of all flesh, and wait in the light... Those who are brought to a pure still waiting upon God in the spirit, are come nearer to the Lord than words are; for God is a spirit, and in the spirit is he worshipped... In such a meeting there will be an unwillingness to part asunder, being ready to say in yourselves, it is good to be here: and this is the end of all words and writings to bring people to the eternal living Word.

Alexander Parker, 1660

2.42　Come with heart and mind prepared. Pray silently as you gather together that you may all be drawn into the spirit of adoration and communion in which fellowship with one another becomes real. Yield yourselves and all your outward concerns to God's guidance, that you may find the evil weakening in you and the good raised up.

Advices, 1964

2.43　'Where two or three', saith our Lord, 'are gathered together in my name, there am I in the midst of them' (Mt 18:20). In these words he ... invites us not only to meet one with another but, in so doing, with himself also... Shall the poor perishing gratifications of sense and self-love, or any inconveniences of a trivial nature, be suffered to prevent our dutiful attendance upon him, in whom alone stands our everlasting interest? Shall a cloudy sky, a little wet, a little cold, a little ease to the flesh, a view to a little earthly gain, or any common incident, furnish an excuse for declining this duty, and thereby depriving ourselves of the blessed advantage, often vouchsafed to the faithful, of enjoying heavenly communion together in spirit with the Lord of life and glory?

Yearly Meeting in London, 1765

2.44　There are times of dryness in our individual lives, when meeting may seem difficult or even worthless. At such times one may be tempted not to go to meeting, but it may be better to go, prepared to offer as our contribution to the worship simply a sense of need. In such a meeting one may not at the time realise what one has gained, but one will nevertheless come away helped.

Berks & Oxon QM Ministry & Extension Committee, 1948

2.45　It is the individual faithfulness of each Friend which is needed if our meetings for worship are to be held to the glory of God. Each one of us must come expecting not only to receive but to be used. This involves a preparation of spirit, but many interpret the phrase

'Come with heart and mind prepared' too narrowly. The preparation needed is the living of our daily lives in constant awareness of the presence of God. In the rush of living we may miss the true Life. We must face realities, however, and try to overcome the practical difficulties which we do encounter. Our lives are sometimes inevitably rushed. This means that we may come to meetings for worship in turmoil or trouble. We may be tired, irritable or sleepy. We should not in such cases turn away from the meeting for worship, but should realise the value of such occasions as training times.

Important though our part of preparation, dedication and faithfulness is, we have always to remember that *our* part is dependent upon that power which comes to us, unlooked-for and undeserved, the power of the grace of God.

Berks & Oxon QM Ministry & Extension Committee, 1947

2.46 Regular attendance at your own meeting, leading to a deeper knowledge of the members and their needs, will contribute to the quality of its corporate life. We recognise and encourage concerned visitation of other meetings and opportunities of worship with those of other communions, but continued casual or undisciplined attendance sometimes at one place of worship and sometimes at another is a source of weakness both to the individual and to the meeting.

1959; 1994

See also 13.20-13.31 Travelling in the ministry and intervisitation

2.47 Does punctuality matter? It is not merely a question of disturbing the peace and quiet of those already assembled... What is on my mind is more than that. If we were coming together to worship individually, each to enter into his or her own private meditation, then it wouldn't much matter whether all arrived by the appointed time. In private meditation the worshippers could each 'settle' separately, training themselves not to be disturbed by latecomers. But if our goal is to achieve a group mystical experience, deepening and enriching our individual experience, then, it seems to me, we need to start the process at the same time.

A 'gathered' Quaker meeting is something more than a number of individuals sitting down together but meditating individually. So long as each sits in meditation in the way one does when worshipping by oneself, the worship will seldom reach that greater depth which a Quaker meeting at its best achieves. The goal of a truly 'gathered' meeting is to become fused into something bigger than the sum of the parts...

As a meeting 'gathers', as each individual 'centres down', there gradually develops a feeling of belonging to a group who are together seeking a sense of the Presence. The 'I' in us begins to feel like 'we'. At some point – it may be early in the meeting or it may be later, or it may never occur at all – we suddenly feel a sense of unity, a sense of togetherness with one another and with that something outside ourselves that we call God.

Thomas R Bodine, 1980

2.48 Heed not distressing thoughts when they rise ever so strongly in thee; fear them not, but be still awhile, not believing in the power which thou feelest they have over thee, and it will fall on a sudden. It is good for thy spirit and greatly to thy advantage to be much and variously exercised by the Lord. Thou dost not know what the Lord hath already done and what he is yet doing for thee therein.

Isaac Penington

2.49 The mind wanders and the will falters again and again... But it is foolish to allow failures in concentration to plunge us into profitless self-condemnation. A mother does not condemn her child who is struggling with many a failure to learn how to walk, but rather she is pleased by each successful effort... I like to believe that God is similarly pleased with our efforts and understanding of our many failures. What matters is whether or not the will, like a compass needle when deflected, is so pivoted that it can swing back to the true direction.

St Francis de Sales is reassuring:

When your heart is wandering and distracted, bring it back quickly to its point, restore it tenderly to its Master's side, and if you did nothing else the whole of your hour but bring back your heart patiently and put it near our Lord again, and every time you put it back it turned away again, your hour would be well-employed.

Thomas F Green, 1952

2.50 At meeting for worship relax and let your baby be with you; my small daughter called it 'the best cuddle of the week' when I couldn't rush off and do something busy. It's not easy for the parents to believe that their child's gurglings actually help the meeting rather than interrupt it. Nonetheless, that is true, and you shouldn't give way to the temptation to take a happily babbling child out of the meeting (though howling is something different!).

Anne Hosking, 1986

2.51 When meeting for worship begins, I like to look around and see who is there, and this normally leads to a feeling of gratitude for the friendship, warmth, and support I've found among Friends. If I know of any difficulties or problems being experienced by anyone present, I would think along these lines. Or perhaps I would think of someone missing from their usual seat, and this might lead me to think of others who were ill, bereaved, anxious or overworked. I might then reflect on my own many and great blessings, and seek direction in using my time and talents. Or I might see someone unemployed, and be led to think of some of our social problems. It's a sort of chain reaction.

Dorothy Marshall, 1987

2.52 When I sit down in meeting I recall whatever may have struck me freshly during the past week. This is in part, initially at least, a voluntary and outward act... It means that the will is given up to service; and it is quite possible to stop everything by taking an opposite attitude. So thoughts suggest themselves – a text that has smitten one during the week – new light on a phrase – a verse of poetry – some incident, private or public. These pass before the door whence shines the heavenly light. Are they transfigured? Sometimes, yes; sometimes, no. If nothing flames, silence is my portion.

John William Graham, 1920

2.53   A score of years ago a friend placed in my hand a little book which became one of the turning points of my life. It was called *True peace*... It had but one thought ... that God was waiting in the depths of my being to talk to me if only I would get still enough to hear his voice.

I thought this would be a very easy matter, and so I began to get still. But I had no sooner commenced than a perfect pandemonium of voices reached my ears, a thousand clamouring notes from without and within, until I could hear nothing but their noise and din. Some of them were my own voice, some were my own questions, some of them were my very prayers. Others were the suggestions of the tempter, and the voices of the world's turmoil. Never before did there seem so many things to be done, to be said, to be thought; and in every direction I was pushed and pulled, and greeted with noisy acclamations of unspeakable unrest. It seemed necessary for me to listen to some of them, and to answer some of them, but God said, 'Be still, and know that I am God'. Then came the conflict of thoughts for the morrow, and its duties and cares; but God said 'Be still'. And as I listened, and slowly learned to obey, and shut my ears to every sound, I found, after a while, that when the other voices ceased, or I ceased to hear them, there was a still, small voice in the depths of my being that began to speak with an inexpressible tenderness, power and comfort.

John Edward Southall, c 1900

2.54   As I silence myself I become more sensitive to the sounds around me, and I do not block them out. The songs of the birds, the rustle of the wind, children in the playground, the roar of an airplane overhead are all taken into my worship. I regulate my breathing as taught me by my Zen friends, and through this exercise I feel the flow of life within me from my toes right through my whole body. I think of myself like the tree planted by the 'rivers of water' in Psalm 1, sucking up God's gift of life and being restored. Sometimes I come to meeting for worship tired and weary, and I hear the words of Jesus, 'Come unto me, all that labour and are weary, and I will give you rest'. And having laid down my burden, I feel refreshed both physically and spiritually. This leads me on to whole-hearted adoration and thanksgiving for all God's blessings. My own name, Tayeko, means 'child of many blessings' and God has surely poured them upon me. My heart overflows with a desire to give him something in return. I have nothing to give but my own being, and I offer him my thoughts, words and actions of each day, and whisper 'Please take me as I am'.

Tayeko Yamanouchi, 1979

Vocal ministry

2.55   Remember that to every one is given a share of responsibility for the meeting for worship, whether that service be in silence or through the spoken word. Do not assume that vocal ministry is never to be your part. If the call to speak comes, do not let the sense of your own unworthiness, or the fear of being unable to find the right words, prevent you from being obedient to the leading of the Spirit. Ask wisdom of God that you may be sure of your guidance and be enabled humbly to discern and impart something of his glory and truth. Pray that your ministry may rise from the place of deep experience, and that you may be restrained from unnecessary and superficial words. Faithfulness and sincerity in speaking, even very briefly, may open the way to fuller ministry from others. Try to speak audibly and distinctly, with sensitivity to the needs of your fellow worshippers. Wait to be sure of the right moment for giving the message. Beware of making additions towards the end of a meeting when it was well left before.

Advices, 1964

2.56   Jane Fenn, a young woman who migrated to Philadelphia in 1712 and became in time a travelling Quaker minister of note, describes sitting in meeting one day and hearing an inner voice declare that she had been chosen for the ministry:

> Yet I must confess, this awful word of Divine command shocked me exceedingly, my soul and all within me trembled at the hearing of it; yea my outward tabernacle shook insomuch that many present observed the deep exercise I was under. I cried in spirit, 'Lord I am weak and altogether incapable of such a task, I hope thou wilt spare me from such a mortification; besides I have spoken much against women appearing in that manner.'

For six or seven months, Jane Fenn continued to resist the command to speak in meeting, until she could withstand the pressure no longer. She stood up to utter a few broken words and returned home rejoicing. Nevertheless, for many years thereafter, she continued to struggle with her own sense of inadequacy when confronted with the growing demands of the Spirit that she not only preach to local meetings, but also travel through the colonies and eventually back to England.

Margaret Hope Bacon, 1986

2.57 I went to meetings in an awful frame of mind, and endeavoured to be inwardly acquainted with the language of the true Shepherd. And one day, being under a strong exercise of spirit, I stood up, and said some words in a meeting, but not keeping close to the divine opening, I said more than was required of me and being soon sensible to my error, I was afflicted in mind some weeks, without any light or comfort, even to that degree that I could take satisfaction in nothing. I remembered God and was troubled, and in the depth of my distress he had pity upon me, and sent the Comforter. I then felt forgiveness for my offence, and my mind became calm and quiet, being truly thankful to my gracious Redeemer for his mercies. And after this, feeling the spring of divine love opened, and a concern to speak, I said a few words in a meeting in which I found peace. This I believe was about six weeks from the first time, and as I was thus humbled and disciplined under the cross, my understanding became more strengthened to distinguish the language of the pure spirit which inwardly moves upon the heart, and taught me to wait in silence sometimes many weeks together, until I felt that rise which prepares the creature to stand like a trumpet, through which the Lord speaks to his flock.

John Woolman, 1741

2.58 For some weeks before this particular Sunday I had been puzzling over and questioning in my mind various problems connected with my work. It was one of those episodes of spiritual upheaval which most of us go through from time to time when we seem to question our normal certainties, poke around the foundations of our normal life and discover to our alarm that some of them are very shaky. I had been in this highly charged state for several weeks.

On this Sunday morning though, I went quietly to meeting with the family, my recent preoccupations submerged by the business of getting us all dressed and breakfasted and to the meeting house on time. But as the minutes ticked by and I sat in the healing peace, I began to be aware that something inside me was formulating a question which urgently needed to be asked. I say 'something inside me' because it seemed at the same time to be both me and not me. I discovered to my horror that this something was urging me to get up and ask my question. My heart was pounding uncomfortably and I began to shiver (I don't know whether this was obvious to those around me; I was certainly aware of this shivering but shyness prevents one from asking afterwards whether these physical symptoms are visible to others). To start with I resisted this prompting. I looked round the room and noticed several Friends before whom I was reluctant to make a fool of myself. I could not get up and speak in front of them. I would rather die first. The shaking and pounding diminished a little as I decided this. But not for long. Soon it started up again, insistent, not to be denied. This time I told myself 'I'll count twenty and then if no one else has spoken I shall have to.' Again a slight abatement of the symptoms. But to no avail. I counted twenty and then fifty and still no one spoke. Now I sat conscious only of this overpowering force which was pushing me to my feet until finally I had to give in to it.

Afterwards I found it difficult to believe that I had spoken. It was all over so quickly. Had I really stood up in front of all those people and testified? Well, hardly testified, but yes, I had been driven by some inner prompting which, for want of a more precise word, one might well call spirit; and yes, I had quaked, most fearfully, with something which was more than just the fear of making a fool of myself before family and friends.

Elisabeth Salisbury, 1968

2.59   Some think, through a mistaken judgment, that they must be doing something every meeting, (like the preachers of the letter, who must either be singing, preaching or praying all the time) and by such a conduct they lose their interest and place in the hearts of friends by too long and too frequent appearing in both preaching and prayer: For the avoiding of which, keep close to thy gift, intently waiting to know thy place, both when to speak and when to be silent; and when thou speakest, begin under a sense of divine influence, whether it be in preaching or praying; and without it, do not either preach or pray.

Samuel Bownas, 1750

2.60   All true ministry springs from the reality of experience, and uses our gifts of heart and mind in its expression. But ministry is not the place for intellectual exercise. It comes through us, not from us. Although we interpret the Spirit it is that Spirit which will lead us to minister. The Spirit will decide which experiences are relevant and which will speak to the condition of the meeting. If you have to decide whether it is right to speak, consider that it isn't. If your words are important the meeting will find them anyway.

Conference: *Exploring the fundamental elements of Quakerism*, 1986

2.61   Ministry should be of necessity, and not of choice, and there is no living by silence, or by preaching merely.

John Churchman, 1734

2.62   In Friends' meetings also, from the fact that everyone is free to speak, one hears harmonies and correspondences between very various utterances such as are scarcely to be met elsewhere. It is sometimes as part-singing compared with unison. The free admission of the ministry of women, of course, greatly enriches this harmony. I have often wondered whether some of the motherly counsels I have listened to in our meeting would not reach some hearts that might be closed to the masculine preacher.

Caroline E Stephen, 1890

2.63   When language is used unthinkingly, without being related to the experience of either the speaker or the listener, it is meaningless. Words are only symbols and when there is no shared experience the symbolism breaks down. When we speak of our own experience, our feelings are always involved. The same is true when we listen to others: we may read into their words meanings which are not intended but which reflect our own emotions. Certain words or kinds of language may arouse such strong emotions that we are only able to relate them to our own experience and not to that of the speaker. Speakers too may be unaware of the effect of their words. The more important and profound the subject matter, the greater the need for sensitivity in choosing our words. This is no excuse for playing safe in what we say, or for not listening to others when what they say makes us uncomfortable.

Conference: *Exploring the fundamental elements of Quakerism*, 1986

2.64   Each Friend who feels called upon to rise and deliver a lengthy discourse might question himself – and herself – most searchingly, as to whether the message could not be more lastingly given in the fewest possible words, or even through his or her personality alone, in entire and trustful silence. 'Cream must always rise to the surface.' True. But other substances rise to the surface besides cream; substances that may have to be skimmed off and thrown away before bodies and souls can be duly nourished. 'Is my message cream or scum?' may be an unusual and is certainly a very homely query. Still it is one that every speaker, in a crowded gathering especially, should honestly face. Some of the dangers of silent worship can best be guarded against by its courtesies.

Violet Holdsworth, 1919

2.65   *In the Life*

My piece was pat and all ready to say,
She rose first. I threw my piece away.
  My well-turned stuff
  Was not so rough
As hers, but easy elegant and smooth.
  Beginning middle end
  It had and point
And aptly quoted prophet priest and poet.
  Hers was uncouth
  Wanting in art
Laboured scarce-audible and out of joint.
  Three times she lost the thread
And sitting left her message half unsaid.

'Why then did thee throw it
Into the discard?'
    Friend,
It had head
(Like this). Hers oh had heart.

Robert Hewison, 1965

2.66   Ministry is what is on one's soul, and it can be in direct contradiction to what is on one's mind. It's what the Inner Light gently pushes you toward or suddenly dumps in your lap. It is rooted in the eternity, divinity, and selflessness of the Inner Light; not in the worldly, egoistic functions of the conscious mind.

Marrianne McMullen, 1987

2.67   To some are granted deeper spiritual discoveries and revelations than to others, but to all, waiting in expectancy, at moments and in some measure is given a sense of the living touch of God. At such moments there may come the kindling of mind and heart which impels obedience to speak under the immediate promptings of the Holy Spirit. This is the ministry of inspiration, the prophetic ministry in the true sense, when the spoken word pierces to the heart of our relationship with God, unveils the living presence of Christ in the midst of the worshipping group and in its separate members, opens to our sight the way we must tread if we would realise that Spirit in and through our ordinary daily activities and find the creative response to the challenges of our time. In ministry of this character and depth something is given in the utterance which is beyond the intellectual and emotional capacity of the human being speaking, but which uses and enhances and transcends the natural gifts, the acquired knowledge, the hard and honest thoughts or the reaches of the speaker's imagination.

There is also the ministry of teaching which combines 'the potency of prayer and thought'. It recalls the meeting to the discoveries of truth, the perception of the acts of God in the lives of individuals. It includes the effort to understand and to interpret the central fact of Jesus Christ and his place in history, and the searchings and findings of men and women down the ages and in our own day as they have sought to relate new discoveries and insights to their understandings of eternal truth.

1967; 1994

2.68 In my young tempestuous days I heard many things in the Friends' meeting that I disliked and some that seemed to me quite false, and I felt the need to answer them. I was taught, and I believe correctly, that to insist on answering there and then would be to destroy the meeting; and that we all sit under the baptising power of the spirit of Truth, which is its own witness. We sit in silence so as not to trip over words; and we trust the good in each other which is from God, so that we may be kept from the evil.

J Ormerod Greenwood, 1980

2.69 A Friends' meeting for worship finds no room for debate or for answering (still less for contradicting) one another; if this is desirable, it will be left for another occasion. And if anything should seem to be spoken amiss, the spiritually minded worshipper will have the wit to get at the heart of the message, overlooking crudity and lack of skill in its presentation, and so far from giving way to irritation at what seems unprofitable, he will be deeply concerned for his own share in creating the right spiritual atmosphere in which the harm fades out and the good grows. Many a meeting has known this power, transforming what might have been hurtful into a means of grace.

A Neave Brayshaw, 1921

2.70 I think that learning to move in the exercise of the meeting, so that one is a part of it, yet taken beyond it and brought to see some new light as a result of it, is most important in creative ministry. The cluster of messages, with a fair interval of silence between each of them to let its message sink in; the cluster that goes on down, with each message deepening and intensifying and helping to light up a further facet of the communication, can be most effective. But for this to happen those sharing in it cannot be in a discussional frame of mind or in a debating stance, or yield to the ruthlessly critical mind, or all is lost and the meeting is pulled into a forum. It can only be done if there is a willingness to be led by each of the ones ministering into a deeper level of what they were not only saying but what they were meaning to say, and perhaps even beyond into what something beneath us all was meaning to have said through what we were saying... When a cluster ministry moves in this way, we all know that we are moving in the life, that we are breaking the cerebral barrier and being released ... and we are ourselves ignited by what is taking place.

Douglas Steere, 1972

2.71   It should be the care of elders to foster the spiritual life of all members and to give caution and advice to Friends who share in the vocal ministry. They should look out for Friends who may be likely to help the ministry and lead them to make their right contribution to the life of their meeting, and to encourage our members to think deeply on the great issues and problems of life and the fundamentals of our faith.

This, however, is not the duty of elders alone; as any Friends may hinder the work of the ministry by a critical or unloving spirit, so their sympathy and prayers for those who speak will help to create an atmosphere in which an inspired and inspiring ministry may grow. A friendly word of thankfulness from one who has been helped is often a great source of encouragement to the minister.

1925; 1959

For more about eldership see chapter 12 Caring for one another

2.72   He had an extraordinary gift in opening the Scriptures. He would go to the marrow of things and show the mind, harmony and fulfilling of them with much plainness and to great comfort and edification... But above all he excelled in prayer. The inwardness and weight of his spirit, the reverence and solemnity of his address and behaviour, and the fewness and fullness of his words have often struck even strangers with admiration, as they used to reach others with consolation. The most awful, living, reverent frame I ever felt or beheld, I must say, was his in prayer. And truly it was a testimony that he knew and lived nearer to the Lord than other men; for they that know him most will see most reason to approach him with reverence and fear.

William Penn writing of George Fox, 1694

2.73   The intent of all speaking is to bring into the life, and to walk in, and to possess the same, and to live in and enjoy it, and to feel God's presence.

George Fox, 1657

Children in meeting

2.74   Children have an uncanny knack of knowing the difference between living ministry, as opposed to words that are injected into the meeting for their good. This is why I feel Friends should at any time avoid deliberately speaking to children, for it usually means speaking down to them. In fact it is an excellent discipline for anyone who speaks in meeting to try to use words and ideas that can be understood by children, and yet speak to the condition of all present, because they arise from the profound depths which, in fact, produce things that are truly simple.

George Gorman, 1973

2.75   We had two daughters who were the only children to attend on Sundays. That they continued to come with us, and still retain affectionate memories of that, is due entirely to the loving care given by Friends in teaching them and making them feel part of the meeting. We need to instruct our children in the widest sense, so that they can use the knowledge we pass on, both in relation to the Bible and to our Quaker heritage... We do our children (not only those biologically ours) a disservice if we do not pass on to them our concerns, beliefs and ideas. It is a mistake to imagine that children taught nothing positive will then be able to evaluate everything for themselves. But we teach them what we have experienced, in the knowledge that they will incorporate it and use it in their own way, accepting or rejecting it for a world that is of their making, not ours. In the life of the Quaker meeting there is a tradition of equality and respect for individuals that I have found to be of pure gold in value. It is expressed in love and affection between the generations. I know that my daughters, now young adults, have truly felt part of the family of the meeting because they have respected and been respected in an atmosphere that is unusual even among Christian churches. When elderly Friends have died, they too have wept because they have valued the companionship of people who saw them as individuals in their own right and gave them a true sense of belonging.

Jean Brown, 1984

2.76 I recall a family weekend, when the children, about twenty-four of them, aged three and upwards, had their own sessions in parallel to the adults. On the first evening, after the getting-to-know-you games, we sat down on the carpet to worship. We lit some candles on the hearth, turned off the lights, asked two children to be elders, and were still. The meeting went on for over a quarter of an hour, and was very deep. Then the two elders shook hands, but the silence continued. After another five minutes, I started a conversation, but no one responded to my cheerful comments. I was the one who had lost touch. When the children did speak, it was slowly, thoughtfully, with long spaces between. This was when I realised that children do minister... That meeting lasted until someone entered the room and interrupted us – about forty minutes.

Anne Hosking, 1984

See also 2.50, 10.09, 10.10, 12.01 paragraph 6 & 19.35

Enriching worship

2.77 The depth of Quaker worship, its richness, its power and its ability to meet the needs of each worshipper as well as the gathered group, depends on the commitment of every participant, and on the way we all come to our meetings with hearts and minds prepared.

Jack Dobbs, 1982

2.78 I think that we suffer from lack of biblical study both individually and in groups; I do not urge that this should be done in the regular gatherings for worship, but rather in groups during the week. To restrict our fellowship to the single hour on Sunday mornings is, under ordinary conditions, to impoverish our times of worship. The over-busyness resulting from the changed and difficult home conditions has, I fear, told on this side of our lives and does need distinct attention.

Joan Mary Fry, 1947

See also 10.07 & 27.33

2.79 Friends are not usually noted for their art and in earlier periods of their history they objected to paintings, theatre, music and novels. But they did adopt one distinctive art form and made it their own – the spiritual journal. It became the characteristic way in which early Friends told the story of their journeys, both their inward pilgrimage and their outward travels. It is from his journal that we learn that John Woolman was not always pacific or self-controlled and had to wrestle with his desire to impose his own will on others. And we take comfort from the fact that self-doubt and uncertainty were part of his journey as they are of ours.

In this century the practice of journal keeping is being explored as a way of becoming aware of the patterns of our inner life, of growing in self-knowledge and discovering our own gifts and possibilities... Keeping a journal is just one way ... of beginning to re-create your life. At its most basic it is a decision that your life has value and meaning and deserves the effort of recollection and reflection. It is also a decision that what you are living and learning is worth recording. That decision has its roots in a very deep layer of gospel truth.

Jo Farrow, 1986

2.80 I have valued most during my time at Woodbrooke the opportunities to participate in worship-sharing groups. I believe that these are of fundamental importance to one's individual spiritual growth and well-being and to the health of the community of which one is an active member. I am developing a capacity to listen more attentively to disclosures of sorrow and joy as others recount to me their spiritual journeys. Tenuous at first is the hope that we will receive understanding in response to our awkward efforts to communicate. Courage grows though as we experience the concern of others touching us where we feel the pain most deeply. Compassionate listening involves the total engagement of the heart. It is through strength and grace that we are enabled to achieve trust and spiritual intimacy.

Kathy Tweet, 1993

2.81 Power of the inner kind increases with use. It is not unusual for telepathy to develop between those who are close to each other in love. Again, prayer groups increase prayer power, and as the bonds of friendship and trust develop, charismatic healing gifts arise. This type of spiritual study and prayer fellowship has been the most precious part of my life for many years. Such groups sustain and bind people together so that when one falls ill, feels depressed or suffers a bereavement, he or she may count upon the friendship of the others. It is this kind of relationship, where there is both giving and receiving at an inner level, which sometimes extends beyond the grave.

Damaris Parker-Rhodes, 1985

2.82 We have seen the need to evolve a meeting that is a preparation for meeting for worship, a meeting which is similarly open, personal and democratic but which is implicitly educational and uses a wide range of modes of interaction. The touchstone of its success is its ability to generate richer fellowship between participants as they come to know each other and themselves in the deepest things. Learning, in this use of the word, is not head and fact learning, but whole-self learning where feelings and spirit find equal room with thinking and reason.

There is no one way of going about meetings for learning; nor is there one content nor one single aspect of self that they might enrich. As well as intuition there is also information; as well as creative listening and role play and music there is also discussion and guidance. But yet all meetings for learning are about growth in that territory of the self which touches on ultimate meanings, about those things which we feel the deepest, about our shadow as much as about our light, about our being accepted and held in the group and not judged for being found wanting, about new community. Such meetings demand as much discipline as meetings for worship or our business meetings.

Alec Davison, 1982

See also 21.31

2.83 The importance, both for ourselves and for our children, of active association with our fellow members in work and worship has led our Society in the past strongly to encourage Friends to live near meetings. We [urge] Friends in fixing their places of residence to bear this in mind. But we are aware that there are many whose duties oblige them to reside where there is no meeting. We do not desire in any way to discourage these from associating in worship with members of other religious denominations. It is our concern that Friends thus situated should [consider holding] meetings of a simple spiritual character with their neighbours, either on first-day or during the week. The world needs this message, and it is one for which many souls are hungering. Where a meeting on first-day may not seem a wise arrangement a quiet hour of worship with neighbours of other religious denominations on a weekday may be found mutually helpful, and may serve to draw away from too great a dependence on the outward in religion.

London Yearly Meeting, 1905

2.84 If we met more often for worship in each other's homes, it would remind us that God is with us in every place, at the kitchen sink and at the table; we should get to know one another more intimately, and could break bread together; the home atmosphere might make it easier to invite our acquaintances to join us; and any increase in numbers would lead to multiplication by cell-division; and an expanding coverage of the community.

David W Robson, 1971

In addition to the regular meeting for worship on Sundays, and/or perhaps other days of the week, meetings are held on particular occasions, such as marriages and funerals. For extracts concerning meetings for worship on particular occasions, see 10.12 for a meeting held in the home of one who is ill, chapter 16 for Quaker marriage procedure, 17.01-17.06 for funerals and 22.44-22.46 for celebration of commitment.

Meetings for church affairs

2.85   The meeting for business cannot be understood in isolation; it is part of a spiritual discipline.

John Punshon, 1987

2.86   Are your meetings for church affairs held in the spirit of worship and dependence upon the guidance of God? Do you take your right share in them? Do you maintain your respect for others as persons however strongly you may differ from their opinions? Do you refrain from using hurtful and provocative language? Are you sufficiently conversant with our Christian discipline to be able, when difficult questions arise, to consider them with an informed mind as well as a loving and tender spirit?

Queries, 1964

2.87   Being orderly come together, [you are] not to spend time with needless, unnecessary and fruitless discourses; but to proceed in the wisdom of God, not in the way of the world, as a worldly assembly of men, by hot contests, by seeking to outspeak and over-reach one another in discourse as if it were controversy between party and party of men, or two sides violently striving for dominion, not deciding affairs by the greater vote. But in the wisdom, love and fellowship of God, in gravity, patience, meekness, in unity and concord, submitting one to another in lowliness of heart, and in the holy Spirit of truth and righteousness all things [are] to be carried on; by hearing, and determining every matter coming before you, in love, coolness, gentleness and dear unity; – I say, as one only party, all for the truth of Christ, and for the carrying on the work of the Lord, and assisting one another in whatsoever ability God hath given.

Edward Burrough, 1662

2.88   We see our meetings for church affairs not as business meetings preceded by a period of worship, but as 'meetings for worship for business'. Ideally the sacred and the secular are interwoven into one piece. Believing that all our business is brought before God for guidance we deprecate all that may foster a party spirit or confrontation. We therefore seek for a spirit of unity in all our decision making.

London Yearly Meeting, 1986

2.89 In all our meetings for church affairs we need to listen together to the Holy Spirit. We are not seeking a consensus; we are seeking the will of God. The unity of the meeting lies more in the unity of the search than in the decision which is reached. We must not be distressed if our listening involves waiting, perhaps in confusion, until we feel clear what God wants done.

London Yearly Meeting, 1984

2.90 What is required is a willingness to listen to what others have to say rather than to persuade them that one's own point of view represents what is right and proper. It also requires restraint. The reiteration of one point by several Friends each in their own way lends no weight to the point. What the meeting must learn to discern is its rightness, not how many people support it...

When conflict comes, as it does, and the temptation to compromise – to seek consensus – is resisted, the sense of divine guidance is unmistakably registered. New possibilities for a way forward which nobody has thought of emerge out of discussion. Postponement and delay settle minds and assist the process of coming to a united mind. Above all, those who take opposing views come to find that the discipline of waiting has mysteriously united them.

John Punshon, 1987

2.91 It has been the experience of this yearly meeting in the past to know that Friends have met in division and uncertainty, and that then guidance has come, and light has been given to us, and we have become finders of God's purpose. This gives us ground for confidence. We shall not be held back by the magnitude of the questions which are to come before us, nor by a sense of our own unworthiness.

London Yearly Meeting, 1936

2.92 The day was Friday, and we were mindful that within a few hours we would be going in separate directions, never to be gathered under the same circumstances again. As we met for worship that morning we were faced with the decision, whether or not to approve the epistle. We had laboured for several hours the day before, and it looked as though preferences for wording and other concerns would make it impossible to approve the final draft.

However, something happened which transformed the feeling of our meeting... [A New England Friend] said something like 'I know that the blood of Christ and the Atonement are very important issues for some Friends, and I don't see anything in the epistle which addresses those convictions...'

In the discussion that followed, [an] evangelical Friend expressed his concern that the number of references to Christ might be difficult for Friends not used to Christ-language. What had begun as an act of loving concern for other Friends transformed the meeting into a unified whole. The discussion had changed from persons wanting to ensure that their concerns were heard to wanting to ensure that the concerns of others were heard and that their needs were met. We had indeed experienced the transforming power of God's love.

Paul Anderson, *Report of the World Gathering of Young Friends*, 1985

The text of the epistle may be found at 29.17

See also chapter 3 General counsel on church affairs

Chapter 3

General counsel on church affairs

INTRODUCTION

3.01 This chapter refers especially to our main meetings for church affairs, and in particular to monthly and preparative meetings. Attendance at these meetings is the right, and indeed the responsibility, of all Friends. The principles governing our Quaker business method, however, are equally relevant to less regular meetings for church affairs held by recognised meetings and to the committees appointed by any of our meetings. Committees should appoint clerks, if this has not been done by the parent meeting, and minutes should be made during the course of each committee meeting. The general advice in this chapter will be helpful in enabling these meetings too to be rightly held.

See also 2.85–2.92

THE SENSE OF THE MEETING

3.02 In our meetings for worship we seek through the stillness to know God's will for ourselves and for the gathered group. Our meetings for church affairs, in which we conduct our business, are also meetings for worship based on silence, and they carry the same expectation that God's guidance can be discerned if we are truly listening together and to each other, and are not blinkered by preconceived opinions. It is this belief that God's will can be recognised through the discipline of silent waiting which distinguishes our decision-making process from the secular idea of consensus. We have a common purpose in seeking God's will through waiting and listening, believing that every activity of life should be subject to divine guidance.

This does not mean that laughter and a sense of humour should be absent from our meetings for church affairs. It does mean that at all times there should be an inward recollection: out of this will spring a right dignity, flexible and free from pomp and formality. We meet together for common worship, for the pastoral care of our membership, for needful administration, for unhurried deliberation on matters of common concern, for testing personal concerns that are brought before us, and to get to know one another better in things that are eternal as in things that are temporal.

3.03   Our meeting communities vary in size and in the circumstances and experience of their members. Sometimes we may need to vary the ways in which we manage our meetings for church affairs in order to make better use of the talents, time and energy of our members. Co-clerkship, for instance, has been beneficial in a number of meetings; sometimes the monthly pattern of business meetings has been varied to good effect. We should be open to learning from the experiments undertaken by other meetings. Being set in an unsatisfactory routine 'because we've always done it this way' may be as detrimental to seeking God's guidance as throwing our traditions to the wind. We are enjoined to live adventurously, but experiment must be grounded in the experience of generations of Friends, which offers us a method, a purpose and principles for the right conduct of our business meetings.

If we sometimes think things are wrong with our meetings for church affairs, it would help us to look at the situation in perspective if we could realise how many troubles arise not from the system, but from our human imperfections and the variety of our temperaments and viewpoints. These meetings are in fact not merely occasions for transacting with proper efficiency the affairs of the church but also opportunities when we can learn to bear and forbear, to practise to one another that love which 'suffereth long and is kind'. Christianity is not only a faith but a community and in our meetings for church affairs we learn what membership of that community involves.

3.04   Our method of conducting our meetings for church affairs is an experience which has been tested over three hundred years. In days of hot contest and bitter controversy the early Friends, knit together by the glorious experience of the Holy Spirit's guidance in all their affairs, came into the simple understanding of how their corporate decisions should be made.

We have learned to eschew lobbying and not to set great store by rhetoric or clever argument. The mere gaining of debating points is found to be unhelpful and alien to the spirit of worship which should govern the rightly ordered meeting. Instead of rising hastily to reply to another, it is better to give time for what has been said to make its own appeal. We must always be ready to give serious, unhurried and truly sympathetic consideration to proposals brought forward from whatever part of the meeting. We should neither be hindered from making experiments by fear or undue caution, nor prompted by novel suggestions to ill-considered courses.

3.05   The right conduct of our meetings for church affairs depends upon all coming to them in an active, seeking spirit, not with minds already made up on a particular course of action, determined to push this through at all costs. But open minds are not empty minds, nor uncritically receptive: the service of the meeting calls for knowledge of facts, often painstakingly acquired, and the ability to estimate their relevance and importance. This demands that we shall be ready to listen to others carefully, without antagonism if they express opinions which are unpleasing to us, but trying always to discern the truth in what they have to offer. It calls, above all, for spiritual sensitivity. If our meetings fail, the failure may well be in those who are ill-prepared to use the method rather than in the inadequacy of the method itself.

It is always to be recognised that, coming together with a variety of temperaments, of background, education and experience, we shall have differing contributions to make to any deliberation. It is no part of Friends' concern for truth that any should be expected to water down a strong conviction or be silent merely for the sake of easy agreement. Nevertheless we are called to honour our testimony that to every one is given a measure of the light, and that it is in the sharing of knowledge, experience and concern that the way towards unity will be found. There is need for understanding loyalty by the meeting as a whole when, after all sides of a subject have been considered, a minute is accepted as representing the discernment of the meeting.

Not all who attend a meeting for church affairs will necessarily speak: those who are silent can help to develop the sense of the meeting if they listen in a spirit of worship.

3.06 The unity we seek depends on the willingness of us all to seek the truth in each other's utterances; on our being open to persuasion; and in the last resort on a willingness to recognise and accept the sense of the meeting as recorded in the minute, knowing that our dissenting views have been heard and considered. We do not vote in our meetings, because we believe that this would emphasise the divisions between differing views and inhibit the process of seeking to know the will of God. We must recognise, however, that a minority view may well continue to exist. When we unite with a minute offered by our clerk, we express, not a sudden agreement of everyone present with the prevailing view, but rather a confidence in our tried and tested way of seeking to recognise God's will. We act as a community, whose members love and trust each other. We should be reluctant to prevent the acceptance of a minute which the general body of Friends present feels to be right.

As a worshipping community, particularly in our preparative and monthly meetings, we have a continuing responsibility to nurture the soil in which unity may be found.

In a meeting rightly held a new way may be discovered which none present had alone perceived and which transcends the differences of the opinions expressed. This is an experience of creative insight, leading to a sense of the meeting which a clerk is often led in a remarkable way to record. Those who have shared this experience will not doubt its reality and the certainty it brings of the immediate rightness of the way for the meeting to take.

3.07 The meeting places upon its clerk a responsibility for spiritual discernment so that he or she may watch the growth of the meeting toward unity and judge the right time to submit the minute, which in its first form may serve to clear the mind of the meeting about the issues which really need its decision. In a gathering held 'in the life' there can come to the clerk a clear and unmistakeable certainty about the moment to submit the minute. This may be a high peak of experience in a meeting for church affairs, but for the most part we have to wrestle with far more humdrum down-to-earth business. It must always be remembered that the final decision about whether the minute represents the sense of the meeting is the responsibility of the meeting itself, not of the clerk.

Sometimes it will be right to leave the decision to a later meeting, but the clerk should bear in mind that this can be the 'lazy' option. Sensitivity is required in recognising when the meeting is really too tired to proceed further. It may be realised that more background work would be beneficial, or that time is needed for everyone to consider the options more carefully. A decision to come back to the subject on a later occasion will then be a positive and important part of the process.

Friends should realise that a decision which is the only one for a particular meeting at a particular time may not be the one which is ultimately seen to be right. There have been many occasions in our Society when a Friend, though maintaining her or his personal convictions, has seen clearly that they were not in harmony with the sense of the meeting and has with loyal grace expressed deference to it. Out of just such a situation, after time for further reflection, an understanding of the Friend's insight has been reached at a later date and has been ultimately accepted by the Society.

We have a responsibility to uphold our clerks in prayer as they try to discern unity in sharply divided meetings. We must not expect to be delivered from differences of opinion – and indeed our life as a religious community would be dull and unprofitable if we were; but we do need to hold firmly to our conviction that divine guidance is there to be found.

PARTICIPATION IN MEETINGS FOR CHURCH AFFAIRS

3.08   Are your meetings for church affairs held in loving dependence upon the spirit of God, and are they vigilant in the discharge of their duties? ... Do you individually take your right share in the attendance and service of these meetings so that the burden may not rest upon a few?

Queries, 1928

3.09   It is not expected that any Friend should attend every meeting or sit upon innumerable committees. Decide what is within your physical and spiritual capacity, and be responsible in your attitude to what you do select. Be as regular, faithful and punctual as possible in your attendance.

All members are entitled to attend their preparative, monthly and general meetings, which are the units of Britain Yearly Meeting's regional organisation, and Yearly Meeting itself. You are encouraged to do so as regularly as you are able, because our business method depends on the widest possible participation by our members. Friends may be appointed to attend monthly and general meetings in order to ensure that enough Friends will be present but this does not excuse or prevent others from being there. It is recommended that those appointed be asked to report back to their own meetings.

When you are appointed to attend a meeting, you attend with local knowledge which may be of assistance: you are not there as a delegate with an inflexible brief to put over on behalf of another body of Friends which is not itself going through the exercise of the meeting.

On taking your seat, try to achieve quietness of mind and spirit. Try to avoid having subcommittees or conversations just as the meeting is about to begin. Turn inwardly to God, praying that the meeting may be guided in the matters before it and that the clerk may be enabled faithfully to discern and record the mind of the meeting.

For regulations on attendance of non-members see 4.05 for monthly meetings, 4.37 for preparative meetings, 5.02 for general meetings, & 6.12 for Britain Yearly Meeting.

3.10   Remember the onerous task laid upon the clerk and do all you can to assist. Submit information about matters to come before the meeting in good time and preferably in writing. Avoid if you possibly can any last-minute messages to the clerk.

Give your whole attention to the matter before the meeting. If you want to speak, try to sum up what you have to say in as few words as possible. Speak simply and audibly, but do not speak for effect. A pause after each contribution will enable what has been said to find its right place in the mind of the meeting. Do not repeat views which you have already expressed. Do not address another Friend across the room but speak to the meeting as a whole. Be ready to submit to the direction of the clerk. Except in very small meetings, those able to stand to speak should do so.

On some matters before the meeting you may feel very strongly. Listen as patiently as you can to all other points of view. Even Friends you consider ill-informed or wrong-headed may make positive or helpful points: watch for them. Do not put into other Friends' mouths things which they did not say. Be certain of your facts. Avoid stating as facts things which are matters of opinion.

Do not take offence because others disagree with you. Be chary of ascribing, even in your mind, unworthy motives to others. Try not to take things personally. Promote the spirit of friendship in the meeting so that Friends may speak their minds freely, confident that they will not be misinterpreted or misunderstood.

Value the meeting as a social occasion. Introduce strangers to one another. Be approachable; be cheerful. If you are an experienced Friend, invite newcomers to come with you. Help them to understand the business and to get to know the membership.

3.11 If, when all that is necessary has been said, the clerk is not ready to submit a minute, uphold those at the table in prayerful silence. If the minute is in general acceptable, do not harass the clerk by raising several minor corrections at once. Do not, under the pretext of altering the minute, raise new matter for discussion or reiterate your original contribution.

CLERKSHIP

3.12 The clerk needs to have a spiritual capacity for discernment and sensitivity to the meeting. In conducting the meeting and drafting minutes on its behalf, the clerk's abilities are strengthened by an awareness of being supported by the members of the meeting. Friends who have not known the unforeseen joy which comes from this experience may gain encouragement from this knowledge, should they be invited to serve. If the clerk's service is under concern in the certainty of God's presence and help in the meeting, then strength beyond her or his normal powers will be given.

The service of the assistant clerk can be of great benefit both to the clerk and to the meeting. The clerk bears the final responsibility for preparing the business, conducting the meeting and drafting the minutes. It is recommended, however, that the assistant clerk be enabled to share in all the clerk's duties as much as possible. Consultation will often help the clerk to come to a right judgment. The assistant clerk will gain experience and maybe the confidence to accept nomination as clerk in due course. Planning for a period of apprenticeship through assistant clerkship can provide for a smooth transition. Some meetings have found that co-clerkship can be highly successful. This may involve two or more Friends, with or without an assistant clerk, and enables Friends' differing abilities and skills to complement each other, particularly when time and energy are at a premium. Such a departure from tradition usually takes place after careful consideration and planning, and can result in a lively and varied interpretation of the clerk's responsibilities.

The following advice to clerks should be seen as being equally relevant to co-clerks and assistant clerks, and to conveners whose responsibilities are similar to those of clerks. (For further information about conveners see 3.21.)

Advice to clerks

3.13   Remember that while you, as clerk, are the servant of the meeting, you do, by your very attitude and your arrangement of the agenda, set the pattern of worshipful listening which should characterise our meetings for church affairs. The meeting is likely to repose great trust in you, and you bear an important responsibility in enabling the meeting to listen and wait for God's guidance in its deliberations. Your experience in the ways of Friends and your understanding of the Quaker business method are very important in helping the meeting to discern God's will and to recognise the way forward. Help Friends to remember that the period of silent worship at the beginning of the meeting prepares for, and opens the way to the consideration of the business; the worship does not finish as the business begins, and the clerks do not shake hands until the close of the business. The meeting has given you a measure of authority which includes an expectation and an acceptance of leadership and firm guidance. At the same time it will usually respond willingly if you find yourself at a loss and ask for help. Above all, it is your responsibility to come with heart and mind prepared.

Do not leave all your preparations to the last minute. Before the meeting discuss the business with your assistant clerk if possible. Check beforehand all facts which may be in question, so as to avoid plunging the whole meeting into fruitless and time-wasting speculation. It will save time in the meeting to bring at least the factual part of your minutes in draft form.

When introducing business into the meeting try briefly to provide sufficient background information to set the meeting purposefully on its course. In the subsequent deliberations you may need to advise on procedure or make a suggestion if none is forthcoming on a routine matter. A very small meeting may wish you to participate on occasion. Remember, however, that your main task is to discern the meeting's united mind and that it may be much harder to do this if you try at the same time to be a participant in the discussion. Be chary, therefore, of making known your own views. You may well find that this very discipline of detachment leads to a new and deeper relationship with the other members of the meeting. If you are deeply involved in a decision to be reached, the meeting should be invited to ask another Friend to act as clerk for the occasion.

3.14   Do not be afraid to ask the meeting to wait while you prepare your minute. You will then usually be able to complete it and have it accepted in that meeting. In some cases you may need to have time for reflection and to bring in a minute after an interval in the meeting.

Make sure that the minute covers all the points on which a decision is required and remember that reference may need to be made to it in the future. Where minutes record the presentation of reports which will be filed with them, it should not usually be necessary to quote the contents at length in the minutes themselves.

You may be required to draft a minute of record concerning a past event, a minute of exercise, which indicates the area and range of the discussion and records the experience or progress of the meeting, or a minute of decision.

Remember that any minute you present is only a draft minute until the meeting has accepted it as its own. If you have drafted alternative decisions, be ready to minute a decision of the meeting which is different from all the possibilities you had in mind. Accept with good grace improvements to your draft made by the meeting. The drafting of a minute is a spiritual exercise. Every clerk needs the full support and attention of the meeting, so that together they may achieve high standards of clarity and accuracy.

3.15 Acceptance of a minute must be a deliberate act. Even if it is not thought necessary to read out the whole of an agreed draft minute again at the moment of acceptance, the meeting must be sufficiently aware of its terms from the preceding exercise to be conscious of uniting to accept it. It is at the moment of accepting each minute that the united meeting allows you to record it as a minute of the meeting. It is good practice for the rough minutes to be signed at the meeting's conclusion. This also gives the clerk authority to sign any fair copy once it is certain it has been correctly transcribed. Very minor amendments such as punctuation and points of style may be made, but any alteration of the sense should be avoided most carefully. It is undesirable that minutes should be prepared afterwards for presentation to a later meeting when the membership may not be the same as that which originally deliberated.

The sending of copies of the relevant minutes to those who are required to take follow-up action after the meeting is the responsibility of the clerk.

You are responsible for the safekeeping of the minutes once the meeting has accepted them. They belong to the meeting, and only the meeting has authority to amend, countermand or supersede them by a subsequent minute. If minor corrections or annotations of a factual nature are necessary, these must be indicated as such in the margins or as footnotes in order to safeguard the integrity of the minutes.

For the safekeeping of records see 4.41-4.43

3.16   Remember that the Friend with particular gifts of judgment is not necessarily the one whose opinion is most needed on all matters; seek to assess the value of individual contributions. Do not forget that the silence of some is often of greater significance than the speech of others.

Be aware, however, that silence does not necessarily mean consent. When conflicting views have been expressed, leave time and opportunity for those who have previously disagreed to indicate whether they are ready to unite with the minute.

When strong division of opinion seems to be threatening the worshipful basis which should prevail in meetings for church affairs, a period of silent and prayerful waiting on the will of God may well have a calming and unifying effect.

3.17   When a Friend accepts an invitation to speak at your meeting, remember your responsibilities towards her or him. Try to ensure that the agenda is arranged to allow adequate scope for the introduction and consideration of the subject at a time when the meeting is not tired or overburdened with other matters. Try also to give the speaker quiet before the meeting, recognising that this service may be costing in nervous energy. If the speaker comes from a distance, be sure to advise her or him about travelling arrangements, including the time and place of arrival, and see that travelling and other expenses are quickly and graciously reimbursed.

3.18   Be careful to maintain a right balance in exercising the authority which the office lays upon you. Use discretion in deciding which matters should be brought before Friends and which may be dealt with by yourself. Beware, however, of the dangers of exceeding your authority in making decisions yourself on matters which should be referred to the meeting. In cases of doubt you may find it helpful to confer with Friends of experience. In the meeting deal courteously but firmly with those who speak at too great length or too frequently stray from the point under discussion. Remember that the right exercise of the clerk's authority is of great service to the meeting in promoting the smooth and expeditious handling of its business.

3.19 In preparing the business for monthly or preparative meeting, you should try to be in regular contact with the various committees of the meeting. It is important that committees report regularly to their parent meeting. It may be possible to save the meeting's time by adequate preliminary discussion. With regard to nominations, for example, you may be able to avoid having to make appointments 'subject to consent'. It is also important that, in minuting appointments, the term of service and the date of termination be clearly stated.

Monthly meeting clerks are advised to be in close touch with elders and overseers, for example, when applications for membership are being considered. More generally, you should be aware of the responsibilities laid upon elders and overseers for the spiritual life of the meeting, for encouraging full participation in meetings for church affairs, and for the right holding of meetings for worship including meetings for church affairs.

Keep a sense of proportion and a sense of humour. Be sensitive to the tempo of the meeting. Do not be over-brisk nor allow matters to drag tediously. Be alert to those who may need encouragement to speak.

3.20 Apart from the preparation and conduct of the business, as clerk you are also responsible for the general administration of the meeting. You need to follow up previously agreed minutes and ensure that tasks undertaken are carried out, that enquiries are dealt with, and that committees are functioning satisfactorily. You may be involved in some committees ex-officio, and by sensitive awareness of the different activities in the meeting, you can help the meeting to function smoothly and steadily. Giving notices and welcoming visitors are important tasks. You need skill in deciding what to include in the notices, and sensitivity to the concerns and interests of members of the meeting.

Think affectionately between meetings of the needs of the community which has appointed you and how they can best be met; ask guidance of God continually in the performance of your task.

Conveners

3.21 The term *convener* is sometimes used as an alternative to *clerk* as, for example, in committees of monthly or preparative meetings, and of elders and overseers, where either term may be used according to local custom and practice. It is often preferred in the case of a group or subcommittee which has been appointed for a task of limited duration and is directly responsible to a more permanent committee or meeting for church affairs. In such a case the convener is expected to perform the functions of a clerk and should conduct meetings of the group in accordance with our Quaker principles and practice.

Alternatively conveners may be appointed in the first instance with the specified responsibility for bringing together the appointed members of a group. It should always be made clear at the outset if this is the intention, since the first job of the convener at the initial meeting will then be to enable the group to appoint a clerk from among its members. When no convener or clerk has been designated, convening the first meeting of a group is by Quaker tradition the responsibility of the Friend named first in the minute setting up the group. It should not be assumed that the convener will necessarily be appointed as clerk.

NOMINATIONS AND APPOINTMENTS

3.22 Now there are varieties of gifts, but the same Spirit; and there are varieties of services, but the same Lord; and there are varieties of activities, but it is the same God who activates all of them in every-one. To each is given the manifestation of the Spirit for the common good. (I Cor 12:4-7)

It is a responsibility of a Christian community to enable its members to discover what their gifts are and to develop and exercise them to the glory of God.

3.23 Much of the work of meetings for church affairs and committees will be undertaken by Friends especially appointed by the meeting or committee responsible for the work, most often on the recommendation of a nominations committee. The process of appointment starts when the meeting identifies the need for a task to be performed. It is good practice for a meeting to have a clear view of the tasks that need to be accomplished on its behalf and to fix the length of service required so that both the meeting and the Friend appointed understand the commitment.

Many of our gifts are latent. A particular appointment may enable one Friend to exercise unsuspected abilities. Other Friends may find themselves overburdened by being appointed to service beyond their capacity and experience. It requires great discernment to know the right moment to ask a particular Friend to undertake or lay down a particular task.

Most appointments should be for either one or three years. It is generally undesirable for someone to hold an appointment for more than six years continuously although there may be exceptions. Meetings should give thought to the training of replacements for existing officers and it will help in this process if those appointed try to give the meeting some notice of wishing to be released from service.

Meetings will differ widely in the appointments they need to make. In some meetings, there may be a shortage of people willing to undertake the work that is needed. In others there may be many who are anxious to serve and some may feel excluded from the busy life of the meeting if not offered appointment. It is important that the whole process be open and clearly understood by all who attend.

3.24 The following suggestions for good practice are intended to apply to all our meetings and committees and to the appointment of Friends and, where appropriate, attenders.

a. In general a nominations procedure should be used when the appointment is to an office in the meeting, or for any other service of importance. Receiving nominations from the body of the meeting is not generally a good method of making appointments.

b. The great responsibility resting on nominations committees and their clerks cannot be too strongly stressed. Nominations committees should be large enough to be representative; impulsive Friends may need to be questioned, whilst the cautious and conservative may need to be encouraged to consider new ideas. The committee needs a balance of experience and age-groups. Members will need to have knowledge of the meeting and be prepared to take pains to understand the qualifications needed for the required appointments. They will need to be clear about the requirements of the office and where appropriate should consult the requesting body. They will also need to be discerning in judgment and tactful in manner. It is important that the members meet in a spirit of worship. Some meetings have found it helpful to survey the gifts of their members in a systematic way.

c. Nominations committees are appointed on behalf of the meeting, and suggestions for their consideration put forward by other members of the meeting may well be helpful to them. Such suggestions are best made directly to members of the nominating group. A nominations committee should act when asked to by its meeting or committee and only in exceptional circumstances on its own initiative.

d. Nominations committees are appointed in many ways. Sometimes names are suggested from the body of the meeting, on other occasions a special committee is asked to bring forward names of Friends to serve on the nominations committee. In some circumstances participating bodies send forward representatives. It is important to ensure openness and to prevent any suggestion of an inner group; thus membership should be for a limited duration. Many meetings retire one third of their nominations committee every year on a rotating basis.

e. A nominations committee should think carefully before bringing forward the name of one of its own members for appointment. Any such nominee should withdraw from the meeting when her or his name is being presented.

f. A nominations committee should meet in a worshipful manner. Committee members will occasionally need to consult each other by telephone, but this should not be the normal means of conducting the committee's business.

g. The nominations committee is not the appointing body and must bring the suggested names to the body for which it acts. Members of this body have the responsibility for approving the names or not and must be given the opportunity to express any doubts they might have. Sometimes it may seem impossible to find someone to serve. Nominations committees should not hesitate to bring their problem back to the meeting to ask for both guidance and practical help.

h. The duration and scope of an appointment should be explained to all who are asked to accept nomination; the approach should not be made casually or acceptance taken for granted. It will be helpful to ask those nominated if they would consent to serve if the meeting required it. When a nominations committee brings forward a name it should not then be necessary to appoint 'subject to consent'. However it is important that it is made absolutely clear that the appointment would be made by the meeting in its discernment and not by the nominations committee. It will be helpful to indicate when the appointment is likely to be made.

i. Those nominated to serve as clerk of a meeting, elder, overseer, treasurer, registering officer or as a member of any nominations committee should be in membership. In case of difficulty the Recording Clerk may be consulted. (For further guidance on the appointment of elders and overseers see 12.07-12.09.)

j. Where two Friends would be expected to work together (e.g. as a clerk and assistant clerk) care should be taken to talk the proposal over informally with them before making any firm approach.

k. When it is decided not to renominate any Friend holding an appointment, care should be taken to convey this information sensitively in person or by letter well before nominations are submitted.

l. Nominations committees should be required to report from time to time on their thinking and their way of working.

3.25 Despite being made prayerfully appointments do not always turn out as planned. It is at the discretion of a meeting to end an appointment at any time if it is necessary to do so. Loving and tender care will be essential. An appointed Friend who finds the service inappropriate should be released.

Responsibility for an appointment does not end when it is made. Having been fully involved in the making of the appointments, the meeting must support and uphold those carrying out the tasks. Some may be disappointed that they themselves were not asked to carry out a particular function; humility and prayerful support for those chosen will be better than a continuing resentment.

Our ability to discern the gifts of others is not perfect and we will recognise an element of God's grace in our deliberations. Be bold; welcome the chance to give opportunities to younger Friends and to those more recently arrived, and encourage those who underestimate their own potential for service.

THE USE OF SMALL GROUPS IN IDENTIFYING NEEDS AND REACHING DECISIONS

3.26   The focus of this chapter has been the working of our Quaker business method through the tried and tested structures of our meetings for church affairs. It is however important to be aware of the contribution that groups other than our meetings for church affairs and their committees can make to our decision-making process. These might include discussion meetings, threshing meetings or meetings for clearness. From time to time a meeting may benefit from looking at itself and identifying specific areas needing attention: pastoral care, outreach, or major changes such as rebuilding or developing premises. The discussion of such matters in small groups, properly constituted, can help to involve the whole meeting and prepare it for decisions which must eventually be taken in the regular meeting for church affairs. Valuable suggestions and solutions may come from individuals who would not feel able to voice them in the more formal meeting. The terms of reference and limits of the group's decision-making responsibility must be made clear at the outset.

For further guidance on the use of small groups see 12.20-12.21; for general guidelines about meetings for clearness see 12.22-12.25; for threshing meetings see 12.26.

For meetings for clearness see also relevant sections:
4.21 on the amicable settlement of disputes;
11.07 in relation to applications for membership;
13.01 on testing personal leadings;
13.08 & 13.11 in the process of discernment of concern;
16.19-16.21 in relation to intentions of marriage.

AUTHORITY FOR PUBLIC STATEMENTS

3.27   Individuals and groups must be careful not to claim to speak for Friends without explicit authority. Any activity or statement made in public which claims to be undertaken in the name of Friends and relating to the corporate life and witness of the Religious Society of Friends must be authorised by the appropriate meeting for church affairs. Any public statement which claims to be given on behalf of Friends in Britain Yearly Meeting as a whole will require the judgment of a more widely representative body than a preparative meeting, monthly meeting or ad-hoc group; it should be considered and agreed by Meeting for Sufferings or by Yearly Meeting before publication. It must be made clear when local initiatives relate solely to local meetings. Similarly, individual Friends or ad-hoc groups should make it clear that they speak only for themselves unless their preparative or monthly meeting has agreed a minute supporting their action.

On occasion it may be necessary for the clerk of a meeting, or another appointed Friend, to take urgent action to correct misleading reports in the press or other misunderstandings in the public domain. This section is not intended to hamper such necessary action undertaken responsibly in the interests of a meeting.

CONCLUSION

3.28   The ensuing chapters contain regulations governing procedure for our various meetings for church affairs. There will inevitably be cases not covered by a particular regulation, and meetings should seek always to appreciate the general principle behind the regulations. Meetings are counselled, however, against too easily admitting exceptions where circumstances do not warrant them, for these regulations are the fruit of the Society's experience in its corporate life. Friends are encouraged to get to know the relevant regulations before taking an active part in meetings for church affairs.

In our meetings for church affairs an effective continuing life can be secured only if there is at least a strong nucleus of Friends attending with regularity, willing to accept responsibility and to give judgments based on informed minds as well as spiritual wisdom. There are few things which tend to destroy interest and loyalty in any business so easily as prolonged and unnecessary discussions on trivia: such discussions are very often provoked and kept up by those who do not trouble to inform themselves adequately of the facts, or who use their occasional attendance to re-open matters already decided. The meeting should expect and encourage its clerk to take firm action in such circumstances.

3.29   There is no justification for wasting precious time in our meetings for church affairs under the excuse or delusion that we may safely do so because it is God's work. But they should be times of enjoyment as well as of hard work, times when we can see old friends and make new ones over tea, when we can be stimulated by other people's ideas and insights as we deliberate together, when we can discover our own gifts and those of other members as we work together. It was said of Gilpin Gregory that 'when his health failed and he was daily seen by his doctor, he would frequently appear at monthly meeting against his doctor's orders and contrary to the advice of his friends, and if remonstrated with he would say, "It does me good; I shall be none the worse for it, and it may be for the last time".' All our meetings for church affairs should be used imaginatively so that they are not 'business' meetings to be attended from duty or neglected with a sense of guilt but real meetings for church affairs which build us up in Christian love – and do us good.

3.30   Keep your meetings in the power of God... And when Friends have finished their business, sit down and wait a while quietly and wait upon the Lord to feel him. And go not beyond the Power, but keep in the Power by which God almighty may be felt among you... For the power of the Lord will work through all, if ... you follow it.

George Fox, 1658

Chapter 4

Monthly meetings and their constituent meetings

MONTHLY MEETINGS

Constitution and functions

4.01   The monthly meeting is the primary meeting for church affairs in Britain Yearly Meeting. It should provide that balance between worship, administration, deliberation, and social life which can make it an enjoyable occasion, building up the spiritual life of its members. The monthly meeting consists of those who are by minute recorded as its members.

4.02   Each monthly meeting shall appoint from its membership a clerk, assistant clerk, treasurer, registering officer (16.10) and nominations committee. It shall appoint a custodian of records or a committee for the purpose (4.41). It may be advisable to appoint an additional assistant clerk to deal with membership matters. Most monthly meetings will also appoint from their membership an appropriate number and distribution of elders and overseers (12.05-12.06). It is important that detailed guidelines be drawn up for the officers appointed by the monthly meeting, so that those who undertake these tasks are fully aware of what is involved. Monthly meeting appointments should be made for a fixed period, generally not more than three years, after which they should be reviewed.

See 3.22-3.25 Nominations and appointments

4.03   The organisation of the monthly meeting will vary, depending on its size. Not all will need to set up a complex committee structure. It is, however, important that certain areas of responsibility be considered carefully. Monthly meeting time can often be used more efficiently if detailed matters can be prepared by a small group.

The meeting should consider whether, in addition to a nominations committee, the following committees are appropriate to its own situation:

> Warden(s) & Premises Committee, where the monthly meeting is the employing body (and see 13.38);
>
> Trust Property (or Finance & Property) Committee, where the monthly meeting owns property (see 15.03-15.05);
>
> Children & Young People's Committee;
>
> Outreach Committee.

The meeting should also consider which matters are appropriately left to the discretion of elders or overseers or the clerks.

4.04   Each monthly meeting shall meet at such frequency, times and places as the meeting itself may direct.

The clerk may arrange for a special monthly meeting to be held if necessary. Such a meeting must be arranged by the clerk if a written request from five members is received. As wide notice as possible of a special monthly meeting should be given in each constituent meeting. Formal notice must be given at the close of each meeting for worship held on the previous Sunday.

4.05   The monthly meeting is open to all members of the meeting. Other Friends should notify their presence to the clerk before the meeting begins and, if drawn to speak, should be sensitive to the fact that it is not their monthly meeting (see also 11.33). Attenders may be present only with permission of the clerk, which should be sought well in advance of the day of meeting. It should be borne in mind that some matters, particularly membership, are confidential and cannot easily be discussed with non-members present.

4.06   Monthly meetings will from time to time have to consider minutes from Yearly Meeting, Meeting for Sufferings or the standing committees through which it works. Other new monthly meeting business will normally come through a preparative meeting or through a monthly meeting committee or a representative of the monthly meeting on another body. It will usually be appropriate for an individual

Friend with a concern to bring that concern to her or his own preparative meeting before approaching the monthly meeting. If the preparative meeting recognises the concern, it should forward a minute to the monthly meeting (see 13.09-13.18).

4.07　The monthly meeting shall keep the following matters under regular review:

a. the right and regular holding of meetings for worship in its constituent meetings (4.38.a);

b. the right ordering of meetings for church affairs within its constituent meetings (4.29-4.32, 4.37, 4.40);

c. the discharge by preparative meetings of their duties (4.38);

d. the appointment and service of elders and overseers; the level and nature of pastoral care in the monthly meeting (12.06, 12.16);

e. the use of *Advices and queries* (1.05-1.07);

f. the maintenance and revision of its official register of members (11.44) and its list of attenders and children not in membership associated with its several meetings for worship (11.45);

g. the revision of the printed list of members, attenders and children not in membership (11.46);

h. the preparation of the annual tabular statement, recording membership changes, marriages and deaths, which is to be forwarded to the Recording Clerk as early as possible in the following year (11.43);

i. the arrangements for forwarding notices of change of address (11.27) and certificates for transfer of membership (11.28-11.32);

j. the proper custody of its records (4.41-4.47) including deeds (15.09);

k. the care of trust property, including the appointment of managing trustees (15.03-15.04) and the right application of capital and income (15.07);

l. the stewardship of financial resources and maintenance of accounts, including those of its committees and its constituent meetings in accordance with the general rules set out in 14.20-14.23 – they must be examined by an independent person (who must satisfy the conditions set out in 14.22) before the annual statement of accounts is considered by the meeting and, if approved, accepted;

m. the supervision (16.11-16.21) and recording (16.51) of marriages according to our usage; the prompt forwarding to the Recording Clerk of the name of any newly appointed registering officer (16.10); any delegation to specific preparative meetings of responsibility for appointing meetings for worship for the solemnisation of marriage (16.27);

n. the provision of advice on funerals (17.07); the appointment of Friends responsible for the arrangement of funerals (17.08); the production and revision of memoranda (17.15) to ensure that a sufficient number of Friends are familiar with the practical arrangements for funerals and memorial meetings in their area (17.14);

o. the supervision and recording of burials (including the interment or scattering of ashes after cremation) in burial grounds belonging to the monthly meeting (15.17, 17.11-17.13); the supervision of the use of gravestones in its burial grounds (15.20); the care of burial grounds (15.10, 15.19); the recording of deaths of members of the monthly meeting (11.47);

p. the maintenance and use of libraries in local meetings (13.40-13.41);

q. the advice to Friends on their outward affairs and the timely making and revision of their wills (4.19);

r. the nomination, where appropriate, in England and Wales, of Quaker prison ministers and the forwarding of their names to the Recording Clerk for submission to the Home Office for appointment (13.48-13.49).

Monthly meetings will, according to particular circumstances, have other areas of responsibility (e.g. local homes for elderly people) and should always keep them under regular review.

Reference should also be made to the following paragraphs concerning other responsibilities of monthly meetings: representation on Meeting for Sufferings (4.14, 7.04-7.06), on representative councils (4.14, 8.12-8.13) and at the Annual Conference of Treasurers (14.16-14.17); attendance at Yearly Meeting (6.09); assistance in the amicable settlement of disputes (4.21); discernment in concern (13.05-13.07 & 13.09-13.18).

4.08   It is important that the monthly meeting give full and prayerful sup-
        port to everyone who is appointed to serve it, whether on its own
        committees, or as a representative on another body, or in an individual
        capacity (see 3.25).

        This is particularly important when the post to be filled involves
        heavy and perhaps lonely responsibility. The roles of registering officer
        (see chapter 16 *Quaker marriage procedure*) and Quaker prison
        minister (13.44-13.51), which both have specialist and legal aspects,
        are good examples, and Friends nominated should be fully aware of
        the responsibilities involved. Monthly meetings are encouraged to
        pay proper attention to the spiritual support and nurture of those
        who give what may be costly although often rewarding service. See
        12.27 for advice on support groups.

Recording and transfer of local meetings

4.09   The monthly meeting shall record by minute any alteration it makes in
        the status of a meeting: recognition, withdrawal of recognition, the
        establishment or discontinuing of a preparative meeting. Copies of such
        minutes shall be forwarded to the Recording Clerk. (See also 4.35.)

4.10   Any transfer of a meeting from one monthly meeting to another,
        including any amalgamation or division of monthly meetings, shall,
        after agreement between the monthly meetings concerned, require
        the sanction of Meeting for Sufferings which shall then inform the
        general meeting(s) concerned.

Pastoral care and outreach

4.11   Each monthly meeting is responsible for nurturing the spiritual
        life of its constituent meetings for worship and for the oversight,
        pastoral care and religious education of people of all ages. See also
        chapter 12 *Caring for one another*. It should consider regularly the
        opportunities available for local outreach and service.

        The potential contribution of meeting house wardens to outreach
        should be borne in mind, particularly when rebuilding and reorgan-
        isation of meeting houses is being considered (see 13.33).

Membership

4.12   Monthly meetings are responsible for membership matters. They
       have the power of admitting new members into the Society and of
       terminating membership, and the duty of keeping the appropriate
       records of membership. (See chapter 11 *Membership*.)

Relationship to other meetings for church affairs

4.13   A monthly meeting shall furnish Yearly Meeting, Meeting for Suf-
       ferings and its general meeting with such nominations or informa-
       tion as may from time to time be required.

4.14   A monthly meeting is required to nominate Friends to serve on Meet-
       ing for Sufferings, the standing representative body of the whole
       yearly meeting (7.04-7.06). This is the main channel of communica-
       tion between monthly meetings and Yearly Meeting, so monthly
       meeting business should give a high priority to preparation of its repres-
       entatives and receiving reports from them. Other opportunities for
       regular involvement with the wider work of Britain Yearly Meeting
       are provided by the appointment of monthly meeting representatives
       to the representative councils of QHS, QSRE and QPS (8.12-8.13).
       The terms of reference of these bodies and the duties of the monthly
       meeting representatives to provide an effective two-way channel of
       communication should be made clear to those being nominated.

4.15   A monthly meeting may communicate formally by minute with its
       constituent meetings, with its general meeting (5.03), with the Meeting
       of Friends in Wales (5.06-5.07) where appropriate, with Yearly
       Meeting (6.04.a, 6.21), with Meeting for Sufferings (7.03) and with
       meetings with which it does business through its representatives
       appointed to joint committees. The monthly meeting has an obliga-
       tion to receive minutes from those bodies. There may occasionally be
       circumstances in which it will be helpful to circulate other minutes
       for information only.

4.16   In considering concerns which their members may bring before
       them, monthly meetings should exercise care to ensure that their

own consideration is adequate and that in forwarding the matter to another meeting they are truly recognising a leading that the subject be considered further. Monthly meetings must beware of evading their own responsibility for reaching a united judgment. This may involve consideration at more than one sitting of the monthly meeting. It might also be wise for a monthly meeting to seek the counsel of its general meeting (5.01) before forwarding a concern to Meeting for Sufferings or Yearly Meeting.

It is essential that before forwarding a concern the monthly meeting should consult at an early stage with the relevant standing committee or department in order to find out what facts and experience can be offered to its consideration of a concern. (See 13.09-13.18.)

4.17   The relationship between monthly meetings, Meeting for Sufferings and its standing committees is delicate and complex.

> If there is sometimes tension in the relationships this is not necessarily unhealthy. It is unhealthy when a matter is shunted from one body to another because a group of Friends lack the spiritual energy and courage to wrestle with a matter which they know may result in uncomfortable plain speaking to a fellow member whose concern, however deeply held, is not shared by the meeting. It is equally unhealthy when any individual or meeting is preoccupied with status, with 'getting things through', with efforts to predetermine how another body shall act. We can only be delivered from these dangers by a constant relearning of the nature of true concern.

> Meeting for Sufferings, 1978

Junior Yearly Meeting

4.18   Monthly meetings have an important relationship with Junior Yearly Meeting, which is the largest national gathering of 16-18-year-old young Friends within Britain Yearly Meeting. This gathering is arranged by QHS (8.07) but is representative of, and its participants financed by, monthly meetings. Most young people have only one opportunity to participate. Being selected as a monthly meeting representative can be a formative and affirming experience, giving these young Friends an opportunity to meet others in their age group and to become more aware of their Quaker identity.

Advice on outward affairs

4.19 Monthly meetings should periodically bring to the attention of members their responsibility for the right ordering of their outward affairs. Such advice on outward affairs has traditionally reminded Friends of the importance of keeping their financial affairs in good order, and of making and revising their wills in time of health. The proper acquisition and use of income, conduct in business and employment and the stewardship of money held for others have also been included, but monthly meetings need not feel themselves limited to these subjects. Monthly meetings also have discretion as to how they discharge this corporate responsibility for advising on individual conduct. Local traditions vary. Some include a regular reminder from overseers in a newsletter, while others address a special letter of counsel on outward affairs to all adult members. Whatever the method preferred, the purpose is the same: to remind members of the monthly meeting of the guidance to be found in our discipline on matters of honesty and integrity (see chapter 20) as they relate to the personal life of every Friend.

Legal action

4.20 Legal action by Friends, and in particular legal disputes between Friends, should if possible be avoided. However, there may arise differences which might best be resolved by obtaining a legal ruling or definition from a court of law. (See 20.67-20.75 *Conflict.*)

Disputes among Friends

4.21 Monthly meetings are recommended to appoint a group of experienced and knowledgeable Friends who would be available to give general assistance in the amicable settlement of disputes. If help from outside the monthly meeting is needed, enquiry should be made of the Clerk of Meeting for Sufferings who may suggest Friends qualified to give it. Techniques of problem-solving, mediation, counselling or meetings for clearness may be appropriate in particular instances where disputants wish to mitigate the consequences of confrontation. It should be borne in mind that Friends were among the pioneers of conflict resolution as a distinct activity and have constantly sought to promote reconciliation in the wider world.

See also 10.21-10.24 Conflict within the meeting *& 20.67-20.75* Conflict.

Right of appeal against decisions

4.22   If a member is dissatisfied with a final decision of a monthly meeting affecting her or him (e.g. if membership has been terminated) and feels that the monthly meeting has acted unjustly, unreasonably or with insufficient knowledge, the member may appeal in writing to Meeting for Sufferings against the decision of the monthly meeting. On receiving such an appeal, the clerk of Meeting for Sufferings shall report this to the monthly meeting and shall request Meeting for Sufferings to appoint five Friends, who should be independent of the monthly meeting concerned, to make all such enquiries as seem to them desirable, from the member concerned and from others having relevant knowledge, to consider and determine whether or not the appeal should be allowed and whether any further recommendations should be made. The decision of the Friends so appointed shall be final: it shall be given in writing to Meeting for Sufferings which shall record the decision in its minutes and communicate it to the parties concerned.

4.23   If a monthly meeting is dissatisfied with a final decision of another monthly meeting, which affects it, the dissatisfied monthly meeting may appeal to Meeting for Sufferings against such decision. The procedure on such an appeal shall be similar to that on an appeal by a member personally, but prior notice shall be given by the dissatisfied monthly meeting to the other monthly meeting concerned before invoking this appeal procedure.

Testimonies concerning deceased Friends

4.24   The possibility of writing a testimony concerning the life and service of a deceased Friend has been a valued part of our tradition. A testimony should not be a formal obituary or eulogy, but should record in thankfulness the power of divine grace in human life.

4.25   *Testimony concerning Hannah Brown (1711?-1779):*

The purpose of a testimony concerning our deceased, worthy Friends [is] intended as a memorial, that they have walked as children of the Light, and of the Day, and to excite those that remain to take diligent heed, and yield obedience to the teachings of the still small voice, that they may follow them as they followed Christ, the great captain of their salvation.

Hertford Monthly Meeting, 1780

4.26   It is the responsibility of the monthly meeting to arrange for the preparation of a testimony, but it is sometimes difficult to be clear during a session of monthly meeting whether a spontaneous request for one is in right ordering. It is suggested that local meetings should write a brief passage for their own records on every member who dies. The writing of a testimony by the monthly meeting should be undertaken on the recommendation of the local meeting or other group such as elders. If a spontaneous suggestion is made during monthly meeting, this should be referred to the local meeting or to a small group for advice. The testimony, when approved by the monthly meeting and signed by its clerk, may be forwarded to the general meeting (see 5.01) or the Meeting of Friends in Wales if appropriate. If the testimony is considered likely to be of benefit to the Society as a whole, it may be forwarded by any of these three meetings to Yearly Meeting. This should not, however, be an automatic decision. Its value as an inspiration to other Friends is not dependent only on its relevance in a wider rather than a local context.

4.27   If a Friend belonged to several monthly meetings during her or his lifetime, it may be appropriate for more than one monthly meeting to contribute to a testimony. Any such meeting should feel free to take the initiative, but should be particularly sensitive to the need to consult beyond its own boundaries. The monthly meetings concerned should agree on which of them should take responsibility for producing the testimony.

It may be right in a few cases for more than one testimony to be written. One or more such testimonies may be from other yearly meetings, in cases where the Friend spent part of her or his life abroad.

PREPARATIVE, RECOGNISED AND NOTIFIED MEETINGS

Definitions

4.28   The monthly meeting may contain a variety of local meetings for worship differing in size and practice. Any group of Friends may meet to worship at any time. The monthly meeting may encourage worshipping groups, as they evolve into distinct meetings for worship, to adopt practical arrangements suited to their local circumstances. For purposes of organisation the meetings for worship within the compass of the monthly meeting are classified as:

Preparative meetings (see 4.29-4.32), which are established meetings for worship, authorised by minute of the monthly meeting, and which conduct their own regular meetings for church affairs;

Recognised meetings (see 4.33), which are also established meetings, authorised by minute of the monthly meeting and holding public worship at least once a month;

Notified meetings (see 4.34), which in some way do not meet the criteria for recognition, but which are nevertheless notified by the monthly meeting to the Recording Clerk.

Each of these meetings is at all times subordinate to its monthly meeting.

Preparative meetings

4.29   Meetings of a certain size and with enough resources will usually be constituted by their monthly meetings as preparative meetings; this is so for the majority of our meetings. Preparative meetings hold a meeting for church affairs before every monthly meeting and it is this preparation that gives them their name. Preparative meetings are expected to undertake certain responsibilities and to fulfil certain functions.

4.30 Some meetings are too small or too recently established to do all that is required of a preparative meeting. Others, which at one time could comfortably sustain a preparative meeting, find that with a shrinking or ageing membership this becomes an encumbrance. They should seek the help of their monthly meeting at an early stage. It may sometimes be right for them to revert to being a recognised meeting, in which case the monthly meeting should assist in an orderly changeover.

4.31 A very large preparative meeting may well unbalance a monthly meeting. Members of such a meeting will need to exercise considerable care with respect to what is preparative meeting and what monthly meeting business. They will need to consider tenderly those in the smaller meetings who may feel distanced from some of the activities of the monthly meeting. Too large a meeting can also cause problems within the meeting itself, with difficulties in pastoral care and in achieving a sense of community. Sometimes when a preparative meeting grows very large it may wish to consider starting a new meeting. Early consultation with the monthly meeting will be in order.

4.32 In a few cases two or more local meetings hold a joint meeting for church affairs. Where this is done regularly, and with the approval of their monthly meeting, these joint meetings for church affairs may be considered to have the same status as those held by a preparative meeting.

On the responsibilities of preparative meetings see 4.37-4.39

Recognised meetings

4.33 Recognition of a meeting, which is by minute of the monthly meeting, gives order to our affairs and enables the monthly meeting to be sure that proper arrangements for worship, pastoral care and financial matters have been made. It is normally given to meetings which have met for at least a year and which hold a public meeting for worship at least once a month. Where a meeting meets these conditions it is encouraged to seek recognition from the monthly meeting in whose area it is held.

Recognised meetings are usually smaller than preparative meetings and so the monthly meeting must take particular care that satisfactory arrangements for eldership, oversight and financial matters are in place. Care should also be taken to preserve links with the monthly meeting and with the wider yearly meeting. Direct assistance from the monthly meeting may be necessary.

On the responsibilities of recognised meetings see 4.40

Notified meetings

4.34   Notified meetings may be listed in the *Book of meetings* for the convenience of Friends, at the request of their monthly meeting. Usually they will in some way not meet the criteria for recognition, perhaps because they meet infrequently. Where such meetings fulfil the criteria for recognition, they are urged to apply for this. They should not be held back from applying for recognition by the mistaken belief that, as recognised meetings for worship, they would have to assume the responsibilities of a preparative meeting.

Sometimes a new meeting will be set up with the encouragement and authority of the monthly meeting. At other times an informal worshipping group may be seeking to become an established meeting. The monthly meeting may well decide to notify such meetings to the Recording Clerk for inclusion in the *Book of meetings*. However such meetings are urged to apply for recognition as soon as the conditions for recognition can be met and monthly meetings are likewise urged to assist in this process.

Changes of status

4.35   Making any change of status is the prerogative of the monthly meeting. All such changes should be recorded in minutes of the monthly meeting and the Recording Clerk informed. If one of its constituent meetings ceases to be a preparative meeting, the monthly meeting must ensure that adequate arrangements are in place for continuing eldership and oversight and for dealing with financial matters (4.33). Sometimes it is necessary to lay a meeting down. This too is the responsibility of the monthly meeting. (See 4.41 *Records*.)

Changes of address

4.36 Much needless work can be saved if all meetings will notify changes of address of meeting officers to the Recording Clerk.

Responsibilities

Preparative meetings

4.37 The membership of a preparative meeting consists of those on the monthly meeting list of members who are attached to that meeting. The meeting for church affairs should be held when most people can attend, non-members attending by permission of the clerk. Most preparative meetings will encourage regular attenders at meeting for worship to participate on suitable occasions. Friends in membership of other meetings may be present, but should notify their presence to the clerk before the meeting begins, and, if drawn to speak, should be sensitive to the fact that it is not their preparative meeting.

Preparative meetings are at all times subordinate to their monthly meeting.

Much helpful advice and experience in exercising the care of the worshipping community is found in chapter 10 *Belonging to a Quaker meeting* and in chapter 12 *Caring for one another*. All members should be familiar both with these parts of our discipline and with chapter 3 *General counsel on church affairs*.

4.38 Preparative meetings differ greatly in size. Thus the scope of work undertaken will vary. The following is a list of responsibilities:

a. to make arrangements for the regular holding of public meetings for worship, which will normally be held at least once a week. Suitable premises will need to be arranged. The monthly meeting must be kept informed of the time at which meeting for worship is held;

b. to use *Advices and queries* (1.05-1.07);

c. to nurture and sustain the spiritual life of the meeting and the pastoral care of those associated with it; to take a special responsibility for the children within its care and for their parents. The continuing religious education of all, including regular attenders as well as members, should be of real concern to the meeting; the welcoming of newcomers is of particular importance;

d. to conduct all its own business and to ensure, by appointment or otherwise, an attendance of local Friends at the monthly meeting (see 10.06); Friends are encouraged to attend monthly meeting and to take a full part in its activities;

e. to make sure that the financial needs of the meeting and the yearly meeting are properly understood by its members and that channels exist for giving in a convenient way. Accounts must be kept in accordance with the general rules set out in 14.20-14.23; they must be examined by an independent person (who must satisfy the conditions set out in 14.22) before the annual statement of accounts is considered by the meeting and, if approved, accepted;

f. to prepare such statistics, returns and reports as are required;

g. to preserve certain records (see 4.42);

h. to consider local outreach; advertising, in conjunction with the monthly meeting, times and places of meetings in the local press and arranging an entry in the telephone directory are a suggested minimum; enquirers should be helped to explore and understand the Society;

i. to appoint correspondents (see 8.14) to QHS, QSRE, QPS and to other bodies as appropriate;

j. to maintain a library and to encourage the reading of Quaker publications;

k. to form links with other churches and faith communities in the area and where possible jointly to undertake service in the community (see 9.14-9.20);

l. to seek to exert a Christian influence in the neighbourhood both as a meeting and in co-operation with others.

A preparative meeting has a duty to report to its monthly meeting on the discharge of its responsibilities.

4.39   For a meeting to carry out its duties and other activities certain appointments will need to be made (see 3.22-3.25 *Nominations and appointments*). The meeting must at least appoint a clerk and a treasurer. A list of those appointments most generally found helpful follows:

a clerk and probably an assistant clerk (3.12-3.20);
a treasurer (13.42-13.43);
a nominations committee;
a premises committee;
doorkeepers;
a children's committee;
a librarian (13.40);
correspondents (4.38.i);
Friends responsible for hospitality and domestic arrangements.

Whilst elders and overseers are appointed by the monthly meeting, much of their service will be within the framework of the local meeting (see 12.06).

Some meetings will have wardens or resident Friends (see 13.32-13.39). Our dealings with those we employ or who live on our premises need care and knowledge.

On other aspects of preparative meetings see 4.29-4.32

Recognised meetings

4.40   Because these meetings are not required to hold regular meetings for church affairs their arrangements may vary according to local circumstances. The monthly meeting should ensure that a convener or clerk is appointed.

In some cases a nearby preparative meeting may take some responsibility for the recognised meeting, acting supportively and encouraging the members of the recognised meeting to take part in its meetings for church affairs. Alternatively the recognised meeting may prefer to have direct dealings with the monthly meeting.

The convener or clerk will keep contact with the clerk of the monthly meeting, handle correspondence and try to see that the members of the meeting do not become distanced from our larger organisation merely because of the status of their own meeting.

A recognised meeting may wish to hold a meeting for church affairs. The convener or clerk should be sensitive to the need for this and be prepared to take the initiative in convening such a meeting.

If a recognised meeting wishes to become a preparative meeting it should apply to the monthly meeting after consulting its supporting meeting if appropriate.

On other aspects of recognised meetings see 4.33

RECORDS

4.41 Monthly and general meetings should appoint a Friend to act as a custodian of their records, or else appoint a committee for the purpose. Monthly meetings should take responsibility for the records of their constituent meetings, ensuring their timely transfer to the custodian of records. They are advised in particular to ensure that the records of any local meeting which has been laid down are collected together. The Library Committee issues notes of guidance for clerks and custodians on the creation, care and custody of records.

4.42 It is advised that the following be preserved in Friends' ownership:

a. minute books of yearly, general, monthly and preparative meetings;

b. minute books of elders and overseers and of standing committees of meetings for church affairs;

c. official registers of members (11.44), printed lists of members and attenders (11.46), marriage registers (16.45), registers of burials (17.12), burial ground plans (15.17), registers of properties and trusts (15.09);

d. such other documents as it is reasonable to expect may be needed for future reference.

The custodian should maintain a full catalogue of records whether kept in meeting house safes or strongrooms elsewhere, and it is advised that monthly meetings should check the contents at least triennially.

4.43   The attention of monthly and general meetings is drawn to the many advantages of depositing older records with an appropriate national, county or municipal record office. Records not in current use, particularly those more than fifty years old, should be considered for deposit on loan. Such documents, deposited under suitable conditions, remain the property of the monthly or general meeting concerned, while benefiting from the care of professional archivists.

4.44   It is the responsibility of monthly meetings to decide which records shall be available to students, whether Friend or non-Friend, and to stipulate the conditions for their release. Many meetings make available records more than fifty years old, subject to exceptions where particular discretion is needed (e.g. overseers' minutes).

4.45   Meetings have sometimes been approached by an outside body and offered the opportunity to put old records on microfilm. This may be primarily for the benefit of those making the offer. The monthly meeting is responsible for deciding whether it would also be of benefit to the meeting and is strongly advised to seek guidance from the Library Committee (see 4.41). The Library Committee (8.20) should be kept informed of decisions made so that the relevant experience may be shared with other monthly meetings.

4.46   Meetings requiring advice or information on the handling of their records are encouraged to get in touch with the Library Committee; they are reminded that it maintains a central catalogue of local meeting records, and that it should be notified of any change in the place where they are deposited.

4.47   Meetings storing information about their members on computers or other electronic devices will be sensitive to the need to protect such information from unauthorised use and must comply with all legal requirements for data protection. Information on achieving this can be obtained from the Recording Clerk.

Chapter 5

General meetings

CONSTITUTION AND FUNCTIONS

5.01 A general meeting shall consist of all Friends who are members of its constituent monthly meetings.

Any transfer of a monthly meeting from one general meeting to another, including any amalgamation or division of general meetings, shall, after agreement between the monthly and general meetings concerned, require the sanction of Meeting for Sufferings which shall inform the meetings concerned.

The main purpose of the general meeting is for conference and inspiration, and for a broad oversight of the life and witness of the Society within its area, considering regularly what is being done and what might be done to extend the service of its members and to reach out to those who are in need of spiritual guidance and friendship (see 12.06). General meetings can also provide an opportunity for those with special responsibilities, such as clerks, treasurers, elders and overseers, to meet for training and mutual support. It is hoped that general meetings will consider making appropriate provision for children and young people when planning their programme. Some make such provision through summer schools as well as during general meeting sessions. General meetings must keep under regular review the well-being of schools and other institutions in their care.

General meetings should find opportunity for consideration of the central work of the yearly meeting, carried out by Meeting for Sufferings through standing committees and departments, and of topics which are under discussion in the Society. Monthly meetings are encouraged to refer to them matters which in their judgment merit wider interchange of view. (See also 4.16.) These matters may include testimonies concerning the life and service of deceased Friends who were members of the general meeting. If a testimony is considered likely to be of benefit to the Society as a whole, it should be forwarded to Yearly Meeting (see 4.24-4.27).

5.02 A general meeting shall appoint from its membership a clerk or clerks and such other officers as may be necessary. Appointments should be made for a fixed period, generally not more than three years, after which they should be reviewed. Alternatively, if preferred, a representative committee may be set up (as under 5.04) to conduct the business of the general meeting, with suitable arrangements made for clerkship at the table.

A general meeting shall meet at such frequency, times and places as it shall determine. It may be desirable to appoint an arrangements committee, representative of the monthly meetings, to have charge of the agenda and arrangements. A general meeting may, at its discretion, allow those not in membership to be present.

5.03 A general meeting may communicate formally by minute with its constituent monthly meetings, with Yearly Meeting (6.21), with Meeting for Sufferings (7.03), and with meetings with which it does business through its representatives appointed to joint committees. The general meeting has an obligation to receive minutes from those bodies. Occasionally there may be circumstances in which it will be helpful to circulate minutes for information. It shall furnish Yearly Meeting or Meeting for Sufferings with such nominations or information as may from time to time be required.

5.04 General meetings as legal entities must remain in existence so that they continue to discharge trusts and other responsibilities. Any general meeting may, however, discontinue holding regular sessions if in its considered judgment and that of its constituent monthly meetings such sessions are thought likely to serve no useful purpose. If its meetings are to be held less frequently than once a year, Meeting for Sufferings shall be informed and a representative committee shall be set up jointly by the constituent monthly meetings to be responsible for the conduct of necessary business, including nominations and appointments. It shall also be responsible for the holding of occasional, or the resumption of regular, sessions of the general meeting should changed circumstances warrant it.

Reference should also be made to 4.41-4.47 Records

SCOTLAND

5.05 The General Meeting for Scotland, although subordinate to Britain Yearly Meeting, acts on behalf of Friends in Scotland in such procedures as may be required by the Scottish legal system, in particular the timely notification of registering officers, on appointment, to the Registrar General for Scotland (16.10); and in dealings with relevant government departments. In this latter regard, the General Meeting for Scotland will be responsible for the nomination of Friends to the Scottish Office, for example to the Scottish Office Home and Health Department for appointment to Scottish prisons as Quaker prison chaplains (13.45). The General Meeting for Scotland acts on behalf of Britain Yearly Meeting in relation to ACTS: Action of Churches Together in Scotland (9.09-9.12).

WALES

5.06 The Meeting of Friends in Wales is not a general meeting a described in 5.01 and does not supplant those general meeting which include parts of Wales. It consists of all Friends who are members in preparative, recognised and notified meetings within Wales other Friends may attend on the same basis as 4.05 prescribes for th attendance at a monthly meeting of Friends who are not members o that monthly meeting. Those not in membership may attend at th clerk's discretion. It has national responsibilities on behalf of Britai Yearly Meeting within Wales. Meeting for Sufferings has laid specifi responsibilities upon it as follows:

    a. representing Britain Yearly Meeting in Wales, including th appointment of Friends to serve on CYTUN and its commi tees (see 9.09-9.12), and in dealings with the Welsh Office an other public and voluntary bodies;

b. facilitating contact between Friends in Wales, including sharing the responsibilities outlined in 5.01 with the general meetings which include parts of Wales;

c. outreach in Wales, including commissioning, translating and publishing Quaker material in the Welsh language, speaking for Friends in Wales where there is a specific Welsh view to be expressed and acting as a reconciler on issues affecting the Religious Society of Friends in Wales and generally within Welsh society;

d. maintaining links with peace organisations which have a particular Welsh interest or orientation, and giving consideration to social issues which have a special bearing on life in Wales, and to the needs of a bilingual society;

e. representing Wales to Britain Yearly Meeting, liaising with yearly meeting committees and departments where appropriate.

The Meeting of Friends in Wales may communicate by minute with Britain Yearly Meeting and its agenda committee, Meeting for Sufferings, the standing committees of the yearly meeting and of Meeting for Sufferings as well as the general meetings which include parts of Wales and their monthly meetings.

The following is a translation into Welsh of 5.06

CYMRU

5.07 Nid yw Cyfarfod y Cyfeillion yng Nghymru yn gyfarfod cyffredinol fel ac y diffinir hwy yn 5.01 ac nid yw'n disodli y cyfarfodydd cyffredinol sy'n cynnwys rhannau o Gymru. Fe gynhwysa yr holl Gyfeillion sydd yn aelodau yng nghyfarfodydd darparol, cydnabyddedig a hysbysiedig o fewn Cymru; gall Cyfeillion eraill fynychu yn unol a 4.05 sy'n pennu presenoldeb mewn cyfarfodydd misol o'r Cyfeillion hynny nad ydynt yn aelodau o'r cyfarfod misol hwnnw. Gall y rhai nad ydynt yn aelodau fynychu ar awdurdod y clerc. O fewn Cymru, mae ganddo gyfrifoldebau cenedlaethol ar ran Cyfarfod Blynyddol Prydain. Gosododd y Cyfarfod Dioddefiannau gyfrifoldebau penodol arno fel a ganlyn:

a. cynrychioli Cyfarfod Blynyddol Prydain o fewn Cymru, gan gynnwys penodi Cyfeillion i weithredu ar CYTUN a'i bwyllgorau (gweler 9.09-9.12), ac mewn perthynas a'r Swyddfa Gymreig a chyrff cyhoeddus a gwirfoddol eraill;

b. hwyluso cysylltiad rhwng y Cyfeillion sydd yng Nghymru, gan gynnwys rhannu'r cyfrifoldebau amlinellir yn 5.01 gyda chyfarfodydd cyffredinol sy'n cynnwys rhannau o Gymru;

c. cyffwrdd ag eraill o fewn Cymru, gan gynnwys comisiynu, cyfieithu a chyhoeddi yn y Gymraeg ddeunydd Crynwrol, siarad ar ran Cyfeillion yng Nghymru lle mae angen datgan llais penodol Cymreig, a gweithredu fel cymodwr ar faterion sydd yn effeithio ar Gymdeithas Grefyddol y Cyfeillion o fewn Cymru ac yn gyffredinol o fewn y gymdeithas Gymreig;

ch. cadw cysylltiad gyda chyrff heddwch sydd, diddordeb neu ogwydd penodol Cymreig, a rhoi sylw i faterion cymdeithasol sydd o bwys arbennig i fywyd yng Nghymru, ac i anghenion cymdeithas ddwyieithog;

d. cynrychioli Cymru i Gyfarfod Blynyddol Prydain, gan gysylltu, phwyllgorau ac adrannau y cyfarfod blynyddol fel sydd addas.

Gall Cyfarfod y Cyfeillion yng Nghymru gysylltu trwy gofnod a Chyfarfod Blynyddol Prydain a'i bwyllgor agenda, Cyfarfod Dioddefiannau, pwyllgorau sefydlog y cyfarfod blynyddol a Chyfarfod Dioddefiannau ynghyd â'r cyfarfodydd cyffredinol sy'n cynnwys rhannau o Gymru a'u cyfarfodydd misol.

Chapter 6

Yearly Meeting

HISTORY

6.01   Our yearly meeting grew out of a series of conferences of ministering Friends, some regional, some national. We may think of that at Swannington in 1654 or Balby in 1656 (the postscript to whose lengthy letter of counsel is so much better known than the letter itself) or Skipton the same year, or the general meeting for the whole nation held at Beckerings Park, the Bedfordshire home of John Crook, for three days in May 1658, and attended by several thousand Friends. This in some ways might be considered the first yearly meeting were it not for the fact that the 1660s, through persecution and pestilence, saw breaks in annual continuity. The meeting in May 1668 was followed by one at Christmastime, which lasted into 1669, since when the series has been unbroken. 1668, therefore, we have traditionally chosen as the date of establishment of London Yearly Meeting. But many (though not all) of the meetings up to 1677 were select, that is, confined to 'publick' (or ministering) Friends: from 1678 they were representative rather than select in character. Minutes are preserved from 1672.

The life of the yearly meeting centred until the mid-nineteenth century on the quarterly meeting answers to the queries and the 'Epistles Foreign and Domestick'. Epistles and travelling ministers between them made the Atlantic community of Friends a reality; smuggling in Cornwall or dissension in Nantucket received equal thought and attention. The education of Friends' children was a recurring theme, and with the establishment of Ackworth (1779) and Sidcot (1808) the reports of boarding schools made increasing claims on the time of the Meeting. The answers (more and more stereotyped) to the queries, lengthy reports and other documents read aloud, the long-winded Friends, the narrow range of interest and minutiae of procedure – all must on occasion have been stifling to the rebels. 'And now for about an hour', wrote a young Friend in 1858, 'the YM talked to points of order. When 5 or 6 courses are mentioned and a good many friends speak to each, it does not seem difficult to spend an hour or more in this way.' 'It is difficult', he added charitably, 'to see how this is altogether to be avoided.'

In fact, however, Yearly Meeting was probably seldom as parochial as the cautious minutes show, and even they point to certain outstanding sessions – the 1783 one on the slave trade, for instance; or that in 1818 on capital punishment. Yearly Meeting was not merely preoccupied with introspective consideration of the state of the Society: it sought to awaken the public conscience. A statement in 1856 on liberty of conscience was translated into half a dozen languages and taken by deputations of concerned Friends to ecclesiastics and statesmen from Madrid to St Petersburg. Petitions to parliament and memorials to the monarch covered a wide range of concern. When in 1842 Caroline Fox with her brother and father called on Carlyle, 'he wanted to know what we were doing at the Yearly Meeting, and what were its objects and functions, and remarked on the deepening observable amongst Friends; but when we told of the letter to the Queen recommendatory of peace in Afghanistan, he was terribly amused. "Poor little Queen! She'd be glad enough to live in peace and quietness if the Afghans would but submit to her conditions".'

'Every Quakeress', wrote Charles Lamb, 'is a lily; and when they come up in bands to their Whitsun-conferences, whitening the easterly streets of the metropolis, from all parts of the United Kingdom, they show like troops of the Shining Ones.' Women Friends had from the seventeenth century taken opportunity during the men's Yearly Meeting to confer together, but it was not until 1784 that a Women's Yearly Meeting was established, with the right to communicate with women's quarterly meetings. From the 1880s some joint sessions of men and women Friends were held, and in 1896 Yearly Meeting decided that 'in future women Friends are to be recognised as forming a constituent part of all our meetings for church affairs equally with their brethren'. Some separate sessions still continued but the Women's Yearly Meeting was laid down in 1907.

After the yearly meeting was constituted on a representative basis in 1678 ministering Friends, and later, elders, found occasion to meet with members of the Second Day Morning Meeting (the weekly gathering of 'ministering Friends in and about the city') at the beginning and the close of Yearly Meeting. This gathering, therefore, assumed a measure of national authority – it issued, for instance, in 1702 'A brief memorial of some necessary things' which was the basis of the advices on ministry – and in 1754 it was constituted as the Yearly Meeting of Ministers & Elders. In 1876 the meeting was enlarged in membership and re-named the Yearly Meeting on Ministry & Oversight, but as part of the egalitarian movement of the late nineteenth century it was decided to discontinue the separate hierarchy of preparative, monthly and quarterly meetings on ministry and oversight, and, in consequence, the Yearly Meeting on Ministry & Oversight last met in 1906. Elders and overseers subsequently met separately for conference.

Until as recently as 1861 Yearly Meeting was in theory composed only of representatives, together with 'such ministering Friends as may be in town, and the correspondents or members of the Meeting for Sufferings'. From the mid-eighteenth century (if not earlier) the doors were in fact open to any man Friend, and much business was in consequence referred to the Large Committee, which was confined to those constitutionally entitled to be there. When at length the Yearly Meeting sessions were opened to all men Friends as a right there was one, at least, who took a mournful view. 'The Yearly Meeting', he wrote, 'will become less and less of a *religious*, and more and more of a merely *popular*, assembly. The fruit of its deliberations, even at its best, will be liable to fall, in an unripe state, as "untimely figs", by a want of constancy and settlement in the *root of life*. There is, besides, great cause to dread, *that the talkative, unstable part in man, which should be silent in the churches, will presume to speak therein with increasing boldness,* bringing forth confusion.'

Whether or not we feel Daniel Pickard's predictions have been justified, we can indeed be thankful that in almost every generation there has been a Right Holding of Yearly Meeting Committee, though the exact title may have varied from one occasion to another. Such a group has the opportunity of deciding whether we need to direct our attention to constitutional change, or to the shortcomings of our human nature. In 1902 John Wilhelm Rowntree and Edward Worsdell applied their minds to the conduct of Yearly Meeting with devastating remarks: 'Discussion confused and futile', 'discussion disproportionate and prolix', 'a demonstration not a conference'. It was two years before this outburst that the first memorandum of agenda had been issued, and it had been agreed to print some reports in advance.

In 1905 Yearly Meeting was held for the first time out of London. Meeting at Leeds it received at its opening session a message from the venerable patriarch J Bevan Braithwaite, who after sixty-four years of unbroken attendance, felt the journey inadvisable. 'Coming together as we do', wrote the Yearly Meeting in its response, 'amid such new surroundings, the thought of the faithful lives of service which have been given in the past to the work of our Society comes with peculiar power and helpfulness to us, and as we listened to thy letter and thought of the long years in which thou wast present during the sittings of the yearly meeting, the desire arose that we might be more faithful in giving ourselves to the work.' We too may re-echo the desire that we may be inspired by those who have gone before us in our yearly meeting but not fettered by their procedures.

In 1994 London Yearly Meeting agreed to change its name to the Yearly Meeting of the Religious Society of Friends (Quakers) in Britain, or in short form, Britain Yearly Meeting. This decision followed a recommendation by Meeting for Sufferings after a consultation with monthly meetings. The new name was chosen to express the identity of the yearly meeting in a more inclusive way, so that friends who were physically distant from London could feel more fully part of the whole. It also reflects more accurately the geographical area which is covered: England, Scotland, Wales, the Channel Islands and the Isle of Man. The new name came into effect on 1 January 1995.

PURPOSE AND FUNCTION

6.02   We did conclude among ourselves to settle a meeting, to see one another's faces, and open our hearts one to another in the Truth of God once a year, as formerly it used to be.

Yearly Meeting in London, 1668

6.03　The intent and holy design of our annual assemblies, in their first constitution, were for a great and weighty oversight and Christian care of the affairs of the churches pertaining to our holy profession and Christian communion; that good order, true love, unity and concord may be faithfully followed and maintained among all of us.

Yearly Meeting in London, 1718

6.04　Yearly Meeting is an occasion when the concerns of one group of Friends or another can be shared with the meeting as a whole, as it seeks God's guidance and relates each particular insight or service to the others brought before it. At different stages of its history its agenda and pattern have been built up in different ways. There was a time when the main exercise related to 'the state of the Society' as revealed by the answers to the queries or, after written replies were discontinued, by triennial reports from quarterly meetings. The twentieth century witnessed a considerable growth in the standing committees of the yearly meeting and increasingly the agenda of Yearly Meeting was built up round their concerns. An Agenda Committee (6.15) is charged with the duty of considering and deciding upon the business to be transacted by the Yearly Meeting. The agenda may comprise:

a. minutes from monthly or general meetings and minutes or memoranda from standing committees of Meeting for Sufferings sharing with the yearly meeting as a whole some concern which has their united support;

b. a summary of the proceedings of Meeting for Sufferings during the year together with such reports as it may forward from committees on their work;

c. epistles received from other yearly meetings, reminding us of our membership in a world family of Friends;

d. subjects initiated by the Agenda Committee (6.15).

6.05　In the course of reflecting on his experience as secretary from 1940 to 1945 of Friends War Victims Relief Committee and Friends Relief Service, Roger Wilson wrote in 1949:

Yearly Meeting is not, in the last resort, made up of a body of experts. People who know a great deal about the matter in hand may do most of the talking, central committee members familiar with the complexities of translating convictions into practical terms may appear to be leading the meeting. But a few halting yet sincere hesitations, uttered by a Friend from a small meeting in a distant county may, in fact, be of more significance in revealing a matter in its true setting than all the sophistication of the committee worthies. Again and again on deep issues it is reality as known and experienced by the simple and single-minded meeting, that does not know too much to have lost its simple faith, that guides the Society; and the central committee or its administrator who knows that its service is, in the end, related to the life of the local meetings in the country, will have a deep respect for the weight of Yearly Meeting.

6.06   No organisation or planning can produce a good Yearly Meeting if those who attend come for an inadequate reason. When the Religious Society of Friends gathers for its annual assembly, it does so because it seeks to come to know the mind of God on the various affairs to be brought forward... We are ordinary people, with the shortcomings of ordinary people, and there is laid upon us the necessity of patience with one another in all our gatherings, and especially in Yearly Meeting, and the willingness to accept the imperfect arising from our human limitations. When therefore we find our Yearly Meeting falling short of the standard which it should reach, whether in worship or in deliberation, it behoves each of us to listen more intently for the voice of the Spirit, and to seek the more earnestly that every contribution, be it by spoken word or in silence, is that which is in accord with the divine leading. In our worship at Yearly Meeting, it is laid upon us with special weight to listen. It is not our ministry that is required in worship, nor our inspiration in deliberations, but we seek to hear the true word of God speaking through our frail humanity and leading us to the place where he would have us be. This is the right holding of Yearly Meeting.

Right Holding of Yearly Meeting Committee, 1960

6.07   *The service and counsel of John Morland (1837-1934):*

His attendance at Yearly Meeting was increasingly prized, and his personality felt to be a permeating influence. To the last his judgment retained its acuteness. How frequently in a few trenchant sentences he has cut through a problem or re-stated confused issues... The precepts laid down by him whilst clerk of Yearly Meeting (1899-1903) were scrupulously observed by himself: 'Do not speak without a sense of the imperative ought; speak audibly, not loudly but clearly; speak shortly.'

Testimony of Mid-Somerset Monthly Meeting, 1934

6.08 *Mary Hughes (1860-1941) comes with heart and mind prepared:*

Anyone who lived with her during April and May knew how intensely Friends' Yearly Meeting was on her mind. It was as important to her as 'going up to Jerusalem'. For weeks beforehand it came into her prayers in the morning, at meal times and with friends. She wished that God's power would be in the meetings, that people would go forth from them with a new vision of God's work for them, a new sensitiveness towards their fellows, especially the distressed.

Rosa Hobhouse, 1949

CONSTITUTION

6.09 Britain Yearly Meeting in session is the final constitutional authority of the Religious Society of Friends in England, Scotland*, Wales†, the Channel Islands and the Isle of Man. Its membership consists of all those who belong to the several monthly meetings in Great Britain, the Channel Islands and the Isle of Man. All members of the yearly meeting have the right to attend and to take part in its deliberations. In order to provide for a due attendance, each monthly meeting is to ensure that a sufficient number of Friends will undertake to be present. Public statements to be made in the name of the Religious Society of Friends in Great Britain, the Channel Islands

---

* On the responsibilities of the General Meeting for Scotland see 5.05.
† On the responsibilities of the Meeting of Friends in Wales see 5.06-5.07.

and the Isle of Man must be authorised by Britain Yearly Meeting or by Meeting for Sufferings (3.27).

Clerks

6.10 The Yearly Meeting shall at its first session appoint, on the nomination of the Committee on Clerks (6.16), a clerk and two assistant clerks. The clerks shall hold office until the first session of the ensuing Yearly Meeting.

Visiting Friends

6.11 Members of the Society not belonging to Britain Yearly Meeting may attend the sessions of the Yearly Meeting on producing a minute o letter of introduction signed by the clerk of their own meeting o otherwise satisfying the clerk of their membership.

Permission to non-members

6.12 Permission for the attendance of non-members at one or more ses sions may be given at the discretion of the clerk, if satisfied that thei presence is likely to be of service to the Yearly Meeting. Such pe mission should be sought well in advance of Yearly Meeting an should be supported by one or more elders to whom the applicant well known. Last-minute requests should not be made.

Time of meeting

6.13 Yearly Meeting shall normally meet in May, but approximately on meeting in four shall be held residentially in the summer. The dat and places at which Yearly Meeting is to be held shall be determin by Meeting for Sufferings on the recommendation of the Year Meeting Agenda Committee. Meeting for Sufferings shall have t power to summon a Special Yearly Meeting.

Yearly Meeting committees

6.14 Work in the intervals of Yearly Meeting is normally entrusted to Meeting for Sufferings, but the following committees are appointed in whole or in part by Yearly Meeting, for continuing work after its conclusion: Agenda Committee, Committee on Clerks.

In order to facilitate the business of Yearly Meeting the following committees shall be appointed at an early session: Nominations Committee, Epistle Drafting Committee, Committee to Examine Minutes. The service of these committees ceases at the close of Yearly Meeting, save only in the case of the nominations committee which shall serve until the first session of the ensuing Yearly Meeting. Additionally Yearly Meeting may appoint, on the nomination of Yearly Meeting Nominations Committee, at an early session two Friends to serve on the Arrangements Committee for the period of Yearly Meeting.

Agenda Committee

6.15 The planning of the agenda for, and the use of the premises during, Yearly Meeting shall be in the hands of the Yearly Meeting Agenda Committee, which shall consult as may be necessary with standing committees, general and monthly meetings, and the Meeting of Friends in Wales. The membership of the Agenda Committee shall be as follows:

   a. the clerk and assistant clerks of Yearly Meeting;
   b. nine Friends appointed by Yearly Meeting for a three-year period on the recommendation of its nominations committee, one third retiring annually though eligible for re-appointment;
   c. nine Friends appointed by Meeting for Sufferings for a three-year period on the recommendation of its nominations committee, one third retiring annually though eligible for re-appointment;
   d. [deleted]
   e. [deleted]
   f. one Friend appointed by Yearly Meeting for a three-year period on the recommendation of Children & Young People's Committee of Quaker Home Service.

The Agenda Committee shall

g. appoint such subcommittees of its members as are from time to time required;

h. appoint annually three or more of its members to serve on the Arrangements Committee;

i. nominate annually Friends to serve as an Epistle Drafting Committee.

Committee on Clerks

6.16 The Committee on Clerks nominates annually to the Yearly Meeting a clerk and two assistant clerks. The Committee on Clerks shall comprise thirteen Friends. Twelve of these shall be appointed by Yearly Meeting on the recommendation of its nominations committee and one (the clerk) on the recommendation of the retiring Committee on Clerks. The committee shall serve for a three-year period. Not fewer than four nor more than six of those retiring shall be nominated for the next ensuing period. No Friend shall serve for more than six continuous years unless one of the twelve appointed members should become clerk, in which case he or she may serve for a maximum of nine continuous years on the committee.

Every third year Yearly Meeting shall instruct its nominations committee to bring to the next ensuing Yearly Meeting the names of twelve Friends to serve on the Committee on Clerks for the three-year period beginning at that Yearly Meeting. The names are to be in the hands of the Recording Clerk in sufficient time for printing in *Documents in advance*.

Arrangements Committee

6.17 The Agenda Committee shall appoint annually three or more of its members who shall, with the clerk and assistant clerks of Yearly Meeting, serve as an Arrangements Committee. Yearly Meeting may at an early session appoint, on the nomination of Yearly Meeting Nominations Committee, two further Friends to serve on this committee for the period of Yearly Meeting.

The Arrangements Committee shall act on behalf of the Agenda Committee between meetings. It shall consider any alterations which may appear to be required in the agenda whether before or during Yearly Meeting, any application received too late for consideration by the Agenda Committee for the use of the premises during Yearly Meeting, and any questions referred to it for the better ordering of the Yearly Meeting. It shall decide which testimonies concerning deceased Friends and epistles from yearly meetings and other Friends' bodies are to be read in the sessions.

Nominations Committee

6.18   The Yearly Meeting shall at its first session appoint some six to eight Friends as a standing nominations committee for any special purposes during the course of the Yearly Meeting, to serve until the beginning of the following Yearly Meeting. The Nominations Committee shall bring forward nominations as requested, and in particular three Friends to serve on the Agenda Committee for the ensuing three years, up to two additional Friends to serve on the Arrangements Committee for the period of the Yearly Meeting, and, every third year, twelve Friends to serve on the Committee on Clerks for the three-year period beginning at that Yearly Meeting. It shall also nominate Friends to fill any vacancies that may have arisen in the Yearly Meeting appointments on these committees. The committee shall also nominate to the Yearly Meeting in which it was appointed a Friend, preferably from among its own members, to serve as clerk of the Nominations Committee of the next ensuing Yearly Meeting.

Epistle Drafting Committee

6.19   The Yearly Meeting shall at its first session appoint, on the nomination of the Agenda Committee, an Epistle Drafting Committee, of which one member shall be named as convener. Yearly Meeting shall, at an appropriate stage in its deliberations, offer guidance on the content of the epistle. The draft of the epistle shall be made available to Friends for written comment and shall be submitted to Yearly Meeting for approval, normally at the beginning of the final session. The epistle as approved shall be read in the concluding session of Yearly Meeting and signed by the clerk.

Committee to Examine Minutes

6.20 The Yearly Meeting shall at its first session appoint not more than ten Friends, who shall arrange a rota whereby two of their number shall examine the minutes of the meeting at the close of each session and correct any slight inaccuracies that may be found. If any substantial alterations appear to be required they are to be proposed at the next session prior to any other business.

Documents

6.21 Any communication to the Yearly Meeting from a general or monthly meeting or the Meeting of Friends in Wales shall be in the form of a minute signed by the clerk of such meeting.

The Agenda Committee, in arranging the subjects to be brought before Yearly Meeting, is encouraged to ask standing committees and general or monthly meetings to express their concerns in concise but lucid memoranda which can be printed as *Documents in advance* and circulated in ample time to allow not only for individual study but for discussion in local meetings. Material should be in the hands of the Recording Clerk in good time for the information of and consideration by the Agenda Committee.

The summary of proceedings of Meeting for Sufferings, together with the reports of its several committees, shall be published, also in advance of Yearly Meeting, as the *Annual report of Meeting for Sufferings and its committees*.

This document, while presented to Yearly Meeting for approval, is a general survey of the work done in the course of the year in the name of Britain Yearly Meeting. It is therefore commended to the attention not merely of those attending Yearly Meeting but of all members of the yearly meeting.

The *Documents in advance* and *Annual report,* together with the *Report and accounts of the Yearly Meeting Fund,* the epistles received from other yearly meetings, testimonies concerning deceased Friends and the printed *Minutes* of Yearly Meeting, form its *Proceedings.*

Chapter 7

Meeting for Sufferings

HISTORY

7.01   The yearly meeting's local organisation was settled in the years 1667-9. The 1670s saw the development of central organisation. Apart from Yearly Meeting (1668), three bodies deserve special mention – the Six Weeks Meeting (1671), Morning Meeting (1673) and Meeting for Sufferings (1675). All were basically meetings of London Friends; all, to a greater or less extent, undertook national responsibilities. The Six Weeks Meeting was the most metropolitan of the three, though even it engaged on occasion in such national business as the wording of the marriage certificate. The Morning Meeting may have had its origin in the 'meeting of ancient Friends' said to have started about 1656 or the general meeting of ministering Friends in and about the city, established in 1661. It comprised men 'publick' (or ministering) Friends in and about the city, and when, later, elders were appointed, men elders became eligible for membership of the Morning Meeting, which met each Monday.

It was the Morning Meeting which took the initiative in calling a conference in October 1675 to consider what steps could be taken to secure redress from sufferings. At that meeting it was agreed 'that certaine friends of this Citty be heere nominated to keep a Constant Meeting about Sufferings 4 times a year, with the day and time of each meeting here fixed and setled'. Twelve Friends, two from each of the London monthly meetings, were then listed with 'as many as are free of the Second dayes morning meeting of publick Friends to meet togeather as aforesaid', and that 'at least one friend of each County be appointed by the quarterly meeting thereof to be in ready-ness to repaire to any of the same meetings at this Citty, at such times as theire urgent occasions or sufferings shall require'. The constitution of Meeting for Sufferings agreed by Yearly Meeting 1702 was set forth as: 'Publick Friends and such that are appointed or approved by the severall Quarterly Meetings of the Countyes & other Countrys that Correspond with this meeting in all Places, and are entred as such in the Correspondent Book.'

The full Meeting for Sufferings was to meet at the beginning of each law term and one quarter of the membership was to meet weekly (each Friday) until the next full meeting. The minutes begin on 22 June 1676. At the outset some eight to ten Friends attended the weekly meetings and the speed with which, backed by information from the quarterly meeting correspondents, the meeting was able to put Friends' case to good effect before members of both Houses of Parliament is indeed impressive. The meeting was not restricted to the efforts to obtain redress in particular 'Cases of Suffering' (though this was the first item in the minutes until about 1750). Yearly Meeting entrusted it with the task of trying to obtain relief from the oath, in which it was successful under the Affirmation Acts of the late seventeenth and early eighteenth centuries. Yearly Meeting likewise asked it to try to secure a reduction of the burden suffered under tithes, which the meeting attempted by the promotion of successive Quakers Tithe Bills in the 1730s. It was the same closely-knit relationship of county quarterly meeting correspondents and London members of Meeting for Sufferings that enabled Friends to campaign with such success in the movement towards the abolition of the slave trade. Meeting for Sufferings, meeting weekly (as it continued to do until 1798), was able with great effect to carry out Yearly Meeting's instructions. So swift and smooth had its organisation become that it would be tempting to describe it as highly efficient parliamentary lobbying. Although it was primarily a London body its effective correspondent system enabled it to speak with an authoritative national voice.

The nineteenth century saw a steady increase in the work of Meeting for Sufferings and a corresponding growth of its committees. The Parliamentary Committee had existed from the early eighteenth century. The Slave Trade Committee of 1783-92 was followed by other and more permanent committees – the 1817 Minden & Pyrmont Committee became the Continental Committee, serving for over 100 years as a link between Friends in Great Britain and small groups on the continent of Europe, in Australasia, in Calcutta, southern Africa and other places; the administrative committees charged with the care of the premises and with printing were supplemented by others responsible for the library and for finance; other committees took up particular concerns of Friends – several undertook successive efforts at relief work, an anti-slavery committee was re-established, in 1888 the Peace Committee was formed, and subsequent committees were set up to express Friends' views on the opium traffic and on betting and gambling.

Alongside this steadily widening stream of interests, the constitution of the meeting was changing. The era of railway travel made it increasingly easy for Friends to attend, and the system of London and country correspondents gave place to that of quarterly meeting representatives. This was reflected in revised constitutions of 1856 and 1883. In 1884 the meeting had an appointed membership of 98 with representatives from all but six quarterly meetings. In 1898 (following a decision of Yearly Meeting 1896) the first women Friends took their seats in Meeting for Sufferings. Anna Littleboy, one of those then appointed recalled thirty years later that 'while kindly and courteously received, it was evident that the presence of women was not exactly welcomed by most of the older members, and the clerk impressed upon them that the meeting was for the conduct of business and not for speeches'.

Perhaps a more drastic change than the admission of women Friends was the laying down in 1901 of the Morning Meeting and the transference of its functions to Meeting for Sufferings. Henceforward the consideration of personal concerns for service overseas and the welcoming of travelling Friends from other yearly meetings was added to already increasing business. Preoccupation with relief work, and still greater growth of the range of Friends' concern added to the length of agenda. The days of the meeting which began at 11 o'clock and was over by a late lunch-time had passed.

The twentieth century therefore witnessed a steady trend of delegation of routine matters to subcommittees, but it also saw a gradual growth in the meeting's function in drawing together and relating to one another the different strands in the yearly meeting's life and service. This process was helped as some of the nineteenth-century 'independent associations' (the Friends Foreign Mission Association and the Friends Tract Association for example) became or were merged with official committees of the yearly meeting, gradually accepting the responsibilities and discipline that this involved. It also became increasingly clear that the distinction between committees of Yearly Meeting and Meeting for Sufferings had outlived its usefulness, and Special Yearly Meeting 1965 agreed that all standing committees should be appointed by Meeting for Sufferings which, in periodic review of their work, would be enabled 'to become more sensitive to the insights of the committees and thus ... promote that knowledge and understanding by means of which both the meeting and the committees should be able more effectively to enter into and to discharge their responsibilities'.

The additional tasks laid on Meeting for Sufferings as 'a central body which can act on behalf of the Society between Yearly Meetings' necessitated, in the words of Special Yearly Meeting 1965, that 'such a body must be representative of Friends both geographically and as to diversity of our membership'. This led to representation from monthly meetings rather than quarterly meetings, to three-year appointments rather than annual, to a change in the day of meeting from Friday to Saturday and, in 1974, to the withdrawal of the automatic right of elders to attend. In furtherance of 'the essential unity of the work undertaken in the name of the Yearly Meeting', staff employed by the Yearly Meeting and by seven separate employing committees were unified and became employees of Meeting for Sufferings. The anomaly remained that while the yearly meeting's essential central services were funded by means of a 'quota' contributed by monthly meetings, standing committees were issuing separate financial appeals which had the effect of competing one with another. The financing of all the central work was unified between 1986 and 1988, placing further responsibility on Meeting for Sufferings for the testing of concern and for the allocation of available resources to the wide variety of religious service undertaken in the name of the yearly meeting.

Thus, albeit in different circumstances, Meeting for Sufferings attempts to fulfil its functions as defined by Yearly Meeting 1833: 'A standing committee of this meeting ... entrusted with a general care of whatever may arise during the intervals of this meeting, affecting our religious society and requiring immediate attention'.

FUNCTIONS

7.02 Meeting for Sufferings is the standing representative body entrusted with the general care of matters affecting Britain Yearly Meeting. Within our church government it deliberates, it makes decisions and it oversees their implementation. The summary of proceedings of

Meeting for Sufferings, which records decisions reached by the meeting and trends in its thinking, is before Yearly Meeting each year for receipt and acceptance.

Meeting for Sufferings informs Yearly Meeting of the structure of standing committees through which it works. Within that framework Meeting for Sufferings appoints committee members, and may appoint new committees from time to time. It may not alter, without the approval of Yearly Meeting, the existence or basic functions of Quaker Home Service, Quaker Peace & Service or Quaker Social Responsibility & Education, which were established by a minute of Yearly Meeting 1976.

The committees and departments, through which Meeting for Sufferings works, shall furnish annual reports on their work and also occasional reports, as requested by the meeting from time to time, on their policy and stewardship. They are reminded of their accountability to the meeting, which they must consult in any of the following circumstances:

a. when proposing to enter upon some major new field of service, or to give up some significant long-term project;
b. when proposing to make some new pronouncement or envisaging a new relationship which involves some important question of principle for Britain Yearly Meeting;
c. when considering major appeals or commitments;
d. when it seems desirable to share with Friends the interpretation of some urgent need or of some unusually significant piece of service;
e. when some concern impinges on the work of other committees or aspects of the yearly meeting's wider work.

Meeting for Sufferings shall determine the dates of Yearly Meeting and where it shall be held (see 6.13). It may summon a Special Yearly Meeting should occasion arise.

7.03 Monthly and general meetings, the Meeting of Friends in Wales and committees of Meeting for Sufferings may communicate with the meeting by minute signed by or on behalf of their clerk. Such meetings or committees may request that Friends other than members of Meeting for Sufferings be allowed to speak to such minutes.

Reference should also be made to the following regulations concerning other responsibilities of Meeting for Sufferings:

3.27, authority for public statements;
4.10, area changes of monthly meetings;
4.16-4.17 & 13.13, concerns;
4.21, assistance to monthly meetings in the amicable settlement of disputes;
4.22-4.23, appeals against monthly meeting decisions;
5.04, discontinuance of regular sessions of general meetings;
6.04.b & 6.21, summary of proceedings for Yearly Meeting;
13.15-13.18, authorisation for religious service away from home;
13.27, minutes of liberation and travelling minutes;
14.12-14.15, estimates, finance and the Yearly Meeting Fund;
16.54, printing and publication of marriage forms.

CONSTITUTION

7.04   Meeting for Sufferings shall comprise the following:

    a. about 170 Friends appointed by the Yearly Meeting on the nomination of monthly meetings (7.06), in accordance with the schedule provided (7.05), serving for triennial periods from Yearly Meetings 1994, 1997, etc;

    b. Friends appointed by the Yearly Meeting on the nomination of certain standing committees of Meeting for Sufferings (7.07), being officers or other named representatives, in accordance with the following schedule:

Quaker Communications Central Committee	2
Quaker Finance & Property Central Committee	2
Quaker Home Service Central Committee	2
Quaker Peace & Service Central Committee	2
Quaker Resources for Service Central Committee	2
Quaker Social Responsibility & Education Central Committee	2
Quaker Committee for Christian & Interfaith Relations	1
Quaker World Relations Committee	1

c. two representatives appointed by the Yearly Meeting on the nomination of Young Friends General Meeting, being officers or others able to speak in the name of YFGM;

d. the clerk and assistant clerk of Meeting for Sufferings, any previous clerk and assistant clerk of the meeting during the remainder of the triennial period in which their service ends, the clerk of Yearly Meeting, and the clerk of Meeting for Sufferings Committee, ex officio;

e. up to ten Friends co-opted by the meeting itself (7.08), the appointments ending at the close of each triennial period;

with the Recording Clerk, the Assistant Recording Clerk, members of the Management Meeting (8.23) and any other staff appointed directly by Meeting for Sufferings, ex officio (see 7.09).

In case of vacancy by death or resignation under (a), (b) or (c) above, the nominating body may forward to Meeting for Sufferings for appointment the name of a Friend to serve for the remainder of the triennial period. Such appointments shall be subject to confirmation by the ensuing Yearly Meeting.

Meeting for Sufferings shall regularly inform the Yearly Meeting of all changes in its membership under (d) and (e) above.

Permission for the attendance of other Friends at a particular meeting may be given at the discretion of the clerk of Meeting for Sufferings.

Monthly meeting representatives

7.05 Each monthly meeting shall make two nominations from its membership for appointment to Meeting for Sufferings. Additional nominations shall be made by larger monthly meetings in accordance with a schedule approved by the Yearly Meeting one year before each triennial appointment, modified as necessary by interim decisions necessitated by the division or amalgamation of monthly meetings. The schedule shall provide for one additional representative for every 300 members or part thereof in excess of 300 (see 7.04.a).

Advice to monthly meetings as to nominations

7.06 In nominating Friends to serve on Meeting for Sufferings, monthly meetings are reminded of the variety and weight of the business which comes before that meeting, which must have the spiritual authority to speak in the name of the yearly meeting.

A responsible sharing in the exercise of the meeting is essential. Britain Yearly Meeting requires Friends to serve on its behalf who are diligent within their own areas in the attendance of meetings both for worship and for church affairs, and able if occasion arises sensitively to interpret the views and judgment of their own monthly meetings to Meeting for Sufferings.

More important, however, is the duty of members to the meeting itself; if it is to reach right judgments it must be served by Friends of spiritual maturity and with a good grasp of our testimonies and structures.

Monthly meetings are therefore encouraged to nominate representatives who are well versed in Friends' business methods through participation at local level. In making nominations monthly meetings should bear in mind the need to balance experience and continuity with the value of fresh insight and wider involvement of the membership of the yearly meeting, and the importance of reporting back as part of the communication between Meeting for Sufferings and monthly meetings.

Committee representatives

7.07 In order that the meeting may have immediately available to it authoritative information about the thinking or action of any of its principal committees which may appear to have a bearing on any subject under consideration, the said committees are asked to ensure that there is a regular attendance of their representatives.

Co-options

7.08 To secure or to retain the service of able and knowledgeable Friends, without disturbing local arrangements for selecting representatives,

Meeting for Sufferings is empowered to co-opt up to ten Friends (see 7.04.e).

Participation of staff in Meeting for Sufferings

7.09 Members of the Management Meeting and other staff attending Meeting for Sufferings (see 7.04) are present in order to be able to provide Meeting for Sufferings with information about their departments and their work, and in order for them to be able to interpret and carry out the decisions of the meeting more effectively.

They are not managing trustees of the Yearly Meeting and are not responsible for the decisions of Meeting for Sufferings.

However, Friends' understanding of the Quaker business method is that God may speak to us through anyone present. Meeting for Sufferings therefore welcomes the full participation of the designated staff in its worship and deliberations.

Meeting for Sufferings, 1994, 1998

Time of meeting

7.10 Meeting for Sufferings shall normally be held on the first Saturday in each month. It may vary its date of meeting as need arises. It has the power to omit meetings. The clerk shall have the power to call a special meeting and at least seven days' notice shall be given to all members of the meeting.

Clerks

7.11 Meeting for Sufferings shall annually appoint Friends to serve as clerk and assistant clerk.

Chapter 8

Committees and departments

INTRODUCTION

8.01 Britain Yearly Meeting in session is the body with ultimate authority for church affairs for Quakers in Britain. The term 'Britain Yearly Meeting' refers also to the combination of the seventy or so monthly meetings that make up the Religious Society of Friends in Britain, and it may be used as well in referring to the work carried out centrally on behalf of the membership. This work is overseen by committees with membership drawn from Friends throughout Britain.

8.02 There are four aspects to the central work of Britain Yearly Meeting:

a. organising and maintaining the yearly meeting itself as responsive to the leadings of the Holy Spirit; this entails calling, briefing and running decision-making meetings with all the facilities necessary for them to work efficiently and effectively, and also conducting relations with other churches and faiths and ecumenical bodies;

b. supporting Friends in their local organisation, by providing services and advice relevant to the current demands of the Quaker community: for example such work may relate to children, elderly people, those getting married, those looking after meeting houses, and those raising funds;

c. raising awareness and developing understanding within and without Britain Yearly Meeting about the basic tenets of Quaker faith and practice, such as spirituality, peace and human rights;

d. putting Quaker thinking into practice in relation to the problems and needs of people at home and abroad: for example through training, conferences, work with those in positions of power, and social and development projects.

8.03 The work of Yearly Meeting and Meeting for Sufferings (see chapters 6 and 7) is in large part carried out by several committees appointed by and responsible to those bodies.

These committees are of two main types. Standing committees are long-term bodies, established for an unlimited duration, whilst ad hoc committees may be set up for a specific purpose as occasion requires and are usually expected to complete their task by a set date. (See also 7.02.)

Most of the work of Meeting for Sufferings is undertaken by standing committees. Six of these are the central committees (see below), which oversee the work of the departments, largely based at Friends House, on behalf of Meeting for Sufferings. There are also a few other standing committees which report directly to Meeting for Sufferings, and these are listed below. The standing committees may delegate certain work to functional committees, and other ad hoc committees or groups may be placed under the umbrella of its standing committees by Meeting for Sufferings. Committees appointed in whole or in part by Yearly Meeting in session are described in chapter 6.

8.04 The diagram shows the committee structure of the yearly meeting at the beginning of 1998 indicating the lines of communication between units. The committee structure has evolved over the life of the Society in Britain, and its organisation reflects the varying degrees of autonomy and the different purposes inherited through this process.

THE SIX CENTRAL COMMITTEES

It is unlikely that the work of the central committees, as described here, will remain unchanged for the next generation. The existence and basic functions of Quaker Home Service, Quaker Peace & Service and Quaker Social Responsibility & Education may not be altered except with the approval of Yearly Meeting (see 7.02) but the more detailed outline of the work of the committees described below may change more frequently according to the emphasis given by the central committees and Meeting for Sufferings. The sections that follow indicate the balance of work at the beginning of 1998.

8.05 **Quaker Communications** exists to support and strengthen local meetings and the yearly meeting as a whole. It does this by helping

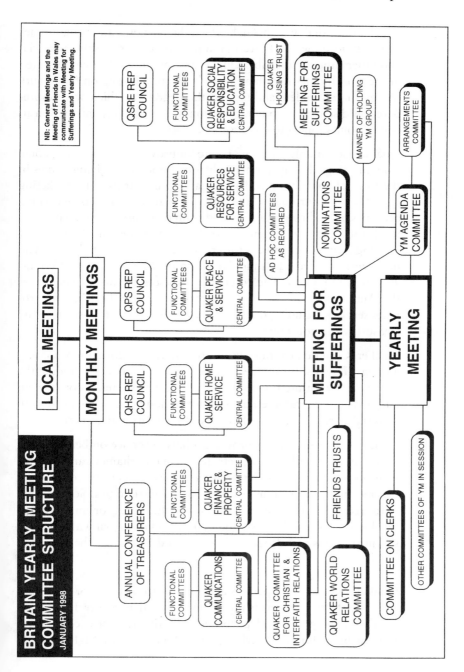

BRITAIN YEARLY MEETING
COMMITTEE STRUCTURE
JANUARY 1998

LOCAL MEETINGS

MONTHLY MEETINGS

MEETING FOR SUFFERINGS

YEARLY MEETING

NB: General Meetings and the Meeting of Friends in Wales may communicate with Meeting for Sufferings and Yearly Meeting.

QSRE REP COUNCIL

FUNCTIONAL COMMITTEES

QUAKER SOCIAL RESPONSIBILITY & EDUCATION
CENTRAL COMMITTEE

QUAKER HOUSING TRUST

MEETING FOR SUFFERINGS COMMITTEE

MANNER OF HOLDING YM GROUP

ARRANGEMENTS COMMITTEE

FUNCTIONAL COMMITTEES

QUAKER RESOURCES FOR SERVICE
CENTRAL COMMITTEE

AD HOC COMMITTEES AS REQUIRED

NOMINATIONS COMMITTEE

YM AGENDA COMMITTEE

QPS REP COUNCIL

FUNCTIONAL COMMITTEES

QUAKER PEACE & SERVICE
CENTRAL COMMITTEE

QHS REP COUNCIL

FUNCTIONAL COMMITTEES

QUAKER HOME SERVICE
CENTRAL COMMITTEE

FRIENDS TRUSTS

ANNUAL CONFERENCE OF TREASURERS

FUNCTIONAL COMMITTEES

QUAKER FINANCE & PROPERTY
CENTRAL COMMITTEE

FUNCTIONAL COMMITTEES

QUAKER COMMUNICATIONS
CENTRAL COMMITTEE

QUAKER COMMITTEE FOR CHRISTIAN & INTERFAITH RELATIONS

QUAKER WORLD RELATIONS COMMITTEE

COMMITTEE ON CLERKS

OTHER COMMITTEES OF YM IN SESSION

to promote a dialogue through which the purposes and programmes of yearly meeting work are developed. It seeks to secure financial and other support to enable Quaker testimonies to be demonstrated in the world: our strength as a yearly meeting resting on the quality of our shared understanding and the degree to which we are prepared in discussion, voluntary action and financial contribution to commit our support to common purposes.

Quaker Communications works to improve and monitor income from meetings, Friends, other individuals and grant-giving bodies in the form of contributions, legacies and grants. It uses its marketing expertise to contribute to the effective planning of income-earning activities, including publishing and conference provision. It sponsors work on legacy development (14.10) and on behalf of the yearly meeting it makes proposals for grant aid to appropriate bodies who may wish to provide funds to support Meeting for Sufferings' approved initiatives. The committee oversees the arrangements for the Annual Conference of Treasurers (see 14.16-14.17), and provides services including the annual schedule (14.08) to assist meeting treasurers and collectors.

Quaker Communications works to improve information sharing amongst Friends. It provides a wide variety of services including the provision of printed material (leaflets, newsletters, books etc); audio-visual programmes; use of information technology; exhibition materials; arranging of conferences, study visits and gatherings.

Quaker Communications provides a liaison service on behalf of the yearly meeting with press, electronic media, parliament and government departments. This work gives witness to current concerns of our meetings and to our historic Quaker testimonies. Some of the work requires partnership with relevant European or international Quaker bodies. Quaker testimonies may lead us to join with others in seeking reforms and also sometimes to stand out against the fashion of the day.

8.06 **Quaker Finance & Property** is accountable to Meeting for Sufferings for the effective stewardship of finance and property for Britain Yearly Meeting's central purposes. The financial service involves responsibility for the Yearly Meeting Fund (see 14.12-14.15) and any associated funds, administration of the Meeting Houses Funds (15.15), receipt and oversight of any special funds given to Britain Yearly Meeting and advice on financial and investment policy. The clerk of the committee is appointed directly by Meeting for Sufferings.

The committee ensures that the accounts of the Yearly Meeting and associated funds are properly prepared, and presents them to Meeting for Sufferings (see also chapter 14 *Finance*). It also undertakes financial resource planning, for which it prepares forecasts and guidelines. Quaker Finance & Property manages the property owned and used by Britain Yearly Meeting and provides advice to local meetings.

For Friends Trusts Ltd see 15.02

8.07 **Quaker Home Service** exists to support and strengthen the life of local meetings, the individuals within them and the yearly meeting as a whole. The ultimate strength of the Society rests to a considerable degree on the quality of spiritual life and pastoral care in its local meetings, and their ability to reach out and welcome enquirers.

The responsibilities of QHS can be summarised under three headings of sustaining the fabric of Quaker life, deepening the spiritual life of Friends and meetings, and promoting outreach at local and national level. These are not ends in themselves, but means of helping to deepen our experience of God's grace and its consequent expression in our lives, whether inwardly or outwardly, individually or corporately. This work is carried out mainly through the empowerment of Friends individually and within their meetings.

QHS offers support, training and the promotion of good practice to those working with children and young people in meetings. The holding of Junior Yearly Meeting is an important part of its work. Together with Woodbrooke, and through Charney Manor and Swarthmoor Hall, Quaker Home Service encourages adult religious learning. The Library Committee (see 8.20) is a functional committee of Quaker Home Service.

QHS offers opportunities for support and learning to those with special responsibilities in meetings, for example elders, overseers, clerks and wardens. It helps develop local and regional networks for pastoral care and the handling of queries and crises. Quaker literature for Friends and for those wishing to learn more about the Society is selected, commissioned and published, and distributed through the Quaker Bookshop. Outreach is promoted by advertising, exhibitions, posters, leaflets and response to enquirers at national level. Regional work is facilitated, and resources developed to help Friends undertake outreach locally and give attenders a deeper and wider view of the Society. QHS encourages awareness of our heritage, particularly through visits to places of historic Quaker interest.

8.08 **Quaker Peace & Service** works with and on behalf of Friends in Britain Yearly Meeting, in association with the Yearly Meeting of Friends in Ireland (see 8.11 and 8.13), where aspects of international affairs and service can best be dealt with centrally. The primary function of QPS is work for peace and against violence. This work is based on faithfulness to the Quaker peace testimony, and our belief that there is that of God in everyone. It entails helping to build the institutions of peace at all levels, from neighbourhood to international. It also involves: changing attitudes and policies concerning violence and weapons of war; encouraging the use of nonviolent alternatives; promoting human rights; and enabling Quakers to witness in ways which include taking action as peacemakers, advocates or reconcilers, discreetly or openly, as appropriate.

In support of this primary function QPS works for peaceful socioeconomic change against poverty and injustice. It advocates human development in harmony with nature, provides a framework of support and discernment for concerned Friends and others to engage in practical activities in areas of conflict, and channels small amounts of material assistance.

QPS seeks ways to identify and give experience to the next generation of Quaker workers, as well as promoting the two-way communication between QPS and Friends who are concerned to act locally or global issues.

The work of QPS is a corporate expression of our experience that the Holy Spirit moves people as individuals and groups to serve and learn from their fellow human beings and to promote peace.

8.09 **Quaker Resources for Service** is entrusted with providing the people and technical resources on which the whole of the yearly meeting's central work relies, within the context of Quaker testimonies to truth, equality, simplicity and peace. It is responsible for personnel and office services and the Friends House restaurant.

The committee maintains and develops policies to enable Britain Yearly Meeting to be a good and effective employer through the recruitment and development of staff. Emphasis is put on the development of a supportive working community in accordance with Quaker values, and on consultation with recognised staff representatives in a spirit of partnership and shared aspirations for the work of the yearly meeting.

The committee helps enable Friends to realise their concerns for personal service in the corporate work of the yearly meeting, including by nominated and other forms of service. The committee co-ordinates nominations procedures for those committees reporting to Meeting for Sufferings, and is responsible for the servicing of Meeting for Sufferings Nominations Committee (see 8.19).

QRS works to ensure that staff and service project workers are provided with the resources, support and development opportunities that will enable them to carry out the work of the yearly meeting effectively. It supplies support services, including information technology, and office and reception facilities, in as creative and cost-effective a manner as possible, and is responsible for ensuring a safe working environment. The committee is also responsible for the occupancy arrangements for the staff employed by Meeting for Sufferings.

8.10 **Quaker Social Responsibility & Education** exists to strengthen Friends' conviction that our spiritual understanding demands expression in society. It encourages exploration of our social testimony as an integral part of our faith. It supports Friends' individual and corporate concerns in meetings, and helps Britain Yearly Meeting to come to an informed judgment about new corporate concerns as well as fostering those which are already recognised. The more deeply we live out our faith, the more surely that faith will be nurtured.

QSRE's purpose is to draw local experience into a whole: the daily experience of Friends must be the foundation of corporate leadings. It provides advice and information to enable Friends to study and pursue religious insights on social and educational questions. Its committees and groups assist Friends to share experience and understanding of particular concerns, supporting or setting up networks and issuing newsletters. It organises practical social projects as opportunities for Quaker corporate witness in local communities.

Concerns are fostered by gathering groups of Friends across the yearly meeting to exchange experience, researching the latest information and reflecting on the spiritual dimensions of the issue. Much of this work is then shared more widely with individual Friends and meetings; some of the insights gained in this work for justice, for truth and for reconciliation are more widely disseminated and are conveyed to government and other institutions. Where appropriate, QSRE joins in or supports work which is carried out ecumenically or by other national and regional organisations.

Constitutions of central committees

8.11   Central committees are accountable to Meeting for Sufferings for the formulation and presentation of policy and for their departments' work, and for budgeting and financial control in consultation with Meeting for Sufferings Committee. Each committee establishes functional committees as required and reviews their work. Each is responsible for establishing an effective nominations committee, working closely with Meeting for Sufferings' nominations committee as appropriate. Each committee is responsible for bringing matters to Meeting for Sufferings and for taking matters referred by Meeting for Sufferings either for consideration with an appropriate representative council (if relevant) or for urgent attention and action.

Quaker Communications, Quaker Finance & Property, Quaker Home Service, Quaker Peace & Service, Quaker Resources for Service and Quaker Social Responsibility & Education each has a central committee, working to terms of reference approved by Meeting for Sufferings. There are between 10 and 25 members serving on each committee, appointed by Meeting for Sufferings on a triennial basis, with any re-appointment subject to a maximum service of three consecutive terms. In addition, Meeting for Sufferings appoints two Friends to Quaker Peace & Service on the recommendation of its nominations committee from names suggested by the Yearly Meeting of Friends in Ireland.

Constitutions of representative councils

8.12 Quaker Home Service, Quaker Peace & Service and Quaker Social Responsibility & Education each has a representative council which provides the department with a two-way channel of communication with Friends in their meetings, the main purposes being educational, inspirational and consultative.

The role of the representative council member is also one of co-ordination and communication, in order to enhance links between local meetings, monthly meetings and the particular department. As detailed discussion of policy and review of working practices is often carried out by central committees in the light of feedback obtained by the representative councils, the role of council members is vital. They should:

a. attend (or arrange for their deputy to attend) each meeting of the representative council – monthly meetings will pay participation fees and reasonable travel expenses;

b. bring to the council news of activities or needs at local level in order to keep the department's work relevant and appropriate;

c. keep their local meetings informed about the breadth and depth of work undertaken by the department and in so doing support the fundraising effort necessary to sustain this work;

d. encourage and support the appointment of correspondents in local meetings and endeavour to meet and talk with them and to pass news of local needs and of relevant resources back and forth;

e. be in touch with any local members of the relevant central committee and include them in consultations with local correspondents;

f. make regular reports to monthly meetings, whether in full session or in special interest groups or through written reports and newsletters.

The Annual Conference of Treasurers (see 14.16-14.17) acts in a similar way to a representative council in relation to Quaker Communications and Quaker Finance & Property.

8.13   Representative council membership comprises:
   a. the appointed representative, or appointed deputy, of each monthly meeting within Britain Yearly Meeting;
   b. two representatives of Young Friends General Meeting;
   c. the members of the relevant central committee;
   d. the clerk of Britain Yearly Meeting and the clerk of Meeting for Sufferings ex officio;
   e. up to ten co-opted members.

In addition, each monthly meeting within the Yearly Meeting of Friends in Ireland is invited to appoint one member to the representative council of Quaker Peace & Service.

The membership is reviewed triennially.

The meeting correspondent

8.14   Local meeting correspondents (4.38.i) receive and distribute news of the work of Britain Yearly Meeting by keeping in touch with Quaker Home Service, Quaker Peace & Service and Quaker Social Responsibility & Education respectively. It is equally important that correspondents send local news to Friends and others elsewhere through these central channels: communication is a two-way process.

Correspondents will receive regular mailings. Quaker Communications Department will provide advice on how to select and present relevant information effectively. The correspondent should agree a working method with the preparative meeting clerk.

The local meeting clerk or convener should send the name of the correspondent, upon appointment, to the appropriate department. It i helpful if the correspondent is also in contact with the appropriate monthly meeting representative council member.

OTHER COMMITTEES OF MEETING FOR SUFFERINGS

Other standing committees directly accountable to Meeting for Sufferings are indicated below.

8.15   **Meeting for Sufferings Committee** supports Meeting for Sufferings in its work, so that the meeting has the time to guide the work and to develop the vision of Quaker witness. The committee is responsible for assisting, by detailed preparation, Meeting for Sufferings in its consideration and discernment of the range, variety, complexity and priorities of the Society's central work. It also considers and recommends policies for the work of Meeting for Sufferings and the management of its implementation. Areas of responsibility also include recommending annually a Britain Yearly Meeting budget for approval by Meeting for Sufferings, dealing with any matter referred from Meeting for Sufferings, undertaking regular monitoring duties and keeping under review any core statement of purpose for the central work of Britain Yearly Meeting.

Membership: at least twelve members of Meeting for Sufferings, appointed from names submitted by its nominations committee. One third of the membership is appointed annually in rotation and a member may be re-appointed for a further period of up to three years. Any member not currently appointed to Meeting for Sufferings will be co-opted to Meeting for Sufferings, within the limitations laid down in 7.04.e, for their period of service on the committee. In addition, the assistant clerk of Meeting for Sufferings and the clerk of Quaker Finance & Property Central Committee serve ex officio. The Recording Clerk, acting as secretary, shall meet with the committee. The committee may, at need, augment its meeting with appropriate members of the staff and with representatives of other committees.

8.16   **Quaker Committee for Christian & Interfaith Relations** is responsible for keeping Britain Yearly Meeting informed of the various movements towards co-operation within the Christian Church and opportunities for interfaith dialogue. Its work and constitution are described in 9.13.

8.17   **Quaker World Relations Committee** maintains contact with other yearly meetings and with Friends World Committee for Consultation and its Europe & Middle East Section. Its work and constitution are described in 9.06.

8.18   **Quaker Housing Trust** was formed in 1967 in response to Friends' concern about the provision of adequate and appropriate housing. The Trust makes grants and loans, and offers advice to charitable organisations providing accommodation, particularly to vulnerable people. Independent of the Yearly Meeting Fund, it is a channel whereby Friends may give or lend money for such provision. It is a registered charity and a company limited by guarantee.

Membership: between seven and twelve trustees appointed for terms of three years by Meeting for Sufferings, names having been submitted by its nominations committee, to form the Council of Management.

8.19   **Nominations Committee** brings forward the names of Friends to serve on committees of Meeting for Sufferings, as clerks of the meeting (7.11), as the meeting's representatives on Yearly Meeting Agenda Committee (6.15), and as representatives to attend yearly meetings abroad. It also suggests names of Friends to serve on bodies on which the meeting is represented (such as the Council of Churches for Britain and Ireland), on ad hoc groups, or to fill other appointments as requested by the meeting.

8.20   **Library Committee** is responsible for the maintenance of the Library at Friends House (comprising books, manuscripts, pictures and other material relating to Quaker thought, testimony and service) and for the proper custody of Britain Yearly Meeting's central archives. It is authorised to accept in the name of Meeting for Sufferings material by gift or on temporary or permanent loan. It provides advice to local meetings on the preservation of records and maintains an index of their whereabouts. (See 4.41-4.47 *Records*.)

Library Committee is a functional committee of Quaker Home Service Central Committee (8.07), but may report direct to Meeting for Sufferings when appropriate.

DEPARTMENTS AND STAFF

The role of staff

8.21 Meeting for Sufferings employs staff in order to service the central work. Most are based at Friends House in London. Our staff provide many of the facilities and much of the expertise required to carry out the yearly meeting's work effectively in a manner consistent with Friends' testimonies and beliefs. Much preparatory, on-going and follow-up work falls to our staff, and they need our support.

The close working partnership between staff and committee members brings a wide range of talents and experience to bear on our work. The role of committee members is to determine the work to be done and to ensure that it is manageable, whilst it is the responsibility of the staff to manage the work. Committee members need to remain free of routine administrative details if they are to have the time to exercise their important decision-making functions. However, committee members also need to be aware of how their decisions might affect, unsettle or fulfil the staff members involved. In turn, members of staff have to be aware of the delicate tension of being in a position of knowledge and ensure that their committees benefit from their experience and preparation whilst being left in a position to make consequent decisions freely.

The Recording Clerk

8.22 The Recording Clerk acts as secretary to Yearly Meeting, Meeting for Sufferings and Meeting for Sufferings Committee and is responsible for servicing these bodies and for ensuring that their work is carried out. As the senior member of staff employed by Meeting for Sufferings, the Recording Clerk's main tasks include maintaining contact with meetings throughout the yearly meeting, leading the

Management Meeting, being line manager of the departmental general secretaries, acting as 'keeper and interpreter' of the regulations laid down in our church government, and representing Britain Yearly Meeting to, and fostering good relations with, outside bodies.

The office of Recording Clerk has widened considerably since it was first established in about 1657. In those early days, the role was largely concerned with the sufferings of Friends, and up to 1703 included serving the Yearly Meeting as clerk. In more recent times, oversight of the management of the departments has become an important function of the Recording Clerk.

The Management Meeting

8.23   The Management Meeting is responsible for overseeing the management and implementation of the work of Britain Yearly Meeting as determined by Meeting for Sufferings and its committees. It is accountable to Meeting for Sufferings Committee, to whom it reports at least annually and submits its minutes; it advises that committee on practical and technical aspects of the work. The Management Meeting is responsible for the cohesion and consistency of the management of the central work, through the co-ordination of the work of individual managers, working to the vision and policies discerned by Meeting for Sufferings.

The meeting is composed of the Recording Clerk and the departmental general secretaries. It meets monthly under the leadership of the Recording Clerk. Members are collectively responsible for all its decisions, acting for Britain Yearly Meeting as a whole as well as the particular departments for which they are responsible.

CONCLUSION

8.24   Each committee and department has arisen and developed in response to a particular need. Each generation of Friends has been faced with a structure in some respects untidy, and we may be thankful for the clear-minded among us who help us, from time to time, to set our house in better order. But order without life does not work and our continual task is to ensure that our structures are in harmony with the changing tides of life in Britain Yearly Meeting.

It is neither possible nor desirable for every Friend to take a detailed interest in the work of every committee. We are, however, called to a broad sympathy with, and understanding of, the extent of the work entrusted to the committees and departments under the guidance of Meeting for Sufferings in the name of the whole yearly meeting.

8.25   The committees and departments whose work has been described were all set up to carry through what Yearly Meeting or Meeting for Sufferings has considered important service which Friends should undertake. It is imperative, therefore, if they are to continue to be sensitive to the concern of the yearly meeting, that there shall be a living and two-way communication between them and local meetings. It is sometimes complained that committees issue statements or initiate policies and work of which local meetings remain largely ignorant or see as some far-distant event, little affecting them. If the complaint is even in part justified, what remedy is open to us? First, let us set our minds to see the committees not as some distant 'they' with documents emanating from an impersonal 'Friends House'. It is we who compose the committees and the document we dislike was, like as not, drafted by Friends in meetings not far from our own.

People are usually preferable to paper, though admittedly some Friends are more effective than others in transmitting experience in a concise and lively way. Friends accepting service on committees, whether by local nomination or not, might usefully share with their monthly meeting the interests and concerns which are claiming their committee's attention. And, since many Friends are diffident to a fault, clerks might seek them out, looking not to mere reporting but to the sensitive sharing of experience.

If committees are to be responsive to changing concern, they must be aware of local judgment, which in turn must be based upon knowledge. It is essential, therefore, that meetings should from time to time review the effectiveness of the ways in which they keep themselves informed of the activities of committees.

Conclusion

Our committees do not live to themselves. Their appointment by and reporting to Yearly Meeting or Meeting for Sufferings reflect their responsibility. As the representatives of monthly meetings on Meeting for Sufferings attempt a disciplined understanding of the total work and witness of the yearly meeting, so the individual pieces of work of different committees will be seen in a right perspective.

Chapter 9

Beyond Britain Yearly Meeting

INTRODUCTION

9.01   Our meetings for church affairs, within the compass of the Yearly Meeting of the Religious Society of Friends in Britain, exist within a variety of contexts. Britain Yearly Meeting is part of the world family of Friends; Britain Yearly Meeting sees itself corporately, and is seen by others, as part of the Christian Church both globally and locally; interfaith dialogue is increasingly part of contemporary religious life. Within the spectrum of Britain Yearly Meeting there is a wide range of individual understandings of these three contexts, but all three will impinge on the life of our meetings. We need to remain aware of the wider relationships involved, and to take them into account in the conduct of our church affairs.

This chapter describes the formal relationships into which Britain Yearly Meeting has entered, their constitutional foundations and the structures which foster those relationships. It also offers advice on some of the implications for our meetings of Friends' ecumenical involvement at different levels, and on how best to address the problems and opportunities which arise.

Friends do not share a single understanding of the nature of the church, or of our place within it; we tend to feel our way into relationships with which we are reasonably comfortable, rather than prescribe a particular arrangement of structures as correct. This places a heavy but necessary responsibility on our meetings for church affairs, at all levels, for the right conduct of their deliberations leading to decisions on their interchurch involvement.

It is hoped that the following paragraphs will help Friends, whatever our differing views of the nature of the church, towards a fuller understanding of the contexts within which our meetings exist, and will guide us in the conduct of our meetings for church affairs when challenged by relationships with other religious bodies.

BRITAIN YEARLY MEETING AND THE WORLD FAMILY OF FRIENDS

9.02 In the world family of Friends there is a rich variety of experience, some of which is unfamiliar to Friends in Britain Yearly Meeting. Some Friends make frequent and joyful use of song and Bible study, and may be led by a pastor; for others silent waiting on God is the basis of worship, from which vocal ministry develops. Many Friends have a vivid experience of personal salvation through the teaching, life, death and resurrection of Jesus Christ; many hesitate to express their deepest spiritual experiences in words. It is important that Friends in Britain Yearly Meeting be aware that we are part of the world Quaker community, that we have a responsibility to learn about Friends in other parts, and that this can be done in local meetings as well as among yearly meetings.

Friends World Committee for Consultation (FWCC)

9.03 All Quaker groups in the world are invited to affiliate themselves to the Friends World Committee for Consultation. Most have done so. FWCC acts in a consultative capacity, serving as a channel of communication between Friends, helping us to explore and nurture our identity as Quakers, so that we can discuss and be faithful to our true place in the world as a people of God. It encourages joint conferences, intervisitation and the collection and circulation of information about Quaker literature, some of which it publishes itself. FWCC is recognised as a non-governmental organisation with consultative status at the United Nations and at some of its agencies. It is therefore able to accredit Quaker representatives to attend UN conferences on issues of Quaker concern, as well as to work on such issues full-time at the Quaker United Nations Offices in New York and Geneva.

9.04 Britain Yearly Meeting is committed to the support of FWCC and in particular of its Europe & Middle East Section (EMES), which has its own secretary and keeps in touch with European yearly meetings as well as Friends in the Middle East and in those European countries which have no yearly meeting. Britain Yearly Meeting contributes financially to FWCC, including EMES. Local meetings are also encouraged to consider how best they might express their support of Friends beyond the boundaries of our own yearly meeting, and enhance our contacts with such Friends.

9.05　Meeting for Sufferings, on the recommendation of its nominations committee, appoints up to seven representatives of Britain Yearly Meeting to serve on FWCC for three years. There will often be value in considering re-appointment for a second three-year term. The representatives are expected to attend the annual meeting of EMES and the triennial meetings of FWCC. They also serve on the Quaker World Relations Committee of Britain Yearly Meeting (see below).

Quaker World Relations Committee (QWRC)

9.06　QWRC is a committee appointed by Meeting for Sufferings to maintain contact with other yearly meetings and with FWCC. It must ensure that the FWCC representatives of Britain Yearly Meeting are well prepared to communicate the concerns of this yearly meeting in the wider Quaker context, and to report fully on the meetings they attend. QWRC is responsible for drawing the attention of Britain Yearly Meeting to issues and concerns raised at world and section meetings of FWCC and for offering suggestions on possible ways to respond.

QWRC acts on behalf of Meeting for Sufferings to prepare letters of greeting to be sent to other yearly meetings. It encourages a lively exchange of interest between Britain Yearly Meeting and FWCC, and intervisitation between this yearly meeting and other yearly meetings.

QWRC is composed of up to fifteen Friends appointed by Meeting for Sufferings, names having been submitted by its nominations committee. In addition the Britain Yearly Meeting representatives to FWCC serve on QWRC ex officio. The membership is reviewed periodically.

Quaker Council for European Affairs (QCEA)

9.07 The European yearly meetings support the Quaker Council for European Affairs, which aims to bring Quaker influence to bear on the institutions of Europe and maintains representatives and support staff in Quaker House, Brussels. A British Committee of QCEA works to increase awareness and to raise funds. Local meetings are encouraged to appoint a British Committee correspondent. Britain Yearly Meeting is committed to the support of QCEA.

Meeting for Sufferings, on the recommendation of its nominations committee, appoints two representatives of Britain Yearly Meeting to serve on QCEA for three years. There will often be value in considering re-appointment for a second three-year term.

BRITAIN YEARLY MEETING AND THE ECUMENICAL MOVEMENT

The historical background

9.08 Britain Yearly Meeting is not a member of the World Council of Churches (WCC). This is because its Basis of Faith was considered by Yearly Meeting in 1940 to require acceptance of a credal formulation. FWCC, being representative of Friends world wide, receives invitations and sends observers to the WCC and some of its constituent bodies. It also sends representatives to the annual meetings of secretaries of Christian World Communions, attended by representatives from the world bodies of the Roman Catholic, Orthodox, Lutheran, Anglican, Reformed, Baptist and many other churches.

Having declined membership of the WCC then in process of formation, London Yearly Meeting took the same position of principle in response to a similar invitation from the nascent British Council of Churches (BCC). In this case, however, it was met by the BCC's decision to extend its Basis of Faith so as to include in its membership those bodies which had previously been associated with the ecumenical movement, thus embracing London Yearly Meeting. Friends continued to play an active part, corporately and individually, in the

BCC from 1942 to 1990; London Yearly Meeting was only precluded, as an associate member after 1965, from voting on amendments to the BCC's constitution. Through the BCC it developed an indirect relationship with the Conference of European Churches. Because of the Conference's credal basis, however, the Yearly Meeting was never a member.

Friends enjoyed full membership of the Scottish Churches Council which had no credal basis. Friends sent observers to the Council of Churches for Wales which did. Both Councils were, like the BCC itself, superseded by 'new ecumenical instruments' in 1990, as set out in the following paragraphs. During the lifetime of the BCC there was no national ecumenical body for England.

Formal relationships and their constitutional foundations

9.09   Britain Yearly Meeting is a member of the Council of Churches for Britain and Ireland (CCBI) and of three national bodies, namely ACTS: Action of Churches Together in Scotland, CTE: Churches Together in England and CYTUN: *Cristnogion ymlaen tuag at undeb* (Christians forward towards unity), Churches Together in Wales. These 'new ecumenical instruments', launched in 1990, have a broader membership than those of 1942-1990. Following Friends' participation in the five-year preparatory process known as 'Not strangers but pilgrims', the Yearly Meeting in 1989 after a difficult exercise decided despite hesitations to apply for full membership of CCBI and the national bodies. Yearly Meeting in 1997 confirmed this decision. Each of the four bodies accepted London Yearly Meeting into membership under a clause (Clause 2b) which appears in each constitution as follows:

> A church, which on principle has no credal statements in its tradition and therefore cannot formally subscribe to the statement of faith in the Basis, may nevertheless apply for and be elected to full membership provided that it satisfies those member churches which subscribe to the Basis that it manifests faith in Christ as witnessed to in the Scriptures and is committed to the aims and

purposes* of the new ecumenical body, and that it will work in the spirit of the Basis.

The Basis reads:

> The Council of Churches for Britain and Ireland is a fellowship of churches in the United Kingdom of Great Britain and Northern Ireland and in the Republic of Ireland which confess the Lord Jesus Christ as God and Saviour according to the Scriptures and therefore seek to fulfil their common calling to the glory of the one God, Father, Son and Holy Spirit.

9.10 The underlying principle of CCBI and the national bodies is the commitment of member churches to one another and to taking seriously the principle that the churches should only do separately what they cannot in conscience do together. Working this out in practice is not always easy and will take time, but it should be one of the underlying principles used in deciding on the work carried out in the name of Britain Yearly Meeting.

9.11 CCBI works through an Assembly and a Church Representatives Meeting, and through associated agencies, commissions and networks. The three national bodies have similar patterns of work. Increasingly Britain Yearly Meeting's committees and departments work directly with their ecumenical counterparts and its members serve on ecumenical groups and committees. It is a principle of CCBI that authority remains rooted in the decision-making bodies of the member churches.

9.12 Meeting for Sufferings appoints Britain Yearly Meeting's representatives to CCBI and CTE; General Meeting for Scotland makes appointments to ACTS; the Meeting of Friends in Wales makes appointments to CYTUN. Representatives report to the appointing body and to the Quaker Committee for Christian & Interfaith Relations.

---

* The *Objects, aims and purposes* of CCBI provide the context within which the *Basis and commitment* are to be understood. The relevant constitutional texts are available on request from the Recording Clerk.

Quaker Committee for Christian & Interfaith Relations (CIR)

9.13   The Quaker Committee for Christian & Interfaith Relations is responsible for keeping Britain Yearly Meeting informed of the various movements towards co-operation within the Christian Church and opportunities for interfaith dialogue, and for responding on behalf of the yearly meeting so that Friends' views on issues of faith and order are represented to other churches and communities of faith.

The Quaker Committee for Christian & Interfaith Relations consists of up to thirty Friends appointed by Meeting for Sufferings, names having been submitted by its nominations committee. The Committee may co-opt a further ten members. The membership is reviewed periodically. The Yearly Meeting of Friends in Ireland (which is a member of the Irish Council of Churches but decided in 1989 not to seek membership of CCBI) appoints a few Friends to keep in touch with the work of the committee.

Local implications

9.14   Britain Yearly Meeting's membership of CCBI does not commit local meetings or individual Friends to any particular course of action with regard to interchurch relationships. However, in 1989 Yearly Meeting asked monthly meetings and general meetings to review the involvement of meetings in local and regional ecumenical activities, encouraging greater participation where need be. The recognition by CCBI member churches of our yearly meeting's non-credal tradition which is implied by Clause 2b (see 9.09) may make it easier to formalise these local relationships.

LOCAL MEETINGS AND ECUMENICAL RELATIONSHIPS

9.15   Local meetings are seeking to develop their religious life in relationship with members of other Christian churches, and with adherents of other faiths and of none. Any local meeting may find itself at some point along a wide spectrum of possible relationships designed to offer increasing degrees of commitment between churches. These range from local councils of churches, through Churches Together in a particular locality, to local ecumenical projects which may involve joint church membership (see 9.18), shared buildings, mutual recognition of ministers or all three.

Interchurch activity especially in England is often assisted by a sponsoring body – a formal association of appropriate church representatives which encourages, assists and oversees ecumenical activity within the boundaries of a city or county. A sponsoring body is enabling, not directive, in nature. Meetings need periodically to review their participation in sponsoring bodies, noting that all the churches have difficulty in matching up their geographical boundaries denominationally and ecumenically.

9.16　Each meeting will decide in its local context the degree of commitment which is appropriate. Friends who are ecumenically active may need reminding of the need not to rush ahead at a pace beyond that at which their meeting as a whole is comfortable. Those who have earlier experiences of belonging to other churches will need to recognise that such churches may change over time in their beliefs and practices. Like Britain Yearly Meeting other churches include within their membership people of very diverse beliefs.

At interchurch meetings Friends are valued for our willingness to uphold Quaker testimonies and leadings as much as for our tradition of listening and openness. But many aspects of Friends' faith and practice are not widely appreciated; misunderstandings may occur when other churches' lack of familiarity with our discipline and structure of church government, and Friends' imperfect knowledge of theirs, produce mismatched expectations or faulty assumptions.

In defining the relationship between churches, the problem of appropriate wording will sooner or later occur. The wording under which London Yearly Meeting became a member of CCBI and the three national bodies (9.09) may be helpful in this regard, but other much simpler forms may be preferable. In negotiating acceptable terms of membership, Friends should hold to our testimony that credal statements can fetter the free action of the Spirit.

See also 27.21-27.26 Creeds

9.17 Meetings may find it useful to check the wording of any local Basis of Faith to which they are invited to subscribe with the Recording Clerk, through whom advice may be obtained in case of need from the Quaker Committee for Christian & Interfaith Relations.

9.18 Membership by a meeting of a particular ecumenical body may be impossible, for example because the wording of its Basis is unacceptably exclusive, or because the mutual recognition of ministers which is involved does not extend to the Quaker understanding of ministry, or because joint membership for all participating churches' members is required. (Such automatic joint membership is unacceptable both because of the practical problems encountered upon transfer into a monthly meeting without the same ecumenical experience, and because, in departing from the principle of the individual application for membership, it is not in accordance with our discipline as set out in chapter 11.) In cases of doubt, reference should be made (as under 9.17) to the Recording Clerk, through whom advice may be obtained. If membership of a particular body proves impossible the meeting will have to consider how its relationships with other churches can be carried forward in different ways. Many practical forms of joint activity, from Christian Aid Week to work on housing and other social issues, are well established and present few if any problems for Friends. Some will wish to go thus far and no farther.

9.19 Our relationships with other churches are likely to involve us in joint religious services of various kinds. Sometimes there will be opportunities to introduce members of other churches to Quaker worship, thereby broadening their ecumenical experience. At other times we may participate in forms of worship which broaden our own. It may be appropriate on some ecumenical occasions for us to arrange meetings for worship which include some programmed elements.

When we find ourselves representing Friends in worship arranged by other churches we may have to make difficult decisions about the extent of our involvement. The difficulty is particularly acute in eucharistic worship, where different forms of eucharistic sharing are now frequently offered and are commonly seen by other Christians as both the means and the end of unity. Friends' testimony is to a corporate life and experience of God which does not depend on the observance of outward sacraments. Abstaining from the outward sacraments does not inevitably follow from this, but is one way of witnessing to it, particularly when the importance of the outward sacraments in building up the life of the church is being stressed.

See also 27.35-27.36 Priesthood *& 27.37-27.44* Sacraments.

9.20   To sum up, meetings find themselves engaged in a variety of local ecumenical arrangements. These entail differing responsibilities and degrees of commitment to joint activity. In a time of rapid change and challenging ecumenical encounters, meetings must give careful thought to the implications of any new relationship into which they are invited to enter. They are under no obligation to enter into any formal arrangement, or to move from one kind of relationship to another. The ferment of new initiatives within and among the churches requires Friends to exercise discretion and discernment while seeking to respond to the promptings of the Spirit. We should be wary of prematurely committing our meeting; as representatives on ecumenical bodies we must be ready, on occasion, to say no even if this disappoints the expectations of the other churches. In giving effect to the concept of churches together in pilgrimage, meetings will go as far and as fast along the ecumenical road as each judges, in its local situation, to be consistent with unity in the meeting, with our understanding and practice of church government, and with Quaker testimonies and integrity.

See also 27.12-27.20.

FRIENDS AND INTERFAITH RELATIONS

9.21   Ecumenical relationships beyond the Christian Church embrace dialogue with other communities of faith. Individual Friends have long been active in interfaith work. Britain Yearly Meeting has not only pursued this work in the context of community relations, but has also come to appreciate the theological issues implicit in interfaith dialogue and the mutual enrichment through interfaith sharing. This has come to be reflected in new emphases in the work of its Quaker Committee for Christian & Interfaith Relations. Britain Yearly

Meeting is a member of CCBI's Commission on Inter-Faith Relations and is represented on the Inter-Faith Network through CCBI.

Friends' experience is that interfaith dialogue can profitably be undertaken locally, where local issues set the agenda of work which can most usefully be done together. Other communities of faith often find our meeting houses acceptable venues for their worship, and meetings are encouraged to find out whether their own premises could be so used. This approach, however, does not mean that Friends should see themselves as theologically neutral. We need to be part of the dialogue, attesting to our own insights and convictions.

Meeting houses may also be used for multifaith worship. The hospitality of worship which Friends can offer through silence may serve as a meeting point for many religious traditions.

See also 27.01-27.11 Friends and other faiths

Chapter 10

Belonging to a Quaker meeting

OUR COMMUNITY

10.01 Our life is love, and peace, and tenderness; and bearing one with
another, and forgiving one another, and not laying accusations one
against another; but praying one for another, and helping one another
up with a tender hand.

Isaac Penington, 1667

10.02 We know the power of God's Spirit at work in the lives of people
within the community of our meetings. These people may have been
drawn into the community by a sudden convincement, a long period
of seeking, or have grown up within it from childhood. We also
know that we are engaged in a life-long growth into faith, and experience a continuing irruption of grace into our lives which demands
and sustains a commitment to a life of discipleship. We recognise this
power at work in people of all ages, races and creeds: a transforming power which can issue in lives of joy, humility and service.

London Yearly Meeting, 1986

10.03 The Religious Society of Friends is organised into local meetings,
each of which should be a community. It is our search for God's way
that has drawn us together. In our meeting we can each hope to find
love, support, challenge, practical help and a sense of belonging. We
should bring ourselves as we are, whatever our age, our strength,
our weakness; and be able to share friendship and warmth.

Some of us now live away from our families; some of us move house
quite often. Although surrounded by others we may be leading isolated and lonely lives. It is important that our meetings welcome newcomers warmly and that we include them in invitations to our
homes.

Our sense of community does not depend on all professing identical beliefs, for it grows from worshipping together, knowing one another, loving one another, accepting responsibilities, sharing and working together. We will be helped by tried and tested Quaker methods and procedures, but the meeting will only live if we develop a sense of community, which includes children and adults alike. If all those who belong to our meeting are lovingly cared for, the guidance of the spirit will be a reality. The celebration and commemoration of life's great events draw us together as we share the occasion and rejoice or mourn with one another.

Our shared experience of waiting for God's guidance in our meetings for worship and for church affairs, together with careful listening and gentleness of heart, forms the basis on which we can live out a life of love with and for each other and for those outside our community.

1994

10.04   *William Charles Braithwaite (1862-1922), a lawyer and banker, was the author of* The beginnings of Quakerism *and* The second period of Quakerism. *He was active in establishing the Swarthmore Lectures and in the transformation of* Christian Doctrine *1883 into the 1921* Christian life, faith and thought.

The life of a religious society consists in something more than the body of principles it professes and the outer garments of organisation which it wears. These things have their own importance: they embody the society to the world, and protect it from the chance and change of circumstance; but the springs of life lie deeper, and often escape recognition. They are to be found in the vital union of the members of the society with God and with one another, a union which allows the free flowing through the society of the spiritual life which is its strength.

William Charles Braithwaite, 1905

10.05   We recognise a variety of ministries. In our worship these include those who speak under the guidance of the Spirit, and those who receive and uphold the work of the Spirit in silence and prayer. We also recognise as ministry service on our many committees, hospitality and childcare, the care of finance and premises, and many other tasks. We value those whose ministry is not in an appointed task but is in teaching, counselling, listening, prayer, enabling the service of others, or other service in the meeting or the world.

The purpose of all our ministry is to lead us and other people into closer communion with God and to enable us to carry out those tasks which the Spirit lays upon us.

London Yearly Meeting, 1986

10.06 The custom of appointing certain named Friends to attend our meetings for church affairs may lead others to the mistaken conclusion that their responsibility for these gatherings is of less importance than that for the meeting for worship. But the privilege of membership implies that every Friend should feel concerned to attend these meetings.

1959

10.07 We must place within the reach of all our adult members advanced religious teaching similar in aim to that which we have seen to be needful for our children. We seek to secure such a general condition of church life that spiritual growth shall be fostered, and a high standard of spiritual intelligence shall be maintained. We are but seeking a rich and well-tilled soil from which every type of ministry shall spring with a robuster growth.

John Wilhelm Rowntree, 1899

See also 2.77-2.78 & 27.33

10.08 After a leisurely and useful preparative meeting, Friends sat at a long table in the children's room to enjoy supper together. We depend on those who till the soil, and tend the produce which forms our daily food, so it was good to remember them in thankfulness and for us to eat in fellowship the food mutually contributed, prepared and served. It was sacramental, in the sense in which Friends so profoundly believe. We spoke of those unable to be present, so that there was a sense of the entire meeting gathering in community.

This feeling of community pervaded the weekend. In preparative meeting the allotment committee reported and outlined plans for an orchard in the upper section of our ground; the fruit may not remain to be gathered by us but the blossoms will gladden everyone. The entire ground is in our care: allotments, burial ground, lawns, and we see it as one unit together with the meeting house which it surrounds. Yet true significance lies not in the grounds and buildings but in the people: those who tend the flowers, the grass and the allotment; members of the poetry group (some of whom gave pleasure by readings after supper); the study groups; the gathering of younger people; those whose activities lie in other places... The gravestones speak of the past, of those who also served the meeting, whose lives are woven into ours, as ours will affect those still to come.

William G Sewell, 1977

10.09   We were meeting in the long sitting-room, and the floor-space was as usual filled by the children. The room was pretty full. Then Sophie's father came and put her in her carry-cot on the floor. She was very young, and we hadn't expected to be greeting her so soon. I looked around the adults, wondering which of us would minister.

At the other end of the room Cathy, aged three, slipped down from her mother's knee. Slowly, carefully, and mostly upright she clambered in and out, past all the other children. She reached the carry-cot and peeped in at the baby. Then she turned and gave everyone a smile of pure delight. Still smiling, without a word, she returned to her mother.

Nobody else spoke either. Sophie had been welcomed into meeting.

William Fraser, 1989

10.10   If we take seriously the nurture of our children in the worshipping group, we must start by re-appraising the whole life of the group. What kind of communication exists between us all? Do we know one another as people sharing joys and sorrows?

Do we have enough confidence in each other to know that our problems as well as our convictions and uncertainties can be shared with understanding? How is the child and the stranger received amongst us? Do we see our young people as individuals we want to know and

care for and do we want to provide opportunities when they can get ⸺
know and care for us? Are they encouraged to feel that they hav⸺
much to give us, that we value them and are the poorer without th⸺
insights and questioning they provide? Are we across all the ages ⸺
community learning together? Do we consciously look for experienc⸺
which can be shared by the whole community? Children and your⸺
people need their own peer groups but are encouragingly appreciativ⸺
of the whole group sharing when they feel an integral part of it ar⸺
can share in situations which deepen relationships and form lastir⸺
friendships. Part of that sharing is learning to know of our past ⸺
Quakers and of our Christian roots but even more necessary is th⸺
sharing of what we as Quakers believe today and how this should h⸺
shaping our lives both individually and corporately. Together we hav⸺
a task in exploring our faith today with all its implications for actio⸺

Peggy McGeoghegan, 1976

10.11   It was said of the early Christians, 'Behold, how they love or⸺
another'. Could this equally be said of us? Or are our meetin⸺
places where newcomers may not always be welcomed, where peop⸺
feel alone? What happens to those who are part of our meeting⸺
Are their lives changed? Do they care more? Love more? What do w⸺
know of one another's lives outside of the meeting? Of one anothe⸺
spiritual journeys? Do we seek to share joys and humour as well ⸺
sorrows, or are we perhaps too near the 'sober-sides' images of po⸺
ular belief? Surely the nurturing of relationships and the response⸺
their breakdown will arise from the willingness of each of us to ent⸺
with imagination and love into one another's lives. If we truly kno⸺
one another then we are likely to be sensitively aware of one anothe⸺
needs. Often it is just being alongside someone; listening; a gent⸺
touch when words cannot be found. Our extreme busyness, and th⸺
pressure and tension of modern life, make it at once more necessa⸺
and at the same time more difficult that our meetings should becon⸺
living and loving communities.

June Ellis, 1986

10.12   It is a good practice and one which has taken place in Friend⸺
meetings I have known, for a small group to hold a meeting for wo⸺
ship in the bedroom of a seriously ill member, who feels that he ⸺

she would like others to come to them in this way. Since we have no set form of service for such occasions or for funerals, it is of great importance that elders and concerned Friends should be sensitively aware of the need of a real 'word of life' to be spoken and should be prepared for such needs and for ministry to the bereaved. I have been a member of more than one loving meeting, but I have to admit that the word I longed for was not spoken to me or my family when we suffered great grief, though much sympathy and kindness were shown to us. I am thankful to say that I have both before and since that time heard it spoken to others.

Ruth Fawell, 1967

10.13 Quakerism need not be defined exclusively as white, Christian and middle-class, and such culture need not be adopted as the culture of those who are convinced. When this does happen the inequalities and unequal power dynamics of our society are reflected in our meetings and in this way Black people are discouraged from fully participating in worship.

Our Society is often blind to the gifts and richness of other traditions and this cultural chauvinism impedes its development. Racism within the Society of Friends is perhaps more damaging because it is unconscious and springs from stereotyped assumptions: 'And no harm is meant by it. Harm may be done but it is never meant'.

Epistle of Black, white, Asian and mixed-heritage Friends, 1991

10.14 Er mai Saesneg fu prif gyfrwng y Gymdeithas yn yr ynysoedd hyn trwy'r blynyddoedd, dylid cydnabod fod rhan o'i bywyd wedi ac yn cael ei fynegi trwy ieithoedd eraill, ac yng Nghymru hefyd trwy'r Gymraeg. Darostyngir traddodiad ein Cymdeithas, ein hanes a'n tystiolaeth os anwybyddir hynny. Yn ddiarwybod bu i rai siaradwyr Cymraeg gael y teimlad iddynt gael eu hymylu. Dylid sicrhau fod y Gymraeg yn cael ei phriod le yng ngwaith a gweithgareddau'r Cyfarfod Blynyddol yng Nghymru.

Cyfarfod Dwyfor, 1994

For a translation of this text into English see page 615

10.15 We know that the spiritual growth of the meeting is inextricably linked to the growth of its life as a community, and that spiritual development is a continuous process for both older as well as the younger members of a meeting. Many young people have had and are having bad experiences in their local meetings, especially the smaller ones, where they often feel patronised, smothered or bored, and where they have found little evidence of a spiritual search amongst the older Friends: in places the Society seems fossilised, locked into the past or a mistaken comfortableness.

Young Quaker, 1985

10.16 For many years the Leaveners was my only contact with the Society of Friends and, despite being a birthright Friend, I would probably have drifted away from Quakers completely without the influence of the Quaker Youth Theatre.

The summer residential projects had a sense of purpose which I did not find at my Young Friends gatherings and used skills which appealed to me personally. Living and working together so closely towards a common goal always bonded the company together well, but in the heady mix of exhaustion and adrenalin caused by the long hours and public performance the intensity of friendships formed was extra special. I came home from these gatherings invigorated and uplifted, filled with the joy and wonder of life that now forms a central part of my spiritual outlook.

The necessary noise and activity of The Leaveners emphasised the quiet and peace of meeting for worship which began and ended each day. More than ever before I learned how Quaker worship is something to be treasured, a real act of sharing.

Nick Putz, 1994

10.17 The spiritual welfare of a meeting is greatly helped if its social life is vigorous, and its members take a warm personal interest in one another's welfare. The pastoral work of the Society is specially committed to the overseers, but our members generally should not allow themselves to feel that they are relieved from responsibility. In the greater events of life, such as marriage, the birth of a child, illness or death, it is our duty and privilege to share in one another's joys and sorrows; and sympathy thus shown is a potent means of binding us in closer fellowship. Those who hold public offices, or are engaged in various forms of social service, should be made to realise that they have the sympathetic support and prayers of their friends in their work. Opportunities might well be found for such Friends to tell of their activities, and receive encouragement and counsel; the other members of the meeting would thus acquire a deeper sense that they are called to a real share in the service.

1925

10.18 To make a safe home for small children, to comfort one person in sorrow, to do one's work as efficiently as possible, to listen with understanding, to be gentle with the old and courteous to the young – these are the humble tasks to which most men and women are called. They build the home or the meeting or the community which is the first step towards the Kingdom of Heaven on earth. The second is to be aware of greater tasks and to be ready to be used in solving them – ready, not worried or anxious or envious, but content to wait, exercising a ministry of prayer to sustain the healers and the reconcilers already at work in their thousands.

Olive Tyson, 1966

10.19 In a true community we will not choose our companions, for our choices are so often limited by self-serving motives. Instead, our companions will be given to us by grace. Often they will be persons who will upset our settled view of self and world. In fact, we might define true community as the place where the person you least want to live with always lives!

Parker J Palmer, 1977

10.20 One of the unexpected things I have learnt in my life as a Quaker is that religion is basically about relationships between people. This was an unexpected discovery, because I had been brought up to believe that religion was essentially about our relationship with God.

If we are sensitive, we find that everything that happens to us, good or bad, can help us to build a vision of the meaning of life. We can be helped to be sensitive by reading the Bible and being open to experience of nature, music, books, painting, sport or whatever our particular interest may be. It is in and through all things that we hear God speaking to us. But I do not think I am alone in my certainty that it's in my relationships with people that the deepest religious truths are most vividly disclosed.

George Gorman, 1982

CONFLICT WITHIN THE MEETING

10.21 There are times of conflict in every meeting when we are required to find and show the love we have for one another and to face our difficulties squarely, for it is only when we work through them, using our meeting for church affairs and other appropriate methods, that we can move forward together. Such conflict may involve a clash of personalities, a difference over the quantity or style of vocal ministry, or issues about the place where meetings for worship are held. Problems may become tangled and one sort of issue may masquerade as another. Care will be required to identify the root cause. Skill, time and great love are needed to overcome these problems, but where they have been openly faced and successfully overcome, meetings have sometimes been much richer for the experience.

The primary responsibility for finding a way to resolve these problems lies with elders and overseers. It may be that the use of a meeting for clearness (see 12.22-12.25) would offer a way forward.

Deep-seated problems are sometimes more easily resolved when an experienced facilitator from outside the situation is called on. Quaker Home Service or monthly and general meetings may be able to suggest Friends with an understanding of how groups and individuals interact with one another and who are able to spend time with a meeting that has got into seemingly insoluble difficulties.

1994

10.22 Part of the creative experience of a community is learning how to deal with conflict when it arises, and Friends are not usually good at this. 'Speaking the truth in love' is a Quaker cliché, but 'papering over the cracks' is the principle more commonly acted upon. Conflict met in 'brokenness' of spirit can take a meeting a long way on its spiritual journey, whereas unresolved it deadens the life. We are a small Society. Clashes have always arisen, just as they arise in any family group. In one sense the members of a family know each other too well, in another sense not well enough. It is impossible to impress one's relations, but they can be a great stand-by in time of need, and it is then that they come to know each other better, if the bond is strong enough.

Joan Fitch, 1980

10.23   One of the realities of our meetings these days is that sometimes two people, whom we have come to know as a couple, are unable to sustain their relationship and decide to separate. However much we may regret it, separations are becoming commonplace in society at large. Quakers are not immune to this affliction and when it happens the event often challenges the meeting in all sorts of unexpected ways. The reasons for the break-up may perplex us and we may feel hurt and unsettled, particularly if the estrangement deprives us of the company of a familiar friend. 'If it could happen to them where will it end?' There may even be a sense of guilt as if somehow the meeting allowed this to happen. 'If only our oversight had been better.' 'After all, Friends should endeavour to uphold the sanctity of the marriage relationship.'

Through all of this we must remember that we are often only bystanders who may not be aware of all the circumstances that led to the breakdown. It is important to affirm our love for *all* those who are directly affected, especially if there are children known to the meeting. The task of supporting an abandoned partner may call for special sensitivity and a willingness to be available during the dark moments. But the need to show our care for the other partner should not be overlooked either. Above all the meeting must try to affirm that of God which is in all of us, whatever our feelings about who is to blame. This is a time for great prayerfulness, unobtrusive caring and gentle support. We must trust that, with grace, we may all find paths to grow, leading us out of the painful experience.

John Miles, 1994

10.24 In our desire to be kind to everybody, to appear united in spirit, to have no majorities and minorities, we minimise our divisions and draw a veil over our doubts. We fail to recognise that tension is not only inescapable, however much hidden, but when brought into the open is a positive good.

Kenneth C Barnes, 1984

See also 4.21 Disputes among Friends, *20.67-20.75* Conflict *& 22.47-22.50* Facing change and difficulty

INDIVIDUAL COMMITMENT

10.25 When we consider the criteria for membership, the two greatest factors are community and commitment. Not just a practical commitment, but a spiritual willingness to grow and learn, out of which our practical commitment will evolve... YFCC [Young Friends Central Committee, which in 1993 became Young Friends General Meeting] has demonstrated that it is possible today for a large Quaker meeting to operate without any formal membership whatsoever. Our membership is more positive: simply our commitment to attend, our willingness to participate as 'Young Friends of the Truth'. In recent years, recognising the importance of oversight has been an essential part in creating the community spirit with which we are now blessed. We feel that the present lack of basic communication in our local meetings can be helped by such work and by the consideration of active Friends... We must be prepared to make ourselves vulnerable and care for each other. We suggest that methods of increasing communication be widely used, so that all active Friends are visited annually by other Friends, to listen to each other and to confirm the spiritual growth in our lives which we so often ignore.

A group of Young Friends, 1986

10.26 One of life's hardest lessons is that there is no justification for expecting that our neighbour is to traverse precisely the same path as that which we ourselves have followed... The difficulty a man has in grasping this truth is increased in proportion as his own experience has been vivid and clearly defined. One who has been lifted out of the horrible pit, has had his feet set upon a rock, and a new song put into his mouth, finds it hard to believe that another who has arrived quietly and without crisis, with no strong consciousness of guilt and no corresponding ecstasy of deliverance, can really be a disciple at all.

William Littleboy, 1916

10.27 Are there not different states, different degrees, different growths, different places? ... Therefore, watch every one to feel and know his own place and service in the body, and to be sensible of the gifts, places, and services of others, that the Lord may be honoured in all, and every one owned and honoured in the Lord, and no otherwise.

Isaac Penington, 1667

10.28 It is often hard to accept that other people have their own valid relationship with God, their own specialness and insights. We are not just disciples – we are disciples together.

Our vision of the truth has to be big enough to include other people's truth as well as our own. We have to learn to love difficult unlovable people. Accepting each other, and each other's relationship with God, let us continue to hold together at our deepest level. We are a forgiven community. Part of the cost of discipleship is living with the other disciples.

Beth Allen, 1984

10.29 *Pierre Ceresole (1879-1945), the Swiss pioneer of work camps and founder of International Voluntary Service, suffered repeatedly as a conscientious objector. He broke with Christian orthodoxy, which he felt no longer believed in its own dogmas, and joined Friends in 1936.*

I feel very strongly ... that the spiritual life absolutely requires that we should not remain isolated. It is this deep need of getting out of a prolonged and dangerous relative isolation which urges me to ask now to be admitted among the Quakers. It is more and more clear to me that it is only in the bosom of a religious family, freely but very strongly constituted, that the individual can render to the world the services it sorely needs and which no politics, not based on a deep inspiration, can hope to organise.

Pierre Ceresole, 1936

10.30 Even if it were possible to be a member of every church at once, there would still be incompleteness; the infinite fullness of God will always exceed our powers of understanding and obedience, even our powers to receive vision and joy. Dual membership for me is not a formula whereby I may find satisfaction because to be both a Friend and a United Reformed Church minister has all the gaps of one tradition filled by the other, though it is certainly a practice in which there is a great and satisfying measure of complementarity. Membership is rather a commitment, and membership of the People of God is a total commitment. But it is a fact of this earthly life that the total claim of God must be expressed in the actual and limited claim of those people with whom in fact life is shared. It has been my tremendous privilege and joy to find myself so committed in two communities, receiving from each more than I could well express and believing I am called to give in each whatever God enables.

Dorothy Havergal Shaw, 1994

10.31 Friends are not about building walls but about taking them down. For us as rural Friends, living many miles from each other and a Quaker meeting, having dual membership is a way of acknowledging our involvement with where we live: with local activities including Christian ones. Our origins have been in other branches of the church, giving experience which we value. Yet we wish to affirm that, for us, waiting on God in the silence of Quaker worship is at the very centre of our lives and the mainspring of our other activities.

Some members of North Northumberland Meeting, 1994

10.32 Why, I ask myself, did I go to worship with those rather small and not very distinguished groups of people? Surely it was that sitting among these quite ordinary people, to most of whom I remained a stranger and a foreigner for some months, I sensed an experience of belonging – of community. A true Friends' meeting for worship drawing individuals with varieties of temperament, talent and background always manages to engender a climate of belonging, of community which is infectious and creative. This experience of 'belonging' has remained with me over the years and it has grown both in intensity and universality... The 'giving out' of such a sense of community is the natural witness of a Quaker meeting which has in it the seed of life and creative experience.

Ranjit M Chetsingh, 1967

10.33   Why am I a Friend? Because Quakerism takes a whole view of life. Everyday living and religion are all of one piece, and we are including, not excluding, in our approach... Over the years the Society has given me continuing friendship. To be human is to be a separate person and, therefore, to know the fact and the mystery of aloneness. Although I find I can make surface contact with people quite readily, I am often lonely and experience stretches of doubt and dryness. Then especially I need friends who will accept a quality of friendship which involves praying for me. By this I mean that they care enough to think of me, to ask themselves if there is any special need of mine they can meet, to commend what they don't know about me to God's wisdom, and when we meet to make me welcome.

Donald Court, 1965

10.34   I suppose the question to ask is not, why am I applying for membership, but, why not sooner than this? All I can say is that I am not a hasty person. I have been considering applying for at least four years. I have felt myself to be part of Friends for so long that it has shocked me, on occasions, to realise that I am not thought of as 'one of us' but rather 'one of them'. I have come to see that how I perceive myself in terms of commitment and belonging is not necessarily how I am perceived. At times this has made me sad. But I can see that I owe it to Friends to make my position clear. If the Society can be thought of as a ship, I would like to be one of the crew, not a passenger, and to be seen like this.

Jai Penna, 1989

Chapter 11

Membership

THE MEANING OF MEMBERSHIP

11.01   'The Kingdom of Heaven did gather us and catch us all, as in a net,'
wrote Francis Howgill in 1663, 'and his heavenly power at one time
drew many hundreds to land. We came to know a place to stand in
and what to wait in.'

Early Friends felt no need for formal membership; they were a community of seekers who recognised in each other a similar hunger, a
similar quest. Seeking the 'hidden seed of God' they were prepared
to recognise it wherever they found it.

The seventeenth century, however, was not an easy time to be a dis-
senter; and Friends, like many others, suffered ridicule, arrest,
imprisonment, fines, distraint of their goods and death. In this harsh
climate it required a degree of personal commitment openly to avow
membership. This, combined with the recognition of a 'heavenly
power' at work, was all that was required.

Today membership may not involve putting liberty, goods or life at
risk but the spiritual understanding of membership is, in essentials,
the same as that which guided the 'Children of the Light'. People still
become Friends through 'convincement', and like early Friends they
wrestle and rejoice with that experience. Membership is still seen as
a discipleship, a discipline within a broadly Christian perspective
and our Quaker tradition, where the way we live is as important as
the beliefs we affirm.

Like all discipleships, membership has its elements of commitment
and responsibility but it is also about joy and celebration. Membership is a way of saying to the meeting that you feel at home, and in
the right place. Membership is also a way of saying to the meeting,
and to the world, that you accept at least the fundamental elements

of being a Quaker: the understanding of divine guidance, the manner of corporate worship and the ordering of the meeting's business, the practical expression of inward convictions and the equality of all before God. In asking to be admitted into the community of the meeting you are affirming what the meeting stands for and declaring your willingness to contribute to its life.

When early Friends affirmed the priesthood of all believers it was seen as an abolition of the clergy; in fact it is an abolition of the laity. All members are part of the clergy and have the clergy's responsibility for the maintenance of the meeting as a community. This means helping to contribute, in whatever ways are most suitable, to the maintenance of an atmosphere in which spiritual growth and exploration are possible for all. It means contributing to the meeting by giving time and energy to events and necessary tasks, and also being willing to serve on various regional or yearly meeting committees and other groups. There is a special responsibility to attend meetings for church affairs, for it is here that the meeting enacts its faith. Membership also entails a financial commitment appropriate to a member's means, for without money neither the local meeting nor the wider structure can function.

Membership does not require great moral or spiritual achievement, but it does require a sincerity of purpose and a commitment to Quaker values and practices. Membership is a spiritual discipline, a commitment to the well-being of one's spiritual home and not simply appearance on a membership roll. The process of application with its personal consideration, writing the letter to the monthly meeting, preparing to be visited and being visited are all part of the spiritual journey: part of the seeking that is so integral to our religious heritage. The membership application process is not only about seeking but also about finding.

The process is an important part of the life of the monthly meeting, too; accepting a new member means not only welcoming the 'hidden seed of God' but also affirming what it is as a community that we value and cherish. Quakers once called themselves 'Friends in the Truth' and it is the finding of this truth that we affirm when we accept others who value it into membership.

CHILDREN'S MEMBERSHIP

11.02 There are three main ways of looking at children's membership, each with solid historical roots in Quaker tradition:

a. you are not a Friend until you make a profession of faith, which you can do only at a mature age and after careful consideration; you must consciously and deliberately decide, declare and commit yourself: something you are unable to do as a child;

b. a child who is brought up within the community of a Friends' meeting is a full member in every sense; children were used by Jesus as patterns of the Kingdom and a child as well as an adult may have deep insights; your religious pilgrimage begins at, or before, birth and at any moment you are at a particular point on the journey;

c. a child may be a full member, but growing up demands confirmation; every one, at a given point of their physical and spiritual growth, should take up their membership for themselves and express it in some of the many forms of service.

11.03 These three approaches have usually been seen as mutually contradictory – if one is right the other two must be wrong. But in reality all three can be right: they express different aspects of membership. Each emphasises something of what it means to be persons shaped by the family and community we are born into, but having to choose our own position in relation to our family and community. Parents should try to recognise that their child may quite properly choose, in the light of the child's own temperament and experience, a way different from the one chosen on her or his behalf, even if that way lies outside the Society. Children, for their part, may recognise that any choice made for them will reflect the temperament and experience of their parents. (See 11.24.)

ACQUISITION OF MEMBERSHIP

11.04 Entry into membership of the Religious Society of Friends is a public acknowledgement of a growing unity with a community of people whose worship and service reflect, however imperfectly, their perception of discipleship and their recognition of the work of the

Holy Spirit in the world. This unity is grounded in the experience of being 'gathered' in the love of God in the silent expectancy of our meetings for worship and in a willingness to surrender ourselves to a corporate seeking for the will of God in such measure as we can comprehend it.

11.05   The membership of any Friend begins when a record to this effect is made in the minutes of a monthly meeting. There are normally two ways in which membership may be acquired:

      a. by personal application (11.07);
      b. by admission on the application of parents or guardians (11.22).

Personal application

To the applicant

11.06   Anybody aged sixteen or over may apply independently for admission into membership: if you are under sixteen the law requires that the application should be accompanied by an indication of your parents' consent. In special circumstances the monthly meeting may require the signature of a parent or guardian.

11.07   Membership is of a specific monthly meeting and only through this do you also become a member of your local meeting and Britain Yearly Meeting. Thus the application is made by writing a letter to the monthly meeting clerk who should at once send you an acknowledgement. Letters of application frequently include some explanation of why it is an applicant feels drawn to the Society but this is not necessary; the letter need be no more than a plain request. Before writing you should consider your reasons for wanting to apply. The meeting's elders or overseers will be happy to spend time discussing any questions or ideas you have and many meetings have discussion groups specifically for applicants. There are also a number of helpful books and the meeting librarian or Quaker Home Service will be able to suggest titles. Some meetings may also use meetings for clearness (12.22-12.25) to consider important issues of this sort.

Once the monthly meeting has received your letter of application it will normally appoint two Friends to visit you. (See also 11.13-11.19.) Being visited is not a test but is designed to provide an opportunity to talk with experienced Friends about the responsibilities of formal membership and the commitment which is implied in the application. The visit may also take place over more than one occasion; speed is not important at this stage, as it is essential that your application be thoroughly considered before a report is made to the monthly meeting.

11.08   *Richard Claridge (1649-1723) of Peel Monthly Meeting had been rector of the parish of Peopleton in Worcestershire for nineteen years when in 1691 he resigned and joined the Baptists. In 1697 he became convinced of the truth as understood by Friends. He recalled his experiences in these words:*

This was the way that Friends used with me, when I was convinced of truth; they came oftentimes to visit me, and sat and waited upon the Lord in silence with me; and as the Lord opened our understanding and mouths, so we had very sweet and comfortable seasons together. They did not ask me questions about this or the other creed, or about this or the other controversy in religion; but they waited to feel that living Power to quicken me, which raised up Jesus from the dead. And it pleased God so in his wisdom to direct, that all the great truths of the Christian religion were occasionally spoken to. Now this was Friends' way with me, a way far beyond all rules or methods established by the wisdom of this world, which is foolishness with God: and this is their way with others that are convinced of the truth.

11.09   The visitors will report to the monthly meeting in writing. The monthly meeting will discuss your application and you will be informed of the meeting's decision by visit, or by a letter from the clerk. The meeting you usually attend will also be informed.

The role of overseers

11.10   Overseers should be sensitive to the needs of attenders and, when the time is right, encourage a consideration of membership. Part of this encouragement, which need not necessarily result in an application, could include the provision of formal or informal discussion groups and suggestions about relevant reading. For those thinking more seriously of applying it may be comforting to know that the letter need be no more than a statement and that the visit is not an occasion to be feared but rather an opportunity for further reflection. Many meetings have found it helpful to present applicants with a copy of our book of discipline or other relevant book. This is sometimes done once an application has been accepted by the monthly meeting and sometimes by the overseers or visitors during the application process; whatever the method or moment selected, it is important for the applicant to become familiar with our discipline.

The monthly meeting: reception of application and appointment of visitors

1.11   Once the letter of application is received it should be acknowledged quickly by the clerk, and the matter placed on the agenda of the next convenient monthly meeting. The appropriate preparative or recognised meeting should also be informed that the letter has been received.

1.12   When the monthly meeting receives an application it should appoint two Friends to act as visitors. As it is not always possible to make the most suitable nominations in the meeting itself, monthly meetings may find it advisable either to ask overseers to nominate one or more of the visitors beforehand or to have a nominations committee for this purpose. One of the visitors should be from a meeting other than that with which the applicant is most closely associated. Great care should be taken to select sympathetic and discerning Friends who also understand the implications of membership.

Friends who are aware of an application may wish to uphold the applicant and the visitors in prayer.

The appointed visitors

11.13   Visiting the applicant has a dual purpose. As a part of the spiritual journey of the person applying, the visit should be a sensitive exchange of thought between seekers; it should provide an opportunity for, and result in, mutual understanding and enrichment. It also serves to provide clear information to help in making the final membership decision. It should not, however, be undertaken in a spirit of examination. Periods of silence at the beginning and end of the time spent together may serve to establish an atmosphere of worship (see 11.08). It may be helpful to both visitors and applicant to meet on more than one occasion.

11.14   The visitors should seek to help the applicant towards a fuller understanding of Quaker faith and practice and the implications of membership, where this is needed. They should ensure that the applicant understands the nature of Quaker worship as a corporate waiting on God where inspiration and guidance may be received. The applicant should understand why we dispense with outward forms and should have considered seriously whether worship without them will be spiritually satisfying. Visitors will need to make it clear that the Society is essentially Christian in its inspiration, although it asks for no specific affirmation of faith and understands Christianity primarily in terms of discipleship.

11.15   One of the important implications of membership is the responsibility each member has for the life of the meeting. Pastoral care, which in many other churches is given in part by a separated ministry, is in our yearly meeting a responsibility shared by all members; and there is the responsibility to give financial support. Meetings for church affairs are also a part of the life of the meeting and applicants should be alive to the reasons we conduct our business the way we do and the importance of playing an active role in it.

11.16   Our theology and practice are inseparable and the visitors will need to find out how far the desire for membership arises from a clear understanding of this rather than from an appreciation of some particular aspect of our practice such as our social witness, our peace testimony or our mostly silent worship.

11.17   Remember that moral and spiritual achievement is not what is required in an applicant: sincerity of purpose is. Complete agreement with all our testimonies is not necessary. It is important for the life of the Society that the applicant is broadly in unity with the views and practices of Friends. Many applicants have too lofty an idea of the Society, and of the quality of the lives of its members. They should be warned of possible disappointment.

11.18   Our membership ... is never based upon worthiness... We none of us are members because we have attained a certain standard of goodness, but rather because, in this matter, we still are all humble learners in the school of Christ. Our membership is of no importance whatever unless it signifies that we are committed to something of far greater and more lasting significance than can adequately be conveyed by the closest association with any movement or organisation.

Edgar G Dunstan, 1956

11.19   It is not the task of the visitors to recommend a course of action regarding a membership application to the monthly meeting, only to provide information on which the monthly meeting can decide. While most cases will present no difficulty it may sometimes become apparent that the application has been premature or even a mistake. Sometimes the visitors may feel that being a Quaker is likely to be only a stage in the applicant's spiritual search, but that membership may yet be right at this point. They should prepare a report for the monthly meeting sufficiently full to enable it to reach a right judgment on the application. Visitors should also be alive to the fact that any sensitive personal information imparted during the visit needs to be handled with great discretion and should be included in the membership report only if the report would be substantially incomplete without it.

The attention of those appointed as visitors is directed also to 10.13, 10.15, 10.25-10.34 & 11.48

The monthly meeting: decisions about membership

11.20 When the report from the visitors comes to the monthly meeting, it should be considered with concern for the right way forward. Some applicants will be readily welcomed into membership. In other cases a delay of some kind may be appropriate. Very occasionally applications may be received from those for whom the Society is clearly not the right spiritual home, or for whom membership would be inappropriate. In these cases a firm decision to refuse the application will be in order. Whatever the decision, the applicant will be informed promptly. Monthly meetings will often appoint Friends to welcome an applicant into membership, but we should remember that when someone is admitted into membership it is the pleasure of all the monthly meeting, and especially of the appropriate local meeting, to welcome them.

11.21 In the procedure for admission into membership exceptional circumstances may need special treatment. Monthly meetings have on occasion taken the initiative in arranging to visit an attender of long standing to see if he or she did not feel spiritually in membership. There have even been instances where a monthly meeting has quite rightly accepted an application without a visit. Nevertheless, monthly meetings should not lightly depart from well-tried practices. Our church government is to be seen not as a code of regulations to meet every conceivable contingency, but as an embodiment of the corporate experience and wisdom of the yearly meeting.

For some Friends' experience of dual membership see 10.30-10.31

Application on behalf of a child

11.22 Parents or those with parental responsibility or guardians who intend to bring up a child in accordance with the religious principles of the Society may apply for admission of that child into membership, while he or she is under the age of sixteen. The application, stating this intention, should be in writing and give the full name and date of birth of the child and be signed by both parents or by those with parental responsibility or guardians. Monthly meetings may, in special circumstances, dispense with the signature of one of the parents.

11.23   On receipt of the application the monthly meeting may appoint Friends to visit the parents or those with parental responsibility or guardians before reaching a decision as to admission into membership. The decision of the monthly meeting is to be conveyed to the parents or those with parental responsibility or guardians in writing. The names of the children so admitted are to be entered on the official register of members with the date of admission and the date of birth, and the appropriate local meeting is also to be informed.

Options available to those admitted on parental application

11.24   Membership acquired on parental application constitutes full membership and the member is under no obligation to confirm it on reaching a certain age. It is entirely valid, however, for a member to wish to indicate a personal acceptance of membership acquired in this way, or to wish to resign and seek re-admission as a 'convinced' Friend. Such requests may be made after much serious thought and monthly meetings should respond carefully, being guided by the spiritual needs of their members rather than by the desire to establish or follow a uniform practice.

11.25   A member whose admission was secured under section 11.22-11.23 may at any time take one of the following courses of action:

a. continue in membership acquired on the application of parents without making any formal statement;

b. indicate personal acceptance of membership acquired on application of parents and have this personal acceptance formally recognised by the monthly meeting (the member may in addition desire the appointment of one or two Friends as visitors);

c. resign from membership and, at the same or some later time, seek admission 'by convincement' under the provisions of 11.06-11.21;

d. resign from membership without further formality since he or she does not consider himself or herself a member.

A member wishing to follow course (b), (c) or (d) shall so indicate in writing to the monthly meeting clerk, whereupon the monthly meeting shall take such action as it thinks appropriate. It should record in its minutes the action taken.

11.26   Overseers should bring these options to the attention of younger Friends on reaching maturity but should be sensitive enough not to press them to make any decision when they might not be ready for it (see 12.13.g).

See also 11.36 Resignation by the individual

TRANSFER OF MEMBERSHIP

Change of address

11.27   On change of address, whether temporary or permanent, of a member or attender to the compass of another monthly meeting (i.e. a new monthly meeting with which the member or attender is most likely to become associated) a notice of change of address, including postcode and telephone number if appropriate, shall be sent immediately to the clerk of the other monthly meeting, who shall at once inform the local overseers. The sending of such notices shall be the responsibility of local overseers (unless the monthly meeting makes alternative arrangements) and the monthly meeting clerk shall in all cases be informed. It is useful if such notices are accompanied by a letter giving such information as might be helpful about the age, occupation, interests, etc of the member or attender. Printed forms for these notices are available from the Recording Clerk.

A notice should be sent even when a member or attender is moving some distance from any meeting or abroad. If the move is to a country where there is no known group of Friends, Friends World Committee for Consultation (FWCC) should be consulted as to where the nearest Friends live so that contact may be made. If it is to an area where several yearly meetings overlap, FWCC may be able to advise on the most useful point of contact.

Transfer procedure

11.28 It is generally best for Friends and for their service to the Society if their membership is in the area in which they reside, so a Friend moving from one monthly meeting area to another should ask either monthly meeting to arrange for transfer of membership. If such a request is not made within three months of leaving a monthly meeting area, a certificate of transfer may be issued on the initiative of that monthly meeting. Alternatively the monthly meeting into the compass of which a member has moved may apply for the certificate. Printed forms for these certificates are available from the Recording Clerk.

11.29 On receiving a certificate for transfer of membership the monthly meeting clerk should immediately inform the local overseers who should get in touch with the Friend if they have not already done so. They are responsible for advising the monthly meeting as to the acceptance of the certificate unless the monthly meeting finds other procedures more appropriate.

The membership is not transferred until the certificate has been accepted by the monthly meeting and a confirmation of that acceptance has been received by the issuing monthly meeting. Printed forms for certificates of acceptance are available from the Recording Clerk.

11.30 If the receiving monthly meeting sees an objection to accepting the certificate it shall return the certificate with as little delay as possible, stating the reasons for its return. This should be done only in exceptional circumstances. Monthly meetings are reminded that, though a Friend may have taken little or no part in the life of the meeting, even for many years, their move may prove an occasion for a renewed participation in the life of the Society. Nevertheless a meeting may properly return a certificate:

a. where it seems clear that the Friend will not become part of the receiving monthly meeting;

b. where in the view of the receiving monthly meeting the Friend is likely to remain, or to become, more closely associated with the issuing monthly meeting or another;

c. where in the view of the receiving monthly meeting the issuing monthly meeting should consider whether termination of membership may not be more appropriate.

11.31 It may be desirable that the overseers of the meeting from which the Friend is moving write to the clerk of overseers of the receiving meeting giving such information in confidence as may be felt to be useful.

11.32 In cases of doubt regarding the address in another yearly meeting to which a certificate should be sent, enquiry should be made of the Recording Clerk, who may also be able to give general information concerning meetings and Friends resident abroad. (See also 11.27 paragraph 2.)

For information on transfer of membership in relation to marriage see 16.52

11.33 If because of special circumstances a Friend's membership is not transferred to the monthly meeting in the area in which the Friend lives, he or she should nevertheless be encouraged to give such service as seems appropriate within that meeting. (See also 4.05 & 4.37.)

SOJOURNING MEMBERSHIP

11.34 Some yearly meetings issue certificates of sojourning membership to their members taking up temporary residence elsewhere. Such certificates are not recognised in Britain Yearly Meeting as sojourning membership forms no part of our discipline. Members of other yearly meetings should follow the advice in 4.05 (when attending a monthly meeting), 4.37 (when attending a preparative meeting) or 6.11 (when attending Britain Yearly Meeting).

See also 13.20-13.27

TERMINATION OF MEMBERSHIP

11.35 The membership of any Friend shall cease when a record to this effect is made in the minutes of the monthly meeting to which he or she belongs. Either the Friend or the monthly meeting may initiate steps leading to the termination of membership. The termination recorded in the minutes of the monthly meeting shall be understood as no more than a record that membership as a spiritual fact has ceased to exist (but see also 11.43).

Resignation by the individual

11.36 Any Friend who has attained the age of sixteen may address a letter of resignation to the clerk of the monthly meeting. Monthly meetings should arrange for such letters to be referred to the local or monthly meeting overseers for advice. Normally a resignation should not be accepted until after a visit on behalf of the monthly meeting. On the acceptance of a resignation the monthly meeting clerk shall immediately inform the Friend concerned.

Termination by the monthly meeting

11.37 Monthly meetings may take the initiative in terminating membership in cases:

    a. where over a prolonged period a Friend has ceased to show any interest in the life of the Society and there seems no reasonable likelihood of renewed participation;

    b. where a Friend's address has been unknown for a period of at least three years and cannot, after a careful search, be ascertained;

    c. where the conduct or publicly expressed opinions of the member are so much at variance with the principles of the Society that the spiritual bond has been broken.

11.38 In the relationship between Friends and their local meetings there may be periods of misunderstanding or strain. Though the main responsibility of pastoral care properly rests, in most monthly meetings, with local overseers, they may not necessarily have the sense of perspective or required skills to reach right judgments in all cases. A proper desire for confidentiality may make local overseers reluctant to bring such matters to monthly meeting overseers, and monthly meetings are therefore urged to see that clear and workable arrangements exist whereby local overseers can bring a few judicious Friends from elsewhere in the monthly meeting into consultation at an early stage in any membership matter which is likely to prove difficult.

11.39 If any Friend, by conduct or publicly expressed views, appears to be denying the Society's beliefs and principles or bringing it into disrepute, and private counsel has proved of no avail, the monthly meeting shall appoint well-qualified Friends to attempt to restore unity. If it appears that advice and counsel are, and are likely to continue to be, without their desired effect, the monthly meeting may record a minute of disunity with the action of that Friend and, in exceptional circumstances, terminate membership.

11.40 Monthly meetings should not normally terminate membership under 11.37 (a) or (c) until after a visit. An official letter inviting the Friend to reply should be issued by direction of the monthly meeting, signed by the clerk and sent to the Friend concerned before a decision to terminate membership under (a) or (c) is reached. On the actual termination of membership the monthly meeting clerk should immediately inform the Friend or Friends concerned, drawing their attention to the right of appeal should they feel aggrieved by the decision of the monthly meeting (see 4.22).

11.41 Pleas for the continuance of formal membership on sentimental grounds should have no place in a religious society, but monthly meetings are reminded that many Friends go through periods, sometimes prolonged, when their association with the life of the meeting is tenuous. Monthly meetings are urged to be very tender in all such cases and to beware of undue haste or unwarranted assumptions in proposals for the termination of membership.

Children

11.42 Letters of resignation on behalf of children who have not attained the age of sixteen should normally be signed by the parents or those with parental responsibility or guardians. Monthly meetings are at liberty in special circumstances to dispense with the signature of one of the parents. Such a resignation should be accepted by the monthly meeting unless in its judgment this is contrary to the best interests of the child. Monthly meetings may also initiate the termination of membership of the children of any Friends whose membership has ceased under 11.36 or 11.37. If it seems likely that any child whose membership has been terminated will continue in association with the meeting, the monthly meeting should transfer the name to the list of children connected with the meeting but not in membership.

Classification for returns

11.43   For tabular statement purposes (see 4.07.h) returns shall be classified under:

a. resignations on the initiative of the member;
b. terminations of membership on the initiative of the monthly meeting;
c. resignations on behalf of children.

Monthly meeting clerks shall complete a footnote stating how many terminations under (b) are in each of the categories in 11.37 and how many under (c) are on the initiative of the monthly meeting. It is therefore important that minutes recording the termination of membership be specific.

RECORDS OF MEMBERSHIP

Official register of members

11.44   Each monthly meeting shall maintain an official register of members and shall appoint a suitable Friend to have care of it. (See 4.47 about data protection.) No alteration shall be made to the register save in accordance with decisions minuted by the monthly meeting. The official register of members shall be examined annually and checked with the monthly meeting minutes by the Friends appointed to prepare or check the tabular statement. The official register may be maintained in loose-leaf form provided that proper precautions are taken. Superseded official registers of members shall be preserved by monthly meetings among their records.

Lists of attenders and children not in membership

11.45   Each monthly meeting shall maintain a list of attenders and of children not in membership associated with its several meetings for worship or shall arrange that such lists shall be kept by overseers. An attender is one who, not being a member, frequently attends a specific meeting for worship.

Printed lists of members, attenders and children not in membership

11.46   It is recommended that in the printed lists of members, attenders and children not in membership the date of birth should be printed and continued until the age of eighteen.

Respecting the essentially private nature of such lists, meetings should exercise care to limit their availability and guard against the risk that they might be put to undesirable use (see 4.47).

Recording of marriages and deaths

11.47   Monthly meetings shall record in their minutes marriages of their members according to our usage. Monthly meetings shall likewise record in their minutes the deaths of their members. It is recognised that some monthly meetings will wish to receive information on deaths in a standard form of their own devising while others may be satisfied with a letter from a close relative or local overseer or be content, in certain circumstances, with an oral report.

On records see 4.42

CONCLUSION

11.48   Friends have often had difficulty with the concept of membership and the definition of its basis. However, in practice, there is rarely any difficulty over particular applications.

In 1966 London Yearly Meeting accepted a new statement on membership after a difficult exercise in which problems of disunity were faced. This statement introduced the membership chapter in *Church government* from 1967 to 1995 and it remains an inspiration to many Friends:

'George Fox and his early followers', wrote Rufus Jones, 'went forth with unbounded faith and enthusiasm to discover in all lands those who were true fellow-members with them in this great household of God, and who were the hidden seed of God.' Our Society thus arose from a series of mutual discoveries of men and women who found that they were making the same spiritual pilgrimage. This is still our experience today. Even at times of great difference of opinion, we have known a sense of living unity, because we have recognised one another as followers of Jesus. We are at different stages along the way. We use different language to speak of him and to express our discipleship. The insistent questioning of the seeker, the fire of the rebel, the reflective contribution of the more cautious thinker – all have a place amongst us. This does not always make life easy. But we have found that we have learned to listen to one another, to respect the sincerity of one another's opinions, to love and to care for one another. We are enabled to do this because God first loved us. The gospels tell us of the life and teaching of Jesus. The light of Christ, a universal light and known inwardly, is our guide. It is the grace of God which gives us the strength to follow. It is his forgiveness which restores us when we are oppressed by the sense of falling short. These things we know, not as glib phrases, but out of the depths of sometimes agonising experience.

Membership, therefore, we see primarily in terms of discipleship, and so impose no clear-cut tests of doctrine or outward observance. Nevertheless those wishing to join the Society should recognise its Christian basis. Words often seem inadequate to convey our deepest experiences, yet words – however imperfect – are necessary if we are to share with one another what we have learned. In *Christian faith and practice* and in the *Advices and queries* we have tried to express those broad principles of belief and conduct on which unity is essential. These find expression in our testimonies, which reflect the Society's corporate insights, and a loyal recognition of this is to be expected, even though precise agreement on every point is not required. We are aware of continual failures in our discipleship, and no one should hesitate, from a sense of unworthiness, to apply for membership.

Membership implies acceptance of responsibility and a sense of commitment. It implies a willingness to be used by God, however imperfect we may feel ourselves to be as his messengers. He will not miraculously deliver us from the trials of temper and temptation, pettiness and pride, which are a part of human nature. In our worship together, and as we learn together in a Christian community, he will help us to overcome the limitations of our nature, to become more fully the people he intends us to be. 'Not as though we had already attained, either were already perfect, but we follow after ... forgetting those things which are behind, and reaching forth unto those things which are before, we press toward the mark for the prize of the high calling of God in Christ Jesus.'

See also chapter 10, Belonging to a Quaker meeting

Chapter 12

Caring for one another

INTRODUCTION

12.01   All of us in the meeting have needs. Sometimes the need will be for patient understanding, sometimes for practical help, sometimes for challenge and encouragement; but we cannot be aware of each other's needs unless we know each other. Although we may be busy we must take time to hear about the absent daughter, the examination result, the worries over a lease renewal, the revelation of an uplifting holiday, the joy of a new love. Every conversation with another Friend, every business meeting, every discussion group, and every meeting for worship can increase our loving and caring and our knowledge of each other.

Loving care is not something that those sound in mind and body 'do' for others but a process that binds us together. God has made us loving and the imparting of love to another satisfies something deep within us. It would be a mistake to assume that those with outwardly well-organised lives do not need assistance. Many apparently secure carers live close to despair within themselves. We all have our needs.

Careful listening is fundamental to helping each other; it goes beyond finding out about needs and becomes part of meeting them. Some would say that it is the single most useful thing that we can do. Those churches that have formal confession understand its value, but confession does not have to be formal to bring benefits. Speaking the unspeakable, admitting the shameful, to someone who can be trusted and who will accept you in love as you are, is enormously helpful.

Plain speaking is a longstanding Quaker testimony. It is not only that we hold a witness to the value of truth but also that straightforwardness saves us from many mistakes and much time wasted. On first acquaintance some Quakers can seem rather brusque; without the conventions of flattery and half-truths, we particularly need to make clear the steadfast love we have for one another.

Caring can take many forms. Some help will be beyond the resources of the local meeting, but it should not be beyond our resources to see when it is needed and to see that it is provided. Often it is what we are rather than anything we do which is of help to others. We should be wary of giving advice: a sympathetic ear, whilst a person finds their own way forward, will usually do more lasting good. Some people may not want to be helped, seeing our concern as an intrusion. Great sensitivity is called for.

The adults in a meeting have a shared responsibility for making a reality of our claim that the presence of children and young people is valued and that everybody's needs and feelings matter. People vary in how comfortable they feel with silent worship; some children, like some adults, take naturally to its disciplines and joys; others have to work at it. Some meetings offer other forms of worship from time to time. In any case it is important that the needs of all age groups are considered when we plan our activities.

12.02   To be without an ordained clergy is not to be without either leadership or ministry. The gifts of the Spirit to us include both. For us, calls to particular ministries are usually for a limited period of time, and those gifts pertain to the task rather than the person. In one lifetime a person may be called to a number of ministries.

London Yearly Meeting, 1986

12.03   With our structure, we risk failures in understanding and transmitting our tradition, and failures in pastoral care. We do not always adequately support one another. When we appoint people to carry out tasks for us, there is a danger of approaching this in too secular a way... We can and must pray for them to receive the necessary gifts and strength from the Spirit.

London Yearly Meeting, 1986

12.04   The great aim of a Christian community is to enable its members to know what their gift is and then to enable them to exercise it to the glory of God. This may sometimes involve a prolonged and perhaps painful exercise before some members come to accept that the gift they have to offer is not the one they thought.

New life from old roots, 1965

ELDERSHIP AND OVERSIGHT

12.05 Some Friends, whether called elders or not, have been looked to for spiritual counsel from the beginning. So in 1653 William Dewsbury proposed that each meeting should appoint 'one or two most grown in the Power and the Life, in the pure discerning of the Truth' to take responsibility for the spiritual welfare of the meeting and its members.

While the nurture of the spiritual life and responsibility for the right holding of meeting for worship continued to rest with 'elders', the more practical aspects of pastoral care were, towards the end of the eighteenth century, assigned to appointed 'overseers'.

Most monthly meetings continue the practice of appointing elders and overseers from their membership to ensure that the needs of the worshipping groups within their compass are met.

Monthly meetings' responsibility for pastoral care

12.06 The responsibility for providing each local meeting with the necessary resources for eldership and oversight rests with the monthly meeting, while much of the ongoing work is carried out in its constituent meetings. Good communication between these meetings and the monthly meeting should be maintained at all times so that items referred by one body to another are attended to and, where necessary, action is taken.

Elders and overseers (where appointed) will only be able to serve well if they are known and accessible to Friends and attenders. Care should be taken that members of a meeting know which of their number are serving for the time being in each capacity.

Meetings of those responsible for eldership and oversight should be called at least once a year by the monthly meeting. Here they can consider the needs of other meetings besides their own as well as the fundamentals of their faith and practice. Here too, newly appointed elders and overseers can learn about the tasks laid upon them and about how these responsibilities are carried out in other meetings. The monthly meeting should ensure that opportunities for consultation and inspiration are made known and appoint representatives to conferences on pastoral care matters, which might also be arranged by general meetings. Meetings are urged to learn about, and make use of, the wide variety of experience and resources available. Guidance on many aspects of pastoral care is available from Quaker Home Service.

Monthly meetings shall keep under regular review the provision of pastoral care in their constituent meetings (see 4.07.d & 12.16). Monthly meetings should seek the forms of eldership and oversight in each constituent meeting that best meet needs (12.15).

Appointment of elders and overseers

12.07　Appointment as elder or overseer does not imply that the Friends concerned are elevated to a higher position but that the meeting recognises that they may have the capacity to serve it in a particular way. Appointments are for a three-year period and may be renewed for a further three years; sometimes it may be necessary or desirable for a Friend to serve as elder or overseer for more than six consecutive years but this should not happen routinely (see 3.23). There is need for adequate continuity but there should be no expectation of continuous uninterrupted service. Care should be taken that newly appointed elders and overseers understand the duties involved. Those who are not to be re-nominated should be informed before new names are submitted to the monthly meeting.

Nominations to these offices are made either by the monthly meeting standing nominations committee or by a special monthly meeting nominating committee, consisting of a group of Friends drawn from the constituent meetings for this purpose. Members should bear in mind that they are not bringing forward names from their preparative meetings for ratification but nominating elders and overseers from the monthly meeting as a whole.

12.08   Beatrice Saxon Snell relates a story from her own experience, which
         reminds us that we are all potentially the instruments of God:

> I had a salutary lesson in sober thinking when I was first asked to
> become an elder. The invitation appalled me; I felt I was not old
> enough, had not been in the Society long enough; I suspected
> strongly that my monthly meeting had asked me on the inad-
> equate grounds of vocal ministry; I read up the appropriate pas-
> sages in *Church government* and felt still more appalled.
> Nevertheless I had been in the Society just long enough to know
> that the group often has a wisdom which can seldom be justified
> on logical grounds but which is, nevertheless, superior to the wis-
> dom of the individual. I therefore went to consult a much respected
> elder of my acquaintance. She and her house were late Victorian;
> she sat on her ugly sofa with the poker up her spine, her feet set
> neatly together and her hands folded in her lap; and she let me talk
> myself out. When I had quite finished she inclined herself slightly
> towards me and said: 'My dear, we have to take what we can get.'
> I have since been convinced that this is a text which ought to be
> framed and hung up over the bed of every elder in the Society: it
> ought to be hung over the bed of every Friend who is tempted to
> refer to the elders as 'they'.

1982

12.09   When asked to consider nomination for this service to the meeting,
         Friends should do so prayerfully and in the knowledge that the task
         will be entrusted to them for a period only. No one should be reluct-
         ant to pass on the responsibility to others when one triennial
         appointment comes to an end.

Once the monthly meeting has made the appointments, the monthly
meeting clerk shall immediately notify every Friend appointed and
shall convene the first meetings of elders and of overseers respectively unless the monthly meeting has adopted other procedures for so
doing. At the first meeting of each group a clerk or convener shall be
appointed, unless the monthly meeting has already appointed one.

The monthly meeting clerk shall transmit to each constituent meeting and to the Recording Clerk the names of elders and overseers

appointed for the next triennial period, and of their respective clerks or conveners, as soon as possible after their appointment.

A monthly meeting may release individual elders or overseers from service, and may make interim appointments, at any time during the triennial period. All such changes are to be notified to each constituent meeting and to the Recording Clerk. It is important that the monthly meeting make known to its members the method by which it wishes to receive nominations for such interim appointments. It may, for example, wish them to be brought forward by its standing nominations committee, or it may prefer to receive nominations from the existing monthly meeting elders and overseers or from the preparative meeting most directly concerned.

A Friend whose membership is transferred from the monthly meeting that made the appointment shall cease upon transfer to be an elder or overseer.

Caring for one another in the local meeting

12.10 The work of eldership and oversight is mainly carried out locally. Those responsible for pastoral care will need wisdom and sensitivity. Their ability to inform, advise and counsel will often be called on. Those invited to serve in either capacity may feel that the challenges sound daunting and that they will not match up to expectations. The meeting will be a source of support to those asked to be elders or overseers. The responsibility of eldership and oversight will bring its own rewards.

Understanding of human personality and motivation gained from a variety of disciplines will be of help in effective pastoral caring. Additionally, it may be necessary to be informed about ways of acquiring skills and, where necessary, to seek information from those qualified to give it. Members of our meetings or those associated with us will often have the required knowledge and experience.

It is important to distinguish between everyone's need to be listened to with sympathetic acceptance, especially when faced with bereavement or other painful situations, and those whose need goes beyond the competence of members of the meeting. It should not be thought of as failure to enlist specialist help from outside the meeting when what is needed cannot otherwise be provided. In all advisory work it is important to recognise that much of it is confidential. If in doubt as to what is confidential and what is not, it is good practice always to check with those involved before passing on any information.

In situations where a meeting for clearness may be appropriate, the individual(s) wishing to call it should consult those responsible for pastoral care in their meeting. An appropriate handbook may be available.

See also 12.22-12.25 on meetings for clearness in general and 16.19-16.21 on meetings for clearness concerning intentions of marriage

12.11   Traditionally the first concern of elders is for the nurture of the spiritual life of the group as a whole and of its individual members so that all may be brought closer to God and therefore to one another, thus enabling them to be more sensitive and obedient to the will of God. So the right holding of our meetings for worship will be their particular care. The chief concern of overseers is with the more outward aspects of pastoral care, with building a community in which all members find acceptance, loving care and opportunities for service.

Though there is a difference of function, much of the work of elders and overseers is of the same nature. It is important that the two groups should at all times work in close collaboration and should, wherever possible, share their common commitment to the service of their meetings. Whether they meet in separate groups or not, they should, from time to time, arrange joint meetings locally as well as in the monthly meeting area.

Responsibilities of eldership

12.12   Some of the responsibilities listed here may be carried out by overseers, or by specially appointed groups or committees, but it is important that elders should see that they are fulfilled. It is laid upon elders:

a. to meet regularly to uphold the meeting and its members in prayer; to guide those who share in our meetings towards a deeper experience of worship; to encourage preparation of mind and spirit, and study of the Bible and other writings that are spiritually helpful; to encourage individual and united prayer in the meeting;

b. to promote the right holding of meetings for worship, remembering that responsibility for the meeting, including the fitness of the ministry, is shared among all the members of the worshipping group;

c. to foster helpful vocal ministry, seeking to discern the needs and gifts both of individual contributors to the vocal ministry and of the meeting as a whole: some Friends may hesitate to risk speaking in meeting because they lack confidence in their own call to speak – they will need encouragement; others may too easily rise to their feet without being clear as to the helpfulness of the message; sometimes it may be necessary to restrain unsuitable ministry;

d. to be responsible for the quiet gathering of the meeting for worship in order, reverence and harmony, for the arrangement of seating and for encouraging punctuality; elders will arrange for the closing of the meeting, normally by shaking hands;

e. to ensure that the basis and method of conducting meetings for church affairs are understood; to accept responsibility for their right ordering (see chapter 3);

f. to take responsibility for the right holding of meetings for worship on special occasions such as marriages (16.31) and funerals (17.08-17.09), and, if memorial meetings are asked for, to make sure that their purpose is clear to those who attend (17.10) – some meetings like to make special arrangements for welcoming new babies or celebrating other events (see also 10.12, 10.17 & 22.44-22.46);

g. to care for individual Friends and attenders, entering with sympathy into their needs; to remember those who are unable to attend our meetings through age, illness or for other reasons; to visit them or where helpful to make special arrangements for meetings for worship in their homes; to take special responsibility for ministry to the dying and comforting the bereaved;

h. to encourage opportunities for all in the meeting to broaden and deepen their knowledge and understanding – this might include learning about the roots and foundations of our faith, becoming aware of the insights of other faiths and being challenged by new ideas, exploring with one another how to deepen our ministry, making opportunities for quiet reflection, increasing our understanding of ourselves and others and acknowledging our share of responsibility where there is conflict and loss;

i. together with overseers, to care for the children and young people associated with our meetings; to listen to what they have to say and to enable them to take as full a part as possible in our life and worship; to ensure there are regular opportunities for their spiritual nurture (see also 12.13.f);

j. together with overseers, to take care of the needs of enquirers and attenders, encouraging them to join in the life of the meeting;

k. to encourage Friends to take responsibility for their rightful part in the life of the community in which the meeting is situated; to welcome to our meetings those who belong to other Christian bodies, to other faiths and to none;

l. to consider the question of vocal ministry in the constituent meetings of the whole monthly meeting area and to give support where there is need for intervisitation.

It is advised that elders keep minutes of their meetings.

For responsibilities of elders in relation to non-members wishing to attend Yearly Meeting see 6.12. On the participation of elders in meetings for clearness see 12.22-12.25 and in meetings for clearness concerning intentions of marriage see 16.19-16.21. See also 12.10.

Responsibilities of oversight

12.13 Some of the responsibilities listed here may be carried out by elders, or by specially appointed groups or committees, but it is important that overseers should see that they are fulfilled. It is laid upon overseers:

a. to encourage attendance at meeting for worship and to make sure that newcomers to the meeting are welcomed and introduced to other members of the worshipping group;

   b. to encourage members to attend meetings for church affairs whenever possible and to take their rightful part in them;

   c. to make opportunities for Friends and attenders to get to know one another so that their diverse needs can be discovered and so that all will become aware of their gifts and experience, which may be of service to the meeting and to the Society – to be valued and needed is an enrichment for all concerned;

   d. together with elders, to take particular care of the needs of enquirers and attenders;

   e. to meet regularly to ensure that the pastoral needs of everyone associated with the meeting are being noticed; to check the membership list frequently, not only for accuracy but also in order to cover unmet needs – each child and young person should be considered as an individual and not solely as a member of a family group;

   f. together with elders, to exercise care over the children and young people associated with the meeting, whether in membership or not, and to see that suitable activities are arranged (see also 12.12.i); to encourage them, where appropriate, to take part in gatherings arranged for young people at local or national level, consulting with parents when appropriate;

   g. to make opportunities to talk with young people whose parents have brought them into membership about whether they wish to confirm it. At this stage they, and young attenders, may like to address a personal application to the monthly meeting and to be visited in the usual way; some may, at this point, wish to resign from the membership acquired for them by their parents (see also 11.24-11.26);

   h. to give advice and information about how to apply for membership both to attenders and to parents who may wish to make application on behalf of their children. Some attenders, either through shyness or because of a feeling of unworthiness, may be holding back from seeking membership; they may need encouragement to apply to the monthly meeting. It will be helpful to remind them that the letter of application to the monthly meeting clerk need not necessarily be more than a statement of the wish for membership, and that when they meet with the Friends appointed as visitors there is opportunity for asking questions and exploring matters of faith rather than examining fitness for membership (see also 11.10);

i. to visit members and attenders who have recently joined the meeting or moved into the area and to visit new-born babies; to see that the regulations on notices of change of address (11.27) and certificates of transfer of membership (11.28-11.31, 16.52) are promptly attended to and that certificates are applied for when not duly received; to advise the monthly meeting on the acceptance or non-acceptance of certificates of transfer;

j. to encourage caring friendship within the Quaker community. Should difficulties between Friends arise, overseers may be able to offer help at an early stage so that misunderstandings may be resolved; overseers are encouraged to make opportunities to talk privately with a Friend whose behaviour and manner of life is inconsistent with a Quaker witness, to explore underlying causes and endeavour to restore harmony (see also 11.38-11.39);

k. to send recommendations to the monthly meeting for the termination of membership in accordance with 11.37-11.41, once every effort has been made to follow up those who have drifted away from the meeting or have not been heard from for several years;

l. to ensure that young members and attenders living away from home are cared for and made welcome; to maintain contact with Friends residing abroad or in other parts of the country;

m. to advise local treasurers, collectors or finance committees, as appropriate, which members and attenders should and which should not receive contribution schedules;

n. to advise Friends who are in financial difficulty or who need help with education or training of their children about ways of obtaining assistance; to ensure that financial help is available, where this is needed, to enable Friends to attend meetings for church affairs and to accept appointments connected therewith;

o. to make sure that those intending to marry understand the principles on which the Society's usage is based and to refer them to the registering officer (see 16.05);

p. to see that sick people and elderly people, whether in their own homes, in hospital or in sheltered housing, are visited and cared for; to seek means of alleviating financial hardship.

Where overseers become aware that an elderly person is no longer able to look after herself or himself, it may be appropriate to offer help in consultation with the person concerned and any relatives or others involved. Overseers should try to be aware of the statutory and voluntary provision of residential and other care in their locality, including Quaker homes;

q. together with elders, to respond to the needs of the bereaved at time of loss; to provide comfort and sympathetic listening, however grief may be expressed.

It is advised that overseers keep minutes of their meetings.

On the participation of overseers in meetings for clearness concerning intentions of marriage see 16.21.b, and in other meetings for clearness see 12.22-12.25. See also 12.10.

Sharing responsibility for pastoral care

12.14 However pastoral care is organised, it is essential that the responsibilities for spiritual, intellectual, emotional, material and physical care for each member of the Quaker community, as listed above, should be given prayerful consideration. As the responsibilities of eldership and oversight overlap in many instances, there should be close co-operation between elders and overseers at all times.

12.15 Some of our meetings are undertaking to care for one another without specially appointed elders and overseers. These meetings need to give careful consideration to the best way of attending to pastoral care without neglecting any of the responsibilities of eldership or oversight outlined above. Thought must be given, for example, to those who attend the meeting only rarely or are housebound.

If a preparative meeting wishes to adopt an alternative method of providing pastoral care, it should take time to work out how the responsibilities would be shared and who would represent the group in meetings for eldership and oversight within the monthly meeting. It should undertake a periodic review of the effectiveness of any procedure adopted.

In some cases Friends may decide that shared oversight works well for them but that they still see advantages in appointing elders to attend to the spiritual nurture of the group. Traditional practices are tried and tested. For some meetings, however, there will be advantages in exploring newer and possibly more appropriate ways of meeting their particular needs.

Any proposals for changes in the way pastoral care is exercised in a meeting or meetings should be taken to the monthly meeting for guidance, support and decision. Monthly meetings should have a particular care for those meetings involved in novel ways of exercising eldership and oversight, both to offer guidance if difficulties or deficiencies arise and to ensure that the benefits of new practices can be shared with other meetings. (See also 4.35.)

12.16   Whether elders and overseers are appointed or not, local meetings should regularly review their spiritual life and its expression in caring. A meeting might like to compile and use a series of queries for this purpose. Such a review could take place every two or three years and might in itself be a form of pastoral care. The process might start in small groups, in which unmet needs could be revealed and confidentiality respected, then move on to an occasion drawing all together. Special attention might need to be given to involving those associated with the meeting who take little part in its regular life because of youth, age, disability or disaffection. (See 4.07.d & 12.06.)

12.17   And all such as behold their brother or sister in a transgression, go not in rough, light or upbraiding spirit to reprove or admonish him or her, but in the power of the Lord, and the spirit of the Lamb, and in the wisdom and love of the Truth, which suffers thereby, to admonish such an offender. So may the soul of such a brother or sister be seasonably and effectually reached unto and overcome, and they may have cause to bless the name of the Lord on their behalf, and so a blessing may be rewarded into the bosom of that faithful and tender brother or sister that so admonished them.

George Fox, 1669

12.18   Nor would we limit the performance of these duties to those who occupy such stations; we are all to watch over one another for good and to be mutually interested one for another, being united together as lively stones in the spiritual building of which the Lord Jesus Christ is the chief corner-stone.

Yearly Meeting in London, 1851

12.19   [Let not] Friends in the station of overseer ... take a limited view of their duties... To them is committed the oversight of the flock, in the love of Christ. [Let them] give themselves to this ... duty in faith and prayer, seeking, in the wisdom of God, to encourage all in the right way of the Lord; to bind up that which is broken; to bring home the wanderers; to visit the sick and the afflicted; and to extend loving care over the young and inexperienced. Desirable as it is that some should be specially entrusted with these duties, an earnest concern has prevailed that all may take their right share in the privilege of watching over one another for good.

Yearly Meeting in London, 1871

SMALL GROUPS

Meeting together in small groups

12.20   As Friends, we know that the quality of our unprogrammed worship is enhanced, and our care of one another is more effective, the better we come to know and understand one another.

We grow closer to one another as a worshipping community develops through regular attendance at meeting for worship, through working together physically or mentally, and in meeting with one another informally. Meeting together in small groups may have its part to play in this process, and may be valuable in helping us to explore and share our spiritual experience. Study and discussion groups provide well-tried opportunities, as do more informal social gatherings.

From time to time it may be helpful for a meeting to look at itself and try to identify specific areas that need attention, such as how to improve pastoral care, how to include attenders and newcomers, or how to improve communication and outreach. While these matters may well be raised in a preparative or monthly meeting, valuable suggestions and solutions may come from individuals who do not always find it easy to voice them in a more formal business meeting. The time given to preparation of heart and mind may also contribute very usefully to the right ordering of our meetings for church affairs. (See also 3.26.)

Elders and overseers may consider it part of their role to review the needs and workings of small groups in their meetings.

Worship sharing and creative listening groups

12.21   Some Quaker meetings have discovered the value of small groups in developing the art of listening to God, to others, and to oneself. Such 'worship sharing' or 'creative listening' groups can provide a setting where all who take part are involved in the process of learning about themselves as well as about others. Here silence, too, can heal and restore. For Quakers this approach fits in naturally with our experience of worship.

The terms 'creative listening' and 'worship sharing' are often used interchangeably, the difference between them being perhaps that the latter comes closer to a meeting for worship with a more pronounced emphasis on the worshipping atmosphere.

Careful preparation is needed to establish the basis of such groups, and there are several publications and sources which may give help. Advice may also be had from Quaker Home Service.

Good practice would normally include: the limitation of the size of the group to a maximum of twelve; beginning and ending the meeting in silence; the requirement of absolute confidentiality; allowing space between contributions; speaking from personal experience; not commenting directly on what another has said; listening with attention; not lapsing into discussion.

It may be that some do not contribute in spoken words. There is a need to respect the possibility that members of the group may not wish to discuss further what they have begun to share in the group. These groups can be particularly useful in allowing us to explore deep and personal thoughts and experiences in a supportive and safe environment.

Meetings for clearness

12.22   In earlier times Friends saw the need for 'clearness' as part of the necessary preparation for marriage. Only after a group of Friends, appointed by the monthly meeting, had established that there was clearness from other conflicting obligations could they recommend the solemnisation of a marriage. In some North American yearly meetings this practice has been maintained and the concept has broadened. It has become a loving and caring exercise on behalf of the meeting. The couple are helped to explore their commitment to God, to one another and to the meeting, to look in depth at the outcome of previous relationships or marriages, to consider their attitudes towards the care of existing or future children and at how the couple can make decisions about their life together. (See also 16.19-16.21 & 12.10.)

12.23   A number of meetings within Britain Yearly Meeting are making use of clearness groups for a variety of purposes. They may be called to prepare a couple for marriage, to test a concern, to make decisions about membership, to consider new forms of service or to seek guidance at times of change or difficulty. Such meetings may sometimes be of help and comfort to the dying.

Sometimes individuals or a family will need help when confronted by difficult choices at turning points in their lives. There may be interpersonal differences that sour relationships, or a meeting may have identified a particularly fraught area of divergence of opinion or belief in its membership. Any of these and similar situations, if they are faced openly and with love, may be tested in an atmosphere of worship. So those concerned may find a way forward.

12.24   By focusing on a particular issue, a meeting for clearness enables everyone present to become 'clear' about possible options and ways forward. Such a meeting may be a matter of private arrangement but if a preparative meeting is to be involved, elders or overseers will normally be consulted. The suggestion for a meeting may come from them or from those seeking clearness. In the case of clearness for marriage the registering officer will in most cases be a member of the clearness group, so that he or she will be in a position to give guidance to the meeting on whether a Quaker marriage should be allowed (see 16.19-16.21).

An elder or an overseer may need to explain the nature and conduct of the meeting to those asking for one. Four or five trusted Friends, not necessarily those closely involved with the matter under consideration, should be invited to participate. Their main qualification will be that they are likely to be able to contribute constructively in the process of discernment.

12.25   Meetings for clearness should be held in a relaxed atmosphere of trust yet a certain degree of formality is helpful. A facilitator should be chosen to assist in clarifying the question or questions being asked. Some groups may decide that notes should be taken. It will have to be made explicit that confidentiality is to be maintained within the group. There is need for listening with undivided attention, for tact, affirmation and love for those seeking clearness.

Each member of the group should have opportunities to question and explore the background to the matter that is to be clarified. It is important not to be diverted by side-issues but to concentrate on exploring options and understanding underlying difficulties. It will take time to reach clearness and periods of gathered worship will be helpful.

The meeting should have an unambiguous ending and should not continue once tiredness sets in. A further meeting or meetings may be needed if the original issue, or practical details, would benefit from further thought. When clearness is reached the group should be laid down.

Threshing meetings

12.26   This term currently denotes a meeting at which a variety of different, and sometimes controversial, opinions can be openly, and sometimes forcefully, expressed, often in order to defuse a situation before a later meeting for worship for business. Originally the term was used to describe large and noisy meetings for convincement of 'the world's people' in order to 'thresh' them away from the world.

Small groups

Support groups

12.27 Friends sometimes undertake, or are asked to undertake, tasks which they find challenging, either on a single occasion or as a continuing commitment. Under these circumstances they may value the support of a small group of Friends. This could be offered by the body requesting the service or it may be requested by the Friend concerned. Membership of the group should reflect the preferences of the Friend to be supported. The group may need to remind itself that its job is not so much to judge the task as to support the Friend carrying it out.

Chapter 13

Varieties of religious service

INTRODUCTION

13.01   It is part of our commitment as members of the Religious Society of Friends that we try to live our lives under the guidance of the Spirit. Whatever the service to which we are called, whether it be great or small, our meeting can uphold us in prayer and other ways.

Our service may be in the home, an unpaid job, a vocation or a lifetime's career. For some there will be service in the local meeting, in one of the many roles that help to make our meetings true Christian communities. Some of these are explained later in this chapter. Britain Yearly Meeting itself offers people opportunities for service both as members of staff and on our various Quaker committees.

Personal leadings can be tested in a variety of ways. Other Friends and those with special responsibilities in the meeting will be ready to listen and to encourage. Where important and difficult decisions have to be made it may be appropriate to ask for a meeting for clearness (12.22-12.25).

Quakers have long been involved in a wide range of action rooted in our faith: in the cause of peace and reconciliation, local, national or international; on behalf of oppressed or deprived people; in furtherance of our testimonies to honesty and integrity. The diversity of Quaker activity has been remarkable. In all these areas, however, there have been particular Friends who have felt themselves at certain times to be singled out to act in response to a spiritual compulsion. This we call concern and we distinguish it from those things that we are concerned about.

Matters which we are 'concerned about' are often very important. They might include changing the way that Britain Yearly Meeting does something or hoping that it will undertake a particular service. These matters are best brought to our meetings for church affairs and dealt with under our well tested business method, as outlined in chapter 3.

CONCERN: FAITH IN ACTION

The Quaker understanding of concern

13.02 Throughout the history of the Religious Society of Friends we have recognised that to anyone may come, at any time, a special inward calling to carry out a particular service. It is characterised by a feeling of having been directly called by God and by an imperative to act.

The ministry which has been carried out 'under concern' is a remarkable record of strength and perseverance in adversity. Many speak of the peace that came to them with the certainty that they were working with God. Recognising concern has also placed an obligation on the meeting which tests and supports it. Friends have on occasion been released from financial considerations and in some cases their families have been cared for whilst they carried out the service required of them.

A concern may arise unexpectedly out of an interest or may creep up on one out of worshipful search for the way forward. It may be in line with current desires and projects or it may cut across them; it may lead to action which is similar to that undertaken by others or it may require a brave striking out into the unknown.

13.03 There is a feeling of being right or fitting associated with the experience of concern:

> There was from the early stages of our discussion a strong sense of the 'rightness' of what we were talking about. The ideas flowed freely, and although we were not conscious of it at the time, we would say now that we were clearly working under guidance.
>
> Barry and Jill Wilsher, writing about the origins in 1978 of the Quaker Peace Action Caravan.

13.04 Others have spoken of a moment of calling, of an overwhelming sense of love and light, leading to a certainty that they must act:

> If you ask me for the important dates they are as follows: meeting for worship several Sundays at Morley, Wilmslow early 1967; Cambridge 22-23 September 1967, at the village of Grantchester where the message came opposite to the war memorial: '*You* shall do it and *I* shall help'. This message was the driving force. Friends were hesitant; some thought it very emotional, others thought it very moving. Only, I knew that that Power would never allow a failure.

> George Murphy writing about the concern which led to the founding of the Bradford University School of Peace Studies in 1973.

Discernment in concern

13.05   Achieving clarity about a concern is a particular exercise in discernment. It is a process that begins with considerable private reflection and the asking of some tough questions. Is this a desire that someone else do something or is it really a call to act oneself? Is this concern in keeping with the testimonies of the Society? Is it genuinely from God?

The discernment process is not confined to solitary reflection. As a Religious Society we are more than a collection of people who meet together – we meet as we do because we believe that gathered together we are capable of greater clarity of vision. It is therefore the practice in our Society for a Friend who, after due consideration, believes that he or she has a concern, to bring it before the gathered community of Friends. This is both a further part of the testing process and an expression of our membership in a spiritual community. It is a recognition of mutual obligations: that of a Friend to test the concern against the counsel of the group and that of the group to exercise its judgment and to seek the guidance of God.

13.06   As a general rule concerns should be brought before a preparative or, where appropriate, monthly meeting. The concern may, if recognised by that meeting as a true leading, then be forwarded to other meetings for consideration by a wider or more specialised group of Friends. It is not appropriate, however, for concerns to be sent forward automatically to another meeting. One part of the discernment process is judging at what point a concern has been considered by all appropriate bodies. Meetings should beware of the risk of using the process of forwarding concerns to avoid their responsibilities (see 4.16-4.17).

Throughout the discernment process there should be one overriding principle before the hearts and minds of all: is this individual or group right to believe that this action or service has been 'laid upon' them by God?

13.07   'Concern' is a word which has tended to become debased by excessively common usage among Friends, so that too often it is used to cover merely a strong desire. The true 'concern' [emerges as] a gift from God, a leading of his spirit which may not be denied. Its sanction is not that on investigation it proves to be the intelligent thing to do – though it usually is; it is that the individual ... knows, as a matter of inward experience, that there is something that the Lord would have done, however obscure the way, however uncertain the means to human observation. Often proposals for action are made which have every appearance of good sense, but as the meeting waits before God it becomes clear that the proposition falls short of 'concern'.

Roger Wilson, 1949

Responsibilities of individuals and meetings

To Friends with concerns

13.08   Friends with a concern should take counsel from experienced members of the meeting, particularly those who may have a different approach to the problem. Consider setting up, or asking for, a support group of trusted Friends (12.27). A meeting for clearness may also be part of the process of discernment (12.22-12.25). Allow the process to take time and do not rush yourself.

At each stage Friends will try to bring their insights to bear. Be prepared for their comments to cause some soul-searching and possible revisions. Be very clear what you are asking of each meeting (see 13.12-13.14).

Occasionally the process of discernment and adoption does not operate as it should, for we are not perfect and sometimes lose the spirit in the letter. We may lose sight of genuine inspiration in the press of daily events and overcrowded agendas. This may happen at any stage in the process and may necessitate re-presentation or presentation in a new format. It is useful to have a support group (12.27) at moments like this.

The role of the meeting

13.09 The importance of the local worshipping group in fostering active concerns cannot be over-emphasised. Where Friends know and trust one another the gifts we all have can be used more fully in obedience to the Inward Light. This is the source from which concerns spring.

The atmosphere of mutual confidence and understanding that fosters concerns also leads naturally to sharing concerns with the meeting. A concern that is brought before a meeting should be considered with the greatest love, kindness and discipline. Much as we like to support our Friends in the things for which they have an unbounded enthusiasm, it is no kindness to recognise as a concern something which has not received the fullest attention possible.

13.10 When a Friend has laid a concern before a monthly or preparative meeting, there should be a chance for questioning and elucidation, after which it is normally the practice for the Friend to withdraw while the matter is being considered. If the concern is recognised the Friend may be given a minute with which to go forward.

It may be determined that the concern is not in harmony with the testimonies of our Society. It should be remembered, however, that:

It is with individuals rather than with communities that new truth originates... While corporate guidance is of great value in controlling individual extravagance, it is a source of great danger to the church if it is opposed to a genuine individual concern.

William Charles Braithwaite, 1909

Both individual and meeting should pay heed to the advice: 'Think it possible that you may be mistaken'.

13.11   It may not always be possible to give adequate consideration to a concern in the course of a normal monthly or preparative meeting, or in the course of a regular committee meeting. The option of a special monthly meeting and/or a meeting for clearness to help work through the issues should be considered (see 12.22-12.25).

13.12   The meeting which has considered a concern needs to be absolutely clear whether it is:

   a. recognising a concern seen as religiously valid;
   b. supporting the concern and accepting responsibility for its furtherance, including financial support where necessary (13.18);
   c. adopting the concern as one it shares, whereupon the concern becomes a concern of the whole meeting;
   d. recognising the concern and forwarding it with its support to a more widely representative meeting;
   e. forwarding it because the meeting is unable to reach a decision on the validity of the calling – in this case however it is likely that further preparation and consideration is preferable to forwarding it to another meeting at this stage;
   f. deciding that the matter before it is not a religiously valid concern.

13.13   Where they are clear that they have recognised a concern, Friends in the meeting will turn their attention to the practical details of its implementation and consequences. It may happen that a meeting recognises a Friend's concern but can see no way in which it can be taken forward or given practical effect at this time. It is then appropriate to hold it over for further consideration when the circumstances are more favourable.

If a concern relates to the corporate life of Britain Yearly Meeting it should be sent forward by the monthly meeting, either to Meeting for Sufferings or to Yearly Meeting (see 4.16).

When service abroad in any capacity is proposed, early consultation with the relevant committees of Britain Yearly Meeting is imperative. Consultation with the Friends World Committee for Consultation and appropriate yearly meetings may also be necessary.

It has already been noted that meetings that support a Friend's concern will sometimes assume the financial responsibility for the concern. Whether or not this is so, they may also consider offering other forms of help such as the use of a car, offers of childcare or the setting up of a support group of people close to the Friend or concern (see 12.27).

When a concern has run its course, consideration should be given to how this may be recognised and acknowledged. A meeting that has supported a concern should be informed when it is seen to be right to lay that concern down. Celebration for the right ending of what was rightly begun may be appropriate.

See also 4.06 & 4.16-4.17

Minutes and finances

13.14 When a Friend applies to a meeting with the object of taking a concern to a more widely representative meeting, any minute agreed should be addressed to that meeting and a copy forwarded without delay to its clerk. A copy should also be given to the Friend or Friends presenting the concern.

When such a concern has been supported or adopted by an appropriate body other than the monthly meeting, it is the duty of the clerk of the supporting or adopting body to send notice at once to the clerk of the monthly meeting of which the Friend is a member. Giving such information promptly enables the monthly meeting to enter with understanding into the Friend's concern, and to offer whatever support seems appropriate (see 12.27).

13.15 When a monthly meeting has encouraged any Friend to apply to Meeting for Sufferings for support in service, it is the duty of the clerk to give notice to the Recording Clerk without delay to enable, where possible, advance notice to be given to members of Meeting for Sufferings.

13.16 Minutes should, when appropriate, make clear the nature and probable duration of the intended service. If long-term service is intended suitable arrangements should be made, by means of a corresponding committee or in other ways, for interim reports to the meeting issuing the minute.

13.17　When a concern is fulfilled the Friend should return the minute to the meeting which has supported the service and the meeting should record the return of the minute.

13.18　If financial help is needed when a Friend travels in the service of the Society, it shall normally be given by the meeting supporting the service. If the service is by invitation the inviting meeting shall normally give it.

OTHER FORMS OF SERVICE

13.19　Within our meetings there are many tasks which need to be performed and many responsibilities to be taken. This volume has details of many of these. For instance clerkship is dealt with in chapter 3 and eldership and oversight in chapter 12. What follows is a fuller description of some of the more specialised forms of service.

TRAVELLING IN THE MINISTRY AND INTERVISITATION

13.20　Travelling to visit and worship with Friends, both within our yearly meeting and beyond, is greatly to be valued. It helps to bind together the family of Friends. London Yearly Meeting endorsed its value in 1925:

> We should take an interest not only in our own particular meetings, but also in other adjacent meetings, especially if they are few in numbers or otherwise in need. The visitation of another meeting in the spirit of Christian fellowship is an act of service, even if unaccompanied by any words of spoken ministry. When carried out under right concern it may bring encouragement and refreshment both to those who visit and those who are visited.

13.21　It should be remembered by all who visit Friends in other yearly meetings that great sensitivity is required. Each yearly meeting is autonomous and each has its own tradition and practice. Do not think yourself a fount of all knowledge just because you are from

Britain Yearly Meeting. Our understanding of Quakerism grew out of the experiences of Friends in the history of these islands. Our assumptions are bound up with our culture, heritage and history. All yearly meetings have changed their practice over time and now have a variety of traditions to draw upon. It is necessary to know the local Quaker tradition as well as the history of the country in order to communicate fully with the Friends you are visiting. Quaker committees concerned with work overseas may be able to give advice and guidance to Friends visiting meetings abroad that will increase the usefulness of their visits.

Travelling in the ministry

13.22   This will usually be preceded by the testing of a concern and its recognition by the monthly meeting to which the Friend belongs. Everything in the previous sections 13.05-13.18 will apply. The Friend concerned may have been given financial support by the sponsoring meeting. Pastoral support has in the past been provided by Friends travelling in pairs, sometimes a younger Friend with an older. There may be circumstances where this practice is still helpful. The minute recognising the Friend's concern should be short enough to be read out after a meeting for worship.

13.23   Friends hoping to travel abroad in this service will be well advised to consult with the relevant departments of Britain Yearly Meeting and with the Friends World Committee for Consultation. After the concern has been recognised, the Friend should contact the yearly meeting(s) within which they intend to travel and be guided by their advice. As noted above it is important to remember that all yearly meetings are autonomous and that traditions and practice vary widely.

13.24   It is vital that Friends hoping to travel in the ministry test their concern thoroughly; we may be reminded of the practice of John Woolman, who travelled in the ministry extensively:

> Having been some time under a religious concern to prepare for crossing the seas in order to visit Friends in the northern parts of England, and more particularly in Yorkshire, after weighty consideration I thought it expedient to inform Friends at our

monthly meeting at Burlington of it, who, having unity with me therein, gave me a certificate. And I afterwards communicated the same to our quarterly meeting, and they likewise certified their concurrence. Some time after, at the General Spring Meeting of Ministers and Elders, I thought it my duty to acquaint them with the religious exercise which attended my mind, with which they likewise signified their unity by a certificate, dated the 24th of third month, 1772, directed to Friends in Great Britain.

13.25   That Quakers could be called to the ministry other than in meeting for worship on Sundays was a new thought to us when, in 1967, a dear American Friend asked us whether we felt we had such a call. Its full significance did not strike us until later; the itinerant or travelling ministry had been the lifeblood of the Society of Friends in its earlier days and had continued into the beginning of the twentieth century. We served our apprenticeship with Lewis and Sarah Benson, travelling mainly in North America. We tried to catch some of their eagerness to bring to everyone the freshness of the message, their humility, their spirituality and their concern to gather all people to Christ, their Teacher. We soon found ourselves travelling with others or alone in Ireland, Scotland, France, Germany and Denmark as well as nearer home, while others ventured as far as Kenya and Australia. What drove all of us was a Christian message that needed to be shared wherever the door opened within or outside the Society of Friends.

Arthur and Ursula Windsor, 1994

13.26   We should be prepared to receive someone sent by another Quaker meeting with as much care as we send someone to travel in the ministry.

It is not enough to send foreign Friends into small groups of Friends who will listen politely to their visitors: they should first know their visitors' culture and tradition in order to receive them with open minds and hearts. Friends in London Yearly Meeting need to discover where they stand individually. As we often do not know the personal theologies of members of our own meetings, how can we prepare our own Friends to listen to others? Yet we must. If Friends world wide are to be a world family of Friends we have to learn to hear and to understand each other.

Quaker World Relations Committee, 1992

Types of minutes

13.27 A Friend released for service, under concern, by her or his meeting is provided with a minute of liberation. This will normally be written by Meeting for Sufferings (see 13.15).

A Friend travelling on Friends' business, or to perform a particular, limited service is provided with a travelling minute. This may be provided either by Meeting for Sufferings or by the monthly meeting. Such a minute may be endorsed by the welcoming meeting.

Letter of greeting

13.28 This is a letter issued by a meeting to one of its members or long-term attenders who is going to travel amongst Friends in other parts of the world for reasons not immediately connected with the service of the Society. In this case the preparative, monthly or general meeting may give the Friend a letter of introduction, signed by the clerk, to take with them. Such a letter is not a minute of authorisation for a particular service and care should be taken to avoid suggesting that it is.

Intervisitation

13.29 We urge Friends, when staying away from home during holiday or on business, to attend a meeting for worship if there is one within reach. Such attendance may well have the effect of strengthening the meeting, and of helping Friends who were hitherto strangers to know one another.

1925, 1994

When visiting meetings in another yearly meeting be careful not to be a burden. Remember the caution in 13.21.

13.30   For over 35 years I have been visiting meetings other than my own. For the last 15 years monthly meeting has given me a travelling minute which is returned annually with its endorsements. I have visited the smaller meetings in my own monthly meeting; I have visited nearby meetings in other monthly meetings and thus kept contact with neighbours who might easily be strangers; when further from home I have sought out smaller meetings which might be encouraged by a visitor, and I am sure that the two or three present have been so encouraged. I have attended special occasions such as the reopening of a refurbished meeting house and rejoiced with those who rejoiced.

The words of John Woolman are in the travelling minute: 'A concern arose … that I might feel and understand their life and the Spirit they live in, if haply I might receive some instruction from them, or they be in any degree helped forward by my following the leadings of Truth amongst them'. John Woolman's hopes have been abundantly fulfilled for me.

Richard Schardt, 1994

13.31   At the very small recognised meeting where I am a member – we have been as few as two at meeting for worship – we welcome visitors from other meetings, whether casual or regular, and look upon them as a source of enrichment. We understand that we in turn can give from our quietly gathered meeting.

Ingrid Williams, 1994

WARDENS

13.32   As Friends, we cannot separate our religious calling from our practical work for the kingdom of God. As Friends concerned for wardenship, we make our contributions in the local community to those who come to our meeting house. We appear to offer our facilities, but in fact we offer our love.

Quaker Home Service conference on wardenship, 1981

13.33   The aim of wardenship is to provide a warm and welcoming atmosphere within the meeting house, to create conditions conducive to worship and to offer a service to the community. Wardenship should be seen as an integrated part of Quaker life and worship, and a responsibility which is shared by the whole meeting. There are unique opportunities for outreach. Many demands are made of wardens who are regularly available; these range from requests for financial and practical support to appeals from those with deep emotional, social or spiritual needs. Wardens acquire a fund of knowledge about the meeting and its place in the neighbourhood and can often help the meeting with initiatives in outreach.

Wardens and meeting houses

13.34   Wardens are appointed to look after some of our meeting houses. In many cases they also live on the premises. The appointment is normally made by the monthly meeting, as the primary meeting for church government, but for practical purposes this responsibility is sometimes delegated to a preparative meeting or to trustees. Wardenship in its present form is a recent development among Friends and arises not for its own sake but from our desire that our meeting houses be more widely used for the benefit of the communities in which they stand.

Just as our meeting houses vary from those in a busy city centre or new town location to historic Brigflatts or Jordans, so their use varies from those which are open throughout the week to a wide range of community groups and commercial lettings, to others where there is little use except for meetings for worship. Consequently the work and conditions of employment of wardens vary enormously.

Employment of wardens

13.35   The employing monthly meeting and the preparative meeting concerned should be quite clear about the terms of employment. Wardens are usually provided with accommodation in or adjacent to the meeting house, but a few are non-resident. Some see wardenship as a service they wish to give, perhaps on early retirement; others regard it as a very worthwhile form of employment. Some wardens are paid as full-time employees, others on a very part-time basis; some receive free accommodation only, whilst others (usually where there is little work involved) make a contribution towards the rent, heating, and other costs. Wardens may also have other employment.

Employing meetings and wardens are reminded that there are laws detailing the formal rights and responsibilities of both employers and employees. QHS Wardenship Committee can provide up-to-date information.

There must be a clear job description which is reviewed regularly. Advertisements should be comprehensive and interviews thorough. A policy of equal opportunities is appropriate. It is essential that the warden or wardens have written terms and conditions of employment linked with a suitable written agreement covering the accommodation provided. Time off and adequate holidays should be agreed and consideration given to pension needs. Rehousing on completion of service requires careful consideration before appointment.

13.36   Work which is rightly the responsibility of office holders and members of the meeting should not be left to wardens, and wardens should not be appointed to those offices which could give rise to a conflict of interest: clerk, assistant clerk, treasurer or managing trustee. There should be clear guidance as to who is responsible for lettings. Ex-officio attendance at premises and wardenship committees is a frequent and helpful practice. Care must be taken to respect the privacy of wardens during their leisure time and not to make unreasonable demands upon their services. Their private accommodation should not be considered as an extension of the meeting house.

13.37   Wardens should not be asked to accept conditions of accommodation and work which most Friends would not tolerate personally. Casually made appointments can lead to misunderstandings and unintended exploitation. Meetings employing a warden are urged to consult with QHS Wardenship Committee, to ensure that good practice is observed in their meeting.

Support for wardens

13.38   Wardens and meetings benefit from the provision of good support. This may be provided by premises committees, wardenship committees or a link Friend or Friends. The needs of the warden should be considered by the employing meeting and reviewed on a regular basis. Wardens may obtain help from QHS Wardenship Committee who organise regular national and regional conferences and specialist training courses, provide a consultancy and information service, and make a handbook available. (See also 12.27 *Support groups.*)

Resident Friends and caretakers

13.39   Much of the above applies also to resident Friends who give general oversight to meeting houses with few outside users, and to caretakers, whose work is often confined to cleaning and preparing rooms for meetings, opening and closing the building and caring for the garden.

LIBRARIANS AND LIBRARIES

13.40   Monthly meetings are required to keep under regular review the maintenance and use of libraries in local meetings (see 4.07.p); they should encourage any meetings which do not have their own library to establish one. The running of the library, however, remains the responsibility of the local meeting. Most local meetings appoint a librarian, who will need the support of the meeting and a budget for the purchase of books. In some meetings this task is shared by a number of Friends. Some monthly meetings draw their librarians together from time to time to share their experience. Help and advice are also available from the Library Committee and from Quaker Home Service.

13.41   A well-stocked and organised library is a powerful aid to the life of the meeting and its outreach. The books can represent a resource for learning about the Religious Society of Friends, about Christianity, the Bible, other world faiths and the social issues of our day. New books can stimulate and challenge as we continue our religious education.

Librarians will find many ways of making the books within their library accessible to Friends and attenders. Some meetings publish reading lists and reviews of recently acquired books in their newsletters. Others will introduce new acquisitions at a preparative meeting or in the notices after meeting for worship. The librarian should be familiar with the contents of the library and be prepared to offer recommendations to those wanting to use it. Book boxes can be obtained from the Quaker Bookshop at Friends House and are a good way of encouraging Friends to enlarge their reading. Other resources than books are available and useful, and librarians may wish to consider including these.

Where there are physical limitations, such as when meeting for worship is held in rented accommodation, imagination and a determination to share our discoveries of helpful books will suggest ways in which the problems may be alleviated.

TREASURERS

13.42 People who perform this task for meetings do a great service. Their work often receives scant attention from other Friends, but without them we could quite simply not operate. They will need to be familiar with numbers but neither accounting skills nor a computer are necessary. More important is sensitivity in helping each member and attender to give what is appropriate, allaying feelings of guilt whilst informing them of the need for money both at a local level and for our central work.

The treasurer is a servant of the meeting, advising and helping but leaving decisions to the meeting itself.

13.43 Every meeting which holds funds or handles money should appoint a treasurer, who should be in membership (3.24.i). Some meetings find it helpful to appoint an assistant treasurer or 'collector' to encourage and assist Friends in their giving. More details can be found in chapter 14, *Finance*.

Whilst continuity and experience are important in financial matters, the appointment of a treasurer should be reviewed triennially and the length of service should not be unduly extended. It is good practice for a meeting to plan ahead for the timely release of its treasurer, possibly appointing an assistant who will prepare to take over the task.

A handbook is available and advice can be sought from the Quaker Finance & Property Department at Friends House. Monthly meeting treasurers are entitled to attend the Annual Conference of Treasurers (14.16-14.17).

PRISON MINISTERS, VISITORS AND CHAPLAINS

13.44   In the early days of the Quaker movement many Friends were imprisoned for their beliefs. Many Friends were imprisoned in this century too, as conscientious objectors to military service. Perhaps because of this there has been a continuing concern for prisoners and the conditions in prisons, exemplified in the work of Elizabeth Fry (see 23.98-23.100), which is continued by others to the present day. The section that follows explains the terms used and the procedures to be followed. It also offers advice to all Friends about supporting those who do this work.

13.45   A **prison minister** (formerly termed a 'visiting minister') is a priest or minister of a recognised religious denomination appointed by the Home Office to a specific institution under the Prison Act 1952 to perform duties of a religious nature inside that particular institution. Quaker prison ministers are included in this definition.

Prison visitors are appointed by the Home Office on the recommendation of the prison governor to befriend a prisoner who has requested visits. Prison visitors have no duties of a specifically religious character. It is important that they are not confused with the Board of Visitors, who have a quite different function.

In **Scotland** different terminology is used to describe the functions outlined in 13.46-13.49. General Meeting for Scotland is responsible for sending to the Scottish Office Home and Health Department our nominations of Friends to serve as prison chaplains. These chaplains have a responsibility for the pastoral care of Friends imprisoned in Scotland and have to operate in liaison with the official prison ministers appointed by the Church of Scotland. In 13.46-13.51 the phrase 'Quaker prison minister' should be read to include Quaker prison chaplains in Scotland.

Quaker prison ministers

13.46 A Quaker prison minister has four tasks: to visit and minister to those in prison who have registered themselves as Quakers; to assist the work of the prison chaplaincy; to be a Quaker presence in the prison, particularly in relation to staff; and to be a channel between the prison service and the monthly meeting, keeping Friends aware of prison issues.

Where it is possible for the Quaker prison minister to arrange an occasional or regular meeting for worship, these can be of great value.

13.47 When prisoners are under restraint or punishment, in segregation or in the hospital wing, they will be in particular need of spiritual comfort and reassurance. The Quaker prison minister has a right and duty in these circumstances to visit a prisoner registered as a Quaker, whether in membership or not, whilst a visit from a prison visitor may not be allowed.

Appointment

13.48 A Friend is recommended for this service by the monthly meeting (4.07.r), which then applies to the particular institution for the nomination to be approved and the appointment made, using a Home Office form obtainable from the Recording Clerk.

13.49 If the nomination is approved, the particular institution informs the Quaker prison minister that a formal appointment has been made. The monthly meeting should then ensure that Quaker Social Responsibility & Education is informed of the appointment. This process may take some weeks. Potential prison ministers should be aware that they will be investigated by the Criminal Records Office.

Preparation and support

13.50 QSRE can offer a newly appointed Quaker prison minister the benefit of knowledge and experience. In the first instance they will send the handbook for Quaker prison ministers published by QSRE. Conferences are held each year which provide information on aspects of penal affairs, but also offer those attending good opportunity to discuss particular problems and to gain the informed support of Friends working in other penal establishments.

13.51 The Quaker prison minister undertakes to bear the monthly meeting's responsibility for ministering to the spiritual needs of prisoners who are registered as Quakers. Prison ministers have their needs too, and it is very important that the monthly meeting should support the Friend doing this demanding work on their behalf. The Quaker prison minister and monthly meeting will probably want to decide amongst themselves how support can best be given (see 12.27) and whether or not it should come from a formally appointed group.

Monthly meetings will find it helpful to encourage Quaker prison ministers to report on their work once a year.

Prison Visitors

13.52 Prison visitors are appointed by the Home Office, or the Scottish Office Home and Health Department, on the recommendation of the prison governor to visit certain prisoners who have asked for visits to be arranged. Their duty is to befriend those they visit. They have no duties of a specifically religious nature and are sometimes required to avoid religious topics. Friends wishing to offer this service should approach the governor of the prison where they wish to serve.

Some Quakers are both prison ministers and visitors. The roles overlap and Quaker prison ministers find themselves moving naturally from one to the other.

13.53 Going into a prison can be intimidating and it may be difficult to find the right way of communicating with those you meet there. It is often hard to know what to say particularly to those serving long sentences or far from home, but if the preparation of the heart is taken seriously the right words will come. Ministry is giving of oneself and allowing others to give to us; our common humanity enables us to minister. Laughter, too, is part of the healing ministry.

COLLEGE CHAPLAINS

13.54 The role and the title of the Friends responsible for the pastoral care of students can vary according to the institution; they may also be called student welcomers, student overseers or student chaplains. These Friends may be appointed either by the monthly meeting or by one of its preparative meetings according to local circumstances. Their role can be the oversight of Quaker students, linking them to the local meeting. If there are Friends on the staff they will usually help. Sometimes the college chaplains may be part of an ecumenical team and their role will extend to all students and staff. The work may need support, both financial and spiritual, from the appointing meeting (see 12.27).

13.55 Work in colleges and universities is an opportunity for outreach. Friends' non-credal approach and openness to new light, from whatever quarter, may be particularly appealing to the enquiring minds of students. Friends should be ready to make Quaker views known as well as providing pastoral care.

There may be opportunities for holding a meeting for worship in a college. In this case local elders should share in responsibility for such a meeting.

Some areas may have several educational institutions and several Friends responsible for pastoral care; local meetings should have an overall responsibility to support all these Friends both practically and spiritually.

Where there is a local Young Friends group this may offer a welcome to younger students who are close to them in age.

13.56   Quaker Home Service offers information and advice to college chaplains and links them together.

Chapter 14

Finance

GIVING FOR QUAKER WORK

14.01 How we raise and administer our financial resources affects both the interrelatedness of our service and the quality of the work itself.

Beryl Hibbs, 1985

The need for money

14.02 Within Britain Yearly Meeting money is needed for:

a. strengthening the life and witness of our local meetings;
b. spreading the message of Friends and interpreting and developing the thought and practice of the Religious Society of Friends;
c. undertaking our service for the relief of suffering at home and abroad;
d. funding the concerns of Friends that our meetings have adopted or agreed to support;
e. providing for the pastoral care of individual Friends, including assistance to those in need and for education;
f. maintaining and developing our meeting houses as places in which to worship and from which to carry our witness into the world;
g. administering and maintaining the organisation of Britain Yearly Meeting.

14.03 Our first financial responsibility is to our own meeting. All Friends and regular attenders should help, in accordance with their means, to meet the costs of having a place for worship and of running the meeting and its chosen activities.

14.04   Our monthly meetings, where our membership lies, are the back-bone of our yearly meeting. These need our financial support so that they may carry out their functions as described in chapter 4.

14.05   Beyond our monthly meeting, funds are required for the wider organisation of Friends and the work we undertake centrally. Without these we would be a scattered collection of small meetings with no coherence or shared witness.

14.06   The concerns of individuals and of groups have led Friends to undertake work which needs the help of permanent staff and of a central organisation. Meeting for Sufferings has many committees and oversees the work of our central departments (see chapters 7 & 8). The work of these committees and departments is financed through the Yearly Meeting Fund (14.12- 14.15).

14.07   It is important that Friends should make themselves aware of the activities which need their support. Details of the work financed centrally are available in publications distributed through meetings by the Quaker Communications Department. The *Report and accounts of the Yearly Meeting Fund* is published each year (6.21).

The schedule

14.08   In most monthly or preparative meetings a contribution schedule is sent to members and regular attenders annually, assisting them in contributing to local funds and the Yearly Meeting Fund, and in directing funds to particular uses, if so desired. Contribution schedules for distribution through meetings are available from the Quaker Communications Department. Meetings are urged, in appointing treasurers, to ensure that they are conversant with the financial needs of Britain Yearly Meeting and are prepared to bring them to the notice of Friends. Local overseers should be consulted as to which members and regular attenders should, and which should not, receive schedules (see 12.13.m). Some meetings have found it best to appoint two Friends, one to undertake the financial administration, the other a collector, who encourages and advises Friends and attenders in their giving.

Contributions can be considerably increased by the use of deeds of covenant and such other tax-effective means as may currently be available (for example Gift Aid), which enable the yearly meeting to benefit at no extra cost to the donor. Such arrangements also have the advantage that those who have a conscientious objection to any part of their taxes being used for military purposes can effectively redirect some tax to the work of the yearly meeting. Leaflets about tax-effective means of giving and advice on fundraising methods may be obtained from the Quaker Communications Department.

See 29.02.

Legacies

14.09   When drawing up a will, Friends are urged to consider bequeathing money for Quaker work. Income from legacies continues to be very important.

14.10   When a legacy is made to Britain Yearly Meeting, or one of its constituent meetings, it is best if Friends Trusts Limited is named as the beneficiary. Any special directions or wishes as to the purposes for which the legacy is to be used should be clearly specified, bearing in mind that any such use must fall within the general charitable purposes and programmes of the yearly meeting. In case the intended purposes do not remain applicable it is advisable not to make such directions or wishes legally binding. In the absence of any directions the legacy will be used for the work of the yearly meeting as a whole. Further advice on the wording of legacies can be obtained from the Quaker Finance & Property Department.

Use of funds

14.11   It is a requirement of legislation governing charitable status that all funds belonging to Britain Yearly Meeting and its constituent meetings, whether held locally or centrally, must be used exclusively to further its charitable purposes. Friends as individuals can contribute to other causes and such contributions can be given to a special collection arranged by a meeting, but there should be no contribution from the funds of the meeting itself.

THE YEARLY MEETING FUND

14.12 The Yearly Meeting Fund is charged with meeting all the central expenses of Britain Yearly Meeting: the administration of the Recording Clerk's Office and the holding of Yearly Meeting, Meeting for Sufferings and their committees; the work of the central departments; the maintenance of Friends House and other yearly meeting properties; the provision of the Library; the central support services for finance, personnel, premises and communications; the expenses of Friends attending Meeting for Sufferings and committees for central work; grants and subscriptions to other bodies and individuals; and such expenses as are authorised from time to time by or on behalf of Yearly Meeting or Meeting for Sufferings.

14.13 The income of the Yearly Meeting Fund is raised from individual contributors and meetings in response to information about the financial requirements for the centrally-funded work of the yearly meeting; from legacy income from Friends and other supporters; also from grants and contributions from sources outside Britain Yearly Meeting, from dividends and interest from investments, and from rents for the commercial offices in Drayton House and other investment properties.

14.14 The Quaker Finance & Property Central Committee is charged with the stewardship of the Yearly Meeting Fund under the direction of Meeting for Sufferings. Bank accounts are kept in the name of Britain Yearly Meeting and cheques are signed by the Recording Clerk or the Finance & Property Secretary or any other person duly authorised by the Quaker Finance & Property Central Committee. Funds which cannot be expended immediately are invested at the discretion of the Quaker Finance & Property Central Committee in accordance with legal constraints and the generally acknowledged ethical testimonies of Friends. Stewardship of the resources of the yearly meeting includes oversight of investments, property and all other assets, and financial resource planning.

14.15 The central committees prepare annual estimates of expenditure and income for the work of their departments within the guidelines agreed by Meeting for Sufferings. These budgets are co-ordinated by the Meeting for Sufferings Committee and presented to Meeting for Sufferings. Once approved the estimated expenditure should not be exceeded in any major degree. New commitments may not be entered into, nor major work laid down, without the authority of Meeting for Sufferings.

Annual Conference of Treasurers

14.16 The Annual Conference of Treasurers is held in order that the financial results of the previous year can be reviewed and budgets for the current year explained. It should be informed of the existing and proposed work of the yearly meeting, the funds available and to be raised, and the methods of fundraising proposed. The Conference is free to consider any aspect of the financing of that work, and may advise Meeting for Sufferings by minute concerning any matter of finance or fundraising. The Conference shall appoint its own committee with appropriate terms of reference and membership.

14.17 The membership of the Conference is as follows: the treasurer for the time being, or other appointed representative, of each monthly meeting, and of Young Friends General Meeting; members of the Conference committee; representatives of central and standing committees; with appropriate members of the Management Meeting in attendance.

See also 8.12

STEWARDSHIP OF OUR FUNDS

14.18 A fundamental principle of this part of our church government is corporate integrity. All Friends share responsibility for upholding this principle. This means that at every level of our church government Friends must be seen to be above reproach in our corporate, as well as our personal, conduct in respect of finance and property. We hold these assets in trust and the way we use and develop them is an important part of our witness. Whether we are formally appointed trustees for a period of service or not, each of us has responsibilities for the provision and stewardship of money, premises and other material resources belonging to the meetings of which we are members.

14.19   Churches have traditionally been trusted to manage their own affairs with minimal supervision from the civil authorities. This self-regulation is, however, being called increasingly into question, as social attitudes change, as abuses committed in the name of religion come to light, and as public bodies such as the Charity Commission take a closer interest in the financial arrangements of all charities. We must be sensitive to the new climate of opinion and accept social expectations which require of us a new openness to scrutiny by outside agencies. So long as our standards of corporate integrity, as well as of personal probity, remain of the highest order we shall have nothing to fear from public interest in our financial arrangements.

See also 20.54-20.66 on personal conduct in financial affairs

Accounts

14.20   All accounts held for meetings, committees and other Quaker bodies in banks and building societies must be held in the name of the meeting, committee or other Quaker body, and not in the name of any individual. The conduct of the account is the corporate responsibility of the account-holding body. It is recommended that the treasurer, the clerk and at least one other Friend should be authorised signatories and this must be recorded in the minutes and certified by the clerk to the bank or building society in which the account is held. All changes of authorisation must be promptly notified under the same procedure, with the clerk certifying the authenticity of the minute. It is good practice to allow cheques to be drawn and withdrawals only made up to a specified amount on the treasurer's authority alone, while cheques and withdrawals of larger amounts require more than one of the authorised signatures. Account-holding bodies are advised to review their arrangements in this regard at regular intervals.

14.21   Treasurers and other Friends particularly involved in the financial administration of their meetings are recommended to make themselves familiar with the detailed advice contained in the *Treasurers' handbook,* obtainable from the Quaker Communications Department.

14.22   In order that financial responsibility is assured, proper accounting records must be kept including all the transactions and the assets and liabilities of the meeting. An annual statement of accounts must be prepared and this must be examined by an independent person who has the requisite ability and practical experience to carry out a competent examination of the accounts before they are considered by the responsible meeting, committee or other Quaker body and, if approved, accepted. If a Friend is appointed he or she should not have been involved in the accounting or property and financial management of the meeting concerned. If the gross income or the total expenditure in any year or in either of the two preceding years exceeds £250,000 (a sum which may be amended by order of the Secretary of State for the Home Office under Section 43 of the Charities Act 1993) then the examination must be carried out by a qualified auditor as defined in the Charities Act 1993.

14.23   Legislation sets out the general provisions for keeping accounts and for their supervision by the Charity Commissioners in England and Wales and by the Lord Advocate in Scotland. The detailed requirements are subject to orders made from time to time by the Secretary of State and further information on these is obtainable from the Quaker Finance & Property Department. It is expected that the report and accounts of each monthly meeting will normally encompass the financial affairs of all its constituent meetings. A copy of the latest accounts must be provided to any member of the public on request. Accounting records must be preserved for at least six years after the end of the financial year to which they relate.

Ethical investment

14.24   Friends are rightly concerned about the effects of their investments (see 20.56-20.57). Those responsible for investments on behalf of Friends should refer to 15.07. A meeting or committee should consider ethical criteria when choosing investments, but in so doing should try not to increase the work of the treasurer, particularly if the amount of money involved is small. A treasurer can usefully seek guidance from the meeting or committee concerned.

Personal liability

14.25 Treasurers and others acting on behalf of a meeting, committee or other Quaker body ought not to be held personally liable for any loss so long as they have acted reasonably, in good faith and on the best advice available to them. It is the responsibility of the meeting, committee or other Quaker body to exercise the necessary care, and in particular to set bounds to the latitude of decision allowed to its treasurer and others acting on its behalf. Indemnification against personal loss and liability cannot be expected if these bounds are exceeded.

14.26 Trustees incur additional responsibilities, some of which impinge on them as individuals. They are answerable at law for the conduct of their trust. Advice on the Quaker understanding of trusteeship is given in the next chapter (15.03-15.05) and in the *Treasurers' handbook*. General guidance on the legal position of trustees will be found in leaflets available from the Charity Commission, or in Scotland the Inland Revenue, and specific advice can be obtained from these bodies when required.

Chapter 15

Property and trusteeship

TRUST PROPERTY

15.01 All property belonging to the yearly meeting is held in trust to be used for its charitable purposes, either generally or for specific uses as determined by the donor. Some property is in the form of land and buildings, the remainder being held in cash and investments. Land and buildings can either be functional, being held by Friends for their own occupation and use (such as meeting houses and offices), or be investment property to produce income. When property is held on a perpetual trust, commonly referred to as an endowment, the capital must not be expended, but only the income it produces.

In legal terms the constituent meetings of the Yearly Meeting of Friends in Britain are charities for the advancement of religion and, as such, are subject to the requirements of the Charities Acts 1992 and 1993, or to the Law Reform (Miscellaneous Provisions) (Scotland) Act 1990. Each meeting in England and Wales should be either registered with the Charity Commissioners or formally recorded and notified by Friends Trusts Limited as an excepted charity. In Scotland each meeting should obtain recognition by the Inland Revenue as a Scottish charity. This will enable the meeting readily to demonstrate its entitlement to the fiscal reliefs available to charities. It will also define the meeting as a charity unit for the purpose of trusteeship of property and for reporting and accounting.

It is possible for individual trusts and preparative or recognised meetings to be separately recorded as charities in their own right and there may be special circumstances where this is appropriate, but it is recommended that the monthly meeting should normally be regarded as the charity unit. This recommendation to record the monthly meeting as a charity embracing all its constituent meetings takes account of the fact that individual membership lies with the monthly meeting and of the advice (see 15.03) that property should be held on behalf of monthly meetings.

The services of the Charity Commission, or in Scotland the Inland Revenue, are available to trustees of charities for advice on all matters; and particularly for the establishment of 'schemes' to facilitate the working of charitable trusts, or to provide for a variation of their objects in cases where the objects for which they were founded have become obsolete or unworkable. The duty is laid on trustees of charities to consider seeking such variations instead of allowing trust income to accumulate unspent. For smaller trusts there are provisions whereby trustees can initiate a merger with another trust or expend capital without the need for a formal scheme.

Friends Trusts Limited

15.02   Friends Trusts Limited is a company which is limited by guarantee and does not have a share capital. It was incorporated in 1923 and is recognised as the trust corporation for The Religious Society of Friends in Great Britain. It is a registered charity, number 237698. The members of the Board of Management are appointed by Meeting for Sufferings and are not remunerated. The clerk of the Quaker Finance & Property Central Committee is a member of that Board ex officio. The registered office of Friends Trusts Limited is at 173 Euston Road, London NW1 2BJ.

The main object of the Company is to act as custodian trustee, where the terms of trust permit, of property and investments situated in any part of the world and held on trust for the benefit of or in connection with the Religious Society of Friends in Great Britain. In general it considers its function as holding, as distinct from managing, property and investments; any decisions, as regards both capital and income, are normally taken by the managing trustees of the meeting or other Quaker body to whom the property belongs, and Friends Trusts Limited then acts entirely on the instructions of such beneficial owner.

For the duties of Friends Trusts Limited in connection with the sale or disposition of meeting houses and other property of which it is custodian trustee see 15.10-15.11

Trustees

15.03   All property and investments belonging to Britain Yearly Meeting
and its constituent meetings must be managed by trustees on behalf
of the meeting or other body concerned, to which reports should be
made at suitable intervals. It is generally advisable that trusts should
be held on behalf of monthly meetings rather than preparative or
general meetings. Where trust property belongs to, or other trusts
are under the care of, preparative meetings, the monthly meeting is
to exercise a general oversight of them.

It is recommended that all property and investments of meetings in
England and Wales should be held in the name of Friends Trusts
Limited as custodian trustee of the Society, and not in the names of
individual trustees. This will relieve meetings of the need to transfer
ownership each time a trustee ceases to act and a new one is appointed.
It means that Friends Trusts Limited will be the legal owner of the
property but that the beneficial ownership and management will
remain with the meeting or other Quaker body concerned. As a trust
corporation Friends Trusts Limited is a permanent legal entity and
this makes it easier for it to effect property transactions and to enter
into legal contracts.

15.04   Where property is held on the terms of a trust deed or Charity Commission Scheme there will be defined arrangements for the appointment of managing trustees. In other cases it is advisable for the
monthly meeting to have a procedure for appointing and maintaining an adequate number of managing trustees, in order to ensure the
proper day-to-day conduct of all the property matters for which the
meeting is responsible.

The managing trustees should be provided with rules or terms of reference which define their duties, the duration of their appointments
and the extent to which they may take decisions without reference
back to their appointing body.

The meeting may make individual appointments or, preferably,
appoint the members for the time being of its finance and property
committee (or of a similar committee) to serve as its managing
trustees ex officio. Appointments as managing trustees should not be

confined to those with long experience of property and financial matters but should be widely representative of the meeting. It is a criminal offence for a person to act as a trustee if he or she has an unspent conviction for any offence involving dishonesty or deception or is an undischarged bankrupt or has been disqualified from being a company director or trustee. Under certain circumstances it is possible for such disqualifications to be waived by the Charity Commissioners.

Among managing trustees, moreover, there should at all times be a sufficient spread of membership to ensure that there is at least one managing trustee belonging to each preparative meeting, to bring local knowledge to managing trustees' deliberations and to facilitate liaison with preparative meetings and their premises committees. Managing trustees may on occasion be invited to make representations on behalf of their preparative meetings, and on other occasions have to interpret to their preparative meetings decisions taken in the best interests of the monthly meeting as a whole. Theirs is not an easy task; but it is a vital one, and plays an important part in our church government by maintaining good relations between monthly meetings and their preparative meetings.

15.05   Managing trustees are expected to conduct their meetings according to the Quaker business method (see chapter 3). Some Charity Commission schemes provide for majority voting but this provision would be exercisable only if trustees could not agree a minute made by their clerk discerning the sense of the meeting. Minutes are to be made in the meeting and accepted and signed in accordance with our church government.

Managing trustees should report to their monthly meeting at least once a year. They should also refer to the monthly meeting in session any major decisions, such as those involving the acquisition, disposal or major alteration of land or buildings.

The powers conferred upon managing trustees should not be delegated by them except in connection with routine matters or those with few or no financial implications. They may, for example, choose to delegate to preparative meetings and their premises committees the interior decoration and maintenance of buildings, and the general upkeep of gardens and burial grounds, subject to specified limits on expenditure which may be incurred without prior permission having been obtained from the managing trustees. Managing trustees should also satisfy themselves that adequate reporting arrangements are in place for them to supervise the exercise of delegated powers, and likewise for preparative meetings and their premises committees to be kept regularly informed of the policies being followed and decisions taken by the managing trustees.

For further information on trusteeship see the Treasurers' handbook

Investment of trust funds

15.06   Except where the trust deed specifically provides otherwise, the powers and duties of trustees are subject to the provisions of the Trustee Investments Act 1961. Full details of its requirements are set out in a leaflet available from the Charity Commission. Broadly, the Act allows trustees to invest a proportion of their funds in the stocks and shares of certain qualifying companies incorporated in the United Kingdom, and also in certain authorised unit or investment trusts. When making any such investment the trustees must obtain written advice from a person whom they believe to be qualified by ability and experience to give such advice.

15.07   Friends will also need to take note of the guidelines issued by Meeting for Sufferings for ethical considerations in the selection of investments. When the fund to be invested is small it is difficult to obtain the necessary spread of investment except by participation in a unit trust or an investment trust; there are several such trusts in which the underlying investments conform to specified ethical criteria but not all of them are acceptable under the Trustee Investments Act 1961. Further information about ethical investment can be obtained by subscribing to the Ethical Investment Research Service (EIRIS), whose address may be obtained from the Quaker Finance & Property Department.

See also 14.24 & 20.56-20.57

Records, trust accounts and property registers

15.08 Friends should ensure that the trusts on which legacies and other gifts are held are recorded in some way that will make future reference easy. A separate account should be kept in the books of the meeting, committee or other Quaker body for each fund held on separate trusts, so as to avoid any inadvertent expenditure of capital or income for a purpose for which it was not intended. All such funds, while being separately identifiable, should be included as an integral part of the annual report and accounts of the meeting, committee or other Quaker body which holds them in trust. Consequently they are subject to the examination, auditing and reporting requirements applicable to such accounts (14.22).

15.09 Monthly meetings and other owning bodies are recommended to maintain a register of properties and similar trusts; this register should note the original purposes of such trusts, any alterations agreed in such purposes, the names of trustees, the method of appointment of new trustees (15.04), and the whereabouts of the deeds and relevant documents. The safe-keeping of these documents should be entrusted to two or more Friends appointed for the purpose and the place of deposit should be known to Friends. It is advised that such registers should be examined at least triennially, being compared with the minutes of the monthly meeting to ensure that any alterations are properly recorded.

Sale and other disposal of property

15.10 Buildings and land held on charitable trusts shall not be mortgaged, sold, leased or otherwise disposed of unless the trustees have first followed the procedure required by law. This normally entails obtaining a written report from a qualified surveyor acting exclusively for the charity, advertising the disposition as advised by the surveyor and being satisfied that the terms are the best that can reasonably be obtained. In certain circumstances, such as disposition to a person connected with the charity, it is necessary to obtain an order from the Charity Commissioners. Further information on the detailed requirements is obtainable from Friends Trusts Limited.

These regulations do not apply in Scotland where there are no restrictions on the disposition of charity land provided that it does not contravene the terms of the trusts. However it is recommended that meetings in Scotland should, as a matter of good practice, follow the procedure outlined above.

Disused burial grounds – especially those where there is no meeting house adjacent – have sometimes proved burdensome to monthly meetings. In such cases the possibility of sale should be considered, with due regard to the use to which the ground would be put. If the land has no immediately realisable value consideration should be given to a lease, possibly at peppercorn rent, to some person or body prepared to maintain it in good condition as an open space. Whilst a burial ground remains in the care of the meeting it is important to see that it is properly maintained and that others do not acquire the land through default. A memorandum is available from the Quaker Finance & Property Department about the disposal of burial grounds and the removal of remains.

Monthly meetings or other owning bodies should consider and endeavour to assess realistically all the circumstances before offering for sale any land or buildings in connection with a meeting house. There have been cases in the past where a small meeting has been revived or one long discontinued has been reopened. It has become increasingly difficult to find suitable sites or existing properties that are available for new meeting houses. This may be an additional reason for retaining existing meeting houses in Quaker ownership, in case one day they may be required again.

England and Wales

15.11 Before selling or leasing land which has been held for a specific purpose, such as a burial ground, it is necessary to give public notice of the intention and to consider any representations made about the proposal. In proceeding with any disposal the owning body and its managing trustees will be under a statutory duty to obtain the best terms available. Where Friends Trusts Limited is the custodian trustee of the property it is required to seal the conveyance or lease and will do so on receipt of the properly minuted instructions of the managing trustees. However the Board of Management of the Trust will need to be satisfied that the required procedure has been followed and that all costs arising in connection with the disposal will be met by the beneficial owner. In the case of a meeting house or other property which has been used for the purposes of the Society the proceeds of sale will form a permanent endowment and the capital must be retained for similar purposes in the future.

Scotland

15.12 The Charities Acts 1992 and 1993 and the remit of the Charity Commissioners do not for the most part apply to charities which are constituted under Scots law. Such charities are subject *inter alia* to the Law Reform (Miscellaneous Provisions)(Scotland) Act 1990. Whilst the recognition of charities in Scotland is carried out by the Inland Revenue and the Lord Advocate, the regulations on trustee-ship and accountability are much the same in substance as those which apply in England and Wales. However the only restrictions on the sale of meeting houses or burial grounds in Scotland and the use of the proceeds of sale are those determined by the trusts on which the property is held.

MEETING HOUSES

Certification and registration

15.13 Meeting houses in England and Wales should be certified as places of worship under the Places of Worship Registration Act 1855. Forms for this can be obtained from the superintendent registrar of births, deaths and marriages for the district in which the meeting house is situated. Such certification will establish the meeting house as a place of worship for the purpose of any legislation where evidence of use of the property is required. Places of public religious worship are exempt from the payment of non-domestic rates and there are sig-nificant concessions for other property used for charitable purposes. In order to ensure that the full entitlement is obtained it is necessary to inform the Local Valuation Office of the Inland Revenue and the rates department of the local authority of the nature and purposes of such property. There is no provision for the registration of places of worship in Scotland and liability to or exemption from rates is governed by the Local Government (Scotland) Act 1991.

Care of premises

15.14 A meeting house should not be regarded primarily in terms of bricks and mortar, or merely seen in relation to potential site value. Its real value derives from the worship and service of the meeting. Even so, our meeting houses no less than our own homes deserve our care, attention and imaginative thought, so that they may be attractive both to ourselves and to others. Care of our premises is an important and sometimes exacting responsibility, which should be exercised by or on behalf of the meeting to which it belongs. Managing trustees and premises committees should be vigilant so that small defects do not pass unnoticed and lead in the future to extensive and costly repairs. It is recommended that premises be inspected at regular intervals by a surveyor or architect. The Advisory Committee on Property, which is accountable to the Quaker Finance & Property Central Committee, can be approached for more detailed advice and the handbook which they publish consulted.

New meeting houses

15.15 In the provision of meeting houses, monthly meetings should, wherever possible, choose sites which allow for the greatest possible use by the whole community. The acquisition of older property for conversion to a meeting house may involve difficulties which should be assessed by a surveyor before purchase is considered by the monthly meeting. In contemplating the building of meeting houses, monthly meetings should have regard to the suitability of the building as a place of worship. Relevant criteria include simplicity of design, soundness of construction, access for people with disabilities and avoidance of extravagance.

Funds are available in suitable cases for making loans or grants, or both, to monthly meetings to meet part of the cost of building new meeting houses; the purchase and adaptation of properties to make them suitable for use as meeting houses; major alterations to existing meeting houses and major repairs to historic meeting houses. Information about the Meeting Houses Funds is obtainable from the Quaker Finance & Property Department.

Use of premises

15.16 Monthly meetings are advised to permit and encourage the use of their meeting houses for educational and other suitable purposes which serve the needs of the people living in their neighbourhood. Such users should be expected to make an appropriate financial contribution to the running expenses and upkeep. It should be borne in mind that the primary purpose of the meeting house is as a place of public worship.

As premises used by the public, meeting houses must meet certain statutory requirements in respect of fire precautions, safety and hygiene. Gas and electrical appliances may need to be certified as correctly installed. All premises must be adequately insured, including third-party and accident insurance as well as buildings and contents insurance; the *Treasurers' handbook* should be consulted for more detailed advice.

In considering the proper use of their meeting houses, monthly meetings should be sensitive to the feelings of the worshipping community, whose members may object to the introduction of alcoholic drinks on to the premises, or to smoking or other practices, by other users of the meeting house which is the meeting's home. Lettings policies should be agreed between monthly meetings and preparative meetings, in respect of particular premises, and conditions made clear to prospective users. The use of Quaker premises by political parties, and by other religious or secular organisations with whose principles or practices Friends might not be in sympathy, will always require careful consideration and full consultation with Friends in the meeting most closely concerned. Particular care must be taken to avoid bookings by 'front' organisations with undesirable aims; the bona fides of new users should be checked. In all cases it is important to ensure that any publicity given to meetings held on

Quaker premises makes a clear distinction between those organised by a meeting, committee or other Quaker body as such, and those for which other groups are responsible, in order to avoid confusion in the public mind.

Meetings and committees involved in the letting of Quaker premises should always bear in mind the need to minimise hurt to individual Friends, division among the membership and erosion of our distinctive Quaker identity.

BURIAL GROUNDS

Record of interments

15.17   Monthly meetings are advised to keep a careful record of their burial grounds and to maintain and regularly review plans of them containing details of the interments (see 4.42.c). The plan of burial plots and record of interments for each burial ground should be cross-referenced, as appropriate, to entries and indexes in the register of burials (see 17.12).

Closed burial grounds

15.18   A clear distinction must be made between those burial grounds which are available for further burials and those which should be regarded as closed, or available only for the interment of ashes. The scattering of ashes is permitted in closed burial grounds (see 17.11-17.13).

Other burial grounds

15.19   Where a meeting has made special arrangements for Quaker burials and interments in burial grounds not in Friends' ownership, it is advised to maintain close liaison with the relevant authority.

Gravestones

15.20   Friends are left at liberty to adopt the use of plain gravestones in any
burial grounds; it being distinctly understood that, in all cases, they
are to be erected under the direction of the monthly meeting; so that,
in each particular burial ground, such uniformity is preserved in
respect to the materials, size, form and wording of the stones, as well
as in the mode of placing them, as may effectually guard against any
distinction being made in that place between the rich and the poor.

Chapter 16

Quaker marriage procedure

INTRODUCTION

16.01 For the right joining in marriage is the work of the Lord only, and not the priests' or magistrates'; for it is God's ordinance and not man's; and therefore Friends cannot consent that they should join them together: for we marry none; it is the Lord's work, and we are but witnesses.

George Fox, 1669

16.02 Thomas Ellwood, recalling his own marriage in 1669, wrote of the value of the meeting for worship: 'We sensibly felt the Lord with us and joining us, the sense whereof remained with us all our lifetime, and was of good service and very comfortable to us on all occasions.'

Early Friends realised the importance of recording marriages which had taken place in a meeting for worship and increasingly recognised their responsibility for reporting such marriages to the authorities. They fervently maintained, however, that marriage was a solemn contract made in the presence of God in the meeting for worship. From the very early days of the Society stress was laid on the need for serious consideration prior to marriage, the clearness of the parties from all other engagements, the publicity given to the intention of marriage and the value of the meeting for worship, in which the declarations were made by the parties in the presence of a number of members of the Society.

The basis of a Friends' marriage remains the same as in the early days of the Society. The simple Quaker wedding where the couple, together with their friends, gather in worship is for Friends the most natural setting for the two concerned to make a commitment to each other in the presence of God. With their declaration they take each other freely and equally as life-long partners, committing themselves to joining their lives together in loving companionship, asking God's blessing on their union. They believe that, whatever stresses and strains may arise in the relationship, these can be resolved if both partners are able and willing to accept and trust each other in a generous spirit. With God's help their love for each other can deepen and change in a lifetime of marriage together.

Britain Yearly Meeting has established certain procedures in the case of a marriage to be solemnised in a Friends' meeting for worship. This is partly to ensure that the legal requirements are observed and the proper records kept. Far more important, however, is the value of the procedure in emphasising to those being married the solemn nature of their undertaking; to the monthly meeting the need to uphold the parties concerned, both during the meeting for worship and thereafter; and to all those concerned, their corporate responsibility for the meeting for worship being rightly held. Couples contemplating marriage should at an early stage seek advice from their registering officer as to the entire procedure.

As a number of those attending the wedding may be unfamiliar with worship based on silence, it is particularly important that there should be a good attendance of Friends who come concerned for the spiritual depth of the occasion. A meeting for worship for the solemnisation of a marriage is held in the same form and spirit as a Friends' meeting for worship at other times. It is an occasion when the parties to the marriage may gain inspiration and help from the meeting, which may continue to be a source of strength to them during their married life. It is also an opportunity for all those who attend the meeting for worship to ask God's blessing on the marriage and support the parties to it in their prayers.

A selection of Friends' views may be found at Marriage and steadfast commitment *22.33-22.50 and* Ending of relationships *22.73-22.79. For seventeenth-century practice see 19.56.*

16.03   We think it right to remind our members of the ancient testimony of our Society, that marriage is not a mere civil contract, but a religious act.

Yearly Meeting in London, 1848

SUMMARY OF PROCEDURE

16.04   Quaker marriage is not an alternative form of marriage available to the general public, but is for members and those who, whilst not being in formal membership, are in unity with its religious nature and witness. Usually, however, one or both of the parties being married will be members or they will be otherwise associated with the Society. Additionally, the Marriage Act 1949 relating to England and Wales places certain limitations on who may be married according to Friends' usage.

16.05   Anyone contemplating marriage according to the usage of Friends should at an early stage apply to the registering officer of the monthly meeting in the area in which it is intended that the marriage should take place. Ideally this should be at least three months before the intended marriage, and it must be not less than six weeks beforehand, to give time for the necessary procedures to take place (see also 16.23-16.27 & 16.33). The couple must complete a declaration of intention of marriage (16.12-16.13 & 16.17). They must also fulfil all the legal requirements for a marriage, including obtaining the appropriate certificates from the registrars of the districts in which they live. Couples may consider the holding of a meeting for clearness as part of their preparation for marriage (16.19-16.21).

Those not in membership need to complete additional requirements, including a discussion with at least two members of the Society and perhaps through the holding of a meeting for clearness, to help the monthly meeting to assess whether there is sufficient unity of understanding, or association with the Society, to allow a marriage according to Quaker usage to go forward (see 16.13). (For the responsibility of overseers in this matter see 12.13.o.)

16.06 Once an application for marriage has been approved, public notice of the intended marriage will be given at the meeting(s) which the couple attend, and the monthly meeting will appoint, or ensure the appointment of, a meeting for worship for the solemnisation of the marriage. A brief explanation at the start of this meeting will generally be given for any of those attending who have not been to a Quaker marriage, or meeting, before. During the course of the meeting the couple will stand if able and exchange declarations of marriage in prescribed words (16.36-16.37). Wedding rings play no formal part in Quaker marriages, but many couples like to give each other rings after they have made their declarations. Neither photography, nor potentially disturbing electronic recording is suitable during the meeting for worship. At an appropriate stage during the meeting a certificate confirming the declaration is signed by the couple and two or more witnesses, and is then read aloud by the registering officer, or other suitable Friend. After the meeting it is customary for all present when the declarations were made to sign the certificate.

16.07 In brief, those to be married must:

    a. apply to the registering officer for their marriage to be solemnised according to the usage of Britain Yearly Meeting (16.12-16.18);

    b. obtain support in writing from two adult Friends for each non-member applicant (16.13);

    c. give notice of intention as required by law in England and Wales to the superintendent registrar and obtain the certificate or licence (16.22-16.26);

    d. give notice of intention as required by law in Scotland and obtain the marriage schedule before marriage and arrange for the legal registration of the marriage after it has been solemnised (16.22-16.26 & 16.46);

The registering officer must arrange for:

    e. the giving of public notice of the intended marriage in the meeting or meetings to which the parties belong or which they usually attend (16.23);

    f. ensuring in England and Wales that the certificate (form D) is in the hands of the superintendent registrar for those intending to marry who are not in membership (16.25-16.26);

g. ensuring that the relevant meeting for church affairs appoints the meeting for worship at which the marriage will take place (16.27-16.30);

h. notice of the intended meeting for worship to be given in accordance with 16.35;

i. the solemnisation of the marriage at the meeting for worship; in England and Wales the registration of the marriage after the meeting, and in Scotland the appropriate signing of the schedule (16.36-16.40 & 16.46).

16.08   No marriage following these procedures can take place which is not authorised by law. The procedure laid down in 16.12-16.18 & 16.22-16.35 must also be completed before the marriage takes place.

OFFICERS

16.09   The officers concerned with the arrangements for marriages are:

a. the clerks and registering officers of monthly meetings: these are officers of the yearly meeting and their names and addresses may be ascertained from the *Book of meetings* or by enquiry among local Friends;

b. the superintendent registrars (England and Wales) or the district registrars (Scotland): these are public officials responsible for registration districts.

Registering officers

16.10   Each monthly meeting shall appoint a suitable Friend as registering officer for the purpose of these regulations, and, in England and Wales, but not in Scotland, to register all marriages that may be solemnised according to the usage of the Society within the monthly meeting. Monthly meetings are advised to review their appointments regularly, normally on a triennial basis. The registering officer shall register only such marriages as are solemnised within the limits of the monthly meeting by which he or she is appointed. On every fresh appointment of a registering officer the monthly meeting making the appointment shall report to the Recording Clerk without delay, by minute signed by the clerk, the name and address of the registering officer newly appointed. The Recording Clerk is required to certify all such appointments in England and Wales to the Registrar General and, for such appointments in Scotland, to the clerk of General Meeting for Scotland who will inform the Registrar General for Scotland.

16.11 The monthly meeting is responsible for the appointment of a meeting for worship for the solemnisation of a marriage, directly or by giving permission to a preparative meeting (see 16.27). The registering officer, acting on behalf of the monthly meeting, is responsible for the acceptance of an application for marriage according to Friends' usage. He or she is also responsible for giving the parties the necessary advice and assistance in relation to the procedure under these regulations, for seeing that all the necessary steps preceding the marriage are completed, and, in England and Wales, but not Scotland, for the registration of the marriage. He or she should feel free to consult the monthly meeting clerk or some other knowledgeable Friend to check that the appropriate forms have been properly completed. Monthly meetings may also appoint from time to time two or three Friends whom the registering officer can consult in cases where he or she feels this necessary or desirable. A handbook for registering officers is available from the Recording Clerk.

All powers and duties given to the clerk of a monthly meeting or preparative meeting shall, in the case of her or his absence or incapacity, be exercised by the assistant or acting clerk of the same meeting.

PREPARATION FOR MARRIAGE

Application

16.12 One of the parties wishing to be united in marriage should apply for a copy of the marriage forms (see 16.54) to the registering officer of the monthly meeting under the auspices of which they wish the marriage to take place. Form A is a joint declaration of intention of marriage, stating the time and place of the meeting for worship at which it is desired that the marriage may be solemnised. If necessary the date and time (but not the place) of the marriage may be omitted when filling in form A, but in such cases particulars should be sent to the registering officer as soon as possible. Before form A is completed the registering officer should be satisfied that there is no evident difficulty in the intended marriage being held at the time and place proposed. Form A should be completed and returned (together with form B and/or C if appropriate) to the registering officer not less than six weeks before the date of the intended marriage. It need not be signed by both parties at the same time or in the presence of each other, but the signature of each of the parties must be attested by one adult witness. The registering officer should meet with both the parties to discuss their application and to give such advice and assistance as may be necessary. If this proves impossible, the registering officer should ask the registering officer of an area convenient for the parties to meet with them. The registering officer should also consider whether there might be advantage in meeting the parties separately.

16.13   If one or both of the parties is not in membership, each party not in membership should in addition complete form B (if a man) or form C (if a woman); these are applications for permission to marry according to the usage of the Religious Society of Friends. Each application must be supported by the written recommendation of two adult members of the Society.

The two adult members are expected to have discussed the application with the parties, even if the applicant(s) is already known to them. If the applicant(s) is not known to them, then a home visit, perhaps to each party not in membership individually, may be appropriate. Alternatively, the discussion could take place within a meeting for clearness (16.19-16.21). The two Friends should be satisfied that each applicant is in unity with our testimony as to the nature of marriage, and has experience of our meetings for worship. They must not be close relatives of either party.

The completed forms B and/or C should be returned together with form A to the registering officer, who will follow the procedure described in 16.18.

Advice to registering officers and monthly meetings

16.14 The registering officer is advised to meet with the applicants at a very early stage, preferably before they complete the marriage forms, so that the Quaker testimony on marriage may be talked over, to ensure that the applicants understand the nature of Quaker worship, our testimony to simplicity and the avoidance of ostentation, and are ready to make their declarations in the form required. The registering officer may find it an advantage to draw one or more other Friends into these conversations, or use a meeting for clearness (16.19-16.21). It is the duty of the registering officer to forward an application for a marriage to the meeting for church affairs which is responsible for appointing a meeting for worship for this purpose (16.27-16.31).

16.15 The registering officer, acting on behalf of the monthly meeting, also has the responsibility for granting permission to non-members to marry according to our usage (see 16.13, 16.16 & 16.18, noting the different procedure between (a) England and Wales and (b) Scotland). The registering officer should be satisfied that care has been taken to ensure that those applying for a Friends' marriage are in unity with our testimony as to the nature of marriage (see 16.01-16.03). It is on this testimony that the claim rests for recognition of our special and privileged procedure.

16.16 Special care should be exercised in the following cases:

a. where neither party is known to the registering officer;
b. where neither party is a member;
c. where either party has had a previous marriage dissolved;
d. where either party has been in a long-term relationship with another person, especially where children are involved.

If the registering officer does not feel able to allow arrangements to proceed without further consideration, in these and other cases where special care is necessary, the matter should be referred to the monthly meeting or to such Friends as may have been appointed for the purpose. The registering officer is advised to take this action where either party has had a previous marriage dissolved, as suggested in 16.17.

Re-marriage of divorced persons

16.17 Monthly meetings should be sympathetic to and understanding of those who wish to marry in a Friends' meeting and who have been divorced. Many in this situation may have experienced a sense of failure in their lives and feel deeply that they have not been able to keep solemn promises they have made in the past. We should all be able to share these feelings, realising the occasions when we have experienced a sense of failure and have not lived up to promises we have made. Whilst in no way departing from our corporate testimony as to the sanctity and life-long nature of marriage, monthly meetings are given discretion whether or not to grant permission to those who wish to re-marry in a Friends' meeting.

In exercising such discretion, monthly meetings will need to be fully satisfied that those who wish to re-marry share this testimony and, except in rare cases, are well known to and associated with the meeting. As recommended by London Yearly Meeting in 1957, monthly meetings might well appoint certain Friends of sound judgment and discretion to consider each application and so assist the meeting in reaching a decision without undesirable discussion of details in the meeting itself. See also 16.19-16.21 and 12.22-12.25 on the use of meetings for clearness.

See also 22.73-22.79 for extracts on the ending of relationships

Permission to non-members

16.18 On receipt of the completed forms A and B and/or C as the case may be, the registering officer, if assenting to the application, shall, if the marriage is to be solemnised in England or Wales, issue form D to the party, or each such party, not in membership and resident in England or Wales. Form D is a certificate granting permission for marriage to be solemnised according to the usage of the Society in Britain. If the parties have to give notice to different superintendent registrars, form D should be issued in duplicate for the party, or each such party, not in membership (see 16.22 & 16.25-16.26). In Scotland the issuing of form D to non-members does not apply to residents.

If the registering officer does not accede to the application he or she shall refer the matter to his or her monthly meeting which may grant or refuse the application at its discretion. If the monthly meeting grants the application, the registering officer shall proceed. If the monthly meeting refuses the application, the clerk shall inform the parties in writing immediately.

The use of meetings for clearness in preparation for marriage

16.19 Some monthly meetings have re-introduced a former practice. On receiving a request for a marriage according to Friends' usage, they offer to appoint a meeting for clearness as part of the preparation involved. They recognise that this may provide an opportunity, for both the couple and those invited to take part, to explore the nature of the commitment that is being contemplated. The small group of Friends and the couple will get to know one another at a deeper level. Prayerful consideration in a relaxed atmosphere is time well spent. It may be of benefit to the couple in later years.

The origin of these meetings was to ensure that the persons contemplating marriage were 'clear' of any encumbrance. Nowadays the name is used to indicate a search for clearness as to whether the proposed course of action is right.

16.20 The proposal to hold a meeting for clearness may be initiated either:

a. by the couple themselves if they are not yet sure whether it is right for them to marry or to ask for a Quaker ceremony. They may want to consider the implications more deeply with a group of Friends prior to formal application. This may or may not involve the registering officer;

b. by the registering officer in the course of initial discussions about marriage procedures. He or she would explain to the couple how such a meeting is called and that it should be viewed as a helpful part of the preparation for marriage rather than an examination as to their fitness for it. The aim of such a meeting is to allow the couple to explore what their commitment will mean to them as they plan their future life together;

c. by the monthly meeting, particularly where there are special circumstances that need careful consideration, or if one or both of those asking for a Quaker marriage are not well known to the meeting (see 16.16).

Whether or not a meeting for clearness is held, all the procedures and requirements outlined in this chapter will have to be carefully considered and complied with.

16.21 The conduct of meetings for clearness is covered in 12.22-12.25. A few special points should be noted in this context:

 a. it will not be appropriate to include close relatives of the couple in the membership of the meeting for clearness;

 b. when an application has been received and it is agreed that a meeting for clearness should be held, at least one elder or one overseer (or experienced Friend, where these officers are not appointed) should be included in the group. In most such cases the registering officer will also join it so that he or she is in a position to give guidance to the monthly meeting as to whether the marriage should be allowed;

 c. any personal matters that are disclosed in the course of the meeting should be regarded as confidential to the group;

 d. subsequently, the registering officer should be in a position to recommend to the monthly meeting whether or not the couple should be allowed to marry according to our usage.

ARRANGEMENTS FOR MARRIAGE

Notice to registrar

16.22 Before a marriage can be solemnised in England or Wales according to the usage of Friends, notice must be given by the parties concerned to the appropriate superintendent registrar and a certificate or certificates obtained. The certificate(s) or certificate and licence, as the case may be, should be obtained from the superintendent registrar(s) for the area(s) in which the parties live, and should be delivered to the registering officer as soon as possible after they are obtained. For marriages in Scotland a marriage schedule is obtained from the registrar for the district in which the marriage is to take place and this should be sent to the registering officer as soon as possible after it has been obtained (see 16.46.b).

Registering officers are strongly advised to have in their possession not less than twenty-four hours before the ceremony the certificate(s) or certificate and licence of the appropriate superintendent registrar(s) in England or Wales, or the appropriate schedule issued by the district registrar in Scotland. In England and Wales marriages may take place in areas other than those in which the certificates or licences were issued, but in Scotland marriages must take place within the area of the district registrar issuing the marriage schedule. In no case can a marriage be solemnised unless the certificate (or certificate and licence) or schedule is produced.

Public notice of intention of marriage

16.23   On receipt of form A the registering officer, if assenting to the application, shall cause public notice of the intended marriage to be given at the close of the usual meeting(s) for worship of which the parties are members, or, if not in membership, which they attend or which is the nearest to their place(s) of residence. Such notice shall be in the terms of, or to the effect of, form E. Form E shall be endorsed by the Friend by whom the notice is given. If the registering officer receives any notice of objection, which must be in writing, he or she shall immediately inform the parties.

Marriages when one or both parties are resident outside Great Britain

16.24   In any case where one, or both, of the parties is resident outside Great Britain, or is not a citizen of the United Kingdom, the registering officer is advised to refer to the superintendent or district registrar for advice as to any additional formalities which may have to be completed, or any modifications which may have to be made to the procedure outlined above. It should be noted that the Isle of Man and the Channel Islands are outside Great Britain.

Marriage by certificate

16.25 a. *Marriages in England and Wales*

If both the parties reside, and have resided for at least seven clear days, in the district of the same superintendent registrar, one of the parties should give notice of the intended marriage in person to the said superintendent registrar. Such notice should be accompanied by the appropriate fee and should be on the prescribed form which will be supplied by the superintendent registrar on application. After the expiration of twenty-one clear days the superintendent registrar will, on application, deliver a certificate stating that the notice required by law has been duly complied with. The superintendent registrar's certificate is valid for twelve months after the entry in the marriage notice book, after which it expires. After expiry, the application must start afresh.

If the parties reside in the districts of different superintendent registrars and have so resided for at least seven clear days, then notice must in like manner be given to each superintendent registrar, and the certificate of each superintendent registrar must be obtained.

If one or both of the parties reside in Scotland, notice must be given to the district registrar(s) of the registration district(s) in Scotland in which each party has her or his usual residence or has been resident for fifteen clear days immediately previous to the giving of such notice, and the certificate(s) of such district registrar(s) must be obtained and will have the same validity as a certificate of a superintendent registrar.

If either of the parties is not in membership, a certificate (form D) in respect of each such party must be produced to each superintendent registrar (for parties resident in England or Wales), or district registrar (for parties intending to marry in England or Wales but resident in Scotland), at the time when such notice is given.

b. *Marriages in Scotland*

In Scotland, under the provision of the Marriage (Scotland) Act 1977, each of the parties to a marriage shall submit to the district registrar a 'marriage notice' accompanied by the prescribed fee and certain documentary evidence. No residential qualification is required. Provided that the other party submits a marriage notice, a party resident in the United Kingdom outside Scotland may submit to the district registrar an 'approved certificate' which will be issued, in the case of England or Wales, by the appropriate superintendent registrar. However, although allowed under the Act, this procedure is more cumbersome than submission of a marriage notice directly to the district registrar, and is, in practice, rarely followed, since a marriage notice is always required for the other party. The district registrar will normally be able to issue a marriage schedule fourteen days after entering the marriage notice, if this means it is being issued less than seven days before the marriage. Provision is made, however, for the issue of a marriage schedule earlier than fourteen days subject to the completion of certain formalities and the approval of the Registrar General.

Marriage by licence

16.26 a. *Marriages in England and Wales*

If the parties desire that the marriage should be by licence, in order to reduce the time required under the procedure by certificate, the following procedure should be adopted in place of that prescribed in 16.25.

Notice should be given to the superintendent registrar of the district in which one of the parties has resided for not less than fifteen days previously. On the next day but one the superintendent registrar may issue a certificate and licence. The parties are liable for the observance of certain formalities and for the payment of additional fees.

If either of the parties is not in membership, a certificate (form D) in respect of each such party must be produced to the superintendent registrar (for those resident in England or Wales), or district registrar (for those marrying in England or Wales but resident in Scotland).

If the parties reside in districts of different superintendent registrars and a licence is granted to one of the parties, it is not necessary to give notice to the superintendent registrar of the district in which the other party resides.

Where the other party resides in Scotland, it is not necessary to give notice to the registrar of the registration district in Scotland in which such other party resides.

b. *Marriages in Scotland*

In Scotland, the Marriage (Scotland) Act 1977 abolished the procedure of marriage by licence in favour of provision for the district registrar supplying, under certain safeguards, a marriage schedule in a period shorter than fourteen days (see 16.25.b).

Although the procedures under (a) and (b) above reduce the time involved in obtaining the necessary documents from the registrar, time must still be allowed for the proper appointment of the meeting for worship and other procedures as described in the following sections

THE MEETING FOR WORSHIP

Appointment of meeting for worship

16.27   A meeting for worship for the solemnisation of a marriage is the responsibility of the monthly meeting within the area of which it is held. It is normally to be appointed by the monthly meeting. The monthly meeting may, however, grant permission to a preparative meeting in its area to appoint meetings for worship for the solemnisation of marriage. Such permission should be given only to a specific preparative meeting or preparative meetings deemed capable of discharging this responsibility, but should not be given generally as a matter of course to all its preparative meetings. Permission should be given only where it is reasonable to expect the attendance of a sufficient number of well-concerned Friends at any such meeting for worship as the preparative meeting may appoint. The monthly meeting should make arrangements for the regular review of the delegation of such permission, which may be withdrawn at any time. Where a meeting for worship for the solemnisation of marriage is desired at a meeting held less frequently than once a week, or where it is proposed to hold a marriage in Scotland at a place where no regular public meeting for worship is held, the appointment shall always be made by the monthly meeting.

16.28   In cases where the monthly meeting is the appointing body and serious inconvenience would be caused if the appointment of a meeting were delayed until the next monthly meeting, the clerk of the monthly meeting may, in consultation with the registering officer and such other Friends as he or she considers appropriate, make the appointment on its behalf. Such action is to be minuted at the next monthly meeting.

16.29   In cases where the preparative meeting is the appointing body, and serious inconvenience would be caused if the appointment of a meeting were delayed until the next preparative meeting, the clerk of the preparative meeting, may, in consultation with the registering officer, arrange for Friends at the meeting concerned to make the appointment at the conclusion of meeting for worship. Such action is to be minuted at the next preparative meeting.

16.30   As soon as possible after the receipt of the completed form A (and forms B and/or C in the case of those applicants who are not in membership), the registering officer shall, through the clerk of the monthly or preparative meeting (as the case may be), bring before it the application for the appointment of a meeting for worship (form F). The meeting shall decide whether a meeting for worship may be appointed at the time and place desired by the parties or at any other time and place which may be mutually convenient. If the certificate(s) or certificate and licence (16.25-16.26) have not been received, the meeting for worship may be appointed subject to the satisfactory completion of these formalities. The registering officer shall inform one of the parties of the decision of the meeting.

16.31   The meeting making the appointment is recommended to ensure, by the appointment of a sufficient number of suitable Friends, that the meeting for worship may be rightly held in accordance with our usage. Marriages are often attended by relatives or friends who have no previous experience of a meeting for worship. The couple may feel it helpful to send invited guests copies of such leaflets as are available on the conduct of marriages, or they may choose to send a letter of their own composing with the invitation, telling guests of the form of worship, the procedure and what is expected of them. Elders have responsibility (12.12.f) for the conduct of the meeting for worship. It is now common practice for them, in consultation with the registering officer and the couple, to arrange for a Friend to give a short explanation of Friends' manner of worship and the proceedings at the outset of the meeting.

Time and place of meeting for worship

16.32   In appointing the time and place of the marriage it is desirable that the registering officer should be consulted in order that he or she may be present. (In cases where the registering officer is unable to be present see 16.47.)

a. *Marriages in England and Wales*

Although Friends' marriages are exempted from certain provisions of the Marriage Act 1949, nevertheless it has been decided by the yearly meeting that marriages shall be solemnised on any day within the hours enacted for marriages generally (between the hours of eight in the morning and six in the afternoon) in a meeting house or other place to which the public has access and where a recognised public meeting for worship is regularly held at least once every calendar month.

For the solemnisation of marriages according to the usage of Friends it is not required that the premises should be registered for marriage, but monthly meetings are cautioned against appointing such meetings for worship, particularly in the case of smaller recognised meetings, unless they are held in premises known locally as places of public worship after the manner of Friends.

There is legislative provision for the solemnisation of marriages in hospitals and private houses when exceptional circumstances exist, that is where one of the persons to be married is seriously ill and is not expected to recover and cannot be moved to a place at which a marriage could normally be solemnised. Any exceptional arrangements require close consultation between the Recording Clerk, the registering officer, and the superintendent registrar.

b. *Marriages in Scotland*

In Scotland a marriage may be solemnised at any hour and place; the use of a meeting house therefore is not obligatory. The meeting for worship has to be specially appointed by or on behalf of the monthly meeting (16.27-16.29). The monthly meeting should be satisfied that there are adequate reasons why the marriage could not be solemnised in a place where a regular public meeting for worship is held, and that a sufficient number of Friends will be able to attend at the time and place proposed to ensure that the meeting for worship is rightly held in accordance with our usage.

16.33   Where one or other of the parties has associations with another church or religious body and wishes to be married according to the procedure of that body as well as by Friends' usage, this may be done in accordance with the law in England and Wales, but only if both legal ceremonies take place separately on the same day. In all other respects, the normal procedure, including registration, should be undertaken, and the two separate legal ceremonies must not be seen to be combined in any way. However, care is needed to ensure that those being so married are in sympathy with Friends' testimony as described in 16.01-16.02. (See 16.07-16.08, 16.13 & 16.18.)

16.34   Some couples may wish to have a meeting for worship in loving support of their marriage either before or after a legal ceremony has taken place elsewhere. In such a case it is important that it is made quite clear that the meeting is not a formal marriage. The wording of any declaration must reflect this. Advice on the procedure in this situation may be had from the Recording Clerk.

Public notice of meeting for worship

16.35   Public notice of a meeting for worship appointed for the solemnisation of marriage shall be given at the place at which it is to be held at the close of the usual meeting for worship last held there before the day of solemnisation. In cases where a marriage is to be held in a meeting house or other premises where a meeting for worship is held less often than once a week, public notice of the meeting for worship for the solemnisation of marriage may be given by placing a notice on the notice board outside the meeting house or other premises a week in advance. If this is not possible, advice should be sought from the Recording Clerk. The registering officer shall ensure that such notice is given (form G).

Declaration

16.36 When the meeting for worship is gathered, the parties at a convenient time shall stand and, taking each other by the hand, declare in an audible and solemn manner, the one after the other in either order, the man saying:

Friends, I take this my friend   [name] to be my wife, promising, through divine assistance, to be unto her a loving and faithful husband, so long as we both on earth shall live.

and the woman in like manner saying:

Friends, I take this my friend   [name] to be my husband, promising, through divine assistance, to be unto him a loving and faithful wife, so long as we both on earth shall live.

The declaration may be prefaced by 'In the presence of God' or 'In the fear of the Lord and in the presence of this assembly'. The phrase 'through divine assistance' may be replaced by the words 'with God's help'. The phrase 'so long as we both on earth shall live' may be replaced by the words 'until it shall please the Lord by death to separate us'. No other changes to the wording may be made.

The declaration must be made in English (but see 16.38), except that in all places where the Welsh tongue is commonly used a Welsh form of the declaration may be used.

The following is a translation into Welsh of 16.36 less the final sentence:

Datganiad

16.37 Pan fo'r cyfarfod i addoli wedi ymgynnull mae'r ddeuddyn, pan fo'n gyfleus, i sefyll, a chan afael y naill yn llaw y llall, i ddatgan yn eglur ac yn ddifrifol, y naill ar ôl y llall, ym mha bynnag drefn y dymunant, gyda'r dyn yn dweud:

Gyfeillion, yr wyf i yn cymryd fy nghyfeilles [enw] yn wraig i mi ac yn addo, trwy gymorth dwyfol, y byddaf iddi hi yn ŵr cariadus a ffyddlon gyhyd ac y byddom ein dau fyw ar y ddaear.

Yn yr un modd y mae'r wraig i ddweud:

Gyfeillion, yr wyf i yn cymryd fy nghyfaill [enw] yn ŵr i mi ac yn addo, trwy gymorth dwyfol, y byddaf iddo ef yn wraig gariadus a ffyddlon gyhyd ac y byddom ein dau fyw ar y ddaear.

Gellir cynnwys, fel rhagymadrodd i'r datganiad, y geiriau 'Ym mhresenoldeb Duw' neu'r geiriau 'Yn ofn Duw ac ym mhresenoldeb y gynulleidfa hon'. Yn hytrach na'r geiriau 'trwy gymorth dwyfol' gellir dweud 'trwy gymorth Duw'. Yn lle'r geiriau 'gyhyd ac y byddom fyw ar y ddaear' gellir defnyddio 'hyd nes y gwêl yr Arglwydd yn dda ein gwahanu trwy angau'. Ni oddefir unrhyw newidiadau eraill.

16.38 If one or other of the parties wishes to make the declaration in any other language then that may be done, but the Registering Officer needs to ensure that an interpreter is present to testify to the words spoken. In addition, the parties concerned should repeat the spoken words to the best of their ability in English.

16.39 If, by reason of an impediment of speech or otherwise, either of the parties is unable to make the declaration distinctly, then the registering officer present at the marriage shall read the declaration audibly and the party shall signify assent to its terms in some clear and unmistakable way so that the registering officer is satisfied that the meeting has understood this assent.

RECORDING OF MARRIAGES

Certificate of marriage

16.40　A certificate prepared beforehand by the parties, with the following wording, is to be signed during the meeting by the man and by the woman with her surname used immediately prior to marriage. Directly after it has been signed by at least two of those present as witnesses, it is to be read audibly by the registering officer or other suitable Friend. Others present at the marriage who have heard the declarations may sign the certificate after the conclusion of the meeting.

It is recommended that the certificate be signed and read either immediately after the declarations have been made, or towards the close of the meeting.

Certificate of marriage

[name]* and   [name]* having
made known their intention of taking each other in marriage and
public notice of their intention having been given, the proceedings
were allowed by the proper officers of
Monthly Meeting of the Religious Society of Friends.

This is to certify that for the solemnisation of their marriage, [name]
and [name] were present at a duly appointed public meeting for worship of the Society at †   this   day of
                    month of the year

Taking each other by the hand,

    [name] declared:

and   [name] declared:

In confirmation of these declarations they have in this meeting
signed this certificate of marriage.

....

....

We having been present at the above marriage have also subscribed
our names as witnesses the day, month and year above written.

....

....

---

* Here insert address or parentage.
† Here should be inserted address of meeting house or other place.

16.41   *Tystysgrif priodas*

Gan i [enw]* a [enw]* fynegi eu bwriad i gymryd y naill a'r llall mewn priodas a gan i'r bwriad hwnnw gael ei hysbysu'n gyhoeddus fe ganiatawyd y gweithrediadau gan swyddogion cymwys Cyfarfod Misol
o Gymdeithas Grefyddol y Cyfeillion.

Hyn sydd i dystio i [enw] a [enw], er dathlu eu priodas, fod yn bresennol mewn cyfarfod addoli cyhoeddus o'r Gymdeithas a benodwyd yn†
ar y dydd o'r mis yn y flwyddyn

Gan gymryd llaw y naill a'r llall,

Datganodd [enw]:

a datganodd [enw]:

Mewn cadarnhad o'r datganiadau hyn maent, yn y cyfarfod, wedi arwyddo'r dystysgrif hon.

....

....

Yr ydym ninnau hefyd, a fu'n bresennol yn ystod y briodas, yn torri ein henwau yma fel tystion ar y dydd, y mis a'r flwyddyn a ysgrifennwyd uchod.

....

....

_____

*Yma doder cyfeiriad neu riaint.
†Yma dylid rhoi cyfeiriad y tŷ cwrdd neu pa bynnag fan y bo.

16.42   Copies of this certificate in scroll or book form may be obtained from Quaker Bookshop at Friends House, but self-made versions are also acceptable.

16.43   The certificate of marriage is to be used only when the procedure has been followed in accordance with the provisions in this chapter.

It should not be used in other circumstances, as, for instance, at a meeting for worship held in conjunction with a marriage not according to our usage.

Registration of marriage

16.44   Immediately after the conclusion of the meeting, the marriage shall, in England and Wales, be registered by the registering officer, as provided in 16.46.a; in Scotland the procedure outlined in 16.46.b shall be followed.

Care and disposal of marriage registers (England and Wales)

16.45   For marriages in England and Wales the requisite marriage register books will be supplied in duplicate to registering officers from the office of the Registrar General, whose address may be obtained from the Recording Clerk or the local superintendent registrar. When the duplicate register books are filled, one of them is to be delivered to the superintendent registrar of the district to which the registering officer has been assigned by the Registrar General; the other is to remain under the care of the monthly meeting, and is to be kept with their other records (4.42). This procedure is not necessary in Scotland, although registering officers there do need to obtain copies of the certificates.

Recording of marriages

Registration procedure

16.46   a. *Marriages in England and Wales*

In England and Wales the legal registration of the marriage is carried out by the registering officer. As soon as possible after the solemnisation of a marriage, the registering officer, having received the proper certificate or licence, and being satisfied that the marriage has been solemnised in accordance with the usage of the Society, shall register, or cause to be registered, the several particulars of the marriage in the duplicate register books. Every such entry shall be signed by the parties married and by at least two witnesses, and by the registering officer.

b. *Marriages in Scotland*

In Scotland the legal registration of the marriage is carried out by the district registrar and not by the registering officer. No marriage may be solemnised unless the parties produce to the registering officer a marriage schedule (16.25.b). Immediately after the solemnisation of the marriage the marriage schedule shall be signed by the parties, by both witnesses, and by the registering officer. The parties shall within three days thereafter deliver the marriage schedule to the district registrar who shall cause the particulars to be entered in the register of marriages kept by her or him.

Provision for absence of registering officer

16.47   Should the registering officer be prevented through illness or absence from home or any other cause from issuing or signing the marriage forms in 16.12, he or she (or failing this the clerk of the monthly meeting) shall be at liberty to appoint any suitable Friend to act for him or her in these respects. It must be emphasised that this should not become a normal manner of proceeding.

If, in England and Wales, the registering officer should be prevented from being present at the solemnisation of the marriage, care shall be taken that the entries be, notwithstanding, duly made and signed by the parties and witnesses. The registering officer, having been satisfied of the regularity of the proceedings, shall afterwards add her or his signature: no person may sign the register in her or his place.

In Scotland, a deputy appointed as above may sign the statutory marriage schedule, and if it is known beforehand that this will be necessary the name of the deputy should be given to the district registrar who issues the schedule.

Certified copies from marriage registers

16.48   For marriages in England and Wales the Registrar General supplies, on request, a book of forms for issuing to an applicant a certified copy of any entry in the marriage registers. A registering officer shall, if required, issue a certified copy of any entry in any of the marriage registers of the monthly meeting by which he or she is appointed. For this an appropriate fee is payable. At least one copy is made for the couple in any case after the marriage. No one but the registering officer may sign a certified copy. In cases of doubt, due to any change of monthly meeting area, the Recording Clerk shall determine which registering officer has authority to certify such a copy.

For marriages in Scotland, application should be made to the district registrar.

Correction of errors

16.49   In filling up the registers (for marriages in England and Wales) great care must be taken that no error is committed. On the discovery afterwards of any error in an entry, the registering officer shall, within one calendar month after such discovery, in the presence of the parties married, or, in the case of their absence, then in the presence of the superintendent registrar of the district, and of two other witnesses (who are respectively to attest to the same), correct the error by entry in the margin without any alteration of the original entry, and he or she shall sign the marginal entry and shall add to it the date when the correction is made. In Scotland, these matters are dealt with by the district registrar.

Registering officers' quarterly returns

16.50 Every registering officer in England and Wales shall make a quarterly return, in January, April, July and October, of a copy of the entries of the marriages that have been registered by her or him in the three calendar months preceding or, if no marriage has been registered by her or him in that period, a certificate that such is the case. This return, with the relevant certificates and licences, shall be delivered to the superintendent registrar of the district to which the registering officer has been assigned by the Registrar General.

Blank forms for these certified copies and nil return certificates are supplied from the office of the Registrar General (whose address may be obtained from the Recording Clerk) or may be available from the local superintendent registrar.

In Scotland, returns are made by the district registrar.

Report of marriages

Report to monthly meetings

16.51 The marriage being solemnised and duly registered, the registering officer shall report the same to the monthly meeting (form H). The monthly meeting shall record by minute the receipt of such report with particulars of the membership of the parties, and the date and registration of the marriage.

In cases where either party is a member of a monthly meeting other than the one under the auspices of which the marriage has taken place, the registering officer of the monthly meeting responsible for the marriage shall report it to the clerk of each such monthly meeting, which shall similarly record the particulars of the marriage by minute.

Transfer of membership on marriage

16.52   A monthly meeting on receipt of a report of a marriage of one of its members shall ask overseers to consult with the Friend, in order that any transfer of membership may be made as soon as possible after the marriage. If any such transfer is required it shall be by certificate for transfer of membership, according to usual practice (11.28-11.33). If it is not possible for a decision to be taken at the time of marriage as to what transfer of membership should be made, the question shall be continued in the care of overseers.

Monthly meeting returns

16.53   At the beginning of each year the forms for the purpose supplied by the Recording Clerk should be returned by monthly meetings listing all marriages that have been solemnised during the previous year under their auspices according to the usage of the Society, or, if applicable, stating none.

16.54   Copies of the forms mentioned in the above regulations, other than those supplied by the office of the Registrar General, will be supplied to registering officers by the Recording Clerk. Meeting for Sufferings is responsible for the printing and publication of these forms, and for any revision of them which may be required from time to time.

Marriages taking place outside Great Britain

16.55   When any members of Britain Yearly Meeting intend to solemnise their marriage outside Great Britain, they are recommended to conform to the usage of our Society in respect of marriage, so far as is possible within the laws of the country and those of our own. They should report their course of procedure and furnish evidence of such a marriage to the monthly meeting(s) in this country to which they belong, and the monthly meeting(s) should record the marriage in its minutes. It should be noted that the Isle of Man and the Channel Islands are outside Great Britain.

Recording of marriages

Membership not acquired by marriage

16.56 A person not in membership shall not acquire by marriage any right of membership of Britain Yearly Meeting, notwithstanding that the other party to the marriage is a member. Meetings are encouraged to make welcome those who become associated with them through marriage to one of their members.

Chapter 17

Quaker funerals and memorial meetings

INTRODUCTION

17.01 Friends should come to a funeral with both heart and mind prepared. We want to experience a deep sense of communion with God and with one another, which we hope will comfort and strengthen those who mourn. There are at least two aims in our worship: to give thanks to God for the life that has been lived, and to help the mourners to feel a deep sense of God's presence.

Hardshaw East Monthly Meeting Elders & Overseers, 1986

17.02 The funerals of Friends should be held in a spirit of quiet peace and trust. Natural sorrow there will be, especially for Friends taken away in youth and in the strength of their days, but often our thought will be one of a great thankfulness for lives which have borne witness to the upholding power of Christ.

1925

17.03 Friends should not adopt any rigid pattern for the conduct of funerals. In some cases it is best to hold, separately from the committal or cremation, a 'meeting for worship on the occasion of the death of our Friend', at a weekend, when Friends are free to attend and there is time for the spirit of quiet trust and dependence on God to overcome natural grief. In other cases the brief meeting for worship at the crematorium is all that is either possible or desired... If Friends really believe that all meetings of every kind are meetings for worship in which the presence of Christ is with them and that they are in unity with the living and the dead, they will not experience difficulties or find the occasion of a funeral imposing a pattern of unbalanced eulogy of the deceased. Arising from a gathered meeting, messages of a general character, even from those who have not known the deceased, will enrich the worship of all who are there.

Berks & Oxon QM Ministry & Extension Committee, 1951

17.04 A feeling of hesitation as to speaking at funerals is most natural, for great wisdom and tenderness are required. On the other hand, these gatherings give opportunities of a very special character, and we urge all on whom the gift of the vocal ministry has been bestowed to consider whether it may not be their duty and privilege to use it on these occasions, even if in some degree contrary to their convenience and inclination. There is also need for the presence of others, and [their] attendance in a loving and sympathetic spirit is a very real service.

Warwickshire North Monthly Meeting Ministry Committee, 1912

17.05 The value of vocal prayer at a funeral can hardly be overemphasised. If offered under guidance it will often touch hearts too much distressed to listen to an address and will bring real comfort. This is above all to be borne in mind where there is some special ground for sorrow, when the anxious mourners may thus be helped to open their hearts to the healing stream of divine love.

Warwickshire Monthly Meeting Elders, 1960

17.06 Quakers do have something very special to offer the dying and the bereaved, namely that we are at home in silence. Not only are we thoroughly used to it and unembarrassed by it, but we know something about sharing it, encountering others in its depths and, above all, letting ourselves be used in it...

People so often talk of someone 'getting over' a death. How could you ever fully get over a deep loss? Life has been changed profoundly and irrevocably. You don't get over sorrow; you work your way right to the centre of it.

Diana Lampen, 1979

PROCEDURE

Conduct of funerals

17.07 Monthly meetings shall satisfy themselves that adequate arrangements are made for advice to be available on the holding of meetings for worship as on other matters in connection with funerals. This responsibility is the subject of a separate section: see 17.14-17.15.

17.08 Quaker funeral arrangements are the responsibility of the monthly meeting (4.07.n). It shall notify its members at regular intervals of the names of those Friends currently appointed to arrange funerals on its behalf.

It is for each monthly meeting to determine, and to keep under review (4.07.n), how these Friends are best chosen. They may be the monthly meeting elders as a group, or a subcommittee of elders, or a funeral arrangements committee constituted in some other way. Alternatively, the monthly meeting may delegate this responsibility to the elders, or to a specially appointed member, of each preparative meeting. What is important is that in each monthly meeting its preferred procedures for arranging funerals are clearly understood and followed.

17.09 The Friends appointed should consult with the relatives of the deceased and with local elders, who take particular responsibility for the right holding of the meeting for worship on such occasions (12.12.f). Sometimes programmed elements may be appropriate in the worship. It is important to be clear at this stage whether a memorial meeting (17.10) is also to be held at a later date. The Friends appointed to arrange a funeral should also promptly inform appropriate Friends in the monthly meeting to ensure an adequate presence at the funeral. Former as well as serving elders and overseers may, for example, be included. They should be chosen for their wise judgment and special concern for the right conduct of such occasions of worship, and the concern should be clearly laid upon them.

Where it is expected that a number present will be without experience of a meeting for worship, it is important for an elder, or another designated Friend, to explain briefly the nature of the meeting for worship and the procedure to be followed.

Arrangements should be made in advance for some Friends to sit at the front of the meeting and for one of them, usually an elder, to take definite responsibility for bringing it to an end. At the close of the meeting for worship, it may be desirable for this Friend to come forward to the relatives, speaking with them and indicating that they should lead the way out.

Among passages which may be suitable to be read at funerals are 21.49-21.73 & 22.93-22.95

Memorial meetings

17.10 It may be right to hold a memorial meeting for worship to give thanks for the life of a Friend who has died. Sometimes, when local circumstances allow little time at the place of cremation or burial, a meeting will be held before or afterwards, allowing time for Friends to travel to or from the crematorium or cemetery. Sometimes a memorial meeting will be arranged at a later date at the convenience of relatives and local Friends. Occasionally a memorial meeting may be held soon after the death but the funeral only much later (for example, when the body has been lost at sea, or donated for medical education and research). The particular circumstances will affect the nature of the occasion and the balance of grief, loss and thankfulness.

Memorial meetings as well as special meetings on the occasion of a funeral demand great sensitivity to individual needs. The memorial meeting for a Friend whose life was lived in the local meeting will spring from and deepen the worshipping community of those Friends. If the deceased was someone whose links with the meeting were less strong, but who was well known in the wider community, the occasion may tend towards greater formality. When non-members are likely to be present, a great responsibility is laid on the local elders to ensure that the meeting is rightly held, and that its purpose is made clear to those who attend (12.12.f).

An elder, or other designated Friend, should be appointed to explain briefly how the meeting will be conducted, how long it is likely to last, and how it will be concluded. The length of the meeting may vary but Friends will be sensitive to the wishes of the relatives as well as to the spiritual condition of the meeting as it moves towards a natural ending.

Burials

Burials in Friends' burial grounds and interment and scattering of ashes

17.11   Monthly meetings possessing burial grounds are to appoint a Friend or Friends authorised to issue on behalf of the monthly meeting(s) an order for burial (or interment or scattering of ashes). Books of blank forms and counterfoils for these may be obtained from the Recording Clerk. No grave is to be made, nor ashes interred or scattered, without such an order.

Immediately after the burial, or interment or scattering of ashes, the order is to be countersigned by a different Friend, witnessing that this has taken place. The countersigned order shall be presented at the next monthly meeting, which shall record the relevant facts in a minute. If the deceased was a member of another monthly meeting, the clerk shall transmit the information to the clerk of that monthly meeting.

Register of burials and interment and scattering of ashes

17.12   After the order for burial (or interment or scattering of ashes) has been presented to the monthly meeting possessing the burial ground, and the clerk has certified that the relevant facts have been recorded in a minute of that meeting, the order now bearing all the signatures required shall be returned to the first signatory and re-attached to its counterfoil. Such completed orders and counterfoils constitute the register of burials (and interment and scattering of ashes) and shall be preserved with the records of the monthly meeting (see 4.42.c). It is open to the monthly meeting, if it wishes, to maintain a register book as well. In any case, entries and indexes in the register should be cross-referenced, as appropriate, to the plan of burial plots and record of burials and interments maintained under 15.17.

In respect of the burial of bodies, the proper maintenance and preservation of a register of burials by the monthly meeting possessing the burial ground is a requirement of Section 1 of the Registration of Burials Act 1864. In respect of the interment or scattering of ashes it is not a legal requirement; but it accords with Quaker practice over the years by ensuring that a full record is kept of the use made of Friends' burial grounds, and that no distinction is made with regard to inclusion in registers between those whose bodies are buried and those whose ashes are interred or scattered.

Burials of non-members and interment and scattering of ashes

17.13 Burials of non-members may be allowed in Friends' burial grounds, but it is hoped that, save in exceptional circumstances, they will be conducted as are the burials of Friends; and likewise the interment or scattering of ashes of non-members. The Friends appointed to arrange meetings for worship on the occasion of a funeral are to exercise discretion as to complying with any application that may be made in such cases. Alternatively, a monthly meeting may entrust this exercise of discretion directly to the Friend or Friends authorised to issue orders for burial (or interment or scattering of ashes), if it judges that they will not feel overburdened by this additional responsibility.

Responsibilities of monthly meetings

17.14 Monthly meetings shall ensure that a sufficient number of Friends are familiar with the practical arrangements for funerals at the particular crematoria and public cemeteries within their compass, as well as for those conducted in their own burial grounds.

It is good practice for those who hold these responsibilities to take counsel together regularly (whether through meetings of elders or otherwise) on the right holding of Quaker funerals and memorial meetings within their monthly meeting.

17.15   Several monthly meetings have produced guidance notes or memoranda of good practice, giving practical advice based on the specific circumstances of each area. This is a convenient way of pooling the local experience of Friends in their conduct of funerals and memorial meetings and keeping it readily available in written form. Monthly meetings are recommended to produce such memoranda for members' use and to keep them up to date. There follows a list of those matters which monthly meetings have found most useful to include:

   a. ways in which appointed office holders may become aware of local custom and practice;
   b. consultations with the family, bearing in mind the wishes of the deceased;
   c. liaison with crematorium staff and funeral directors. Particular care should be taken to clarify points where Quaker expectations may differ from what is assumed to be normal practice;
   d. the need for firm and sensitive direction during the funeral. Those present, particularly distressed mourners, will welcome clear guidance on how to proceed;
   e. consideration of the length of the meeting for worship;
   f. the presence of those not accustomed to our form of worship and the need to include them, allay their anxieties and preserve the integrity of the meeting;
   g. the opening and closing of the meeting for worship;
   h. the use of prepared ministry;
   i. burials: the conduct and form of any meeting by the graveside;
   j. policy regarding the minister's fee normally charged by funeral directors in the account rendered to the estate, bearing in mind that it is not Friends' practice to accept a fee for ministry;
   k. an indication that Friends should consult this chapter in conjunction with the memorandum produced by their monthly meeting.

CONCLUSION

17.16   There is laid on all who are present the responsibility to translate their prayers for comfort and support into thoughtful, kindly and sustained actions that will continue to help those who have lost a loved one to face life anew with courage, and to adapt themselves to their new circumstances.

George Gorman, 1973

See also 15.17-15.20 Burial grounds, *21.49-21.58* Death *& 22.80-22.95* Bereavement.

Chapter 18

Faithful lives

Our church government would be an empty shell without the living expression of our faith provided by generations of individual Friends. Our custom of writing testimonies to the grace of God as shown in the lives of Friends provides us with a wealth of material showing ordinary Friends living out their faith from day to day. These testimonies show us that, whatever our circumstances, God can be present with us, and they encourage us each to be faithful to our own calling.

Our discipline and structures do not exist by themselves. The life of our Society is made up of the lives of its members. The faithfulness of our Society consists in the faithfulness of each and all of us. And none of us can expect 'the Society' to be more faithful, more committed, more loving, than we ourselves are prepared to be.

18.01 *Joseph Bevan Braithwaite (1818-1905) was a leading Friend in the latter part of the nineteenth century, yet in his youth he came close to resigning his membership. Before doing so he thought it right to attend the Yearly Meeting of 1840 throughout and form his own judgment. His mind was changed by the reading of the testimonies to the lives of deceased Friends, as he records:*

I listened with an open mind to all that passed, whilst I was at the same time writing a pamphlet explaining my views in opposition to Friends... But I heard the testimonies [concerning] deceased ministers and was ashamed and self-condemned for my harsh judgment... I had been enabled through unutterable mercy to accept the Lord Jesus Christ as my Saviour; now I saw somewhat of His unspeakable preciousness as 'the Good Shepherd' and 'Counsellor' of His people, 'always, even unto the end of the world'.

The following testimonies and memoirs provide examples of Friends over three centuries being faithful to their leadings. (For current practice see 4.24-4.27)

18.02   *Testimony concerning Elizabeth Hooton (1600?-1672) by George Fox:*

She was a serious, upright-hearted woman to the Lord and received his Truth several years before we were called Quakers... She was moved of the Lord to go to New England, taking her daughter with her, to desire the persecuting priests and magistrates to take away the laws for imprisoning, spoiling of goods, whipping, branding with hot irons and cutting off the ears of Friends and putting them to death; and instead of that they whipped her and her daughter very cruelly and put them out of their jurisdiction. And she was moved of the Lord to go again, and then the magistrates of Boston passed sentence of death upon her and about 27 or 28 more, and kept them close prisoners, and we got an order from King Charles the Second and hired a ship to carry it over that they might have a trial before the king, upon which they set them at liberty though they did not take away the persecuting laws...

Many prisons this poor Elizabeth Hooton was cast into only for serving and worshipping God and declaring the Truth, and about the year 1671 she travelled with me and others to Barbados and ... to Jamaica and being a weak ancient woman and zealous for the Lord and his Truth, she died in the Lord and is blessed and at rest from her labours and her works follow her.

She was convinced at Skegby in Nottinghamshire and held meetings at her house where the Lord by his power wrought many miracles, ... confirming people of the Truth which she there received about 1646, and fulfilled her ministry and finished her testimony about 1672...

She was a godly woman and had a great care laid upon her for people to walk in the Truth that did profess it, and from her receiving the Truth she never turned her back on it, but was fervent and faithful for it till death.

1690

18.03   *Testimony concerning Thomas Ellwood (1639-1713):*

He was greatly respected by his neighbours for his services amongst them; his heart and doors were open to the poor, both sick and lame, who wanted help, and had it freely, taking care to provide things useful for such occasions ... often saying, he mattered not what cost he was at, to do good.

He was an early comer to meetings, seldom hindered by weather (though he lived three miles distant) when bodily weakness did not hinder. The monthly meeting was held at his house about forty years, and he always looked very kind and courteous on Friends, when they came there, and took care and notice of the meanest, who came in sincerity.

Upperside Women's Monthly Meeting, 1714

18.04   *Testimony concerning Christopher Story (1648-1720):*

He suffered imprisonment and spoiling of goods with much patience, which proved to be his lot pretty early, by wicked men who became informers, seeking his ruin, with many others; yet the Lord preserved him in faithfulness, and brought him clean through all these exercises. He stood firm in his testimony against the anti-christian yoke of tithes, that none might be unfaithful therein, either in paying or in receiving them. And, having a gift beyond many in the government of church affairs, he exercised the same in much wisdom and prudence, and laboured diligently for the peace of the church, and to keep out everything that might appear to cause strife and debate. He had an excellent gift of healing and making up of breaches.

Carlisle Monthly Meeting, 1721

18.05   *Testimony concerning Joshua Barber (1660-1732):*

He was greatly beloved by the generality of the meeting he belonged to, for his good example, steady walking, and impartial judgment, even among his nearest Friends, as well as others. When he thought there was occasion for advice, he dealt in great plainness with all, where he was concerned, as he found his way open in the truth, so that he became a terror to evil-doers, though a comfort to them who did well.

Brighouse Monthly Meeting, 1733

18.06   *Testimony concerning Abiah Darby (1717-1794):*

She was a tender sympathiser with those afflicted, whether in body or mind, and an eminent example of Christian benevolence to those who are stewards of the good things of this life, being rich in good works, ready to distribute, willing to communicate, feeding the hungry, clothing the naked, visiting the sick, and also at sundry times, under an especial apprehension of duty, the condemned and other prisoners in different jails.

Shropshire Monthly Meeting, 1795

18.07   *Testimony concerning William Coles (1743-1815):*

Our beloved friend was a man of few talents and did not possess the advantages of a liberal education; but having been favoured with the watchful care and instruction of religious parents and when very young yielding obedience to the visitations of Divine Love, he grew up in piety and virtue, and became an encouraging example of true Christian simplicity, humility, meekness, self-denial and universal charity.

When called to the work of the ministry, as he was animated with the Spirit of Christianity, and filled with a well-tempered zeal for the promotion of Truth and Righteousness, so in the exercise of his gift he was reverent in his deportment; and his communications evinced that he was well instructed in the school of Christ.

To advanced age he was industriously employed in procuring the means of subsistence; and with but a very moderate supply of the things of this life was contented and thankful, showing at the same time a disposition to generosity and hospitality.

Buckinghamshire Quarterly Meeting, 1816

18.08   *Memoir of Elizabeth Fry (1780-1845) by two of her daughters, Katherine Fry and Rachel Cresswell:*

It was her conviction that there is a sphere of usefulness open to all. She appreciated to the full the usual charities of gentlewomen, their visits to the sick and aged poor and their attention to the cottage children, but she grieved to think how few complete the work of mercy by following the widow or disabled when driven by necessity to the workhouse, or caring for the workhouse school, that resort of the orphaned and forsaken...

She heard of thousands and ten thousands of homeless and abandoned children wandering or perishing in our streets. She knew that attempts were made to rescue them and that unflinching men and women laboured and toiled to infuse some portion of moral health into that mass of living corruption... She encountered in the prisons every grade and variety of crime: the woman bold and daring and reckless, revelling in her iniquity and hardened in vice, her only remaining joy to seduce others; ... the thoughtless culprit, not lost to good and holy feeling nor dead to impression from without; and lastly the beginner, she who from her deep poverty had been driven to theft or drawn by others into temptation. Elizabeth Fry marked all these and despaired of none amongst them. Here again ... a crying need existed for influence, for instruction, reproof and encouragement. But it was not to all she would have allotted *this* task, though she could never be persuaded but that in every instance women well qualified for the office might be found to care for these outcasts of the people.

1847

18.09 *Testimony concerning Hannah Chapman Backhouse (1787-1850):*

It was early impressed upon her mind that it was her duty on all occasions to adopt the language and simple dress of a 'Friend'. She has been frequently heard to allude to this period of her experience; she did not make the change in a spirit of blind conformity, or as a mere matter of expediency; but after having reflected seriously on the basis of our practice in these respects: and her unswerving stability herein arose from her being deeply and thoroughly convinced that, as it regards plainness of speech, it had its origin in a righteous principle of truth-speaking and Christian integrity; and that our testimony against the vain and ever varying fashions of the times, in dress and other matters, is the result ... of that true liberty of soul in which the lowly disciple of Christ ... is led to manifest in all his conduct and demeanour that he has no desire to be conformed to this world.

Darlington Monthly Meeting, 1851

18.10   *Memorial concerning Joseph Bewley (1795-1851):*

Humility was a conspicuous trait in the character of Joseph Bewley; for although he had acquired considerable influence among his brethren, he sought no pre-eminence. 'A meek and quiet spirit', united with kindness of heart and equanimity of temper, obtained for him the love and esteem of a large circle of relatives and friends. He was naturally diffident and retiring, and seemed to feel himself restrained from taking much part in public affairs, and to consider that a narrower path of duty was assigned to him. But his desires for the welfare of his fellow-men, and his sympathies for the sorrowing and afflicted, were not circumscribed by the bounds of religious association. His heart was open to feel for the sufferings of every class; and his pecuniary means were liberally but unostentatiously employed in the alleviation of distress, and in contributing to increase the comforts of those whose resources were limited. The wide-spread affliction, resulting from the general failure of the potato crop in 1846, called forth in his mind feelings of deep commiseration for his famine-stricken countrymen. He originated the movement for their assistance which led to the formation of the 'Friends' Relief Committee'; and, as one of its secretaries, he devoted himself with unwearied assiduity to the arduous endeavour to alleviate the distress which then so extensively prevailed.

Dublin Monthly Meeting, 1852

18.11   *A memoir of William Dent (1778-1861):*

The writer recalls in his school days the tall spare figure of a venerable Friend who regularly attended Yorkshire Quarterly Meetings. It was evident that he lived in the wholesome deliberate air of the country. His Quaker garb was spotlessly neat. His face spoke of indwelling light and peace with all mankind. When words came they were few and weighty. It is told how he would drive fourteen miles to a Friends' meeting to worship. On one such occasion he rose, and said, 'God is love', and then sat down again. It is believed no listener forgot that sermon. He and his family were known to be of the salt of the earth; but what could a plain tenant farmer accomplish in a small village aloof from the life of the world? At the time when he settled in it several of the houses were in an insanitary condition; the labourers had no gardens to speak of, the children had no school, but there was a public house for the parents. When at four score years his call came to go up higher he left a village where every cottage was a healthy home, where all able-bodied labourers wishing for an allotment could have one. The public house had gone and a good village school had been established. For many years the schoolmistress had lived in his house. A Bible Society anniversary in his big barn was the annual festival and Eirenicon of the district. It may fairly be said that the whole neighbourhood was slowly uplifted by the coming of one quiet life into its midst.

1913

18.12   *Testimony concerning John Henry Barlow (1855-1924):*

Resolute but cautious, judicial and yet sympathetic, a man of quiet strength and almost stern gravity, and yet with a very tender spirit beneath apparent severity, a man slow to take the initiative, yet vigilant and constant in the discharge of responsibilities which were laid upon him – such was John Henry Barlow... His character and his faith qualified him to render invaluable service to the Society as clerk of [London] Yearly Meeting from 1913 to 1919. During these troubled and perplexing years when feelings were often strained and patience nigh to breaking point, when new elements of enthusiastic life were beginning to emerge in the Society, John Barlow showed himself to be a true leader, by promoting real harmony without compromise. 'He had a great gift in knowing, during those difficult war years, just when the Meeting had got to a place where it might step quite swiftly into a region higher and clearer than itself realised it was yet ready for, and he helped it to take the step by offering minutes which, while they did not compromise, did not on the other hand rouse factious opposition nor lead to subsequent reaction by any over-stressing or labouring of words'.

Warwickshire North Monthly Meeting, 1924

18.13   *Mary Hughes (1860-1941) was a daughter of Judge Thomas Hughes, author of* Tom Brown's schooldays. *In her late thirties she started to live in the East End of London. She identified herself completely with those around her, sharing their poverty, their privations and their lack of opportunities for cleanliness. She joined the Society of*

Friends in 1918 and Friends long remembered the stirring of conscience that was felt in Yearly Meeting when her white-haired, red-cloaked figure was present:

The longest journey Mary Hughes made was in spiritual conception. In her youth she ... took part in work on behalf of the poor and unfortunate. You drove to that work in a carriage and when the work was done you drove back to a beautiful house... Mary Hughes was never a one for condemning the way in which other people lived their lives; she was too busy with the way in which she chose to lead her own. If she had ever consciously wondered why this way, which she saw in her youth, was not satisfactory to her, she could have found the answer ... in those words *when the work was done*. It became clear to her that what she had to do could never be *done,* not even for an hour. Her life itself must be her work, but it could be her work only if it were lived in the appropriate circumstances. She didn't want to *visit* the poor. She wanted to be *with* the poor and to be poor herself...

She had no set schemes. She founded no institution. Neither did Jesus... 'He went about doing good.' So did Mary Hughes... It was a question of being rather than of doing. You trusted to the contagion of goodness rather than to homily or sermon. Necessarily, such a personality, linked as it was to endless sources of spiritual strength, became a magnet, and there again one hears the echo of an old phrase: 'I will *draw* all men unto Me.' As this magnet drew the poor and dispossessed, there was plenty to do; and Mary Hughes went about the doing of it in her own idiosyncratic way... She never turned down man or woman who had duped or bamboozled her. It was in the nature of things that the world contained sinners, and she wished above all to live close to the nature of things. This she could confidently do because of her belief that the overriding reality is spiritual. She would have thought herself most faithless if a few sinners had shaken her... Burning with shame, radiant with love, she set her course and followed it... The whole point of her life will be missed unless we can share her faith that 'the things that are seen are temporal, the things that are unseen are eternal'. Looked at from that point of view, this shabby and sometimes verminous woman becomes one of the few, 'of whom the world is not worthy'.

Howard Spring, 1949

18.14   *Testimony concerning Mary Ann Stokeley (1869?-1941):*

Mary Ann Stokeley was associated with Ratcliff Meeting from her earliest years. Born and bred in Stepney, within a stone's throw of the old Ratcliff Meeting House in Brook Street (now Cable Street), she first attended the Sunday School at the age of four, and thereafter made her spiritual home with Friends. Very short in stature and of comparatively frail physique, she knew poverty at first hand, and was never able to earn an adequate wage. Yet despite her physical and educational disadvantages, for many years she was responsible for a Sunday School class of rowdy Stepney girls, to whom she gave of her best.

Mary Stokeley did not apply for membership of our Society until she reached middle life, after many years as an attender. Her attendance at meeting for worship was regular and punctual and she took an interest in all the concerns of her preparative and monthly meetings. Very conscious of her own limitations, her part was a silent one, but she was amazingly faithful to the tiny meeting to which she belonged. Our Friend was not a 'oncer' – for many years she was in the meeting house morning, afternoon and evening every first-day. It was indeed the centre of her life.

During the air raids in the last war she was repeatedly pressed to leave the district, but she preferred to share the danger with her own kith and kin, and there can be no doubt that the anxiety of the time shortened her life. Ratcliff Meeting was reduced to one or two, yet up to her last illness she was in her place every first-day morning with unfailing regularity. Faithfulness was indeed the keynote of her life, and an example to us all.

That our Friend should, out of her poverty, have left us a substantial legacy is truly humbling. She lived in one room, enjoyed none of the refinements which most of us consider essential for a reasonable life, and might well have spent the money on comforts in her last years. But she preferred to leave her money to the religious fellowship of which she was so humble and unobtrusive a member.

Ratcliff & Barking Monthly Meeting, 1955

18.15 *Testimony concerning Joseph E Southall (1861-1944):*

Towards any form of pretence, hypocrisy, shallow or muddled thinking, he was merciless. He had a shattering way of evoking the memory of George Fox at the most inconvenient moment... Gatherings of Friends were often put upon their mettle by a summing up from Joseph Southall, and many were the sharp encounters which reminded us of simple but vital principles in danger of being smothered by more material concern. And then, the battle over, who has not seen him shaking hands with his late adversary over a cup of tea, beaming through his half-moon spectacles with the world's most celestial twinkle in his eyes, the clear parchment pallor of his face broken into what would have been the smile of a benevolent old gentleman had it not somehow been pointed with the wit of a Joseph Southall.

Warwickshire Monthly Meeting, 1945

18.16 *Testimony concerning Jessie Ritch (1896-1951):*

We do not forget that our Friend was not without her human foibles; these indeed endeared her to us all the more, as we realised that she was no plaster-saint but compounded of the same elements as ourselves. Her enthusiasms were sometimes short-lived, but even when, as sometimes happened, she asked to be relieved of some piece of service taken up under concern, the result was often that others were drawn to share what had been of her originating.

Sutton Preparative Meeting, 1952

18.17 *Testimony concerning Lucy E Harris (1873-1962):*

Lucy E Harris ... trained as a doctor... She sailed for China almost at once, one of the first doctors to be sent by Friends... No situation daunted Lucy Harris. Fighting between war-lords was rampant after the Chinese Revolution of 1911 and it was inevitable that she should meet and have trouble with some of these unpleasant characters. Her utter fearlessness in dealing with such difficulties sprang from her deep faith in God, not a cosy belief that nothing dangerous would happen to her, but a firm belief that in whatever did happen she would have the presence of God with her... Two war-lords with their followers were lined up on each side of the river. Lucy Harris, a tiny slightly-built woman possessing a firm, strong, clear voice, stood in a boat in the middle of the river, shouting to them, insisting that they stop their fighting and go their separate ways. They turned themselves about and went. On another occasion wounded had been crowded into her hospital from one of the battles of the opposing bandits. The successful one demanded that they should be handed over to him. Quite apart from the fact that the wounded men were her patients, she knew that this would mean instant death to them. She refused to hand them over.

Hertford & Hitchin Monthly Meeting, 1963

18.18   *Testimony concerning Annie Morris (1900-1980):*

Annie and Edward Morris shared the common lot of many Lancashire people – hardship and poverty. [After Edward died in about 1950 Annie] went back to the mill to work once again at the job she knew so well – weaving...

About this time Westhoughton Meeting sharply declined in numbers. As her contemporaries died one by one, eventually Annie Morris remained as the only active member of Westhoughton Meeting, and for thirty years she served as an overseer. Although suffering from rheumatoid arthritis, Annie Morris took upon her frail shoulders the responsibility of maintaining the life of the meeting. It was a great sadness to her, not only to see the decline of the meeting but the decay of the meeting house. As months and years passed, the meeting house became unsafe, but Annie, although in poor health, continued to hold meeting for worship alone. This was a time of great sadness but she remained invincibly faithful to her belief in the goodness of God.

Eventually, first one and then another joined Annie in meeting for worship in the cold damp meeting house. Soon there were about ten people attending...

She died on the 14th September 1980. She had been attending Westhoughton Meeting for more than seventy years – a faithful Friend.

We thank God for the lovely, faithful, tender spirit that was Annie Morris.

Hardshaw East Monthly Meeting, 1980

18.19   What Katie [Riley] was is written in the hearts of all who loved her. Her hospitality was phenomenal, the neat little house and garden providing rest and beauty. She delighted in helping her guests to relax, showing them lovely books or pictures, serving meals daintily. It seemed a joy to her to live for others, and she regularly visited the lonely, the elderly and the sick. She sent little notes of love, always decorated with an appropriate drawing, and hundreds of such messages are treasured by many people. If someone ill or housebound needed her, Katie would go for weeks or even months to stay with them, though it was a real sacrifice, as she loved her own home and meeting best.

Pleasaunce Holtom, 1981

18.20   *The 1959 edition of* Christian faith and practice *contained an introduction to its opening chapter which has become much loved amongst Friends, as much for the charm of its language as for its content. We would not now write such a passage, with its heavy emphasis on men, and with women being remembered for 'the beauty of their person as well as character'; moreover, some Friends omitted in 1959 now find a place. Yet we wish to keep this passage for its reminder of the many Friends, just as worthy to be mentioned as those in this book, who however have not found a place, and for its warning of our failures which is just as necessary now as when it was written.*

The Society of Friends might be thought of as a prism through which the Divine Light passes, to become visible in a spectrum of many colours; many more, in their richness, than words alone can express.

George Bradshaw made railway time-tables to the glory of God, John Bellows made dictionaries, Daniel Quare made clocks; but these we cannot quote. The labourer in the fields, the housewife sweeping her room, the faithful tradesman, have left few memorials. Scholars like Thomas Hodgkin, Frederic Seebohm and Rendel Harris have their memorials elsewhere. No voice speaks here for the long line of scientists that began before John Dalton, and stretches on after Arthur S Eddington. Let no one think, because we have omitted them, that we could forget the Quaker seamen: Robert Fowler, Thomas Chalkley, Paul Cuffee the negro captain, and all their gallant band. There is no word from the masters of industry – the Darbys of Coalbrookdale, Richard Reynolds, Joseph Rowntree or George Cadbury; or from those pioneers of social protest – John Lilburne the Leveller, John Bellers, Peter Bedford or Alfred Salter of Bermondsey. Here are no pictures of the women whom we remember for the beauty of their person as well as character – Gulielma Penn and Esther Tuke; or such glorious old men as William Tuke (who in his sixties founded York Retreat) or Theophilus Waldmeier (who in his sixties founded the Lebanon Hospital); or our children James Parnell, little Mary Samm, and those who kept the meeting while their elders lay in gaol.

Even of the ministers there are few enough: George Fox, but not Richard Farnsworth, that 'man of parts and Champion for the Truth'; John Woolman, but not Anthony Benezet; Stephen Grellet, but not his friend and travelling companion, William Allen; Elizabeth Fry, but not Deborah Darby who foretold her career of mercy. We have shown persecution endured and overcome in seventeenth-century England and New England, but not in nineteenth-century Norway or twentieth-century Germany. Though the field of Quaker concern has stretched across the world, we have had for the most part to stay at home, naming but one or two of a great company beyond seas. If we could have shown Rachel Metcalfe mothering her orphans from her invalid chair; or George Swan, the boy from the fairground, playing his concertina through the villages of India – if only we could have shown them all!

But then in honesty we should have had to reveal also the extent of our failure; the light dimmed in narrow hearts and creeds, the baptism of grace lost in timidity and torpor, the corrosion of arrogance and self-satisfaction – for we have known these, too. May the light prevail over the darkness; may those who are here speak for all the children of the Light, to the needs of other times as well as to their own.

Chapter 19

Openings

In this chapter we tell the story of the origins of our Religious Society. The experiences, insights and 'openings' of Friends in the seventeenth century set out the framework and purpose of the Society and give an authoritative point of reference. But it is not just history, even though it is historical, for the openings also set a direction and point into the future.

At a time of political and religious turmoil, early Friends as a people were gathered, guided and ordered by God. From their experience of the immediacy of the presence of Christ sprang the form of worship and the way of life which became the distinctive testimonies of Friends, and which were upheld with courage in the face of great persecution. From the need to make provision for those suffering and the need to set boundaries to individual behaviour, came the insights into 'Gospel Order' and the setting up of meetings for church affairs which were also meetings for discipline.

As we look at these openings – both beginnings and insights – we are not telling a full history. We are telling those parts of the story which explain and illuminate the identity of our yearly meeting as it is now, as it interprets its origins in the Light now given to it, and as it is called by the same Inward Teacher to find, in differing times and circumstances, the same Truth.

A GATHERED PEOPLE

19.01 *George Fox (1624-1691) was born in Fenny Drayton in Leicestershire. As a young man he was shocked by the failure of those who professed themselves to be Christians (professors) to live up to their Christian standards.*

When I came towards nineteen years of age, I being upon business at a fair, one of my cousins, whose name was Bradford, being a professor and having another professor with him, came to me and asked me to drink part of a jug of beer with them, and I, being thirsty, went in with them, for I loved any that had a sense of good, or that did seek after the Lord. And when we had drunk a glass apiece, they began to drink healths and called for more drink, agreeing together that he that would not drink should pay all. I was grieved that any that made profession of religion should offer to do so. They grieved me very much, having never had such a thing put to me before by any sort of people; wherefore I rose up to be gone, and putting my hand into my pocket, I took out a groat and laid it down upon the table before them and said, 'If it be so, I'll leave you'. So I went away; and when I had done what business I had to do, I returned home, but did not go to bed that night, nor could not sleep, but sometimes walked up and down, and sometimes prayed and cried to the Lord, who said unto me, 'Thou seest how young people go together into vanity and old people into the earth; and thou must forsake all, both young and old, and keep out of all, and be as a stranger unto all'. Then, at the command of God, on the 9th day of the Seventh Month [September], 1643, I left my relations and broke off all familiarity or fellowship with young or old.

Journal, 1643

19.02   *This disillusionment drove George Fox from home in search of spiritual help, and during the next four years he turned without success to one person after another.*

Now after I had received that opening from the Lord that to be bred at Oxford or Cambridge was not sufficient to fit a man to be a minister of Christ, I regarded the priests less and looked more after the dissenting people... As I had forsaken all the priests, so I left the separate preachers also, and those called the most experienced people; for I saw there was none among them all that could speak to my condition. And when all my hopes in them and in all men were gone, so that I had nothing outwardly to help me, nor could tell what to do, then, oh then, I heard a voice which said, 'There is one, even Christ Jesus, that can speak to thy condition', and when I heard it my heart did leap for joy. Then the Lord did let me see why there was none upon the earth that could speak to my condition, namely, that I might give him all the glory; for all are concluded under sin, and shut up in unbelief as I had been, that Jesus Christ might have the pre-eminence who enlightens, and gives grace, and faith, and power. Thus, when God doth work who shall let [ie hinder] it? And this I knew experimentally.

Journal, 1647

19.03   I was under great temptations sometimes, and my inward sufferings were heavy; but I could find none to open my condition to but the Lord alone, unto whom I cried night and day. And I went back into Nottinghamshire, and there the Lord shewed me that the natures of those things which were hurtful without, were within in the hearts and minds of wicked men... And I cried to the Lord, saying, 'Why should I be thus, seeing I was never addicted to commit those evils?' And the Lord answered that it was needful I should have a sense of all conditions, how else should I speak to all conditions; and in this I saw the infinite love of God. I saw also that there was an ocean of darkness and death, but an infinite ocean of light and love, which flowed over the ocean of darkness. And in that also I saw the infinite love of God; and I had great openings.

Journal, 1647

19.04   Now the Lord God hath opened to me by his invisible power how that every man was enlightened by the divine light of Christ; and I saw it shine through all, and that they that believed in it came out of condemnation and came to the light of life and became the children of it, but they that hated it, and did not believe in it, were condemned by it, though they made a profession of Christ. This I saw in the pure openings of the Light without the help of any man, neither did I then know where to find it in the Scriptures; though afterwards, searching the Scriptures, I found it.

Journal, 1648

19.05   *During the next three or four years, George Fox travelled through the East Midlands, and the East and West Ridings of Yorkshire and encountered religious groups of several kinds. In one group at Mansfield he met the former Baptist preacher Elizabeth Hooton (1600?-1672): 'a tender people and a very tender woman', he wrote later in his Journal. She was among his first 'convincements' and was the first woman to play a prominent part in the movement, suffering much in the Quaker cause, both in Britain and overseas. (A part of his testimony concerning her is to be found at 18.02.)*

Elsewhere, George Fox met others who would prove to be significant. Late in 1651 William Dewsbury (1621-1688) described his own spiritual state as follows:

About the time when I was eight years of age, of my natural birth, the Word of the Lord came unto me. 'I created thee for my glory, an account thou must give to Me for all thy words and actions done in the body', which word enlightened my heart and opened the book of conscience in me... Then I ceased from my vain conversation ... and began to read the Scriptures and books, and mourn and pray to a God I knew not where he was... They said he was above the skies, calling it Heaven, but I felt the hand of the Lord within me, executing justice upon the wicked in me, and what way ever I turned to seek him in observations, thither the flaming sword turned ... to keep the way of the tree of life and executed the righteous justice of God upon me.

Then it pleased the Lord to order my friends to put me to keep the sheep, where I was retired from company, so my mind was kept in my mournful estate, where my great ease was in mourning to a God I knew not... [But] I could find no peace in that worship of God the world hath set up, as in receiving the bread and wine, which they told me was the seals of the covenant... Then I durst join no more in their practice in singing David's conditions, which they called Psalms, for the light in my conscience let me see the evil of my heart, that I was not in David's condition.

There was much speaking of God, but I met with none that could tell me what God had done for their souls, in redeeming them from the body of sin which I groaned under, and [which] separated me from the presence of God.

19.06   *In 1652, George Fox journeyed towards the north-west:*

As we went I spied a great high hill called Pendle Hill, and I went on the top of it with much ado, it was so steep; but I was moved of the

Lord to go atop of it; and when I came atop of it I saw Lancashire sea; and there atop of the hill I was moved to sound the day of the Lord; and the Lord let me see atop of the hill in what places he had a great people to be gathered.

19.07 *George Fox found the 'great people' to the north in and about Sedbergh and Preston Patrick. Journeying on from there he came to Swarthmoor Hall near Ulverston, the home of Thomas Fell (1598-1658) and his wife Margaret (1614-1702). She later described his visit:*

In the year 1652 it pleased the Lord to draw him [George Fox] toward us... My then husband, Thomas Fell, was not at home at that time, but gone the Welsh circuit, being one of the Judges of Assize, and our house [Swarthmoor Hall] being a place open to entertain ministers and religious people at, one of George Fox his friends brought him hither, where he stayed all night. And the next day, being a lecture or a fast-day, he went to Ulverston steeplehouse, but came not in till people were gathered; I and my children had been a long time there before. And when they were singing before the sermon, he came in; and when they had done singing, he stood up upon his seat or form and desired that he might have liberty to speak. And he that was in the pulpit said he might. And the first words that he spoke were as followeth: 'He is not a Jew that is one outward, neither is that circumcision which is outward, but he is a Jew that is one inward, and that is circumcision which is of the heart'. And so he went on and said, How that Christ was the Light of the world and lighteth every man that cometh into the world; and that by this Light they might be gathered to God, etc. And I stood up in my pew, and I wondered at his doctrine, for I had never heard such before. And then he went on, and opened the Scriptures, and said, 'The Scriptures were the prophets' words and Christ's and the apostles' words, and what as they spoke they enjoyed and possessed and had it from the Lord'. And said, 'Then what had any to do with the Scriptures, but as they came to the Spirit that gave them forth. You will say, Christ saith this, and the apostles say this; but what canst thou say? Art thou a child of Light and hast walked in the Light, and what thou speakest is it inwardly from God?'

This opened me so that it cut me to the heart; and then I saw clearly we were all wrong. So I sat me down in my pew again, and cried bitterly. And I cried in my spirit to the Lord, 'We are all thieves, we are all thieves, we have taken the Scriptures in words and know nothing of them in ourselves'... I saw it was the truth, and I could not deny it; and I did as the apostle saith, I 'received the truth in the love of it'. And it was opened to me so clear that I had never a tittle in my heart against it; but I desired the Lord that I might be kept in it, and then I desired no greater portion.

1694

19.08   *Francis Howgill (1618-1669), one of the Westmorland Seekers, described the sense of communion engendered among these early Friends:*

[We] were reckoned, in the north part of England, even as the outcasts of Israel, and as men destitute of the great knowledge, which some seemed to enjoy; yet there was more sincerity and true love amongst us and desires after the living powerful presence of God than was among many in that day who ran into heaps and forms but left the cross behind them. God out of his everlasting love did appear unto us, according to the desire of our hearts, who longed after him; when we had turned aside from hireling-shepherds' tents, we found him whom our souls loved; and God, out of his great love and great mercy, sent one unto us, a man of God, one of ten thousand, to instruct us in the way of God more perfectly; which testimony reached unto all our consciences and entered into the inmost part of our hearts, which drove us to a narrow search, and to a diligent inquisition concerning our state, through the Light of Christ Jesus. The Lord of Heaven and earth we found to be near at hand, and, as we waited upon him in pure silence, our minds out of all things, his heavenly presence appeared in our assemblies, when there was no language, tongue nor speech from any creature. The Kingdom of Heaven did gather us and catch us all, as in a net, and his heavenly power at one time drew many hundreds to land. We came to know a place to stand in and what to wait in; and the Lord appeared daily to us, to our astonishment, amazement and great admiration, insomuch that we often said one unto another with great joy of heart: 'What, is the Kingdom of God come to be with men? And will he take up his tabernacle among the sons of men, as he did of old? Shall we, that were reckoned as the outcasts of Israel, have this honour of glory communicated amongst us, which were but men of small parts and of little abilities, in respect of many others, as amongst men?' And from that day forward, our hearts were knit unto the Lord and one unto another in true and fervent love, in the covenant of Life with God; and that was a strong obligation or bond upon all our spirits, which united us one unto another. We met together in the unity of the Spirit, and of the bond of peace, treading down under our feet all reasoning about religion. And holy resolutions were kindled in our hearts as a fire which the Life kindled in us to serve the Lord while we had a being, and mightily did the Word of God grow amongst us, and the desires of many were after the Name of the Lord. O happy day! O blessed day! the memorial of which can never pass out of my mind. And thus the Lord, in short, did form us to be a people for his praise in our generation.

19.09 *In 1653 James Nayler (1617?-1660), in his examination before the justices at Appleby, described the experience that led to his throwing in his lot with Friends:*

I was at the plough, meditating on the things of God, and suddenly I heard a voice saying unto me, 'Get thee out from thy kindred, and from thy father's house'. And I had a promise given with it, whereupon I did exceedingly rejoice that I had heard the voice of that God which I had professed from a child, but had never known him... And when I came at home I gave up my estate, cast out my money; but not being obedient in going forth, the wrath of God was upon me, so that I was made a wonder to all, and none thought I would have lived. But after I was made willing, I began to make some preparation, as apparel and other necessaries, not knowing whither I should go. But shortly afterwards going a gate-ward with a friend from my own house, having on an old suit, without any money, having neither taken leave of wife or children, not thinking then of any journey, I was commanded to go into the west, not knowing whither I should go, nor what I was to do there. But when I had been there a little while, I had given me what I was to declare. And ever since I have remained not knowing today what I was to do tomorrow... [The promise was] that God would be with me, which promise I find made good every day.

19.10   *Elizabeth Halhead was married to the much travelled, much impris-oned Friend Miles Halhead (1614?-pre 1681). Before she too became a Quaker she is reputed to have said,* I would to God I had married a drunkard, I might have found him at the alehouse; but I cannot tell where to find my husband. *Faithfulness to God's call was not con-venient, and the cost was often borne by families.*

19.11   *James Nayler became a leader amongst Friends, but in 1656 was sent to trial on a charge of blasphemy after entering Bristol on horse-back whilst his followers spread garments before him and cried out, 'Holy, holy, holy, Lord God of Israel'. He steadily maintained that 'he denied James Nayler to be Christ, but Christ was in him'. He was severely punished and imprisoned. Reflecting on his experiences he wrote:*

The lower God doth bring me, and the nearer to himself, the more doth this Love and Tenderness spring and spread towards the poor, simple and despised ones, who are poor in spirit, meek and lowly Suffering Lambs, and with those I choose to suffer, and do suffer, wherever they are found.

19.12   *In 1659 he sought to be reconciled with George Fox, from whom he had become estranged, but was rebuffed. William Dewsbury was at last instrumental in bringing a reconciliation, and James Nayler resumed his Quaker service, 'living in great self-denial and very jeal-ous of himself'.*

In 1660, after his release, he set out on foot for the north, intending to go home to his wife and children. On the way, he was robbed and bound, and found towards evening in a field. He was taken to a Friend's house near King's Ripton, where he died. These were some of his last words:

There is a spirit which I feel that delights to do no evil, nor to revenge any wrong, but delights to endure all things, in hope to enjoy its own in the end. Its hope is to outlive all wrath and con-tention, and to weary out all exaltation and cruelty, or whatever is of a nature contrary to itself. It sees to the end of all temptations. As it bears no evil in itself, so it conceives none in thoughts to any other. If it be betrayed, it bears it, for its ground and spring is the mercies and forgiveness of God. Its crown is meekness, its life is everlasting love unfeigned; it takes its kingdom with entreaty and not with contention, and keeps it by lowliness of mind. In God alone it can rejoice, though none else regard it, or can own its life. It's conceived in sorrow, and brought forth without any to pity it, nor doth it murmur at grief and oppression. It never rejoiceth but through sufferings; for with the world's joy it is murdered. I found it alone, being forsaken. I have fellowship therein with them who lived in dens and desolate places in the earth, who through death obtained this resurrection and eternal holy life.

19.13   *From the north the new movement had in 1654 spread to London and the south. Among the converts were Mary Penington (1625?-1682), widow of Sir William Springett. Before she had heard of Quakers she had been uneasy about having her infant daughter 'sprinkled'. In 1654 she married Isaac Penington, and they found peace in worship with Friends, though still 'exercised against taking up the cross to the language, fashions, customs, titles, honour, and esteem in the world'. We know of her feelings from her* Experiences *which she compiled between 1660 and 1680:*

My relations made this cross very heavy; but as at length I happily gave up, divested of reasonings, not consulting how to provide for the flesh, I received the strength to attend the meetings of these despised people which I never intended to meddle with, but found truly of the Lord, and my heart owned them. I longed to be one of them, and minded not the cost or pain; but judged it would be well worth my utmost cost and pain to witness such a change as I saw in them – such power over their corruptions. I had heard objected against them, that they wrought not miracles; but I said that they did great miracles, in that they turned them that were in the world and the fellowship of it, from all such things. Thus, by taking up the cross, I received strength against many things which I had thought impossible to deny; but many tears did I shed, and bitterness of soul did I experience, before I came thither; and often cried out: 'I shall one day fall by the overpowering of the enemy'. But oh! the joy that filled my soul in the first meeting ever held in our house at Chalfont. To this day I have a fresh remembrance of it. It was then the Lord enabled me to worship him in that which was undoubtedly his own, and give up my whole strength, yea, to swim in the life which overcame me that day. Oh! long had I desired to worship him with acceptation, and lift up my hands without doubting, which I witnessed that day in that assembly. I acknowledged his great mercy and wonderful kindness; for I could say, 'This is it which I have longed and waited for, and feared I never should have experienced'.

19.14   *Isaac Penington (1616-1679) wrote:*

At last, after all my distresses, wanderings and sore travails, I met with some writings of this people called Quakers, which I cast a slight eye upon and disdained, as falling very short of that wisdom, light, life and power, which I had been longing for and searching after... After a long time, I was invited to hear one of them (as I had been often, they in tender love pitying me and feeling my want of that which they possessed)... When I came, I felt the presence and power of the Most High among them, and words of truth from the Spirit of truth reaching to my heart and conscience, opening my state as in the presence of the Lord. Yea, I did not only feel words and demonstrations from without, but I felt the dead quickened, the seed raised; insomuch as my heart, in the certainty of light and clearness of true sense, said: 'This is he; this is he; there is no other; this is he whom I have waited for and sought after from my childhood, who was always near me, and had often begotten life in my heart, but I knew him not distinctly, nor how to receive him or dwell with him'.

But some may desire to know what I have at last met with. I answer, 'I have met with the Seed'. Understand that word, and thou wilt be satisfied and inquire no further. I have met with my God, I have met with my Saviour, and he hath not been present with me without his Salvation, but I have felt the healings drop upon my soul from under his wings. I have met with the Seed's Father, and in the Seed I have felt him my Father; there I have read his nature, his love, his compassions, his tenderness, which have melted, overcome and changed my heart before him.

What shall I say? I have met with the true peace, the true righteousness, the true holiness, the true rest of the soul, the everlasting habitation which the redeemed dwell in.

19.15 *Isaac and Mary Penington were friends of the Ellwood family and Thomas Ellwood (1639-1713) first experienced Quaker worship at their home. He here describes his second meeting for worship:*

I had a desire to go to another meeting of the Quakers, and bid my father's man inquire if there was any in the country thereabouts. He thereupon told me he had heard at Isaac Penington's that there was to be a meeting at High Wycombe on Thursday next. Thither therefore I went, though it was seven miles from me, and, that I might be rather thought to go out a-coursing than to a meeting, I let my greyhound run by my horse-side. Being come to the house ... I saw the people sitting together in an outer room, wherefore I stept in and sat down on the first void seat, the end of a bench just within the door, having my sword by my side and black clothes on, which drew some eyes upon me. It was not long ere one stood up and spake, whom I was afterwards well acquainted with (his name was Samuel Thornton), and what he spake was very suitable and of good service to me; for it reached home, as if it had been directed to me.

As soon as ever the meeting was ended and the people began to rise, I, being next the door, stept out quickly and, hastening to my inn, took horse immediately homewards; and, so far as I remember, my having been gone was not taken notice of by my father.

This latter meeting was like the clinching of a nail, confirming and fastening in my mind those good principles which had sunk into me at the former... And now I saw that, although I had been in a great degree preserved from the common immoralities and gross pollutions of the world, yet the spirit of the world had hitherto ruled in me and led me into pride, flattery, vanity and superfluity, all which was naught. I found there were many plants growing in me which were not of the Heavenly Father's planting, and that all these, of whatever sort or kind they were or how specious soever they might appear, must be plucked up.

Now also did I receive a new law, an inward law superadded to the outward – the law of the spirit of life in Christ Jesus – which wrought in me against all evil, not only in deed and in word, but even in thought also, so that everything was brought to judgment and judgment passed upon them all. So that I could not any longer go on in my former ways and course of life, for when I did judgment took hold upon me for it.

So that here began to be a way cast up before me to walk in, a direct and plain way, so plain that a wayfaring man how weak and simple soever ... could not err while he continued to walk in it; the error coming by his going out of it. And this way, with respect to me, I saw was that measure of Divine Light which was manifested in me, by which the evil of my doings, which I was to put away and to cease from, was discovered to me.

1659

19.16   *Commitment, however, involved not only attendance at worship, but also acceptance of those testimonies that had come to be held by Quakers as a whole. Thomas Ellwood soon found his new convictions put to the test:*

A knot of my old acquaintance [at Oxford], espying me, came to me. One of these was a scholar in his gown, another a surgeon of that city... When they were come up to me, they all saluted me, after the usual manner, putting off their hats and bowing, and saying, 'Your humble Servant, Sir', expecting no doubt the same from me. But when they saw me stand still, not moving my cap, nor bowing my knee, in way of congee to them, they were amazed, and looked first one upon another, then upon me, and then one upon another again for a while, without a word speaking. At length, the surgeon ... clapping his hand in a familiar way upon my shoulder and smiling on me said, 'What, Tom, a Quaker!' To which I readily, and cheerfully answered, 'Yes, a Quaker.' And as the words passed out of my mouth I felt joy spring in my heart, for I rejoiced that I had not been drawn out by them into a compliance with them, and that I had strength and boldness given me to confess myself to be one of that despised people.

1659

19.17   *From 1655 the movement spread to mainland Europe, the West Indies, and the mainland of North America. Marmaduke Stevenson here describes his call to service:*

In the beginning of the year 1655, I was at the plough in the east parts of Yorkshire in Old England, near the place where my outward being was; and, as I walked after the plough, I was filled with the love and presence of the living God, which did ravish my heart when I felt it, for it did increase and abound in me like a living stream, so did the life and love of God run through me like precious ointment giving a pleasant smell, which made me to stand still. And, as I stood a little still, with my heart and mind stayed upon the Lord, the word of the Lord came to me in a still, small voice, which I did hear perfectly, saying to me in the secret of my heart and conscience, 'I have ordained thee a prophet unto the nations', and, at the hearing of the word of the Lord, I was put to a stand, seeing that I was but a child for such a weighty matter. So, at the time appointed, Barbados was set before me, unto which I was required of the Lord to go and leave my dear and loving wife and tender children; for the Lord said unto me, immediately by His Spirit, that He would be as an husband to my wife and as a father to my children, and they should not want in my absence, for He would provide for them when I was gone. And I believed the Lord would perform what he had spoken... So, in obedience to the living God, I made preparation to pass to Barbados in the Fourth Month [June] 1658. So, after some time that I had been on the said island in the service of God, I heard that New England had made a law to put the servants of the living God to death if they returned after they were sentenced away, which did come near me at that time; and, as I considered the thing and pondered it in my heart, immediately came the word of the Lord unto me, saying, 'Thou knowest not but that thou mayst go thither.'

But I kept this word in my heart and did not declare it to any until the time appointed. So, after that, a vessel was made ready for Rhode Island, which I passed in. So, after a little time that I had been there, visiting the seed which the Lord had blessed, the word of the Lord came to me, saying, 'Go to Boston with thy brother William Robinson', and at His command I was obedient and gave up to His will, that so His work and service may be accomplished. For He had said unto me that He had a great work for me to do, which is now come to pass. And, for yielding obedience to and for obeying the voice and command of the everlasting God, which created heaven and earth and the fountain of waters, do I, with my dear brother, suffer outward bonds near unto death.

And this is given forth to be upon record, that all people may know who hear it, that we came not in our own wills but in the will of God. Given forth by me, who am known to men by the name of Marmaduke Stevenson, but have a new name given me, which the world knows not of, written in the book of life.

19.18 *The Massachusetts legislature had enacted that every Quaker within its jurisdiction should be banished on pain of death. In June 1659 William Robinson, Mary Dyer and Marmaduke Stevenson came into the colony 'Boston's bloody laws to try'. They were banished but returned and were condemned to death. The two men were hanged.*

Mary Dyer was reprieved and again banished but she returned once more in May 1660. This time there was no reprieve:

Then Mary Dyer was brought forth, and with a band of soldiers led through the town, the drums being beaten before and behind her, and so continued that none might hear her speak all the way to the place of execution, which was about a mile. Thus guarded, she came to the gallows, and being gone up the ladder, some said to her, that, if she would return [home] she might come down and save her life. To which she replied, 'Nay, I cannot, for in obedience to the will of the Lord I came, and in His will I abide faithful to death'... Then one mentioned that she should have said, she had been in Paradise. To which she answered, 'Yea, I have been in Paradise these several days'... Thus Mary Dyer departed this life, a constant and faithful martyr of Christ, having been twice led to death, which the first time she expected with an entire resignation of mind to the will of God, and now suffered with Christian fortitude, being raised above the fear of death through a blessed hope and glorious assurance of eternal life and immortality.

After Mary Dyer's death a member of the General Court uttered one of those bitter scoffs which prove the truest of all epitaphs: She did hang as a flag for others to take example by.

A GUIDED PEOPLE

The experience of being gathered by God leads into the experience of being guided by God. This was not just the experience of individuals, important though this is. The key to the development of Quakerism is the understanding of corporate guidance which tests and informs individual leadings. At the heart of this is the meeting for worship where Christ, the Inward Light, is present and is met. Fox often wrote that Christ has come to teach his people himself. From this teaching comes Quaker faith and practice.

19.19   *Thomas Camm (1641-1707) recalled a meeting of the Westmorland Seekers at Preston Patrick in 1652:*

Thither George Fox went, being accompanied with John Audland and John Camm. John Audland would have had George Fox to have gone into the place or pew where usually he or the preacher did sit, but he refused, and took a back seat near the door, and John Camm sat down by him, where he sat silent waiting upon God about half an hour, in which time of silence Francis Howgill seemed uneasy, and pulled out his Bible and opened it, and stood up several times, sitting down again and closing his book, a dread and fear being upon him that he durst not begin to preach. After the said silence and waiting, George Fox stood up in the mighty power of God, and in the demonstration thereof was his mouth opened to preach Christ Jesus, the light of life and the way to God, and saviour of all that believe and obey him, which was delivered in that power and authority that most of the auditory, which were several hundreds, were effectually reached to the heart, and convinced of the Truth that very day, for it was the day of God's power. A notable day indeed never to be forgotten by me, Thomas Camm, ... I being then present at that meeting, a school boy but about 12 years of age.

19.20   *Edward Burrough (1632 or 1633-1663) wrote:*

While waiting upon the Lord in silence, as often we did for many hours together, with our minds and hearts toward him, being stayed in the light of Christ within us from all thoughts, fleshly motions and desires, we received often the pouring down of the spirit upon us, and our hearts were made glad and our tongues loosened, and our mouths opened, and we spake with new tongues, as the Lord gave us utterance, and his spirit led us, which was poured upon sons and daughters.

19.21   *Robert Barclay (1648-1690), who wrote the first systematic exposition of Quaker theology, shows how knowledge comes from worship:*

Not by strength of arguments or by a particular disquisition of each doctrine, and convincement of my understanding thereby, came [I] to receive and bear witness of the Truth, but by being secretly reached by [the] Life. For, when I came into the silent assemblies of God's people, I felt a secret power among them, which touched my heart; and as I gave way unto it I found the evil weakening in me and the good raised up; and so I became thus knit and united unto them, hungering more and more after the increase of this power and life whereby I might feel myself perfectly redeemed; and indeed this is the surest way to become a Christian; to whom afterwards the knowledge and understanding of principles will not be wanting, but will grow up so much as is needful as the natural fruit of this good root, and such a knowledge will not be barren nor unfruitful.

19.22   *From this experience of worship comes the Quaker understanding of the church as being formed and led by the spirit. George Fox wrote:*

We need no mass for to teach us, and we need not your common prayer, for the Spirit that gave forth the scriptures teacheth us how to pray, sing, fast, and to give thanks... The true faith changeth not, which is the gift of God, and a mystery held in a pure conscience... Our faith, our church, our unity in the Spirit, and our Word, at which we tremble, was in the beginning before your church-made faiths, and our unity, church and fellowship will stand when they are all ended.

19.23   *Robert Barclay wrote:*

In a true church of Christ gathered together by God, not only into the belief of the principles of Truth but also into the power, life and Spirit of Christ, the Spirit of God is the orderer, ruler and governor, as in each particular, so in the general. And when they assemble together to wait upon God, and worship and adore him; then such as the Spirit sets apart for the ministry, by its divine power and influence opening their mouths ... these are thus ordained of God and admitted into the ministry; and their brethren cannot but hear them, and receive them. And so this is not monopolised by a certain kind of men, as the clergy ... and the rest to be despised, as laity; but it is left to the free gift of God to choose any whom he sees meet thereunto, whether rich or poor, servant or master, young or old, yea male or female.

19.24 *Friends related that understanding of their faith to the scriptures, but they grounded their faith on the Spirit which had given forth the scriptures. George Fox at Nottingham in 1649 was listening to a minister who told the people*

that the scriptures were the touchstone and judge by which they were to try all doctrines, religions, and opinions, and to end controversy. Now the Lord's power was so mighty upon me, and so strong in me, that I could not hold, but was made to cry out and say, 'Oh, no, it is not the scriptures', and was commanded to tell them God did not dwell in temples made with hands. But I told them what it was, namely, the Holy Spirit, by which the holy men of God gave forth the scriptures, whereby opinions, religions and judgments were to be tried; for it led into all Truth, and so gave the knowledge of all Truth.

It is significant that Fox, after justifying women's meetings by abundant quotation from scripture, concluded with the words: If there was no scripture ... Christ is sufficient.

The Light

The Inward Light is the light of Christ. It is a universal Light, which can be known by anyone, of either sex, of any age, of whatever religion.

19.25 *Women were to play a full part in the life of the church alongside men. Elizabeth Bathurst (1655?-1685) wrote in* The sayings of women ... *in several places of the Scriptures:*

We find many renowned women recorded in the Old Testament, who had received a talent of wisdom and spiritual understanding from the Lord. As good stewards thereof they improved and employed the same to the praise and glory of God ... as male and female are made one in Christ Jesus, so women receive an office in the Truth as well as men. And they have a stewardship and must give account of their stewardship to their Lord, as well as the men. Therefore they ought to be faithful to God and valiant for his Truth upon the earth, that so they may receive the reward of righteousness.

1683

19.26   *The Light was seen in children. George Fox recalled his experience when in 1653 he was imprisoned in Carlisle:*

And whilst I was in the dungeon a little boy, one James Parnell, about fifteen years old, came to me, and he was convinced and came to be a very fine minister of the word of life, and turned many to Christ.

See also 19.35 on the faithfulness of children

19.27   *Mary Fisher (1623?-1698), after travelling to preach to the Great Turk, testified to this universal Light:*

Now returned into England ... have I borne my testimony for the Lord before the king unto whom I was sent, and he was very noble unto me and so were all that were about him ... they do dread the name of God, many of them... There is a royal seed amongst them which in time God will raise. They are more near Truth than many nations; there is a love begot in me towards them which is endless, but this is my hope concerning them, that he who hath raised me to love them more than many others will also raise his seed in them unto which my love is. Nevertheless, though they be called Turks, the seed of them is near unto God, and their kindness hath in some measure been shown towards his servants.

19.28   *William Penn (1644-1718) was a politician, a courtier, a theologian, a prolific writer and the founder of the colony of Pennsylvania. In 1693 he wrote:*

The humble, meek, merciful, just, pious, and devout souls are everywhere of one religion; and when death has taken off the mask they will know one another, though the divers liveries they wear here makes them strangers. This world is a form; our bodies are forms; and no visible acts of devotion can be without forms. But yet the less form in religion the better, since God is a Spirit; for the more mental our worship, the more adequate to the nature of God; the more silent, the more suitable to the language of a Spirit.

19.29   *The Light leads to holiness. George Fox wrote:*

So as man and woman come again to God, and are renewed up into his image, righteousness and holiness by Christ, thereby they come up into the Paradise of God, the state which man was in before he fell, and into a higher state than that, to sit down in Christ that never fell.

19.30   *Isaac Penington expressed it in different language:*

The sum and substance of true religion doth not stand in getting a notion of Christ's righteousness, but in feeling the power of endless life, receiving the power, and being changed by the power. And where Christ is, there is his righteousness.

19.31   *And in a general epistle of 1667 George Fox wrote:*

They that offered in the Jews' temple were to wear the holy garments. So are you to do that are the true Christians, and are called a royal priesthood. What! are all true Christians priests? Yes. What! are women priests? Yes, women priests. And can men and women offer sacrifices without they wear the holy garments? No. What are the holy garments men and women must wear? The fine linen and they must go in white. What! is this the priest's surplice? Nay ... it is the righteousness of Christ, which is the righteousness of the saints, this is the royal garment of the royal priesthood, which everyone must put on, men and women.

19.32   *This statement comes in George Fox's letter to ministers which he sent in 1656 when he was in prison in Launceston in Cornwall. It was written down for him by Ann Downer (1624-1686) who had walked from London to help him. Later she was a very influential Friend in the women's meetings in London.* George Fox wrote:

Friends,

In the power of life and wisdom, and dread of the Lord God of life, and heaven, and earth, dwell; that in the wisdom of God over all ye may be preserved, and be a terror to all the adversaries of God, and a dread, answering that of God in them all, spreading the Truth abroad, awakening the witness, confounding deceit, gathering up out of transgression into the life, the covenant of light and peace with God.

Let all nations hear the word by sound or writing. Spare no place, spare not tongue nor pen, but be obedient to the Lord God and go through the world and be valiant for the Truth upon earth; tread and trample all that is contrary under.

Keep in the wisdom of God that spreads over all the earth, the wisdom of the creation, that is pure. Live in it; that is the word of the Lord God to you all, do not abuse it; and keep down and low; and take heed of false joys that will change.

Bring all into the worship of God. Plough up the fallow ground... And none are ploughed up but he who comes to the principle of God in him which he hath transgressed. Then he doth service to God; then the planting and the watering and the increase from God cometh. So the ministers of the Spirit must minister to the Spirit that is transgressed and in prison, which hath been in captivity in every one; whereby with the same Spirit people must be led out of captivity up to God, the Father of spirits, and do service to him and have unity with him, with the Scriptures and with one another. And this is the word of the Lord God to you all, and a charge to you all in the presence of the living God: be patterns, be examples in all countries, places, islands, nations, wherever you come, that your carriage and life may preach among all sorts of people, and to them; then you will come to walk cheerfully over the world, answering that of God in every one.

The testimonies

The experience of Friends was that the Light led them into an understanding of the Christian life and the way it was to be lived. We express the principles they discovered in terms such as Truth, Equality, Simplicity, and Peace. However, these are not abstract qualities, but vital principles of life. Early Friends expressed them in the ways of action which they called the testimonies, and for which they were prepared to suffer and to die.

19.33   *Yet William Dewsbury could say:*

For this I can say, I ... joyfully entered prisons as palaces, telling mine enemies to hold me there as long as they could: and in the prison-house I sung praises to my God, and esteemed the bolts and locks put upon me as jewels, and in the Name of the eternal God I always got the victory, for they could keep me there no longer than the determined time of my God.

If any one has received any good or benefit through this vessel, called William Dewsbury, give God the glory; I'll have none, I'll have none, I'll have none.

1688

Truth

'Truth' is a complex concept; sometimes the word is used for God, sometimes for the conviction that arises from worship, sometimes for the way of life.

19.34   *Witnessing to Truth involved the keeping up of public meetings for worship, whatever the penalties involved. In 1675, during a time of great persecution, a 'solemn general meeting of many faithful friends and brethren', issued the following advice:*

It hath been our care and practice from the beginning that an open testimony for the Lord should be borne and a public standard for truth and righteousness upheld in the power and Spirit of God by our open and known meetings, ... so it is our advice and judgment that all Friends gathered in the name of Jesus keep up these public testimonies in their respective places, and not decline, forsake or remove their public assemblies, because of times of suffering as worldly, fearful and politic professors have done because of informers and the like persecutors; for such practices are not consistent with the nobility of the truth and therefore not to be owned in the Church of Christ.

19.35   *In Bristol in 1682:*

On the 7th of the month called July, they dispersed the meeting which then consisted chiefly of children; for the men and women being generally in prison, the children kept up their meetings regularly, and with a remarkable gravity and composure: it was surprising to see the manly courage and constancy with which some of the boys behaved on this occasion, keeping close to meetings in the absence of their parents, and undergoing on that account many abuses with patience... On the 30th, in the afternoon, about fifty-five were at the meeting, when Helliar, with a twisted whalebone-stock, beat many of them unmercifully, striking them violent blows on their heads, necks and faces, few of them escaping without some marks of his fury...

He also [on 13 August] sent eleven boys and four girls to Bridewell, till a Friend engaged for their appearance next day before the deputy mayor, who endeavoured both by persuasions and threats to make them promise to come at no more meetings; but the children in that respect were unmoveable: wherefore they were sent to Bridewell again, Helliar, to terrify them, charging the keeper to provide a new cat of ninetails against next morning. Next day at the Tolzey he urged the justices to have them corrected, but could not prevail. The boys and girls were mostly from ten to twelve years of age. Their names were Samuel Gibbon, William Miller, Joseph James, Elias Osborne, Tabitha Jones, Jonathan Jones, William Fry, Joseph Watkins, Rachel Mears, William Day, Samuel Watkins, James Randy, Martha Watkins, Martha James and James Wheeler.

19.36   *Witnessing to Truth also involved preaching. Katherine Evans (d 1692) and Sarah Chevers were imprisoned for three years in the prison of the Inquisition in Malta, for their preaching.*

And in the greatest of our afflictions we could not say in our hearts, 'Father, would thou hadst not brought us here!' but cried mightily to our God for power to carry us through whatsoever should be inflicted upon us, that the Truth of our God might not suffer through our weakness. And the Lord did hear us ... and carried us on with all boldness, and made our foreheads as flint ... that whensoever we were brought forth upon trial, all fear was taken away, that we stood as iron gates.

1662

19.37 *Friends also saw Truth as demanding honest, simple speech, and a refusal to acknowledge double standards by taking oaths. George Fox wrote:*

They gave me the book to swear on, and the book saith, Swear not at all: But I told them, if they could prove that after Christ Jesus and his apostles had forbidden men to swear, they had allowed it, I would swear. Thus I said, and my allegiance lies in truth and faithfulness, not in swearing, and so should all your allegiance lie, if you did well. I do not deny swearing upon some account, and own it upon others, but I deny it, because Christ and the apostle have said, I should not swear at all.

19.38 *Margaret Fell was imprisoned and was made liable to lose all her property for her refusal to take an oath of loyalty to the king.*

The same justices sent for me to Ulverston, where they were sitting, and when I came there they asked me several questions, and seemed to be offended at me for keeping a meeting at my house, and said, They would tender me the oath of allegiance. I answered, They knew I could not swear, and why should they send for me from my own house, when I was about my lawful occasions, to ensnare me, what had I done? They said, If I would not keep meetings at my house, they would not tender me the oath. I told them I should not deny my faith and principles for any thing they could do against me, and while it pleaseth the Lord to let me have an house, I would endeavour to worship him in it. So they caused the oath to be read, and tendered it to me, and when I refused it, telling them, I could not swear for conscience-sake, Christ Jesus having forbid it, they made a *mittimus*, and committed me prisoner to Lancaster Castle, and there George Fox and I remained prisoners until next assizes, and they indicted us upon the statute for denying the oath of allegiance, for they tendered it to both of us again at the assizes, and the indictments were found against us.

So they passed sentence of Præmunire upon me which was that I should be out of the King's protection and forfeit all my estate, real and personal, to the King and imprisonment during life. But the great God of heaven and earth supported my spirit under this severe sentence, that I was not terrified but gave this answer to Judge Turner, who gave the sentence, 'Although I am out of the King's protection, I am not out of the protection of the Almighty God'.

1664

See also Oaths and affirmation 20.48-20.53

Equality

19.39 *From Truth sprang the testimonies that indicated equality between people. Brigflatts Friends wrote about Gervase Benson (c 1604-1679):*

And the said Gervase became greatly serviceable upon many accounts for the promotion of Truth, labouring in the work of the gospel of which he was made an able minister, appointing meetings in fresh places... And many were convinced by his ministry, which was sound and weighty, and his conversation answerable, being an example of humility in all things, notwithstanding the height and glory of the world that he had a great share of, so that none (scarce) was more plain in apparel and furniture of his house, conforming to the simplicity of the Truth, and in testimony against all the vain titles of the world that his former station might have given him. He generally styled himself husbandman, notwithstanding that he had been a colonel, a justice of peace, mayor of Kendal, and was commissary in the archdeaconry of Richmond before the late domestic wars, yet as an humble disciple of Christ, downed those things.

19.40 *Thomas Ellwood committed himself to being a Quaker when he declined to return 'the vain salutations of the world'. He maintained the testimony against hat honour, and the testimony to plain language:*

The sight of my hat upon my head made [my father] presently forget that I was that son of his, whom he had so lately lamented as lost; and his passion of grief turning into anger, he could not contain himself; but running upon me, with both his hands, first violently snatcht off my hat, and threw it away; then giving me some buffets on my head, he said, Sirrah, get you up to your chamber...

But as this hat-honour (as it was accounted) was grown to be a great idol, in those times more especially, so the Lord was pleased to engage his servants in a steady testimony against it, what suffering soever was brought upon them for it. And though some, who have been called into the Lord's vineyard at latter hours, and since the heat of that day hath been much over, may be apt to account this testimony a small thing to suffer so much upon, as some have done, not only to beating, but to fines, and long and hard imprisonments; yet they who, in those times, were faithfully exercised in and under it, durst not despise the day of small things; as knowing that he who should do so, would not be thought worthy to be concerned in higher testimonies...

But whenever I had occasion to speak to my father, though I had no hat now to offend him, yet my language did as much; for I durst not say 'You' to him; but 'Thou', or 'Thee', as the occasion required, and then would he be sure to fall on me with his fists.

See also 15.20 Gravestones, 19.25, 19.31 & 20.27-20.36

Simplicity

19.41 *Plainness of dress also sprang from following Truth. Joan Vokins (d 1690) wrote to her children in 1686:*

Be careful and take heed that you do not stain the testimony of Truth that you have received, by wearing of needless things and following the world's fashions in your clothing and attire, but remember how I have bred you up.

19.42 *It brought with it difficulties. Thomas Chalkley (1675-1741) recalled his experience in the 1680s:*

When between eight and ten years of age, my father and mother sent me near two miles to school, to Richard Scoryer, in the suburbs of London. I went mostly by myself to school; and many and various were the exercises I went through, by beatings and stonings along the streets, being distinguished to the people (by the badge of plainness which my parents put upon me) of what profession I was; divers telling me, 'Twas no more sin to kill me, than it was to kill a dog'.

19.43 *A letter from Isaac Penington in 1665 re-echoes Thomas Ellwood's reminder that we must not despise 'the day of small things' (Zech 4:10):*

Do not look for such great matters to begin with; but be content to be a child, and let the Father proportion out daily to thee what light, what power, what exercises, what straits, what fears, what troubles he sees fit for thee; and do thou bow before him continually in humility of heart... Thou must join in with the beginnings of life, and be exercised with the day of small things, before thou meet with the great things, wherein is the clearness and satisfaction of the soul. The rest is at noonday; but the travels begin at the breakings of day, wherein are but glimmerings or little light, wherein the discovery of good and evil are not so manifest and certain; yet there must the traveller begin and travel; and in his faithful travels ... the light will break in upon him more and more.

19.44 *As with any other testimony, there was always the danger of degenerating into legalism, a preoccupation with outward detail rather than the inner springs of action. Late in her life, Margaret Fox urged Friends to* stand fast in that liberty wherewith Christ hath made us free (Gal 5:1). *See 20.30-20.31 for examples of Margaret Fox's advice.*

See also 20.27-20.36

Peace

19.45　*The conviction came to one Friend after another that war was inconsistent with Truth. William Dewsbury wrote:*

At that time did the wars begin in this nation, and the men called ministers cried, 'Curse ye Meroz, because they went not forth to help the Lord against the mighty'. Then I was willing to give my body to death, in obedience to my God, to free my soul from sin, and I joined with that little remnant which said they fought for the gospel, but I found no rest to my soul amongst them. And the word of the Lord came unto me and said, 'Put up thy sword into thy scabbard; if my kingdom were of this world, then would my children fight', which word enlightened my heart and discovered the mystery of iniquity, and that the Kingdom of Christ was within, and the enemies was within, and was spiritual, and my weapons against them must be spiritual, the power of God. Then I could no longer fight with a carnal weapon against a carnal man, and returned to my outward calling, and my will was brought in subjection for the Lord to do with me what his will was.

19.46　*In June 1660 Margaret Fell delivered to Charles II a paper directed to the king and both houses of parliament making clear the corporate testimony of Friends 'against all strife and wars':*

We are a people that follow after those things that make for peace, love and unity; it is our desire that others' feet may walk in the same, and do deny and bear our testimony against all strife, and wars, and contentions that come from the lusts that war in the members, that war in the soul, which we wait for, and watch for in all people, and love and desire the good of all... Treason, treachery, and false dealing we do utterly deny; false dealing, surmising, or plotting against any creature upon the face of the earth, and speak the truth in plainness, and singleness of heart.

See 24.04 for the corporate version of this testimony

19.47　*Corporate testimony depends on individual faithfulness. An individual will be faithful through a recognition of the testimony and a searching of the heart to see what steps are required. The following anecdote depends on oral tradition, but it has played so large a part in Quaker thinking that it is included here:*

When William Penn was convinced of the principles of Friends, and became a frequent attendant at their meetings, he did not immediately relinquish his gay apparel; it is even said that he wore a sword, as was then customary among men of rank and fashion. Being one day in company with George Fox, he asked his advice concerning it, saying that he might, perhaps, appear singular among Friends, but his sword had once been the means of saving his life without injuring his antagonist, and moreover, that Christ had said, 'He that hath no sword, let him sell his garment and buy one.' George Fox answered, 'I advise thee to wear it as long as thou canst.' Not long after this they met again, when William had no sword, and George said to him, 'William, where is thy sword?' 'Oh!' said he, 'I have taken thy advice; I wore it as long as I could.'

Samuel Janney, 1852

See also chapter 24 Our peace testimony

19.48   *A Testimony of William Penn concerning early Friends:*

They were changed men themselves before they went about to change others. Their hearts were rent as well as their garments, and they knew the power and work of God upon them... And as they freely received what they had to say from the Lord, so they freely administered it to others. The bent and stress of their ministry was conversion to God, regeneration and holiness, not schemes of doctrines and verbal creeds or new forms of worship, but a leaving off in religion the superfluous and reducing the ceremonious and formal part, and pressing earnestly the substantial, the necessary and profitable part, as all upon a serious reflection must and do acknowledge.

1694

AN ORDERED PEOPLE

The danger for any spirit-inspired religion is individualism carried to excess. In the seventeenth century, this was seen amongst those called Ranters. Friends, too, ran this risk. What preserved them was the discovery of 'gospel-order', the setting up of meetings for church affairs where individual insight was tested against the insight of the gathered group. A series of meetings for church affairs, some local, some regional or national, had developed from 1654 onwards, though it was during the years 1667-1669 that George Fox journeyed throughout the country, creating from a series of ad-hoc meetings a regular structure of monthly and quarterly meetings as part of a yearly meeting for the whole nation.

19.49 All the men's monthly meetings were settled in the glorious order of the gospel, and that all in the power of God might seek that which was lost, and bring again that which was driven away, and might cherish the good and reprove the evil.

George Fox, 1668

19.50 *A system grew up where by and large men and women Friends held separate meetings for church affairs, a practice which continued until the end of the nineteenth century. Some meetings were held jointly, and some Friends objected to the existence of women's meetings altogether. George Fox defended them:*

For man and woman were helpsmeet in the image of God ... in the dominion before they fell; but after the Fall ... the man was to rule over his wife; but in the restoration by Christ, into the image of God ... in that they are helpsmeet, man and woman, as they were in before the Fall.

19.51 *The type of business dealt with by such meetings had already been established. George Fox described the general meeting at Skipton in April 1660, attended by Friends 'out of most parts of the nation':*

And justices and captains had come to break up this meeting, but when they saw Friends' books and accounts of collections concerning the poor, how that we did take care one county to help another, and to provide for our poor that none of them should be chargeable to their parishes, etc, and took care to help Friends beyond the seas, the justices and officers were made to confess that we did their work and Friends desired them to come and sit with them then. And so they passed away lovingly and commended Friends' practice.

19.52 *In 1659 the Box Meeting of women Friends was set up in London. George Fox wrote:*
And when I came to Gerard Roberts' house about 8 in the morning there came in Sarah Blackbury to complain to me of the poor and how many poor Friends was in want. And the Lord had showed me what I should do in his eternal power and wisdom. So I spoke to her to bid about 60 women to meet me about the 1st hour in the afternoon at the sign of the Helmet at a Friend's house, and they did so accordingly: such as were sensible women of the Lord's truth and fearing God. And what the Lord had opened unto me I declared unto them concerning their having a meeting once a week every second-day, that they might see and inquire into the necessity of all Friends who was sick and weak and who was in wants, or widows and fatherless in the city and suburbs.

19.53 *The sense of responsibility for one another might lead to unexpected paths, as is shown by the letter of 1662 to the mayor and sheriffs of London, signed by thirty Friends concerned for the seven-score Quakers then imprisoned in Newgate:*

And if no other way can be found for their relief, if they may not have the liberty to follow their occasions for some weeks, or until such time as you shall call for them, which we desire on their behalfs, and are here already to give our words, that they shall become prisoners again as you shall appoint them: And if no other way can be found, then we, a certain number of us, do present our bodies to you, offering them freely to relieve our afflicted and oppressed brethren, and are ready to go into their places, and to suffer, as prisoners in their room, for your security, that so many of the poorest of them, as we are here, may have their liberty to go about their needful occasions, whether it be for some weeks, or until you shall call for them, as you see meet in your wisdom. All which we do in humility of heart, and sincerity of our minds, and in the fear of God, and love to our brethren, that they may not perish in prison, and in love to you, that innocent blood and oppression may not come upon you, but be prevented from ever being charged against you.

19.54 *Rebecca Travers (1609?-1688), writing to George and Margaret Fox in 1676, commented on the situation as she then saw it:*

The ancient love among some of the brethren waxes cold, and self love and the too much love of this world stains our pristine glory, when it was said, even by our enemies, they so love one another that we shall never be able to break them. The women's meetings are accompanied with the power and presence of the Lord as ever – our service great, and our supply faileth not.

19.55 *A letter 'From the women Friends in London' in 1674 described the tasks of women's meetings:*

Dear sisters ... our services are: to visit the sick and the prisoners that suffer for the testimony of Jesus ... relieving the poor, making provision for the needy, aged and weak, that are incapable of work; a due consideration for the widows, and care taken for the fatherless children and poor orphans ... for their education ... and putting them out to trades... Also the elder women exhorting the younger in all sobriety, modesty in apparel, and subjection to truth ... and to stop tatlers and false reports and all such things as tend to division amongst us, following those things which make for peace and reconciliation and union; also admonishing such maids and widows as may be in danger ... either to marry with unbelievers or to go to the priest to be married ... that we may answer our duty herein, we meet every Second-day ... that none may stand idle ... for our services still increase many ways. But chiefly our work is, to help the helpless in all cases, according to our abilities.

19.56 *Both men's and women's meetings had a share in the oversight of marriage, great care being taken that all was in good order before the couple were liberated for their marriage. In 1688 the Women's Yearly Meeting at York issued A testimony for the Lord and his Truth:*

Friends, be not concerned in reference to marriage, out of God's fear, but first wait to know your Maker to become your husband and the bridegroom of your souls... O Friends! This state is happy, and blessed are they that attain it and live in it; the Lord is not unmindful of them, but in his own time, if he see it good for them, can provide meet-helps for them. Then will your marriage be honourable, being orderly accomplished with the assent of parents and the unity of Friends and an honour to God and comfort to your own souls.

19.57   *Wiltshire Quarterly Meeting in 1678 set down advice on the conduct of meetings for church affairs:*

For the preservation of love, concord and a good decorum in this meeting, 'tis earnestly desired that all business that comes before it be managed with gravity and moderation, in much love and Amity, without reflections or retorting, which is but reasonable as well as comely, since we have no other obligation upon each other but love, which is the very bond of our society: and therein to serve the Truth and one another; having an eye single to it, ready to sacrifice every private interest to that of Truth, and the good of the whole community.

Wherefore let whatsoever is offered, be mildly proposed, and so left with some pause, that the meeting may have opportunity to weigh the matter, and have a right sense of it, that there may be a unanimity and joint concurrence of the whole. And if anything be controverted that it be in coolness of Spirit calmly debated, each offering their reasons and sense, their assent, or dissent, and so leave it without striving. And also that but one speak at once, and the rest hear. And that private debates and discourses be avoided, and all attend the present business of the Meeting. So will things be carried on sweetly as becomes us, to our comfort: and love and unity be increased: and we better serve Truth and our Society.

19.58   *This practical advice must be seen in the context of Friends' sense of the corporate guidance of God:* Friends are not to meet as people upon town or parish business but are to wait upon the Lord. *Thus the named officer of the meeting was not to preside but to record, to be a clerk. William Penn wrote in 1694:*

In these solemn assemblies for the church's service, there is no one presides among them after the manner of the assemblies of other people; Christ only being their president, as he is pleased to appear in life and wisdom in any one or more of them; to whom, whatever be their capacity or degree, the rest adhere with a firm unity, not of authority, but conviction, which is the divine authority and way of Christ's power and spirit in his people: making good his blessed promise, that he would be in the midst of his, where and whenever they were met together in his name, even to the end of the world.

See also 2.85-2.92 Meetings for church affairs *& chapter 3* General counsel on church affairs

A CONTINUING STORY

19.59   *Before the end of the seventeenth century, most of the early Friends, the 'First Publishers of Truth', had died. Convincements continued, but there was also a new generation of Friends, children of the early Quakers. William Penn addressed them:*

And now, as for you, that are the children of God's people, a great concern is upon my spirit for your good: and often are my knees bowed to the God of your fathers for you, that you may come to be partakers of the same divine life and power, that has been the glory of this day; that a generation you may be to God, an holy nation, and a peculiar people, zealous of good works, when all our heads are laid in the dust.

O! you young men and women, let it not suffice you, that you are the children of the people of the Lord; you must also be born again, if you will inherit the kingdom of God.

Wherefore, O ye young men and women, look to the rock of your fathers: there is no other God but him, no other Light but his, no other grace but his, nor Spirit but his, to convince you, quicken, and comfort you; to lead, guide, and preserve you to God's everlasting kingdom. So will you be possessors as well as professors of the truth, embracing it, not only by education, but judgment and conviction; from a sense begotten in your souls, through the operation of the eternal Spirit and power of God in your hearts ... that, as I said before, a generation you may be to God, holding up the profession of the blessed truth in the life and power of it.

19.60   *Samuel Bownas (1676-1753) was one of these second generation Friends. The incident he here recounts took place in 1696 when he was about twenty years old. He later became a travelling minister.*

Now to return to my apprenticeship, I had a very kind, loving master and mistress, and I had meat enough and work enough but had little consideration about religion nor any taste thereof. On First-days I frequented meetings and the greater part of my time I slept, but took no account of preaching nor received any other benefit, than being there kept me out of bad company, which indeed is a very great service to youth ... but one First-day, being at meeting [at Brigflatts, near Sedbergh], a young woman named Anne Wilson was there and preached: she was very zealous and fixing my eye upon her, she with a great zeal pointed her finger at me uttering these words with much power, viz: 'A traditional Quaker; thou comest to meeting as thou went from it, and goes from it as thou came to it but art no better for thy coming; what wilt thou do in the end?' This was so pat to my then condition that like Saul I was smitten to the ground as it might be said, but turning my thoughts inwards, in secret I cried, 'Lord, what shall I do to help it?' And a voice as it were spoke in my heart, saying 'Look unto me, and I will help thee'...

I saw by experience wherein my shortness had been in being contented and easy with a form of truth and religion, which I had only by education, being brought up in plainness of both habit and speech; but all this though very good in its place, did not make me a true Christian; I was but a traditional Quaker, and that by education only and not from the Scriptures because they were a book sealed to me. And I now saw plainly that education though never so carefully administered would not do the work ... there was no other way but this, viz by the Spirit of Christ alone (John 10:1-3), to attain to true faith, which works by love and gives victory over our infirmities and evil deeds, working such a change in us that we can in truth from experience say we are born from above.

By 1700 our yearly meeting had become a settled organisation, with established procedures and an expected way of life. Friends were able to worship freely, though still barred from the English universities and from political life. They were becoming 'a peculiar people', marked out by their dress and speech, yet their separateness from the surrounding culture may have helped them to preserve testimonies such as the practice of the equality of women with men.

The eighteenth century saw a 'Quietist' period, when completely silent meetings became normal. In the nineteenth century there was an evangelical revival, with a heavy dependence on the scriptures literally interpreted. Throughout these periods also there was a steady growth in social concern for the poor, for prisoners, for slaves; a steadfast adherence to testimonies against war and tithes; and many examples of individual and corporate faithfulness, of lives lived in the light of the gospel.

During the second half of the nineteenth century educational opportunities opened up for Friends, for women as well as men. Many of the outward marks of the testimonies, such as plain dress, began to fall into disuse. In the last decade of the century two major events occurred which shaped the yearly meeting as it now is. In 1895 the Manchester Conference introduced liberal theology into the yearly meeting's thinking and led to mechanisms for educating the yearly meeting in its own tradition. In 1896 the Yearly Meeting decided that its men's and women's meetings should meet together and that women should be admitted into membership of Meeting for Sufferings.

Since then the yearly meeting has changed from comprising mostly those born into the Society to being largely made up of newcomers. For all of us there is still a need to be 'convinced', to make the tradition our own, so that we may know the same divine life and power, and open our lives to the same transforming Truth.

19.61   The Truth is one and the same always, and though ages and generations pass away, and one generation goes and another comes, yet the word and power and spirit of the living God endures for ever, and is the same and never changes.

Margaret Fell

Chapter 20

Living faithfully today

THE SOURCE OF OUR STRENGTH

20.01   I ask for daily bread, but not for wealth, lest I forget the poor.
I ask for strength, but not for power, lest I despise the meek.
I ask for wisdom, but not for learning, lest I scorn the simple.
I ask for a clean name, but not for fame, lest I contemn the lowly.
I ask for peace of mind, but not for idle hours, lest I fail to hearken
    to the call of duty.

Inazo Nitobe, 1909

20.02   *Job Scott (1751-1793) of Rhode Island travelled widely in the min-*
istry. His Journal (see 21.51 & 22.36) is one of the treasures of the
Quietist period.

Our strength or help is only in God; but then it is near us, it is *in us*
– a force superior to all possible opposition – a force that never was,
nor can be foiled. We are free to stand in this unconquerable ability,
and defeat the powers of darkness; or to turn from it, and be foiled
and overcome. When we stand, we know it is God alone upholds us;
and when we fall, we feel that our fall or destruction is of ourselves.

Journal of Job Scott, 1751-1793

20.03   *The poetry of John Greenleaf Whittier (1807-1892), a Massachusetts*
journalist and anti-slavery campaigner, continues to find a place in
modern hymn-books, far beyond the boundaries of the Religious
Society of Friends. In The brewing of soma, of which the following
are the final stanzas, the Quaker poet asks forgiveness for the Chris-
tian tendency to fall back on artificial stimulants to spiritual experi-
ence, which he likens to the drug-induced ecstasies of primitive
religion in 'the childhood of the world' and contrasts with the true
inspiration which we may experience in silent waiting upon God.

Dear Lord and Father of mankind
   Forgive our foolish ways!
Reclothe us in our rightful mind,
   In purer lives thy service find,
In deeper reverence, praise.

In simple trust like theirs who heard
   Beside the Syrian sea
The gracious calling of the Lord,
Let us, like them, without a word,
   Rise up and follow thee.

O Sabbath rest by Galilee!
   O calm of hills above,
Where Jesus knelt to share with thee
The silence of eternity
   Interpreted by love!

With that deep hush subduing all
   Our words and works that drown
The tender whisper of thy call,
As noiseless let thy blessing fall
   As fell thy manna down.

Drop thy still dews of quietness,
   Till all our strivings cease;
Take from our souls the strain and stress,
And let our ordered lives confess
   The beauty of thy peace.

Breathe through the heats of our desire
   Thy coolness and thy balm;
Let sense be dumb, let flesh retire;
Speak through the earthquake, wind, and fire,
   O still, small voice of calm!

1872

20.04   When work does not turn out as was expected or intended, do not
let it depress you. If you are working from a right motive, and doing
your best under the guidance of a loving Father in heaven, your
work cannot be and is not failure... Remember that the Lord never

lays work upon His people that He does not give them strength or ability to perform, and if it please Him in the working out of His great purposes that life shall be sacrificed or cut short in the midst of the work, be assured that the work will not permanently suffer from such a cause.

Joseph John Armistead, 1913

20.05 The people whom I know who live a truly nonviolent life are in touch with the source of power, call it what you will; the Light, the seed, God, the holy spirit. Many others of us find this wellspring when we need it, and lose it again, find it and lose it, find it and lose it. Regrettably, I am one of the latter. When I have something very difficult to face that I know I can't cope with, then I turn desperately to the source. One of the things I find most infuriating about myself is that I often let the contact go when the emergency is over and flounder along without it for months on end when my everyday existence could be transformed by it. It is as if I opened the blinds in my house for only an occasional hour when – for example – I had an important visitor, or a cable arrived, or I had to sweep up some broken glass; and afterwards allowed the blinds to fall closed again. So that for ninety-per-cent of the time I bumble around, do my housework in semi-darkness, strain my eyes trying to read and can scarcely discern the features of those to whom I talk. More than anything I want to learn to live in the Light. So I think, anyway, but in fact I perhaps don't altogether want to take the demands involved, don't want to see all the dust in my life.

Jo Vellacott, 1982

20.06 Some among us have a clear sense of what is right and wrong – for themselves personally if not for everyone else. They have a reassuring certitude and steadiness which can serve as a reference point by which others may navigate. There are others who live in a state of uncertainty, constantly re-thinking their responses to changing circumstances, trying to hold onto what seems fundamental but impelled to reinterpret, often even unsure where lies the boundary between the fundamental and the interpretation...

Please be patient, those of you who have found a rock to stand on, with those of us who haven't and with those of us *who are not even looking for one*. We live on the wave's edge, where sea, sand and sky are all mixed up together: we are tossed head over heels in the surf, catching only occasional glimpses of any fixed horizon. Some of us stay there from choice because it is exciting and it *feels like the right place to be*.

Philip Rack, 1979

20.07   Later on I was meditating, imagining Light and Love surrounding the world leaders as they gathered: 'Free them from fear', I asked ... but then I couldn't go on. I realised that all I could honestly ask was for myself to be freed from the fear which only an hour ago had threatened to ruin my day. All I could do was to come to terms with my own brokenness and make peace with myself and then with my immediate environment. And remembering the conflicts and problems in my life at that moment, even that seemed beyond me.

Susan Lawrence, 1984

20.08   Prayer is an exercise of the spirit, as thought is of the mind. To pray about anything is to use the powers of our spirit on it, just as to think clearly is to use our mental powers. For the best solution of every problem, the best carrying out of every action, both thought and prayer are necessary... To pray about any day's work does not mean to ask success in it. It means, first to realise my own inability to do even a familiar job, as it truly should be done, unless I am in touch with eternity, unless I do it 'unto God', unless I have the Father with me. It means to see 'my' work as part of a whole, to see 'myself' as not mattering much, but my faith, the energy, will and striving, which I put into the work, as mattering a great deal. My faith is the point in me at which God comes into my work; through faith the work is given dignity and value. And if, through some weakness of mine, or fault of others, or just 'unavoidable circumstances', the work seems a failure, yet prayer is not wasted when it is unanswered, any more than love is wasted when it is unreturned.

Mary F Smith, 1936

20.09   Over the years many Friends have told me that they no longer need regular daily prayer. I don't want to suggest that I am a better man or that there is only one way but simply that this has not been my experience. I am not emotionally strong, and the expected, and even more the unexpected, needs of patients, students, colleagues, family, friends and strangers leave me empty and exhausted. I could not face the next day without a time in which life is renewed. I shall not describe this in detail. The essence is regularity and time – time to reach down to the level where I can begin to see myself and my work straight, where that strength we call love can break through my anxiety and teach me how to respond instead of react, where I am not ruled by conscience but by Jesus the true man within; the level where I can accept my whole nature and forgive myself and others... Prayer alone can reopen the road to the spirit, blocked repeatedly by busyness, self-importance, self-indulgence, self-pity, depression or despair.

Donald Court, 1970

20.10 The place of prayer is a precious habitation: ... I saw this habitation to be safe, to be inwardly quiet, when there was great stirrings and commotions in the world.

John Woolman, 1770

20.11 Love silence, even in the mind... Much speaking, as much thinking, spends; and in many thoughts, as well as words, there is sin. True silence is the rest of the mind; and is to the spirit, what sleep is to the body, nourishment and refreshment.

William Penn, 1699

20.12 Like many people, I had given up the practice of prayer as I had learned it when young, for it seemed to me at best a convention, at worst a superstition. It was George Gorman, in *The amazing fact of Quaker worship*, who helped me to see that I do in fact pray. When I go up to kiss my sleeping children and linger with them, in quietness and love, that is prayer. There is a wordless unity of God, myself, my children, a sense of gratitude and reverence, awareness of my need for strength, shame for my failings, a promise to try again.

Exercise is good for us; prayer is the right kind for the spirit. As with physical exercise there are many kinds, to do by yourself or with

other people, at different intervals, with different aids. It takes time
and commitment to develop the right kind for each one of us.

Anne Hosking, 1984

20.13   There were three separate occasions when heart-felt disturbances
called me back to prayer. One was entirely joyful: sitting up in bed
early one summer morning nursing my week-old first child, looking
out on the sunshine and being swept into a feeling of miraculous
oneness with all creation and able to thank a real God with the
whole of my being.

The second was in great contrast. The winter after my husband's
death, when I was physically stretched to the limit caring single-
handed for six young children and emotionally in a state of bleak
torpor, I came across Simone Weil's *Waiting on God* and in a chapter called 'The love of God and affliction' recognised my own condition. I could not claim that I knew the worst that she, in her utterly
clear and ruthless style, was describing, but it was near enough, and
knowing that someone else recognised it brought a certain comfort.
But most important, she showed a place for God in the shape of the
crucified Christ, and part of my misery for some time had been the
blank absence of any sense of the presence of God...

The third experience, some years later, concerned a friend who was
extremely ill. She was one of the few really good people I had ever
known, and I saw her in great distress. When I reached home from
the hospital I went to my room and tried to lay myself alongside her
suffering and bring us both before God. In the depth of affliction I
had sometimes felt like Job; now I found myself wrestling like Jacob.
This last episode began the process of break-up which led on by slow
degrees to a time when I knew I had to try to pray again; not just in
dire immediate need but as a basis for daily living.

Joan Fitch, 1980

20.14   Those of us known as 'activists' have sometimes been hurt by the
written or spoken implication that we must be spending too little
time on our spiritual contemplative lives. I do know many atheists
who are active to improve the lot of humankind; but, for those of us
who are Friends, our attendance at meeting for worship and our

silent prayerful times are what make our outer activity viable and effective – if it is effective.

I have similarly seen quieter Friends hurt by the implication that they do not care enough, because they are not seen to be 'politically active'. Some worry unnecessarily that they may be doing things of a 'less important' nature, as if to be seen doing things by the eyes of the world is the same thing as to be seen doing things by the eyes of God... I suggest that we refrain from judging each other, or belittling what each is doing; and that we should not feel belittled. We cannot know the prayers that others make or do not make in their own times of silent aloneness. We cannot know the letters others may be writing to governments, similarly... We were all made differently, in order to perform different tasks. Let us rejoice in our differences.

Margaret Glover, 1989

20.15   In its history the Society of Friends has produced many people whose lives of conspicuous service have profoundly influenced their times. John Woolman, Elizabeth Fry, Joseph Sturge and many others would have made for themselves no claim to a special dedication to service, but they were none the less able, out of the depth of their love for their fellows, to take great opportunities that came to them. Their service sprang directly out of their religious faith, but this faith was itself stimulated and fostered by the religious atmosphere in which they lived. To this atmosphere the lives of many Friends, now nameless and unknown, contributed by their faithfulness in inconspicuous service, and so made it possible for the greater spirits to grow to their full stature.

Gerald Littleboy, 1945

20.16   Our testimonies arise from our way of worship. Our way of worship evokes from deep within us at once an affirmation and a celebration, an affirmation of the reality of that Light which illumines the spiritual longing of humanity, and a celebration of the continual resurrection within us of the springs of hope and love; a sense that each of us is, if we will, a channel for a power that is both within us and beyond us.

Lorna M Marsden, 1986

20.17 Testimonies are not imposed on members of the Society of Friends, but they are re-affirmed corporately and re-expressed sufficiently often to be both a challenge and a way of living for most Friends. They are part of our distinctive witness. They do not make it any easier to live a life of faithfulness to God's leadings, for they give rise to many dilemmas and compromises as we live in a society which is often based on other presuppositions. We cannot help being immersed in it even whilst trying to change its norms. Finding ways of expressing the testimonies that are relevant to present times is a continuing challenge. Such expressions will not necessarily seem practical, tactful, sensible, expedient or in line with some current vogue of thinking, for they are based on what seems right in an absolute sense of inner conviction.

Chris Lawson, 1987

20.18 Ever since I first came among Friends, I was attracted to the testimonies as an ideal. I wanted to belong to a church which made the rejection of warfare a collective commitment and not just a personal option. I admired a simplicity, a devotion to equality, and a respect for others which reflected what I already knew of Christ. In a deceitful world I warmed to those who did not swear oaths and strove to tell the truth in all circumstances. But this was a beginning in the spiritual life. The seed that was sown in my mind and my politics struck root in my soul and my faith.

The choice of the word 'testimony' is instructive. The testimonies are ways of behaving but are not ethical rules. They are matters of practice but imply doctrines. They refer to human society but are about God. Though often talked about they lack an authoritative formulation...

A 'testimony' is a declaration of truth or fact... It is not an ejaculation, a way of letting off steam or baring one's soul. It has a purpose, and that is to get other people to change, to turn to God. Such an enterprise, be it in words or by conduct and example, is in essence prophetic and evangelical.

John Punshon, 1987

For the development of the testimonies in the seventeenth century see 19.33-19.48

20.19 It is not necessary that we should know all mysteries before we begin to follow Christ. To some of us much that is taught of His person and His work may not be clear, but so it was with the early disciples. They did not understand at first the mystic union with their Master to which they were called, but they followed Him, and as they followed, there was gradually unfolded to them the fullness of His love and life. If we begin where they began, and follow as they followed, we shall end where they ended, in adoring love.

London Yearly Meeting, 1909

20.20 For a Quaker, religion is not an external activity, concerning a special 'holy' part of the self. It is an openness to the world in the here and now with the whole of the self. If this is not simply a pious commonplace, it must take into account the whole of our humanity: our attitudes to other human beings in our most intimate as well as social and political relationships. It must also take account of our life in the world around us, the way we live, the way we treat animals and the environment. In short, to put it in traditional language, there is no part of ourselves and of our relationships where God is not present.

Harvey Gillman, 1988

20.21   It is in my heart to praise thee, O my God;
        let me never forget thee,
        what thou hast been to me:

    In the night, by thy presence in the
        day of trial when I was beset in darkness,
        when I was cast out as a wandering bird,
        and when I was assaulted with strong temptations,
        then thy presence in secret did preserve me,
        and in a low estate I felt thee near me.

    When the floods sought to sweep me away
        Thou set a compass for them,
        how far they should pass over;

    When my way was through the sea,
        and when I passed under the mountains
        there was thou present with me;

When the weight of the hills was upon me
   thou upheld me, else had I sunk
   under the earth;

When I was as one altogether helpless,
   when tribulation and anguish was upon me
   day and night, and the earth
   without foundation;

When I went on the way of wrath,
   and passed by the gates of hell,
   when all comforts stood afar off,
   and he that is mine enemy had dominion;
   when I was cast into the pit,
   and was as one appointed to death;
   when I was between the millstones,
   and as one crushed with the weight
   of his adversary,

As a father thou was with me
   and the rock of thy presence.

James Nayler, 1659

20.22   *Luke Cock (1657-1740), a butcher by trade, and a noted singer, was a young man living in North-East Yorkshire when he was convinced. The following extract reports in his own idiom a sermon he gave at York in 1721:*

Necessity, Friends, outstrips the law: necessity has made many people go by the Weeping Cross... I remember I was yonce travelling through Shrewsbury, and my Guide said to me: 'I'll show thee the Weeping Cross.' 'Nay', said I, 'thou need not; I have borne it a great while'. Now this place that he showed me was four lane ends.

I remember when I first met with my Guide. He led me into a very large and cross [place], where I was to speak the truth from my heart – and before I used to swear and lie too for gain. 'Nay, then,' said I to my Guide, 'I mun leave Thee here: if Thou leads me up that lane, I can never follow: I'se be ruined of this butchering trade, if I mun't lie for a gain.' Here I left my Guide, and was filled with sorrow, and went back to the Weeping Cross: and I said, if I could find my good

Guide again, I'll follow Him, lead me whither He will. So here I found my Guide again, and began to follow Him up this lane and tell the truth from my heart. I had been nought but beggary and poverty before; and now I began to thrive at my trade, and got to the end of this lane, though with some difficulty.

But now my Guide began to lead me up another lane, harder than the first, which was to bear my testimony in using the plain language. This was very hard; yet I said to my Guide, 'Take my feeble pace, and I'll follow Thee as fast as I can. Don't outstretch me, I pray Thee.' So by degrees I got up here.

But now I was led up the third lane: it was harder still, to bear my testimony against tithes – my wife not being convinced. I said to my Guide, 'Nay, I doubt I never can follow up here: but don't leave me: take my pace, I pray Thee, for I mun rest me.' So I tarried here a great while, till my wife cried, 'We'se all be ruined: what is thee gang-ing stark mad to follow t'silly Quakers?' Here I struggled and cried, and begged of my Guide to stay and take my pace: and presently my wife was convinced. 'Well,' says she, 'now follow thy Guide, let come what will. The Lord hath done abundance for us: we will trust in Him.' Nay, now, I thought, I'll to my Guide again, now go on, I'll follow Thee truly; so I got to the end of this lane cheerfully...

My Guide led me up another lane, more difficult than any of the for-mer, which was to bear testimony to that Hand that had done all this for me. This was a hard one: I thought I must never have seen the end of it. I was eleven years all but one month in it. Here I began to go on my knees and to creep under the hedges, a trade I never forgot since, nor I hope never shall. I would fain think it is unpossible for me to fall now, but let him that thinks he stands take heed lest he fall.

I thought to have had a watering: but ye struggle so I cannot get you together. We mun have no watering tonight, I mun leave you every yan to his own Guide.

20.23   *George Fox wrote to Friends in November 1663, during the time of much persecution:*

Sing and rejoice, ye Children of the Day and of the Light; for the Lord is at work in this thick night of Darkness that may be felt: and Truth doth flourish as the rose, and the lilies do grow among the thorns, and the plants atop of the hills, and upon them the lambs doth skip and play. And never heed the tempests nor the storms, floods nor rains, for the Seed Christ is over all and doth reign. And so, be of good faith and valiant for the Truth.

20.24 How does Jesus speak to us today? Does his closeness to God challenge you to put what you have learnt from worship into daily practice?

Questions and counsel, 1988

20.25 Incomparably the most important thing is that each one of us should be sensitive to the call of God to ourselves and not spend time in passing judgment on the lives of others. To some the call will be to adopt the witness of great simplicity, perhaps to live in an Indian village or in a London slum. To others the most important thing will be to maintain our ancient testimony against 'fightings with outward weapons, for any end, or under any pretence whatever'. But perhaps most will be called to the humdrum tasks of serving an employer supremely well, or running a house, bringing up a family, keeping the peace with difficult neighbours, serving the community in little things – the tasks which, because they are simple, are in fact most difficult to do with dedication... Our duty is to be sensitive to what God is asking us to do, and not to dissipate our energies trying to be absolutists in several directions at once.

Industry and the Social Order Conference, 1958

20.26 To me, being a Christian is a particular way of life, not the unquestioning acceptance of a particular system of theology, not belief in the literal truth of the Virgin birth, or the Resurrection and Ascension, but being the kind of person that Jesus wanted his followers to be and doing the things he told them to do...

Nor, it seems to me, can you live a Christian life unless, like Jesus, you believe in the power of goodness, of justice, of mercy and of love; unless you believe in these so strongly that you are prepared to put them to the acid test of experiment; unless these constitute the real meaning of life for you, more important than life itself, as they were for Jesus.

Kathleen Lonsdale, 1967

SIMPLICITY AND EQUALITY

20.27 The heart of Quaker ethics is summed up in the word 'simplicity'. Simplicity is forgetfulness of self and remembrance of our humble status as waiting servants of God. Outwardly, simplicity is shunning superfluities of dress, speech, behaviour, and possessions, which tend to obscure our vision of reality. Inwardly, simplicity is spiritual detachment from the things of this world as part of the effort to fulfil the first commandment: to love God with all of the heart and mind and strength.

The testimony of outward simplicity began as a protest against the extravagance and snobbery which marked English society in the 1600s. In whatever forms this protest is maintained today, it must still be seen as a testimony against involvement with things which tend to dilute our energies and scatter our thoughts, reducing us to lives of triviality and mediocrity.

Simplicity does not mean drabness or narrowness but is essentially positive, being the capacity for selectivity in one who holds attention on the goal. Thus simplicity is an appreciation of all that is helpful towards living as children of the Living God.

Faith and practice, North Carolina Yearly Meeting (Conservative), 1983

20.28 It is our tender and Christian advice that Friends take care to keep to truth and plainness, in language, habit, deportment and behaviour; that the simplicity of truth in these things may not wear out nor be lost in our days, nor in our posterity's; and to avoid pride and immodesty in apparel, and all vain and superfluous fashions of the world.

Yearly Meeting in London, 1691

20.29 Personal pride does not end with noble blood. It leads people to a fond value of their persons, especially if they have any pretence to shape or beauty. Some are so taken with themselves it would seem that nothing else deserved their attention. Their folly would diminish if they could spare but half the time to think of God, that they spend in washing, perfuming, painting and dressing their bodies. In these things they are precise and very artificial and spare no cost. But what aggravates the evil is that the pride of one might comfortably supply the needs of ten. Gross impiety it is that a nation's pride should be maintained in the face of its poor.

William Penn, 1669

See also 19.39-19.40 Equality *& 23.32-23.46* Discrimination and disadvantage

20.30   *In 1698 Margaret Fox, then in her late eighties, felt that this testimony was fast degenerating into a preoccupation with the way Friends dressed, the colours they wore, and the furniture used in their houses.*

It's a dangerous thing to lead young Friends much into the observation of outward things which may be easily done. For they can soon get into an outward garb, to be all alike outwardly. But this will not make them into true Christians: it's the spirit that gives life.

20.31   We are now coming into that which Christ cried woe against, minding altogether outward things, neglecting the inward work of Almighty God in our hearts, if we can but frame according to outward prescriptions and orders, and deny eating and drinking with our neighbours, in so much that poor Friends is mangled in their minds, that they know not what to do, for one Friend says one way, and another another, but Christ Jesus saith, that we must take no thought what we shall eat, or what we shall drink, or what we shall put on, but bids us consider the lilies how they grow, in more royalty than Solomon. But contrary to this, we must look at no colours, nor make anything that is changeable colours as the hills are, nor sell them, nor wear them: but we must be all in one dress and one colour: this is a silly poor Gospel. It is more fit for us, to be covered with God's Eternal Spirit, and clothed with his Eternal Light, which leads us and guides us into righteousness. Now I have set before you life and death, and desire you to choose life, and God and his truth.

Margaret Fox, 1700

20.32   The Creator of the earth is the owner of it. He gave us being thereon, and our nature requires nourishment, which is the produce of it. As he is kind and merciful, we as his creatures, while we live answerable to the design of our creation, are so far entitled to a convenient sub-sistence that no man may justly deprive us of it. By the agreements and contracts of our fathers and predecessors, and by doings and proceedings of our own, some claim a much greater share of this world than others: and whilst those possessions are faithfully improved to the good of the whole, it consists with equity. But he who, with a view to self-exaltation, causeth some with their domestic animals to labour immoderately, and with the monies arising to him therefrom, employs others in the luxuries of life, acts contrary to the gracious design of him [the Creator] who is the true owner of the earth; nor can any possessions, either acquired or derived from ancestors, justify such conduct.

John Woolman, 1763

20.33   Were all superfluities and the desire of outward greatness laid aside, and the right use of things universally attended to, such a number of people might be employed in things useful, as that moderate labour with the blessing of Heaven would answer all good purposes relat-ing to people and their animals, and a sufficient number have time to attend to proper affairs of civil society.

John Woolman, 1763

20.34   If John Woolman's approach is the right one for the Society of today it is not enough to go over our own behaviour in detail, cutting a bit here and pulling back a bit there; we must be concerned with our and society's attitude to life as a whole, to 'live answerable to the design of our creation'.

Michael Lee, 1976

20.35   Is our concern for simplicity relevant to our concern for the national economic situation? If we think of simplicity in terms of doing with-out certain things, of voluntarily reducing our standard of living, I believe this is almost irrelevant at the economic level in view of the scale of the world's need.

If we think of simplicity as a spiritual quality which incidentally sim-plifies our life styles then I believe it has relevance. This kind of sim-plicity goes straight to the heart of things and puts first things first, is needed to rectify our distorted values, to help us accept changes in our pattern of living. As this simplicity grows in our hearts and bears fruit in our lives, we may learn and help others to learn that the really abundant life is not to be found in the clutter of material complexity, but in simplicity.

L Hugh Doncaster, 1976

20.36 I wish I might emphasise how a life becomes simplified when dominated by faithfulness to a few concerns. Too many of us have too many irons in the fire. We get distracted by the intellectual claim to our interest in a thousand and one good things, and before we know it we are pulled and hauled breathlessly along by an over-burdened programme of good committees and good undertakings. I am persuaded that this fevered life of church workers is not wholesome. Undertakings get plastered on from the outside because we can't turn down a friend. Acceptance of service on a weighty committee should really depend upon an answering imperative within us, not merely upon a rational calculation of the factors involved. The concern-orientated life is ordered and organised from within. And we learn to say No as well as Yes by attending to the guidance of inner responsibility. Quaker simplicity needs to be expressed not merely in dress and architecture and height of tombstones but also in the structure of a relatively simplified and co-ordinated life-programme of social responsibilities.

Thomas R Kelly, 1941

See also 23.53-23.70 Work and economic affairs & *24.50-24.52* Right sharing of the world's resources

Moderation and abstinence

20.37 It being discoursed that the common excess of smoking tobacco is inconsistent with our holy profession, this meeting adviseth that such as have occasion to make use of it do take it privately, neither in their labour or employment, nor by the highways, nor in alehouses nor elsewhere too publicly.

Hardshaw Monthly Meeting, 1691

20.38   As temperance and moderation are virtues proceeding from true religion ... we beseech all to be careful of their conduct and behaviour, abstaining from every appearance of evil; and as an excess in drinking has been too prevalent among many of the inhabitants of these nations, we commend to all Friends a watchful care over themselves, attended with a religious and prudent zeal against a practice so dishonourable and pernicious.

Yearly Meeting in London, 1751

20.39   The world is a dark enough place still for too many. It can ill spare even the poorest rushlight candle of cheerfulness or the smallest fire of fellowship. We must not put out the glimmer of light which shines for so many still today through the tavern windows, unless we can put a better in its place. We need the light of a brighter cheerfulness, and the glow of a warmer fellowship.

T Edmund Harvey, 1931

20.40   Many yearly meetings hold very strong testimonies against any use of tobacco or alcohol. Within Britain Yearly Meeting some Friends advocate total abstinence from alcohol, others counsel moderation. Those who smoke tobacco, drink alcohol or abuse other substances risk damage to their own health, and may hurt or endanger other people. Such use can deaden a person's sensitivity and response to others and to God. Consider whether you should avoid these products altogether, discourage their use in others, especially young people, and refrain from any share in their manufacture or sale. Maintain your own integrity and do not let social pressures influence your decisions.

1994

20.41   For those trapped in substance abuse, such advice [as in 20.40] may seem hollow. Commonalities exist between addictive behaviours with these substances and other compulsive actions such as in the areas of eating disorders, gambling, overwork and physical abuse. The causes go deep and may not be fully understood, but the resulting pain, fear, desperation and denial, damaging the abuser and all around that person, need to be supportively recognised. A meeting community should be ready to listen non-judgmentally, offer information about sources of help, refuse to enable people to continue in harmful patterns, and continue to offer an environment free from addictive practices.

Faith and practice, Baltimore Yearly Meeting, 1988

20.42 Friends, whatever ye are addicted to, the tempter will come in that thing; and when he can trouble you, then he gets advantage over you, and then you are gone. Stand still in that which is pure, after ye see yourselves; and then mercy comes in. After thou seest thy thoughts, and the temptations, do not think, but submit; and then power comes. Stand still in that which shows and discovers; and then doth strength immediately come. And stand still in the Light, and submit to it, and the other will be hushed and gone; and then content comes.

George Fox, 1652

HONESTY AND INTEGRITY

20.43 Are you honest and truthful in word and deed? Do you maintain strict integrity in your business transactions and in your relations with individuals and organisations? Are you personally scrupulous and responsible in the use of money entrusted to you, and are you careful not to defraud the public revenue?

Queries, 1964

20.44 Integrity is one of the virtues for which Quakers in the past have been praised. It is a quality worth having, but it is doubtful if it can be reached by self-conscious effort or by adherence to a principle... Integrity is a condition in which a person's response to a total situation can be trusted: the opposite of a condition in which he would be moved by opportunist or self-seeking impulses breaking up his unity as a whole being. This condition of trust is different from the recognition that he will always be kind or always tell the truth. The integrity of some Dutch Friends I have met showed itself during the war in their willingness to tell lies to save their Jewish friends from the Gestapo or from starvation.

Kenneth C Barnes, 1972

20.45   The Quaker testimony to truthfulness is central to the practice of its faith by members of the Religious Society of Friends. From the beginning Friends have believed that they could have direct and immediate communication with God which would enable them to discern right ethical choices. They soon experienced common leadings of the Spirit which became formalised into testimonies... Arising from the teaching of Jesus as related in the writings of John and James: 'Let your yes mean yes and your no mean no', Quakers perceived that with a conscience illuminated by the Light, life became an integrated whole with honesty as its basis.

From time to time ... adherence to factual truth can give rise to profound dilemmas for Quaker Peace & Service workers if they are in possession of information which could be used to endanger people's lives or give rise to the abuse of fundamental human rights... Some of us are clear that in certain difficult circumstances we may still uphold our testimony to truthfulness while at the same time declining to disclose confidences which we have properly accepted. Such withholding of the whole truth is not an option to be undertaken lightly as a convenient way out of a dilemma. We all accept that ultimately it is up to an individual's own conscience, held in the Light, to decide how to respond.

Quaker Peace & Service, 1992

20.46   A neighbour ... desired me to write his will: I took notes, and, amongst other things, he told me to which of his children he gave his young negro: I considered the pain and distress he was in, and knew not how it would end, so I wrote his will, save only that part concerning his slave, and carrying it to his bedside, read it to him, and then told him in a friendly way, that I could not write any instruments by which my fellow-creatures were made slaves, without bringing trouble on my own mind. I let him know that I charged nothing for what I had done, and desired to be excused from doing the other part in the way he proposed. Then we had a serious conference on the subject, and at length, he agreeing to set her free, I finished his will.

John Woolman, 1756

20.47   To conform a little to a wrong way strengthens the hands of such
        who carry wrong customs to their utmost extent; and the more a
        person appears to be virtuous and heavenly-minded, the more power-
        fully does his conformity operate in favour of evil-doers... While we
        profess in all cases to live in constant opposition to that which is
        contrary to universal righteousness ... what language is sufficient to
        set forth the strength of those obligations we are under to beware
        lest by our example we lead others wrong?

        John Woolman, 1763

        See also 19.01 & 20.22

Oaths and affirmation

20.48   Throughout their history Friends have refused to take oaths; and
        they underwent much hardship before provision was made by
        statute allowing them to affirm.

        1967

20.49   And they gave me the Book, and I took it and was turning to a place
        that was against swearing, and they took it from me again and bid
        me say after the clerk. So I told them, if they would prove that Christ
        and the apostles commanded to swear after they had forbidden it,
        give us scripture for this, and we would swear. It was Christ's com-
        mand that we should not swear.

        George Fox, 1664

        See also 19.37 & 19.38

20.50   The deeper meaning of simplicity can be seen in the stand of Friends
        against the taking of oaths. Friends believe that their word should be
        accepted at any time among all persons and thus [uphold] the right
        to stand simply on their own word rather than swearing on the Bible
        or before God, a witness which has gained recognition in modern
        legal practice.

        Faith and practice, North Carolina Yearly Meeting (Conservative),
        1983

England and Wales

20.51 The opportunity to bear witness to our ancient testimony against oaths will come to most Friends only on the rare occasions when they have to give evidence, serve on a jury or act in some other legal capacity. It is none the less a testimony to be cherished. The occasion of making an affirmation can be spiritually enriching and stands in a long and honourable tradition.

Evidence given by a person who affirms is legally of equal value with 'sworn' evidence. So is any other action performed or duty undertaken following affirmation, including jury service. This principle that 'a solemn affirmation shall be of the same force and effect as an oath' (section 5 (4) of the Oaths Act 1978) applies in all circumstances; another example is the affidavit sworn when applying for a grant of probate, which may equally be replaced by affirmation.

It is of assistance to let the clerk of a court know in advance of an intention to affirm, though there is no obligation to do so. The right to affirm is now absolute, with no requirement to state a reason for preferring affirmation to the swearing of an oath.

The form of oral affirmation prescribed in all places and for all purposes where an oath is or shall be required by law is as follows: 'I, [name], do solemnly, sincerely and truly declare and affirm': and then follows the substance of the affirmation. A witness may affirm, for example, that 'the evidence I shall give shall be the truth, the whole truth and nothing but the truth' or 'that I shall tell the truth'; a juror in a criminal trial 'that I will faithfully try the defendant(s) and give (a) true verdict(s) according to the evidence', and in civil proceedings 'that I will well and truly try the issues joined between the parties and a true verdict give according to the evidence'.

Written affirmations are also admissible, for example under section 6 of the Oaths Act 1978, or in other legal capacities as appropriate. Every affirmation in writing shall commence: 'I AB of X do solemnly and sincerely affirm', and the form in lieu of jurat shall be 'affirmed at X this ... day of ... 19../20.. before me [name]'.

1967; 1994

The following is a translation into Welsh of 20.51

20.52   Dim ond ar yr achlysuron prin pan fo raid iddynt roddi tystiolaeth,
bod yn aelod o reithgor neu weithredu mewn unrhyw sefyllfa
gyfreithiol arall, y daw cyfle i Gyfeillion arddel ein tystiolaeth
hynafol yn erbyn cymryd llwon. Y mae, serch hynny, yn dystiolaeth
i'w choleddu. Gall y profiad o gadarnhau fod yn brofiad sydd yn
un ysbrydol gyfoethog ac mae iddo draddodiad hen a pharchus.

Mae unrhyw dystiolaeth a roddir gan berson sydd yn cadarnhau o'r
un gwerth cyfreithiol â thystiolaeth dan 'lw'. Mae hynny hefyd yn wir
am unrhyw weithredoedd neu ddyletswyddau yr ymgymerir â hwy o
ganlyniad i gadarnhau, gan gynnwys gwasanaethu ar
reithgor. Mae'r egwyddor yma fod 'i gadarnhad difrifol yr un grym
a'r un effaith â llw' (adran 5(4) o Ddeddf Llwon 1978) yn gymwys
ym mhob amgylchiad; enghraifft arall yw'r affidafid dan lw wrth
wneud cais am grant profiant, pryd y gellir ei wneud trwy gadarnhad.

Mae o gymorth os gadewir i glerc y llys wybod ymlaen llaw am y
bwriad i gadarnhau ond nid yw'n angenrheidiol gwneud hynny. Mae'r
hawl i gadarnhau bellach yn un absoliwt heb unrhyw angen i fynegi'r
rheswm dros ddewis gwneud hynny yn hytrach na chymryd llw.

Ffurf y cadarnhad llafar a bennir ymhob lle ac i bob pwrpas lle bo
neu lle bydd llw yn ofynnol yn ôl y gyfraith yw'r canlynol: 'Yr wyf
i [enw] yn datgan a chadarnhau yn ddifrifol, yn ddiffuant ac yn
ddidwyll': ac yna fe ddilyn sylwedd y cadarnhad. Gall tyst
gadarnhau, er enghraifft, y bydd 'y dystiolaeth a roddaf y gwir, yr
holl wir a'r gwir yn unig' neu 'y byddaf yn eirwir'; rheithor mewn
prawf trosedd 'y profaf yn fyddlon y diffynnydd (diffynyddion) a
rhoi rheithfarn gyflawn (rheithfarnau cyflawn) yn ôl y dystiolaeth,
ac mewn gweithrediadau sifil 'y profaf yn iawn ac yn deg y
materion mewn dadl rhwng y pleidiau a rhoi rheithfarn gyfiawn yn
ôl y dystiolaeth'.

Mae cadarnhau ysgrifenedig hefyd yn dderbyniol, er enghraifft yng
nghyswllt adran 6 o Ddeddf Llwon 1978, neu, pan fo'n addas
mewn amgylchiadau cyfreithiol eraill. Dylai pob cadarnhad
ysgrifenedig ddechrau: 'Yr wyf i AB o X yn cadarnhau yn ddifrifol
ac yn ddiffuant', a'r ffurf yn lle jiwrat fydd 'cadarnhawyd yn X ar y
...... dydd o ...... 19—/20— ger fy mron [enw]'.

1967; 1994

Scotland

20.53   In Scotland there is a long tradition of affirmation, so there has not been the same need for a distinctive Quaker witness as in England and Wales. The information and advice given in 20.51 is equally valid in Scotland. The Oaths Act 1978 applies in Scotland as well as in England and Wales.

1994

Conducting business

20.54   From its earliest days our Society has laid great stress on honesty and the payment in full of debts justly incurred. Though social conditions have undergone great changes over the years of our Society's history, so that much of the advice given in the past may seem out of date, it is well to remind ourselves that the principles underlying the advice have not changed. Since we believe that all people are the children of God, we cannot take advantage of others by any form of dishonesty, whether in buying or selling goods, in business or privately, or as employees by failing to give an honest return in labour for the pay we receive. When we have received goods or services, we shall be punctual in making payment of the price agreed on, and we shall not attempt to evade our proper obligations to the community by way of taxation.

1959; 1994

20.55   As Christians, all we possess are the gifts of God. Now in distributing it to others we act as his steward, and it becomes our station to act agreeable to that divine wisdom which he graciously gives to his servants. If the steward of a great family, from a selfish attachment to particulars, takes that with which he is entrusted, and bestows it lavishly on some to the injury of others, and to the damage of him who employs him, he disunites himself, and becomes unworthy of that office.

John Woolman, 1763

Sources and use of income

20.56   The guiding principle which Friends should keep in mind in making an income, whether by work or by investment, should be the good of others and of the community at large, and not simply of themselves or their own family. Friends should, even at the risk of loss, strive to be strictly honest and truthful in their dealings; should refuse to manufacture or deal in commodities that are hurtful, and should be vigilant against obtaining an undue profit at the cost of the community. If Friends are investing, thought should be given, not only to security and the rate of interest, but to the conditions under which the income is produced and the effect which the investment may have on the welfare of all, through social or environmental impact, at home or elsewhere. In spending income, Friends should consider how their actions affect society and whether such expenditure upon themselves and their family is to the advantage of the community as a whole. Friends should also consider whether there is a reasonable relation between the labour expended on producing the things they buy and the real satisfaction yielded by their use.

1925; 1959; 1994

See also 4.19 Advice on outward affairs. *For guidance on ethical investment see 14.24 & 15.07*

20.57   We believe that, as Quakers, we should put our whole lives under the guidance of the Spirit. This should determine our choices as individuals and as a Society between saving and spending and the way in which savings are invested. We are led to choose investments that benefit the community at large and not just ourselves and our families or small groups; to be strictly honest and truthful; and to refuse to deal in products or services which are hurtful to individuals or to society as a whole. We should only invest in accordance with our principles.

Young Friends Central Committee, 1980

20.58   The love of money is apt to increase almost imperceptibly. That which was at first laboured after under pressure of necessary duty, may, without great watchfulness, steal upon the affections, and gradually withdraw the heart from God. The danger depends not upon how much a man has, but upon how much his heart is set upon what he has, and upon accumulating more.

Yearly Meeting in London, 1858

20.59 Friends should know their income and live within it, not hesitating to seek advice if difficulties threaten. In the interest of those they love and as an example of honest citizenship Friends are advised to avoid entangling themselves in heavy commitments by unwisely obtaining goods on credit. Anxiety for the future, however, should not lead Friends to withhold what should rightly be expended for the needs of the family or other dependents or devoted to the service of others.

1925; 1959; 1994

20.60 Encourage a spirit of Christian bountifulness. Let all ... cultivate from early years a true liberality according to their means; it should be a joy to the Christian to support wise efforts to promote the good of others.

1925; 1959

Gambling and speculation

20.61 Gambling disregards our belief that possessions are a trust. The persistent appeal to covetousness evident, for example, in football pool propaganda is fundamentally opposed to the unselfishness which was taught by Jesus Christ and by the New Testament as a whole. The attempt, which is inseparable from gambling, to make a profit out of the inevitable loss and possible suffering of others is the antithesis of that love of one's neighbour on which Jesus insisted.

1959; 1994

20.62 We are faced at every hand with enticements to risk money in anticipation of disproportionate gain through gambling. Some governments employ gambling as a means of raising revenue, even presenting it as a civic virtue. The Religious Society of Friends continues to bear testimony against betting, gambling, lotteries, speculation, or any other endeavour to receive material gain without equivalent exchange, believing that we owe an honest return for what we receive.

Faith and practice, Baltimore Yearly Meeting, 1988

20.63　So much has the public conscience been warped from the living Truth that a man who has acquired wealth by operations on the Stock Exchange is spoken of as having 'made' his money regardless of whether any useful purpose has been served. One who identifies the status quo with the divine law regards such an accession of wealth as something to be accepted with thankful heart like manna from heaven. True enlightenment would show that, if nothing has been given in return, the wealth so gained has been misappropriated and the whole transaction, though sanctioned by law and custom, is, in its essence, a violation of the eighth commandment.

In our *Advices* [1931] we are warned against commercial speculations of gambling character, and we are told to 'remember how widespread and diverse are the temptations to grow rich at the expense of others'. The faithful observance of this advice points the way to an issue greater than personal rectitude with regard to gambling. It should lead to an examination of the system which permits or encourages these abuses, and to a demand for drastic changes.

Shipley N Brayshaw, 1933

See also 23.53-23.70 Work and economic affairs

Care of money held for others

20.64　Friends who hold moneys on behalf of others should have regard to the importance of the proper safeguarding and wise administration of such moneys. It is important that, where possible, a separate bank account be used which is not in the name of a single individual. Particular care should be taken to keep proper accounts which should be examined, if necessary by a qualified auditor, once a year.

1959; 1994

See also 14.20-14.24

Wills

20.65   When death occurs, difficulties are encountered where an unsatisfactory will or no will at all has been made. It is therefore recommended that Friends should make wills in time of health and should obtain professional advice. Wills should be reviewed from time to time, as due to change of circumstances it may be wise for new wills to be made.

It should be remembered that in English law a will is automatically revoked on a marriage (unless the will is specifically made in contemplation of such marriage) and on divorce provisions in a will in favour of a spouse normally cease to have effect. Under Scots law a will may be revoked by the birth of a child, but neither marriage nor divorce has the effect of revoking a will. In all the above circumstances it is important that a new will should be made.

In choosing executors, care should be taken not to overburden those who are to act, particularly where continuing trusts may be involved. Friends who have responsibility for children should make provision for their care, appointing guardians and trustees as necessary. Where there is more than one parent the will should cover the possibility of their dying at the same time. Finally, the place where the will may be found should be made known to those likely to be directly responsible.

1967; 1994

20.66   Let Friends in making their wills have a strict regard to justice and equity, and not be actuated by caprice and prejudice, to the injury of those who may have a reasonable expectation from their kindred and near connections. Let none (although occasion may have been given or taken) carry any resentment to the grave, remembering that we all stand in need of mercy and forgiveness. Friends are advised not to make large bequests to relatives or others who do not need them; and to remember the pressing claims of religious and social concerns.

Friends are advised, on the one hand, to make their wills as simple as possible, avoiding complicated provisions; and, on the other hand, to consider carefully circumstances which may arise after their decease, so that due provision may be made for all who ought to benefit under the will, even should births, marriages or deaths occur, which the testator had not anticipated.

1782; 1911

See also 4.19 Advice on outward affairs

CONFLICT

20.67 And all Friends take heed of jars and strife, for that is it, which will eat out the Seed in you; therefore let not that harbour in your bosoms, lest it eat out the good in you, and ye come to suffer in your own particulars. Therefore dwell in love and life, and in the Power and Seed of God, which is the honourable, royal state.

George Fox, 1656

20.68 I have heard some Friends deny their anger in a silent 'peace' where there is no understanding of each other. Such Friends are angry but by their silence the progress of world peace has stood still. If we are angry we know how wars develop. It does not matter who's wrong. What matters is that we care enough to talk to each other.

How do we become reconciled to each other if we are asunder? All I can say is to go up to that person and say what is in your heart; that their ways are hurting but you still love them. But this takes time and not many people like to look in a person's face and find out who they are. So we miss the reconciliation and do not have the experience – that we *cared*. Given that, then we will know who we are and find relief in tears we all should share. This is where peace starts.

Sue Norris, 1982

20.69 If someone we love does have a bad temper, we try to avoid the circumstances that provoke it. If it is so easily provoked that we cannot avoid it, the soft answer may have to include, then or later, a quiet but firm reproof, for their own sake as well as ours. But very often our ability to co-operate peacefully with our family, our neighbours, and our fellow-workers does depend upon our knowing how, with courtesy, to refuse to be drawn into particular types of discussion or to take sides on questions which arouse needless passions. We may do this in particular when we know that they have violent prejudices which we do not share, but which we are not likely to be able to remove by argument. Or when the dispute is about a matter of fact that could easily be determined by experiment or by consulting a work of reference.

All these are the small change of everyday life, but they count for happiness in living together as persons, and they are a pointer to happiness in living together as nations.

Kathleen Lonsdale, 1957

20.70 Where any have received offence from any other, first to speak privately to the party concerned, and endeavour reconciliation between themselves; and not to whisper or aggravate matters against them behind their backs, to the making parties, and the breach wider.

Yearly Meeting in London, 1692

20.71 Conflict happens, and will continue to happen, even in the most peaceful of worlds. And that's good – a world where we all agreed with one another would be incredibly boring. Our differences help us to learn. Through conflict handled creatively we can change and grow; and I am not sure real change – either political or personal – can happen without it. We'll each handle conflict differently and find healing and reconciliation by different paths. I want nonetheless to offer three keys, three skills or qualities which I've found helpful from my own experience.

The first skill is *naming:* being clear and honest about the problem as I see it, stating what I see and how I feel about it. What is important about these statements is that I own them: 'I see', 'I feel' (not 'surely it is obvious that ...', 'any right thinking person should...'). This ability to name what seems to be going on, is crucial to getting the conflict out into the open, where we can begin to understand and try to deal with it.

Such a skill is dangerous. It can feel – indeed, it can be – confrontational. It feels like stirring up trouble where there wasn't any problem. It needs to be done carefully, caringly, with love, in language we hope others can hear. We need to seek tactfully the best time to do it. But it needs to be done.

The second skill is the skill of *listening*: listening not just to the words, but to the feelings and needs behind the words. It takes a great deal of time and energy to listen well. It's a kind of weaving: reflecting back, asking for clarification, asking for time in turn to be listened to, being truly open to what we're hearing (even if it hurts), being open to the possibility that we might ourselves be changed by what we hear.

The third skill is the skill of *letting go*: I don't mean that in the sense of giving up, lying down and inviting people to walk all over us, but acknowledging the possibility that there may be other solutions to this conflict than the ones we've thought of yet; letting the imagination in – making room for the Spirit. We need to let go of our own will – not so as to surrender to another's, but so as to look together for God's solution. It's a question of finding ways to let go of our commitment to opposition and separation, of letting ourselves be opened to our connectedness as human beings.

If we are to do any of these things well – naming, listening, letting go – we need to have learned to trust that of God in ourselves and that of God in those trapped on all sides of the conflict with us. And to do that well, I find I need to be centred, rooted, practised in waiting on God. That rootedness is both a gift and a discipline, something we can cultivate and build on by acknowledging it every day.

Mary Lou Leavitt, 1986

20.72   It is advised that, in all cases of controversy and difference, the persons concerned therein either speedily compose the difference between themselves or make choice of some faithful, unconcerned, impartial Friends to determine the same; and that all Friends take heed of being parties with one or another.

1833

20.73 Let Friends everywhere be careful that all differences about outward things be speedily composed, either between themselves, or by arbitrators; and it would be well that Friends were at all times ready to submit their differences, even with persons not of our religious persuasion, to arbitration, rather than to contend at law.

1833

20.74 When legal action is required in separation or divorce, this should be the simplest process available consistent with the complexity of the problems involved in the unravelling of a marriage and the need for the best legal advice. Try to avoid rancour or undue parade of differences. Mediation and conciliation services can often help in the adjustment of such matters and this avoids disputatious procedures in court.

1994

See also 4.20-4.21 & 22.73

20.75 I come back again and again in my own mind to this word Truth. 'Promptings of love and truth' – these two sometimes seem to be in conflict, but in fact they are inseparable. If we are to know the truth, we must be able to see with unclouded eyes, and then we will love what is real and not what is duty or fancy. Once when I was in the middle of a difficult exercise of Quaker decision-making, I wailed to an older and wiser Friend, 'How can I speak the truth in love when I feel no love?' Her reply was, 'Unless you speak the truth there never will be love'.

Alison Sharman, 1986

See also 10.21-10.24 Conflict within the meeting & 4.21 Disputes among Friends

Chapter 21

Personal journey

YOUTH

21.01   While I was too young to have any religion of my own, I had come
to a home where religion kept its fires always burning. We had very
few 'things', but we were rich in invisible wealth. I was not 'chris-
tened' in a church, but I was sprinkled from morning to night with
the dew of religion. We never ate a meal which did not begin with a
hush of thanksgiving; we never began a day without 'a family gathering' at which mother read a chapter of the Bible after which there
would follow a weighty silence. These silences, during which all the
children of our family were hushed with a kind of awe, were very
important features of my spiritual development. There was work
inside and outside the house waiting to be done, and yet we sat there
hushed and quiet, doing nothing. I very quickly discovered that
something real was taking place. We were feeling our way down to
that place from which living words come, and very often they did
come. Some one would bow and talk with God so simply and quietly
that He never seemed far away. The words helped to explain the
silence. We were now finding what we had been searching for. When
I first began to think of God I did not think of Him as very far off.
At a meeting some of the Friends who prayed shouted loud and
strong when they called upon Him, but at home He always heard
easily and He seemed to be there with us in the living silence. My
first steps in religion were thus *acted*. It was a religion which we *did*
together. Almost nothing was *said* in the way of instructing me. We
all joined together to listen for God, and then one of us talked to
Him for the others. In these simple ways my religious disposition
was being unconsciously formed and the roots of my faith in unseen
realities were reaching down far below my crude and childish surface
thinking.

Rufus Jones, 1926

21.02 When I was about seven years old, I announced that my favourite text was 'Hitherto hath the Lord helped me'. The elders were amused, but I am not so sure that it was funny after all. The distance from one birthday to the next seems infinite to a small child, and 'the thoughts of youth are long, long thoughts'. Looking back over many years, I fancy my choice now would be much the same. I am not prepared, here and now, to analyse and define the reasons, but I can only say that this quiet certainty has run all through my life linking up babyhood and youth and middle age with the latest stretch of the road and 'hitherto', though sometimes almost slipping through one's fingers, that golden thread has never wholly escaped my grasp.

Elizabeth Fox Howard, 1943

21.03 And you, young convinced ones, be you entreated and exhorted to a diligent and chaste waiting upon God, in the way of his blessed manifestation and appearance of himself to you. Look not out, but within... Remember it is a still voice that speaks to us in this day, and that it is not to be heard in the noises and hurries of the mind; but it is distinctly understood in a retired frame. Jesus loved and chose solitudes, often going to mountains, to gardens, and sea-sides to avoid crowds and hurries; to show his disciples it was good to be solitary, and sit loose to the world.

William Penn, 1694

21.04 [Our] work is based on the thought that 'What you have inherited from your forefathers you must acquire for yourselves to possess it'. That is to say that each generation of young Friends by its experiments must discover for itself the truths on which the Society is built if it is to use those truths and to continue and enlarge the work of the Society. Hence the occasional separate meetings of younger Friends and our desire to have means of expressing corporately our own experience.

Young Friends Committee, 1926

21.05 Occasionally, reassuring memories drift across my consciousness during my times of weakness. One of these is an impromptu meeting for worship that took place during a Leaveners' tour of Moscow. It was the time of *perestroika* and great change, everything we did was 'the first' and we were constantly in the limelight. By the fourth day we were emotionally shattered, we needed a break. We sought out some quiet together as a company, hidden away in a small derelict room on the top floor of a college building away from the constant attention of our new friends. Our meeting was charged with emotion; we cried, we laughed, we ministered, we healed. Every person (Quaker or not) ministered and together we re-forged our shattered emotions. That meeting was momentous in my spiritual development, and always reassuring when I am low.

Roger Davies, 1994

21.06 Junior Yearly Meeting gave us the opportunity to step back and look at our lives from a different perspective. As Quakers we are often preoccupied with global issues and as young people we are only too often preoccupied with the pressures of work. We had the space to stop, to listen and to think about ourselves...

Through our discussions we recognised our anxieties and fears. We realised that we are individuals and that we are alone but, as part of a loving community, to be alone does not necessarily mean to be lonely. We discovered that it is acceptable to have confused feelings, to be different, to do things our own way. We should not feel guilty when we are wrong, and appreciate that there must be room for mistakes. There are people who want us to be exactly as we are.

Epistle of Junior Yearly Meeting, 1991

See also 10.16, 21.19 & 22.66-22.71

KNOWING AND ACCEPTING OURSELVES

21.07 It is by our 'imperfections' that we move towards each other, towards wholeness of relationship. It is our oddities, our grittiness, the occasions when we hurt or are hurt, that challenge us to a deeper knowledge of each other. Our sins have been said to be stepping-stones to God.

Kenneth C Barnes, 1985

21.08   We are all, yes, I believe, *all* a mixture of good and bad, and we are not always good at recognising in this magpie mixture what is bad and what is good. Our need is to accept ourselves as a whole, and offer that whole to God, leaving it to God 'unto whom all hearts are open, all desires known, and from whom no secrets are hid' to evaluate the good and bad in us. The glorious miracle is that, if we can do this, God can still use us, with all our faults and weaknesses, if we are willing to be used.

The knowledge that I am usable, and sometimes used, is to me a source of love and gratitude and strength far deeper even than joy and happiness.

Anna Bidder, 1978

21.09   My life has been one of great vicissitude: mine has been a hidden path, hidden from every human eye. I have had deep humiliations and sorrows to pass through. I can truly say I have 'wandered in the wilderness in a solitary way, and found no city to dwell in'; and yet how wonderfully I have been sustained. I have passed through many and great dangers, many ways – I have been tried with the applause of the world, and none know how great a trial that has been, and the deep humiliations of it; and yet I fully believe it is not nearly so dangerous as being made much of in religious society. There is a snare even in religious unity, if we are not on the watch. I have sometimes felt that it was not so dangerous to be made much of in the world, as by those whom we think highly of in our own Society: the more I have been made much of by the world, the more I have been inwardly humbled. I could often adopt the words of Sir Francis Bacon – 'When I have ascended before men, I have descended in humiliation before God.'

Elizabeth Fry, 1844

21.10   In this century we have been newly filled by the conscious knowledge of our own darkness – that we carry this darkness within us. We no longer need to project our darkness outward into demons or scapegoats – or, if we do, we know we are evoking disaster. It is by encounter with our own darkness that we recognise the light. It is the light itself which shows us the darkness – and both are summoned within us.

Lorna M Marsden, 1983

21.11 Those who have difficulty in accepting the idea of a personal shadow as far as they themselves are concerned, whose knowledge of human nature is two-dimensional (that is, without depth), all too easily think that morality attaches to feelings, that hateful, hostile, cruel or greedy feelings are immoral. They do not, perhaps, realise that the feelings that arise in us are neither moral nor immoral, but neutral. The supreme importance of morality is the way we choose to act on our feelings. And we shall not be free to choose if we do not know what they are.

Jack H Wallis, 1988

21.12 Trouble of soul can teach us things that raptures never could – not only patience and perseverance, but humility and sympathy with others.

Edward Grubb, 1933

21.13 When we descend from our towers, and come out from our sanctuaries, and take our place in ordinary homes, and workshops, and are surrounded and jostled by our fellow-creatures, we find that our sensitive souls shrink from some of these contacts: that this man humbles our pride, and that one offends our aesthetic sense: that this woman takes our words amiss, and that one misconstrues and resents our actions. It is so much easier to feel enthusiasm for humanity, than to love our immediate neighbours.

Phyllis Richards, 1948

21.14 We know, with varying degrees of acceptance into awareness, our own weaknesses, and there is a tendency to think that others – who seem, on the surface, to be very sure and confident – do not struggle in the way we do. But many of those who appear to cope and be strong and tireless are indeed very different behind their masks. We are all wounded; we all feel inadequate and ashamed; we all struggle. But this is part of the human condition; it draws us together, helps us to find our connectedness.

June Ellis, 1986

21.15 I have found in my life that from time to time when revelling in new-found joys or faced with decision, problem or grief, there must be for me a listening ear. Even if my listener says little but sheds over me a feeling of rejoicing with me, of being alongside me as I strive, of sorrowing with me in my hour of distress, then I can better appreciate or face the situation. I believe this is true for most of us. There are moments when we need one another. If this sometimes unuttered cry is answered, then truly we meet, and do not grope or slip past each other. But if two individuals share at an even deeper level from out of their own experience in their search for ultimate reality in life, then the divine in the human shines through and a new creation is born for both.

Margaret S Gibbins, 1969

21.16 *In a speech at the end of the United Nations Decade of Women, in 1985, Alice Wiser said:*

Each of us is responsible for our own actions and our own reactions. We are not responsible for someone else's actions and reactions. This is very important for women especially because most women have been taught that they are responsible for the happiness of everyone in their family. They are taught that all family unhappiness and discord is their fault. But responsibility rests within each individual.

21.17 True Godliness don't turn men out of the world, but enables them to live better in it, and excites their endeavours to mend it: not hide their candle under a bushel, but set it upon a table in a candlestick.

William Penn, 1682

21.18 Do you cherish that of God within you, so that love may grow in you and rule your life?

Questions and counsel, 1988

21.19 When I left school I set out into the world determined that nothing as small as the Society of Friends would hold me. 'I want the real world', I said. 'Friends are good people, aunts and uncles and cousins, they are friends of the family to whom I must always be polite. They do not drink or smoke or swear, they do not lose their tempers. They do not love money, they do not worship success (well, only a little bit), they do not compete, they do not gamble, they do not fight. They do not do what they want to do. If they want to do something very much they deeply suspect it is not the right thing to do. But I am not like that at all. I would like to drink and smoke, to make money, to be successful. I want to fight and to win; I want to please myself, to enjoy myself, to be myself. I am talented and clever and malicious; I will escape, for I am clearly not a Quaker, and find out what it is I am. I am no-one's daughter and no-one's grand-daughter', I said defiantly, 'I am myself.' And I marched down Shaftesbury Avenue waving my banner with only a casual glance at Westminster Meeting House.

What I am telling is a classic story but we must admit that every cliché contains profound truth and a story is classic because so many people recognise it as true. 'Father' I said, 'give me my inheritance and I will go out and seek a fortune.' So I took my inheritance and went out and spent it. When it was all gone I came to myself and, finding myself somewhat diminished, faced with demands I found difficult to fulfil, I went to meeting.

'Here I am', I said.

'That's all right.'

'Just for a bit of a sit-down.'

'Whatever you need.'

'You mustn't expect anything from me,' I said, 'I can only bring a need.'

'Whatever you have.'

Dorothy Nimmo, 1979

21.20   Isolation of spirit ... comes to most – perhaps all of us – at one time or another. There are times in our lives when the tides of faith seem far out, times of dryness, times when we do not feel the comfort and guidance of God's hand. At such times we may stay away from meeting feeling that it does not give us the spiritual help that we need; or it may be that we continue to go and are to outward appearance actively engaged on the meeting's life and business, while, within, we feel the agonies of isolation and the longing for light to lighten our darkness. I can think with thankfulness of Friends who have brought light to my darkness – perhaps a single sentence, a friendly letter, a walk on the downs: their help was perhaps given unconsciously, but it was because they were sensitive to God's leadings that they were able to do it. Do we seek to be the channels of God's love and caring? 'Caring matters most.'

Edward H Milligan, 1951

LIVING A FULL LIFE

21.21   The art of living must be studied, as must every art. It calls for imagination, so that every advance, every change, is not merely a difference, but a creative act. Achievement, at any level above the lowest, calls for courage to hold on, in spite of current moods, and for exacting self-discipline. The art of Christian living calls for the same self-preparation; but its reward is not merely aesthetic satisfactions. The soul, hungry for God, is fed. Life itself takes on new meaning. Thus it is that we break from the confines of the prisons we have built about ourselves. Thus it is we are brought into the freedom of the Kingdom of God which, every day, through the wide world, is being realised in the hearts of men.

Horace B Pointing, 1946

21.22   There is, it sometimes seems, an excess of religious and social busyness these days, a round of committees and conferences and journeyings, of which the cost in 'peaceable wisdom' is not sufficiently counted. Sometimes we appear overmuch to count as merit our participation in these things... At least we ought to make sure that we sacrifice our leisure for something worthy. True leisureliness is a beautiful thing and may not lightly be given away. Indeed, it is one of the outstanding and most wonderful features of the life of Christ that, with all his work in preaching and healing and planning for the Kingdom, he leaves behind this sense of leisure, of time in which to pray and meditate, to stand and stare at the cornfields and fishing boats, and to listen to the confidences of neighbours and passers-by...

Most of us need from time to time the experience of something spacious or space-making, when Time ceases to be the enemy, goad-in-hand, and becomes our friend. To read good literature, gaze on natural beauty, to follow cultivated pursuits until our spirits are refreshed and expanded, will not unfit us for the up and doing of life, whether of personal or church affairs. Rather will it help us to separate the essential from the unessential, to know where we are really needed and get a sense of proportion. We shall find ourselves giving the effect of leisure even in the midst of a full and busy life. People do not pour their joys or sorrows into the ears of those with an eye on the clock.

Caroline C Graveson, 1937

21.23   Jesus's question in the Sermon on the Mount: 'If ye salute your brethren only, what do ye to excess?' *What do ye to excess?* How often he showed his approval of extravagant generosity when it arose from a simple and pure impulse of the heart. He defended the act of the woman who broke the alabaster box of precious ointment so that she might pour it over his feet. 'If thy brother ask of thee thy coat, give him thy cloak also' – in other words, more than he expects to receive. In his parable of the Prodigal Son, the father does not wait to welcome his son at the door of the house; he runs to meet him, and it is the *best* robe which he puts on him. It is this excess, this extravagance, which we find in God's love for us, that for me shows the meaning of the word 'Grace'.

It is for this grace that we pray; that we, too, may love to excess even though it may appear foolish in the eyes of the world.

Phyllis Richards, 1949

21.24   All our senses are given to us to enjoy, and to praise God. The smell of the sea, of the blossom borne on the wind, of the soft flesh of a little baby; the taste of a ripe plum or bread fresh from the oven, the feel of warm cat's fur, or the body of a lover – these are all forms of thanksgiving prayer. I am sure that it is as wrong to fail to delight in our bodies as it is to misuse them through excess. Not to be a glutton does not mean that we may not delight in good food: not to be ruled by lust does not mean that we must not enjoy the exquisite pleasures of sex: not to be slothful does not mean that we must never lie in the sun, not doing, just being. When Jesus said, 'I am come that they might have life, and that they might have it more abundantly',

I do not think He was speaking only of spiritual life – I think He meant us to have positive delight in all the good things in this wonderful world which his Father created.

Bella Bown, c 1980

21.25 Perhaps the most neglected of all the advices is that we should live adventurously. If there is one wish I would pray the Spirit to put into our Christmas stockings, it is warmth, openness, passion, a bit of emotion that doesn't mind making a fool of itself occasionally.

Gerald Priestland, 1977

21.26 It is 'life' only that can lead to life, and no forms are availing without it. Seek the life in all things, and cherish it by all authorised means.

Hannah Kilham, 1831

See also chapter 22 Close relationships

CREATIVITY

21.27 A sudden concentration of attention on a rainy August morning. Clusters of bright red berries, some wrinkled, some blemished, others perfect, hanging among green leaves. The experience could not have lasted more than a few seconds, but that was a moment out of time. I was caught up in what I saw: I became a part of it: the berries, the leaves, the raindrops and I, we were all of a piece. A moment of beauty and harmony and meaning. A moment of understanding.

Ralph Hetherington, 1975

21.28 There is a daily round for beauty as well as for goodness, a world of flowers and books and cinemas and clothes and manners as well as of mountains and masterpieces... God is in all beauty, not only in the natural beauty of earth and sky, but in all fitness of language and rhythm, whether it describe a heavenly vision or a street fight, a Hamlet or a Falstaff, a philosophy or a joke: in all fitness of line and colour and shade, whether seen in the Sistine Madonna or a child's knitted frock: in all fitness of sound and beat and measure, whether the result be Bach's Passion music or a nursery jingle. The quantity of God, so to speak, varies in the different examples, but His quality of beauty in fitness remains the same.

Caroline C Graveson, 1937

21.29   *Robin Tanner (1904-1988), for much of his life an inspector of education responsible for arts and crafts in primary schools, was himself a gifted teacher and an artist of great distinction.*

The history of the protest of early Friends against excess and ostentatious superfluity is fascinating. It is easy to ridicule their apparent denial of the Arts; yet it must be admitted that, certainly visually, out of it there was born an austere, spare, refreshingly simple beauty... What is hopeful is that in the Society there is no finality; we can laugh at ourselves and go on learning. As long as we are given to constant revision there is hope for us. Special pleading for the Arts is no longer needed. They are not viewed, as they once were, as a distraction from God. Rather they are seen as a manifestation of God.

Robin Tanner, 1966

21.30   *A hesitation about the traditional policy of the Society towards the arts was expressed by Elizabeth Fry in 1833:*

It appears to me to be one important means of helping the human mind in a healthy state, that in recreations which are needful for it, it should be trained as much as possible to look to those things that bring profit as well as pleasure with them. My observation of human nature and the different things that affect it frequently leads me to regret that we as a Society so wholly give up delighting the ear by sound. Surely He who formed the ear and the heart would not have given these tastes and powers without some purpose for them.

21.31   The acceptance of the practice of music as a legitimate activity for Friends has been difficult because of the clear views expressed by early Friends. Solomon Eccles, a professional musician from a family of musicians, tried to burn his 'virginals, fiddles and all' and when the crowd tried to prevent him 'I was forced to stamp on them and break them to pieces [because I saw] a difference between the harps of God and the harps of men.' Similarly our founder, George Fox, says in his Journal that he was 'moved to cry also against all sorts of music ... [for it] burdened the pure life, and stirred people's minds to vanity.' With such a strong lead it took Friends until 1978 before Ormerod Greenwood could name this attitude an apostasy. Now we can say that Friends do not merely accept music, but that composing, performing and listening to music are, for many, essential parts of their spiritual lives. Evidence for this can be found in the experience of the Leaveners. The Quaker Youth Theatre has not only delighted but challenged us; and the first performance by the Quaker Festival Orchestra and Chorus of *The gates of Greenham* in the Royal Festival Hall in 1985 produced the largest British Quaker gathering – musical or otherwise – this century. Acceptance of music has gone through a number of stages: firstly it became acceptable for Friends to practise it in their daily lives; secondly they felt able to practise it together; and thirdly they have felt able to include it in their worship. There are a number of meetings now which recognise that music beforehand, whether listening or singing together, can help Friends prepare their hearts and minds; and some Friends feel that to perform in worship, whether spontaneously or in a prepared way, can enable the meeting to reach the deep centre which characterises meetings held in the light. Friends now acknowledge that we can hear God's harps being played through 'the harps of men'.

John Sheldon, 1994

21.32   Along the paths of the imagination the artist and mystic make contact. The revelations of God are not all of one kind. Always the search in art, as in religion, is for the rhythms of relationships, for the unity, the urge, the mystery, the wonder of life that is presented in great art and true religion.

Horace B Pointing, 1944

21.33   *Waldo Williams (1904-1971), who joined Friends in 1953, was one of the foremost Welsh poets of the twentieth century. His poem 'Mewn dau gae' finds a place here, not because it reflects on creativity, but as a vivid example of the power of words to evoke the deep mysteries of life.*

Mewn dau gae

O ba le'r ymroliai'r môr goleuni
Oedd a'i waelod ar Weun Parc y Blawd a Parc y Blawd?
Ar ôl imi holi'n hir yn y tir tywyll,
O b'le deuai, yr un a fu erioed?
Neu pwy, pwy oedd y saethwr, yr eglurwr sydyn?
Bywiol heliwr y maes oedd rholiwr y môr.
Oddifry uwch y chwibanwyr gloywbib, uwch callwib y cornicyllod,
Dygai i mi y llonyddwch mawr.

Rhoddai i mi'r cyffro lle nad oedd
Ond cyffro meddwl yr haul yn mydru'r tes,
Yr eithin aeddfed ar y cloddiau'n clecian,
Y brwyn lu yn breuddwydio'r wybren las.
Pwy sydd yn galw pan fo'r dychymyg yn dihuno?
Cyfod, cerdd, dawnsia, wele'r bydysawd.
Pwy sydd yn ymguddio ynghanol y geiriau?
Yr oedd hyn ar Weun Parc y Blawd a Parc y Blawd.

A phan fyddai'r cymylau mawr ffoadur a phererin
Yn goch gan heulwen hwyrol tymestl Tachwedd
Lawr yn yr ynn a'r masarn a rannai'r meysydd
Yr oedd cân y gwynt a dyfnder fel dyfnder distawrwydd.
Pwy sydd, ynghanol y rhwysg a'r rhemp?
Pwy sydd yn sefyll ac yn cynnwys?
Tyst pob tyst, cof pob cof, hoedl pob hoedl,
Tawel ostegwr helbul hunan.

Nes dyfod o'r hollfyd weithiau i'r tawelwch
Ac ar y ddau barc fe gerddai ei bobl,
A thrwyddynt, rhyngddynt, amdanynt ymdaenai
Awen yn codi o'r cudd, yn cydio'r cwbl,
Fel gyda ni'r ychydig pan fyddai'r cyrch picwerchi
Neu'r tynnu to deir draw ar y weun drom.
Mor agos at ein gilydd y deuem –
Yr oedd yr heliwr distaw yn bwrw ei rwyd amdanom.

O, trwy oesoedd y gwaed ar y gwellt a thrwy'r goleuni y galar
Pa chwiban nas clywai ond mynwes? O, pwy oedd?
Twyllwr pob traha, rhedwr pob trywydd,

Hai! y dihangwr o'r byddinoedd
Yn chwiban adnabod, adnabod nes bod adnabod.
Mawr oedd cydnaid calonnau wedi eu rhew rhyn.
Yr oedd rhyw ffynhonnau'n torri tua'r nefoedd
Ac yn syrthio'n ôl a'u dagrau fel dail pren.

Am hyn y myfyria'r dydd dan yr haul a'r cwmwl
A'r nos trwy'r celloedd i'w mawrfrig ymennydd.
Mor llonydd ydynt a hithau a'i hanadl
Dros Weun Parc y Blawd a Parc y Blawd heb ludd,
A'u gafael ar y gwrthrych, y perci llawn pobl.
Diau y daw'r dirháu, a pha awr yw hi
Y daw'r herwr, daw'r heliwr, daw'r hawliwr i'r bwlch,
Daw'r Brenin Alltud a'r brwyn yn hollti.

Waldo Williams, 1956

For a translation of this text into English see page 615

21.34   One of the most vivid experiences [of individual worship] on my part was sitting quietly for at least an hour before a picture by the Dutch painter Vermeer, and absorbing its sheer beauty... The room was crowded with people, but I was oblivious of them, as I was equally oblivious of the passage of time. As a result of this act of concentration the vision of this particular masterpiece is indelibly stamped on my mind which has forever been enriched by it. I know that my ordinary acts of seeing and observation have been sharpened by that experience. There was drawn from me an acknowledgement of the greatness of the artist and his painting and I caught, with awe, the light of his inspiration and creativeness. Further, something was given to me that I can only describe as, literally, a transcending of the normal everyday world. This quite simple secular act was for me a truly worshipful experience.

George Gorman, 1973

21.35   Worshippers are like the spokes of a wheel. The nearer they come to the centre of all Life the nearer they are to each other. Having reached the centre they become united in a single life through the creative love of God.

Howard H Brinton, 1931

21.36   I believe in the powers of ordinary men and women; in their immense potentialities; in their capacity to rise higher than themselves; in their essential creativeness; in them as artists. I do not believe in the 'chosen few': I believe in us all.

I believe we were brought into this world to live and to enjoy it; to take out of it all that, in our full stature, we are able. I believe it then falls to every person to reach that state of fecundity and richness that makes him long to put back into life something uniquely his own.

I believe and glory in the uniqueness of every child and every man and woman. I believe that it is that uniqueness that above all needs to be cherished, protected, nourished and helped to grow and flower and come to fruition. Our job is to discern and to promote this uniqueness. In greater or lesser degree we each bear the privileged responsibility for using the artist in us. Yes: I believe in having the best of both, of all, worlds!

I believe that everyone should be successful. I believe, therefore, in the giving and accepting of praise. Praise and appreciation are necessary to us all. I believe that if all is well with the human element in our environment we are prepared to make the sustained effort that is necessary to ensure success.

I believe in work. I believe in play. On the whole I see no distinction. Let us not be afraid of work! Play – games – poetry – music – movement – all the Arts, are unnecessary yet absolutely essential. They make possible the impossible and reconcile the irreconcilable.

I believe in the absolute necessity for the arts. Man cannot live by bread alone.

Robin Tanner, 1963

21.37   'What's that on the shelf?' my artistic friend asked. 'A turbine blade. I designed it', I replied proudly.
'Oh', she said.

Visiting three weeks later she asked, 'Why is that still there?'
'Because I think it's beautiful.'
'Oh', she said.

My friend enthused over the beauty of a cathedral, a Rembrandt, a Turner, a sonnet. I find none in a cathedral, little in Rembrandt or poetry, a lot in a Turner.

I find great beauty in Concorde, a Norton, a modern suspension bridge, in calculus and a good computer program – especially if I have written it! She little or none. I thrill to the sound of a racing car, the sight and smell of a machine shop, the noise and balletic movement of men and machine shaping white hot steel in a forge – and in my turbine blade. She does not.

We could both be moved to tears by mountains, Beethoven, Britten, clouds ... and by friendship.

Graham Clarke, 1994

21.38 In a broadcast Good Friday meditation given by an ex-colleague I was surprised to hear him speaking about the way in which listening to Bach's Brandenburg Concertos had been the crucial factor in his recovery from a near fatal heart attack. He said that whenever he listened to them, on the Sony Walkman his son had given him, at whatever time of day or night, he could feel the atoms in his body rearranging themselves in response to the glorious order and freedom of Bach's music. From the moment he began to listen to them his healing had begun.

For weeks after hearing that meditation I found myself reflecting on the way in which music acts as a restorative for me. I listened to the Brandenburg Concertos again and was aware of the stimulation to my own central nervous system. But then I noted that Frank Sinatra singing 'New York, New York', or Shirley Bassey singing 'Don't cry for me Argentina' could have a similar effect. The raw energy of Tina Turner singing could, if I gave myself up to the rhythm, produce a responding surge of energy in me. I understand that students doing tests after listening to Mozart are reported to have better scores than when they do the tests without the warm-up.

The Holy Spirit can indeed restore us to health (or stimulate us to work well) through the medium of music as well as prayer or antibiotics! And why, indeed, should I be surprised that this is so? Creativity is the gift that we were given on the eighth day of creation. In naming and re-making the world we are co-workers with God, and whether we are making a garden or a meal, a painting or a piece of furniture or a computer program, we are sharing in an ongoing act of creation through which the world is constantly re-made.

Jo Farrow, 1994

21.39   As a teenager I first really knew about the Spirit within me when I danced. Here was a way at last of stilling the thoughts, questions and reasonings in my head, and just being. My body became alive in response to the music and my emotions were unlocked. I knew a joy and openness that was new to me.

As an adult I still find spontaneous free movement to music a religious experience; emotions and reactions come from deep within me and not through conscious thought. To dance in this way with others – meeting and sharing without words but with open receptiveness – is an uplifting experience.

Jennifer Fishpool, 1991

21.40   I feel that the creation of poetry is not unlike the upsurging of words in a Quaker meeting. First, heart and mind must be prepared – and the emotional and mental preparation for art is something which few non-artists realise. Then there is the waiting, perhaps for months, because poetry cannot be forced: it is an act of imagination, not of will ... and then at last comes the moment of certainty, accompanied usually by some physical action, and the words begin to flow.

Clive Sansom, 1965

21.41   It is in the workshop and at the bench that an insight into the soul of wood craftsmanship can be truly gained. There are tools, there is the wood – rude planks, ungarnished, their surface scored with the saw. Between them, and without which each is useless, must come the soul and spirit of the designer and craftsman; the deft hands prompted by an alert mind; the knowledge attained only through years of study and service; the creative instinct and ability that will, by the correct use of the tools, transform the mere plank into a thing of usefulness and beauty – possibly a joy for ever... It was at the lathe, when a youth, that I first realised the charm of line, the contour that flows continuously on, diminishing and enlarging, though separated by ornamental members... Those who have studied woodcraft for half a century find themselves still learning and quite unable to pack all their knowledge into a nutshell for the convenience of a beginner. The training is not that of the university; it is, however, quite as exacting in its own way and so merits equal recognition and respect, and it is encouraging to note that this idea is slowly gaining ground. The woodworkers of a century ago added to their carpentry the dignity of craft; this is why the examples of their handiwork that remain are treasured. Let it not be assumed that it is merely because such work is old that it is appreciated so highly. Even a slight study will reveal the artist mind that prompted the hands, the perception that had grasped the principles of design, the certain knowledge in its decisive finish. There is the secret of its permanent inspiration, its power to soothe and charm.

Walter Rose, 1938

See also 23.53-23.70 Work and economic affairs

21.42 Today Science is rediscovering the creative mystery of the universe. The old self-assurance is largely gone. Within the first quarter of the twentieth century a revolution has taken place. The laws of mechanics no longer explain all things. The intellect of man has become aware of something strange and unpredictable at the very heart of existence. Matter and radiation have assumed a complexity which was hardly guessed at in the eighteen hundreds. The exploration of the minute structure of matter seems to take us as far into the unknown as does the exploration of the farthest reaches of space.

Howard H Brinton, 1931

GETTING OLDER

21.43 If we are getting older it will be harder to acknowledge that we have not been called to spectacular service, that we are unlikely now to make a stir in the world, that our former dreams of doing some great healing work had a great deal of personal ambition in them.

A great many men and women have had to learn this unpalatable lesson – and then have discovered that magnificent opportunities lay all around them. We need not go to the ends of the earth to find them; we need not be young, clever, fit, beautiful, talented, trained, eloquent or very wise. We shall find them among our neighbours as well as among strangers, in our own families as well as in unfamiliar circles – magnificent opportunities to be kind and patient and understanding.

This is a vocation just as truly as some more obviously seen as such – the vocation of ordinary men and women called to continual, unspectacular acts of loving kindness in the ordinary setting of every day. They need no special medical boards before they embark on their service, need no inoculation against anything but indifference and lethargy and perhaps a self-indulgent shyness. How simple it sounds; how difficult it often is; how possible it may become by the grace of God.

Clifford Haigh, 1962

21.44 Here is the unfailing attraction of the life in Christ. It is a life which even to old age, is always on the upgrade; there is always something calling for a joyful looking forward; it is a life where, across each revelation of God's grace as it comes to us is written, in letters of gold, Thou shalt see greater things than these. It gives full scope ... to our desire for high adventure. No conceivable life can be so interesting, so stimulating, as that which we live in Christ.

William Littleboy, 1917

21.45 We must be confident that there is still more 'life' to be 'lived' and yet more heights to be scaled. The tragedy of middle age is that, so often, men and women cease to press 'towards the goal of their high calling'. They cease learning, cease growing; they give up and resign from life. As wisdom dawns with age, we begin to measure our experiences not by what life gives to us, not by the things withheld from us, but by their power to help us to grow in spiritual wisdom.

Evelyn Sturge, 1949

21.46 Those of you who are kept by age or sickness from more active work, who are living retired lives, may in your very separation have the opportunity of liberating power for others. Your prayers and thoughts go out further than you think, and as you wait in patience and in communion with God, you may be made ministers of peace and healing and be kept young in soul.

London Yearly Meeting, 1923

21.47
Who is this old woman I have to live with now?
All my previous life I've lived with myself,
Not always comfortably I admit,
Still we got along.

You see we shared the same habits, myself and I.
For instance – we both thought and moved fast.
This stranger uses a stick – creeps along,
Drops things, can't pick them up.
Slow at picking up a point too.
I lose my patience with her.

Myself and I would work, play and sleep at nights
After crammed days. She sits and sits.
Kind people say,
'I'll come and see you soon dear'.
'Isn't she wonderful' they say.
I don't think so. Sometimes I think...
Well, you know what I mean!
(Others think so too,
Otherwise they wouldn't be so kind to the old thing.)
The worst of it is, it seems I'm stuck with her.
God knows how I'll manage,
But as he knows, perhaps he'll see to it.

Katharine Moore, 1983

21.48 I am convinced it is a great art to know how to grow old gracefully, and I am determined to practise it... I always thought I should love to grow old, and I find it even more delightful than I thought. It is so delicious to be *done* with things, and to feel no need any longer to concern myself much about earthly affairs... I am tremendously content to let one activity after another go, and to await quietly and happily the opening of the door at the end of the passage-way, that will let me in to my real abiding place.

Hannah Whitall Smith, 1903

DEATH

21.49 I am glad I was here. Now I am clear, I am fully clear... All is well; the Seed of God reigns over all and over death itself. And though I am weak in body, yet the power of God is over all, and the Seed reigns over all disorderly spirits.

George Fox, shortly before his death, 1691

21.50 *Testimony concerning Abigail Watson (1684-1752):*

About a year before she died, she was sensible her departure drew nigh, for she found no engagement on her mind to travel abroad, as she frequently had done, when of ability, but said, 'She found her work was done and nothing in her way,' so was made quite easy and only waited for the salvation of God 'who', she said, in a reverent, thankful frame of mind, 'had been with her all her life long, and now I shall sing, sing, sing.'

National Half-year's Meeting in Dublin, 1753

21.51 I feel, and I wish you to feel for and with me, after the Rock of eternal life and salvation; for as we are established thereon, we shall be in the everlasting unity, which cannot be shaken by all the changes of time, nor interrupted in a never-ending eternity... We cannot approve or disapprove by parts the works of Omnipotence rightly. We must approve the whole and say, Thy will be done in all things... The desire of my heart is the great blessing of time and the consolation of eternity ... let self be of no reputation; trust in the Lord, and he will carry thee through all.

Job Scott, shortly before his death, 1793

21.52 I longed to be told for sure that we (for I was afraid for myself as well as for those I loved) would not die, not really. What I wanted was undeniable proof of the immortality of my personality.

Over the next few years, the fear stayed with me, as the dark side of love. Then my mother died. I felt the expected grief, remorse at my failings as a daughter, anger at illness and waste, and all the many emotions bereavement normally arouses.

But the fear of personal annihilation was met by the knowledge that 'Death is not the end. Your mother still loves you and you can go on loving her.' I don't know how I 'heard' those words: there was no vision, no voice, no particular moment or place. I do know that the day after she died, I told my husband what I had 'heard'.

Anne Hosking, 1980

21.53   Saturday morning, making chocolate clusters,
And you with chocolate
All smeared around your rosy mouth,
Looking very comical
Turned to me and said,

'Will your body
Come back again, Grannie,
After you are dead?'

'No, not this body,' I reply,
Putting a cluster
Neatly shaped,
Upon the baking tin between us.
'But I'll be around all right,
Hovering somewhere, laughing with you,
Feeling quite near
As Grandpa does with me.'

Your thoughts had very nearly
Moved elsewhere but, satisfied,
'That's OK' you said.

Ruth Fawell, 1976

21.54   Death is not an end, but a beginning. It is but an incident in the 'life of the ages', which is God's gift to us now. It is the escape of the spirit from its old limitations and its freeing for a larger and more glorious career. We stand around the grave, and as we take our last, lingering look, too often our thoughts are there; and we return to the desolate home feeling that all that made life lovely has been left behind on the bleak hillside... Yet the spirit now is free, and the unseen angel at our side points upwards from the grave and whispers, 'He is not here, but is risen'. The dear one returns with us to our home, ready and able, as never before, to comfort, encourage, and beckon us onward.

William Littleboy, 1917

21.55 To my dearest Helen, my Brothers and my Friends: why grieve? I grieve not, I promise you. I am more than ready to go. Life should mean achievement, in great things and in small. Without achievement life has neither virtue nor relish; I can achieve nothing more here but, beyond, I believe I shall. I do not fear death... The dying itself may be unpleasant; being dead, that foolish description we use, that must be otherwise. An excellence; a fulfilment. God is purpose, order, power, but, forget it not, *love* also, else where comes love? Love is the force that drives all else. If life has taught me anything, it is that love is, of all things, eternal. Love is of God, my God, therefore it is eternal and cannot die; here is the greatest comfort in creation. Love straddles the hurdle we call death and I, who have loved you all, I take it with me and its chain will link us to eternity. This is what I would say to you all: 'I am content'.

Bob Lindsay, 1989

21.56 I believe it is of real value to our earthly life to have the next life in mind, because if we shut it out of our thoughts we are starving part of our spiritual nature – we are like children who fail to grow up – none the finer children for that. Not only do we miss much joy in the earthly life if we imagine it to be the whole of our existence, but we arrive on the further shore with no knowledge of the language of the new country where we shall find ourselves unfitted for the larger life of the spirit. George Fox urged Friends to 'take care of God's glory'. That is a motto for all spheres known and unknown.

Joan Mary Fry, 1955

21.57 If we ... have not prepared ourselves in some measure for dying, what have we been doing? To face up to the fact of death gives a fuller awareness of God-given life...

About a dozen years ago I became critically ill and I have a vivid memory of looking down on my self on the bed; doctors and nurses worked on that body, and I felt held in such secureness, joy and contentment, a sense of the utter rightness of things – I was held in the hands of God. The crisis passed and I was filled with wonder at the newness of life...

Soon after, I had radical surgery followed by many months of slow recovery with repeated setbacks and further operations. There were times when truly *out of the depths I cried*; I had no reserves of strength left, either physical, emotional or spiritual, but I never completely lost the memory of being held and the wonder at being alive. Gradually the wounds healed: old griefs as well as disease and operations...

Can we face up to the fact of death? Can we prepare ourselves in some measure for dying? I feel I have to try and tell you of my experience and the understanding it brought me – however personal and limited. From the closeness to my own dying, I know *God is*. Death is not a negation of life but complements it: however terrible the actual dying, life and death are both parts of the whole and that wholeness is in God. I still fight the conventional words of 'resurrection and life everlasting' but I know that after Jesus died the overwhelming certainty of his presence released his disciples from fear. I believe eternal life is in each moment of life, here and now; the real tragedy is not how or when we die but if we do not live the life we are given to our full potential.

Jenifer Faulkner, 1982

21.58   *Walter Martin (1929-1989) retired from his post as General Secretary of Quaker Peace & Service in 1982 after contracting motor neurone disease. In 1988 he wrote:*

Over the last few years I have become very much aware of the supremacy of the spirit over the body in principle, but although I have failed to achieve this idea in practice my real self, namely the spiritual, has been considerably enhanced... Morale and spirits remain high because God has strengthened my faith, for I feel that it is simply the start of a new life. But I do get upset when I think of my relatives and friends who will grieve for me, so pray regularly that God give them the strength to overcome their grief with time.

I have learned that it is best not to concentrate on my troubles but to think about and pray for others... I feel privileged to share in the attitude of the Apostle Paul when he says: 'In whatsoever condition I find myself therewith to be content.'

See also 22.80-22.95 Bereavement *& chapter 17* Funerals and memorial meetings

SUFFERING AND HEALING

21.59 Pain isolates one. It pervades everything; blackens the sky, pushes other humans away, reduces music and poetry and the outside world to dullness; grinds on and on endlessly.

Some say that Christianity is a morbid religion, over-emphasising a Christ tormented on a cross. I can only say that even as a child I could sometimes comfort myself in pain by remembering his suffering... It was Jesus the man, enduring agonising pain in terrible loneliness, who spoke to my condition and brought me sometimes much needed consolation.

Joan Fitch, 1988

21.60 Death hangs a long way off. Do I just wait
And pass my youth through to my greying days
In petty pastimes, and misery for ways
Of life I dare not hope to live? My gait
Is twisted and my speech uncouth. I hate
The pity and the distance set around
By those who see and dare not know, so bound
By other's expectations. Am I too late
To live; to study how to learn; to try
And fail yet seek another way to give,
To gain myself? In this exchange the dry
Desert of my poverty may flower – live
In ways undreamed – and the pain of fading
Hopes will disappear in life's rich trading.

Jonathan Griffith, 1977

21.61   *Bernard Brett (1935-1982) had severe cerebral palsy; he joined Friends in Colchester and worked tirelessly to help others.*

At some times I have felt very definitely the guiding hand of God, steering my life in certain directions and this is a very wonderful and rich feeling. Yet at other times, and for quite long periods, I have known the empty loneliness and even despair which comes from depression. Everything seems dry and arid, and friendships which at other times are a source of joy seem empty and meaningless. There are times when God and my personal faith seem to be completely beyond my reach or understanding. These are frightening times, because the work or activities I seek to do have no apparent value or reason. Life seems an endless struggle and the prospect of having to live within the extreme limitations of my disabilities, with the knowledge that with the passing years they will become rather worse than better, is a daunting thought. There are some mornings when I wake up during times of depression when I simply want to cease living.

21.62   *The old age of William Penn (1644-1718):*

His memory was almost quite lost, and the use of his understanding suspended; so that he was not so conversible as formerly; and yet as near the Truth, in the love of it, as before... His mind was in an innocent state, as appeared by his very loving deportment to all that came near him: and that he still had a good sense of Truth was plain, by some very clear sentences he spoke in the Life and Power of Truth, in an evening meeting we had together there; wherein we were greatly comforted; so that I was ready to think this was a sort of sequestration of him from all the concerns of this life which so much oppressed him; not in judgment, but in mercy, that he might have rest, and not be oppressed thereby to the end.

Thomas Story, 1714

21.63   I was sixteen – alone in the world in a strange sense – utterly friendless – ill and away from boarding school (where I was not happy, but perhaps happier than at home) for nine months at a stretch...

I had not slept at all for three long weeks. The doctors refused to give me sleeping pills or send me to hospital as I was so young. I pleaded in vain for sleeping pills or hospital, and failing I gathered up my courage to face an intolerable situation quite alone.

I contemplated suicide. Though I did not fear it, I knew, young and disturbed though I was, that it would grieve my adoptive parents terribly, and perhaps some of the girls and staff at my boarding school would be upset...

I thought long and with strange sixteen-year-old maturity. I was no longer a child, though my parents treated me as if I were three, and I had been reading Plato in Greek for about two years.

I decided against suicide. It would be cowardly anyway. I prayed for sleep and health and friends – especially one dear friend. That prayer was absolutely answered beyond my wildest dreams many years later when I was 51. It was worth waiting for. Since I was small I have had the Chinese attitude to time, that time passes imperceptibly and the joys of life are worth waiting for.

Hilary Pimm, 1983

21.64   *John Woolman (1720-1772) of Mount Holly, New Jersey, restricted his business interests for reasons of conscience; he travelled widely in the ministry especially to urge Friends to give up the ownership of slaves. His Journal (see especially 2.57, 13.24, 20.46 & 27.02) has become a religious classic.*

In a time of sickness with the pleurisy, a little upward of two years and a half ago, I was brought so near the gates of death that I forgot my name. Being then desirous to know who I was, I saw a mass of matter of a dull gloomy colour between the south and the east, and was informed that this mass was human beings in as great misery as they could be, and live, and that I was mixed in with them, and henceforth might not consider myself as a distinct or separate being. In this state I remained several hours. I then heard a soft, melodious voice, more pure and harmonious than any voice I had heard with my ears before; and I believed it was the voice of an angel who spake to other angels. The words were *John Woolman is dead.* I soon remembered that I was once John Woolman and being assured that I was alive in the body, I greatly wondered what that heavenly voice could mean. I believed beyond doubting that it was the voice of an holy angel, but as yet it was a mystery to me.

I was then carried in spirit to the mines where poor oppressed people were digging rich treasures for those called Christians, and heard them blaspheme the name of Christ, at which I was grieved for His Name to me was precious. Then I was informed that these heathens were told that those who oppressed them were the followers of Christ, and they said amongst themselves, 'If Christ directed them to use us in this sort, then Christ is a cruel tyrant'.

All this time the song of the angel remained a mystery; and in the morning my dear wife and some others coming to my bedside, I asked them if they knew who I was, and they telling me I was John Woolman, thought I was only light-headed, for I told them not what the angel said, nor was I disposed to talk much to anyone, but was very desirous to get so deep that I might understand this mystery.

My tongue was often so dry that I could not speak till I had moved it about and gathered some moisture, and as I lay still for a time, at length I felt divine power prepare my mouth that I could speak, and then said, 'I am crucified with Christ, nevertheless I live, yet not I, but Christ liveth in me. And the life I now live in the flesh, is by faith in the Son of God, who loved me and gave Himself for me.' Then the mystery was opened, and I perceived there was joy in heaven over a sinner who had repented, and that that language, *John Woolman is dead*, meant no more than the death of my own will.

John Woolman, 1772

21.65 Art thou in the Darkness? Mind it not, for if thou dost it will fill thee more, but stand still and act not, and wait in patience till Light arises out of Darkness to lead thee. Art thou wounded in conscience? Feed not there, but abide in the Light which leads to Grace and Truth, which teaches to deny, and puts off the weight, and removes the cause, and brings saving health to Light.

James Nayler

21.66 Sometimes religion appears to be presented as offering easy cures for pain: have faith and God will mend your hurts; reach out to God and your woundedness will be healed. The Beatitude 'Blessed are they who mourn, for they shall be comforted' can be interpreted this way too, but the Latin root of the word 'comfort' means 'with strength' rather than 'at ease'. The Beatitude is not promising to take away our pain; indeed the inference is that the pain will remain with us. It does promise that God will cherish us and our wound, and help us draw a blessing from our distressed state.

S Jocelyn Burnell, 1989

21.67   *Release*

I was terrified I'd break down.
I did.
It didn't matter.

Rosalind M Baker, 1986

21.68   Andrew's dying was messy. We had to live with increasing weakness and incontinence, with pain, and with the irritations and discomforts of so many infections. We had to fight through it all, still holding hands, still loving.

Such things are hard, but few dyings are easy. Struggling with pain, fighting fear, mourning losses are indeed part of living. These do not make living with AIDS unique...

Let me say now that we have met only love from Friends – yet there are some to whom I have still not told the whole truth about Andrew's death...

There are times in meetings for worship when I have sat shaking with the call to minister from our experience of living with HIV and AIDS, yet I have held back. I have held back because I have been afraid. Afraid that Friends will not hear my ministry for that word AIDS; afraid I might break the unity of meeting or might break friendships I cherish. I still do not know if these fears are justified, but they are real. Facing AIDS can be a chance to grow in the things of God, but it has also torn lives apart.

I loved Andrew. He died after living with AIDS. These are facts of my life. They are facts of the life of the Religious Society of Friends. In our living and loving and dying I have found much to cherish as well as much that hurts, found growth as well as loss. My hope is that together we can share these things, together hold them in worship, prayer and love.

Iain Law, 1991

21.69   We have many devices to protect ourselves from sadness – naturally enough it is a distressing feeling...

And yet sadness ... is a very noble feeling if we bear it with dignity and render it into a sacrament. To try to run away from the awareness of the pain of sadness is tantamount to thinking of light without shadow; or love without the anxiety of possible separation; or life without death.

Fortunato Castillo, 1978

21.70   *Damaris Parker-Rhodes (1918-1986) studied Eastern mysticism and the holistic approach to health; her experience of cancer of which she died, brought her fresh insights into the Christian symbols with which she had been brought up.*

Following the operation all sense of God disappeared, and anyone who came to my bedside (and the love and visiting I received was one of the great treasures of my life) I asked to take my hand and mediate God's love to me. In fact healing and prayer surrounded me on every hand, although I myself felt cut off in complete inner aridity except when actually held in the inner place by someone taking my hand and praying.

1985

21.71   My first experience of healing came when I was very ill for many weeks with lung and respiratory problems and in an extremely physically weak condition. Whilst fighting for each very painful breath I began to think I might not recover and lay in a twilight world of sleep, pain and exhaustion but yet knowing 'Thy will be done'. It would have been so easy to let life slip at this point, but it was exactly then that I felt a surge of energy go through my body and I knew that it was right for me to to be given more time on earth and that I would recover. It felt as if I was being 'ticked off' for lacking faith. As that energy passed through me I remembered clearly and strongly a very dear member of my meeting and wondered if she was praying for my recovery. I continued to hold on to her image in my mind and began to feel the strength returning to my body. She later told me she had indeed prayed for me daily and had sometimes been joined by other Friends for intercession. I knew experientially I had been upheld in God's healing light and power and it is this experience which has made me so convinced of the healing ministry. I know there may be more mundane, matter-of-fact explanations for my recovery but *in extremis* and in great need I was reaching for far more than the mundane.

Joolz Saunders, 1994

21.72   When people ring us up for healing, they often ask, 'Are you Christians?' or, 'Do you believe in Jesus and the God of love?' We reply that we do believe in these things, and ask them what they believe in. Whatever they say, we can truthfully tell them, 'Fine! Come for healing. We won't try to change your beliefs. Healing can only make you a better Anglican, Catholic, Hindu, Buddhist, Jew, Atheist or whatever you are.' (Even better Quakers.)

In addition to its many religious forms, Healing also includes many arts and sciences. There is the art of listening, the art of smiling, the art of empathy, of knowing just what people need, and not rushing in to offer help that is not suitable. Then there is the healing that comes through prayer in its various forms, through the laying on of hands, through music and dance, painting and colour, through communion with and understanding of the world of nature, and through friendship.

Jim Pym, 1990

21.73   As we open ourselves to become the channel of God's healing grace we shall find that healing is given to those who pray as well as to those for whom we are praying.

Jack Dobbs, 1984

See also 2.81

Chapter 22

Close relationships

22.01   Love is the hardest lesson in Christianity; but, for that reason, it should be most our care to learn it.

William Penn, 1693

FRIENDSHIP

22.02   Our name, the Religious Society of Friends, suggests that we think of ourselves not only as Friends in the Truth, which the early Quakers saw themselves to be, but also as a society of friends, prizing friendship highly and recognising its value for the religious life.

In our intimate relationships, as in the wider community of our meeting, openness to one another can open us to the Holy Spirit and enable us to acknowledge that of God in our own hearts and in those of our friends.

1994

22.03   We are called to obedient love even though we may not be feeling very loving. Often it is through the performance of loving acts that loving feelings can be built up in us. We may start with small, perhaps very tiny steps. It is only as we begin to allow Christ's love to act in and through us that it can become a part of us.

Sandra Cronk, 1983

22.04   Throughout life, rejoice in every aspect of friendship. Blessed indeed are those who enjoy a rich diversity of friends and who participate in many varying relationships. We all have the capacity of being sons and daughters, sisters and brothers, uncles and aunts, wives and husbands, metaphorically if not through blood-relationships. As well we are all both teachers and learners, both thinkers and workers, both employees and employers, nurses, parents and neighbours. We are most fortunate in being friends and lovers. True friendships grow in depth, understanding and mutual respect, as friends value 'that of God' in one another.

Elizabeth Seale Carnall, 1981

22.05   There is a part of us which from childhood is absolutely alone. When we fall in love we imagine we have found an ultimate assuagement of loneliness. This is not so. In a true marriage or a near friendship what in fact is found is a companion in loneliness.

Damaris Parker-Rhodes, 1977

22.06   I wonder whether we do not need to rediscover the possibilities of a friendship in which the deepest areas of experience may be shared. Certainly that kind of openness seems to have existed in earlier generations among a group who were very significant in the life of the Society. Until this century it was not uncommon for Friends to travel in the ministry, following a real sense of leading in this direction. Often they went out in pairs, one older, one younger. The study of their travels shows, I think, that their friendship became one in which they could open to one another their struggles and failures, their hopes and visions, when they became for each other the way through to the presence of God. On their journeyings, too, they met with Friends in their homes, seeking times for worship and prayer together, sometimes with whole families, sometimes with individuals. In this way they shared help on the inner journey with those with whom they met.

Christopher Holdsworth, 1985

22.07   I came to realise that the best way to deepen my love of God was to use my experience of the love in my everyday life in all its variety, subtlety and uncertainty. Getting on with those I love is often a business demanding patience, discretion, tact and understanding. It gets complicated sometimes. It also gets strained, occasionally to the breaking point. But without expression it is barren. I show my love in the things I do, and I also show it by words of endearment.

These things are all part and parcel of one another. This is what worship should be like. This is the idiom in which we should speak to God.

John Punshon, 1987

22.08 Sensitivity is the art above all that we need to cultivate. I feel this with great force because I am still trying to learn it. I recall with sadness my insensitivity years ago to the difficulties of one of my closest friends. His marriage was breaking up and although I saw him regularly during the period, I was completely unaware of his unhappiness. With such a lesson in my background, I should have learnt by now – yet I still manage to tread hard on tender toes. All this makes me even more certain that if we are to speak to others, we first need to learn to listen to them with sensitivity.

George Gorman, 1981

22.09 Have you ever sat with a friend when in the course of an easy and pleasant conversation the talk took a new turn and you both listened avidly to the other and to something that was emerging in your visit? You found yourselves saying things that astonished you and finally you stopped talking and there was an immense naturalness about the long silent pause that followed. In that silent interval you were possessed by what you had discovered together. If this has happened to you, you know that when you come up out of such an experience, there is a memory of rapture and a feeling in the heart of having touched holy ground.

Douglas Steere, 1955

22.10 In friendship we are beyond law and obedience, beyond rules and commandments, beyond all constraint, in a world of freedom. But did not Jesus say, 'Ye are my friends if ye do whatsoever I command you'? Yes, he did. We, on our side, are apt to miss the quiet humour of his paradoxes. 'These are my commandments,' he goes on, 'that ye love one another'.

In other words, the friendship of Christ is realised in our friendships with one another. His command is that we rise above commandments, and therefore his obedience is perfect freedom. Make service your centre, with its laws and duties and self-sacrifice, and life is a bondage. Make friendship the centre and life is freedom.

John Macmurray, 1942

SEXUALITY

22.11   Human sexuality is a divine gift, forming part of the complex union of body, mind and spirit which is our humanity. The sexual expression of a loving relationship can bring delight, joy and fulfilment.

For many, a life-long faithful relationship gives the opportunity for the greatest personal development and for the experience of sexual love which is spiritual in its quality and deeply mysterious. Others may find fulfilment in different ways. Whatever the moral climate, a sexual relationship is never purely a private matter without consequences for wider human relationships. Its effect on the community, and especially on children, must always be considered. Sexual morality is an area of challenge and opportunity for living our testimonies to truth, nonviolence, equality, integrity and love.

In our *Advices* of 1964 we are reminded:

No relationship can be a right one which makes use of another person through selfish desire.

1994

22.12   Our sexuality is an integral part of our being human, giving warmth and power to all our loving. Yet it is difficult for us to love both fully and wisely; too easy often to be niggardly and cautious in giving of ourselves, or grasping and selfish in satisfying our desires. These failures will lead to stress and conflict; but painful as they are, such experiences can still be a means of growth in understanding and an eventual strengthening of a relationship.

Elizabeth Seale Carnall, 1981

22.13   No doubt from the earliest days of Christianity there have been men and women for whom the sexual relationship was illumined and deepened by the Christian message of love, for whom it expressed a true equality, an equal-sided valuation and respect, for whom coitus was an expression of tenderness and unity, not merely the gratification of animal urges. But it is one of the great tragedies of history that not until recent times has this implication of Christianity found public expression...

Sexual activity is essentially neither good nor evil; it is a normal biological activity which, like most other human activities, can be indulged in destructively or creatively. Further, if we take impulses and experiences that are potentially wholesome and in a large measure unavoidable and characterise these as sinful, we create a great volume of unnecessary guilt and an explosive tension within the personality. When, as so often happens, the impulse breaks through the restriction, it does so with a ruthlessness and destructive energy that might not otherwise have been there. A distorted Christianity must bear some of the blame for the sexual disorders of society.

Towards a Quaker view of sex, 1963

22.14 In the journey through life, as we grow and mature, live singly or in a relationship with others our sexuality will grow, develop and change. Our sexual needs, drives and fantasies will be different at different stages in our life – as a teenager, a partner, a parent, an older person. Our sexuality is, throughout, an expression of ourselves. It is an integral part of our humanity and as such is subject to the leadings of the spirit. We should therefore give thanks for our sexuality and seek to nurture it both within ourselves and in our loving relationships.

Bill Edgar, 1994

22.15 It is the nature and quality of a relationship that matters: one must not judge it by its outward appearance but by its inner worth. Homosexual affection can be as selfless as heterosexual affection, and therefore we cannot see that it is in some way morally worse.

Homosexual affection may of course be an emotion which some find aesthetically disgusting, but one cannot base Christian morality on a capacity for such disgust. Neither are we happy with the thought that all homosexual behaviour is sinful: motive and circumstances degrade or ennoble any act...

We see no reason why the physical nature of a sexual act should be the criterion by which the question whether or not it is moral should be decided. An act which (for example) expresses true affection between two individuals and gives pleasure to them both, does not seem to us to be sinful by reason alone of the fact that it is homosexual. The same criteria seem to us to apply whether a relationship is heterosexual or homosexual.

Towards a Quaker view of sex, 1963

22.16   We affirm the love of God for all people, whatever their sexual orientation, and our conviction that sexuality is an important part of human beings as created by God, so that to reject people on the grounds of their sexual [orientation] is a denial of God's creation... We realise that our sexual nature can be a cause of great pain as well as great joy. It is up to each one of us to recognise this pain, ... to reach out to others as best we can, and to reflect on our own shortcomings in loving others... We need to overcome our fear of what is strange or different, because we are all vulnerable; we all need love.

Wandsworth Preparative Meeting, 1989

22.17   I was once asked by a young man with end-stage AIDS whether he would be acceptable to God, since he was a homosexual. I shall never forget the look on his face. I could not answer that depth of despair with pious phrases about the inward light or that of God in everyone... It is impossible to address AIDS without addressing sexuality... Being taught that one's innate bodily responses and sexuality are sinful does not give one a good basis for building loving, creative, intimate relationships. This is a problem for some heterosexuals too. Very many people with illnesses such as HIV and AIDS feel alienated, outcasts, cut off from normal human society. In the face of the losses, actual or potential, which pile up in the course of illness – loss of health, of strength, of work, of sex, of income, of friends, of home, of independence, of choice, of life itself – one can quickly feel stripped of everything that gives one any sense of self-worth. It is but a short step from this to feeling that AIDS is God's punishment. Yet the gospel (good news) is that enlightened Christian teaching is about a God who suffers alongside us, and helps us to transcend loss and suffering.

Gordon Macphail, 1989

22.18   Where there is genuine tenderness, an openness to responsibility, and the seed of commitment, God is surely not shut out. Can we not say that God can enter any relationship in which there is a measure of selfless love? – and is not every generalisation we make qualified by this?

Towards a Quaker view of sex, 1963

22.19   The Yearly Meeting has struggled to find unity on this [subject of sexuality], which comes so close to the personal identity and choices of each one of us. We are still struggling for the words which will help us, so that we may come to know the balance which allows us both to deal with the personal tensions of our own response to sexuality and also to see ourselves as all equal in the sight of God.

The extracts in this section are an anthology of the evolving experience of Friends and meetings. While our own [individual] experience does not identify with every extract, we recognise, in love, the Friend whose experience is not our own. We pray for ourselves, that we may not divide but keep together in our hearts.

London Yearly Meeting, 1994

SHARING A HOME OR LIVING ALONE

22.20   Do you try to make your home a place of friendliness, refreshment and peace, where God becomes more real to all who live there and to those who visit it?

Queries, 1964

22.21   There are many ways of living together in a household where commitment and loving care are essential ingredients. For example: the care for an ageing parent by a daughter or son; brothers and sisters who live together for longer than many married couples; friends who share a home for many years; partners who, without the frame work and legal protection of marriage, nevertheless love and care for one another for the rest of their lives.

Whether the foundation of the shared home is marriage or not, the essence of good relationships remains the same. They hold within them commitment, acceptance, sharing and trust. These qualities help develop the difficult skill of giving others both enough space to grow at their own speed and also security, so that the vulnerability engendered by growth and change does not lead to possessiveness.

Many Friends living alone have made their homes a place of wel come and support for those who need warmth and friendship. It is often their own experience of being alone that has helped them to understand and to listen with love.

1994

22.22   *At the age of 16 William Caton, an early member of the Swarthmoor household, wrote in 1652 of the love that enfolded all who became part of Margaret Fell's home:*

Truly willing we were to sympathise and bear one with another, to be helpful one unto another, and in true and tender love to watch over one another. And, oh the love, mercy and power of God, which abounded to us, through us and among us; who shall declare it? And hence came that worthy family to be so renowned in the nation, the fame of which spread much among Friends. And the power and presence of the Lord being so much there with us, it was as a mean to induce many, even from far, to come thither, so that at one time there would have been Friends out of five or six counties... I was cherished and encouraged in the way of life by my entirely beloved friend Margaret Fell, who as a tender-hearted nursing-mother cared for me and was tender of me as if I had been one of her own chil dren; oh, the kindness, the respect and friendship which she showed me ought never to be forgotten by me.

22.23   *Testimony concerning Amy Lewis (1893-1951):*

In 1920 [Amy and Warren Lewis] joined the Society of Friends, and some years later moved to Eccles to establish the home which is inseparable from Amy Lewis's life and work. She did not allow her outside activities to impoverish her home, but rather enriched all her service with the generous warmth of her family life. She and her husband have shown us that under the exacting conditions of our modern world it is possible to build a new kind of Swarthmoor Hall; the outward circumstances may be different but the spirit is the same... Things were never easy materially, and faith and works, conjoined to prayer, were their principal resources. As the years went by, countless men and women, young and old, came to this home to talk out their problems and to share in its blessings.

Hardshaw East Monthly Meeting, 1951

22.24   In the busy years of home life the parents are upheld and strengthened by their dependence upon God and upon one another; the efficient running of the home, the simple hospitality, the happy atmosphere, are all outward signs of this three-fold inner relationship. Home-making is a Quaker service in its own right. It should be recognised as such and a proper balance preserved, so that other activities – even the claims of Quaker service in other fields – should not be allowed to hinder its growth.

1959

22.25   There is something quite special about relationship with one's grandchildren, perhaps most of all in earlier childhood, when one slips into the garden of Eden with them for a spell. I don't even want to analyse what is so happy-making about this two-way relationship, although I constantly dwell upon it as one of the remarkable bonus joys of these later years of life. It is an experience that I have tasted for more than twenty years now, with six very different variations on the same theme.

Ruth Fawell, 1987

22.26   Friends do not take readily to being cared for. 'Caring matters most' has been quoted to us when seeking direction during our active years. But many of us will find that we ourselves are in need of full care in our old age. This will not be easy. It calls for 'a different kind of living', as one Friend commented when answering questions about experience in a home for the elderly. Uprooted from familiar well-loved things, of house and neighbours, released from stabilising responsibilities (however small), there will be adjustments to be made.

But there are compensations and opportunities. Loss of physical well-being can bring a new experience of the strength of the Spirit which can overcome pain and suffering. A new and fuller understanding of prayer can come, given the time to study and practise how to pray. And in the experience of living in a Home with others, a deep sense of sharing the darkness and the light can lead to a sense of community not known before. Finally, living close to physical death (our own and that of others), we come to recognise death as a natural and often welcome event. Yet another movement of growth into the fullness of the knowledge of God.

Margaret L McNeill, 1990

22.27   *In 1989 Rachel Rowlands wrote of her experience of living in the Quaker Community at Bamford, Derbyshire:*

This idea of people having sufficient separate space – the families with their self-contained units, single people in individual bedsits and a flat – stems from early discussions when we recognised that many communities founder through lack of breathing space and privacy. There is still much scope for 'being communal': twice-daily meeting for worship, four o'clock tea in the main kitchen, looking after other people's children, borrowing this, lending a hand with that, communal housework, a shared meal followed by house meeting each Friday evening, entering into each other's joys and sorrows, celebrating birthdays, gardening, developing new skills together in work on the roof or down the manhole...

We are called to recognise each other's boundaries, strengths and weaknesses, to be assertive and learn to handle conflict constructively. We struggle to face, rather than evade, our conflicts and this has recently been the focus of our 'Mary' meetings, which, named after a facilitator who helped us initially, are the one type of meeting which everyone makes a firm commitment to attend. As meeting for worship is the cornerstone of our spiritual life, so these meetings are for the nitty-gritty of living together.

22.28   It is surely the fear of the unknown which holds Friends back. I am a heterosexual, married for 23 years, mother of children, and divorced. Only since moving to London have I come to have as close friends same-sex couples or singles, many of them members of the Society of Friends. As a divorcee I, like them, do not fit into the 'norm', and the hospitality, support and sheer caring I have received from them has often been in sharp contrast to that of 'straight' couples, who often seem too busy, or too embarrassed, to ask me to their homes in the evenings. I had many of the preconceptions others have. Thank God I have learnt differently, although I still undoubtedly make gaffes, as ignorance still dogs my words. Ignorance is excusable, but intolerance? Having known at first hand the desperate loneliness of being on one's own, I can still only guess at the loneliness of many isolated lesbians and gays.

Margaret Glover, 1988

22.29   God's love is ministered to most people through the love of our fellow human beings. Sometimes that love is expressed physically or sexually. For me and my lover John, God's love is given through our homosexual relationship. In common with other people who do not have children to raise, we are free from those demands to nurture other vital things. This includes our meeting and the wider Society of Friends.

We both draw on our love a great deal to give us the strength and courage to do the things to which God calls us... Our spiritual journey is a shared one. Sometimes the pitcher needs to be taken back to the fountain. In order to grow, I need my church to bless and uphold not just me as an individual, but also our relationship.

Gordon Macphail, 1989

The single life

22.30   The amount of solitude which is attainable or would be wholesome in the case of any individual life is a matter which each of us must judge for himself... A due proportion of solitude is one of the most important conditions of mental health. Therefore if it be our lot to stand apart from those close natural ties by which life is for most people shaped and filled, let us not be in haste to fill the gap; let us not carelessly or rashly throw away the opportunity of entering into that deeper and more continual acquaintance with the unseen and eternal things which is the natural and great compensation for the loss of easier joys. The loneliness which we rightly dread is not the absence of human faces and voices – it is the absence of love... Our wisdom therefore must lie in learning not to shrink from anything that may be in store for us, but so to grasp the master key of life as to be able to turn everything to good and fruitful account.

Caroline E Stephen, 1908

22.31 Singleness is a state in which many of us find ourselves... Some of us choose, for various reasons to remain single – an absorbing career perhaps or the care of others which we feel demands all we have to give and in which we find fulfilment. We all need to love and be loved and for some of us this need is met, and can be met, in all sorts of nourishing ways. We need to look for these ways and then recognise them with joy when they come to us.

For others of us though, this way would not be of our choosing and sometimes the path we tread is hard, barren and stony. There is for us an ache inside which does not go away. We long to be someone's nearest and dearest. We would like to have demands made upon us, to be needed, to be important for someone else's happiness and well-being. For some of us celibacy is a hard road – we long to be touched, caressed and for sexual union. What, we wonder, are we to do with the gift of our sexuality? In today's society we confuse sexuality with sex and fall into the trap of thinking we must have a sexual partner in order to express our sexuality. This is not true. Our sexuality belongs to us and there are many ways of expressing and taking delight in it.

We may fall into another trap – that of imagining that life with a partner is all bliss! Our partnered Friends will soon put us right on this, whilst rejoicing in all the good a happy partnership can bring.

All of us, partnered or single, need to feel that we belong, that we are valued and included – we need affirmation and recognition of who and what we are – we need, in our meeting especially, to make sure that this happens.

Jennifer Johnson, 1990

22.32 Many of us, widows or widowers, divorced or separated, homosexual and heterosexual, bachelors and spinsters, will be living alone for at least part of our lives. Some may still be grieving over the loss of a loved one, and whether that loss is caused by death or by separation, the need may be to have time in which to rediscover oneself as a single yet whole person, with needs and strengths, potentialities and achievements. Another may be enjoying freedom from commitment to another, but feel guilty about being self-centred. Yet others may be perplexed, even tormented, by their sexual drives and fantasies, and may be seeking ways of sublimation. Some may still feel the wounds of an earlier broken relationship and fear to take further risks, or may have experienced at one remove the tensions and hurts of an unhappy marriage. Some may have doubts about their own capacity to give happiness to a married partner or may have romantic ideas of finding the perfect partner, while yet others do not know why, without making any conscious choice, they have remained single. But underlying all these differences there is the common need to love and be loved.

Some Westminster Friends, 1990

MARRIAGE AND STEADFAST COMMITMENT

See also chapter 16 Quaker marriage procedure

22.33 Marriage is a context for a relationship, not a guarantee of its quality. The choice of a partner and the decision to marry are crucial, and meetings may be able to help in the process of discernment and the counselling of couples.

In marriage a private relationship becomes public, and thereby receives legitimacy, practical support and blessing from social institutions and the worshipping group. Above all, marriage gives at present the most accepted framework for the raising of children in a secure environment.

The institution of marriage is sometimes questioned, but a life-long loving relationship, whether within that framework or not, is nonetheless a cherished ideal. We have to acknowledge that the social climate and our attitudes towards marriage have undergone profound changes in the course of the twentieth century. Close relationships other than marriage have become common and their value increasingly recognised. There is a greater openness about the strains of marriage, and the pain of separation and divorce is now common in our Society.

Whilst believing that marriage is different and special, we recognise the value of other relationships and the single state. Those who choose to marry make a conscious choice that this is the right framework for their commitment.

Much of what earlier generations of Friends have thought and written about 'marriage and the Quaker home' can be applied more widely. The wisdom and experience of earlier Friends are valued even when their language and concepts are perceived as exclusive by today's standards.

1994

22.34   I met my husband-to-be, Kenneth Boulding, in the spring of 1941, at the very gathering at which I was taken into membership by the Religious Society of Friends... During our whirlwind courtship (sedately conducted at subsequent Quaker gatherings) I caught glimpses of a new understanding of what family might mean in an era when war clouds were shadowing the world. Not yet twenty-one I was overwhelmed by Kenneth's idea that through our marriage we were to found a colony of heaven. In that summer before our marriage, I had the awed feeling that I had somehow to reconstruct myself to be a person worthy of such a venture. I was so unready! The summer was already programmed. I was enrolled in a civilian training programme for women, designed to ready us for service in war-torn areas of Europe. At the training camp I struggled to prepare myself for the double task of marriage and community service. I prayed a lot. Could I be ready in time? I know now ... that one is never ready for the next step in life's journey. We learn what we need to know on the road itself.

In joining the Society of Friends that spring forty-six years ago, I committed myself to becoming a peacemaker. But I didn't know very much about peace-making. Kenneth Boulding, ten years older, served as a teacher-companion-guide. Entering the marriage we both saw our task as creating a home of peace from which to help to build a more peaceful world. When the impatiently awaited babies finally started coming in 1947, the practice of peace in the home became more difficult and challenging than when there were only two of us. But we knew we had to practise at home what we wanted for the world.

Elise Boulding, 1989

22.35   Never marry but for love; but see that thou lovest what is lovely. He that minds a body and not a soul has not the better part of that relation, and will consequently [lack] the noblest comfort of a married life.

Between a man and his wife nothing ought to rule but love... As love ought to bring them together, so it is the best way to keep them well together.

A husband and wife that love one another show their children and servants that they should do so too. Others visibly lose their authority in their families by their contempt of one another; and teach their children to be unnatural by their own examples.

Let not enjoyment lessen, but augment, affection; it being the basest of passions to like when we have not, what we slight when we possess.

Here it is we ought to search out our pleasure, where the field is large and full of variety, and of an enduring nature; sickness, poverty or disgrace being not able to shake it, because it is not under the moving influences of worldly contingencies.

Nothing can be more entire and without reserve; nothing more zealous, affectionate and sincere; nothing more contented and constant than such a couple, nor no greater temporal felicity than to be one of them.

William Penn, 1693

22.36   Having felt thee abundantly near this evening, I am free to write what revives for thy perusal, hoping it may be useful towards our rightly stepping along through time together. And first, dearly beloved, let me tell thee, that however short I may be of strict adherence to the Light of Life; yet it is my crown, my chiefest joy, to feel the holy harmonious influences and inshinings of the love of Jesus my Saviour upon my soul; and I feel that without this I must be miserable indeed. I also believe that the true enjoyment of the marriage union consists eminently in both being engaged to draw near to the Lord, and to act in his counsel; which I not only wish, but in a good degree expect, may be our happy case. If it should, though we have as it were a dry morsel to partake of, as to the things of this life; yet we may joy in the Lord, and rejoice in the God of our salvation.

Job Scott, 1780

22.37 To choose as a life partner one who shares your interests and enthusiasms, who makes a good friend as well as a good lover – whose personality and freedom you respect, who shares the belief that marriage is a religious act, and that the love that unites man and woman is part of the great love of God – these are some of the foundation stones of a happy marriage.

Ruth I Midgley, 1950

22.38 About this time we read the landmark publication of British Friends called *Towards a Quaker view of sex*... I think there is great validity in the insight of that pamphlet that what makes a relationship sinful is exploitation, not whether it is legal. We all know that a great deal of exploitation goes on in legal marriages. What makes any relationship, any action, right is caring – caring for the other person, for things, for the earth, and for oneself. George and I put words from Walt Whitman in our marriage ceremony to express what we wanted our marriage to be: 'a union of equal comrades'. I think that is a right goal for any relationship, not only between consenting adults, but between children and adults. George and I have been together forty-two years – we became engaged on February 22, 1935. Sometimes when I tell young people that I found marriage liberating, they respond, 'You've got to be kidding.' But it is true. We have kept the goal of being a union of equal comrades, granting each other space to be ourselves and to grow towards wholeness.

Elizabeth Watson, 1977

22.39 At the time of our marriage, early in the third decade of this century, we were not so knowledgeable about our sexuality as young people are today, although I suspect, as scientists, we knew as much, or more, than most people of our generation. This meant, however, that in early married life there was a definite period of adjustment before we were happily, and with mutual satisfaction, settled in our ways. Quite early we began to realise that however important the attractions of sex were, we were very dependent on other interests to unite us. We were fortunate to have such interests in common, which developed and made ever increasing demands on us, influencing the course of our lives. Wasn't it Saint-Exupéry, so widely read in our youth, who impressed on us that true love does not consist of gazing into each other's eyes, but turning faces outward together to face the world?

William G Sewell, 1982

22.40   *Testimony concerning Jessie Gadsden (1912-1990):*

Jessie and her companion Mary Mills were among a handful coming to Bewdley Meeting in the late 1950s when it was an allowed once-a-month-in-summer meeting for worship. When this small group of Friends were determined on a renewed preparative meeting, Jessie and Mary would be there early on Sunday pushing a murderously heavy hand-mower amongst the graves recently uncovered from three or four feet of grass and nettles.

Over the years her contribution to the home and life she shared with Mary was constant and faithful. It was a partnership and Jessie's support for Mary's dedicated work in school and in Guides seemed as unquestioning as Mary's was as the second pair of hands in Jessie's flower and vegetable garden.

This was Jessie's real world... But she always left the greenhouse or the bushes graciously for a caller at any time. 'Here's ...' Mary would call from her part of the garden, and no-one felt unwelcome. Their cakes and Jessie's home-made bread (not to mention gifts of vegetables, flowers and fruit!) made it hard for us to stay away.

Worcestershire & Shropshire Monthly Meeting, 1990

22.41   Marriage, says the Christian, is for life; and the wedding is a declaration that it is so. It is a fearsome declaration to make, and without the grace of God, arrogant and absurd...

This is why the wedding is an act of worship, and not merely a formal indication in a register office: because the Christian, saying these terrible things, dare not just nod them off before a clerk; but must come and put his vows into the hand of God, trusting that God will hold [the couple] where He wants them held. To turn a wedding into worship is to recognise that marriage is bigger than we are; that it is not just a pleasant arrangement we have made for our own convenience, but a vocation into which we have been drawn by nature and by God.

The truth is that very few marriages remain all the time, day and night, summer and winter, pleasant or convenient. We have to give things up for each other: sometimes hobbies and pastimes, habits of spending, friends. Some glib talkers about marriage say that we do not need to 'give up': we must enrich each other's lives, not rob them. But this is unreal... If we mean business about marriage, we shall throw a good deal overboard in painful but decisive abandon; we shall bring along with us whatever is shareable, and a few things that are not; and we shall discover new things that we never did alone, but which we can start together and use as the basis for 'mutual society, help and comfort, in prosperity and adversity'... Then the Christian knows he is committed, that he is in it for good or ill; and in a curious way the situation is lightened by the knowledge.

Harold Loukes, 1962

22.42   Love is the will to nurture life and growth in oneself and in another... Love is personal; it is the sacred trust of living things. Likewise, love is neither need nor dependency. 'I need you' is not the same as 'I love you'. Need as the basis of a relationship may lead one person to suffocate another through demands. Need may drive me to manipulate, intimidate, or coerce you into fulfilling me.

Love is so vastly different! It is freeing; it acknowledges the separateness of the beloved. It treasures the unique otherness of the beloved that is each one's contribution to the relationship. Love calls for submission and sacrifice. It does not seek to possess, but rather to empty itself in nurture of the loved one.

Donald A Green, 1982

22.43 Marriage is to be taken seriously, but not always in grim earnest; its problems take perspective from fun, adventure and fulfilment, and joy and sorrow are mingled together. We rejoice in success, but we must also be glad that we can console each other in failure. 'With my body I thee worship' is to many a blessed phrase: but while some find a perfect physical relationship easily, others reach it the hard way, and it is not less precious for that. It is wonderful never to quarrel, but it means missing the dear delight of making it up. Children bring joy and grief; some will have none and will miss both the grief and the joy. For some, there is a monogamy so entire that no other love ever touches it; but others 'fall in love' time and time again, and must learn to make riches of their affection without destroying their marriage or their friends. Let us thank God for what we share, which enables us to understand; and for the infinite variety in which each marriage stands alone.

We thank God, then, for the pleasures, joys and triumphs of marriage; for the cups of tea we bring each other, and the seedlings in the garden frame; for the domestic drama of meetings and partings, sickness and recovery; for the grace of occasional extravagance, flowers on birthdays and unexpected presents; for talk at evenings of the events of the day; for the ecstasy of caresses, for gay mockery at each other's follies; for plans and projects, fun and struggle; praying that we may neither neglect nor undervalue these things, nor be tempted to think of them as self-contained and self-sufficient.

1959

Celebration of commitment

For Quaker marriage procedure see chapter 16

22.44 According to George Fox the joining in marriage is God's work and that of no one else. Having found Friends rather late in life, when we were both approaching the age of sixty, the fact that in a Quaker marriage, partners marry each other appealed immensely to us and we so wished that this could have been our experience. Would it be possible to re-take our vows within a meeting for worship, we wondered? The elders of our meeting were approached and they could see no reason why, as part of the spoken ministry, we should not rise when we felt the time was right and make our commitment to each other using the words of the marriage ceremony but replacing the word 'take' with 'take again'. So on the first day of the ninth month 1991, exactly forty years to the day since we had been through a marriage service, we re-took our vows within a Quaker meeting for worship.

For us this was a wonderful experience. Several Friends felt moved to speak and after the meeting there were tears and hugs all round.

Don Grimsditch and Doris Mitchell-Grimsditch, 1994

For George Fox's words referred to here see 16.01

22.45 We recognise that many homosexual people play a full part in the life of the Society of Friends. There are homosexual couples who consider themselves to be married and believe that this is as much a testimony of divine grace as a heterosexual marriage. They miss the public recognition of this in a religious ceremony even though this could have no legal significance.

We have found the word 'marriage' difficult but we are clear that we have a responsibility to support all members of our meetings and to uphold them in their relationships. We can expect that some committed homosexual couples will ask their meetings for a celebration of their commitment to each other. Meetings already have the means whereby meetings for worship can be held for this purpose but we recognise that many find this a difficult matter. The acceptance of homosexuality distresses some Friends.

Meetings may well find it easier to consider this matter in connection with specific relationships rather than in the abstract, but we believe that meetings may be helped if something of the exercise of this meeting is shared with them.

Meeting for Sufferings, 1987

22.46 My partner and I decided we could not legally marry but were being led instead to have a 'celebration of commitment'. We came to this decision after a great deal of thought, and testing by family, (F)friends and our meeting. What seemed essential to us was the public witnessing of a commitment made before God by one's worshipping community who then also took a responsibility to uphold it. The form our relationship took had to be true to our inner conviction about equality, justice, honesty, openness and love. We could not participate in something that explicitly placed us above others in a hierarchy of worth. Neither could we ignore the valid criticisms raised by both homosexual people and the women's movement about the nature of the legal and conventional institution of marriage in our society.

We ended up having a wonderful 'celebration of commitment'. There was a warmth of overt, public support and acceptance at the meeting for worship for what we were doing and all its implications, not only for homosexual Friends but also in affirming the value of mutual spiritual ties in the face of devaluing legally binding ones. A number of (F)friends have told us how, for the first time in their lives, they had been made to feel truly included in such an event. For some it has made a huge difference in their relationship with their meeting in general.

We exchanged promises in the following words: 'I Alison/Mark choose to weave the strands of my life with those of yours, Mark/Alison, as a lifelong companion and a faithful lover. I am passionately committed to you, to us, and to our growth in God. I will dance with you, cry with you, laugh with you and pray with you. I know this won't be always easy but, with God's help, I will celebrate with you this gift that we have been given. Friends, I make this declaration before you and before God.'

Alison Davis and Mark Hughes, 1994

Facing change and difficulty

22.47   Finding a true and faithful loving relationship may well be the greatest experience of our lives. It is in close relationships that we are helped to understand both ourselves and our partners, and to change and grow, emotionally and spiritually. Such relationships are, however, challenging as well as fulfilling, and the fulfilment does not come without the challenge. Tension can be either the source of learning and growth or the cause of hostility and the breakdown of relationships. Responding to the Holy Spirit, both individually and together, we may grow through problems and pain as well as shared joys and interests, and find deeper understanding.

1994

22.48   True love is proven when the loved one begins to be not only the mysterious beckoner of destiny, but becomes also the occasion of dull indubitable duty. At a frontier of life when one partner begins to say to him or herself: 'How can I love any longer? But I must love', then sometimes steadfastness and faith have power to nurse into existence the new being needed as companion and lover. What a triumph when old love is transformed into a deeper surer new love which can accept more fully what each has, and the pair find a rebirth together in those things which are eternal, and through this a renewal of their everyday living.

1959

22.49   Unfaithfulness is not necessarily physical. There is a kind of mental or spiritual adultery which can damage all three people concerned. Hard as it is to forgive physical unfaithfulness, it is equally hard, and sometimes harder, to forgive an apparently innocent friendship between one partner and a third person if it creates a sense of exclusion and deprivation, and destroys the confidence, respect and affection promised in marriage.

Towards a Quaker view of sex, 1964

22.50   Some situations which cause pain or suffering are avoidable, so part of our learning must be to analyse the situation and see if this is such a case. If it is, we must try to prevent it happening again. But perhaps the most painful situations are those that are apparently beyond our control. Another part of our learning is to recognise that there is unfairness, uncertainty, fear, loneliness and hurt in this world; learning to accept that this is the nature of the world can, of itself, be painful.

Initially we may be able to do little, bound up in an acute, self-centred pain. As we try to cope with the anger, the pain and grief that come through some unhappy experience, we can learn a lot about the less-well-articulated, darker sides of our personality. These darker aspects should not be ignored. Although we tend to equate evil with darkness, we should remember that in the plant world roots grow in the dark. Darkness (and shadows) are as much a part of the natural order as light.

S Jocelyn Burnell, 1989

See also 10.23

PARENTS AND CHILDREN

The gift of children

22.51 Take the decision to have children joyfully, even though it is a hard one to take consciously, for many adaptations will be necessary for both partners. Consider carefully what each parent's responsibilities will be and how you will share the various tasks of childcare and domestic life. Freedom to step aside from the career path for a while may be valued by either partner, or the traditional roles may be cherished, or both parents may agree to share work in the home and outside it equally.

Elizabeth Seale Carnall, 1981

22.52 Our lives have recently been transformed by the birth of a baby daughter. Nothing we read or were told could prepare us for the total revolution in our lives which the arrival of this beautiful spirit into our midst has brought. I feel that I am living on a new plane since the muffled kicks and hiccups of pregnancy were revealed to be a perfect and wonderful human being...

That moment of timelessness and joy was like a glimpse of heaven, seen through the miracle of birth ... with the endless possibilities for discovery, growth and love for all three of us.

Peter Wallis, 1987

22.53   The birth of a baby to a couple is, if all goes well, a joyful experience. It is also a time of tremendous change for the parents, who will be taking on new roles and responsibilities. Not everyone will find the transition an easy one. The exclusive relationship between the couple has to change as together they develop new parenting skills. All parents hope for a 'perfect' child, so it can be a grave disappointment if the child should be handicapped in some way. It may not only result in their grieving for the future they will not now have but can also make them feel emotions such as guilt or anger, however irrational these feelings may seem to be. Similarly a miscarriage or stillbirth needs to be acknowledged and mourned for in the same way as any other death of a loved one. The birth of another child does not wipe out the sorrow for the child which was lost. And some couples will not have children at all. In a small minority of cases this will be by choice, but for others it may be a life-long affliction.

Loraine Brown, 1985

Difficult decisions in pregnancy

22.54   There are many reasons why a person may consider an abortion. Friends in this yearly meeting have no united view on abortion in general, nor is there agreement on principles. Understandably there has been little open sharing of experience, and therefore, sadly, almost no public discussion among Friends. As a result many individuals face a decision without feeling able to call on the practical and spiritual support of a gathered meeting or small group, without the help of Friends in seeking the Light. If a Friend asked in desperation, 'Where is God in all this? What can I do?' what could we say? We need accounts of personal experience that may offer starting points for a corporate search for that Light.

Anne Hosking, 1994

22.55   I once read in a feminist philosopher's work that only pacifists could logically be opposed to abortion since only they took an absolutist approach that it is always wrong to take life. But what if you are both a pacifist and one who believes that women should have a right to make choices about their own lives? Since we live in a society that both expects women to take responsibility for children and yet provides little financial or emotional support, how can we insist that a young woman takes on the burden of an unwanted child, or even the physical and emotional stress of bearing a child for adoption?

These could have remained theoretical questions. But life is not like that. A member of my family became pregnant and a decision had to be made quickly, within twenty-four hours. A baby was not intended, neither of the young people concerned had financial resources, a child would affect the establishment of at least one, if not two careers. I was the sole financial support of the family, so that I too could not care for a child.

It was clear to me then, it was clear to all of us, that an early abortion was the right answer. That does not mean that abortion itself is right, but that when human beings get into situations where every choice is wrong, then courageous and responsible decisions have to be made, and the consequences lived with.

I am still sure that in the circumstances the right choice was made. It was made by the person who had to live with the consequences, and it was made with family support. In a sense, an unborn child carried for all of us the costs of being a broken family in a broken world. But when I see and hold other peoples' babies, there is in my heart a grief which I cannot share, since it is not my secret, for the grandchild I never had and shall never know.

Anonymous, 1990

22.56   Modern genetic techniques place us in dilemmas not experienced by previous generations. When, after years of trying to conceive, I found I was expecting a baby, I insisted that it have its chromosomes checked. This was not because I thought that anything was wrong, but because I believed it to be irresponsible knowingly to bring a severely handicapped child into the world.

When the bad news came a decision had to be made quickly. I knew that even if it was born, my child would probably live for less than six months, unable to feed normally. Perhaps we would be advised to leave it in the hands of hospital staff to await its fate. Meanwhile I faced the rest of a pregnancy, supposedly a happy time, constantly telling people and convincing myself that my child was not going to be healthy. There would be no joyful preparation of cradle, clothes and toys for us. I also knew that the majority of babies with serious abnormalities abort naturally in the early part of pregnancy; but this time nature had left me to make the cruel choice.

With family support, I decided to end the pregnancy. I never saw my child – I was afraid to. There was no funeral, indeed to this day I do not know what happened to the body. We were left bereft: of the normal child we had longed for, of the child I had carried within me for those months, and, after a long waiting, of the possibility of another child. These griefs were hidden; we were not offered professional support; a pacifist among pacifists, I did not feel able to ask my meeting for theirs. Friends do not discuss the subject of abortion easily.

Then, from the darkness, came our miracle child, healthy and much loved. But I still look at those of an age that my first one would be now, and I feel the wound will never close.

Jane Heydecker, 1994

22.57 However one views it, and for whatever reason it is carried out, an abortion is a deliberate taking of a potential life. The arguments around the right to life versus the right to choose do little to help those who believe in personal morality yet whose religion lays down no hard and fast rules about moral issues such as abortion.

As a nurse who was asked to become involved in the procedure of therapeutic abortion I was forced to decide. My final decision, made after much heart-searching, was to say 'No'. As a result I had to move to a less conveniently placed hospital, but my decision was accepted and at no time was my livelihood threatened.

The right of medical personnel to choose not to become involved in the procedure of therapeutic abortion is enshrined in law. In my case I used my right to choose, but this left me with a dilemma. Where should I stand on another's right to choose to have an abortion? My choice was respected and my rights maintained. My responsibility had to be to respect another's choice and maintain their right to my compassion and understanding. To do less would make my decision nothing more than a pious declaration which ignored the very real pain suffered by many women who decide to have an abortion.

Pauline Condon, 1994

22.58 Faced with an unexpected and unwanted pregnancy Friends will no doubt consider the options open to them earnestly and prayerfully. The chosen course of action will not always be the same as each instance requires its own solution. Among the options is the possibility of having the baby and letting it be adopted. With loving counselling a mother can come to see that this course of action gives her baby the prospect of development within a loving family. It can give great joy to the adopting family. It is a solution which, if carried through in a spirit of love for the baby, can be an uplifting and positive one, emancipating the mother from feelings of sadness and guilt, and enabling the child to know that its mother was concerned to do the best she could for it.

More than twenty years ago we adopted a child. We and our three other children will always be grateful to the girl who not only carried and bore that child in spite of the difficulties, but had the courage to give the baby away. We hope that one day they may be able to meet again and she will know what a charming, talented and hard-working child she gave life to, and the great joy she gave to another family. It is not something we often speak of as we do not wish to add to the pain of others who make a difficult choice. We hope that Friends will always remember this option when involved with an unwanted pregnancy.

Anonymous, 1994

22.59 Although my wife had repeatedly expressed her aversion to babies and the idea of maternity even before we were married, I had lived in the hope and expectation that if 'it' happened, her feelings would change. After about eleven years 'it' did happen, accidentally and unplanned, and I waited for the transformation but in vain. My wife's distress at her condition was painful to bear and although I persuaded her to seek counselling, she saw abortion as the only way.

My feelings were very mixed. My yearning for parenthood was acute, yet, if I had been in her position, I would want to decide for myself what happened to my body, so I tried to give her all the support I could. Also the talk was all about 'battered babies' at that time, and as I could not bear the thought of exposing our child to the risk of maternal rejection, I saw that an abortion was inevitable.

The weather as I remember (for all this happened about twenty years ago) was perfect, bright and sunny when I took her to the hospital, a few miles away from where we lived. And the next day I went to work as usual, although my thoughts were far away. Late in the morning the strangest feeling came over me, a sense of intense desolation and emptiness, but at the same time a conviction that all was well and that my child was safe.

I found out later that the feeling occurred at the time my wife said she went down to the theatre and although the timing could have been coincidence and I could have been suffering a reaction to emotional strain, some would regard it as a spiritual experience. All I know is that it was comforting as well as painful and helped me to come to terms with my grief.

Anonymous, 1994

Pressures on parents

22.60   We recognise the new freedom and equality of those marriages in which both parents are able to pursue careers and to share the duties of the home. We are proud to think that in the past, by liberating women in the ministry and encouraging them in service, we have helped to create this pattern. But we know, too, that it brings its own tensions and dangers. If parents pursue their own interests and vocations (however worthy) without consideration for their families, the children will suffer. There are times when family calls must be put before all others, even those of our Society. We do not believe that rules of conduct can be strictly laid down, but we beg parents to be ready, in this as in other ways, to sacrifice monetary advantage, the pleasure of liberty, or the interests of their professional life, in order to preserve and build the family.

1959

22.61　I remember the time when I first instituted 'Mother's quiet time'. There was family resentment and I had feelings of trepidation and guilt. No, I would not come to the door, I would not settle a quarrel, I would not answer the phone, I was going to be all by myself without interruption! This started with a meagre half an hour and finally stretched into a much longer period, becoming an important ingredient in my lifestyle. It seemed to make the whole ensuing day more relaxed and less under pressure of feeling hyperactive.

Damaris Parker-Rhodes, 1985

22.62　I think parents need to be aware of how vital it is to leave everything to answer a young child's reaching out to you to 'come quickly' to share a sunset or the beauty of a discovered wild flower, or the trick of the pet dog, or to listen with full attention, no matter what seems prior on your agenda, when children burst into the house from school eager to have you listen to a tale of woe or a triumph they have experienced during the day. There is little question that if as a parent we have not taken the time really to listen to children when they are young, listened not only to their words but to their feelings behind the words, they are unlikely to want to come with their sharings in later life. Learning to listen to each other in families can help to make us better listeners to others and to the Inner Guide.

Dorothy Steere, 1984

22.63　Our children are given to us for a time to cherish, to protect, to nurture, and then to salute as they go their separate ways. They too have the light of God within, and a family should be a learning community in which children not only learn skills and values from parents, but in which adults learn new ways of experiencing things and seeing things through young eyes. From their birth on, let us cultivate the habit of dialogue and receptive listening. We should respect their right to grow into their own wholeness, not just the wholeness we may wish for them. If we lead fulfilling lives ourselves, we can avoid overprotecting them or trying to live through them... The family is a place to practise being 'valiant for the truth'. We can live lives of integrity, letting both 'yes' and 'no' come out of the depth of truth within us, careful of the truth in all our dealings, so that our words and our lives speak the same message. We cannot expect our children to be honest with us or anyone else if they hear us stretching the truth for convenience or personal gain. They are quick to catch such discrepancies. Moreover, we should trust them enough to be honest with them about family problems – disasters, serious illness, impending death. It is far harder on children not to know what is wrong.

Elizabeth Watson, 1980

22.64 'Write about the joys, traumas, challenges, insights or revelations of being a Quaker parent' said the letter in *The Friend*. Well, I've seen all those in the last sixteen years. Joy was there on becoming an adoptive parent, trauma on discovering our daughter's severe medical condition. The challenge came when adopting again and the revelations when knowing that sometimes we just could not cope.

Learning how to be an effective parent goes on and on, a learning which for me has been very revealing and given me insights into those parts of me which I did not care to discover. My experience has not been an easy one, but yet I feel very privileged to have been allowed to bring up someone else's children...

How should I have reacted when feeling angry, frustrated and physically exhausted? Those elements of gentleness, compassion and understanding which I want to apply have flown out of the window. No wonder I had times of great guilt feelings. Entrusted with the care of children not born to you gives a heightened sense of responsibility and the feeling that you must 'get it right', while always being more conscious of the approval of others. Adoption need not always bring difficulties and can be and is a wonderful experience. I feel very close to my children, perhaps closer than some parents feel to their natural children. I have tried to give them a sense of warmth and belonging, a feeling that they are loved and respected. They both know about their adoptions and if and when the time comes when they wish to know more than we can tell them about their backgrounds, I hope we shall be able to help and support them. Our extended family has always been totally supportive of our children, which has helped them to 'belong' through their growing years. Over the years too, we have come to see that the Meeting supported us like an extended family, propping us up in times of need and being available with advice and care.

Juliet Batten, 1994

The needs of children

22.65 Difficult and painful divorces; an alcoholic parent; the death of a small child or of a parent – how do children cope with these situations? Adults who find them difficult believe that children need to be protected from them. Are children indeed more robust than we think? Perhaps children are enabled to cope when they see that adults are coping.

But other 'difficult questions' will face children and us parents. How can we prepare children to withstand the drug abuse culture? To resist inappropriate touching and sexual abuse? Children need to be lovingly warned at an early age about possible dangers without filling them with fears about the future.

Perhaps more importantly, is there a Quakerly way of coping with the strong feelings of anger and guilt that can be aroused by family relationships, particularly when they are going wrong? Just being able to admit to having angry feelings can be strengthening. Is there a Quakerly way of discussing difficult issues within the family and of reaching decisions, perhaps in a 'family meeting' set in the context of worship? The family is a system in which each member needs to be allowed to assert her or his needs and have them met in the loving interaction of family life.

Douglas and Jenny Butterfield, 1986

22.66 Small babies cling to the mother's breast. They need comfort, warmth and cherishing, yet they can equally kick and scream to demonstrate their independent will. From the cradle to maturity the desire to belong and, at the same time, the need to assert our independent existence are in constant tension as we discover new facets of ourselves. At first a child sees the world as an extension of itself, but it learns quite quickly that other people have to be taken into account – either because parent figures enforce obedience or because the child wants to please those who nurture and bring it up. Whether the early environment is loving and caring or whether the child feels unwanted or rejected, each stage of growth is accompanied by joy and painful set-backs, by love and sometimes violent feelings of hatred or rage. A child that feels it is understood and loved will find it easier to develop inner security...

Development of personality is a continuing process – never completed. A child may be clear about its needs and wants, but then come the often tumultuous years of adolescence, of coming to terms with new and powerful sexual drives. Teenagers begin to realise themselves as separate and different from parents and friends. It is no easy task to live up to ideals and at the same time to accommodate rival claims and impulses. It is at this time that Quaker children often experience particular difficulties in adjusting to a world beyond their own home where values, standards and expectations are different from those they have grown up with. Do we try to understand the difficulties, stresses and failures of our growing children and make them fully aware that, come what may, they are still loved? This does not mean that we give them unlimited licence. They still need an adequate framework within which it is safe to experiment and rebel.

Rosalind Priestman, 1985

22.67 I am a product of multi-faceted parenting. I can boast about five parents and numerous other individuals and institutions that shaped me throughout my childhood and adolescence. As an adult approaching thirty I am only just beginning to recognise the riches of my experience, the pain and the joys. I long to talk to and read of others who have not been products of a nuclear family. We need to develop ways of supporting each other towards an understanding and acceptance of a chaotic family history...

My time with my foster parents provided me with a crucial stability and predictability into which each of my parents descended periodically to take me out or to take me on holiday. I was very confused as to who were my real parents, at one point being convinced that my foster family were, and these visitors were imposters. I cannot look back on that time as happy. I increasingly recognise and remember that I was a very unhappy child full of powerful feelings of needs which I felt I could not express for fear of losing what security I did have. These feelings are only now beginning to surface in consciously identifiable ways.

So on to boarding school, which very much became my parent... I wonder if some of the teachers there realised the full power of their 'parenting' and shaping me as an individual. There the Quaker philosophies planted themselves firmly into my personality as guiding lights. I was led into Quaker activities such as workcamps and the Leaveners. These became a vital part of my parenting as I began to feel part of an extended family, with a coherence, loving acceptance and creativity that met many of my still undefined but strongly felt needs...

I recognise that my experiences are not unique, although the specific combination may be. What I want to do is to allow myself all the feelings and thoughts that I may have repressed, both negative and positive, so that I may celebrate and mourn my lack and my experience of parenting.

Caroline Jones, 1994

22.68   It was only after working with 'Questabout' that I realised how hard it is to be a Quaker teenager. Young people are thrown together at school with all sorts of people, whereas their parents may well be able to move in a selected circle. The rules of social intercourse in schools are usually not as refined as in the office. While Dad and Mum may work beside people with whom they disagree, politeness will prevent too much overt friction; the boy or girl from a Quaker family in an area where the majority of people have more conservative attitudes may be made to feel very isolated. Not many people will be challenged to a fight at the office, but many Quaker teenagers have to defend daily a peace testimony which they may not yet have worked through for themselves. It is here that support from older Friends not in the immediate family can be vital.

Hugh Pyper, 1986

22.69   Parents will normally expect their children to be heterosexual, to provide them with '2.1 grandchildren' and share proudly in the conventional marriage pattern. Hence the shock of knowledge of homosexuality can be very real, and acceptance and love are not often an immediate reaction.

Yet the gay person desperately needs this reassurance and understanding, and longs for the parents to embrace them, and to extend this feeling to their partners as well; to be accepted and treated in the same happy way that would be accorded to a heterosexual relationship. For the gay person, coming to terms with the knowledge that they are gay in a world that is mainly heterosexual is difficult. The way is fraught with bigoted people, barriers of discrimination, hostility, sneers and even violence. Above all, they need support, love and complete acceptance in a joyful secure understanding from those close to them outside the gay community, from friends and relations, families including sisters and brothers and, in the case of Quakers, from Friends and meetings.

Arthur Hardy, 1989

Letting go

22.70 We cannot hope to transfer more than a little of our wisdom to our young people – if wisdom it is. We have increasingly to stand back as they grow older, knowing that the problem is passing out of our hands. They go off to college – or to live in a flat of their own, that aim and delight of so many young people. At last they have privacy, freedom from supervision and criticism, independence – but they are now fully exposed to all that we fear. Often they have much more self-confidence than is justified ('I can take care of myself'), and they little know that to avoid disaster they must avoid the circumstances in which the first sequence of events takes place. Many are carried headlong into sexual experiences that they did not intend or foresee.

This is the moment of disengagement, when parents must tell themselves that the young people are no longer their children and that they are outside their discipline. The decisions made by the young men and women mustn't be clouded by confusion with parental emotions ('How can you bear to hurt your mother?'). Parents cannot help being anxious, but they must bear that in themselves, not project it. They cannot live their children's lives for them.

It is also the moment for parents to tell themselves that their children are not alone. They are in the hands of God. God does not offer any kind of perfection in the actual circumstances of life, nor freedom from exposure to evil. Nor will parents ever be able – if they are honest – to look back over their experience of parenthood without being conscious of imperfections in their own understanding and handling of their children.

Kenneth C Barnes, 1960

22.71   We help [our children] not by futile attempts to 'keep them in the Society' (they must make their own explorations), but by recognising their own full stature as God's children. If we, the important adults in their lives, respect their integrity, their capacity to worship and experience God, then they will respect it too. If we share the skills that we are learning, then they will practise them too. If we are truly touched by God in worship, and realise that we can all, both young and old, open up to God, then we have made a good foundation. A lot else will follow, in the children's religious education, but God comes first.

Anne Hosking, 1984

22.72   Children who are brought up in freedom, who rightly make their own lives, do not naturally all separate themselves, but return, coming and going at their convenience to their old home. Their parents discover in time that instead of having children and grandchildren to love and care for, it is they themselves who are possessed by their children and their children's children. It is a reversal of earlier relationships that may lead so naturally to the happy closing of long married life.

William G Sewell, 1982

ENDING OF RELATIONSHIPS

22.73   Grieving is a proper and common response to any significant loss. It may be particularly difficult when the loss being mourned is not immediately obvious. It might, for example, be the death of love or the end of commitment in a relationship whose outward form continues; or the relationship which is ending may never have been made public. A meeting whose members know each other well may be a source of real support at times of crisis. Feeling valued as a member of the meeting and having the opportunity to continue giving service at such times can be very important to somebody whose life is disintegrating. We must be aware that it may, for a time, be beyond our capacity to help those who are grieving.

When ending a relationship entails breaking up a shared home, and especially when children are involved, it is important to consider the feelings of all those affected. Thoughtfulness cannot dissolve irreconcilable differences but loving attention may help to generate creative solutions even in unpromising circumstances.

Appropriate financial arrangements will have to be made by the partners for each other and for any dependents. It is essential that these arrangements are properly and clearly made, registered and kept. Against a background of loss of trust, this will not be easy but responsible financial conduct can assist all parties towards the slow process of rebuilding lives.

It should be borne in mind that the law on these topics is itself developing all the time and up-to-date professional advice should be obtained.

1994

See also 4.20-4.21, 10.23 & 20.74

22.74   Changes in ourselves and others may lead to relationships coming to an inevitable end. Whether the loved one is removed by death or by separation, the time of re-adjustment is stressful and difficult. We need time to mourn. We all know of the heartache and sometimes the liberation that divorce brings. We encounter these experiences in the Quaker community of our local meeting just as much as in our families and neighbourhood. There are many single-parent families and reconstituted families with step-children, where all those who are involved have been touched and deeply affected by the events that led up to the crisis and what followed. As a result, there are many people who are in great need of imaginative and ongoing support from their meeting. There will be feelings of bereavement, as of losing part of themselves, of loneliness, frustration, resentment and anxiety. This may lead to depression and an acute feeling of isolation, but it is then that we often discover new strengths in ourselves, and the value of true friendship... The ability to forgive and to accept the forgiveness of others may be the doorway that leads to new beginnings.

Rosalind Priestman, 1985

22.75   We need to encourage an understanding of, and action upon, our marriage testimony. This suggests three consequences for our meetings: we have to take greater care of those preparing for marriage;

we have to encourage the strengthening and enriching of all marriages; and we have to consider how to help those whose marriages are in crisis to deal with their spiritual responsibilities. This ... means having an understanding of our faith and of how we can reconcile the highest ideals with human failure. We must not give up the ideals just because acting on them is difficult. So we cannot say that the breaking of marriages is right. The attempt to reconcile, to forgive, to start again, must always be of first priority. However, from time to time, there may be situations where a couple have genuinely tried but have come to feel that their marriage is no longer sustainable. At this point, we have to recognise that Christianity places people and their needs before the keeping of rules. The question must become, what is now the most loving way forward for the family? It may be that the answer is ... separation or divorce. This must be an occasion for sorrow and grief at failure, but also of hope for new life. The role for members of the meeting may be to provide support and reassurance that they too discern that a right decision has been reached.

However, where people are married and especially where there are children, the commitment to be loving and faithful cannot be cancelled but has to be renegotiated for a new situation. The partners still have a responsibility to each other, to care about and support each other... Too many divorces result in hostility and bitterness. Where there has been a decision to part, couples may need help in determining what love for each other will mean in the future. Clearness committees, and perhaps a meeting for worship to mark a divorce and to make a new commitment to lifelong friendship, may be ways.

'Chris', 1986

22.76   If a couple have failed, and broken away, and suffered; and if there comes into their lives a new hope of building a home, and they approach it responsibly, gravely; then it is surely right ... to stand by them in love and sympathy and hold them up before the Lord. If this is not so, then 'sins-in-marriage' become a special sort of unforgivable sin, beyond the reach of the grace of God. But as any married couple know, 'sins-in-marriage' are easy to commit and hard to avoid. Other sins, like robbing a bank, are easier to avoid, yet are open to forgiveness...

The Quaker view is that this forgiveness is part of God's intention, and that the business of the Church is not to judge but to inspire and sustain: not to say to a quarrelling couple, 'We shall not bless you if you drift apart', but 'We will try to help you now in your quarrel. And if you fail we will still try to help you to find God's will for you then.' It is thus that the sanctity of marriage is asserted, rather than in the denial of a new start.

Harold Loukes, 1962

22.77   Years after my husband had left me and our children I was very ashamed at how much private anger and resentment I still felt towards him. I confessed this to a very dear Friend, Maria Bruce, who was surprised and said: 'But your anger and resentment have sustained you – without them you might have sunk into depression or despair. So don't be ashamed of them – you have used them to good purpose.' I never felt either guilt or anger again.

Anonymous, c 1980

22.78   For me the certain realisation of God came at the time of the breakdown of my marriage. The unthinkable had happened and I seemed to be at my lowest state physically and mentally. There seemed to be no present and no future but only a nightmare of dark uncertainty. One distinct message reached me: to 'go under' was out of the question, I could only start again, learn from my mistakes and take this second chance at life that I had been given. I found a strength within I did not know I had, and I believe now that it came from the prayers and loving support of so many people round me.

This rebirth was for me a peak experience, the memory of which is a constant reassurance in times of emptiness and doubt. Facing the future, even with a sure faith, is not easy. I am cautious at every step forward, taking time and believing I shall be told where to go and what to do. Waiting patiently and creatively is at times unbearably difficult but I know it must be so.

'For the vision is yet for an appointed time, but at the end it shall speak, and not lie: though it tarry, wait for it: because it will surely come.' (Hab 2:3)

Jennifer Morris, 1980

22.79   When a divorced or widowed person wishes to remarry it is a time for rejoicing. Remarriage is a new commitment to the ideal of life-long partnership and it takes much faith, strength and courage to remarry following the traumatic loss of a spouse. While there are many differences between losing a partner by death and by divorce there are also basic similarities and problems. Anger, hurt, resentment, loneliness, feelings of failure, unreal expectations are only a few of the spectres from the past which may haunt a remarriage. Realistically coming to grips with problems and seeking solutions before the wedding may give a remarriage the solid base it needs.

Family Life Sub-committee of New England Yearly Meeting, 1985

See 16.17 & 16.19-16.21

BEREAVEMENT

22.80   Maybe we face the fact of death for the first time when someone near and precious to us dies, and we then wake up to wrestle spiritually with the feelings of anger, dismay and acute deprivation that take us by surprise and question our hard-won faith. Or we may be called upon to stand by another person suffering great grief in bereavement. It is through such experiences that we struggle towards an attitude of our own towards death, so that we can speak from where we stand, and from the acceptance of the strange and paradoxical nature of death as of life.

Ruth Fawell, 1987

22.81   Loneliness after loss is a bitter and unproductive fruit that generally has to be eaten, skin, stone and all. Meanwhile the table bearing the accustomed spiritual refreshment has vanished, as though it never existed.

In the immediate shock of loss there is help. Friends rally, nature supplies an anaesthetic, the doctor offers valium. The crux comes later, just when you supposed the worst was past: companions consider the crisis over and return to their own affairs; the first sharp sting has worn off, and you will have decided to give up drugs. You have no idea what is lying in wait.

But now the real battle begins, the formidable adjustment has to be made. The caring and the sharing will never come back, at least in their past form, and a cold, apparently comfortless, independence has to be shaped to create a life of value. The temptation is to look round for a substitute for the one lost – but people grieving are not their normal selves, they are off balance and their judgment is impaired. A new companionship, if it is to be, is like happiness: no good searching for it, if it arrives it will be as a by-product.

The other temptation is to shirk experiencing the loss to the full when the time has come. A readiness and an openness to the approach of that dark night are necessary. Easy to fill the conscious mind with work, or a contrived 'pleasure-seeking', or do-gooding. The unconscious is preparing the pit, and down into it you will eventually be driven. Better go willingly, with all your armour on. For this is in fact the training ground of your spirit, where you will learn how much, through your own pain, you have to offer to others. And so the first and greatest step out of the dark place becomes recognisable: self-absorption begins to give way to empathy with a world of suffering you previously didn't know existed. People in the first shock of grief will be drawn to you, and you, no longer a newcomer to that world, will have found your listening skills.

As to that delicious and sustaining food you were accustomed in happier times to peck at, why, there it is again, and you haven't recognised it. The former sustenance was only fit for children, and has been replaced by helpings of insight appropriate to your increased maturity.

Margery Still, 1990

22.82   I thought back to my own times of sadness. They had been acute and I had prayed for relief. But gradually I had felt towards the awareness that there was a harsh reality about pain and sadness more tangible than words and phrases. To write about pain is to run into the danger of wrapping up sadness in words and pushing it outside. But sadness had brought home to me that all wisdom fails, all books are empty, in the face of the inescapable experience of pain. Sadness has its own authority.

It built a bridge to others. But to do this the pain had to be accepted, acknowledged as a companion. If pain brought bitterness and an irresistible desire to blame others and punish them, then it was isolating. If it was accepted as a personal burden, it opened a door to the souls of others seeking answers to the mystery of suffering.

I was also made aware that when I had met other people of different faiths or of none, who seemed to know the same experience of loss and bewilderment and search below the level of words and creeds, then we found that, despite differences, we were strangely at one.

Could this be the path to a new sense of unity, the community of those who had known pain, and thence had found depth, so that creeds and traditions became but signposts to an acceptance of sadness and an entry into a depth where we found harmony with each other? Was this the way forward to a deeper unity with people of other religions or indeed of none? Perhaps we could start with the simple discovery that words divide and sadness unites.

Robert Tod, 1989

22.83   The good minister who spoke at the baby's funeral service said, 'Do not be afraid of crying for him, because tears of love are able to heal the wounds of love. Such wounds are not healed by forgetting, but by remembering in such a way that memories are healed. The saints of old were wise when they spoke of tears as a gift, a healing flood to wash clean the soul.'

And God shall wipe away all tears from their eyes ... blessed are they that mourn for they shall be comforted. But there is no comfort now, there are only the empty arms and the empty cot. How are we to live with this emptiness which will never be filled, the broken promise of a life that never unfolded? ...

Anger, there is so much anger. Anger for a life denied is a wholesome healing anger. And if part of that is anger at a God who we thought was kind, and who now brutally turns his back, then so be it...

A God we cannot be honest with is no God. If we bow the head and say, Thy will be done, when our heart is aflame with protest, we only increase our own pain. Better to rail, rail on God at the passing into night of this small sweet innocence than to assume unreal acceptance. And then, with small steps, treading the way of sorrows, we may gradually, or perhaps with blinding suddenness, look up from the dark road and see – see that He has been treading the Way with us, holding us when we faltered, giving us the strength to go hesitatingly forward.

Sheila Bovell, 1988

22.84   *The following experience relates to the death of his son Lowell at the age of 11, while Rufus Jones was on a visit to England in 1903:*

The night before landing in Liverpool I awoke in my berth with a strange sense of trouble and sadness. As I lay wondering what it meant, I felt myself invaded by a Presence and held by Everlasting Arms. It was the most extraordinary experience I had ever had. But I had no intimation that anything was happening to Lowell. When we landed in Liverpool a cable informed me that he was desperately ill, and a second cable, in answer to one from me, brought the dreadful news that he was gone. When the news reached my friend John Wilhelm Rowntree, he experienced a profound sense of Divine Presence enfolding him and me, and his comfort and love were an immense help to me in my trial... I know now, as I look back across the years, that nothing has carried me up into the life of God, or done more to open out the infinite meaning of love, than the fact that love can span this break of separation, can pass beyond the visible and hold right on across the chasm. The mystic union has not broken and knows no end.

22.85   It was just five words on a quiet Sunday afternoon that changed our lives: 'Your son has been killed'. An unbelievable, shocking message. I was split into two parts, half knew what had to be done but the other half was paralysed. I should never see my son again, never hear him speak, never touch him and never tell him our news. Never, never, never – what a terrible word! Never again do what I so much loved. What a hellish thought. Never again tell him by a smile and a wink how much I loved him. Never, oh hateful word. My heart was cut out and I was overwhelmed by grief...

It is hard to find consolation in the written word, but it is there. Dear William Penn: 'And this is the comfort of the good, the grave cannot hold them...' We grasp at that hope and then, when quite unprepared, there is a feeling, a presence which cheers the heart. Yes, I am sure our son is still hereabouts...

Somehow in the depths I feel sure that life is continuous through the grave. It is like a stitch of embroidery which appears above the canvas, runs along and is seen, then dips back below out of sight. The thread, the wool is continuous and only appears to disappear. Indeed I had a strong feeling that only humans need starts and finishes, beginnings and endings. In the real spiritual world there are no starts and ends, all space, time and life are boundless and eternal. This feeling has been so strong it is now a great support...

It is impossible now to watch the news unmoved, to see repeated daily all over the world tragedies and weeping parents. We must suffer in this world if we are to understand the suffering of others. One must pluck this lesson of understanding from the icy pain of grief.

Peter Tatton-Brown, 1989

22.86 Losing a child is devastating. When that child, at any age, finds life so unbearable that he destroys himself, for the mother who conceived, carried and then bore him the pain is terrible.

We each have to find our own way through such experiences, and these ways will vary. Always first is the help given through the love and understanding of those closest to us, and those near enough to suffer with us...

Thank heaven this first desolation doesn't last for ever, nor do the various physical ills one can be afflicted by when grieving, and family and friends eventually become real again, and their love and care a comfort...

In the extreme need of early days the hills brought their healing. I went out again on my solitary walks, not able ... to reach the tops, but with my eyes on their strength and their changing beauty. And in time ... they brought joy – joy that in a mysterious way is the other side of the coin from pain.

Joan Fitch, 1988

22.87 On the morning of Frances' death, as I stood by her bedside, I made a secret resolve somewhere deep in my being which has only recently come to the surface. I made an agreement with God that from that day onward, everything I have to say about God, everything I have to say theologically, has to stand with me by Frances' bedside. If it cannot stand at the side of death, if it cannot stand by the side of a fifty-five-year-old woman who wanted to live to see the trees again, it had better not stand at all because it is probably not worth very much.

Zoe White, 1988

22.88 My father chose to end his life, after three years of chronic pain and illness which increasingly robbed him of his faculties. Towards the end of his life he came to resent medical science, which provided oxygen for sixteen hours a day to keep him alive. His life was being unnaturally prolonged and he felt he had a right to end it when his pain and suffering became intolerable.

During the years of his illness I saw my father change from caring parent to dependent child; a brave man, overwhelmed by pain and immobility, became a broken man. Yet in those years of caring I came to know my father in a way I had never done when I was a child. I had long discussions with him, gave him treats, took him to his favourite places; an opportunity to give to someone who had given so much to me.

My meeting helped sustain me. My father was constantly on our healing list. I was surrounded with love and support when I came to meeting with tears of frustration and despair. After his death, meeting helped me to celebrate his life and supported me in my grieving and recovery from emotional exhaustion. I can now see my father's decision as an act of courage.

Vivien Whitaker, 1994

22.89   Few things make us feel more inadequate than being faced with another's grief. Although every grief is unique yet there are feelings common to many or all griefs. It helps us to be ready to stand by someone in [their] loss if we know a little of what to expect... Grieving is a necessary and arduous task. It should not be a state but a process; but the griever needs courage and support from others to go right through it and not get 'stuck' at some point.

Death comes in so many forms. Some deaths leave us sad for a time but do not really upset the balance of our lives, especially if the death was of an elderly person, quietly rounding off a full and happy life... Whilst waiting a long time for an expected death can be a great strain, it does give the people involved time to adjust and work through some of their feelings. On the other hand, sudden death can bring an overwhelming shock. The survivors are left with a great sense of the precariousness of existence; the experience can be shattering, a permanent alteration of life. Some are broken by it completely, and in the desire to help it is as well to be aware of this possibility.

However much a death has been expected and prepared for, it is still a shock when the moment comes. This shock produces a numbness at first which is merciful. It may enable the bereaved person to carry out the practical tasks which follow a death. But it may not. If we are sensitive we will see what help the bereaved person needs... How often we hear people say in those early days, 'She is being marvellous'. But this stage passes, and a period of great inner chaos can follow... [The] loss of one's partner can be one of the severest forms of psychological stress. The emotions can be quite overwhelming. Some say it feels like insanity...

Slowly life can be found to have meaning again, and at the heart of that meaning lies the word 'love'. 'Growth into true life', wrote one widow, 'lies in love of one another. We have the choice of letting grief shadow our lives or growing from it.' This healing love is beyond us and within us, and continually seeks us out. Those whose privilege it has been to come right through grief know this in a deep and personal way. They can in their turn reach out to others in distress. The true meaning of the word 'compassion' is 'suffering together with someone'. Perhaps they have discovered for themselves that the sense of the absence of God which came with the depression made them know how much they need God.

Diana Lampen, 1979

22.90 *Margaret Torrie, with the help of her husband, Alfred, and others, founded CRUSE in 1958 to help widows and their families. Its work helped to change social attitudes towards widowhood and to break through the existing taboos on death. She later wrote from her experience of the counselling service thus established:*

There are clearly-marked signposts which, if followed, lead the way to recovery. First there has to be the wish, however transient, to find the way to better things. It is the beginning of hope, that basic ingredient for all life. From there, confidence and belief develop, and the certainty that in spite of all evidence to the contrary, good is in us and around us offering support. In such a situation of positive thinking we cease to be dreamers and accept fully our present lot. It is the material from which we are to build our future, whether long or short in time... The remarkable discovery we can make is that love has not deserted us, and that it is available to us now in a new way. Our own willingness to love and to give in the world about us is the secret of recovery and the new beginning.

1970

22.91 After we passed our eightieth birthdays, we had to admit that the days of our autumn had arrived. We had lived together long lives of interest and adventure; in many ways we knew they were complete. Younger folk were coming along to take our places. Life was good and we still enjoyed it; but we recognised that each day was a bonus, to be accepted with grateful thanks. As the fires of life sank lower, we knew that the bonus days must end, and the life-long partnership must close. When after increasing weakness the time came for my wife to leave us, grief was lost in the joy of a life well lived and thankfulness for the many years it had been shared with mine.

William G Sewell, 1982

22.92 On the occasion of a funeral, words of comfort and reassurance may be found in the Bible and other spiritually profound writings, including those of Friends. The reading of an appropriate passage chosen with sensitivity to the bereaved and the circumstances of their bereavement, can minister to the varied needs of those present and deepen the quality of their worship.

1994

See 17.01-17.10

22.93 There are lives so rounded and crowned by their completed deeds of love, that death seems to have appeared in the fulness of their prime only to consecrate them for ever; others stand apart from human ties in a solitude which makes time seem of little consequence, and the grave a not unfamiliar country... We do not know to what unfathomable necessities the times and seasons of life and death may correspond; and as little do we know, in looking at each other's lives, what may be unfolding or what may be concluded, as seen from within. That which seems to others a cutting short of activity, may be to ourselves the laying down of arms no longer needed; our eyes may see the haven, where our friends can see only the storm; or if we cannot see a fitness in the time of our death, is that a strange thing in such a life as this?

Caroline E Stephen, 1908

22.94 Love bridges death. We are comrades of those who are gone; though death separate us, their work, their fortitude, their love shall be ours, and we will adventure with hope, and in the spirit and strength of our great comrade of Galilee, who was acquainted with grief and knew the shadows of Gethsemane, to fight the good fight of faith.

John Wilhelm Rowntree, 1905

22.95 The truest end of life, is to know the life that never ends. He that makes this his care, will find it his crown at last. And he that lives to live ever, never fears dying: nor can the means be terrible to him that heartily believes the end.

For though death be a dark passage, it leads to immortality, and that's recompense enough for suffering of it. And yet faith lights us, even through the grave, being the evidence of things not seen.

And this is the comfort of the good, that the grave cannot hold them, and that they live as soon as they die. For death is no more than a turning of us over from time to eternity. Death, then, being the way and condition of life, we cannot love to live, if we cannot bear to die.

They that love beyond the world cannot be separated by it. Death cannot kill what never dies. Nor can spirits ever be divided that love and live in the same Divine Principle, the root and record of their friendship. If absence be not death, neither is theirs.

Death is but crossing the world, as friends do the seas; they live in one another still. For they must needs be present, that love and live in that which is omnipresent. In this divine glass, they see face to face; and their converse is free, as well as pure.

This is the comfort of friends, that though they may be said to die, yet their friendship and society are, in the best sense, ever present, because immortal.

William Penn, 1693

See also 21.49-21.58 for extracts on facing death & chapter 17 Quaker funerals and memorial meetings

Chapter 23

Social responsibility

FAITH AND ACTION

23.01 Remember your responsibility as citizens for the government of your town and country, and do not shirk the effort and time this may demand. Do not be content to accept things as they are, but keep an alert and questioning mind. Seek to discover the causes of social unrest, injustice and fear; try to discern the new growing-points in social and economic life. Work for an order of society which will allow men and women to develop their capacities and will foster their desire to serve.

Advices, 1964

23.02 True godliness don't turn men out of the world but enables them to live better in it and excites their endeavours to mend it... Christians should keep the helm and guide the vessel to its port; not meanly steal out at the stern of the world and leave those that are in it without a pilot to be driven by the fury of evil times upon the rock or sand of ruin.

William Penn, 1682

23.03 We know that Jesus identified himself with the suffering and the sinful, the poor and the oppressed. We know that he went out of his way to befriend social outcasts. We know that he warned us against the deceitfulness of riches, that wealth and great possessions so easily come between us and God, and divide us from our neighbours. The worship of middle class comfort is surely a side-chapel in the temple of Mammon. It attracts large congregations, and Friends have been known to frequent it. We know that Jesus had compassion on the multitude and taught them many things concerning the Kingdom. He respected the common folk, appealed to them and was more hopeful of a response from them than from the well-to-do, the clever and the learned. Yet he never flattered the workers, never fostered in them feelings of envy and hatred, and never urged them to press for their own interests ruthlessly and fight the class-war to the finish. He called them to love their enemies and to pray for them that despitefully use them. Yet the very fact that he appealed to the humble and meek leads up to ... 'the discovery that the blessing and upraising of the masses are the fundamental interest of society'. In brief, he makes us all ashamed that we are not all out in caring for our fellow-men.

H G Wood, 1958

23.04   The duty of the Society of Friends is to be the voice of the oppressed but [also] to be conscious that we ourselves are part of that oppression. Uncomfortably we stand with one foot in the kingdom of this world and with the other in the Eternal Kingdom. Seldom can we keep the inward and outward working of love in balance, let alone the consciousness of living both in time and in eternity, in timelessness. Let us not be beguiled into thinking that political action is all that is asked of us, nor that our personal relationship with God excuses us from actively confronting the evil in this world. The political and social struggles must be waged, but a person is more and needs more than politics, else we are in danger of gaining the whole world but losing our souls.

Eva I Pinthus, 1987

23.05   Evils which have struck their roots deep in the fabric of human society are often accepted, even by the best minds, as part of the providential ordering of life. They lurk unsuspected in the system of things until men of keen vision and heroic heart drag them into the light, or until their insolent power visibly threatens human welfare.

William Charles Braithwaite, 1919

23.06   'Politics' cannot be relegated to some outer place, but must be recognised as one side of life, which is as much the concern of religious people and of a religious body as any other part of life. Nay, more than this, the ordering of the life of man in a community, so that he may have the chance of a full development, is and always has been one of the main concerns of Quakerism.

Lucy F Morland, 1919

23.07   *The testimony of Marsden Monthly Meeting concerning John Bright (1811-1889), who was a member of parliament for over 40 years and held ministerial office, shows how he carried the calm strength of his religious faith into his political life.*

His deep sense of responsibility in the sight of God, and his intense human sympathy were the most powerful influences in drawing him from business into public life; and his natural nervousness was thus overcome by his sympathetic nature taking up the cause of the poor and the wronged. Of his public speeches it might be said, *he believed and therefore he spoke*. His aim was not popularity or party triumph, but the hope of advancing the cause of Truth and Right so far as he saw it...

Although at one time there were grave doubts in the minds of many Friends as to whether it was desirable for members of our Society to engage in active political life ... it has been evident in John Bright's case that he entered upon it under a deep sense of duty, and that he endeavoured to carry his Christianity with him into all his public life.

23.08   'Two sins have my people committed; they have forsaken me, a spring of living water, and they have hewn themselves cisterns, cracked cisterns that can hold no water' (Jer 2:13). I know of no better description of the world we live in than that. We have forgotten that we need the life-giving water of the holy spirit if the material element of the world in which we live is not, sooner or later, to turn into dust and ashes; and we have developed social institutions which cannot hold or channel the life-giving water anyway...

As Christians we need to see ourselves as God's plumbers, working on tanks and channels for the living water that can quicken the daily life of men, women and children... Jesus taught us about patterns of living that make for wholeness as we and our neighbours care for one another and build one another up. And all the patterns that Jesus showed us of cisterns and channels of caring and service challenge the patterns of mammon that offer quicker and more showy results, but that end in the debris of a possessive society that allows the living water to run away into the sand. Good plumbers build to last; they don't fall for fashions that rust and fade and crack.

Seventeenth-century Friends were good plumbers. In and out of season, in and out of jail, in and out of court, counting house and farmstead, our Quaker forebears challenged the conventions of the day – in politics, in commerce, in the law, in the established church, in social etiquette, in education, in attitudes to war, poverty and crime. In face of the sterile institutions of their day they found living answers about the ways in which men and women might go about their business of living together.

Roger Wilson, 1976

23.09 We are all the poorer for the crushing of one man, since the dimming of the Light anywhere darkens us all.

Michael Sorensen, 1986

23.10 We need both a deeper spirituality and a more outspoken witness. If our spirituality can reach the depths of authentic prayer, our lives will become an authentic witness for justice, peace and the integrity of creation, a witness which becomes the context for our prayer. Out of the depths of authentic prayer comes a longing for peace and a passion for justice. And our response to violence and injustice is to pray more deeply, because only God can show us the way out of the mess that the world is in. And only God gives us the strength to follow that Way.

Gordon Matthews, 1989

CORPORATE RESPONSIBILITY

23.11 We are not for names, nor men, nor titles of Government, nor are we for this party nor against the other … but we are for justice and mercy and truth and peace and true freedom, that these may be exalted in our nation, and that goodness, righteousness, meekness, temperance, peace and unity with God, and with one another, that these things may abound.

Edward Burrough, 1659

23.12   The word 'testimony' is used by Quakers to describe a witness to the living truth within the human heart as it is acted out in everyday life. It is not a form of words, but a mode of life based on the realisation that there is that of God in everybody, that all human beings are equal, that all life is interconnected. It is affirmative but may lead to action that runs counter to certain practices currently accepted in society at large. Hence a pro-peace stance may become an anti-war protest, and a witness to the sacredness of human life may lead to protests against capital punishment. These testimonies reflect the corporate beliefs of the Society, however much individual Quakers may interpret them differently according to their own light. They are not optional extras, but fruits that grow from the very tree of faith.

Harvey Gillman, 1988

23.13   Seeking to live at all times in a divine order of life, Quakers have always counted social service part of Christianity. In fidelity to the genius of their inward experience, they have set themselves the task of developing their own spiritual sensitiveness to the light of truth; and have then resolutely confronted the unawakened conscience of the world with the demands of the new light, and have borne witness to it with undaunted patience. This has resulted in progressive enlightenment for themselves, and in the slow but sure triumph of many of the causes of which they have become champions. The reform of the criminal law, the improvement of prisons, the suppression of the slave-trade and of the institution of slavery, the abolition of the opium traffic, the protection of native races, the repeal of the state regulation of vice, the emancipation of women, have all been powerfully helped to victory – however incomplete – by Quaker action on these lines, side by side with that of other noble-hearted reformers. Other great ills, patent or latent in our civilisation, have yet to be overcome, perhaps have yet to be perceived; the old philanthropy has to deepen into something more vital if the full demands made by the teaching of Christ are to be obeyed; but the faithful following of the Light that illumines the alert conscience still seems to many of us the truest way for securing this deeper experience and for recognising and combating the evils that menace social and international life.

William Charles Braithwaite, 1919

SOCIAL JUSTICE

23.14 Our gracious Creator cares and provides for all his creatures. His tender mercies are over all his works; and so far as his love influences our minds, so far we become interested in his workmanship and feel a desire to take hold of every opportunity to lessen the distresses of the afflicted and increase the happiness of the creation. Here we have a prospect of one common interest from which our own is inseparable, that to turn all the treasures we possess into the channel of universal love becomes the business of our lives...

Oppression in the extreme appears terrible: but oppression in more refined appearances remains to be oppression; and where the smallest degree of it is cherished it grows stronger and more extensive. To labour for a perfect redemption from this spirit of oppression is the great business of the whole family of Christ Jesus in this world.

John Woolman, 1763

See also 20.32 & 20.34

23.15 Reduce and simplify your material needs to the point where you can easily satisfy them yourself, so that those who live for the Spirit and claim to live for it do not correspondingly increase the material burden weighing on other people, cutting them off from the possibility or even the desire to develop their spirit also.

How will the world be better off if, in developing your spiritual life, you make the material life of others that much more burdensome, and if, like in the movement of scales, as you rise yourself towards the eternal, you make other people descend by the same degree, away from him, beyond him? You have only introduced or confirmed an inequality and an injustice, without increasing the total of the Spirit.

Pierre Ceresole, 1937

See also 25.13

23.16 *The war of 1914-18 made Friends more vividly aware of the close connection between war and the social order. Nine months after the outbreak of war London Yearly Meeting was impressed by the* *words of John Woolman:* May we look upon our treasures, the furniture of our houses, and our garments, and try whether the seeds of war have nourishment in these our possessions. *After three years' exercise of mind eight 'Foundations of a true social order' were adopted. They were not intended as rules of life but as an attempt to set forth ideals that are aspects of eternal Truth and the direct outcome of our testimony to the individual worth of the human soul. Though they proclaimed the ending of 'restrictions' of sex, they spoke of God as Father and human beings as men and brothers, as was conventional in their time.*

i. The Fatherhood of God, as revealed by Jesus Christ, should lead us toward a brotherhood which knows no restriction of race, sex or social class.

ii. This brotherhood should express itself in a social order which is directed, beyond all material ends, to the growth of personality truly related to God and man.

iii. The opportunity of full development, physical, moral and spiritual, should be assured to every member of the community, man, woman and child. The development of man's full personality should not be hampered by unjust conditions nor crushed by economic pressure.

iv. We should seek for a way of living that will free us from the bondage of material things and mere conventions, that will raise no barrier between man and man, and will put no excessive burden of labour upon any by reason of our superfluous demands.

v. The spiritual force of righteousness, loving-kindness and trust is mighty because of the appeal it makes to the best in every man, and when applied to industrial relations achieves great things.

vi. Our rejection of the methods of outward domination, and of the appeal to force, applies not only to international affairs, but to the whole problem of industrial control. Not through antagonism but through co-operation and goodwill can the best be obtained for each and all.

vii. Mutual service should be the principle upon which life is organised. Service, not private gain, should be the motive of all work.

viii. The ownership of material things, such as land and capital, should be so regulated as best to minister to the need and development of man.

23.17   *Joseph Rowntree (1836-1925) was a cocoa manufacturer who studied the problems of poverty and of drink. He was in advance of his times in recognising the dangers inherent in sentimentally motivated charity. He devoted much of his own wealth to establishing three trusts to carry forward his concern for Quaker witness and for research and political action to make possible necessary changes in society.*

Charity as ordinarily practised, the charity of endowment, the charity of emotion, the charity which takes the place of justice, creates much of the misery which it relieves, but does not relieve all the misery it creates.

1865

23.18   Much of current philanthropical effort is directed to remedying the more superficial manifestations of weakness and evil, while little thought or effort is directed to search out their underlying causes. The soup kitchen in York never has difficulty in obtaining financial aid, but an enquiry into the extent and causes of poverty would enlist little support.

Joseph Rowntree, 1904

23.19   Are you working towards the removal of social injustices? Have you attempted to examine their causes objectively, and are you ready to abandon old prejudices and think again? Do you, as disciples of Christ, take a living interest in the social conditions of the district in which you live? Do you seek to promote the welfare of those in any kind of need and a just distribution of the resources of the world?

Queries, 1964

Poverty and housing

23.20   It was an initiative by Harriett Wilson some twenty years ago that led to the formation of the Child Poverty Action Group. She brought her concern about poverty in Britain to the Social & Economic Affairs Committee (one of the predecessors of Quaker Social Responsibility & Education) who organised a meeting of about twenty concerned people at Toynbee Hall... During the meeting the decision to form the group simply made itself. I was then asked whether the Society of Friends would sponsor it. As I stood up to reply I was in a deep dilemma. I could not escape the awe-inspiring feeling that history was being made; it was right for the Society to have brought those concerned together, but it was not for us, as a small religious body, to undertake the political operations which would obviously be needed to achieve the group's objective.

In the event the CPAG was formed as a non-denominational charitable body. It has grown into one of the most effective pressure groups in the country, and one of the ways by which Friends could help to alleviate the undoubtedly increasing poverty would be to support the group.

Apart from campaigning for a better deal for the poor generally, the Child Poverty Action Group advises people on how to make sure that they get the welfare provisions to which they are entitled; and the group brings test cases to that end.

Richard Allen, 1984

23.21   *A public statement by the Religious Society of Friends (Quakers) in Britain agreed in session at London Yearly Meeting 22-25 May 1987:*

Quakers in Britain have felt called to issue this statement in order to address a matter of urgent national priority to promote debate and to stimulate action.

We are angered by actions which have knowingly led to the polarisation of our country – into the affluent, who epitomise success according to the values of a materialistic society, and the 'have-leasts', who by the expectations of that same society are oppressed, judged, found wanting and punished.

We value that of God in each person, and affirm the right of everyone to contribute to society and share in life's good things, beyond the basic necessities.

We commit ourselves to learning again the spiritual value of each other. We find ourselves utterly at odds with the priorities in our society which deny the full human potential of millions of people in this country. That denial diminishes us all. There must be no 'them' and 'us'.

We appreciate the stand taken by other churches and we wish to work alongside them.

As a Religious Society and as individuals we commit ourselves to examine again how we use our personal and financial resources. We will press for change to enable wealth and power to be shared more evenly within our nation. We make this statement publicly at a time of national decision [a general election] in the hope that, following the leadings of the Spirit, each one of us in Britain will take appropriate action.

23.22   If we do not have the sense that selfishness is right, we may yet be carried along by the prevailing social currents to behave as though we do. More insidiously, we may seek material well-being for those we love, and thus achieve a sort of displaced selfishness. We may need to examine what we really believe, and in the light of that we can address questions about personal conduct. The main question for us who are comfortable is whether we use our positions of comparative power to arrogate to ourselves more than our reasonable share of the resources of the world. If so we should try to redistribute what we can, to live in a more responsible way. For those who are poor, a different question arises: what is selfish materialism, and what is proper aspiration?

We cannot take more than our share of finite resources unless we have the power so to do. Poverty and powerlessness are bound up with each other. Poverty leads to powerlessness, and powerlessness leads to poverty.

Martin Wyatt, 1988

23.23   We need to see the problem of homelessness as only one end of a spectrum of evil that has the massive subsidies to owners at the other. It is a problem that will be as difficult and painful to solve as slavery. Slavery as an evil shared many of the qualities of the present housing situation – it benefited the wealthy, created an underclass and denied them human rights. The solution was painful, for abolition often required that slave owners abandon their investment with no recompense. To change our attitudes to housing will be no less of a challenge to us than slavery was for the reformers, not only because institutional evil is hard to recognise but also because so many of us benefit personally from the present situation.

We must first understand the present system and become clear about the extent of right and wrong that it contains. If we could achieve this, we could first work towards a consensus on goals and then, I hope with other churches, start on the secular arguments.

This is a challenge that the Society, and indeed other churches, must face. If we fail to address the roots of an issue in which most of us are unwittingly part of the problem, we will need to look very carefully at the claims we make about our contribution in the world.

Richard Hilken, 1992; 1993

Slavery

23.24   It is the sense of this meeting, that the importing of negroes from their native country and relations by Friends, is not a commendable nor allowed practice, and is therefore censured by this meeting.

Yearly Meeting in London, 1727

23.25   *By 1772 the Yearly Meeting's concern had extended to the holding of slaves by anybody:*

It appears that the practice of holding negroes in oppressive and unnatural bondage, hath been so successfully discouraged by Friends in some of the colonies, as to be considerably lessened. We cannot but approve of these salutary endeavours, and earnestly intreat they may be continued, that, through the favour of Divine Providence, a traffic so unmerciful and unjust in its nature to a part of our own species made equally with ourselves for immortality may come to be considered by all in its proper light, and be utterly abolished, as a reproach to the Christian profession.

John Woolman was present at this Yearly Meeting. The experience which, sixteen years earlier, had led to his concern in this matter is described in 20.46

23.26 *Yearly Meeting 1822 accepted 'An address to the inhabitants of Europe on the Iniquities of the slave trade, issued by the Religious Society of Friends':*

The arguments of the Christian, like the religion from which they are derived, are plain and simple, but they are in themselves invincible. The gospel of our Lord Jesus Christ is a system of peace, of love, of mercy, and of good-will. The slave trade is a system of fraud and rapine, of violence and cruelty... That which is morally wrong cannot be politically right.

23.27 It has probably come as a shock to many Friends to learn that slavery still exists in many parts of the world, either in its usually understood form or as forced labour which is akin to slavery... The prime need, as a preliminary action, is the gathering together of accurate information on all aspects of this important problem... Though the powers of the British Government to deal with potential slavery or slave trading are now much more circumscribed, we would encourage any efforts they are able to make through international channels to bring to an end this deplorable traffic in the lives of members of the world family.

London Yearly Meeting, 1958

23.28 Quakers gradually led the way in the great reform which has now been largely achieved. A legal judgment of 1772 declared that if slaves arrived in England they became free. These pioneers against slavery were heretics, outside the normal confines of our great religious institutions, but what a debt and the churches owe to these heretics who, nevertheless, liberated the spiritual wind which sent them forward to explore territories beyond the limited horizon of their age.

We are involved in an intense perpetual struggle within the mind of man. If wars begin in the mind of men, so does slavery. When I was in the Yemen some four or five years ago, before the present [1962-67] civil war began and before Egypt sent some 70,000 troops into that country, I talked at some length with the late Imam, the Crown Prince and others about the slavery I knew existed there, and I myself saw in the early morning the old women sweeping the streets and was told that they were slaves. I glanced up at the edifice at the top of the hill wherein there were scores of boys kept as hostages by the Imam. Again, a form of slavery.

When I was some years ago in Northern Nigeria I knew that those who could do so maintained harems, which surely is another form of slavery. When I read letters from time to time from a friend in South Africa who now finds every excuse for the permanent subjugation of black South Africans, I know that her mind is essentially still subscribing to slavery. When in South Carolina I talked to a Baptist deacon and he stated that all would be peaceful in his part of America were it not for 'darned agitators', I knew again that he was virtually, although a Christian, endorsing a form of slavery. Further, when we all remember the repression of human liberty in certain European states, then we know that the Anti-Slavery Society and its purpose, which is defined as the protection of human rights, has only partially fulfilled its mission...

[There] are indications of real advances. Let us take courage and inspiration from them, but let us also appreciate how much still has to be done.

Reginald Sorensen, 1966

23.29   In the 1970s children could still be found picking crops in pesticide-soaked fields of the USA, labouring on building sites in Mexico, in sweat-shops in the East End of London, being injured in factory accidents in Italy, making carpets in Turkey, assembling plastic toys in Hong Kong, labouring as unofficial sub-employees in Indian factories, and working in agriculture almost everywhere. Even the nineteenth-century chimney boy has his twentieth-century equivalent – boys employed on Saturdays to crawl through and clean factory air ducts...

The attitudes which have perpetuated child labour are likely to remain a fundamental problem; attitudes which treat particular groups, such as women and children, as subservient and expendable and which respond with violence even to non-violent movements towards reform... The all too frequent cruel exploitation of child labour is a scandal. It is doubly a scandal when it co-exists with massive adult unemployment. What is needed now is a concerted effort to launch a wide-ranging programme of reform.

James Challis, 1979

Torture

In 1961 Amnesty International was established on the initiative of a small group, which included a Quaker, Eric Baker, to take up the cause of prisoners of conscience: men and women imprisoned for their religious, political or other beliefs or opinions, who had not used or advocated the use of violence. It became increasingly evident that many such prisoners were being subjected to torture. In 1974, in Documents in advance *and at Yearly Meeting, Eric Baker introduced a session on the subject, which was subsequently selected for special study at the Friends World Committee for Consultation Triennial meeting in 1976.*

23.30   Can torture ever be justified? Once chattel slavery was considered an economic and social necessity; nevertheless it has now been abolished in most regions of the world. This has happened at least in part because of the revulsion which this offence to human dignity aroused. Should not torture arouse the same revulsion?

Torture is not just a sporadic occurrence in this country or that, but a moral contagion which has spread throughout the world, even to governments which have been proud of their record of civilised behaviour. Torture is not only systematic physical ill-treatment but may also involve the misuse of psychology and other sciences and technologies.

Is this evil one that will arouse us to action as our Society was once aroused by the evil of slavery?

London Yearly Meeting, 1974

23.31   It is a matter of grave anxiety that torture and secret imprisonment are being used by many governments, anti-government groups, and others to extract information, to suppress criticism, and to intimidate opposition, so that throughout the world countless numbers of men, women and children are suffering inhuman treatment. We believe in the worth of every individual as a child of God, and that no circumstances whatsoever can justify practices intended to break bodies, minds and spirits.

Both tortured and torturer are victims of the evil from which no human being is immune. Friends, however, believe that the life and power of God are greater than evil, and in that life and power declare their opposition to all torture. The Society calls on all its members, as well as those of all religious and other organisations, to create a force of public opinion which will oblige those responsible to dismantle everywhere the administrative apparatus which permits or encourages torture, and to observe effectively those international agreements under which its use is strictly forbidden.

Friends World Committee for Consultation, 1976

Discrimination and disadvantage

23.32 I have never lost the enjoyment of sitting in silence at the beginning of meeting, knowing that everything can happen, knowing the joy of utmost surprise; feeling that nothing is preordained, nothing is set, all is open. The light can come from all sides. The joy of experiencing the Light in a completely different way than one has thought it would come is one of the greatest gifts that Friends' meeting for worship has brought me.

I believe that meeting for worship has brought the same awareness to all who have seen and understood the message that everyone is equal in the sight of God, that everybody has the capacity to be the vessel of God's word. There is nothing that age, experience and status can do to prejudge where and how the Light will appear. This awareness – the religious equality of each and every one – is central to Friends. Early Friends understood this and at the same time they fully accepted the inseparable unity of life, and spoke against the setting apart of the secular and the sacred. It was thus inevitable that religious equality would be translated into the equality of everyday social behaviour. Friends' testimony to plain speech and plain dress was both a testimony of religious equality and a testimony of the unacceptability of all other forms of inequality.

Ursula Franklin, 1979

23.33 Guided by the Light of God within us and recognising that of God in others, we can all learn to value our differences in age, sex, physique, race and culture. This enables mutual respect and self-respect to develop, and it becomes possible for everyone to love one another as God loves us. Throughout our lives, we see ourselves reflected in the facial expressions, verbal comments and body-language of others. We have a responsibility to protect each other's self-respect.

Because of their commitment to social concerns, some Quakers may find it inconceivable that they may lack understanding of issues involving racism. Jesus stressed the unique nature and worth of each individual. It is unreasonable to expect assimilation or to ignore difference, claiming to treat everyone the same. This denies the value of variety, which presents not a problem, but a creative challenge to live adventurously.

Personality, sex, race, culture and experience are God's gifts. We need one another and differences shared become enrichments, not reasons to be afraid, to dominate or condemn. The media have increased our knowledge of the world, but we need greater self-awareness if our actions are to be changed in relation to the informa-tion we receive. We need to consider our behaviour carefully, heeding the command of Jesus that we should love our neighbours as we love ourselves.

Meg Maslin, 1990

23.34 *Testimony concerning Dorothy Case (1901-1978):*

In the mid-50s, West Indians started coming to this country in great numbers, and Dorothy had more and more of their small children in her nursery. With two Friends from Streatham Meeting, Dorothy joined a Racial Brotherhood Association started by the Mayor of Lambeth and a West Indian Brixton resident. The Association could not find premises suitable for a community centre, largely because of colour prejudice, and, when the Mayor left the district, the once flourishing association nearly collapsed. But largely through the determination of Dorothy and the two Streatham Friends, it was revived, Dorothy agreeing to become secretary. To find premises was always the problem and in 1958 Dorothy wrote: 'Last year I felt that if we *didn't* function somehow, we'd had it, and as I'm keen on cricket, I booked a pitch on the Common and collected a few of the West Indian fathers of babies at my nursery, and their friends. It surpassed all our expectations and we had a wonderful season.' When winter came, although they only had two small basement rooms, they functioned as best they could as a true community centre. At this time Dorothy had helpful contacts with the International Centre and with Friends Race Relations Committee of which she was a member from 1964-1974, sharing her particular concerns for the West Indian community in Lambeth with it and, as race relations correspondent, with her meeting. A former member of Westminster Meeting recalls that Dorothy was a source of inspiration to her West Indian neighbours, standing by them in difficult situations, and offering them encouragement at all times.

Purley & Sutton Monthly Meeting, 1978

23.35   This year's Junior Yearly Meeting has made us hope that the concentrated love we have experienced could be spread over the world; but it has also alerted us to the harsh realities of racism.

We recognise that racism is more complex than simply black and white – it is part of a wider problem of prejudice involving sexism and religious bigotry. In this context, we were particularly alerted to the situation in Northern Ireland which, like racism, exhibits institutional and [personal] prejudice.

We urge Friends throughout the world to examine their responsibilities in this light.

Epistle from Junior Yearly Meeting, 1988

23.36   At the centre of Friends' religious experience is the repeatedly and consistently expressed belief in the fundamental equality of all members of the human race. Our common humanity transcends our differences. Friends have worked individually and corporately to give expression to this belief. We aspire not to say or do anything or condone any statements or actions which imply lack of respect for the humanity of any person. We try to free ourselves from assumptions of superiority and from racial prejudice.

We must constantly ask ourselves whether we are living up to these ideals, not only in international relations but also in our individual and corporate relationships within Britain – which has become and will remain multiracial and multicultural. To liberate ourselves from pervasive attitudes and practices of our time and social environment requires new perceptions and hard work.

There is incontrovertible evidence that people who belong to ethnic minority groups, especially those who are readily identifiable by their appearance, are subject to a variety of disadvantages. They face more obstacles than others, first, in gaining education commensurate with their abilities, and then in securing employment which reflects their qualifications. They are less likely to be promoted, and often earn less than others with similar abilities. As a result of legislation passed by both Labour and Conservative governments which restricts the right to live and work in Britain, people from ethnic minorities may be asked to justify their claim to equal rights by anyone in authority at any time. In addition to discrimination, intended or unintended, by employers and by the law, our fellow-citizens are often subjected to abuse, harassment and violence.

The Religious Society of Friends has a duty to play its part in ending these abuses. Being aware of injustice and doing little about it condones that injustice. Friends kept slaves until John Woolman persuaded them that it was wrong to do so. Should we not ask ourselves if we are in a parallel situation today?

Discrimination also takes more subtle forms. It may occur, and feelings may be hurt, by unthinking assumptions and lack of sensitivity. Being a Friend does not confer automatic protection against this, either as giver or receiver. In our dealings with members of minority groups in our daily lives and also within the Religious Society of Friends we may sometimes be less thoughtful and sensitive than we should be.

Meeting for Sufferings' Statement of Intent on Racism, 1988

The use of language in the passage above gives the mistaken impression that in 1988 all Friends in Britain were white. By 1994 we were aware that such usage was exclusive and were committed to inclusive expression, based on respect and celebration of diversity among Friends in Britain.

23.37 Having a severe disability in my experience meant almost total isolation from my peers during my teens and early twenties. I could not talk with them or go out with them and this had a drastic effect on my confidence and self-respect. I suffered agonies of repressed sexual longing.

I was lucky. I had the means to recover unavailable to great numbers of young disabled people. As I found vehicles I could drive my contacts widened and I could exercise my freedom, responsibility and keen intelligence but it took long years of learning to catch up on normal life...

In some circles it is quite impossible for me to get an honest opinion about what I think and do. Any trivial achievement is regarded with awe and anything approaching normality is quite inconceivable. If I committed some frightful social blunder, they would nod their heads and make irrelevant excuses for me.

Enough of such things. You soon 'forget' them; but deep within you burns a clear impression of profound inferiority; of unacceptability; of a need to apologise for even being the miserable wretch that you are and for needing that minimum of help you dare to require. When all this is added to a very real and terrifying social immaturity, where can you begin to hope? ...

Many people, much less disabled than me, accept the role society imposes, hating themselves and their handicaps, hating to ask for help, hating friendly curiosity and concern, hating to admit to what they feel they are.

All this is a terrible indictment of society but it is not an indictment of the individual. Each of them, including myself, is only echoing the fear and hurt about disability and about their own minds and bodies that they received when they were young. Young children, left alone, will look, enquire, accept, and sometimes even care, without prompting.

Everyone must learn to be glad of what they really are and must feel able to ask for the necessary help to fulfil themselves. We are all in this together, handicapped or not. We all need help to be ourselves.

Jonathan Griffith, 1981

23.38 *Carol Gardiner has lived with multiple sclerosis for many years. In 1989 she wrote about her realisation that she did not have enough reserves of spiritual and physical energy at that time to go to a residential Yearly Meeting, and so it was not accessible to her.*

Our Religious Society includes a considerable number of people who to some degree live with disabilities, and we generally present quite a good record of considering their needs and attempting to cater for them – a consideration born of our conviction that there is 'that of God' in every person. But we should ask ourselves continually if this consideration is being maintained and whether it goes far enough. If we really mean that there is that of God in everyone, then it behoves us to look with creative, loving imagination at the condition of every human being. This includes listening to what they say, and the words they choose to say it, and also listening for what they do not or cannot say. It does not mean listening to what someone else says supposedly on their behalf.

23.39 Too long have wrongs and oppression existed without an acknowledged wrongdoer and oppressor. It was not until the slave holder was told 'Thou art the man' that a healthy agitation was brought about. Woman is told the fault is in herself, in too willingly submitting to her inferior condition, but like the slave, she is pressed down by laws in the making of which she has no voice, and crushed by customs which have grown out of such laws. She cannot rise therefore, while thus trampled in the dust. The oppressor does not see himself in that light until the oppressed cry for deliverance.

Lucretia Mott, 1852

23.40 We have been reminded vividly that women live under cultural, political, and economic oppression. All humanity is lessened by it; we are unwilling to tolerate its perpetuation, and must continue to work for justice and peace in the world...

We hope that we will act as leaven in our local meetings, churches, and yearly meetings, so that Quaker women everywhere will be encouraged by our new understanding. As we grow in solidarity with one another, enriched by how we express our faith, we will all be enabled to surmount the cultural, economic and political barriers that prevent us from discerning and following the ways in which God leads us. We honour the lives of our Quaker foremothers as patterns which help us recognise our own leadings. Their commitment, dedication, and courage remain as worthy standards. May our lives be used as theirs were to give leadership to women everywhere to be vehicles of the love of God. We share a deep love for all creation, and cry with the pain of its desecration. We must realise we are part of the natural world and examine our lives in order to change those attitudes which lead to domination and exploitation.

Friends, we are called into wholeness and into community, women and men alike, sharing the responsibilities God has given us, and assuming the leadership we are called to. We begin where we are, in our homes and meetings or churches, our work and communities, celebrating the realisation of the New Creation.

Epistle of the First International Theological Conference of Quaker Women, 1990

23.41   The oppression of the working-classes by existing monopolies, and the lowness of wages, often engaged my attention; and I have held many meetings with them, and heard their appeals with compassion, and a great desire for a radical change in the system which makes the rich richer and the poor poorer. The various associations and communities tending to greater equality of condition have had from me a hearty God-speed. But the millions of down-trodden slaves in our land being the greatest sufferers, the most oppressed class, I have felt bound to plead their cause, in season and out of season, to endeavor to put my soul in their souls' stead, and to aid, all in my power, in every right effort for their immediate emancipation. This duty was impressed upon me at the time I consecrated myself to that gospel which anoints 'to preach deliverance to the captive', 'to set at liberty them that are bruised.' From that time the duty of abstinence so far as practicable from slave-grown products was so clear, that I resolved to make the effort 'to provide things honest' in this respect. Since then our family has been supplied with free-labor groceries and, to some extent, with cotton goods untainted by slavery.

In 1840, a World's Anti-slavery Convention was called in London. Women from Boston, New York and Philadelphia were delegates to that convention. I was one of the number; but, on our arrival in

England, our credentials were not accepted because we were women. We were, however, treated with great courtesy and attention, as strangers, and as women, were admitted to chosen seats as spectators and listeners, while our right of membership was denied – we were voted out. This brought the Woman question more into view, and an increase of interest in the subject has been the result. In this work, too, I have engaged heart and hand, as my labors, travels, and public discourses evince. The misrepresentation, ridicule, and abuse heaped upon this as well as other reforms do not, in the least, deter me from my duty. To those whose name is cast out as evil for the truth's sake, it is a small thing to be judged of man's judgment.

Lucretia Mott

23.42 I am still concerned that there are not many women exercising leadership in government, industry and education... However, this is not a straightforward issue for me. I want to see women fully represented at all levels of society, and yet I share the misgivings that many feminists have for the hierarchical way in which leadership is traditionally exercised.

The Society of Friends seems a good place to explore this dilemma since it has, since the early days, attempted a more truly democratic and participative way of working than has been customary in society at large. This was one of the factors that first attracted me to Friends, as it seems to be an expression of the recognition that we are all equal in our shared humanity. Sexism does violence to this important insight, as it does to individuals of either sex who are seeking to find themselves and express themselves in the world...

I am not saying that the oppressive effects of sexism are never felt within the Society of Friends, for we are all members of the wider society and affected by its attitudes. There are Friends who think that catering should be the preserve of women and that matters of finance are best understood by men. There have been times within Friends' circles when I have felt hurt by these attitudes, as I have no doubt unwittingly wounded others. But I have found the Society's commitment to truth an encouragement and challenge to my own strivings for integrity, and I give thanks for that.

Pauline Leader, 1986

23.43   As male and female are made one in Jesus Christ, so women receive an office in the Truth as well as men, and they have a stewardship and must give an account of their stewardship as well as the men...

Elizabeth Bathurst, 1685

23.44   The language in which we express what we ... say is of vital importance; it both shapes and reflects our values. One result of the emphasis on plain speech by early Friends was to challenge the class hierarchy of the day. The emphasis on non-sexist language by present-day feminists is likewise a challenge to hierarchy, in this case the sex hierarchy, which women have brought into the Light by naming it – patriarchy... Our Quaker tradition enables us to recognise that our choice of language, and our reaction to the choice that others make, reveals values which may otherwise stay hidden.

Having in mind that much Christian teaching and language has been used to subordinate women to men, bear witness to our experience that we are all one in the Spirit and value the special characteristics of each individual. Remember that the Spirit of God includes and transcends our ideas of male and female, and that we should reflect this insight in our lives and through our ministry.

Are you working, in all aspects of your life, towards a better understanding of the need for a different balance between the sexes in their contribution to our society? Do you recognise the limitations which are placed on women and men by assigning roles to them according to gender, and do you attempt to respond instead to the needs and capacities of the individual? Do you recognise and encourage the many ways in which human love may be expressed?

Quaker Women's Group, 1982; 1986

23.45   All of us [Young Friends for Lesbian and Gay Concerns] have suffered discrimination or isolation because of our sexuality. We are all both angry and sad about the discrimination we face in everyday life, whether it consists of being unable to talk to work colleagues about a partner, or having to hide our sexuality in order to keep a job. The consequences of such necessary dishonesty can be very destructive both personally and for society.

Tessa Fairweather, 1993

23.46 I have been greatly exercised for some time by the image we like to present of ourselves (albeit with beating of breasts) as a white, middle-class, well-educated group of heterosexual people, preferably in stable marriages with children that behave in socially acceptable ways. I do feel that this is a myth. The danger of such myths is that we exclude many potential Quakers who feel they cannot/do not live up to the image or who feel that such a group is not one with which they wish to be associated. Sadly, many of us within the Society who do not fit in feel marginalised and second-class.

Another effect is that many problems faced by a large proportion of people are seen as separate: people who are poor, facing oppression, living in poor housing, experiencing prejudice are the 'others'. This enables us to be very caring but distant (and sometimes patronising) and also makes it difficult to be conscious of prejudice behind some of the normally accepted assumptions of our society/Society, such as that people who are unemployed are a different group from those who have employment; that poor people are poor ... because they are not as bright or as able as the rest of us or because their limited homes did not give them the opportunities that a good Quaker home would have done; that children living in single-parent families are automatically deprived by that very fact.

Until we as a Religious Society begin to question our assumptions, until we look at the prejudices, often very deeply hidden, within our own Society, how are we going to be able to confront the inequalities within the wider society? We are very good at feeling bad about injustice, we put a lot of energy into sticking-plaster activity (which obviously has to be done), but we are not having any effect in challenging the causes of inequality and oppression. I do sometimes wonder if this is because we are not able to do this within and among ourselves.

Susan Rooke-Matthews, 1993

See also 10.13, 23.21, & 29.15

THE INDIVIDUAL AND THE COMMUNITY

23.47   Compassion to be effective requires detailed knowledge and understanding of how society works. Any social system in turn requires
men and women in it of imagination and goodwill. What would be
fatal would be for those with exceptional human insight and concern to concentrate on ministering to individuals, whilst those
accepting responsibility for the design and management of organisations were left to become technocrats. What is important is that
institutions and their administration be constantly tested against
human values, and that those who are concerned about these values
be prepared to grapple with the complex realities of modern society
as it is.

Grigor McClelland, 1976

23.48   God comes to us in the midst of human need, and the most pressing
needs of our time demand community in response. How can I
participate in a fairer distribution of resources unless I live in a community which makes it possible to consume less? How can I learn
accountability unless I live in a community where my acts and their
consequences are visible to all? How can I learn to share power
unless I live in a community where hierarchy is unnatural? How can
I take the risks which right action demands unless I belong to a community which gives support? How can I learn the sanctity of each
life unless I live in a community where we can be persons not roles
to one another?

Parker J Palmer, 1977

23.49   Many of us live in the more prosperous areas of large cities, or within
commuting distance of them. The accumulated decisions we make,
together with the accumulated decisions of all our neighbours, help
to determine what life is like for the people who live in the inner
areas of those cities, and in the large isolated housing estates on their
edges. Decisions about where to live, what forms of transport to use,
where to spend money, where to send children to school, where to
work, whom to employ, where to obtain health services, what to
condone, what to protest about, business decisions, personal decisions, political decisions – all these have an effect. Our first and

greatest responsibility is to make those decisions in the knowledge of their effect on others.

Nationally we have to face up to the fact that deprived areas are distinguished as much by personal as by collective poverty, and that the only way to tackle personal poverty is to let people have more money. More money for some inevitably means less for others. Are we willing to press for this?

Martin Wyatt, 1986

23.50   How can the people of Ordsall, where I work, become our neighbours, our sisters and our brothers, especially when we do not know them personally? It is only through prayer and political action that we can affirm our love and demonstrate in the flesh that we do see that of God within them...

We have a variety of strategies for passing by on the other side: we manage not to know about such things, by living elsewhere and averting our eyes and hearts from information which might trouble us; some of us imagine that Biblical morality only enjoins us to direct personal charity towards those we encounter, having nothing to do with justice, with political action to change unjust structures. (A strange love this, which would shelter a Jew but ignore the struggle to prevent the rise of Nazism.) More often we claim that whilst in principle love does also require us to work for the removal of the causes of injustice, such work is in practice so complex that Friends cannot become involved corporately; it should be left to Friends individually as they think fit...

Complexity, however, may depend on whether we are the well-fed or the hungry. Our delicate refusal to dirty our hands in political turmoil may itself be another way of passing by on the other side. Change seems most complicated and controversial to those who do not personally need it. Would we be so delicate if we were Black South Africans? But surely, you may say, we don't face such fundamental injustices.

No, we don't. And yet – come and meet the people in Ordsall with me. You will sense inequality tangibly; you will become aware of the huge range of opportunities which you have and they do not; you will understand the struggle to make ends meet, the problems of debt, ill-health, premature ageing and death, and the hopelessness which is the experience of many. The answers may not be simple: the bureaucratic welfare state did also create some of the problems. But to see the unbridled pursuit of individual self-interest as a solution is grotesque as well as immoral.

Jonathan Dale, 1987

23.51   *Testimony concerning Stephen Henry Hobhouse (1881-1961):*

He soon ceased to attend church services and resigned from the University Rifle Corps on pacifist grounds. He also resolved never to accept the position in the world to which he was the heir, that of a wealthy landowner and country squire...

Although from childhood far from strong in health, Stephen Hobhouse was again and again led to take a difficult course required of him by his conviction of divine leading, whatever the cost to himself... Disturbed by the contrast between the luxurious comfort which he sometimes experienced in visiting the homes of wealthy Friends, and the hard lives of ordinary working people in those days (fifty years ago) he took a small flat in a block of workers' dwellings in a poor part of London because he felt that his discipleship of Jesus called him to share their life as much as he could, and also to open the eyes of his comfortable friends to the way in which the great majority of people had to live.

Hertford & Hitchin Monthly Meeting, 1961

See also 18.13 (concerning Mary Hughes) & 24.52 (concerning Douglas Smith)

23.52   I think I have wasted a great deal of my life waiting to be called to some great mission which would change the world. I have looked for important social movements. I have wanted to make a big and important contribution to the causes I believe in. I think I have been too ready to reject the genuine leadings I have been given as being matters of little consequence. It has taken me a long time to learn that obedience means doing what we are called to do even if it seems pointless or unimportant or even silly. The great social movements of our time may well be part of our calling. The ideals of peace and justice and equality which are part of our religious tradition are often the focus of debate. But we cannot simply immerse ourselves in these activities. We need to develop our own unique social witness, in obedience to God. We need to listen to the gentle whispers which will tell us how we can bring our lives into greater harmony with heaven.

Deborah Haines, 1978

Work and economic affairs

23.53 It was once possible to argue that economic affairs might, like total abstinence, slavery or spiritual healing, be a field of particular interest to groups of Friends. We can now see that the economic order is not a peripheral concern, but central to the whole relationship between faith and practice. This is not a claim that, say, the interest in peace and international relations ought now to take a secondary place in our thoughts and prayers. Still less is it a demand that the Society should cease to be first and foremost a religious body, or to say that it should in any way neglect its spiritual foundations in favour of more good citizenship. It is rather that economic affairs are now so central to our whole existence that no other aspect of personal relationships or individual life-styles can now be looked at without first understanding what it means in terms of our national wealth, incomes, and their distribution.

David Eversley, 1976

See also 24.50-24.52

23.54 Part of understanding life and one's place in life is to form a 'right' relationship with things. The philosophy of the industrial revolution is to 'direct the forces of nature for the use of man' (following the words of the charter given to the engineering profession in 1821). Now, to seek mastery is not to gain a 'right' relationship. The latter requires sensitivity and yields wisdom along with an adequacy of power. The search for mastery alone yields a power that corrupts faster than it is mastered.

Jim Platts, 1976

23.55 When I was a teenager and beginning to think about a career, my father advised me to choose between working with people and working with things, and I sensed an implied judgment that working with people was more worthy.

In the event, the decision was made for me when I married a self-employed engineer with no interest in the record-keeping side of his business. We now work very happily together from home, designing and supplying special purpose machinery to the brush industry. We deliberately keep our business small and more or less manageable. We are not interested in the financial dealings, stocks and shares, investments and take-overs which the press seems to regard as the essence of business.

I see the basis of industry as being a global network of barter, a mutual dependency, a contract of trust for the supply of the necessities and luxuries of life. The opportunities of industry are as large as the needs of the world's people. Every object we use has to be designed, manufactured and sold by someone. It is an honourable occupation to apply one's talents to the marketplace. One person's need becomes another's opportunity, his livelihood, his dignity. 'Working with things' is not devoid of scope for a spiritual attitude...

Perhaps a function of industry is to reflect that of God that is creation and glory. We can be creative in our small way in God's image; we can work in partnership with God, combining natural and human resources; we can extract order from chaos.

Rachel Jackson, 1990

23.56 Employers today, more and more, are demanding total commitment from their employees, often to the detriment of the employees' health and ability to participate in family and community life. People are facing decisions about giving all their energy to their company and having nothing left for themselves or anyone else. Some have the courage to opt for a more balanced approach to life and work, where paid employment has an important place, but also allowing sufficient leisure time to be an active parent, to enrich family and community relationships and replenish their own spiritual reserves. I hope that meetings will support those who make such decisions and help them in any adjustments to their life that they have to make.

Jane Stokes, 1992

23.57 *In the aftermath of the Second World War, Quakers began experimenting with democratic forms of economic enterprise. The best known case is probably Scott Bader, a synthetic resin and polymer manufacturing company in Wollaston, Northamptonshire. The original company was founded in 1920 and organised along orthodox lines of corporate authority by Ernest Bader, who joined the Society of Friends in 1943. During the 1940s he and his family decided to re-organise his firm upon stewardship principles. In 1951 he and his co-founders gave 90% of their shares to the Scott Bader Commonwealth, a company limited by guarantee and a registered charity, inviting employees to become members; in 1963 they gave the remaining 10% of their shares to the Commonwealth.*

Power should come from within the person and the community, and be made responsible to those it affects. The ultimate criteria in the organisation of work should be human dignity and service to others instead of solely economic performance. We feel mutual responsibility must permeate the whole community of work and be upheld by democratic participation and the principle of trusteeship.

Common-ownership of our means of production, and a voice in the distribution of earned surplus and the allocation of new capital, has helped in our struggle towards achieving these aims.

The Commonwealth has responsibilities to the wider national and international community and is endeavouring to fulfil them by fostering a movement towards a new peaceful industrial and social order. To be a genuine alternative to welfare capitalism and state-controlled communism, such an order must be non-violent in the sense of promoting love and justice, for where love stops, power begins and intimidation and violence follow. One of the main requirements of a peaceful social order is, we are convinced, an organisation of work based on the principles outlined here, a sharing of the fruits of our labours with those less fortunate instead of working only for our own private security, and a refusal to support destructive social conflict or to take part in preparations for war.

Scott Bader Corporate Constitution, 1963

23.58   *Testimony concerning Arthur Basil Reynolds (1903-1960):*

Arthur Basil Reynolds ... had that strong sense of the indwelling spirit of God which perforce claimed kinship with everything good and of enduring value in other men and in the world at large. He worked for the continuity of the good life; and to preserve what was good from the past, to hold fast and perpetuate what was good in the present and to work for the hope of good in the future. He was a man of creative imagination, a craftsman with vision and courage who delighted in the work of his hands and was able to inspire others with the same spirit. He had the seeing eye and the unerring hand to translate the vision into actuality. As he walked the countryside a twig in the hedge would suggest a shape of grace and gaiety and his penknife would speedily produce a dancing figure of elfish beauty. All that he touched witnessed to this creative power.

His training as a cabinet-maker was put to use in the workshops at Brynmawr during the unemployment and distress of the depression, when he worked with Friends and others to provide employment and thus to bring renewed hope and self-respect to the mining community. He became manager of the Brynmawr Furniture Makers, an undertaking that successfully produced worthy and beautiful furniture.

Hereford & Radnor Monthly Meeting, 1961

23.59   *Testimony concerning Percy Cleave (1880-1958):*

By occupation, he was a barber, and on moving into this district in 1937 from Swindon, he first took a shop in Wallington, and later one in a poor part of Croydon. Not all who went there did so for a shave or a haircut, but to enjoy its friendly atmosphere, and to talk to Percy. 'I am sure,' said a friend of his, 'that as Percy rubbed oil into a customer's hair, he blessed him.' This would have been natural, since he desired all his actions to be sacramental. He was very positive in his relationships with others, and took a lively interest in all their doings... He was a man whom adversity had refined. It was often surprising when talking to him, to hear of the multitudes of troubles he and his wife had borne. He had accepted the changes and chances of this life, but had not forgotten them, and so could sympathise with those who were still struggling. He had great insight, and was able to see to the heart of a problem. Since he was in a small way of business which barely brought in sufficient money, he had a hard time which persisted until his retirement, when he sought so to arrange his life, that others could speak to him at leisure and without hurry. It was then that he ministered to some families of Friends by going to their homes and cutting their hair. It was pleasant to see him starting on the littlest ones and proceed in order to the adults. To have Percy cut your hair was a grace.

Kingston Monthly Meeting, 1958

23.60   *Testimony concerning Joan Frances Layton (1908-1990):*

Her early education was unconventional and irregular. Nevertheless, she obtained a place at Bedford College, where she read English, French, Latin and Spanish. These stood her in good stead when she started work as a secretary in Covent Garden market. She then obtained a post in the City but, unable to reconcile her work there with her beliefs, she returned to the market amongst 'real people' whose admiration and respect she won, and remained with them for the rest of her working life.

Southampton & Portsmouth Monthly Meeting, 1990

23.61   It remains to speak of the Way of Service, as it concerns the conduct of our ordinary work and business. Nowhere is the practical working of our faith put to a severer test, yet nowhere is there a nobler and more fruitful witness to be borne. Business in its essence is no mere selfish struggle for the necessities and luxuries of life, but 'a vast and complex movement of social service'. However some may abuse its methods for private ends, its true function is not to rob the community but to serve it. But, in the fierce competition which is so marked a feature of the present day, it has become very difficult, some would say impossible, for those engaged in business to be wholly faithful to Christ. Christianity is challenged in the shop and in the office.

We have been touched with keen sympathy for our friends, whether employers or employed, who find themselves in this strait. We cannot here deal fully with this question, but we are sure there is an answer to the challenge, and that the light which shines upon the Way of Life, and gives us the distinction of things inwardly, will guide us to the answer...

Christianity is tested, not only in the shop and in the office, but also in the home. In the standard of living adopted by the home-makers, in the portion of income devoted to comforts, recreations and luxuries, in willingness to be content with simplicity, the members of a household, both older and younger, may bear witness that there is a Way of Life that does not depend on the abundance of the things possessed.

London Yearly Meeting, 1911

23.62 The attempt to identify and apply Christian values in practice is a struggle laid upon each generation. As new knowledge, new methods, new technologies arise, so is the condition for the operation of conscience altered and advanced.

To list the attributes of Christian quality would be to repeat much of the Sermon on the Mount. They can be summed up as personal integrity combined with compassion. Such quality can shine out in the work situation as in the social and religious life... It is characterised by the refusal to put up with the second best; a capacity to take infinite pains with other people; especially is it shown in the constant effort to seek higher standards beyond the traditional practices or those provided for in regulations.

Edward W Fox, 1969

23.63 One of the aspects of parenthood which I enjoy most is putting my mind to trying to solve all sorts of problems. I get a big thrill out of designing gadgets which will make life a little more comfortable. I love to get to work on a thoroughly neglected garden or room and put it right again. I find great satisfaction in being consulted about other people's problems and helping to sort them out. I have come to the conclusion, therefore, that this is the area in which I shall both find my main direction and satisfy my needs to be creative, practical and supportive. If, rather than concentrating on one particular job or career, I apply myself to tackling the many problems that come my way, I am sure that my life will be more than adequately filled with work that I 'most need to do and the world most needs to have done'. Thus I shall have found my vocation or mission. It will not mean that all the problems will get solved, of course, or that those which do will be solved satisfactorily every time, but I am sure that it will mean that my relationships with other people will improve and that both the giving and the taking of love will come easier to me.

Helen Edwards, 1992

23.64   There is much work to be done which is not paid, but which is vital, desperately undervalued, and undertaken to a large extent by women. I refer, of course, to caring for children and/or elderly disabled relatives and homemaking. The work itself is often hard, stressful, mundane and repetitive, unseen and unacknowledged, with low status. We need a transformation of our attitudes to this work, giving it all the esteem it deserves. Experience of running a household teaches innumerable management skills, but these skills are often not perceived by employers as useful to them. Self-image is extremely poor in this group, not because they do not make a contribution but because their contribution is not appreciated.

Another reason for the low self-image of this group is one of the primary indicators of status in our society – income. Caring for a family is unpaid and therefore low status... We must value the work done by carers in a domestic situation because it is essential to the wellbeing of individuals and the community; bringing up the next generation should never be undervalued...

Related to the unpaid caring work carried out in many families is the voluntary work on which our communities depend which is, by definition, unpaid. Without volunteers many of the statutory services would be overwhelmed...

Voluntary work gives the sense of being able to give something – whether in time, money or expertise – and that is precious to the person doing the giving. The feeling of having contributed, the satisfaction of a job lovingly done, is the reward. We should not regard voluntary work as of less value because it is unpaid and the rewards intangible, nor should we exploit the goodwill of volunteers...

Whichever sphere of activity we are involved in, we have to be responsive to the Spirit's leadings and try to put into practice our deepest beliefs, for our faith is a 24-hour-a-day, 7-day-a-week faith, which is not excluded from our workplace, wherever that may be. Everything in the end can be distilled to relationships – our relationships with each other and the earth. Our work must benefit our relationships rather than damage them, and we must ensure that neither the earth nor other people are exploited. Caring, not exploitation, is the key.

Jane Stokes, 1992

23.65 Large numbers of people desperately need, not only the honest, just and sympathetic administration of material assistance, but counselling and caring from skilled but warm persons, who for the most part can only be provided through an institutional framework, whether statutory or voluntary. But social workers themselves often face an uphill struggle, working with people on whom society has imposed burdens which for one reason or another they have found too heavy for them. These burdens may be lifted or lightened by the social worker, but they might never have been imposed in the first place if we had better and wiser architects and town planners, legislators and civil servants, broadcasters and advertising people, personnel managers and supervisors, economists and sociologists.

Grigor McClelland, 1976

23.66 For some it is right to give their whole lives explicitly to concrete forms of service, but for most their service will lie 'in the sheer quality of the soul displayed in ordinary occupations'. Such ordinary occupations are sometimes an essential contribution to the liberation of another person for wider service, and in any case, the inspiration of a dedicated life lived in simple surroundings, though often untraceable, may be profound in its reach.

Gerald Littleboy, 1945

23.67 We can neither deny nor ignore the fact that our self-respect and our sense of being useful are closely bound up with the ability to hold down a job. Unemployment not only results in a lowering of living standards, it also induces a feeling of insecurity, of being unwanted, that we no longer have a place in the community. The fear of unemployment causes more unhappiness and does more to lower self-confidence than any other element in life. The sense of security, so necessary to inner well-being, will never be sustained by a welfare system or any society which ignores these facts. Any percentage rate of unemployment can never be other than an index of human misery and desperate uncertainty; this applies not only to the unemployed persons but to their dependants also. Thus any economic system which possesses an inbuilt tendency to reduce human involvement in its day-to-day engagements is both unnatural and unkind.

George Clarke, 1973

23.68   The poor without employment are like rough diamonds, their worth is unknown.

John Bellers, 1714

23.69   Unemployment is in truth an astonishing evil and calm acquiescence therein is discreditable... The stoic endurance of privation in times of shortage is noble, but poverty caused by enforced idleness, and in the presence of plenty, is so glaring an injustice that no man should accept it tamely.

Shipley N Brayshaw, 1933

23.70   We are in a new situation which demands new thinking. Advanced technology is producing techniques which will affect every field of human activity and can displace many people who at present have little opportunity of alternative work. We need to be far more ambitious and resourceful in our thinking. Technology alleviates the repetitive and mundane nature of many people's jobs. We need to approach the situation positively as an opportunity to promote new business and industrial ventures, to back initiatives from workers and trade unions, exploring alternative uses of the intricate technology of armaments to find ways of promoting service jobs related to inner-city renewal, or to help with unmet social needs. The solution of our energy problems may also serve to provide new opportunities for employment. We must look for revolutionary approaches which can promote the sharing of the gains and benefits of new technology and a far greater awareness of the need to accept the concept of equity.

We have been asked to see those in the midst of our community who are suffering from unemployment as well as to look for new solutions. John Bellers reminded Friends that God would not send his angels to solve our problems; it is we who must seek the solutions with God's guidance, and we who must do the job.

London Yearly Meeting, 1978

Education

23.71 Then I came to Waltham and established a school there for the teaching of boys, and ordered a women's school to be set up at Shacklewell to instruct young lasses and maidens in whatsoever things were civil and useful in the creation.

George Fox, 1668

23.72 This meeting do desire that, where Friends can, they would get such schools and schoolmasters for their children, as may bring them up in the fear of the Lord and love of his truth, that so they may not only learn to be scholars, but Christians also; and that all parents will take the same care at home that such reproof, instructions, counsel, and example may be constantly continued in their respective families, that so from the oldest to the youngest, Truth may show itself in its beauty and comeliness to God's glory and all his people's comfort.

Bristol Yearly Meeting, 1695

23.73 Our experience [is] that God speaks to and works through children as well as adults. Religious education needs to respect, affirm and value children's insights.

The Quaker understanding of Christianity includes:

The experience that it is possible to have both a strong faith commitment and an open mind, to take other positions seriously without trivialising them, and to value the people who differ from ourselves.

The belief that the same God known through Christianity is also present in other faiths. The study of other faith positions is therefore important, not only for its own sake, but as a contribution towards humility before the mystery of truth.

The experience that valuable worship can be held in a multifaith context, especially when silence is the basis for prayer. We would assert that school worship which shows respect for other faith positions by presenting them with accuracy and sympathy is, by our definition, Christian.

The belief in the equality of all human beings of whatever sex, race, class or age. This is firmly grounded in God's love for each individual, rather than in social fashion. This requires policies, not of equal opportunities (which redistribute inequality) but of equality, and implies that schools be reorganised for co-operation rather than competition, and for affirming people in their successes rather than their failures.

Janet Scott, 1988

23.74 The Quaker emphasis in education probably lies in non-violence, in participation, and in caring. Not only to run the school without violence, but to produce young people who will feel a concern to reduce the level of violence in the world. Not to impose the aims of the school on the pupils, but to lead them to their own acceptance of these aims, to a share (however small) in its running, and a pleasure in its successes. To find that of God in every pupil.

'This is the true ground of love and unity,' wrote Isaac Penington in 1659, 'not that such a man walks and does just as I do, but because I feel the same Spirit and life in him, and that he walks in his rank, in his own order, in his proper way.' This marvellous statement by an early Friend of the value of individualism surely commands our assent today. The school which respects every pupil as an individual will try to teach each one what he (or she) needs to learn, to draw out his unique talents, to understand his proper way, whether he is studying or misbehaving. 'This is far more pleasing to me,' Penington continues, 'than if he walked just in that track wherein I walk.'

Quakers and their schools, 1980

23.75 To confirm the deepest thing in our students is the educator's special privilege. It demands that we see in the failures of adolescence and its many confusions, the possibility of something untangled, clear, directed. It asks us to sustain that faith through a multiplicity of discouraging experiences and indeed to find within those experiences the grounds for hope. It requires us to love freely, readily, unconditionally but truly – without relaxing our standards or compromising ourselves – because to do that would be to disappoint and disillusion – a sure means of stunting the student's growth. Above all, we must water the ground of the student's being with faith in that deepest self – to do so constantly, tirelessly, patiently – and to love enough to know what one should demand from the student in response and how and when to ask it.

Barbara Windle, 1988

23.76 The capacity to listen is something which is greatly needed and is an important part of our education, something which has to be worked at constantly. We so easily fall into a pattern of imagining we know what someone else is going to say to us. Sometimes this is the case, but more often than not we have made up our mind, and received a message which may be completely erroneous and precludes a true understanding. We must have all experienced the circumstances in which a child tries to make himself understood and in which we have prejudged what is his meaning. In that case we never meet. There is one occasion which stands out very clearly in my life when a youngster kept coming up to me and I answered what I thought the question was going to be; at the end of a week she stood resolutely between me and the door clutching a piece of paper asking if she could discontinue my lessons. All that time I had been answering an unasked question and missing the point of contact. This is something which most of us do all too often in one way or another: we have a duty to try to help each other to communicate. We must endeavour to meet each other's minds and we must attempt to achieve not only sympathy but empathy.

D June Ellis, 1981

23.77 To 'know oneself' as a teacher implies acknowledging one's weaknesses, source of prejudices and tendencies to stereotype. It involves accepting one's effect on pupils and their parents. Diagnosing a child's learning needs involves risking being wrong. We can only see clearly and risk being wrong when we have a high level of self-esteem and when we love ourselves enough to be open.

To acknowledge those aspects in ourselves and our own practice which hinder an understanding of the learner's needs is difficult. Yet when we can do this, we are given the strength to respond lovingly to others, recognising that of God in everyone, which for Quakers, is what meeting the needs of the individual is all about.

Sarah Worster, 1988

23.78   We seek to affirm in each child at school, each member of the meeting, each person we meet in our daily lives, the person that he or she may with God's help grow to be. We are all the merest infants in God's world, struggling to stand upright and walk unaided, trying in vain to articulate our halting thoughts and feelings. We stumble and fall. We give way to self-pity and shame. God hauls us to our feet again and makes sense of our childish babble, never ceasing to believe in what we may ultimately become. Do we do the same for our children and one another? We have a responsibility to follow Pierre Ceresole's dictum: 'Speak to every child as if you were addressing the utterly truthful upright individual which under your guidance he may one day become'. Our Quaker witness demands of us that we 'respect children very much more than they respect themselves'.

When we find ourselves teaching – as we *all* do in our relationships within meeting – can we draw upon that respect for one another and faith in one another's potential that will enable the other to feel taller and more capable? At Rufus Jones's memorial meeting one of his students simply said: 'He lit my candle'. That is a high aim for us all to aspire to in educating ourselves and our young people.

Barbara Windle, 1988

23.79   I may reach God through Keats, you by Beethoven, and a third through Einstein. Should not education to the Christian mean just this – enlarging and cultivating the country of God; and the subjects on any school timetable be thought of as avenues to an increasingly fuller life in God, or, to change the metaphor, windows, each of which gives a new view of the Kingdom of Heaven? ... This may seem a fantastically idealised view of what happens in a school, especially in these days of examinations, but is there any other open to the religiously-minded teacher? Is the commercial side of school and college life, the exchange of intellectual wares for examination results, so many facts and opinions for so many marks, which is so terribly dominating nowadays, to be allowed to weaken the allegiance of the young to knowledge and beauty as bringers of God to mortal men? No examination has yet been devised the passing of which will guarantee wisdom or culture. For these are slow-growing breeds, matters of character as well as of intellect and sentiment, the outcome of long exposure to the influences of truth and beauty.

Caroline C Graveson, 1937

23.80   Increasingly we see education as part of living rather than as preparation for living, and the motivation for educating ourselves and others grows more intrinsic than extrinsic. At Woodbrooke, which in some respects I still think is a prototype for much modern adult education, we have tried to build a small community to which people come in response to their own need for reflection or new skills or time to read; where proper attention is paid also to the needs of the neighbourhood; where staff and students and domestic workers and gardeners address each other without titles; where teachers and learners often exchange roles; where qualifications for entry are the ability to follow some courses, the wish to study, and the will to make community work; where the tasks are largely self-chosen; where conversation is expected between all age-groups between 18 and 80; where differences of nationality are seen as enrichment rather than as barriers (for one of the tasks of education is the enjoyment of diversity); where the rewards are existential, being visible chiefly in renewed courage or energy or the ability to re-launch oneself or to perform more adequately some of those unpaid services that make up the fabric of society. Of course we do not succeed all the time. But failure is also what we have to educate ourselves for – the humiliating, stimulating experiences of failures that we and our students must learn to use as stepping-stones rather than to deplore as obstacles.

William Fraser, 1973

23.81   To watch the spirit of children, to nurture them in Gospel Love, and labour to help them against that which would mar the beauty of their minds, is a debt we owe them; and a faithful performance of our duty not only tends to their lasting benefit and our own peace, but also to render their company agreeable to us. A care hath lived on my mind, that more time might be employed by parents at home, and by tutors at school, in weightily attending to the spirit and inclinations of children, and that we may so lead, instruct and govern them, in this tender part of life, that nothing may be omitted in our power, to help them on their way to become the children of our Father who is in heaven.

John Woolman, 1758

23.82   When I taught my children how to do many things I ensured that they would have skills to give them abilities, enjoyment and health. What I think I chiefly taught them was that I was right and they were wrong. When I hear them teaching their friends how to play games I realise just how much I bossed them around. In seeking to pass on our values to our children I think we largely waste our time. They will pick up our values from us by the way we live and the assumptions that underpin our own lives.

John Guest, 1987

23.83   If children are to be instructed in the groundwork of true religion, ought they not to discover in those placed over them, a lively example of its influence? Or ought they to see anything in the conduct of *others,* which would be condemned in *them,* were they in similar circumstances? Of what importance, then, is it for guardians of children, to rule their own spirits. For when their tempers are irritable, their language impetuous, their voices exerted above what is necessary, their threatenings unguarded, or the execution of them rash, however children may for a time suffer under these things, they are not instructed thereby in the groundwork of true religion.

Friends Educational Society, 1841

23.84   Friends' peace testimony challenges us all to be peace educators. We may not all be teachers, but we are all communicators, and we all need to be learners. Peace education should be seen as an integral part of our peace testimony. But it is essentially something one does, and not something one talks about... Learning, to be educated, means changing one's behaviour, and peace education therefore aims at changing our own individual behaviour... We communicate our values by the manner of our lives, but how many of us negate the peaceful attitudes we fervently profess by our own aggressive behaviour?

Eva I Pinthus, 1982

23.85   I feel peace education is about teaching children to discover that they have the power to change things they see are wrong and developing the imagination to find alternative responses to conflict. This is not an objective for a course called 'Peace' on the timetable. It must permeate all our teaching. For we cannot teach one thing and act another. If we teach children to feel their own power we must be ready for them to criticise the school itself. In order to survive we must begin to teach them to challenge authority, our own included.

This means that there are likely to be conflicts. And conflicts are to be welcomed as opportunities for growth. Too often conflict leads to violence and aggression because we are trapped in a mentality which expects every conflict to be resolved by a victory for one party. But victory for one implies of necessity defeat for the other and therein lies the seed of further conflict.

Teachers are optimists. We would not be teachers if we did not have confidence in the future and in humankind. We trust that given the right opportunities children will grow up into responsible adults capable of making good choices and of saving the world from disaster. Perhaps the most important thing we can do today is to transmit to our pupils that sense of hope. The prevailing mood is one of pessimism and despair. 'Why should I work hard when I won't be able to get a job anyway?' 'Why should I plan for a future which may never happen?' 'What difference can I make to decisions of governments?'

The two qualities which are most important to children of today are hope and imagination. Hope to believe they can change the world they live in and imagination to find ways to do so.

Janet Gilbraith, 1986

See also 24.54

FRIENDS AND STATE AUTHORITY

23.86 For conscience' sake to God, we are bound by his just law in our
hearts to yield obedience to [authority] in all matters and cases actively
or passively; that is to say, in all just and good commands of the king
and the good laws of the land relating to our outward man, we must
be obedient by doing ... but ... if anything be commanded of us by the
present authority, which is not according to equity, justice and a good
conscience towards God ... we must in such cases obey God only and
deny active obedience for conscience' sake, and patiently suffer what
is inflicted upon us for such our disobedience to men.

Edward Burrough, 1661

23.87 *After the bombardment of Alexandria in 1882, John Bright, in
explaining his resignation from the Government, said to the Commons:*

The House knows that for forty years at least I have endeavoured to
teach my countrymen an opinion and doctrine which I hold, namely,
that the moral law is intended not for individual life only, but for the
life and practice of States in their dealing with one another. I think
that in the present case there has been a manifest violation both of
International Law and of the moral law, and therefore it is impossible
for me to give my support to it.

23.88 We have ... in our Quaker history a lesson for our own lives of the
meaning of Christian citizenship. You can see there a two-fold
strand constantly interwoven: one, respect for the state as representing authority in the community: and the other, desire to serve the
community through the state and in other ways, but along with that,
the desire above all to serve the Kingdom of God: this means that we
must be willing, when loyalty to the Kingdom of God demands it to
refuse the demands of the state and show the highest loyalty to the
state and the best citizenship by refusing demands that are wrong,
because it is only in that way that the conscience of our fellow citizens
can be reached, and in the end a better law come into being.

T Edmund Harvey, 1937

23.89   *From a statement presented to London Yearly Meeting by a committee appointed by young men of enlistment age present at Yearly Meeting 1915:*

Christ demands of us that we adhere, without swerving, to the methods of love, and therefore, if a seeming conflict should arise between the claims of His service and those of the State, it is to Christ that our supreme loyalty must be given, whatever the consequences. We should however remember that whatever is our highest loyalty to God and humanity is at the same time the highest loyalty that we can render to our nation.

23.90   *Statement issued by Meeting for Sufferings in 1917, after the issue of a regulation requiring the submission of pamphlets to the Censor during the World War:*

The executive body of the Society of Friends, after serious consideration, desires to place on record its conviction that the portion of the recent regulation requiring the submission to the censor of all leaflets dealing with the present war and the making of peace is a grave danger to the national welfare. The duty of every good citizen to express his thoughts on the affairs of his country is hereby endangered, and further we believe that Christianity requires the toleration of opinions not our own, lest we should unwittingly hinder the workings of the Spirit of God.

Beyond this there is a deeper issue involved. It is for Christians a paramount duty to be free to obey and to act and speak in accord with the law of God, a law higher than that of any state, and no government official can release men from this duty.

We realise the rarity of the occasions on which a body of citizens find their sense of duty to be in conflict with the law, and it is with a sense of the gravity of this decision, that the Society of Friends must on this occasion act contrary to the regulation, and continue to issue literature on war and peace without submitting it to the censor. It is convinced that in thus standing firm for spiritual liberty it is acting in the best interests of the nation.

23.91   We are deeply uneasy about the increasing secrecy which permeates our process of government. We see this in the 1989 Official Secrets

Act, which no longer allows the defence of the right of disclosure in the public interest. We have been led to the conviction that, despite a culture of state secrecy, we must strive to bring about openness in our country. Secrecy bolsters power and leads to deceit and the abuse of power. At times a sensitive reticence is required but, in working in the spirit of love and trust rather than fear, we seek to discern the boundary between that reticence and secrecy.

London Yearly Meeting, 1990

See also 29.11

Conscription

23.92   *On the passing of the Military Service Act 1916, London Yearly Meeting minuted:*

We take this, the earliest opportunity, of reaffirming our entire opposition to compulsory military service and our desire for the repeal of the Act. War, in our view, involves the surrender of the Christian ideal and the denial of human brotherhood; it is an evil for the destruction of which the world is longing; but freedom from the scourge of war will only be brought about through the faithfulness of individuals to their inmost convictions, under the guidance of the spirit of Christ.

Our position is based upon our interpretation of the teaching of Jesus Christ. We regard the central conception of the Act as imperilling the liberty of the individual conscience – which is the main hope of human progress – and as entrenching more deeply that militarism from which we all desire the world to be freed... Our lives should prove that compulsion is both unnecessary and impolitic. They should manifest a sense of duty not less strong than that which has driven many whom we respect (and some even of our own members) into the fighting forces. We can identify ourselves to the full with the griefs of our nation in which few hearts are not torn by suffering or harrowed by suspense. We pray that in steadfast conformity to the path of duty we may be set free to serve – to give to the community the fullest service of which we are capable – each one in the way of God's appointing.

23.93 Compulsory military service is sometimes claimed as a duty attaching to citizenship. But it is not true social service. On the one hand it is part of the attempt to maintain peace by force, and on the other it is training in methods that are contrary to the highest moral standards recognised by man... The training of men to kill each other is a violation of the sacredness of personality for it is a crime against that of God in every man. It requires an inhumanity and a blind obedience that is a negation of responsible service to our fellow men. It demands much that in private life is recognised as anti-social and criminal... Christ bids us love our enemies; governments bid us kill them. The conscript is, in effect, required to endorse war in advance.

Meeting for Sufferings, 1945

See also 24.14-24.16 Conscientious objection to compulsory military service

Crime and punishment

23.94 The terrible sufferings of our forebears in the prisons of the seventeenth century have given us as a people a special interest in the management of prisons and the treatment of crime. George Fox protested to the judges of his day 'concerning their putting men to death for cattle and money and small matters'; and laid before them 'what a hurtful thing it was that prisoners should lie so long in jail'; showing how 'they learned wickedness from one another in talking of their bad deeds'.

There is, however, much work still to be done, in creating a right understanding of the nature and causes of crime, and in emphasising the need for redemptive treatment rather than retributive punishment. Society is in measure responsible for the criminal, a fact which emphasises the duty of meeting moral failure by redemptive care. Evil can only be finally overcome by good.

1911; 1925; 1959; 1994

23.95 The essential idea behind these first tentative criticisms [of early prison conditions by George Fox and William Penn] was a completely new one: that imprisonment should be looked on as a means of reforming criminals and not merely punishing them. No man is ever utterly lost, and however deep he is sunk in evil, the only just approach to him is to work for his recovery. This principle led John Bellers, the earliest Friend to pay serious and systematic attention to social reform, to plead for the abolition of the death penalty [in 1699]. Society had done enough for its own protection, he argued, when it had rendered a murderer harmless by putting him in prison; if it did more it was acting in a spirit of revenge.

Harold Loukes, 1960

23.96   The real security for human life is to be found in a reverence for it. If the law regarded it as inviolable, then the people would begin also so to regard it. A deep reverence for human life is worth more than a thousand executions in the prevention of murder... The law of capital punishment while pretending to support this reverence, does in fact tend to destroy it.

John Bright, 1868

23.97   *At a time when a Bill was before Parliament for the abolition of the death penalty for murder:*

We feel that we should at this time declare once again our unwavering opposition to capital punishment. The sanctity of human life is one of the fundamentals of a Christian society and can in no circumstances be set aside. Our concern, therefore, is for all victims of violence, not only the murderer but also those who suffer by his act.

The sanctioning by the State of the taking of human life has a debasing effect on the community, and tends to produce the very brutality which it seeks to prevent. We realise that many are sincerely afraid of the consequences if the death penalty is abolished, but we are convinced that their fears are unjustified.

London Yearly Meeting, 1956

23.98   *Elizabeth Fry (1780-1845) was born into the Gurney family in Norwich. She committed herself to a religious life following the visit of William Savery of Philadelphia when she was seventeen. She devoted herself to work for prison reform (see 18.08 & 26.40). In 1827 she wrote of this work:*

Much depends on the spirit in which the visitor enters upon her work. It must be in the spirit, not of judgment, but of mercy. She must not say in her heart *I am more holy than thou,* but must rather keep in perpetual remembrance that '*all* have sinned and come short of the Glory of God'.

23.99 There was no weakness or trouble of mind or body which might not safely be unveiled to [Elizabeth Fry]. Whatever various or opposite views, feelings or wishes might be confided to her, all came out again tinged with her own loving, hoping spirit. Bitterness of every kind died; when entrusted to her, it never reappeared. The most favourable construction possible was always put upon every transaction. No doubt her failing lay this way; but did it not give her and her example a wonderful influence? Was it not the very secret of her power with the wretched and degraded prisoners? She always could see hope for everyone; she invariably found or made some point of light. The most abandoned must have felt she did not despair for them, either for this world or another; and this it was that made her irresistible.

Priscilla Buxton, 1847

23.100 In the evening Martha Savory, my mother [Mary Dudley] and I went to Newgate [Gaol], where we met Elizabeth Fry, Peter Bedford and Edward Harris. We saw about fifteen poor men under sentence of death, who soon collected round us and stood with the most becoming and quiet attention, whilst my mother was engaged to preach the gospel of reconciliation... The two especially who had but a few hours to live, were encouraged to cast themselves upon the mercy and forgiveness of an all-gracious God whose power and goodness are the same as when they were manifested to the thief upon the cross... They wept freely, and though not able to *say* much, we fully believe they *felt*. It was difficult to tear ourselves from such a scene, and we turned from these poor sufferers under the feeling of indignant repugnance to the sanguinary nature of those laws which put so little value upon human life, and adjudge punishments so disproportioned to and so unlikely to prevent the renewal of crimes.

Elizabeth Dudley, 1818

23.101   Imprisonment ... offers some protection to society by removing the offender. But consider how limited that protection is compared to what it could be. It puts the offender against property into a place where he is deprived of opportunities to practise the social rules about property; it puts the violent man into a subculture which is governed by violence; it puts the defrauder into a power system where corruption is rife; it puts the sexual offender into a place where sexual relief is only obtainable by substitutes; ... it puts those who need to learn to take control of their lives into a situation where all significant choices are made for them; and it puts the offender who is likely to reform into a milieu where most of the influences on him or her are criminal ones.

John Lampen, 1987

23.102   We believe in overcoming evil with good. We must speak and act from our own inner light to the inner light in all others as Jesus did. He showed and taught love, respect and concern for all, particularly those rejected by others, reaching out to the good in them.

Causing deliberate hurt to another person because that suffering is thought to be of benefit in itself, we believe is not a Christian response. Punishment in this sense not only harms the punished but also degrades those who inflict it, and is a barrier to the working of God's love within us.

Whether it be in the family, the school, the workplace or the wider community the intentional use of pain and suffering cannot be the best way to resolve differences, or gain the cooperation of people or restrain those who harm themselves or others.

To do away with punishment is not to abandon safety and control or to move towards disintegration, disorder and lawlessness. A non-punitive approach will not remove the need in some circumstances for restraint or secure containment, but it does mean that restraint and containment should be carried out in a life-enhancing spirit of love and care.

Nor in general does this loving approach have lesser expectations or demand less responsibility than does the infliction and acceptance of punishment. In personal relationships and in the broader context of community and international affairs a positive response to aberrant or destructive behaviour through reconciliation, restitution and reparation may take longer but it will be more likely to encourage the good in all parties, restore those who are damaged, reduce resentment and bitterness, and enable all those involved to move towards fuller integration.

Six Quakers, 1979

23.103   Reconciliation in its basic form occurs between two people face to face... But we must be clear that reconciliation, in the sense of meeting, comprehending, and working to prevent the future following the pattern of the past, is not always possible. The demand for justice, the desire for revenge, may prevent it. Quakers in particular seem to have a horror of revenge as a motive. We need to remember that, in the interests of social harmony, law-abiding citizens have voluntarily surrendered their rights of retaliation to the state. It may be true that when the state takes revenge, nothing constructive has been achieved. But it is also true that if not even this is done, the hurt remains with the person who has been wronged. Where the burden of suffering is clearly on one side, the burden of wrong-doing on the other, it is a kind of insult to tell the victim that he or she should be reconciled. We are told that there is no peace without justice. How are we to meet the claims of justice without forging the next link in the chain of hurt?

Restitution ... accepts the reality of what has happened and the right of the sufferer to 'have something done about it'. It accepts that the perpetrator is in most cases feeling guilty, or at least humiliated to have been detected. But it offers him or her an opportunity to regain the good opinion of the sufferer and the community, and to be seen as a person who can give as well as take away, who can right wrongs as well as cause them... When I was working with deviant and deprived children, and almost all disciplinary matters were decided by the whole community on a basis of putting things right, I was able to see how the victims feel supported and protected by this approach. It was moving to see how much they wanted to accept the evidence of contrition, how much they wanted to forgive. Provided that we could ensure that it worked effectively, those who had been hurt were satisfied; it was outsiders, not directly involved, who became angry and told me that this was a sentimental option which did not face the realities of injustice. They were afraid of pain, hurt, violence, and the breakdown of order; and their fear made them violent. Those who had already experienced this breakdown recognised that restitution offered them a way out.

John Lampen, 1987

Those who have looked for a more forthright statement of a Quaker view on a subject which concerns them deeply, may experience some disappointment at not finding it here. However we hope that Friends will appreciate that this may be because Friends are still searching for a corporate view, or because we have not been able to find a suitable extract, or because this book cannot hope to cover every aspect of human affairs.

Some individual Friends have provided the challenge which has led the Society to consider a subject more deeply. Often we have been able to make corporate statements on issues such as war and poverty which challenge ourselves as well as the larger society. Sometimes we can suggest how we should set about seeking a remedy, but often we have to realise that in such a book as this we cannot hope to provide detailed consideration leading to any definitive statement. Indeed we have to beware of putting forward our corporate findings too dogmatically. We must humbly admit our own failings, and then work and pray that we may be led to find a way forward.

Chapter 24

Our peace testimony

THE CORPORATE TESTIMONY

The Peace Testimony is probably the best known and best loved of the Quaker testimonies. Its roots lie in the personal experience of the love and power of Christ which marked the founders of the Quaker movement. They were dominated by a vision of the world transformed by Christ who lives in the hearts of all. Friends sought to make the vision real by putting emphasis on Christian practice rather than primarily on any particular dogma or ideological system. Theirs was a spontaneous and practical religion. They recognised the realities of evil and conflict, but it was contrary to the spirit of Christ to use war and violence as means to deal with them.

The Peace Testimony has been a source of inspiration to Friends through the centuries, for it points to a way of life which embraces all human relationships. The following extracts trace the source of the Peace Testimony in the experience of the founders of the Quaker movement and illustrate its evolution over three hundred and fifty years in response to a changing world. As a Society we have been faithful throughout in maintaining a corporate witness against all war and violence. However, in our personal lives we have continually to wrestle with the difficulty of finding ways to reconcile our faith with practical ways of living it out in the world. It is not surprising, therefore, that we have not always all reached the same conclusions when dealing with the daunting complexities and moral dilemmas of society and its government.

In the closing years of the twentieth century, we as Friends face a bewildering array of social and international challenges, which have widened the relevance of the Peace Testimony from the issue of peace and war between states to the problems of tensions and conflicts in all their forms. Thus we are brought closer to the witness of early Friends, who did not draw a hard and fast distinction between the various Quaker testimonies, but saw them as a seamless expression of the universal spirit of Christ that dwells in the hearts of all.

24.01 I told [the Commonwealth Commissioners] I lived in the virtue of that life and power that took away the occasion of all wars... I told them I was come into the covenant of peace which was before wars and strife were.

George Fox, 1651

24.02 Whoever can reconcile this, 'Resist not evil', with 'Resist violence by force', again, 'Give also thy other cheek', with 'Strike again'; also 'Love thine enemies', with 'Spoil them, make a prey of them, pursue them with fire and the sword', or, 'Pray for those that persecute you, and those that calumniate you', with 'Persecute them by fines, imprisonments and death itself', whoever, I say, can find a means to reconcile these things may be supposed also to have found a way to reconcile God with the Devil, Christ with Antichrist, Light with Darkness, and good with evil. But if this be impossible, as indeed it is impossible, so will also the other be impossible, and men do but deceive both themselves and others, while they boldly adventure to establish such absurd and impossible things.

Robert Barclay, 1678

24.03 A good end cannot sanctify evil means; nor must we ever do evil, that good may come of it... It is as great presumption to send our passions upon God's errands, as it is to palliate them with God's name... We are too ready to retaliate, rather than forgive, or gain by love and information. And yet we could hurt no man that we believe loves us. Let us then try what Love will do: for if men did once see we love them, we should soon find they would not harm us. Force may subdue, but Love gains: and he that forgives first, wins the laurel.

William Penn, 1693

The early statements of the Society's corporate witness set out the basic principles of the peace testimony and served to distinguish Quakers from those suspected of plotting to overthrow the established authorities.

24.04   Our principle is, and our practices have always been, to seek peace, and ensue it, and to follow after righteousness and the knowledge of God, seeking the good and welfare, and doing that which tends to the peace of all. All bloody principles and practices we do utterly deny, with all outward wars, and strife, and fightings with outward weapons, for any end, or under any pretence whatsoever, and this is our testimony to the whole world. That spirit of Christ by which we are guided is not changeable, so as once to command us from a thing as evil, and again to move unto it; and we do certainly know, and so testify to the world, that the spirit of Christ which leads us into all Truth will never move us to fight and war against any man with outward weapons, neither for the kingdom of Christ, nor for the kingdoms of this world.

And as for the kingdoms of this world, we cannot covet them, much less can we fight for them, but we do earnestly desire and wait, that by the word of God's power and its effectual operation in the hearts of men the kingdoms of this world may become the kingdoms of the Lord and of his Christ, that he might rule and reign in men by his spirit and truth, that thereby all people, out of all different judgments and professions might be brought into love and unity with God and one with another, and that they might all come to witness the prophet's words, who said, 'Nation shall not lift up sword against nation, neither shall they learn war any more'. (Is 2:4; Mic 4:3)

Declaration to Charles II, 1660

Margaret Fell's earlier expression of these ideas may be found at 19.46

After the first wave of enthusiasm had spent itself, the Society of Friends settled and became organised. Henceforth there was greater emphasis on specific Quaker testimonies which distinguished Friends from the rest of the community. The Peace Testimony gradually became institutionalised, reflecting the preoccupations of succeeding generations and their perceptions of world affairs. It found expression in more formal and reasoned statements as well as in the vivid personal witness of Friends. The formal statements reflected different experiences of war and violence through the centuries, but the kernel of faith remained unchanged.

For further passages from the seventeenth century see 19.45-19.47

24.05 *Issued by Yearly Meeting in London 1744, during the War of the Austrian Succession:*

We entreat all who profess themselves members of our Society to be faithful to that ancient testimony, borne by us ever since we were a people, against bearing arms and fighting, that by a conduct agreeable to our profession we may demonstrate ourselves to be real followers of the Messiah, the peaceable Saviour, of the increase of whose government and peace there shall be no end.

24.06 *Issued by Yearly Meeting in London 1804, 1805, during the Napoleonic Wars:*

Most, if not all, people admit the transcendent excellency of peace. All who adopt the petition, 'Thy kingdom come', pray for its universal establishment. Some people then must begin to fulfil the evangelical promise, and cease to learn war any more. Now, friends, seeing these things cannot be controverted, how do we long that your whole conversation be as becometh the Gospel; and that while any of us are professing to scruple war, they may not in some parts of their conduct be inconsistent with that profession! ... Friends, it is an awful thing to stand forth to the nation as the advocates of inviolable peace; and our testimony loses its efficacy in proportion to the want of consistency in any... And we can serve our country in no way more availingly, nor more acceptably to him who holds its prosperity at his disposal, than by contributing, all that in us lies, to increase the number of meek, humble, and self-denying Christians.

Guard against placing your dependence on fleets and armies; be peaceable yourselves, in words and actions, and pray to the Father of the Universe that he would breathe the spirit of reconciliation into the hearts of his erring and contending creatures.

24.07 *Issued by Yearly Meeting in London 1900, during the South African War:*

We believe that the Spirit of Christ will ultimately redeem national as well as individual life. We believe further that, as all church history shows, the human means will be the faithful witness borne by Christ's disciples. It has been well said: 'It seems to be the will of

Him, who is infinite in wisdom, that light upon great subjects should first arise and be gradually spread through the faithfulness of individuals in acting up to their own convictions.' This was the secret of the power of the early Church. The blood of the Christians proved a fruitful seed. In like manner the staunchness of early Friends and others to their conscientious convictions in the seventeenth century won the battle of religious freedom for England. We covet a like faithful witness against war from Christians today.

24.08   *Issued by London Yearly Meeting 1915, during the First World War:*

Meeting at a time when the nations of Europe are engaged in a war of unparalleled magnitude, we have been led to recall the basis of the peace testimony of our religious Society. It is not enough to be satisfied with a barren negative witness, a mere proclamation of non-resistance. We must search for a positive, vital, constructive message. Such a message, a message of supreme love, we find in the life and death of our Lord Jesus Christ. We find it in the doctrine of the indwelling Christ, that re-discovery of the early Friends, leading as it does to a recognition of the brotherhood of all men. Of this doctrine our testimony as to war and peace is a necessary outcome, and if we understand the doctrine aright, and follow it in its wide implications, we shall find that it calls to the peaceable spirit and the rule of love in all the broad and manifold relations of life.

Thus while love, joy, peace, gentleness and holiness are the teaching of the life and death of our Lord, it is to these that we are also impelled by the indwelling of the Divine in men. As this spirit grows within us, we shall realise increasingly what it is to live in the virtue of that life and power which takes away the occasion of all wars.

24.09   *Issued by London Yearly Meeting 1943, during the Second World War:*

All thoughtful men and women are torn at heart by the present situation. The savage momentum of war drags us all in its wake. We desire a righteous peace. Yet to attain peace it is claimed that, as Chungking, Rotterdam and Coventry were devastated, so the Eder and Moehne dams must needs be destroyed and whole districts of Hamburg obliterated. The people of Milan and Turin demonstrate for peace but the bombing continues. War is hardening our hearts.

To preserve our sanity, we become apathetic. In such an atmosphere no true peace can be framed; yet before us we see months of increasing terror. Can those who pay heed to moral laws, can those who follow Christ submit to the plea that the only way is that demanded by military necessity?

True peace involves freedom from tyranny and a generous tolerance; conditions that are denied over a large part of Europe and are not fulfilled in other parts of the world. But true peace cannot be dictated, it can only be built in co-operation between all peoples. None of us, no nation, no citizen, is free from some responsibility for this situ-ation with its conflicting difficulties.

To the world in its confusion Christ came. Through him we know that God dwells with men and that by turning from evil and living in his spirit we may be led into his way of peace. That way of peace is not to be found in any policy of 'unconditional surrender' by whomsoever demanded. It requires that men and nations should recognise their common brotherhood, using the weapons of integrity, reason, patience and love, never acquiescing in the ways of the oppressor, always ready to suffer with the oppressed. In every country there is a longing for freedom from domination and war which men are striving to express. Now is the time to issue an open invitation to co-operate in creative peacemaking, to declare our willingness to make sacrifices of national prestige, wealth and standards of living for the common good of men.

24.10 *Public statement of the Yearly Meeting of Aotearoa/New Zealand, 1987, at a time when many Friends were making submissions to a committee established by their government to review defence policy:*

We totally oppose all wars, all preparation for war, all use of weapons and coercion by force, and all military alliances: no end could ever justify such means.

We equally and actively oppose all that leads to violence among people and nations, and violence to other species and to our planet.

Refusal to fight with weapons is not surrender. We are not passive when threatened by the greedy, the cruel, the tyrant, the unjust.

We will struggle to remove the causes of impasse and confrontation by every means of nonviolent resistance available.

We urge all New Zealanders to have the courage to face up to the mess humans are making of our world and to have the faith and diligence to cleanse it and restore the order intended by God.

We must start with our own hearts and minds. Wars will stop only when each of us is convinced that war is never the way.

The places to begin acquiring the skills and maturity and generosity to avoid or to resolve conflicts are in our own homes, our personal relationships, our schools, our workplaces, and wherever decisions are made.

We must relinquish the desire to own other people, to have power over them, and to force our views on to them. We must own up to our own negative side and not look for scapegoats to blame, punish, or exclude. We must resist the urge towards waste and the accumulation of possessions.

Conflicts are inevitable and must not be repressed or ignored but worked through painfully and carefully. We must develop the skills of being sensitive to oppression and grievances, sharing power in decision-making, creating consensus, and making reparation.

In speaking out, we acknowledge that we ourselves are as limited and as erring as anyone else. When put to the test, we each may fall short.

We do not have a blueprint for peace that spells out every stepping stone towards the goal that we share. In any particular situation, a variety of personal decisions could be made with integrity.

We may disagree with the views and actions of the politician or the soldier who opts for a military solution, but we still respect and cherish the person.

What we call for in this statement is a commitment to make the building of peace a priority and to make opposition to war absolute.

What we advocate is not uniquely Quaker but human and, we believe, the will of God. Our stand does not belong to Friends alone – it is yours by birthright.

We challenge all New Zealanders to stand up and be counted on what is no less than the affirmation of life and the destiny of humankind.

Together, let us reject the clamour of fear and listen to the whisperings of hope.

24.11   The peace testimony is about deeds not creeds; not a form of words but a way of living. It is the cumulative lived witness of generations of Quakers... The peace testimony is not about being nice to people and living so that everyone likes us. It will remain a stumbling block and will itself cause conflict and disagreement. The peace testimony is a tough demand that we should not automatically accept the categories, definitions and priorities of the world. We look to the Spirit, rather than to prescriptive hypothetical statements. The peace testimony, today, is seen in what we do, severally and together, with our lives. We pray for the involvement of the Spirit with us, that we may work for a more just world. We need to train to wage peace.

London Yearly Meeting, 1993

PERSONAL WITNESS

24.12   The emphasis on personal action, which in the case of war means abstention, inevitably raises the problem of where one draws the line. In the total wars of the first half of this century, Quakers accepted non-combatant service with the armed forces, served in an independent but uniformed Friends Ambulance Unit, relieved the sufferings of civilian war victims, did alternative civilian service of 'national importance' at home, went to prison for refusing any service which might assist the war effort, even fire-watching. Some refused to pay taxes. There are no formal rules laid down for Quaker conduct in such circumstances, other than to follow the Light of Christ.

Wolf Mendl, 1974

24.13   We had been talking for an hour and a half with a clergyman neighbour, and afterwards I sat by the fire and thought. He had maintained that war has not as yet been grown out of, and that God still uses it as a means of training His children. As I thought over this, old thoughts and memories awoke from sleep. I remembered the familiar words about William Penn's sword – 'Wear it as long as thou canst': and it seemed clear to me that if William Penn had given it up from self-interest or cowardice, or for any reason short of the 'witness of God in his own soul', he would have been wrong. And then the thought extended itself from the life of one man to the life of mankind, and I remembered a sentence in the Epistle to Diognetus: 'What the soul is in the body, that Christians are in the world'. Then I seemed to see that war cannot rightly come to an end from self-interest or cowardice or any worldly reason but only because men and women, by one and one, without waiting for the others, have become loyal to the spirit of Christ.

Marion C Fox, 1914

Conscientious objection to compulsory military service

Compulsory military service was introduced during the two World Wars and Friends, among others, appeared before tribunals to justify their stand as conscientious objectors.

24.14 I was asked to be at the Tribunal in Manchester by 11 am on Tuesday, i.e. yesterday. I was there with Joyce and my witness well before time but they spent so long over the men in front of me that my case did not appear until immediately after lunch. Despite the gruelling time they had given the applicants in the morning, they gave me a very kind hearing. I felt very excited and worked up so when the chairman asked me the leading question, Why do you object to civil defence, I asked to be allowed to sit for a few moments in quietness while I gathered myself. When I felt ready I told them simply what I had experienced of the love of Jesus and how I felt that I was called to answer to the spiritual suffering in the world. They listened very quietly and only asked me how I intended to put into practice what I had learned and then, how my plans for going to China were progressing and then they seemed satisfied. I felt very young and child-like in talking to them. Their decision was to register me unconditionally on the register of COs. All over in about 20 minutes.

Looking back and realising how very easily things might have gone the other way the only explanation which both Joyce and I can see is that it is a miracle of God, helped by the prayers and loving thoughts of my friends.

I do not feel that I have yet grasped the whole significance of what has happened but I do see that it has placed an even greater responsibility upon me to follow what I really feel to be God's calling for it is in that trust that the community has freed me.

Eric Baker, 1941

24.15   I have sometimes been asked what were my reasons for deciding on that refusal to register for war duties that sent me to Holloway Jail 22 years ago. I can only answer that my reason told me that I was a fool, that I was risking my job and my career, that an isolated example could do no good, that it was a futile gesture since even if I did register my three small children would exempt me. But reason was fighting a losing battle. I had wrestled in prayer and I knew beyond all doubt that I *must* refuse to register, that those who believed that war was the wrong way to fight evil must stand out against it however much they stood alone, and that I and mine must take the consequences. The 'and mine' made it more difficult, but I question whether children ever really suffer loss in the long run through having parents who are willing to stand by principles; many a soldier had to leave his family and thought it his duty to do so. When you have to make a vital decision about behaviour, you cannot sit on the fence. To decide to do nothing is still a decision, and it means that you remain on the station platform or the airstrip when the train or plane has left.

Kathleen Lonsdale, 1964

24.16   On my third or fourth attendance at the Sunday service with Friends, an American young Quaker who was on the staff of the American Friends Service Committee working in Tokyo came to talk about his own experiences of having been a conscientious objector during World War II and about the ideas of CO in relation to Quaker beliefs. It really was an epoch-making shock to me to know such a thing as CO existing in this world. I had never heard nor dreamed anything like that even though I had been brought up in a devout Christian family. This person had lived 'love your enemy' in the US at the same time that I had been caught up with the mad notions of nationalism and of winning the 'Holy War' in Japan...

Quaker worship gave me time and space to dissolve my hard shell of self-centredness to be sensitive to discern things with fairness and unaffected by prejudice. I felt the need to be faithful to truth instead of relying on existing judgment. The idea of conscientious objection based on the philosophy of non-violence struck me and was proved to me to be fair, reasonable and Christian. I concluded that it must be the way to take for me and for Japan who had heart-rending experiences of defeat in war and of two nuclear disasters. This became my conviction and I was glad when I realised Japan had declared itself by its new constitution to be a unique CO nation, stating clearly in article 9 of the constitution that it would abolish fighting forces for ever.

One day in Tokyo Local Court, I had an opportunity to make a statement to witness why I felt it necessary to resist tax-payment for military expenditures, saying, 'With military power we cannot protect our life nor keep our human dignity. Even if I should be killed, my way of living or dying to show my sympathy and forgiveness to my opponents, to point to the love of God shown by Jesus Christ on the cross and by his resurrection, will have a better chance to invite others to turn to walk rightly so that we humankind may live together peacefully.'

Susumu Ishitani, 1989

Conscientious objection to taxation for military purposes

24.17   *From time to time the British crown asked the governing bodies of the colonies to support its military ventures in America by levying taxes towards its wars. This proved to be a problem for the Quaker members of the Pennsylvania Assembly as well as for individual Friends. Some Friends in both England and America paid such taxes but John Woolman became uneasy, so he wrote in his Journal:*

Yet there was in the deeps of my mind a scruple which I never could get over... I all along believed that there were some upright-hearted men who paid such taxes, but could not see that their example was a sufficient reason for me to do so, while I believed that the spirit of Truth required of me as an individual to suffer patiently the distress of goods rather than pay actively.

1755

See 14.08

24.18   The action of withholding the military proportion of our taxes arose
for us from our corporately held testimony that 'the Spirit of Christ,
which leads us into all truth, will never move us to fight and war
against any man with outward weapons, neither for the kingdom of
Christ, nor for the kingdoms of this world'. This testimony may at
times lead to resisting the demands of the state, when a higher law
(i.e. God's inner law) makes its first claim on us. We also need to be
conscious that, if we offend against accepted law, we may have to
take the consequences of our action.

Arthur and Ursula Windsor, 1992

24.19   *In March 1982 Meeting for Sufferings considered the request by
some London Yearly Meeting employees that the part of their
income tax attributable to military purposes should be diverted to
non-military uses. Tax was withheld from October 1982 until, in
June 1985, the Appeal Court ruled that the action was unlawful.
Meeting for Sufferings then decided to pay the tax withheld since the
law had been tested as far as possible. At the same time it made a
submission to the European Commission of Human Rights on the
grounds of the right to freedom of thought, conscience and religion;
in July 1986 the Commission ruled the case inadmissible. Yearly
Meeting returned to the matter in 1987 (see 29.10). The following
letter to the Inland Revenue in 1991 records some of the dilemmas
of Meeting for Sufferings in seeking to further the concern:*

The Religious Society of Friends has, since its beginnings in the seventeenth century, borne witness against war and armed conflict as
contrary to the spirit and teachings of Christ. We have sought to
build institutions and relationships which make for peace and to
resist military activity. The horrific nature of modern armaments
makes our witness particularly urgent. The Gulf War involved the
substantial use of expensive modern weapons and technology,
demonstrating that today it is the conscription of our money rather
than our bodies which makes war possible.

For many years members of the Religious Society of Friends have
been exercised about how we might be true to our historic peace testimony while still obeying the laws of our country. You will know that
we have appealed through the courts and ultimately to the European

Commission of Human Rights for recognition of the right of conscientious objection to paying taxes for military purposes...

Since losing the appeal we have paid in full the income tax collected from our employees. In recent months we have considered whether we can continue to do this, but after very careful consideration have decided that for the time being we must do so. The acceptance of the rule of law is part of our witness, ... for a just and peaceful world cannot come about without this. However we do wish to make it clear that we object to the way in which the PAYE system involves us in a process of collecting money, used in part to pay for military activity and war preparations, which takes away from the individual taxpayer the right to express their own conscientious objection. This involvement is incompatible with our work for peace.

24.20　On my last appearance in court [for withholding war tax], having already sent in my defence on grounds of conscience, backed by the Genocide Act, Geneva Convention, etc, I felt I wanted to make a more general statement about the fact that we have not used the United Nations as we should to settle disputes, or given sufficient support to it and its ... agencies. So I wrote a statement, gave copies to my faithful supporting Friends and other pacifists and handed a copy to the Judge, asking if I might read it. He listened attentively to what I read, as his comments afterwards showed, though of course his verdict was the usual refusal. It seems important to me to get the understanding of judges so that they will give serious consideration to our point of view and might eventually influence a change in the law, though they always say that is not their business.

Joan Hewitt, 1992

See also 29.10

THE DILEMMAS OF THE PACIFIST STAND

24.21　I speak not against any magistrates or peoples defending themselves against foreign invasions; or making use of the sword to suppress the violent and evil-doers within their borders – for this the present estate of things may and doth require, and a great blessing will attend the sword where it is borne uprightly to that end and its use will be honourable ... but yet there is a better state, which the Lord hath already brought some into, and which nations are to expect and to travel towards. There is to be a time when 'nation shall not lift up sword against nation; neither shall they learn war any more'. When the power of the Gospel spreads over the whole earth, thus shall it be throughout the earth, and, where the power of the Spirit takes hold of and overcomes any heart at present, thus will it be at present with that heart. This blessed state, which shall be brought forth [in society] at large in God's season, must begin in particulars [that is, in individuals].

Isaac Penington, 1661

24.22 Because of their personal experience and convictions, [early] Friends did not deny the reality of evil and of conflict. Nor did they equate conflict with evil. They were well aware of the suffering which a non-violent witness could bring in an imperfect world. This is in contrast to those who identify peace with the absence of conflict and value that above all things. It is the latter who have given modern pacifism its bad name and have led their critics to refer to them contemptuously as 'passivists'. The failure to take evil and conflict into account as elements in our human condition and an obsession with the need for peace and harmony have led pacifists badly astray... Christian pacifists [are] not exempt from the temptation to sacrifice others for the sake of peace.

Wolf Mendl, 1974

24.23 *Corder Catchpool (1883-1952) served in the Friends Ambulance Unit during the First World War, but on the introduction of conscription he returned to England to give his witness as a conscientous objector and was imprisoned for more than two years; later he worked for reconciliation, especially with Germany. He told the Court Martial which sentenced him at Dovercourt on 28 March 1918:*

There is hardly a moment when my thoughts are not with the men in France, eager to help the wounded by immediate human touch with their sufferings. This I was privileged to do during nineteen months spent at the Front with the Friends Ambulance Unit from October 1914 to May 1916, when it was still possible to give voluntary service. At times the impulse to return to this work becomes almost irresistible. May God steady me, and keep me faithful to a call I have heard above the roar of the guns. By the feverish activity of my hands, I might help to save a fraction of the present human wreckage. That would be for me no sacrifice. It costs far more to spend mind and spirit, if need be, in the silence of a prison cell, in passionate witness for the great truths of Peace. That is the call I hear. I believe that only spiritual influence will avail to free the world at last from war, to free the soldiers' little ones and confused struggling humanity itself from all that men and women are suffering now. I honour those who, in loyalty to conscience, have gone out to fight. In a crisis like the present it would be unbecoming to elaborate the reasons which have led me to a course so different. Today a man must act. I believe, with the strength of my whole being, that standing here I am enlisted in active service as a soldier of Jesus Christ, who bids every man be true to the sense of duty that is laid upon his soul.

24.24   Now, in the war, I do not think that any of us could doubt the colossal quality of the evil represented by Nazi philosophy. And I do not think that, in political terms, it was possible to contemplate coming to any sort of political compromise with it... Speaking personally as a Christian pacifist, I had a far deeper sense of spiritual unity with those of my friends in the fighting services who, detesting war as deeply as I did, yet felt that there was no other way in which they could share in the agony of the world, than I had with those pacifists who talked as if the suffering of the world could be turned off like a water tap if only politicians would talk sensibly together. Where men have sinned as grievously and as long as we have done in our social and international relations with one another, there can be no easy end to the consequences... We could not engage in warlike activity in the hope of relieving the suffering of the Jews or of other oppressed peoples in Europe and Asia. We had, somehow, to try to participate in their suffering and to express the conviction that it is ultimately the power of suffering in love that redeems men from the power of evil.

Roger Wilson, 1949

24.25   Conscientious objection is not a total repudiation of force; it is a refusal to surrender moral responsibility for one's action.

Kenneth C Barnes, 1987

24.26   Friends are not naïve enough to believe that such an appeal 'to that of God' in a dictator or in a nation which for psychological or other reasons is in an aggressive mood will necessarily be successful in converting the tyrant or preventing aggression. Christ was crucified; Gandhi was assassinated. Yet they did not fail. Nor did they leave behind them the hatred, devastation and bitterness that war, successful or unsuccessful, does leave. What can be claimed, moreover, is that this method of opposing evil is one of which no person, no group, no nation need be ashamed, as we may and should be ashamed of the inhumanities of war that are perpetrated in our name and with our support.

Kathleen Lonsdale, 1953

PRACTICAL EXPRESSIONS OF OUR PEACE TESTIMONY

As Friends we have never been satisfied that corporate statements and personal witness are enough. We have always sought to give a practical expression to our faith. Action has taken various forms and has included public protest, the relief of suffering, reconstruction and the removal of the causes of war through mediation, reconciliation, disarmament, building the institutions of peace, promoting social justice, and getting at the roots of conflict and violence in our personal behaviour.

Public protest

24.27   I do not wish to deny that on April 4th, the anniversary of the death of Martin Luther King, I was inside the Faslane Submarine Base, and that I was there as a deliberate act. However, I pled guilty to the charges because had I done otherwise I would have been guilty of far greater crimes against my conscience and against humanity.

If I may, I would like to outline very briefly the reasons for so acting, not so much as mitigation of guilt, but rather as a declaration of intent, for as long as those bases remain, I must continue to act as my conscience guides.

My charge is that I entered a protected area without authority or permission. My claim is that I had authority – the authority of my Christian conviction that a gospel of love cannot be defended by the threatened annihilation of millions of innocent people. It can never be morally right to use these ghastly weapons at any time, whether first, or as unthinkable retaliation after we ourselves are doomed.

I acted also with the authority of the nameless millions dying of starvation now because we choose to spend £11.5 billion on Trident whilst a child dies every 15 seconds.

I am further authorised by my 13-year-old Vietnamese god-daughter whose guardian I am. She was adopted and brought to Scotland to take her away from the unspeakable horror of the Vietnam war. If all that I have done is to bring her closer to the nuclear holocaust, I stand convicted by her of the most cynical inhumanity.

I am charged under an Act giving control and disposal of land to the Queen, the Lords Spiritual and Temporal, the Commons assembled in Parliament and eventually the Secretary of State. I believe the world is God's creation. This beautiful, delicate world in all its infinite wonder is threatened with extinction. That to me is blasphemy.

And so, out of love, love of my god-daughter, love of my world, I had to act. If I see that base at Faslane as morally wrong and against my deepest convictions – as wrong as the gas chambers of Auschwitz, as wrong as the deliberate starvation of children – then by keeping silent, I condone what goes on there.

On April 4th, I made a choice. I chose to create the dream of another way. My only crime is not working hard enough, or long enough, or soon enough towards the fulfilment of the dream. If my actions were a crime, then I am guilty.

Helen Steven, 1984

24.28   *The following is the testimony of a Friend who participated in the vigil, inspired and sustained by women, against the cruise missile base at Greenham Common in the 1980s.*

I stood at the fence one night in September, feet rooted to the muddy ground, hands deep in my pockets, watching through the wire that flat ravaged land that is now never dark, never quiet, imagining through the fence a field of bracken and scrub, a field of flowers, a field of corn, a field of children playing. Red police car, blue lights flashing, 'What are you doing, then, love? Not cutting the fence are you?' 'No, just praying at it.' A soldier with a dog walks up and down inside, suspicious, watching me watching him. 'Good evening.' 'Good evening.' I wait, not knowing what I'm waiting for. The kingdoms of the Lord? A hundred yards to my left, women cut the wire, roll away the stone, and walk through into the tomb. No angels greet them; no resurrection yet.

Yet still women witness to that possibility, the possibility that something may be accomplished which in our own strength we cannot do. Women waiting, watching, just being there, behaving as if peace were possible, living our dream of the future now. 'Why do you come here? Why do you keep coming?' – a soldier near Emerald camp on an earlier visit – 'It's no use, there's nothing you can do, what do you women think you can do by coming here? The missiles are here, you won't change anything, why do you come?' We come to watch, we come to witness, we come with our hands full of ribbon and wool, flowers and photos of loved ones, hands full of poems and statements and prayers, hands full of hope and the knowledge that such hope is impossible to rational minds. I come to be with the women who live here, the dykes, the dropouts, the mothers and grandmothers, angels with countenances like lightning, I come to talk with the police, the soldiers, men who might be gardeners standing by the tomb; I come to meet the Christ in them.

A member of the Quaker Women's Group, 1986

Relief of suffering

Since the early 1800s British Friends have assisted the victims of war and famine. In 1871 the Friends War Victims Relief Committee was formed to help those whose homes and livelihood had been devast-ated in the Franco-Prussian war. This committee adopted as its badge the black and red Quaker star which is now the symbol of Quaker Peace & Service.

24.29   On occasions of public calamity Friends' post must be the care of the poor and the relief of distress.

William Allen, 1812

24.30   Most relief work begins with some obvious need. But almost always there is, behind the physical need, something much less concrete, a damaged or lonely or hopeless or hungry spirit, and relief work which does not penetrate to this level, directly or indirectly, con-sciously or unconsciously, and make some contribution to healing is a job only partially done... Inspired relief workers cease to be external agents; like Woolman they have a sense of being 'mixed' in with suf-fering mankind: unselfconsciously they become part of the chaos, the misery and the perplexity in which they move, and yet they nei-ther accept nor are degraded by the situation. Because of their cer-tainty of the will of God for them they are not frightened to find themselves in the centre of the world's evil, and because of their experience of the love of God, they have the patience and the under-standing to speak to the condition of their fellows. They do not go about looking for a job to do. They are drawn by their divinely-rooted imagination to the service of God and their fellows in a way that the Lord wills. A relief organisation, then, ought to be a corpo-rate body capable of both commonsense and imaginative action, combined with a natural ability to convey to others a sense of inner peace and stability, surviving outward chaos and yet not divorced from it.

Roger Wilson, 1949

24.31   *Through the organisation of international work camps and social projects, Friends have sought to combine their ministry of relief with their ministry of reconciliation:*

There are no barriers of race, national feeling, custom, climate or culture which cannot be broken down by the method of Woolman and St Francis – the method of self-identification with the need of the poorest, even in distant lands, by means of hard manual work done at his side for his benefit. It remains to apply this method, and this idealism, to the international situation in Europe today... The influence of such work will no doubt be entirely negligible as regards the international situation, as the influence of Woolman seemed to be in his own lifetime... But failure does not matter. All that matters is that the right way should be tried; and if the Christian religion means anything at all, the right way is the way of self-identification with the poorest, the way of appeal to the friendliness in others by means of active and practical friendliness in ourselves, the way of unostentatious service... The original international fellowship of Christianity was founded in this way, as barriers of every kind – language, nationality, race, sex, class – were broken down through the literal following of the command for this august sacrament of menial service, as instituted by Christ at his last supper with his disciples.

John S Hoyland, 1936

Reconciliation and mediation

24.32　Reconciliation, in the biblical sense, is not about ideologies or beliefs but about people, their relationship and response to God, and their relationship and response to each other. God was in Christ, reconciling the world to himself, and he calls each of us to a ministry or vocation of reconciliation.

Sydney Bailey, 1980

24.33　All forms of non-violent resistance are certainly much better than appeasement, which has come to mean the avoidance of violence by a surrender to injustice at the expense of the sufferings of others and not of one's self, by the giving away of something that is not ours to give. This meaning of appeasement, the buying of peace for ourselves temporarily by pandering to international blackmail, has rightly come to be despised and to be regarded as an encouragement to aggressors and despots. It should be distinguished sharply from the admission, which personal or international integrity might sometimes demand, that we have made a mistake or have ourselves done wrong, and are ready to make open amends or to reverse our policy. No considerations of national or international prestige should prevent the correction of error when it is realised. This is a *sine qua non* in the search for truth, and is evidence of strength and not of weakness of personal or of national character, even when it means temporary humiliation.

Kathleen Lonsdale, 1953

24.34   *The following extracts are taken from an address in 1958 entitled 'Christians in a divided world' by Margarethe Lachmund, a German Friend who had intimate knowledge of conditions in both East and West Germany. In discussing the problem of Communism for Christians, she could truly state 'I therefore do not speak on this subject theoretically, but from insight gained through personal experience and personal contact with people and conditions on both sides':*

Is Christianity capable of contributing to the overcoming of tensions and showing a way to their solution? I am convinced that we can find a clear, positive answer by investigating how Christ himself met the tensions of his time; for him tensions which separate people simply do not exist. Jesus knows no fear, nothing holds him apart from other people. His fearlessness, however, flows from his communion with God. But this communion with God can be achieved by all men. Thus he sees in the other man only his brother, his neighbour. Next to the love of God, the commandment 'Love thy neighbour as thyself' is for Jesus the most essential of all commandments.

Such a concept does not mean that opposite views are abolished... On the contrary, they [remain distinct and] must not be veiled – that would be untruthful. The courage for clarity and the strength to stand up for truth are repeatedly demanded of us. However, the secret lies in the way in which truth is spoken. If it is spoken with contempt, bitterness or hatred, it results in bitterness; if, however, truth is spoken in love, the door to the other's heart can slowly open so that the truth can perhaps have some effect...

We can help to ease the tensions and live within them in the right way if we fulfil simultaneously Christ's two commandments – the commandment to love and the commandment to speak truth. A synthesis of these two must be found. Out of fear, we may betray truth;

out of bitterness or self-righteousness we may betray love. A desire for peace without truthfulness is worthless and does not bring about peace; without love truth has no effect because it is not heard.

24.35 *Adam Curle was the first professor in the School (later Department) of Peace Studies, established in 1973 largely through Quaker initiative, in the University of Bradford.*

I have often been asked how we handle the fact that peacemaking involves having a relationship, often a close relationship, with people who are committed to violent solutions to their problems. Do we tell them we disapprove of what they are doing or urge them to repent and desist? And if we don't, how do we square this with our principles? For my part I reply that I would never presume to criticise people caught up in a situation I do not share with them for the way in which they are responding to that situation. How could I, for example, preach to the oppressed of Latin America or Southern Africa? Nevertheless, I explain that I do not believe in the use of violence as either effective or moral; my job is to try to help people who can see no alternative to violence to find a substitute...

I am as much concerned with the human condition in general as with specific conflicts, which often represent only the tip of a pyramid of violence and anguish... I am concerned with all the pain and confusion that impede our unfolding and fulfilment. Often, of course, circumstances force us to focus on extreme examples of unpeacefulness. However, if we were to limit our attention to these, we would be neglecting the soil out of which they grow and would continue to grow until the soil were purified. In this sense the social worker, the teacher, the wise legislator, or the good neighbour is just as much a peacemaker as the woman or man unravelling some lethal international imbroglio.

1981

24.36 I do not know whether Quakers have special aptitudes or skills as mediators, but they tend to sympathise with both sides in an international dispute, as both are usually victims of past mistakes. Because Quakers believe that there is that of God in all people to which others may respond, they not only hope for the best but they expect the best, believing that bad situations are likely to get better with the input of a little honest goodwill. And because they consider that force nearly always creates more problems than it solves, Quakers feel impelled to do what is possible by reason and persuasion to resolve conflicts involving or threatening armed force.

Sydney Bailey, 1984

24.37 *Sue Williams and her husband, Steve, were Quaker Peace & Service Representatives in Belfast, where they worked for reconciliation in a divided community.*

Establishing pacifist credentials has taken us collectively a long time, and entailed quite some suffering. How can a group without hierarchy or creed demonstrate that it will not participate in war and 'fighting with outward weapons'? Only when individuals, one after another, across time and space, live out their convictions, so that choices made in different situations still seem to come together as a pattern. Amazingly, we are now widely known as people who will not fight in wars. Not only this, we are almost as widely known for having intervened in wars to try to alleviate suffering on all sides...

Beyond the general notion of pacifism, the situation here has lent a special urgency to our reputation for harmlessness. By this I mean that, as a Friend, I am not only unwilling to serve as a soldier, but unwilling to take up arms in my private capacity. This may not sound like much, but it puts me in a special relationship to political leaders here: they believe that I will not kill them. And they don't believe that of everyone they meet. More to the point, they accept that I don't want them dead, even when I disagree with them. And this too is something they cannot take for granted. It is surprisingly freeing for all of us. I'm sure they don't want to kill me, either. So I feel free to agree with them sometimes, disagree sometimes, without worrying about who else I agree or disagree with in the process, and taking for granted that neither of us wishes to kill the other.

1988

24.38 Mediation is not an easy task. It requires of us an exceptional willingness to listen, to lay aside self, and to enter into the minds of those in dispute. We must not try to find acceptance for our own solution to the conflict, but rather act as the ground in which, with our help, others can work out their answers. A few people are natural mediators; most of us can learn the skills if we feel called to that service.

Friends' opposition to all forms of violence imposes on them the responsibility to seek alternative responses to conflict and injustice. Mediation is one method which can be offered or suggested.

Sue Bowers, 1991

Disarmament

24.39   *During the American War of Independence, the Quaker whaling community on the island of Nantucket suffered heavily from both sides for their neutrality. William Rotch, one of their leaders, had in a disused warehouse a consignment of bayonets which had been taken from muskets which he had accepted twelve years earlier in quittance of a debt, and sold as fowling pieces. In 1776 the bayonets were demanded from him by the Americans.*

The time was now come to endeavour to support our testimony against war, or abandon it, as this very instrument was a severe test. I could not hesitate which to choose, and therefore denied the applicant. My reason for not furnishing them was demanded, to which I readily answered, 'As this instrument is purposely made and used for the destruction of mankind, I can put no weapon into a man's hand to destroy another, that I cannot use myself in the same way.' The person left me much dissatisfied. Others came, and received the same denial. It made a great noise in the country, and my life was threatened. I would gladly have beaten them into 'pruning hooks', but I took an early opportunity of throwing them into the sea.

A short time after I was called before a committee appointed by the court then held at Watertown near Boston, and questioned amongst other things respecting my bayonets.

I gave a full account of my proceedings, and closed it with saying, 'I sunk them in the bottom of the sea, I did it from principle. I have ever been glad that I had done it, and if I am wrong I am to be pitied.' The chairman of the committee Major Hawley (a worthy character) then addressed the committee and said, 'I believe Mr Rotch has given us a candid account, and every man has a right to act consistently with his religious principles, but I am sorry that we could not have the bayonets, for we want them very much.' The Major was desirous of knowing more of our principles on which I informed him as far as he enquired. One of the committee in a pert manner observed, 'Then your principles are passive obedience and non-resistance.' I replied, 'No, my friend, our principles are active obedience or passive suffering.'

24.40   Our conviction is that Christianity has this to say to the world: 'Your reliance upon armaments is both wrong and futile. Armaments are the weapons of organised violence and outrage. Their use is a denial of the true laws of good living. They involve the perpetuation of strife. They stand in the way of the true fellowship of men. They impoverish the peoples. They tempt men to evil, and they breed suspicion and fear and the tragic results thereof. They are therefore not legitimate weapons in the Christian armoury, nor are they sources of security.'

You cannot foster harmony by the apparatus of discord, nor cherish goodwill by the equipment of hate. But it is by harmony and goodwill that human security can be obtained. Armaments aim at a security in isolation; but such would at best be utterly precarious and is, as a matter of fact, illusory. The only true safety is the safety of all, and unless your weapon of defence achieves this work, or works towards this, it is a source of antagonism and therefore of increased peril.

All Friends Conference, 1920

24.41   We in Great Britain have decided to make hydrogen bombs. If a major war breaks out the temptation to use them will be very great. We are warned by our scientists that their use will involve not only the most terrible suffering now, but unknown consequences for succeeding generations who will pay the penalty for our sin. We believe that no one has the right to use these weapons in his defence or to ask another person to use them on his behalf. To rely on the possession of nuclear weapons as a deterrent is faithless; to use them is a sin.

Meeting for Sufferings, 1955

24.42　We are, I trust, steadfast in emphasising hope not fear as the driving force for disarmament. I doubt whether it is even a successful tactic, to motivate people by playing on their fear of death and destruction in a nuclear war; fear can as well engender paralysis as frenzied activity. But even if it were successful, that would not make it right. Quaker approaches to disarmament have largely avoided the temptation to appeal to fear. It is important that we continue to resist that temptation. To place the emphasis instead on hope, and the positive achievements we associate with disarmament, does not mean embracing a shallow optimism. It means relating our hopes for disarmament, our hopefulness, to the Christian understanding of hope, which is something much more profound.

Nicholas A Sims, 1985

Building the institutions of peace and social justice

24.43　We have to ask ourselves at the outset whether the Society of Friends, or indeed any branch of the Christian Church, has any call to concern itself with the sordid realities of international affairs ... There are politicians who would answer with a contemptuous 'No', in the mistaken belief that morals are totally irrelevant to politics. In this they grossly belittle the nature of their political calling which loses all validity if it abandons the attempt to translate moral principles into practical action. The Christians who tell us that politics are irrelevant to morals are on surer ground, since Christian hope is not founded upon political peace; if it were it could never have survived the 2,000 years of wrong which it has had to endure since it was first proclaimed. We cannot but regret the tribulation, the nakedness, the peril and the sword, but we cannot forget that 'in all these things we are more than conquerors through Him that loved us', and that the Christian message is to be proclaimed in all circumstances, even when hell itself seems to have broken loose. Such was the experience of Rendel Harris when, after his ship had been torpedoed in the Mediterranean, he landed with others at Alexandria in a state of 'Apostolic one-stage-from-nudity', to be met at the Customs House with the irrelevant, political question, 'Have you anything to declare?'; he felt that the only possible answer in the circumstances was, 'We declare unto you glad tidings'. All too often, the question put to us by politics cannot be answered in any other way.

J Duncan Wood, 1962

24.44   *In* An essay towards the present and future peace of Europe, by the establishment of a European diet, parliament or estates, *published in 1693, William Penn envisaged constitutional arrangements for a United States of Europe.*

Now if the sovereign princes of Europe, who represent that society or independent state of men that was previous to the obligations of society, would for the same reason that engaged men first into society, viz, love of peace and order, agree to meet by their stated deputies in a general diet, estates, or parliament, and there establish rules of justice for sovereign princes to observe one to another; and thus to meet yearly, or once in two or three years at farthest, or as they shall see cause, and to be styled, the Sovereign or Imperial Diet, Parliament or State of Europe; before which sovereign assembly should be brought all differences depending between one sovereign and another that cannot be made up by private embassies before the sessions begin: and that if any of the sovereignties that constitute these imperial states shall refuse to submit their claim or pretensions to them, or to abide and perform the judgment thereof, and seek their remedy by arms, or delay their compliance beyond the time prefixed in their resolutions, all the other sovereignties, united as one strength, shall compel the submission and performance of the sentence, with damages to the suffering party.

24.45   *In 1925, the following questions were included in a section of our book of discipline on the League of Nations as showing some of the tests by which Friends might judge the League and its actions. These questions still indicate the criteria by which the international organisations of today may be assessed:*

Has it promise of becoming a league of all nations? Does it reflect the aspirations towards human brotherhood that are growing up among men and women in all nations? Does it stand for justice and mercy? Is it relying upon intelligent public opinion and on the consent of its members, rather than on fear or on threats of coercion?

Does its moral authority increase or diminish? Is it working for the welfare, material and spiritual, of men and women, and not in the interests of powerful groups or tyrannical authorities? Is it bringing the light of day into places of deceit and corruption? Is it helping to succour the needy, to release those who are in bonds, to give light to those who are in darkness? Is it fostering co-operation? Does it show by its deeds a recognition of the truth that all men, whatever their colour or creed or class may be, are children of one Father?

24.46   Though rejecting on principle the provisions for coercion incorporated in the charter [of the United Nations], we must support the present organisation, the only peaceful meeting place for West and East, in its positive work of negotiation and functional co-operation, knowing well how imperfect and provisional its machinery still is. As citizens in a democracy we must urge our Government to do everything for the improvement of that machinery, and we may well take the idea of a world federation as a guiding principle for such improvement.

It is most important to use and develop the provisions of the charter for peaceful change of the status quo, so that fair and just conditions are created, which the nations are prepared to uphold. It is true that this is more a matter of will than of machinery; our aim must be to strengthen both the good will of nations and international machinery.

Konrad Braun, 1950

24.47   *Extracts from a statement issued by the Quaker Council for European Affairs in 1987:*

Our vision of Europe is of a peaceful, compassionate, open and just society, using its moral influence to encourage other countries and peoples towards the same goals. It is of a community of peoples which acts towards individuals and other communities as we would have others act towards us. As Quakers we seek to be sensitive to that of God in others and in ourselves, whose needs have the same validity as our own. Hence the right sharing of the world's resources is central to our thinking...

[We envision] a non-threatening Europe, committed to the non-violent resolution of conflict. As Quakers we are committed to peace, but we cannot eliminate conflict. It can be minimised by reducing tension, by not posing threats to others (not only military, but also economic and cultural threats) and by seeking to understand the attitudes of others. Where conflicts arise, we can seek a nonviolent resolution by working for reconciliation...

We look forward to an economy which is conservationist, balanced in respect of growth, and sensitive to the needs and situations of other countries, not selling arms to others. We have only one world, and our present wasteful consumption of non-renewable resources and damage to the biosphere must stop. This requires alternative economic strategies, which are driven by need, not greed. The European economy should take positive account of the economies of other countries and not exploit their weaknesses. The selling of arms exploits such a weakness, and is morally indefensible.

24.48   [Our] understanding of the nature of the development process has altered. We are now increasingly aware that the Western development model, in which many had such confidence, is based on rampant exploitation of both people and the physical environment, is not fulfilling the real needs of many of our own citizens, and threatens the survival chances of human beings in poorer countries. Not only is it an inappropriate and impossible model for others to follow, it is itself responsible for exacerbating many of the problems it purports to solve. It has become increasingly apparent to [us] that new understandings and a change of heart within our own nation are an essential prerequisite to international reforms which might serve the interests of the most vulnerable nations and people.

Quaker Peace & Service, 1988

24.49   People matter. In the end human rights are about people being treated and feeling like people who matter. We are reminded graphically of violations of human rights far away and near at hand. In ignorance or knowingly we all violate human rights. We are all involved in the exercise of power and the abuse of power.

The multitude and complexity of the problems of oppression and injustice often seem to overwhelm us. We can do something. Friends are already working in a variety of ways: through international bodies, through voluntary organisations and by personal witness. Those who can give something of their lives to human rights require our support and we can look for opportunities to help those in need around us.

At the international level we affirm our support of Friends World Committee for Consultation and other bodies in ensuring that the standards and ideals of the UN Universal Declaration of Human Rights are attained, that the world does not slip backwards.

Above all we must take risks for God: look around us to the people who need help; listen to those who experience oppression; engage in the mutual process of liberation.

London Yearly Meeting, 1986

Right sharing of the world's resources

24.50 We have thought of the widespread exploitation of economically under-developed peoples, and of those industrial and other workers who are also exploited and heavily burdened. We must therefore work for a larger measure of liberty in political and economic life. For not only is this at the heart of the Christian message, but we have seen that peace stands on a precarious footing so long as there is unrelieved poverty and subjection. Subjection, poverty, injustice and war are closely allied. This situation demands sweeping political and economic changes; and we are convinced that the hope of freedom does not lie in violence, which is at its root immoral, but in such changes as may be brought about by fellowship and mutual service.

London Yearly Meeting, 1937

24.51 *After more than thirty years and a second world war, London Yearly Meeting in 1968 moved beyond statements, to a call for positive sacrificial action conceived as a corporate witness by Friends to prompt action by the country as a whole:*

The World Conference of Friends held in 1967 asked yearly meetings throughout the world to consider the right use of the world's resources.

We know that the world's resources are neither developed to the full nor used to the best advantage. The inequality in the distribution of goods and services between nations and between individuals within nations stares us in the face.

If we are to face these issues aright we are called to re-examine our whole way of life. At the personal level we must ask ourselves how we spend our time, and how we use the talents God has given us in earning a living, remembering that in spending we are asking others to use their resources in our service.

As members of the Society of Friends we must ask the same question about the resources of our Society: as members of a nation and of the community of nations we must be alive to the fact that ours is among the richer countries of the world, yet devotes but a small fraction of the national income to help the less developed countries.

We commend to the further consideration of Friends ... the continuing need for personal service. We are concerned from this session to ask all Friends who feel able to do so to give a further one per cent of their income to helping the poorer nations.

24.52   *The 1% Fund, established by London Yearly Meeting in 1968, operated for just over twenty years. Even in the first flush of enthusiasm fewer than 1,500 persons or households supported it and by 1989 it had fewer than 500 subscribers. Though the proceeds it raised were put to good use in the developing world, the yearly meeting had failed to respond to the call to demonstrate to the Government that the public would support more taxation for international aid.*

Yet there were individual Friends who wished to make a sacrificial witness. After a lifetime of service to others, Douglas Smith, warden of Settle Meeting House, inherited a legacy which would have given him security and comfort in his old age. The following statement was left with his papers; at his request it was published in 1981 after his death:

Much of our present affluence in Britain was built on the cheap labour, inadequate food, poor housing, poor medical and social services and almost non-existent education of the people of our former Empire. When they demanded their freedom, we cleared out, leaving them almost totally unfitted for stable self-government and without adequate capital to develop their own resources.

Every one of us in Britain, even the poorest, has reaped benefits of many kinds from the misery and poverty in our Empire. We are all deeply in debt. Governments, trade unions, politicians and churches have talked loud and long about justice and the brotherhood of mankind. We have handed over to them our personal responsibility to achieve these aims, but with tragic lack of success.

Now we must act; take new and revolutionary action at the level of our *personal* responsibility to give back to the world's poor the wealth of which we have robbed them and are still robbing them. Unless *we* take our Christian responsibility for closing the gap between our comfort and their misery, we shall blunder deeper and deeper into world-wide disasters – and probably to self-destruction.

For fifty years these injustices have weighed on my conscience. Then in 1979 I acquired considerable wealth, and immediately I was faced inescapably with the Christian challenge to repay as much as possible of the wealth which Britain had taken from the world's poor. I gave away almost all the money to charities and trusts working in the former British possessions. This brought me to the financial level of the old-age pensioner, but with no regret. The pension leaves us room for happiness, contentment and laughter. Compared with an Indian or African peasant, our pensioner is princely rich.

The personal responsibility which we hand over to governments, trade unions, committees and churches has failed to banish world poverty. I hope this statement will lead others to think deeply of their individual responsibility towards all the world's problems and to take action *now*, sacrificially – guided by the Christian spirit of deep caring.

See also chapter 25 Unity of creation *& 23.53-23.70* Work and economic affairs

THE PERSONAL ROOTS OF CONFLICT AND EDUCATION FOR PEACE

24.53   It should be the goal of understanding to pierce first through the thin layer of superficial familiarity and then through the hard rock of differing customs, habits and beliefs to discover the real humanity that lies beneath. National, racial and religious differences have not destroyed our common humanity, but they have given it different faces which may tempt us to forget that all the things that really matter, life and death, birth and love, joy and sorrow, poetry and prayer, are common to us all. The sense of our common humanity is latent within us, but only occasionally do we appreciate it as a living reality, as when at times of great stress we are upheld by strangers of an alien creed and tongue. Then the inward eye is opened and we see humanity standing above all nations, more humble, more patient and far more enduring than all the kingdoms of this earth. This is the ultimate justification for our peace-making.

J Duncan Wood, 1962

24.54   Conflict is a part of life, a necessary result of the varying needs, aims and perspectives of individuals and communities. It is part of our daily experience, both directly and through television and other news media. The ethos of the home, school or workplace will provide some rules (spoken and unspoken) for handling conflict situations. However, these often contradict each other and the pressures from friends and peer groups can work against the 'official' ways of handling conflict. Society educates young people at best haphazardly and at worst quite destructively as far as conflict is concerned. From an early age, people are led to think that conflicts should be settled by someone in authority: the parent, the teacher, the headteacher, the gangleader, the policeman, the judge, the boss, the president. If there is nobody to arbitrate, then the 'strongest' will 'win' and the 'weaker' will 'lose'. Traditionally, little encouragement has been given to young people to take responsibility for resolving conflicts, to look for 'win-win' solutions. Yet the way in which young people learn to respond to conflict will have a pervasive effect both on the quality of their personal lives and on the prospects for society as a whole. Affirming the personal value of each individual, encouraging mutual respect and consciously developing the skills and attitudes involved in creative conflict resolution must be regarded as an important educational priority.

Sue Bowers and Tom Leimdorfer, 1990

See also 20.67-20.75 Conflict *& 23.84-23.85*

OUR VISION

24.55 In place of a process which trusts technology and mistrusts humanity, we must learn and live out a process that builds trust between people and their institutions... From the earliest days of Friends, we have known that safety cannot be defended in our own strength, but only in God's... And we don't have to do it with tools of our own fashioning, ever more elaborate technological juggling acts, ever more devastatingly destructive bombs... [We can] learn to lay down carnal weapons, practising with weapons of the spirit: love, truth-saying, nonviolence, the good news of God's birth and rebirth among us, imagination, vision, and laughter.

No one ever said it would be easy, no one promised it wouldn't hurt. This way of life, this trusting one another and trusting God, is no impermeable shield, guaranteed to protect us by cutting us off, building barriers, keeping the bad things and the bad people out. It's messy, muddly and sometimes painful – but the other way, the search for some kind of mechanical invulnerability, for some kind of scientific guarantee against physical death, that way I am sure lies the death of the Spirit. We know the choice – we've known it all along – and we make it every day... 'I call heaven and earth to witness against you this day, that I have set before you life and death, blessing and curse. Therefore choose life, that you and your descendants may live (Deut 30:19).'

Mary Lou Leavitt, 1987

24.56 *In 1920 the Society of Friends had its first World Conference, held in London as soon as possible after the First World War. In 1937, when the world was so plainly drifting toward a second and more terrible conflict, it was decided to hold another conference, this time in the United States. Rufus Jones was asked to preside over the meetings. He accepted, but the Conference loomed before him as an ordeal. He wrote to Violet Holdsworth:*

In regard to the World Conference, I sincerely hope for good results, but I have become a good deal disillusioned over 'big' conferences and large gatherings. I pin my hopes to quiet processes and small circles, in which vital and transforming events take place. But others see differently, and I respect their judgment.

1937

24.57 The follower of Jesus is to discover and then promote the Kingdom of God. That Kingdom has two tenses: it is already here, in each one of us; and it is still to come, when God's goodness becomes a universal norm. We are to live now 'as if' the Kingdom of God were already fulfilled.

Peace begins within ourselves. It is to be implemented within the family, in our meetings, in our work and leisure, in our own localities, and internationally. The task will never be done. Peace is a process to engage in, not a goal to be reached.

Sydney Bailey, 1993

24.58 Our consideration of international affairs has brought us into the presence of human tragedies, for which only the things of the spirit can offer consolation. They are the bricks of which the institutions of peace must be built, 'oft with bleeding hands and tears'... But tears do not always blind. We may shed them to wash the windows of the spirit that with a clearer vision and a surer sympathy we may take up again our unfinished task of declaring the glad tidings.

J Duncan Wood, 1962

24.59 Mothers for Peace was the brainchild of two 85-year-old Quakers, Lucy Behenna and Marion Mansergh. Taking to heart the message on a Quaker poster, 'World peace will come through the will of ordinary people like yourself', they put their life savings into a scheme to send groups of peacemakers to visit the two superpowers – the USA and the Soviet Union. Mothers were chosen because they have a special affinity with one another and a common desire to secure a safe and peaceful world for their children. The first visits to the US and the Soviet Union occurred simultaneously in 1981. In April and May 1982 return visits were paid by American and Soviet mothers who toured Britain in three groups, meeting all together in London for the final three days.

Mothers for peace, 1983

From this beginning the work has continued and extended, involving women from many countries and cultures.

24.60   The first Friends had an apocalyptic vision of the world transformed by Christ and they set about to make it come true. The present generation of Quakers shares this conviction of the power of the spirit, but it is doubtful whether it will transform the world in our lifetime, or in that of our children or children's children. For us it is not so important when the perfect world will be achieved or what it will be like. What matters is living our lives in the power of love and not worrying too much about the results. In doing this, the means become part of the end. Hence we lose the sense of helplessness and futility in the face of the world's crushing problems. We also lose the craving for success, always focusing on the goal to the exclusion of the way of getting there. We must literally not take too much thought for the morrow but throw ourselves whole-heartedly into the present. That is the beauty of the way of love; it cannot be planned and its end cannot be foretold.

Wolf Mendl, 1974

Chapter 25

Unity of creation

25.01   The produce of the earth is a gift from our gracious creator to the inhabitants, and to impoverish the earth now to support outward greatness appears to be an injury to the succeeding age.

John Woolman, 1772

25.02   Our planet is seriously ill and we can feel the pain. We have been reminded of the many ways in which the future health of the earth is under threat as a result of our selfishness, ignorance and greed. Our earth needs attention, respect, love, care and prayer.

In comfortable Britain we are largely insulated from the effects of the environmental crisis. It is the poor of the world who suffer first.

As a Religious Society of Friends we see the stewardship of God's creation as a major concern. The environmental crisis is at root a spiritual and religious crisis; we are called to look again at the real purpose of being on this earth, which is to till it and keep it so as to reveal the glory of God for generations to come.

It is a stony road ahead but our faith will uphold us; the power to act is God's power which is mediated through each of us as we give and receive support one from another. We can all listen if we will to the sounds of the earth, tuning into it with joy.

London Yearly Meeting, 1988

25.03   My children were having a hard time. Really bad – I mean drugs, sex gone wrong, quite unable to fit in anywhere for the time being. Yet now they have come through it... I felt desperate with guilt.., but as time passed I came to see that what had happened was not entirely our fault, as parents. It was also that they were inheritors of social guilt and social pain. Our children are the first generation to grow up facing the possibility of the end of our species. Perhaps it is partly the planet crying out in us? Perhaps the violated earth needs to cry and feel desperation in us?

Damaris Parker-Rhodes, 1982

25.04 All species and the Earth itself have interdependent roles within Creation. Humankind is not *the* species, to whom all others are subservient, but one among many. All parts, all issues, are inextricably intertwined. Indeed the web of creation could be described as of three-ply thread: wherever we touch it we affect justice and peace and the health of all everywhere. So all our testimonies, all our Quaker work, all our Quaker lives are part of one process, of striving towards a flourishing, just and peaceful Creation – the Kingdom of God.

Audrey Urry, 1994

25.05 I was early convinced in my mind that true religion consisted in an inward life wherein the heart doth love and reverence God the Creator and learns to exercise true justice and goodness not only toward all men but also toward the brute creation; that as the mind was moved on an inward principle to love God as an invisible, incomprehensible being, on the same principle it was moved to love him in all his manifestations in the visible world; that as by his breath the flame of life was kindled in all animal and sensitive creatures, to say we love God ... and at the same time exercise cruelty toward the least creature ... was a contradiction in itself.

John Woolman, 1772

25.06 If it is right that we should show love and compassion for people, surely it is right that we should extend our love and compassion to animals, who can feel fear and experience pain in much the same way as humans. They may not be able to speak, but we can certainly see fear in their eyes and demeanour. I feel that being a vegetarian is a natural progression from being a pacifist and a Quaker.

Vera Haley, 1988

25.07 As to our own planet which God has given us for a dwelling place, we must be mindful that it is given in stewardship. The power over nature that scientific knowledge has put into our hands, if used in lust or greed, fear or hatred, can bring us to utter destruction. If we choose life we may now feed the hungry, clothe the naked, and heal the sick on a world scale, thus creating new conditions for spiritual advancement so often till now prevented by want. Many of our resources – of oil, of coal and of uranium – are limited. If by condoning waste and luxury we overspend the allowance God has given us, our children's children will be cheated of their inheritance. Limited too is the annual bounty of nature. The material foundation of our life is the tilling of the earth and the growing of food... We must conserve the goodness of the soil and not exploit it.

We must guard, too, the abundance and variety of untamed nature, and not forget the spiritual resources available to us in the continued existence of unoccupied lands. Modern civilisation perpetually threatens our awareness of the true nature of our being which in the presence of the wild we can more easily retain or at length recapture. Year by year silence and solitude are growing more needful, yet harder to obtain, and contacts, by this means, with the mind of the Creator more tenuous. To conserve nature is thus again a contribution to the fuller life of mankind.

Norfolk, Cambs & Hunts Quarterly Meeting, 1957

25.08   This is a marvellous world, full of beauty and splendour; it is also an unrelenting and savage world, and we are not the only living things prone to dominate if given the chance. In our fumbling, chaotic way, we do also make gardens, irrigate the desert, fly to the moon and compose symphonies. Some of us are trying to save species other than ourselves...

We have no reason to be either arrogant or complacent: one look at the stars or through a microscope is sufficient to quell such notions. But we have to accept our position in the world with as much grace, responsibility and fortitude as we can muster, and try to grow up to our mission of love in this tangle of prospects and torments.

Pamela Umbima, 1992

25.09   I want to list ten controlling principles for the outward expression of simplicity. They should not be viewed as laws but as one attempt to flesh out the meaning of simplicity into twentieth-century life. First, buy things for their usefulness rather than their status. Second, reject anything that is producing an addiction in you. Third, develop a habit of giving things away. De-accumulate. Fourth, refuse to be propagandised by the custodians of modern gadgetry. Fifth, learn to enjoy things without owning them. Sixth, develop a deeper appreciation for the creation. Seventh, look with a healthy scepticism at all 'buy now, pay later' schemes. Eighth, obey Jesus' injunction about plain, honest speech. Ninth, reject anything that will breed the oppression of others. Tenth, shun whatever would distract you from your main goal.

Richard J Foster, 1979

25.10   Our adoption of the [World Council of Churches'] concern for Justice, Peace and the Integrity of Creation grows from our faith and cannot be separated from it. It challenges us to look again at our lifestyles and reassess our priorities and makes us realise the truth of Gandhi's words: 'Those who say religion has nothing to do with politics do not know what religion means.' The earth's resources must be conserved and shared more equitably and, as we are an integral part of creation, this is our responsibility.

London Yearly Meeting, 1989

25.11   As consumers, producers and investors, or as travellers, readers and campaigners we can be active in support of the Two Thirds World. Our use of energy connects us directly to the greenhouse effect and to world food supplies. Our bank interest rates link us to the debt burdens which are forcing many countries to destroy their environment to produce cash crops and foreign currency. Our ability to acquire knowledge gives us the chance to act as a mouthpiece on behalf of the environment and the poor who are suffering most from its destruction. Indeed we have the responsibility to use that knowledge wisely.

Ruth Tod, 1990

25.12   We live in a part of the world where the dominant motivation is material self-interest, justified by the concept of personal freedom. In these circumstances, the rich get richer and the poor, for the most part, become comparatively poorer. This offends our moral sensibility and, at the practical level, the process of material growth cannot in any event go on indefinitely. We must find some way in which we in the West can change our dominance in setting the style of the world's living from one motivated by self-interest into one in which material resources are made available according to need. We know a good deal about this kind of distribution in particular situations but have not yet any effective idea about how to embody compassion into the essential structure of our society. This demands both thought and personal commitment at the level of where we are, not taking refuge simply in telling those with political power what they should do. We must be aware in all humility that it is we who are sinning in accepting the elevation of self-interest and that it is we who must move towards another form of motivation. What are we doing to proclaim our joyful acceptance that our living standards are going to have to drop; what are we doing to join with other Christians and concerned fellow-citizens to proclaim the vulgarity of our affluent style of living; what are we doing to find ways of influencing the way in which our fellow-citizens think and act, be they our neighbours or elected and appointed representatives, to recognise the need for change?

London Yearly Meeting, 1975

25.13   That the sweat and tedious labour of the farmer, early and late, cold and hot, wet and dry, should be converted into the pleasure of a small number of men – that continued severity should be laid on nineteen parts of the land to feed the inordinate lusts and delicate appetites of the twentieth, is so far from the will of the great Governor of the world, ... [it] is wretched and blasphemous.

William Penn, 1669

25.14   We are building towards the climax of crisis. The spiritual crisis is folding into the ecological crisis and the ecological crisis is folding into the economic crisis. As Christians, it seems to me, we are now required to critically assess the capital driven market economy and identify it as a false religion, a fabulously productive but ultimately destructive system bringing closure on God's goodness in creation and bringing a creeping atheism to the soul. To look this system straight in the eye and call it to account is a critical test of Biblical faith.

Challenging market economics with a Biblical sense of the goodness of God in creation is to join a spiritual struggle. Faith in God, solidarity with the suffering poor and all other forms of life demands that we take a stand and say, 'This destruction must stop.' We must be perfectly clear about the implications of undertaking this responsibility. It is more than just setting up household recycling bins, growing organic vegetables or riding a bike to work. It is more than a talking job. It is a renovation which will change everything: the way we do business, the way we eat, the way we travel, the houses we build, the products and services we can expect and the prices we pay for them, the way we feel about trees and the way we worship God.

Keith Helmuth, 1990

25.15   Our testimonies against war and inequality have been aimed at persuading people, and reminding ourselves, as to where their wealth lies: in the discovery of a common identity and a common cause with other human beings. Those testimonies apply in the same way to our treatment of our natural environment which, as Augustine said, is itself like a 'commonwealth', in which every creature in its own way serves the interests of the others. The difference now is that the commonwealth of people and the commonwealth of the earth have become inseparably interrelated and interdependent – have become in fact one new commonwealth of life. Our thinking about God and the world and the way we live in relation to them must now give recognition to that fact.

Rex Ambler, 1990

See also 20.27-20.36, 21.42, 23.40, 29.04-29.07 & 29.18

Chapter 26

Reflections

EXPERIENCE OF GOD

As we reflect on our experience, intimations emerge about the nature of God. In this we are helped by the experiences of others which enlighten our path. We remember Nayler in his suffering testifying to 'a spirit which delights to do no evil nor to revenge any wrong' and Barclay when he first went to Friends' meetings, feeling the evil weakening in him and the good being raised up. We recall those who have been upheld by love, or filled with joy, or called to commit their lives to service, or who have sensed a divine reality in the wonder of the world or in the depths of being or in the hardest challenges of life.

26.01   Take heed, dear Friends, to the promptings of love and truth in your hearts, which are the leadings of God.

Advices, 1964

26.02   After this I returned into Nottinghamshire again and went into the Vale of Beavor... And one morning, as I was sitting by the fire, a great cloud came over me and a temptation beset me; but I sat still. And it was said, 'All things come by nature'; and the elements and stars came over me so that I was in a manner quite clouded with it. But inasmuch as I sat, still and silent, the people of the house perceived nothing. And as I sat still under it and let it alone, a living hope arose in me and a true voice, which said, 'There is a living God who made all things'. And immediately the cloud and temptation vanished away, and life rose over it all, and my heart was glad, and I praised the living God.

George Fox, 1648

26.03 Now I was come up in spirit through the flaming sword into the paradise of God. All things were new, and all the creation gave another smell unto me than before, beyond what words can utter.

George Fox, 1648

26.04 *Caroline Fox (1819-1871) wrote in her journal at the age of 21, of 'the struggle through which a spark of true faith was lighted in my soul':*

The first gleam of light, 'the first cold light of morning' which gave promise of day with its noontide glories, dawned on me one day at meeting, when I had been meditating on my state in great depression. I seemed to hear the words articulated in my spirit, 'Live up to the light thou hast, and more will be granted thee.' Then I believed that God speaks to man by His Spirit. I strove to lead a more Christian life, in unison with what I knew to be right, and looked for brighter days, not forgetting the blessings that are granted to prayer.

1841

26.05 *Emilia Fogelklou (1878-1972), here recalls her own experience at the age of 23. She had been put in charge of the religious instruction in a progressive school in Gothenburg at a time when she was oppressed by the failure of her search for the reality of God; she was filled with despair, almost to the point of suicide, and felt she was 'just a shell, a shell empty of life'. (She writes of herself in the third person.)*

But then one bright spring day – it was the 29th of May 1902 – while she sat preparing for her class under the trees in the backyard of Föreningsgatan 6, quietly, invisibly, there occurred the central event of her whole life. Without visions or the sound of speech or human mediation, in exceptionally wide-awake consciousness, she experienced the great releasing inward wonder. It was as if the 'empty shell' burst. All the weight and agony, all the feeling of unreality dropped away. She perceived living goodness, joy, light like a clear, irradiating, uplifting, enfolding, unequivocal reality from deep inside.

The first words which came to her – although they took a long time to come – were, 'This is the great Mercifulness. This is God. Nothing else is so *real* as this.' The child who had cried out in anguish and been silenced had now come inside the gates of Light. She had been delivered by a love that is greater than any human love. Struck dumb, amazed, she went quietly to her class, wondering that no one noticed that something had happened to her.

26.06   *Rufus Jones described the experience which his friend John Wilhelm Rowntree had in 1894:*

Just as he was entering young manhood and was beginning to feel the dawning sense of a great mission before him, he discovered that he was slowly losing his sight. He was told that before middle life he would become totally blind. Dazed and overwhelmed he staggered from the doctor's office to the street and stood there in silence. Suddenly he felt the love of God wrap him about as though a visible presence enfolded him, and a joy filled him, such as he had never known before. From that time ... he was a gloriously joyous and happy man. His physical limitations have all along been turned into inward profit. His long, hard battle with a stubborn disease which was attacking the very citadel of his powers – his sight, his hearing and his memory – has only made him more heroic and gentle.

26.07   *Hilda Clark (1881-1955), a doctor, wrote in 1908 of her experience when her sister-in-law died in childbirth:*

I am thinking of those lovely fine days when Cara sat with me for hours sewing her little things. I feel as if my whole life might be better and more use to others from those two days, but what an awful price it is to pay. Do you know, I actually felt that it was 'better' somehow than those awful hours with those two poor creatures in the maternity hospital, when one's heart felt like ice within one, because one realised the tragedy with one's brain, and not with one's heart. And if I ever have to hold such a cold hand and feel such a death stricken pulse, I think a little of the love I have for Cara will go out to the victim, whoever it may be ... No, justice is of the Spirit, not of the outside world – but our understanding is so wrapped up in outward things that we can only grow spiritually by applying spiritual things to material ones – therefore we must be just though Nature is not.

One thing I understand now is that one's intellect alone won't pull one through, and that the greatest service it can perform is to open a window for that thing we call the divine spirit. If one trusts to it alone it's like trusting to an artificial system of ventilation – correct in theory but musty in practice. How I wish it were as easy to throw everything open to the spirit of God as it is to fresh air.

26.08   About two years ago on an April morning I felt ill at ease and unhappy. Life was difficult and the burden of the war weighed upon me. I climbed the steep path at the entrance of one of our public parks and stood beneath some cherry trees that fringe the crest of the bank. A fresh wind blew dark clouds across the green-blue sky. The white blossom shone and glistened in the sunlight. As I stood relaxed and still, I had the illusion that I was enveloped in light. I had the feeling that the light and I were one. Time and space slipped from me. All awareness of details vanished. A sense of unity with the world entered into me. I was tranquillised and steadied by the beauty, the stability of Nature. I do not suppose that I learnt anything that was new to me during this experience. But I believe I was taught something and that something happened in me. I returned to my work tranquil, and strengthened in faith and hope by my experience.

Howard Collier, 1943

26.09   *J Rowntree Gillett (1874-1940) was a banker who gave up his business in the First World War on pacifist grounds and devoted his life to religious and social services.*

Brought up in a house where Jesus Christ was loved and honoured, I can never remember a time when his claims on me were not more or less a living issue, and although on attaining manhood I wandered for many years in a maze of doubt and unrest, nevertheless that issue remained. Just thirteen years ago I became convinced that God was a living reality and had revealed himself to humanity in the character and personality of Jesus Christ. From that time I dedicated myself to him and have tried to lead men and women into a realisation of God's love and care for them.

c 1918

26.10 I am by temperament a sceptic. But, at my feeblest, I am conscious of a power of choice, of a better and a worse. This 'ought' is my insignia of personality. Directly I admit that my life might be better than it is I have a sense of failure and feel a need of help from something or someone outside myself. This sense and this need are to me the meanings of the terms 'sense of sin' and 'need of salvation'. I recognise absolute moral or, rather, spiritual values, quite beyond reason or argument; very often indeed contradicting reason and flouting even scientific law... I am not going to wait until I have fathomed all mysteries and secret lore before I begin to live. It has been my good fortune often to be in company with great souls, who have not only helped me in my intellectual quest for truth about religion, but have always encouraged me to strive towards experience, towards belief in religion. Fitfully and falteringly and with repeated failures I have tried to 'mind that which is pure' in me to guide me to God.

Francis H Knight, 1945

26.11 Whenever we are driven into the depths of our own being, or seek them of our own will, we are faced by a tremendous contrast. On the one side we recognise the pathetic littleness of our ephemeral existence, with no point or meaning in itself. On the other side, in the depth, there is something eternal and infinite in which our existence, and indeed all existence, is grounded. This experience of the depths of existence fills us with a sense both of reverence and of responsibility, which gives even to our finite lives a meaning and a power which they do not possess in themselves. This, I am assured, is our human experience of God.

John Macmurray, 1967

26.12 So one approaches, by efforts which call for the deepest resources of one's being, to the condition of true silence; not just of sitting still, not just of not speaking, but of a wide awake, fully aware non-thinking. It is in this condition, found and held for a brief instant only, that I have experienced the existence of something other than 'myself'. The thinking me has vanished, and with it vanishes the sense of separation, of unique identity. One is not left naked and defenceless, as one is, for example, by the operations of the mind in self-analysis. One becomes instead aware, one is conscious of being a participant in the whole of existence, not limited to the body or the moment... It is in this condition that one understands the nature of the divine power, its essential identity with love, in the widest sense of that much misused word.

Geoffrey Hubbard, 1974

26.13 My experience came after many years of doubting and uncertainty. It came to me one evening, alone in the sitting room at home. It came at a moment when God, who through many people and events over a period of several months had been pursuing me, put his hand on my shoulder. I had to respond – yes or no. It was unequivocal, inescapable and unconditional. It was also completely unemotional; I was stone cold sober – no heavenly visions or lumps in the throat. It was a challenge to the will, a gift of faith for me to reject or accept – and I accepted.

Roy Farrant, 1974

26.14 If anyone had told me in the summer of 1979 that within three years I should be unable to walk, speak, write by hand and feed myself, then surely I would have gone to pieces emotionally and perhaps spiritually. After all, I had just enjoyed a vigorous walking holiday in North Wales, descending from Snowdon by the difficult Crib Goch route... Since hearing the diagnosis, I have been struggling to come to terms with the implications of this illness – no, 'struggling' is the wrong word, for as my physical power has waned, so faith has been wonderfully strengthened... I feel surrounded and upheld by God's love.

Walter Martin, 1984

26.15 In silence, without rite or symbol, we have known the Spirit of Christ so convincingly present in our quiet meetings that his grace dispels our faithlessness, our unwillingness, our fears, and sets our hearts aflame with the joy of adoration. We have thus felt the power of the Spirit renewing and recreating our love and friendship for all our fellows. This is our Eucharist and our Communion.

London Yearly Meeting, 1928

WAYS OF SEEKING

26.16   In its early days our Society owed much to a people who called themselves Seekers: they joined us in great numbers and were prominent in the spread of Quakerism. It is a name which must appeal strongly to the scientific temperament. The name has died out, but I think that the spirit of seeking is still the prevailing one in our faith, which for that reason is not embodied in any creed or formula.

Arthur S Eddington, 1929

26.17   I should like to change the name 'seekers' to 'explorers'. There is a considerable difference there: we do not seek the Atlantic, we explore it. The whole field of religious experience has to be explored, and has to be described in a language understandable to modern men and women.

Ole Olden, 1955

26.18   It is because the learning process is continued throughout life that Friends are seekers as well as finders – not one or the other, but both. One only has to think of the need for a continual search for fresh language, unsoiled by use, to know that we must, if we care about truth, continue to be seekers. We may have a firm hold on old truth ourselves, but unless we are eager to find new ways of expressing it we may be unable to speak the word of life to others just when they most need it.

Ruth Fawell, 1987

26.19   God is revealed to individuals through models suited to their temperaments and abilities; to communities through models suited to their culture. Nor will the interpretation of these models always be the same. Each one is only a guide to the truth that is greater than them all yet accessible in the nearest and simplest way... As our experience widens we are brought closer to aspects of God which we did not understand before. But we are compelled to respect the experience and response of others. If there is no one model of the truth and if no model is essential then there is no basis for authoritarianism or heresy-hunts. Our own vision is widened by the vision of others.

Janet Scott, 1980

26.20   The advice to be open to new light from wherever it may come is one of the reasons why the Quakers have continued to answer that of God in everyone. The trust they showed in the living Christ was their strength 300 years ago, as it is today, though we do not all use the same words. A living truth, if it is to stay alive, must speak to the conditions of the times. Once it is tied up in concise terms, bound by the words used and thought to be the last word, it is already on the decline. Life means growth – and death. We should not cling to words that have lost their life. We cannot force ourselves to believe something which does not ring true for us. Christianity used to survive because of the empty tomb; now Christianity survives in spite of the empty tomb. Great truths survive throughout history, clad in the clothes that are right for the times. A change of garb is inevitable if the truth is to be acceptable. But it is only in the trappings – the bare naked truth remains for all to feel, to acknowledge and express.

Jean West, 1988

26.21   It ought to be recognised that at the present time, at least in this country, the real danger is not from a too narrow, cramping and militantly dogmatic theology, but rather from an inveterate haziness of mind, a half-heartedness and general belittlement of the importance of true thinking in religion. And the final outcome of this is the assumption ... that Christianity may indeed reasonably claim to be 'good', that is, to put forward an elevated ethical standard and an edifying moral idealism, but makes and can make no claim to be 'true'. I do not think it likely that terms like 'theology', 'dogma' and 'creed' will ever evoke enthusiasm among members of the Society of Friends. But it ought to be possible to allay what almost amounts to a phobia with regard to them.

John W Harvey, 1947

26.22   We know that as individuals we have no adequate check upon the development of mere notions within our minds; and so we insist upon the discipline of the worshipping community in which mere waywardness of mind or individualism will be seen for what it is. And we know that the stimulus and personal interchange of the religious community will enable the individual to rise to a greater clarity of perception than would be possible for him alone.

Kenneth C Barnes, 1960

26.23   It is difficult for us to reconcile the two ideas of God as a loving Father and as the Creator of all things, because of the existence of cruelty and undeserved suffering in Nature itself. Jesus apparently did take for granted the idea that God controlled the rising of the sun and falling of the rain and had made us male and female. It makes me long to have him here now so that I could ask him some of the questions that his disciples didn't ask him. In fact I find that I am talking to him in my mind and that it is a great deal more profitable than talking to myself; even though it is, in one sense, talking to myself; and even though I don't get the answers to the questions that puzzle me. But that doesn't worry me now, because I have learned, as a scientist, how much I don't understand. I have learned too that when a scientist encounters two apparently irreconcilable ideas, these are the stepping stones to new knowledge.

Kathleen Lonsdale, 1962

26.24   It is often supposed that science and religious belief are incompatible. Indeed, a dichotomy does exist between some traditional views of God's interaction with the universe and science's perception of natural laws. If we only use God to fill the gaps wherever a rational explanation has not been found, God's role must diminish as scientific understanding grows. A 'God of the gaps' is inevitably a rather small God. However, the immanence of God in our world may be appreciated through Science as vividly as through the Arts. Many scientists daily experience God through their work: in the elegance and sophistication of natural design or the beauty and harmony revealed in certain theories. The growing body of scientific knowledge demands a continuous re-thinking of what is meant by 'Creator' but our greater understanding magnifies rather than diminishes our appreciation of God.

Science and religion have much in common. They are communal activities and involve a search for some greater truth. The sharing of ideas is fundamental to both. The discipline of science can make a valuable contribution to religious thought; critical honesty, the willingness to abandon old ideas and modes of thought when fresh insight demands it and the centrality of experience as an arbiter of truth are as important in one as in the other. In both the scientific and religious searches for truth, the implications of current beliefs are explored to see where they lead. Beliefs are not just safe ledges in an uncertain reality, but rather handholds from which further heights can be reached.

Eleven Quaker scientists, 1989

26.25 As a teenager I looked for proof of the existence of God, but soon realised that there would be none. I chose to adopt as a working hypothesis a belief in God, and to go on from there. I have not felt the need to revise that hypothesis – yet. I believe in a powerful, all-knowing God, but a caring and a forgiving God. I believe he says to us: 'All right, you've got life, get on with it, live it! I am there behind to guide you, to help you live it; but don't expect me to interfere to make life smooth for you – you are old enough to stand on your own two feet.'

From what I have learnt as an astronomer I believe that the Universe evolved itself without any active participation from God, and it seems reasonable to me that the world continues, at least on a grand scale, to evolve by itself – that God does not directly interfere with the running of the world; but that he does through people and their attitudes...

I believe that we are God's agents in this world and that he may require things of us. A lot of my effort goes into trying to understand what God expects of me. I do this by trying to maintain an orientation towards God – to live my life in the spirit – to bring my whole life under the ordering of the spirit of Christ – to acknowledge my discipleship.

S Jocelyn Burnell, 1976

26.26 You say: 'But with the best will in the world, I can't get to the point of believing in God.' Well then, if you want to believe in him, if you feel something great behind it all and not just words, well, work for God, and you will see not only that it comes to the same thing as believing in him, but something infinitely more alive, more real, more powerful which fills you and satisfies you more than anything you might vaguely imagine under the name of 'real and living faith' – a reality, a life and not words.

Pierre Ceresole, 1935

26.27   It's a funny thing about God, which I still haven't understood. If you say with all your heart: He isn't there, then oddly he isn't. He seems to withdraw. In the same way, just not noticing produces the same results. He doesn't come thrusting himself into your life if you don't want him there. (I recognise that some people will want to say that's exactly how God came to them, but I think this is a different matter.) Yet if we say: God, I need you, then he moves closer to us. If we start the conversation, surprisingly it does not simply seem to fade into empty space. A sense of presence gradually begins to make itself felt.

Now I really don't know how I'm going to convince you of that. I also hear people telling me: I've tried that and it doesn't work. And that's also perfectly true, as we all painfully know from our own experiences. I know it's true and a very blank feeling it is when we have it. Yet I also know that the presence of God is as real, as the absence is negating. I begin to recognise that ultimately it is not for any intellectual reasons that I believe in God, nor even possibly as a result of my emotional state, but simply from the growing sense that when I call he answers.

I don't find it easy to write this, for I also need to overcome the sense that you will find what I say faintly ridiculous. However it seems worth the risk, because the alternative is rather bleak – that there is, after all, no converse with God, because we do not begin the conversation. All I want to say is that once the conversation begins, one does not want it ever to stop.

Tony Brown, 1984

26.28   From early on, too, I became aware that the movement into a place where in an ineffable way God became real, was not dissimilar from what went on when I entered into the space of imagination. That kind of space was one which attracted me from as far back as I can go in memory, whether it was opened up by someone reading to me, or when I was older by my reading to myself, or by games which drew open that part of me. And I sense that what went on when we sat round the table for reading after breakfast, or when I said my prayers before getting into bed, or when we went to worship on Sundays, belonged to the same kind of experience. Other ways into that space which opened up very early were through music, both listening to it and making it, and through the beauties of the world. Obviously now I realise that there are differences, a sense of the presence of God is not just the result of the use of imagination, or attending to something lovely, but the thing which is germane for me now is that inner space of various kinds has called my attention and has been a large and enlivening place.

Christopher Holdsworth, 1985

26.29   If we set our hearts on goodness as a personal goal, it means that we have to ignore or suppress all the other parts of ourselves that do not fit into our ideal of goodness. That was what George Fox had already done and he was actually shocked when, on the first part of his inward journey, he came upon the dark and unacceptable parts of himself. Like Simone Weil, the twentieth century mystic, he found that he knew from the inside a potential for all possible crimes. His fantasies were guided by no one but himself, but he quickly made the acquaintance of the things inside him that could be bestial, murderous and depraved. Instead of slamming the door of his consciousness, as many of us do when we come on the less acceptable bits of our inner world, he went on through them, understanding that he would not be of any use to others if he did not acknowledge in himself the impulses to kill, to lust or cheat or indulge his more primitive passions. If he had not had the courage to accept what he discovered, he would never have made the discovery that sets Quaker spirituality apart from the narrow righteousness of the Puritans. He found that, having faced and acknowledged his dark self, he came upon a more liberating truth at the heart of himself.

He experienced the moment of enlightenment which enabled him to trust the creative and intuitive part of himself and know that it could not be obliterated by the dark side... He spoke of 'the ocean of darkness and the ocean of light'. Both are symbols of the unconscious and of the contradictions and polarities of our being – our dark negativities and our shining possibilities.

Jo Farrow, 1984

PERCEPTIONS OF TRUTH

26.30   What is love? What shall I say of it, or how shall I in words express its nature? It is the sweetness of life; it is the sweet, tender, melting nature of God, flowing up through his seed of life into the creature, and of all things making the creature most like unto himself, both in nature and operation. It fulfils the law, it fulfils the gospel; it wraps up all in one, and brings forth all in the oneness. It excludes all evil out of the heart, it perfects all good in the heart. A touch of love doth this in measure; perfect love doth this in fullness.

Isaac Penington, 1663

26.31   I do believe that there is a power which is divine, creative and loving, though we can often only describe it with the images and symbols that rise from our particular experiences and those of our communities. This power is part and parcel of all things, human, animal, indeed of all that lives. Its story is greater than any one cultural version of it and yet it is embodied in all stories, in all traditions. It is a power that paradoxically needs the human response. Like us it is energised by the reciprocity of love.

It wills our redemption, longs for us to turn to it. It does not create heaven and hell for us, but allows us to do that for ourselves. Such is the terrible vulnerability of love.

Harvey Gillman, 1988

26.32   Perhaps more wonderful still is the way in which beauty breaks through. It breaks through not only at a few highly organised points, it breaks through almost everywhere. Even the minutest things reveal it as well as do the sublimest things, like the stars. Whatever one sees through the microscope, a bit of mould for example, is charged with beauty. Everything from a dewdrop to Mount Shasta is the bearer of beauty. And yet beauty has no function, no utility. Its value is intrinsic, not extrinsic. It is its own excuse for being. It greases no wheels, it bakes no puddings. It is a gift of sheer grace, a gratuitous largesse. It must imply behind things a Spirit that enjoys beauty for its own sake and that floods the world everywhere with it. Wherever it can break through, it does break through, and our joy in it shows that we are in some sense kindred to the giver and revealer of it.

Rufus Jones, 1920

26.33 To apply the term 'God' (in the Christian sense) is to say that we perceive intuitively a connection between the marvels of the natural world, the moral law, the life of Jesus, the depths of the human personality, our intimations about time, death and eternity, our experience of human forgiveness and love, and the finest insights of the Christian tradition. To deny the existence of 'God' is to say that we cannot (yet) see such connections. But even the word 'God' is not an essential tool for grasping them.

John Lampen, 1985

26.34 It is not an accident that throughout the centuries women have provided the core of Christian worship. Although, in order to fulfil the Divine Will at that particular place and time, Jesus was born as the son of Joseph, when he passed out of time into eternity surely sex was transcended. Might we not gain also if the male image of the Lord Almighty were replaced in our imagination by a conception more in line with Julian's vision of the Mother-Christ, the dual emblem of the mystery of creative love?

Katharine Moore, 1978

26.35 All my life I've heard, 'God is love', without understanding what was meant. Recently I've come to feel that in a very real way G-d/ess *is* the love that flows in and between and among us. The ebb and flow of my commitment to love, to peace, to harmony makes G-d/ess stronger or weaker in my heart.

Sometimes the web feels like G-d/ess' body, her vast cosmos, of which we are an inextricable part. The web is also the love that flows through creation, from G-d/ess, from us, from everywhere. The web is an affirmation and comfort, support and clear-naming. The web is harmony, proving to me by its fleeting, fragile appearances that peace can happen. Most of all, for me, the web is friendship.

That the web exists is my faith. Spinning at it, dancing along it and calling others into it are my ministry. Ripping it or withdrawing into isolation and despair are my sins. Articulating my faith is hard enough; living it is often beyond me. But we are all connected. Strength seeps in from everywhere and amazing things happen. The sense of participation and communion sweeps over me like ocean waves.

At the end of the article from which this extract is taken, the writer explained her use of 'G-d/ess':

I've yet to find a term that describes how I feel about the divine. 'The Spirit' comes close, and so, sometimes, does 'Goddess'. 'G-d/ess' attempts to convey the difficulty of naming the divine. The dash is an old Jewish practice meant to show the impossibility of confining the divine in a word. The single 'd' and feminine suffix are to show that I don't experience the goddess as different from or inferior to what folks generally refer to as God.

Rose Ketterer, 1987

26.36   *As the Yearly Meeting in 1994 struggled to find unity on whether 26.35 should have a place in our book of discipline, Jo Farrow wrote:*

In the seventeenth century the first generation of Friends shocked many of their Christian neighbours. In trying to express their experiences of God – within them, as spirit, inward light, seed, inward teacher – they used words and phrases which sounded strange and audacious to their contemporaries. They spoke of their experiences of being drawn into community with one another using metaphors and analogies which were both new and old at the same time. 'The kingdom of God did gather us all in a net...' wrote Francis Howgill, trying to express the sense of relief and excitement which was theirs when they discovered one another and became aware of how deeply they had been drawn together as they struggled to articulate their experiences of the Spirit. In much the same way many women today are discovering a need to express their spirituality in ways which seem as strange to some Friends as the expressions of early Quaker spirituality did to those who first heard them. Rose Ketterer is a member of Haddonfield Friends Meeting, New Jersey. She writes of her attempts to reclaim a more womanly understanding of the divine.

26.37   Religion is living with God. There is no other kind of religion. Living with a Book, living with or by a Rule, being awfully high-principled are not in themselves religion, although many people think they are and that that is all there is to it. Religion has got a bad name through being identified with an outward orderliness. But an outward orderliness can be death, dullness and masochism. Doing your duty may be admirable stoicism; it isn't religion.

To find religion itself you must look inside people and inside yourself. And there, if you find even the tiniest grain of true love, you may be on the right scent. Millions of people have it and don't know what it is that they have. God is their guest, but they haven't the faintest idea that he is in the house. So you mustn't only look where God is confessed and acknowledged. You must look everywhere, to find the real religion. Nor must you look, in others or in yourself, for great spooky visions and revelations. Such visions and revelations come to many, a great deal oftener than we think; and to those to whom they come they are sun, moon and stars. But in most people who know God, and in all such people most of the time, living with God is not an apparition but a wordless and endless sureness. Like the silence of two friends together. Like the silence of lovers.

God is waiting to live like that in every single person in the world.

Bernard Canter, 1962

26.38   God for me is the whole; and 'in him I live and move and have my being'... Since I am a person God must be in some measure personal. But the universe is full of other energies, and so God is other than personal too. With Gerard Manley Hopkins I sense that he is 'past all grasp, God'; and yet with Tennyson I am sure that 'Closer is He than breathing, and nearer than hands and feet'. This is so infinitely wonderful and mysterious that my natural human conceit is checked, I see myself in perspective, and worship becomes a rational response. Reverence for the world, for life, for man, leads on inescapably to reverence for the whole which I call God.

Donald Court, 1965

26.39   True faith is not assurance, but the readiness to go forward experimentally, without assurance. It is a sensitivity to things not yet known. Quakerism should not claim to be a religion of certainty, but a religion of uncertainty; it is this which gives us our special affinity to the world of science. For what we apprehend of truth is limited and partial, and experience may set it all in a new light; if we too easily satisfy our urge for security by claiming that we have found certainty, we shall no longer be sensitive to new experiences of truth. For who seeks that which he believes that he has found? Who explores a territory which he claims already to know?

Charles Carter, 1971

26.40   I do not know the course I am to run, all is hid in mystery, but I try to do right in everything... Look up to true religion as the very first of blessings, cherish it, nourish and let it flourish and bloom in my heart; it wants taking care of, it is difficult to obtain. I must not despair or grow sceptical if I do not always feel religious. I felt God as it were, and I must seek to find Him again.

Elizabeth Fry, 1798

26.41   What is my religion? My friends, my teachers, my God. And who is my God? He speaks within me; if I mishear, my friends correct me; if I misdo, I look to Jesus Christ. How then am I taught? I hear in the silence, I ponder in solitude, and I try in the noisy crowd to practise it. What do I learn? To put gaiety before prudence, grace before pleasure, service before power. What am I commanded? To seek patience in suffering, humility in success, steadfastness always. What is forbidden me? To reject another's love, to despise another's wisdom, to blaspheme another's God. And to what purpose? To help others, that we may enter the Commonwealth of Heaven together, each to find our Being in the Whole.

Frederick Parker-Rhodes, 1977

THE LIGHT THAT SHINES FOR ALL

26.42   Now the Lord God has opened to me by his invisible power how that every man was enlightened by the divine Light of Christ; and I saw it shine through all, and that they that believed in it came out of condemnation and came to the Light of Life, and became the children of it, but they that hated it and did not believe in it were condemned by it, though they made a profession of Christ. This I saw in the pure openings of the Light, without the help of any man, neither did I then know where to find it in the Scriptures, though afterwards, searching the Scriptures, I found it. For I saw in that Light and Spirit, which was before Scripture was given forth, and which led the holy men of God to give them forth, that all must come to that Spirit, if they would know God or Christ or the Scriptures aright, which they that gave them forth were led and taught by.

George Fox, 1648

26.43   The heart of the Quaker message does not lie in a doctrine expressed in abstract terms, but in an experience of power and grace, known in our hearts and also related to the structure of the universe; also known individually and recognised as belonging to all. At the same time this universal spirit is focused and made personal in Jesus in a way which makes it appropriate to speak of the Universal Light as the Light of Christ. It is from this double emphasis on universal and Christ-like that the Quaker message starts. It is these two elements, held firmly together, which provide the coherence and unity of Quakerism.

L Hugh Doncaster, 1972

The Light of Christ

26.44   If you would know God and worship and serve God as you should do, you must come to the means he has ordained and given for that purpose. Some seek it in books, some in learned men, but what they look for is in themselves, yet they overlook it. The voice is too still, the Seed too small and the Light shineth in darkness. They are abroad and so cannot divide the spoil; but the woman that lost her silver found it at home after she had lighted her candle and swept her house. Do you so too and you shall find what Pilate wanted to know, viz., Truth. The Light of Christ within, who is the Light of the world and so a light to you that tells you the truth of your condition, leads all that take heed unto it out of darkness into God's marvellous light; for light grows upon the obedient. It is sown for the righteous and their way is a shining light that shines forth more and more to the perfect day.

William Penn, 1694

26.45   Christ has not conquered to excuse us, but that we should follow his steps.

Job Scott, 1792

26.46   The New Testament clearly sets out Christ as fully human and as fully divine. The writers are conscious of no difficulty or contradiction involved in this position. It seemed to them the most natural thing in the world. Probably the sense of contradiction only arises in our minds through ignorance of what is meant by personality. We set divinity over against humanity, on the assumption that so much added to the one must be so much subtracted from the other. Some have so emphasised Christ's divinity as to leave no room for his humanity, while others have done just the reverse. It seems so easy to solve the problem by cutting the knot: either say that Christ was absolute God or that he was ordinary man. But this does not solve the problem, for either solution fails to take account of many of the facts. The difficulty is to get a conception of Jesus that is true to all the facts – of one who was the incarnate Son of God and yet (perhaps we should say 'and therefore') was truly man. It is a pity that we insist on using the terms 'humanity' and 'divinity' as though they implied opposition. May we not rather say that Jesus 'shows us the divine life humanly lived and the human life divinely lived'?

Yorkshire Quarterly Meeting, 1919

26.47   If you allow me to have Christ simply as a friend, he may become what you call God; if you force him on me as God, he cannot become a friend.

Pierre Ceresole, 1920

26.48   I am far from having arrived at the mount of vision where so many more faithful disciples have stood, above all mists of doubt: yet to think of Christ has meant again and again a parting in the clouds through which a beam of light comes gleaming. Sometimes that light has shone into my vision reflected from word or deed of some man or woman who themselves have been illumined by the same Lord; sometimes the echo of his words in the New Testament; the impress of what he did, above all of what he was, and is and will be, has brought the help I needed. I do not understand more than a very little of that life; there are passages in the gospels which puzzle me; I know there may be in the narrative things imperfectly reported or misunderstood by those who heard him. But there he remains, and life goes forth from him still into our lives, bringing hope and forgiveness and healing, a new vision and a new spirit.

T Edmund Harvey, 1949

26.49　'I and the Father are One'. That means to me that I think of God in terms of Jesus Christ, that I pray to Jesus as representing the Father to my consciousness, or to the Father as I see him in Jesus. Carry that thought to Calvary itself. See in the crucifixion not merely a martyr's death, not merely a passing gleam of God's love, certainly not a sacrifice to God carrying a legal significance, but in truth the flashing into light of an eternal fact, the nature of God's relation to sin, of the pain we inflict on his heart by our own wrongdoing. Here is the wonderful dynamic of the cross. God calls you to him. He shows you his suffering, he shows you the hatefulness of the sin that caused it, and, in showing you his love, shows you the punishment of alienation from him, the hell of the unrepentant, in which we must remain until repentance opens the gate for the prodigal and gives entrance to the free forgiveness and love of the Father's house. In Jesus, in his life and his death upon the cross, we are shown the nature of God and the possibilities that are within our reach. We are shown the world as the Father sees it, are called to live in harmony with his will and purpose, to hate the sins that made him mourn, to scale the barrier of sin and discover that the way of penitence lies open and direct to the Fatherly heart. No legal bargain, but a spiritual conflict, an inward change, the rejection of the living death of sin, the choice of the new birth, of the purified self, the conversion from a low and earthly to a high and spiritual standard of life and conduct – here you have the practical conditions of salvation, and in the active, free and holy love of God, ever seeking entrance, ever powerful if we but yield the gateway of our heart, is the substance of the Gospel.

John Wilhelm Rowntree, 1904

26.50　We can respond to the Christ-event in such a way that we see Jesus as a symbol of God, a concrete example of divine being and action. When we do this, though we make statements focused on Jesus, we are in fact trying to talk about God. Using this symbol we can talk about God as helpless and humble, sharing human vulnerability with us. We can see the brokenness of God, the giving up of power in order to take on pain and mortality; the creativity of love which remakes hope out of despair, promise out of sin; the incarnation of the divine in the human, making all of life sacred; the fusion of holiness with life; the divine self-offering. Using this symbol we can talk about comfort; about the light that shines in the darkness; about the certainty of love and joy. We can see the presence of God in every aspect of our lives, so that whatever our situation it is shared and understood. Using this symbol we can above all see God in our fellow-humans and thus be called to service. In every homeless child, every refugee, every criminal or outcast, every worker or preacher, those in authority and those without it, there is a child of God, one who is precious and loved.

Janet Scott, 1980

26.51　The central perceptions of Christianity remain as a source of perennial wisdom without which we sink into non-life. Incarnation, the cross, repentance, forgiveness, resurrection – these unfashionable words express the deep realities of the human condition. At the time of our origin the first Friends relinquished the excrescences and the exterior trappings by which the churches obscured the central vision. When we read George Fox and are shaken by a power and a passion which we apparently have lost, what we should seek is not an impossible return to the historical moment which fostered such convictions but to see in the terms of our own very different, though also chaotic, times what the centrality of Christ can mean to us now.

Lorna M Marsden, 1985

26.52   If we try to imagine ourselves in the position of the first disciples, we would have to think of ourselves as strictly monotheistic Jews, believing in the one God, Jehovah, the creator. As they associated with Jesus, they gradually came to recognise more and more in him: first the special rabbi who taught with authority and not as the scribes; then the Christ, the holy one of God; finally the affirmation of Thomas: 'My Lord and my God'. What a terrible thing for a Jew to have said – and yet, somehow, that was the effect of the impact Jesus made. And then, after his earthly life was finished, these same disciples and their friends were aware of the continuing life of his spirit among them, encouraging, guiding and sustaining them. In short, they had a three-fold experience of one reality: they knew God the father; they knew the person of Jesus who was so identified with him that Thomas could burst out with his great affirmation; and they knew the continuing inspiration of the spirit which they identified with him.

L Hugh Doncaster, 1963

26.53   I cannot explain the mystery of how someone who is a human being just as I am can also be worshipped. And yet the more real the mystery has become for me, it isn't that Jesus has become more like God, but that all my brothers and sisters have. It is through him that I recognise God in my neighbour – through Jesus I've discovered the uniqueness of everyone. And there was in him a quality of willingness to be defeated and destroyed by his enemies and to go on loving them, that alone made possible a new quality of life afterwards.

Paul Oestreicher, 1981

26.54   We make our guesses at the nature of God, and we are often like my small daughter who said, 'My mind goes round and round when I want to think about God, but I can think about Jesus.' To me Jesus is a window through to God, a person who in terms of personality, in a way that can be grasped by our finite minds, shows what mercy, pity, peace are like in human life. I turn to the Jesus of the New Testament – to his healing word, his freedom from anxiety, his outreaching insight, to him as a whole person – not to imitate him but to let him live and grow in my life...

I do not pray to him – I look at him, dwell upon him, love him. But it is the presence of the God he worshipped of which I am conscious as I look at the night sky, the sleeping child and the rose. When I listen in the quietness and when I pray, it is to God that I listen and pray. And since personality is the highest value that I know in life, since all truth comes to us through the medium of human minds and thoughts, I am not surprised that God too comes to me in terms of personality. I can well understand how to many Christians Christ comes as a tangible figure, a Son of God in a special unique way, even though that is not the way he comes to me. Every word that comes to our lips is a symbol and the symbol of the father God has been sanctified by Jesus' use of it as well as by how it has been used throughout the Bible. We have much to learn about the image of fatherhood and from the growing and developing idea of God in the Old Testament. Now we may be beginning to learn about God the mother as well.

Ruth Fawell, 1987

26.55   Jesus the Jew of Nazareth, ... to me, puts a question mark and an exclamation mark to everything. It is not a matter of saying 'Jesus is the answer'. It would be true and more useful to say that Jesus is the question. Here the questions of action and achievement, of God and humanity, are brought to a focus in the paradox of triumph on a cross, of God dying as a man, of a man living as God. Here the question mark which death and suffering put against the love and joys of this world is itself confronted with a question: 'Death, where is thy sting?' And in the light of this, we are faced with the question: 'Who do you say that I am?' I have found, too, that it is easy to side-step the challenge of Jesus. The history of the early church and the growth of the creeds, which are such red rags to Quakers, is precisely the attempt of the church not to lose sight of this paradox, this knife edge, this scandal. Constantly, people wanted to make things easier to grasp and more comfortable to live with by stressing the human side of Jesus at the expense of the divine or vice versa. No one would deny that the attempt to encapsulate the truth about Jesus in words is bound to fail, but the achievement of those years was to keep the tension that he embodies alive so that it has resonance now, instead of opting for an easier answer.

Hugh Pyper, 1986

26.56 The resurrection, however literally or otherwise we interpret it, demonstrates the power of God, to bring life out of brokenness; not just to take the hurt out of brokenness but to add something to the world. It helps us to sense the usefulness, the possible meaning in our suffering, and to turn it into a gift. The resurrection affirms me with my pain and my anger at what has happened. It does not take away my pain; it still hurts. But I sense that I am being transfigured; I am being enabled to begin again to love confidently and to remake the spirit of my world.

S Jocelyn Burnell, 1989

26.57 I decided long ago that God was not the most 'powerful' thing in the universe. He much more resembles a barefoot Galilean prophet speaking in up-country dialect, followed by tax-gatherers, fishermen and prostitutes, who becomes a nuisance and ends up (very properly) by being crucified while the guards dice for his clothes – more to pass the time than because the garments are worth anything. It is not because God is powerful that I worship him; if he is powerful it is in some dimension that I don't know anything about, which we can agree (if you like) to call eternity...

No, the moment when I love God is at the moment when the Galilean prophet was watching his followers melt away and suspected that Simon Peter the fisherman would soon be off too, back to his nets. 'Wilt thou also go away?' he asks Simon; but mercifully Simon is too stupid to see the point of the question, or to take his chance to get out. 'Lord, to whom should we go? Thou hast the word of eternal life.' That's it, the obscure, futile shaky thing, as feeble as a baby in a stable, that's what I worship.

J Ormerod Greenwood, 1973

26.58 For two thousand years there has been emphasis on the Yang aspects of Christ, that is on the amazing teacher, healer and master of all spiritual power, he who rebuked the winds and the waves and told his disciples they had only to believe and mountains could be uprooted and set down in the seas. This over-emphasis upon the power aspect of the spirit has resulted ... in domination of the planet. But because intuitive reverence has been missing we have unwittingly set about destroying the living and healing processes which actually hold the world together.

The Yin or feminine aspect of the Christ now awaits our discovery. This is the Christ in the second period of the Gospel story. He who, echoing his mother's receptivity to the divine, in the garden of Gethsemane prayed, 'Nevertheless, not as I will but as thou wilt.' Just here in the rending of the material, which the cross betokens, a new invasion of spirit into matter occurs. This is the Christ, agonisingly separated from spirit, who by his receptivity makes possible a fresh flow of impregnation from the divine, right down into the depths of nature and into humanity.

Damaris Parker-Rhodes, 1985

26.59   An awareness of older, lonely Friends grew in me with many hours spent visiting, and I felt able to volunteer for work with the Children's Meeting, which I really enjoyed. Living where we did near all the symptoms of inner-city decay and change I had ample opportunity to feel the needs of those around us. This process of awareness culminated when I rather simply and naïvely asked God for a deeper understanding of Christ. I think I expected something rather comforting and lovely. Instead all the world's suffering was gathered up in a moment and pressed upon me. It was quite searing, quite devastating. The experience gave me an understanding of Jesus as one deeply involved in our suffering and pain, actually experiencing it too, that God is not remote but that *God is with us.* Truly Emmanuel.

Rosamond Robertson, 1990

26.60   Those of us who cannot yet personally witness to the experience of direct encounter with the living Christ can only at our peril deny the truth of the experience to which others testify; just as those who do feel this experience are on equally dangerous ground when on account of it they claim that they alone possess the sole route to that God whom Jesus of Nazareth defined as spirit and whose kingdom he once likened to a house with many mansions. Respect for the validity of personal encounter with the spirit of God, subjected to the check of corporate discipline, is part of the essence of our Quaker witness. Thus, though both our practices of worship and our theological understandings now differ widely, these variances may be accepted as elements within the direct, continuing development of the spirit of Jesus, the sensing of which was at the heart of the original Quaker experience.

Richard Rowntree, 1987

The Universal Light

26.61　There is a principle which is pure, placed in the human mind, which in different places and ages hath different names; it is, however, pure and proceeds from God. It is deep and inward, confined to no forms of religion nor excluded from any where the heart stands in perfect sincerity. In whomsoever this takes root and grows, of what nation soever, they become brethren.

John Woolman, 1762

26.62　The light for which the world longs is already shining. It is shining into the darkness, but the darkness does not apprehend it. It is shining into the darkness, but the darkness is not overcoming it. It is shining in many a soul, and already the new order has begun within the kingdom of the heart. It is shining in many a small group and creating a heavenly-earthly fellowship of children of the light. It will always shine and lead many into the world of need, that they may bear it up into the heart of God.

Thomas R Kelly, 1941

26.63　The light that shines into man's heart is not of man, and must ever be distinguished both from the conscience which it enlightens and from the natural faculty of reason which, when unsubjected to its holy influences, is, in the things of God, very foolishness. As the eye is to the body, so is conscience to our inner nature, the organ by which we see; and as both light and life are essential to sight in the natural eye, so conscience as the inward eye cannot see aright without the quickening and illumination of the Spirit of God.

Yearly Meeting in London, 1879

26.64 Wrth roi pwyslais ar y Goleuni oddimewn nid ydym yn dyneiddio crefydd yn ormodol. Nid ein goleuni ni ydyw; ei dderbyn yr ydym ni. A ni ynghanol ein profiadau gyda'n cyd-ddynion, daw rhyw oleuni sydd yn peri i'r profiadau hynny edrych yn wahanol. Dywedwn, yn drwsgl, mai'r Goleuni Oddimewn sydd yn peri'r cyfnewidiad, a chredwn mai oddiwrth Dduw y daeth. Sut y gwyddom nad ydym yn ein twyllo ein hunain? Yn y pen draw nid oes gennym ddim ond ein profiad ein hunain i bwyso arno. Yn y pen draw nid oes gan un a dderbynio'r grefydd fwyaf traddodiadol ddim ond ei brofiad i bwyso arno.

Waldo Williams, 1956

For a translation of this extract into English see page 617

26.65 This central affirmation, that the Light of the Christ-like God shines in every person, implies that our knowledge of God is both subjective and objective. It is easy to misconstrue 'Inner Light' as an invitation to individualism and anarchy if one concentrates on the subjective experience known to each one. But it is an equally important part of our faith and practice to recognise that we are not affirming the existence and priority of your light and my light, but of the Light of God, and of the God who is made known to us supremely in Jesus. The inward experience must be checked by accordance with the mind of Christ, the fruits of the Spirit, the character of that willed caring which in the New Testament is called Love. It is further checked by the fact that if God is known in measure by every person, our knowledge of him will be largely gained through the experience of others who reverently and humbly seek him. In the last resort we must be guided by our own conscientiously held conviction – but it is in the last resort. First we must seek carefully and prayerfully through the insights of others, both in the past and among our contemporaries, and only in the light of this search do we come to our affirmation.

L Hugh Doncaster, 1972

26.66 We may seem at times to take God for granted. But we know the beyond in our midst; we rely on grace, on God's free, sustaining, creative and lively action as we rely on the air we breathe and the ground we walk on.

London Yearly Meeting, 1986

26.67   We misunderstand the truth of the Inward Light if we imagine that
it means a present inspiration independent of the past. Fox claimed
that he had a word from the Lord as sure as any of the Apostles ever
had. We join him in affirming our faith in the contemporary inspiration of the Holy Spirit. But Fox could never have made his claim if
he had not recognised the word of the Lord which came to the
Apostles.

H G Wood, 1951

26.68   The Inner Light does not lead men to do that which is right in their
own eyes, but that which is right in God's eyes. As the Light is One,
so its teaching is ultimately (though not superficially) harmonious.
In actual experience, it is not found that souls truly looking to the
Inner Light as their authority will break away from each other in
anarchy.

Ellen S Bosanquet, 1927

26.69   There is no easy optimism in the Quaker view of life. Fox had no
illusions about sin; but he asks us to deal with it in a new way. When
early Friends likened God's gift to a 'Seed' they did not think of it as
growing inevitably into a noble tree. They were fully aware of the
influences that might arrest its growth. Fox never regarded the con-
quest of sin as a casual undertaking. But with astonishing psychological insight he laid the whole emphasis of his method not on the
sin but on the light that revealed it. By implication he was criticising
those who were so obsessed with the fallen state of man that they
stayed their eyes on man's wickedness rather than on the means of
his redemption. To contemplate evil is a poor way of becoming
good... Fox assures his friends that light will come on conditions.
These conditions were well laid down by Isaac Penington in the
darkness of Reading gaol: 'We were directed to search for the least
of all seeds and to mind the lowest appearance thereof, which was its
turning against sin and darkness; we came by degrees to find we had
met with the pure living eternal Spirit.'

The practice of minding 'the lowest appearance' of the Seed involves
a steady discipline. We must face the austerity as well as accept the
joy of life if we are to grow. The method of this discipline is beauti-
fully and most practically suggested in George Fox's oft-repeated

instruction, 'Mind that which is pure in you to guide you to God.' Here Fox displays a deep psychological insight, born of his own personal struggle. We are to use the little that we have to make it more. We are to tend the small Seed and help it to grow.

Edgar B Castle, 1961

26.70 Give over thine own willing, give over thy own running, give over thine own desiring to know or be anything and sink down to the seed which God sows in the heart, and let that grow in thee and be in thee and breathe in thee and act in thee; and thou shalt find by sweet experience that the Lord knows that and loves and owns that, and will lead it to the inheritance of Life, which is its portion.

Isaac Penington, 1661

26.71 If you build upon anything or have confidence in anything which stands in time and is on this side eternity and [the] Being of beings, your foundation will be swept away, and night will come upon you, and all your gathered-in things and taken-on and imitated will all fail you... Why gad you abroad? Why trim you yourselves with the saints' words, when you are ignorant of the life? Return, return to Him that is the first Love, and the first-born of every creature, who is the Light of the world... Return home to within, sweep your houses all, the groat is there, the little leaven is there, the grain of mustard-seed you will see, which the Kingdom of God is like; ... and here you will see your Teacher not removed into a corner, but present when you are upon your beds and about your labour, convincing, instructing, leading, correcting, judging and giving peace to all that love and follow Him.

Francis Howgill, 1656

26.72 To you who are seekers, to you, young and old who have toiled all night and caught nothing, but who want to launch out into the deeps and let down your nets for a draught, I want to speak as simply, as tenderly, as clearly as I can. For God *can* be found. There *is* a last rock for your souls, a resting-place of absolute peace and joy and power and radiance and security. There is a Divine Center into which your life can slip, a new and absolute orientation in God, a Center where you live with Him and out of which you see all of life through new and radiant vision, tinged with new sorrows and pangs, new joys unspeakable and full of glory... The reality of Presence has been very great at times recently. One knows at first hand what the old inquiry meant, 'Has Truth been advancing among you?'

Thomas R Kelly, 1941

26.73   I would hesitate to claim that I receive direct guidance from God – I do not hear a divine voice that tells me what to do. But I do have a sense that I am being drawn to take one course of action rather than another. The guidance, however, arises from a countless number of experiences, influences, attitudes and disciplines which I have accumulated over the years and upon which I have reflected. So certain types of action seem to be my natural response to particular circumstances. In them all the sense of the presence of God is real and immediate but it is not unmediated.

George Gorman, 1973

26.74   What manner of spirit are we of? Have we any connection with the spirit which descended on the upper room, sounding like 'a mighty rushing wind'? Do we look to be swept out of our comfortable existence by an invading power which comes, as Jesus said, no one knows whence? Or do we look rather for a gentler movement within? Do we say, it was this Spirit of God which breathed into our human clay to make us living souls? It is there, in our humanity, but mixed with passions which confuse its purpose, limited by the tunnel vision of the self. Occasionally a blinding flash may come from without and someone is jolted forwards; but the Spirit's normal method is a quiet insistence, a still small voice barely audible amid the turbulence of earthquake, wind and fire.

Stephen Allott, 1981

26.75   For some time now I have thought of God in more pantheistic terms than I suppose is true of most of my Quaker brothers and sisters. To me, God is something about the universe, something about the depth in each of us.

We've never talked about it in the meeting but this difference in thinking doesn't seem to matter in what we share. We visit the prison in Richmond together, give shelter to runaway teenagers, aid those who are resisting the war. We come together and wait quietly to regain our sense of what lies deepest in us, of the things most important to us. Then when we each of us speak and listen from this condition of mind and heart we somehow understand and are bound together in ways that are healing and empowering.

To me, these are the things that are prayer and revelation and encounter with that which is holy. And when I find something like them beyond the meeting and its membership there too I sense a unity of being. These are the things which, for me, any thought of God must have to do with. How thankful I am that this seems so surely to be true for the others with whom I share the silences, the concerns, the activities of this meeting that I love so well.

Anonymous, 1970

26.76 Within the Society of Friends we have our own problems with the traditional language of Christian spirituality... There are those who can comfortably talk in Christian language, because they experience it deeply as expressing truth and reality as they perceive it. For them it is not 'just a language'; it *is* the truth. The words used are inseparable from the underlying truths, the stories, the tradition, the nature of God as revealed in Jesus. There is no 'gap' between their experience of faith, their beliefs and the language used by the Christian tradition. There are those who just cannot use that language at all, because for them it precisely does not express their deepest truths, and may in fact be felt to deny or even violate them. For these people, their deepest experiences of spiritual reality, as they have encountered it, cannot be encompassed by a language that has acquired so many historical accretions and distortions that it has become at best meaningless and at worst a falsification of truth. So they must grapple with the equal inadequacy of contemporary language to express the depths of their searching.

Pam Lunn, 1990

26.77 In this day and age the place where Friends find their unity is in the kind of God they worship. Their apprehension of the relationship of Jesus Christ to God embraces every orthodox and unorthodox shade of theology from unitarian to trinitarian; but whether we regard Jesus ... as God himself or as the supreme revealer of God to man, it is the same kind of God: a spirit of peace, truth, love and redeeming power. We need to feel the influence of this Spirit in our lives rather than to argue about our different modes of apprehending him. Directly we begin to chide each other for orthodoxy or unorthodoxy, we cease to be the catholic body we are; for the logical end of such chiding is sanctions and the excluding of the weaker body by the stronger. Let us keep our different modes of apprehension and remember always that it is the same God we serve, revealing himself to each according to his faith, his openness and his need.

Beatrice Saxon Snell, 1961

26.78 It is not opinion, or speculation, or notions of what is true, or assent to or the subscription of articles or propositions, though never so soundly worded, that ... makes a man a true believer or a true Christian. But it is a conformity of mind and practice to the will of God, in all holiness of conversation, according to the dictates of this Divine principle of Light and Life in the soul which denotes a person truly a child of God.

William Penn, 1692

Chapter 27

Unity and diversity

FRIENDS AND OTHER FAITHS

27.01 The humble, meek, merciful, just, pious, and devout souls are everywhere of one religion; and when death has taken off the mask they
will know one another, though the divers liveries they wear here
makes them strangers.

William Penn, 1693

27.02 Love was the first motion, and then a concern arose to spend some
time with the Indians, that I might feel and understand their life, and
the Spirit they live in, if haply I might receive some instruction from
them, or they be in any degree helped forward by my following the
leadings of Truth amongst them. And as it pleased the Lord to make
way for my going at a time when the troubles of war were increasing and when by reason of much wet weather travelling was more
difficult than usual at that season, I looked upon it as a more
favourable opportunity to season my mind, and bring me into a
nearer sympathy with them. And as mine eye was to the great Father
of Mercies, humbly desiring to learn what his will was concerning
me, I was made quiet and content.

John Woolman, 1763

27.03 Can we settle the question, 'Is the Society of Friends Christian or
not?' In the historical sense the answer is Yes: but that does not pre-
clude the possibility that we may now be called to a new and wider
perception of the Truth. We have the witness of the Society itself, as
well as the example of Jesus, against turning yesterday's inspiration
into today's dogma. Today's world-wide knowledge of people and
their religions does present a challenge which our universalists are
right to try to meet – just as our Christians are right to remind us
that the insights of the past must not lightly be thrown away. It may

be valuable to live for a while in the tension between the universal and the specific; and if so, there may be a special vocation here through which our Society (with its tradition of respect for the divine Seed in everyone) can minister to the church at large. Or it may be that a synthesis is possible, once we can agree on what is essential to being a Christian.

John Lampen, 1985

27.04 We have acquired a much greater understanding of non-Christian religions from newcomers who have settled in this country since the end of World War II and this has increased the sympathy and respect of many Friends for these faiths. This broader approach to religion has led to an affirmation by 'universalist' Friends that no one faith can claim to be a final revelation or to have a monopoly of the truth and to the rejection of any exclusive religious fundamentalism whether based in Christianity or any other religion.

The ferment of thought in this post-war period has produced a wide variety of beliefs in our Religious Society today and not a little mis-understanding on all sides. Intolerance has reared its head. Some Friends have voiced objections to the use of Christian language in meetings for worship and for business; others have been told that there is no place for them in our Religious Society if they cannot regard themselves as Christians. It has become quite customary to distinguish between 'Christians' and 'universalists' as if one category excluded the other.

This situation has led many Friends to suppose that universalist Friends are in some way set over against Christocentric Friends. This is certainly not the case. Universalism is by definition inclus-ivist, and its adherents accept the right to free expression of all points of view, Christocentric or any other. Indeed, in London Yearly Meeting there are many universalists whose spiritual imagery and belief are thoroughly Christocentric.

From the beginning the Quaker Christian faith has had a universal dimension. George Fox saw the Light 'shine through all' and he identified it with the divine Light of Christ that 'enlightens every man that comes into the world' (John 1:9). He pointed out, as did William Penn in greater detail, that individuals who had lived before the Christian era or outside Christendom and had no knowledge of the Bible story, had responded to a divine principle within them. In these terms, all Quaker Christians are universalists. Obedience to the Light within, however that may be described, is the real test of faithful living.

Alastair Heron, Ralph Hetherington and Joseph Pickvance, 1994

See also 26.43

27.05   The church [is] no other thing but the society, gathering or company of such as God hath called out of the world and worldly spirit to walk in his light and life... Under this church ... are comprehended all, and as many, of whatsoever nation, kindred, tongue or people they be, though outwardly strangers and remote from those who profess Christ and Christianity in words and have the benefit of the Scriptures, as become obedient to the holy light and testimony of God in their hearts... There may be members therefore of this Catholic church both among heathens, Turks, Jews and all the several sorts of Christians, men and women of integrity and simplicity of heart, who ... are by the secret touches of this holy light in their souls enlivened and quickened, thereby secretly united to God, and there-through become true members of this Catholic church.

Robert Barclay, 1678

27.06   I have assumed a name today for my religious principles – Quaker-Catholicism – having direct spiritual teaching for its distinctive dogma, yet recognising the high worth of all other forms of Faith: a system, in the sense of inclusion, not exclusion; an appreciation of the universal and the various teachings of the Spirit, through the faculties given to us, or independent of them.

Caroline Fox, 1846

27.07   *Henry T Hodgkin (1877-1933) played a leading part in the Friends Foreign Mission Association and the Student Christian Movement, and in founding the Fellowship of Reconciliation. He worked as a missionary in China and came to appreciate the validity of other witnesses to God than the Christian one.*

By processes too numerous and diverse even to summarise, I have reached a position which may be stated in a general way somewhat like this: 'I believe that God's best for another may be so different from my experience and way of living as to be actually impossible to me. I recognise [a change] to have taken place in myself, from a certain assumption that mine was really the better way, to a very complete recognition that there is no one better way, and that God needs all kinds of people and ways of living through which to manifest himself in the world.'

This has seemed to carry with it two conclusions which greatly affect conduct. One is that I really find myself wanting to learn from people whom I previously would have regarded as fit objects for my 'missionary zeal'. To discover another way in which God is operating – along lines it may be distasteful or dangerous to me – is a large part of the fun of living. The second direction in which conduct is influenced is the deliberate attempt to share the life and interests of others who are not in my circle ... [for] in such sharing I can most deeply understand the other's life and through that reach, maybe, fresh truths about God.

1933

27.08 The city of Birmingham, England, where I live, is one of the most racially and religiously mixed communities in Europe. It has a stimulating, challenging and exciting atmosphere. On one occasion, at a big interfaith gathering, I was being very Quakerly and very enlightened. The discussion was about prayer, and I confessed that it was my habit to pray anywhere and that I could do so sitting comfortably in a chair. A devout Muslim woman in the conference was shocked at what she saw as my easygoing familiarity with God, my lack of respect, my denial of my own human dignity. When you think of God, she said, there is only one possible response. It is to go down on your *knees*.

I recognised the truth in what she said and have acted on it ever since, though I regret I have not yet been brave enough to kneel in the meeting house. That will come. From this unnamed woman I learned something of Islam – submission to God – in a way that no Christian had ever taught me. But the words are immaterial. It was not the Mosque or the Qur'an addressing me, but the living God I know in Christ speaking through her.

John Punshon, 1987

27.09 As for me, Jesus is a man so great that you may call him the only begotten Son of God, or Divine. We may call His Spirit Love, Light, Truth or Way. Yet that Spirit is so universal and eternal, that I cannot but believe that it has been prevailing everywhere, more or less in all religions, even from before the birth of the historic Jesus, and I believe that it is living more or less in all human beings in the world. This is why Jesus says all that he has taught us is our Father's and not Jesus' own.

Yukio Irie, 1959

27.10 Remember Jesus' answer to the woman of Samaria: 'Neither on this mountain nor in Jerusalem will you worship the Father... God is spirit, and those who worship him must worship in Spirit and in Truth.' In the depth of meditation, in the gathered meeting we rise above all limitations. Gone are the concepts of Quakerism and Vedanta. Gone are the ideas of being a Christian or a Hindu. All these concepts are valid on their own level. They have their place, but they are transcended when we merge our minds in Spirit. I believe this is what Jesus and all the other World Teachers wanted us ultimately to do.

Swami Tripurananda (Jonathan Carter), 1979

27.11 'What think ye of Christ?' is central both in our relationships with other religions and in our relationship with one another within the Society of Friends... We are truly loyal to Jesus Christ when we judge the religious systems of the world by the standard which he himself used: 'Not everyone that saith unto me, Lord, Lord ... but he that doeth the will of my Father'. Every tree is to be known by its fruits: not by its dead wood or thorns or parasites, but by the fruit of its own inner life and nature. We all know the fruits of the Spirit and recognise the beauty of holiness in our own ancestral tree... The flowers of unselfish living may be found growing in other people's gardens and ... rich fruits of the Spirit may be tasted from other people's trees. They spring from the same Holy Spirit of Truth, the same Seed of God, whose power moves us through Christ.

Marjorie Sykes, 1957

FRIENDS AND THE CHRISTIAN CHURCH

27.12 The unity of Christians never did nor ever will or can stand in uniformity of thought and opinion, but in Christian love only.

Thomas Story, 1737

27.13 Even in the apostles' days Christians were too apt to strive after a wrong unity and uniformity in outward practices and observations, and to judge one another unrighteously in those things; and mark, it is not the different practice from one another that breaks the peace and unity, but the judging of one another because of different practices...

And oh, how sweet and pleasant it is to the truly spiritual eye to see several sorts of believers, several forms of Christians in the school of Christ, every one learning their own lesson, performing their own peculiar service, and knowing, owning and loving one another in their several places and different performances to their Master, to whom they are to give an account, and not to quarrel with one another about their different practices (Rom 14:4). For this is the true ground of love and unity, not that such a man walks and does just as I do, but because I feel the same Spirit and life in him, and that he walks in his rank, in his own order, in his proper way and place of subjection to that; and this is far more pleasing to me than if he walked just in that track wherein I walk.

Isaac Penington, 1660

27.14 What, then, is the focus for Christian unity? It must be Jesus, who calls us not into structures but into discipleship and to follow him in his way. Can we not know that we are one in him when we are faithful to his calling and when we exercise towards one another that greatest gift of love? Can we not rejoice in our diversity, welcoming the opportunities to learn from each other? Can we not seek a recognition of each other's ministries as the work of the same Spirit? That Spirit can, if we are ready to adventure, lead us into ways we have not known before.

London Yearly Meeting, 1986

27.15   A rich variety of expression and of practice is to be expected as the Life streams through disciples of every race and clime and condition... It does not press men into a rigid mould of thought or action; rather it would pour its own joy into every mould of humanity. We have sought unity through agreement in doctrines and institutions; and the track of Church history, like some new road through the desert, is strewn with the parched skeletons of our failures.

William Charles Braithwaite, 1919

27.16   We may picture God as weaving a pattern with the lives of men and women. We can glimpse but small fragments of the whole design; in moments of inspiration we can see more clearly, while the saints see most of all. Through it there runs a Quaker strand. It may be only a single thread but it is not insignificant, for without it the pattern would be marred. Yet that thread of itself does not make the whole design. The Society of Friends is but a part of the Christian Church, and the measure of truth which it possesses may only rightly be considered in relation to the whole. The work of the Church in the world today is surely not something to be carried out in miniature by each part, but it is a mighty whole to which each should contribute according to its special gifts and strengths.

William G Sewell, 1946

27.17   Historically our Society stands in the Christian tradition; ... we unite in the desire that Friends everywhere should share in the life and fellowship of the wider Christian community and co-operate as fully as possible in its work... Many of us value opportunities for worship and service with our fellow Christians. No one can measure the debt we owe to the influence and inspiration and leadership of many of our fellow Christians, to the stimulus and fellowship some of us have known in inter-church groups and inter-denominational movements. And there is, too, the valuable service rendered by Christian scholars and thinkers for which we are profoundly thankful.

Friends World Conference, 1952

27.18   For the Church ... is really the people – the children and followers of God. Manses and moderators, sermons and synods are the mere packaging of this people, perhaps inevitable, anyway historical, but not to be mistaken for the thing itself. The thing itself, the believing and worshipping people, has two important characteristics which the individual Christian must never forget. The Church is a community, and it is a continuity... Quakers may be an experimental sect – both in the modern sense of pushing forward the frontiers of faith, and in the older sense of insisting upon experience as the basis of their faith – but if we are honest we must admit that we build upon the foundations laid for us over many centuries by the Church.

Gerald Priestland, 1982

27.19   Secreted within the organism that is the historical Christian faith, there is a mystical and spiritual tradition which uses metaphor, symbol, image and art to come to terms with the questions thrown up by the lifestyle and religious commitment that it has made and to which it remains loyal.

It could be that the modern ecumenical movement is essentially such a quest for meaning through spirituality. Catholics wanting to take communion with Methodists, or Quakers willing to take communion with anybody, are left in no doubt that they are departing from the party line. One sometimes needs a strong conscience to practise unity against the wishes of one's denominational authorities. But hard though it is to see it sometimes, the old, hierarchical, entirely male, theological style of church leadership is weakening. The real ecumenical movement is found among people who have experienced unity, and the universal faith is found there. But this universal faith lives in a way of life, rather than a set of beliefs.

John Punshon, 1987

27.20   The spirit of the ecumenical movement far transcends its rather regressive concern for agreement on beliefs. It is concerned rather more for the realisation of unity in worship, in discipleship, in community and in a common response to the social challenges of our time. In this concern Friends can be wholly one. Our rejection of formal agreements should therefore be balanced by a positive affirmation of a unity of another kind, a unity of spirit, of search and of struggle. For us, real unity between Christians will arise from the honest communication of our faith to each other in our own specific situations, spirit to spirit, and it will take form in lives lived together and work done together. It will be a unity that includes without also excluding, which preserves the core faith without also pruning off the distinctive interpretations.

Rex Ambler, 1989

Creeds

27.21 Creeds are milestones, doctrines are interpretations: Truth, as George Fox was continually asserting, a seed with the power of growth, not a fixed crystal, be its facets never so beautiful.

John Wilhelm Rowntree, 1904

27.22 All Truth is a shadow except the last, except the utmost; yet every Truth is true in its kind. It is substance in its own place, though it be but a shadow in another place (for it is but a reflection from an intenser substance); and the shadow is a true shadow, as the substance is a true substance.

Isaac Penington, 1653

27.23 We do not in the least deprecate the attempt, which must be made, since man is a rational being, to formulate intellectually the ideas which are implicit in religious experience... But it should always be recognised that all such attempts are provisional, and can never be assumed to possess the finality of ultimate truth. There must always be room for development and progress, and Christian thought and inquiry should never be fettered by theory... Among the dangers of formulated statements of belief are these:

  a. they tend to crystallise thought on matters that will always be beyond any final embodiment in human language;

b. they fetter the search for truth and for its more adequate expression; and

c. they set up a fence which tends to keep out of the Christian fold many sincere and seeking souls who would gladly enter it.

Particularly in these days we need to be on our guard against these dangers. Multitudes of people are being shaken out of their comfortable beliefs by the terrific experiences through which the world is passing, and are seeking a secure basis for their faith. And some are finding a Reality which is much too great to be confined within the narrow limits of a creed.

True basis of Christian unity, 1917

27.24   Rejection of creed is not inconsistent with being possessed by a living belief. We have no creed in science, but we are not lukewarm in our beliefs. The belief is not that all the knowledge of the universe that we hold so enthusiastically will survive in the letter; but a sureness that we are on the road. If our so-called facts are changing shadows, they are shadows cast by the light of constant truth. So too in religion we are repelled by that confident theological doctrine which has settled for all generations just how the spiritual world is worked; but we need not turn aside from the measure of light that comes into our experience showing us a Way through the unseen world. Religion for the conscientious seeker is not all a matter of doubt and self-questionings. There is a kind of sureness which is very different from cocksureness.

Arthur S Eddington, 1929

27.25   The Quaker objection to credal statements is not to beliefs as such but to the use of an officially sanctioned selection of them to impose a uniformity in things where the gospel proclaims freedom. 'Credo' is the Latin for 'I believe'. The meaning of the word is debased if you confine it to an act of the will giving intellectual assent to articles of faith. It is much better translated as 'I commit myself to...' in the sense that one is prepared to take the full consequences of the beliefs one has adopted. One adopts not so much a set of propositions as the discipline of working out in one's life and experience the consequences of the truth one has espoused. The value of the beliefs lies solely in their outworking. This I take to be the heart of the original Quaker message.

John Punshon, 1978

27.26 This is the truth which we know and try to live … that every person is capable of response to the divine Spirit; that this Spirit, or Light, or God reaches out to each one directly and freely; that if we follow the leadings of this Spirit faithfully we are led out of sin into unity with the divine will; that this unity leads us into love of and care for all humankind, who are our kin; that what the Spirit shows us is living truth which cannot be fettered by words.

Janet Scott, 1980

The Bible

27.27 And the end of words is to bring men to the knowledge of things beyond what words can utter. So, learn of the Lord to make a right use of the Scriptures: which is by esteeming them in their right place, and prizing that above them which is above them.

Isaac Penington

27.28 From these revelations of the Spirit of God to the saints have proceeded the Scriptures of Truth, which contain:

a. a faithful historical account of the actions of God's people in divers ages, with many singular and remarkable providences attending them;

b. a prophetical account of several things, whereof some are already past, and some are yet to come;

c. a full and ample account of all the chief principles of the doctrine of Christ, held forth in divers precious declarations, exhortations and sentences, which, by the moving of God's Spirit, were at several times and upon sundry occasions spoken and written unto some Churches and their pastors.

Nevertheless, because they are only a declaration of the fountain and not the fountain itself, therefore they are not to be esteemed the principal ground of all truth and knowledge, nor yet the adequate, primary rule of faith and manners. Yet, because they give a true and faithful testimony of the first foundation, they are and may be esteemed a secondary rule, subordinate to the Spirit, from which they have all their excellency and certainty: for as by the inward testimony of the Spirit we do alone truly know them, so they testify that the Spirit is that Guide by which the saints are led into all truth: therefore, according to the Scriptures the Spirit is the first and principal Leader.

Robert Barclay, 1678

27.29 A host of scholars have been at work for centuries to discover and understand the Jesus of history, and with strangely divergent results. The great quest still goes on and I seek to learn from it. But I cannot separate the Lord and Master of the first disciples from his risen spirit and personality which has gone on unfolding itself to those who seek him, healing, renewing, inspiring, redeeming and guiding.

Thus I try to keep in touch with his life and message given first in Palestine, with the impact of his life and personality on the early disciples, as day by day I read a portion of the New Testament; I try, too, to learn something of what his spirit has enabled others to be down all the ages since, from the study of the lives of the saints, both canonised and uncanonised, and by reading some of their writings. In the life of many who would not be called saints, and some even who might not be thought of as good men or women, I find flashes of light which to me are sparks or gleams from the light of Christ. I know that my own thoughts of God, my experience, my clumsy and imperfect prayer, are all penetrated by what Jesus Christ has meant to me. In doubts and difficulty his faith in God's love, his willingness to face even the awful burden of the cross and all that it involved, are a constant stay, bringing renewal of faith and of hope.

T Edmund Harvey, 1949

27.30 As a book containing foundation documents of both the Jewish and Christian religions, the Bible has, of course, unique historical value, both faiths having contributed richly to the world's culture and public life. Again, our Quaker forerunners' use of the Bible to nurture and check the working of Light Within was both wise and profitable. So it is for us. Yet the Bible's supreme value resides in the power of its finest passages as expressions of vital religion which is both personally and socially transforming.

What kind of approach to the Bible leads to that discovery? An intelligent analytical and critical approach has its rightful place. We then stand over the Bible as subjects investigating an object. An inversion of this subject-object relationship is, however, possible. We then approach the Bible not mainly to criticise, but to listen; not merely to question, but to be challenged, and to open our lives penitentially both to its judgments and to its liberating gospel.

Pathways to God are many and varied. Friends, however, along with a great company of other seekers, have been able to testify that this receptive personal response to the biblical message, and especially to the call of Jesus, leads to joyous self-fulfilling life, and to a redemptive awareness of the love and glory of God.

George Boobyer, 1988

27.31   How much the Bible has to teach when taken as a whole, that cannot be done by snippets! There is its range over more than a thousand years giving us the perspective of religion in time, growing and changing, and leading from grace to grace. There is its clear evidence of the variety of religious experience, not the kind of strait-jacket that nearly every church, even Friends, have sometimes been tempted to substitute for the diversity in the Bible. To select from it but a single strand is to miss something of its richness. Even the uncongenial and the alien to us is happily abundant in the Bible. The needs of men today are partly to be measured by their difficulty in understanding that with which they differ. At this point the Bible has no little service to render. It requires patient insight into the unfamiliar and provides a discipline for the imagination such as today merely on the political level is a crying need of our time.

Further the Bible is a training school in discrimination among alternatives. One of the most sobering facts is that it is not on the whole a peaceful book – I mean a book of peace of mind. The Bible is the deposit of a long series of controversies between rival views of religion. The sobering thing is that in nearly every case the people shown by the Bible to be wrong had every reason to think they were in the right, and like us they did so. Complacent orthodoxy is the recurrent villain in the story from first to last and the hero is the challenger, like Job, the prophets, Jesus and Paul.

Henry J Cadbury, 1953

27.32   If we no longer believe in the Bible in the old way, what do we now believe? This question must be put to each one of us, and we have to find an answer. Knowledge of the Bible is very important, but it is unnecessary for us to accept it as infallible or as a legal document; we must think and judge for ourselves, listening to that which speaks to our innermost being.

The Bible is not sacrosanct. It comes from times very different from our own with a different concept of man. It does not contain the absolute literal truth, but it can teach us the truth of life. Dogma is the language of theology. I do not set any limits for my thought in seeking truth in intellectual honesty. But more important than anything else is an anchorage in the divine which is to be found in the depth of every human being; it cannot be formulated in words but must be expressed in life and in relations with our fellow men.

Jesus is the most important person in the Bible, not because the Bible or the churches proclaim it, but because he gave men a new concept of God.

Elsa Cedergren, 1982

27.33   Personal experience makes me think that Bible study is more rewarding undertaken by a group than in solitude... A group may pool their insights and reactions, their knowledge, doubts and stumbling-blocks, and together arrive at greater understanding (of themselves as well as of the Bible) than they could ever have done separately... Though the purpose of study should be serious (indeed without a fundamental seriousness a group will not last for long), surely it need not be over-solemn. The Bible is a human book, and you will find everything human somewhere in it, including humour. We must be prepared for conflict; some of the truth we discover may be unpalatable; and it is essential that we do not cheat, but keep on looking for the truth.

Joan Fitch, 1980

27.34   We understand the Bible as a record arising from ... struggles to comprehend God's ways with people. The same Spirit which inspired the writers of the Bible is the Spirit which gives us understanding of it: it is this which is important to us rather than the literal words of scripture. Hence, while quotations from the Bible may illuminate a truth for us, we would not use them to prove a truth. We welcome the work of scholars in deepening our understanding of the Bible.

London Yearly Meeting, 1986

See also 26.42

Priesthood

27.35   The priesthood of all believers is a foundation of our understanding of the church. Our own experience leads us to affirm that the church can be so ordered that the guidance of the Holy Spirit can be known and followed without the need for a separated clergy... The Spirit in which the apostles lived, ... which was poured out at Pentecost on all the church, young and old, women and men, continues in our experience to empower all members of the church in a variety of ministries.

London Yearly Meeting, 1986

27.36   Just as Quakers do not limit the service of God to certain times, or places, or people, so they do not have a set-apart priesthood... There is no need for any specific person to be designated prophet, priest, or church leader. Quakers would say that if people are open to the power of love and light in their lives then they will themselves become prophetic and priestly, and will not need to follow the external authority of church leaders. They will become empowered to be themselves, to find God in their hearts and to serve other people.

Harvey Gillman, 1988

See also 10.05, 12.02 & 19.31

Sacraments

27.37 Jesus, when he took up the little children and said, 'Of such is the Kingdom of Heaven', was speaking of Jewish children, who, according to the Jewish custom, would not have been baptised, and the Quaker position is really summed up in the words 'John indeed baptised with water, but ye shall be baptised with the Holy Spirit'. It is the inward change, the inward purification, the spiritual fact and not the outward symbol, that belongs in truth to the Kingdom of God. Neither in the refusal to baptise nor to take the supper do Friends set forth a negation. They assert, on the contrary, the positive truth that the religious life is the inward life of the spirit. But no place or time can limit its action, nor any symbol adequately express it.

John Wilhelm Rowntree, 1902

27.38 Alongside Friends' stress on the primacy of God's action, we set great store by the centrality of ordinary experience. We agree with the witness of the universal church that mystical experiences are attested by the moral quality of people's lives. The whole of our everyday experience is the stuff of our religious awareness: it is here that God is best known to us. However valid and vital outward sacraments are for others, they are not, in our experience, necessary for the operation of God's grace. We believe we hold this witness in trust for the whole church.

London Yearly Meeting, 1986

27.39 To Fox and the early Friends the whole of life seemed sacramental, and they refused to mark off any one particular practice or observance as more sacred than others. They took the same stand with regard to Sunday, or First Day; it was not in itself more holy than Saturday or Monday; every week-day should be a Lord's Day. Their whole attitude was gloriously positive, not negative. They were 'alive unto God' and sensed him everywhere.

We do not say that to observe the sacraments is wrong, but that such observance is not essential to wholehearted Christian discipleship and the full Christian experience. We do not judge our fellow Christians to whom the outward sacraments mean so much. Rather do we wish, by prayerful fellowship with them, to be led unitedly with them to a deeper understanding of what underlies those sacraments, and so to share a richer experience of the mind of Christ.

Gerald K Hibbert, 1941

27.40 The Quaker conviction is that the operation of the Spirit outruns all our expectations. We acknowledge that the grace of God is experienced by many through the outward rite of baptism, but no ritual, however carefully prepared for, can be guaranteed to lead to growth in the Spirit. A true spiritual experience must be accompanied by the visible transformation of the outward life. Our understanding of baptism is that it is not a single act of initiation but a continuing growth in the Holy Spirit and a commitment which must continually be renewed. It is this process which draws us into a fellowship with those who acknowledge the same power at work in their lives, those whom Christ is calling to be his body on earth.

London Yearly Meeting, 1986

27.41 We would assert that the validity of worship lies not in its form but in its power, and a form of worship sincerely dependent on God, but not necessarily including the words and actions usually recognised as eucharistic, may equally serve as a channel for this power and grace. We interpret the words and actions of Jesus near the end of his life as an invitation to recall and re-enact the self-giving nature of God's love at every meal and every meeting with others, and to allow our own lives to be broken open and poured out for the life of the world.

London Yearly Meeting, 1986

27.42 Many of the testimonies and practices established by early Friends have survived only in part. One which has almost died out in Britain is the naming of days and months by number instead of by names of pagan origin. It is rare now to hear 'first day' instead of 'Sunday' or 'third month' instead of 'March', though the practice is still acceptable.

Another testimony held by early Friends was that against the keeping of 'times and seasons'. We might understand this as part of the conviction that all of life is sacramental; that since all times are therefore holy, no time should be marked out as more holy; that what God has done for us should always be remembered and not only on the occasions named Christmas, Easter and Pentecost.

This is a testimony which seems to be dying of neglect. Many Friends, involved with family and the wider society, keep Christmas; in some meetings, Easter and its meaning is neglected, not only at the calendar time but throughout the year. What I would hope for is neither that we let the testimony die, nor that we keep it mechanically. I hope for a rediscovery of its truth, that we should remember and celebrate the work of God in us and for us whenever God by the Spirit calls us to this remembrance and this joy.

Janet Scott, 1994

27.43 We need to guard against under-valuing the material expressions of spiritual things. It is easy to make a form of our very rejection of forms. And in particular, we need to ask ourselves whether we are endeavouring to make all the daily happenings and doings of life which we call 'secular' minister to the spiritual. It is a bold and colossal claim that we put forward – that the whole of life is sacramental, that there are innumerable 'means of grace' by which God is revealed and communicated – through nature and through human fellowship and through a thousand things that may become the 'outward and visible sign' of 'an inward and spiritual grace'.

A Barratt Brown, 1932

27.44 I personally believe that there is a quality in the bareness of Christian Quakerism, which may act as a bridge between the past and the future, allowing space for Friends to dare to search within... To be a Quaker is by no means to say goodbye to myth, ritual and symbol, but rather to find myself set free to discover them as the very essence of the way I now experience... Quakers are bridge people. I remain on that bridge, part of my roots reaching back into the Christian past and part stretching forward into the future where new symbols are being born.

Damaris Parker-Rhodes, 1985

See also 26.15

Chapter 28

Sharing the Quaker experience

28.01 The very simple heart of the early Quaker message is needed as much to-day as it ever was... The really universal thing is a living experience. It is reached in various ways, and expressed in very different language... The common bond is in the thing itself, the actual inner knowledge of the grace of God. Quakerism can only have a universal message if it brings men and women into this transforming knowledge. The early Friends certainly had this knowledge, and were the means of bringing many thousands of seekers into the way of discovery. In virtue of this central experience, the Quaker movement can only be true to itself by being a missionary movement.

Henry T Hodgkin, 1916

28.02 When you come to your meetings ... what do you do? Do you then gather together bodily only, and kindle a fire, compassing yourselves with the sparks of your own kindling, and so please yourself ... ? Or rather do you sit down in the true silence, resting from your own will and workings, and waiting upon the Lord, with your minds fixed in that Light wherewith Christ has enlightened you ... and prepares you, and your spirits and souls, to make you fit for his service?

William Penn, 1677

28.03 Now I was sent to turn people from darkness to the light that they might receive Christ Jesus, for to as many as should receive him in his light, I saw that he would give power to become Sons of God, which I had obtained by receiving Christ. And I was to direct people to the Spirit that gave forth the Scriptures, by which they might be led into all Truth, and so up to Christ and God, as they had been who gave them forth. And I was to turn them to the grace of God, and to the Truth in the heart, which came by Jesus, that by this grace they might be taught, which would bring them into salvation, that their hearts might be established by it, and their words might be seasoned, and all might come to know their salvation nigh.

George Fox, 1648

28.04 When I grew to about thirteen years of age, I began to discover something about me, or in my mind, like the heavenly anointing for the ministry; for the Lord had revealed His word as a hammer and had broken the rock in pieces in my living experience; and I was contrited under a sense of power and love; saying even vocally when alone, 'Lord, make me a chosen vessel unto Thee'... With respect to my first appearances [in ministry, when about seventeen years old]... I shrunk from it exceedingly; and often have I hesitated, and felt such a reluctance to it, that I have suffered the meeting to break up without my having made the sacrifice: yea, when the word of life in a few words was like a fire within me... It pleased the Lord to call me into a path much untrodden, in my early travels as a messenger of the Gospel, having to go into markets and to declare the truth in the streets... No one knows the depth of my sufferings and the mortifying, yea, crucifying of my own will, which I had to endure in this service; yet I have to acknowledge to the sufficiency of divine grace herein... At Bath I had to go to the Pump Room and declare the truth to the gay people who resorted there. This was a time very relieving to my sorely exercised mind. In these days and years of my life I was seldom from under some heavy burden, so that I went greatly bowed down; sometimes ready to say, 'If it be thus with me, O Thou who hast given me a being, I pray Thee take away my life from me'... In the year 1801, I wrote thus: 'O heavenly Father, Thou hast seen me in the depth of tribulation, in my many journeyings and travels... It was Thy power which supported me when no flesh could help, when man could not comprehend the depth of mine exercise... Be Thou only and for ever exalted in, by and through Thy poor child, and let nothing be able to pluck me out of Thy hand.'

Sarah Lynes Grubb, 1832

See also 2.55

28.05 An apprehension has seized upon my mind this morning, that after having finished the little books I am preparing for the children of

Sierra Leone, it will be my duty to attempt the introduction of them myself into that country and the neighbourhood, and even to attempt the reduction of unwritten languages. I would not go merely under a profession of opening a school or schools, but to proceed to the religious instruction of the children, for my heart feels an engagement towards them that cannot possibly be fulfilled without going there.

Hannah Kilham, 1817

28.06   Jesus saw the truth that men needed and he thought it urgent that that truth should be proclaimed. That trust is handed on to us, but it is a responsibility from which we shrink. We feel that we have a very imperfect grasp of the meaning of the Gospel. Perhaps, after all the earnest seeking of the Church, we are only beginning to see the tremendous implications of it. We dimly see that this Gospel, before it has finished with us, will turn our lives upside down and inside out. Our favourite Quaker vice of caution holds us back. We have much more to learn before we are ready to teach. It is right that we have much to learn; it is right to recognise the heavy responsibility of teaching; but to suppose that we must know everything before we can teach anything is to condemn ourselves to perpetual futility.

George B Jeffery, 1934

28.07   'Have you anything to declare?' is a vital challenge to which every one of us is personally called to respond and is also a challenge that every meeting should consider of primary importance. It should lead us to define, with such clarity as we can reach, precisely what it is that Friends of this generation have to say that is not, as we believe, being said effectively by others.

Edgar G Dunstan, 1956

28.08   We live in a rationalist society that has shed the security of dogmas it found it could not accept, and now finds itself afraid of its own freedom. Some look for an external authority, as they did of old; but in this situation there are many who cannot just go backwards. They ask for an authority they can accept without the loss of their own integrity: they ask to be talked to in a language they can understand... With these people our point of departure is not a mighty proclamation of Truth, but the humble invitation to sit down together and share what we have found, in the spirit of Woolman setting out on his Indian journey, 'that I might feel and understand their life, and the spirit they live in, if haply I might receive some instruction from them.' We approach them without pressure to accept a statement, or with proselytising zeal, but with 'love as the first motion'.

Harold Loukes, 1955

27.02 gives a fuller version of John Woolman's account

28.09   Outreach is for me an invitation to others to join us in our way of worship and response to life which are so important to us that we wish to share them. At the simplest level this means supplying information about meetings, Friends to contact, and basic beliefs, all of which should be given accurately, clearly and if possible attractively. In the second stage outreach offers to others, through meetings, personal contact and literature, the experience and truth which Friends have found for themselves through three centuries and which impel us just as strongly today. It is different from some forms of evangelism in that it does not use mass emotional appeal, idiosyncratic demands or autocratic compulsion but only the persuasion of insight, humanity and good sense. It does not depend on rewards or threats, but on the active acceptance of those who see it as truth.

Edrey Allott, 1990

28.10   Many of the people who come to us are both refugees and seekers. They are looking for a space to find their authenticity, a space in a spiritual context. It is a process of liberation. Some discover what they need among Friends, others go elsewhere. This gift of the sacred space that Friends have to offer is a two-edged sword. It is not easy administratively to quantify; it leads to ambiguity. It demands patient listening; it can be enriching and challenging to our complacency. It is outreach in the most general sense and it is a profound service. It may not lead to membership and it may cause difficulties in local meetings. But if someone comes asking for bread, we cannot say, sorry we are too busy discovering our own riches; when we have found them, we'll offer you a few. Our riches are precisely our sharing. And the world is very, very hungry.

Harvey Gillman, 1993

28.11   Only such writings as spring from a living experience will reach the life in others, only those which embody genuine thought in clear and effective form will minister to the needs of the human mind. A faith like Quakerism should find expression in creative writing born of imagination and spirit, and speaking in universal tones that will be understood by many who fail to understand the common presentations of Christianity. It is no disrespect to truth to present it in forms that will be readily understood.

1925

28.12   Sharing the Quaker message today does not mean sharing it [only] in English. It means carrying it in French, from Burundi Yearly Meeting to Madagascar. Or standing in Kenya, telling of your faith as a Bolivian Friend in Aymara to be translated into Spanish and then into English and then whispered into Luragoli for the old Friend in the back row! Those who carry the Quaker message today are not only those who worry about whether sanctions against South Africa are right or wrong. Quakers today are the victims of violence and racism in Soweto. Quakers today are not simply watching pictures of famine on their televisions; they are farming the inhospitable altiplano in Bolivia; they are facing drought in Turkana.

Val Ferguson, 1987

28.13   The Quaker Tapestry is a series of over seventy embroidered panels illustrating the history and experiences of Friends. It sprang from an idea in a children's class in a Somerset meeting in 1981, and has been made by many hands in many meetings. It is a new way of sharing Quaker insights through exhibitions in Britain, Ireland and other countries. It is now on permanent exhibition at Kendal Meeting House.

The following line drawing is a reproduction of one of the cartoons used to plan the tapestry panels.

1623 MARY FISHER 1698

one of the many women "publishers of the truth"

"the World, East + West, was their parish"

1657

for God's Spirit dwelt in every man.

1652 ELIZ. HOOTON

YORK GAOL

CAMBRIDGE MARKET 1653

'OLD' ANNE AUSTIN

1655

BOSTON MASS.

MARY DYER 1660

This panel, *Mary Fisher*, illustrates the work of the 'first publishers of truth', as the first Friends who left home to witness to the Light were called. (For an extract from the writing of Mary Fisher, see 19.27.)

Our book of discipline tells how Friends try to live by the leadings disclosed in worship and prayer. The early Friends believed that they had rediscovered true Christianity and that they had a duty to tell the world. They travelled widely, 'publishing the truth', first throughout Britain and then overseas, even approaching the sultan of Turkey.

Now, however, most of the journeys from Britain Yearly Meeting are to do service work: teaching, reconciling, helping with development. There are many small groups of Friends who owe their origin to the spirit reflected in those doing such work, who 'let their lives speak'. Evangelical meetings in some parts of the world lay great emphasis on missionary work, as British and Irish Friends did in the past, and as a result there are many thousands of Friends of the programmed tradition in countries such as Kenya and Bolivia. It is part of our service to try to communicate the faith that we have tested in experience. We long to reach out to those who may find a spiritual home in the Society; we do not claim that ours is the only true way, yet we have a perception of truth that is relevant to all if, as we believe, the light to which we witness is a universal light. Each meeting must find its own way of sharing the Quaker experience, each Friend remember 'that we are each the epistle of Yearly Meeting'.

Chapter 29

Leadings

What shall we hand on? Where is the Spirit now leading us? In this book we have seen how we have been gathered, guided and ordered for more than three hundred years. We shall want both to keep the rich openings we have inherited and to be open to continuing guidance in changing circumstances. This will only be possible if we heed the promptings of love and truth which we trust as the leadings of God.

Individually and corporately Friends are seeking new ways of expressing our testimonies to equality and social justice, to the building of peace, to truth and integrity in public affairs, and to simplicity in a lifestyle that reflects our renewed understanding of our relationship with all creation.

As we try to respond to new leadings we often cannot discern what will remain important and what will be seen as ephemeral. There will be tensions as we wrestle with our diverse perceptions and convictions, and tensions can be creative. Our hope and our experience is that when we are faithful we shall be rightly led.

29.01 How can we walk with a smile into the dark? We must learn to put our trust in God and the leadings of the Spirit. How many of us are truly led by the Spirit throughout our daily lives? I have turned to God when I have had a difficult decision to make or when I have sought strength to endure the pain in dark times. But I am only slowly learning to dwell in the place where leadings come from. That is a place of love and joy and peace, even in the midst of pain. The more I dwell in that place, the easier it is to smile, because I am no longer afraid.

If we dwell in the presence of God, we shall be led by the spirit. We do well to remember that being led by the spirit depends not so much upon God, who is always there to lead us, as upon our willingness to be led. We need to be willing to be led into the dark as well as through green pastures and by still waters. We do not need to be afraid of the dark, because God is there. The future of this earth need not be in the hands of the world's 'leaders'. The world is in God's hands if we are led by God. Let us be led by the Spirit. Let us walk with a smile into the dark.

Gordon Matthews, 1987

29.02   *Following consideration of priorities in financing the work of London Yearly Meeting in 1992, Meeting for Sufferings minuted:*

The ground of our work lies in our waiting on and listening for the Spirit. Let the loving spirit of a loving God call us and lead us. These leadings are both personal and corporate. If they are truly tested in a gathered meeting we shall find that the strength and the courage for obedience are given to us. We need the humility to put obedience before our own wishes.

We are aware of the need to care for ourselves and each other in our meetings, bearing each others' burdens and lovingly challenging each other.

We also hear the cry of those in despair which draws out our compassion. We know the need to speak for those who have no voice. We have a tradition of service and work which has opened up opportunities for us. But we are reminded that we are not the only ones to do this work. Not only can we encourage a flow of work between our central and our local meetings; but we must recognise the Spirit at work in many bodies and in many places, in other churches and faiths, and in secular organisations.

When we look at our past we can see the length of time needed for transformation. We are a small church with the pretensions to change the world. But first we have to let God change us – to empower us to be better Friends, and more active in our own work. We should not be creating structures to work for us, but empowering each other to do the work laid on each of us. However we plan ... the Spirit is unchanging and will always lead us... All is interconnected, worship with action, wisdom with love.

We must look to our meetings, to our love for each other, and our corporate discipline. We must look to ourselves, to speak of our lives and to let our lives speak. Above all we must look to the Truth. We have an Inward Teacher who teaches, guides and commands us. When we know what we have to do, how to do it will come.

29.03   We seem to be at a turning point in human history. We can choose life or watch the planet become uninhabitable for our species. Somehow, I believe that we will pass through this dark night of our planetary soul to a new period of harmony with the God that is to be found within each of us, and that S/he will inspire renewed confidence in people everywhere, empowering us all to co-operate to use our skills, our wisdom, our creativity, our love, our faith – even our doubts and fears – to make peace with the planet. Strengthened by this fragile faith, empowered by the Spirit within, I dare to hope.

Pat Saunders, 1987

29.04   It is said that all great movements progress through three stages: ridicule, discussion, adoption. For the anti-vivisection movement the stage of ridicule is passing, the stage for discussion has begun. Will the Religious Society of Friends condemn vivisection before or after its abolition? Our yearly meeting at present is not a participant in this unfolding humane drama but a silent spectator to it... Should a search for unity with the anti-vivisection movement not be our concern?

Ralph Rowarth, 1994

29.05   We recognise the enormous powers of newly developing genetic engineering techniques to change living matter with speed and scope hitherto unthinkable. Recent applications of bio-engineering to plant and animal species have benefited mainly people in materially wealthy countries at the expense of the materially poor, and of global biodiversity. Continuation of these technologies and their extension to human beings highlights the need for Friends to affirm that the intrinsic value of all life forms is not restricted to their utilitarian functions, and that the richness of human diversity should never be reduced to the level of a commodity or made subject to market forces. The potential of genetic technologies for good and ill requires humility, wisdom, and lovingkindness, and also the capacity to know when to stop. We Friends need to bring our own diverse gifts to help ensure that research into and application of genetic technologies do not proceed without consideration for justice, democracy, and respect for the dignity and well-being of all.

Amber Carroll and Grace Jantzen, 1994

29.06   *In reflecting on time spent working in Vietnam in the early 1970s, Helen Steven wrote:*

Perhaps our most positive contribution to peace-making was to affirm and value Vietnamese culture in the face of the appalling destruction which we saw around us.

I believe that it is this fundamental respect for 'that of God' in everyone which is at the heart of all true development. On my return home I was horrified by our cultural, material and spiritual arrogance. I believe that it is profound arrogance which initiates aid programmes which force western methods of education, medicine or agriculture on people with traditions longer than our own; it is arrogance to assume that any political system or social or economic structure must be maintained and defended no matter how many people are bombed, napalmed or tortured in the process. Surely arrogance drives us to rape and destroy the earth's scarce resources to fuel and protect the needs of one generation in one corner of the globe. And supreme arrogance to believe that we have the monopoly of spiritual truth.

I came home from Vietnam convinced that the real task of development lies at home at our own door.

1987

29.07   We are all one, in a subtle but most significant way, one in the sense of being interdependent. I would not be as I am without you; you would not be as you are without me. At one level this is not difficult to understand. I realise how much I am the product not only of my parents' genes, but also of their emotional and intellectual influence which derived, in turn, from the ambience of their own family life, culture and education. And I am the product of my schooling, the intellectual ideas which have shaped my thoughts, my friends, my wife, my children – all of whose lives I, in turn, am helping to create.

This is easy to grasp. It is also easy to grasp how, for example, our tastes and addictions influence people far outside our range of knowledge. For instance, whether I prefer tea to coffee for breakfast affects the economy of, say Sri Lanka or India, Kenya or Colombia. And this means that the lives of millions of people I have never met are affected. The whimsy of my taste buds may lead to the bankruptcy or the prosperity of nations, to revolutions or oppressions. Who knows? All we can be sure of is that everything we do, say or think cannot help having an impact on the totality, the All of which we form a part.

Adam Curle, 1992

29.08   We Quakers say we have no creed. We almost do! For nearly all of us would say we believe in 'that of God in everyone'.

How easy that is to say. How difficult to live! If we mean it, we have to live it. That is why some of us in Northern Ireland do speak to the men of violence. It does not mean we agree with what they do. It does mean believing in the good that is in everyone and in the potential for growth and change that is in us all.

Some of our closest friends used to be involved in violence and have changed. I have learnt so much from them and their courage in changing, and I am encouraged to believe that anyone can change.

Diana Lampen, 1991

29.09   We have to take responsibility in our own countries for the trade in weapons, which will continue unless we intensify our actions against it. Let us do this together as an international body. Let us picture where Jesus Christ would be in this matter. What would he be saying about the trade in weapons? I often have to remind myself of this, and I even try to remind some of my colleagues in the Australian Senate – well, what would Jesus be saying about this or that – and it pulls them up a bit short, I can tell you.

He would be there, he would be working with us, he would be arguing and doing everything in his power to ensure that this trade, which is totally immoral, was stopped as soon as possible. It's a big job, Friends, but Quakers have often taken on a prophetic role in the past. We should be glad of the example of the slave abolitionists and remember their strength, their courage, their witness, and do likewise now.

Jo Vallentine, 1991

29.10   We are trustees of a long tradition which has sought to bring our religious convictions into the world 'and so excite our endeavours to mend it'. We are trying to live in the virtue of that life and power that takes away the occasion of all wars.

Fundamentally, taxation for war purposes is not a political or a fiscal issue. We are convinced by the Spirit of God to say without any hesitation whatsoever that we must support the right of conscientious objection to paying taxes for war purposes. We realise that we live in a world where it is impossible to see clearly the final consequences of the actions we might initiate from this Meeting. Nevertheless we are impelled by our vision of a peaceful and loving society.

We ask Meeting for Sufferings to explore further and with urgency the role our religious society should corporately take in this concern and then to take such action as it sees necessary on our behalf. We know that this is only one further step in our witness to the Truth, to which we are continually summoned. We go forward in God's strength.

London Yearly Meeting, 1987

29.11   What we have heard on the degree of secrecy which permeates our national institutions brings out in us fear, shock, distress and dilemma at the level of deviousness and distortion that flows from this. The vast security apparatus extends through the whole fabric of society. As a Religious Society we have an historic message of love which will conquer the fear which lies at the base of this increasing secrecy.

We need to uphold those who experience persecution and harassment as a result of this secrecy. We must also ask ourselves: 'Just how truthful are we?' Recognising the sincerity of those of opposing views, we are reminded of the need for our whole lives to be in harmony, so we can speak powerfully to others.

Conference on 'The secret state', convened by Warwickshire Monthly Meeting, 1989

29.12 Early Friends were inclined to address the monarch or ambassadors negotiating a peace treaty. Friends are now more likely to address those involved in the work of international institutions, like the UN or the European Economic Community, although letters are still written to the Prime Minister, and recently British Friends addressed the monarch. It might also be argued that power in today's world has shifted from governments to global financial interests, and it is there that Quaker efforts should be directed.

Our primary objective in speaking truth to power on social and economic issues, especially on the problem of world poverty, should be the interests of the poor. Our role is to remind the rich and privileged, including ourselves, of the challenge to surrender privilege.

Cecil R Evans, 1987

29.13 We have thought and felt deeply about the disgrace that there is poverty in our wealthy country. So long as any one person in our midst can say 'I exist, but I'm nothing' the longing for a more just social order will persist. The truth is that we are all hurt and need healing. There is a spiritual poverty among both rich and poor... If we are to be whole, we can no longer ignore the divisions created by idolising wealth, success and power. A key to a deep-rooted response to poverty is to throw away the illusion that the rich alone have much to offer and to grasp the reality that we all have much to gain from one another.

London Yearly Meeting, 1987

29.14 Quakers believe that the same God who is graciously present with us is also known in other religions of the world, and by all who are 'humble, meek, merciful, just, pious and devout'. An encouraging aspect of the Inter-Church Process has been its lively awareness of Britain as a multi-faith community... But beyond the other faiths, there is a whole people of God, the whole of humanity. We affirm, with the Swanwick [inter-church] declaration, that 'the world with all its sin and splendour belongs to God.' ... The gospel-imperative for the church is to serve the people of God, and most especially 'these least'. The hungry, the homeless, the sick and the prisoners abound in Britain today: the world cries out for justice and peace.

Meeting for Sufferings, 1988

29.15   We recognise and celebrate what we as Black, Asian and mixed-heritage Friends [in Britain] bring to the Society and with pride we affirm our rich positive contributions. However, we find spoken and unspoken assumptions that because we are Black people we are economically needy, socially deprived, culturally disinherited and spiritually in need of Quaker instruction. We experience isolation both physical and spiritual within our meetings. It is not just a matter of numbers but without the active commitment to promote diversity within the Society of Friends it will continue to be difficult to foster a true experience of a spiritual community.

As Black and white Friends we recognise the importance of our children's needs to know and value themselves and the world around them with the love and support of a settled and secure family environment. We must all strive to ensure that race is not a barrier to our children's success. We need to look honestly and openly at the structure of our meetings and seek to broaden our experience of other enriching forms of worship. Quakerism enables us to face both the glory and the seemingly unfaceable in ourselves. Let us do so now – together.

Epistle of Black, white, Asian and mixed-heritage Friends, 1991

29.16   *At the World Conference of Friends in 1991, Val Ferguson asked:*

Does anything unite this diverse group beyond our common love and humanity? Does anything make us distinctively Quaker? I say yes. Each of us has different emphases and special insights, but wherever Friends are affirming each other's authentic experience of God, rather than demanding credal statements, we are being God's faithful Quakers. Wherever we are seeking God's will rather than human wisdom, especially when conflict might arise, we are being faithful Quakers. Wherever we are affirming the total equality of men and women, we are being God's faithful Quakers. Wherever there is no division between our words and our actions, we are being faithful. Whenever we affirm that no one – priest, pastor, clerk, elder – stands between us and the glorious and mystical experience of God in our lives, we are faithful Friends. Whether we sing or whether we wait in silence, as long as we are listening with the whole of our being and seeking the baptism and communion of living water, we will be one in the Spirit.

29.17 *Over 300 Young Friends from 34 countries, 57 yearly meetings, and 8 monthly meetings under the care of Friends World Committee for Consultation, met at Guilford College, Greensboro, North Carolina in July 1985, to envisage the future of the Religious Society of Friends and to see how their lives should speak within that vision.*

We have come together from every continent, separated by language, race, culture, ways we worship God, and beliefs about Christ and God... We have been challenged, shaken up, at times even enraged, intimidated, and offended by these differences in each other. We have grown from this struggle and have felt the Holy Spirit in pro-grammed worship, singing, Bible study, open times of worship and sharing, and silent waiting upon God.

Our differences are our richness, but also our problem. One of our key differences is the different names we give our Inward Teacher. Some of us name that Teacher Lord; others of us use the names Spirit, Inner Light, Inward Christ or Jesus Christ. It is important to acknowledge that these names involve more than language; they involve basic differences in our understanding of who God is, and how God enters our lives. We urge Friends to wrestle, as many of us have here, with the conviction and experience of many Friends throughout our history that this Inward Teacher is in fact Christ himself. We have been struck this week, however, with the experi-ence of being forced to recognise this same God at work in others who call that Voice by different names, or who understand differ-ently who that Voice is.

We have often wondered whether there is anything Quakers today can say as one. After much struggle we have discovered that we can proclaim this: there is a living God at the centre of all, who is available to each of us as a Present Teacher at the very heart of our lives. We seek as people of God to be worthy vessels to deliver the Lord's transforming word, to be prophets of joy who know from experience and can testify to the world, as George Fox did, 'that the Lord God is at work in this thick night'. Our priority is to be receptive and responsive to the life-giving Word of God, whether it comes through the written word – the Scriptures, the Incarnate Word – Jesus Christ, the Corporate Word – as discerned by the gathered meeting, or the Inward Word of God in our hearts which is available to each of us who seek the Truth.

This can be made easier if we face the truth within ourselves, embrace the pain, and lay down our differences before God for the Holy Spirit to forgive, thus transforming us into instruments of healing. This priority is not merely an abstract idea, but something we have experienced powerfully at work among us this week.

Our five invited speakers presented vivid pictures of economic, ecological and military crisis in this world today. We acknowledge that these crises are in fact only a reflection of the great spiritual crisis which underlies them all. Our peace testimony inspires us, yet we move beyond it to challenge our world with the call for justice. We are called to be peacemakers, not protestors.

It is our desire to work co-operatively on unifying these points. The challenges of this time are almost too great to be faced, but we must let our lives mirror what is written on our hearts – to be so full of God's love that we can do no other than live out our corporate testimonies to the world of honesty, simplicity, equality and peace, whatever the consequences.

We pray for both the personal and inner strength as well as the corporate strength of a shared calling/struggle that will empower us to face all the trials that we will necessarily encounter. We have no illusions about the fact that to truly live a Christian life in these cataclysmic times means to live a life of great risk.

We call on Friends to rediscover our own roots in the vision and lives of early Friends whose own transformed lives shook the unjust social and economic structures of their day. They treasured the records of God's encounters with humanity found in the Bible, and above all, the life and teachings of Jesus Christ. And we call upon Friends across the earth to heed the voice of God and let it send us out in truth and power to rise to the immense challenge of our world today.

29.18 And now at this critical point in time, when our outdated world view no longer satisfies, comes this breakthrough: science and mysticism speaking with one voice, the rediscovery of our own (Christian) creation-centred and mystical tradition, and the recognition of the spiritual wisdoms of the native traditions. All uniting and all challenging in a profound way our narrowly drawn boundaries.

Are we willing to open ourselves to this wider vision, to cease our urge to control and dominate, to listen instead to our hearts, to recognise again the integrity and sacredness of this planet which we have so abused? This means entering into a new relationship with 'our Mother the Earth', it means seeing ourselves again in a cosmic context, a larger perspective, which includes fire-ball, galaxy, planet, and all other life forms.

If we can move from our 'human-sized' viewpoint and look instead from the cosmic viewpoint, there is a sudden and dramatic widening of the lens through which we look. Redemption is seen to be for all creation, and our human story, far from being diminished, is incorporated in the whole drama of an emerging universe.

Grace Blindell, 1992

29.19 Therefore, dear Friends, wait in the Light, that the Word of the Lord may dwell plentifully in you.

William Dewsbury, 1675

English translations of passages in Welsh

10.14 Although English has been the main medium of the Society in these islands through the years, it should be recognised that part of its life has been, and is, expressed through other languages, and in Wales also through the medium of Welsh. Our Society's tradition, our history and our witness are demeaned if that is ignored. Some Welsh speakers have been made, unwittingly, to feel marginalised. The rightful place of the Welsh language in the work and activities of the yearly meeting in Wales should be secured.

Dwyfor Meeting, 1994

21.33 Where did the sea of light roll from
Onto Flower Meadow Field and Flower Field?
After I'd searched for long in the dark land,
The one that was always, whence did he come?
Who, O who was the marksman, the sudden enlightener? The roller of the sea was the field's living hunter.
From above bright-billed whistlers, prudent scurry of lapwings,
The great quiet he brought me.

Excitement he gave me, where only
The sun's thought stirred to lyrics of warmth,
Crackle of gorse that was ripe on escarpments,
Hosting of rushes in their dream of blue sky.
When the imagination wakens, who calls
Rise up and walk, dance, look at the world?
Who is it hiding in the midst of the words
That were there on Flower Meadow Field and Flower Field?

And when the big clouds, the fugitive pilgrims,
Were red with the sunset of stormy November,
Down where the ashtrees and maples divided the fields,
The song of the wind was deep like deep silence.

Who, in the midst of the pomp, the super-abundance,
Stands there inviting, containing it all?
Each witness's witness, each memory's memory, life of each life,
Quiet calmer of the troubled self.

Till at last the whole world came into the stillness
And on the two fields his people walked,
And through, and between, and about them, goodwill widened
And rose out of hiding, to make them all one,
As when the few of us forayed with pitchforks
Or from heavy meadows lugged thatching of rush,
How close we came then, one to another –
The quiet huntsman so cast his net round us!

Ages of the blood on the grass and the light of grief
Who whistled through them? Who heard but the heart?
The cheater of pride and every trail's tracker,
Escaper from the armies, hey, there's his whistling –

Knowledge of us, knowledge, till at last we do know him! Great
was the leaping of hearts, after their ice age.
The fountains burst up towards heaven, till,
Falling back, their tears were like leaves of a tree.

Day broods on all this beneath sun and cloud,
And Night through the cells of her wide-branching brain –
How quiet they are, and she breathing freely
Over Flower Meadow Field and Flower Field –
Keeps a grip on their object, the fields full of folk.
Surely these things must come. What hour will it be
That the outlaw comes, the hunter, the claimant to the breach,
That the Exiled King cometh, and the rushes part in his way?

Translation by Tony Conran

616

26.64   By emphasising the Inner Light, we do not humanise religion too much. It is not our light – we receive it. As we are in the midst of experiences with our fellow beings, a light will come that causes those experiences to look changed. We say, in a clumsy way, that it is the Inner Light that has caused the transformation and we believe that it came from God. How do we know that we are not deceiving ourselves? In the end, we have nothing but our own experience to rely upon. In the end, even the one who accepts the most traditional religion has nothing but his own experience to rely on.

Notes on the history of the text

Within two generations of the establishment of the Yearly Meeting held in London the need was felt by Friends up and down the country for a digest of the counsel on practice and government which was contained year by year in its epistles and other minutes and documents. In 1738, therefore, the yearly meeting approved such a compilation, issued under the title of *Christian and brotherly advices given forth from time to time by the Yearly Meetings in London, alphabetically digested under proper heads* – a manuscript volume made available to the clerks of quarterly and monthly meetings.

Additions were circulated to these meetings from time to time during the eighteenth century, but the need for a printed volume was increasingly felt, and in 1782 the text of *Christian and brotherly advices* was entirely revised and brought up to date, being printed the following year as *Extracts from the minutes and advices of the Yearly Meeting of Friends held in London from its first institution*. It is pertinent to recall that since that time a revision has been undertaken by the yearly meeting almost once in every generation until the present day, the 1782 *Book of extracts* (as it was popularly called) being revised in 1801 and a supplement being approved in 1822.

A more substantial revision was undertaken in 1833 and resulted in *Rules of discipline* printed the following year. Besides substantial alterations in the counsel on practice and government, a long introduction 'On the origin and establishment of our Christian discipline' was written for the occasion by Samuel Tuke, and four extracts were subjoined to the preface 'from approved documents of the Society, issued at different periods, and declaratory of its views, in reference to some of the fundamental doctrines of the Christian faith'. A supplement to this revision was approved in 1848.

In 1861 a further substantial revision was undertaken. The old alphabetical subject arrangement was abandoned in favour of a more logical order of chapters, which were grouped in three parts, *Christian doctrine*, *Christian practice*, and *Church government*. The doctrinal extracts included as a part of the preface in 1833 were thus supplemented, and the whole incorporated as an integral part of the book.

There was a further revision in 1883 entitled *Book of Christian discipline*, the last occasion on which the book was revised as a whole and issued in a single volume. The history of subsequent revisions and editions of the three parts of the book is complex, and it is beyond the purpose of this note to enter into all the details, or to relate successive revisions to the changing climate of thought within the Society.

It became increasingly clear in the later nineteenth century that, because of the number and frequency of alterations in the detailed regulations, *Church government* would need more frequent re-issue than the two other parts. Apart from any interim revised editions containing incidental alterations, thorough revisions were approved by London Yearly Meeting in 1906, 1917 and 1931. *Christian practice* meanwhile had undergone two revisions approved by Yearly Meeting in 1911 and 1925, while the 1883 *Part I, Christian doctrine,* was substantially revised and re-cast in a form approved by Yearly Meeting 1921, the title being altered to *Christian life, faith and thought.*

In 1955 Yearly Meeting agreed to the revision of the 1921 *Christian life, faith and thought,* and the 1925 *Christian practice.* The revised text was approved by the yearly meeting in 1959 and was printed in one volume entitled *Christian faith and practice in the experience of the Society of Friends.* Yearly Meeting approved the revision of *Advices and queries* in 1964 and of *Church government* in 1967: these were published in a single volume.

In 1986 a committee was appointed to revise both *Christian faith and practice* and *Church government.* A draft text was submitted to Yearly Meeting 1994, as *Documents in advance* volumes 2 and 3. That Yearly Meeting, after making a number of changes and additions to the draft, approved a final text to be published in 1995 under the single title *Quaker faith and practice: the book of Christian discipline of the Yearly Meeting of the Religious Society of Friends (Quakers) in Great Britain.*

Sources and references

In this book the extracts have been printed with the minimum of information judged necessary for an adequate understanding of them. The author's name or that of the corporate body responsible has been given, together with some indication as to when, and if relevant in what circumstances, the passage was written. The date normally is that of the first separate publication of a work within the author's lifetime: this may, or may not, be the exact year in which the work in question was written. In some places, notably several journals of Friends, the date given is that of the incident recounted, irrespective of whether the passage was written at that time or later in the author's life. Dates appearing in square brackets [ ], following pre-1752 (Old Style, Julian calendar) dates, are New Style dates, according to the Gregorian calendar; for an explanation of the differences between the two, and complications resulting from Friends' use of numbers rather than names of months, see George Fox, Journal, ed J L Nickalls, 1952, pp xiii-xiv. The giving of a date alone indicates approval by the Yearly Meeting in the year shown as a part of a revision of the book of discipline. In chapters 3-9 and 11-17 where no date is given, the text was written by the 1994 Revision Committee and approved by the Yearly Meeting. Some extracts are compiled from two or more sources and in such cases two references are given, separated by a semi-colon, unless the passage from the secondary source is inconsequential in length, in which case a note to the effect is given in the following references.

From 1668 Friends in England, Wales and Scotland met for their annual meeting for discipline in London. This yearly meeting was referred to as 'the Yearly Meeting of the People called Quakers, held in London' or a similar phrase. From 1900 official publications used the form 'London Yearly Meeting' both for the event and for the institution, even though after 1905 Yearly Meetings were held outside London every four years or so. Yearly Meeting 1994 agreed (minute 49) that from 1 January 1995 the yearly meeting would be known as 'the Yearly Meeting of the Religious Society of Friends (Quakers) in Britain, or, in short form, Britain Yearly Meeting'. Extracts from the period before 1900 are attributed to 'Yearly Meeting in London' and from 1900 to 1994 to 'London Yearly Meeting'.

In the text of the book the aim has been to give a faithful and accurate representation of the author's intention. Spelling is, in general, modernised. Punctuation and capitalisation have normally been brought into line with modern practice, though in words relating to God the usage of the original author has often been followed. Words and dates not in the original are included in square brackets [ ] and omissions are indicated by three dots (...) unless the omission is of a single word or short phrase making no material alteration to the purport of the text. Dots of omission have not been shown where the passage has a large number of such omissions: in such cases a note to this effect is given in the following references. In the list of sources LSF as a location indicates the Library of the Religious Society of Friends, London and 'Yearly Meeting' indicates the Yearly Meeting of Friends held in London before 1900.

The detailed references which follow are intended to guide readers to the sources; if this list leads to a fuller study of the works from which the extracts have been taken, it will have achieved one of its purposes. Biographical introductions, preambles and notes in italics have been drafted by the 1994 Revision Committee and are not listed, except where they contain quotations.

Some extracts are taken from works written by a number of Friends working in collaboration; where it has been possible to identify an author individually responsible for a passage, this has been done. Writers of extracts published anonymously or pseudonymously have also been identifed where possible. Sources of quotations (whether identified as such by inverted commas or not) within the text have normally been given.

INTRODUCTION

p 16 Epistle of World Gathering of Young Friends, Greensboro, North Carolina, 1985, *London Yearly Meeting Proceedings*, 1986, pp 226-227.

p 17 Minute 21 of London Yearly Meeting 1978, *London YM Proc*, 1978, pp 312-313.

ADVICES & QUERIES

1.01 ¶5 Quotation from postscript to the letter from the meeting of elders at Balby, 1656, as printed in William Charles Braithwaite, *Beginnings of Quakerism*, 1912, p 311.

1.02 Quotation at end from 'Exhortation to Friends in the ministry', from Launceston prison, 1656, in George Fox, *Journal*, ed J L Nickalls, 1952, p 263.

1.04 ¶1 Introductory quotation from Yearly Meeting manuscript minutes vol 1 (1672-1693), p 115.
¶4 Quotation from John Griffith, *Journal*, 1779, p 294; the phrase was used by Joseph White of Pennsylvania.
¶7 Quotation from Doris N Dalglish, *The people called Quakers*, 1938, p 61.

APPROACHES TO GOD – WORSHIP AND PRAYER

2.01 Drafted by 1967 and amended by 1994 Revision Committee.

2.02 Caroline E Stephen, *Quaker strongholds*, 1890, pp 11-13; 1923 edn, pp 3-4.

2.03 George Gorman, *The amazing fact of Quaker worship (Swarthmore lecture)*, 1973, p 149.

2.04 *Memoirs of...Daniel Wheeler*, 1842, p 71 (entry for 4 ix 1818).

2.05 Ellis Pugh, *Annerch ir Cymru iw galw oddiwrth y llawer o bethau at yr un peth...*, [undated], p 99; translated as *A salutation to the Britains, to call them from the many things, to the one thing needful...*, 1732, pp 191-192.

2.06 Ruth Fawell, *Courage to grow*, 1987, p 6.

2.07 Thomas F Green, *Preparation for growth (Swarthmore lecture)*, 1952, p 17; 1989 edn, p 14.

2.08 Unidentified contributor to Quaker Women's Group, *Bringing the invisible into the light (Swarthmore lecture)*, 1986, p 51.

2.09 Robert Davis, 'Worship and ministry', in Gerald K Hibbert, ed, *Studies in Quaker thought and practice*, pt 2, 1933, p 49.

2.10 Thomas R Kelly, *A testament of devotion*, 1941, pp 29-30; 1949 edn, p 27.

2.11 Drafted by 1925 and amended by 1994 Revision Committee.

2.12 Pierre Lacout, *God is silence*, translated from the French by John Kay, 1970, pp 9, 26; 1985 edn, pp 8, 18; 1993 edn, pp 20, 41.

2.13 William Penn, *Fruits of a father's love*, 1726, ch 2, §27, pp 47-48; repr as 'The advice of William Penn to his children' in William Penn, *A collection of the works*, 1726, vol 1, p 899; *Select works*, 1782, vol 5, p 448.

2.14 Epistle of Yearly Meeting 1884, *YM Proc*, 1884, p 38; the last sentence is from the epistle of Yearly Meeting 1886, *YM Proc*, 1886, p 33.

2.15 Letter of 4 vii 1895 to 'a correspondent', in *John Bellows: letters and memoir*, 1904, p 261.

2.16 Rufus M Jones, 'The spiritual message of the Religious Society of Friends', in Friends World Conference 1937, *Report of Commission I*, p 13.

2.17 Unpublished writing by Rachel Needham, 1987.

2.18 Letter of George Fox to lady Claypole, 1658, in George Fox, *Journal*, ed J L Nickalls, 1952, p 346.

2.19 Joseph Besse, *A collection of the sufferings of the people called Quakers*, 1753, vol 2, pp 217-218.

2.20 Query 6, 1964.

2.21 Elfrida Vipont Foulds, *The candle of the Lord (Pendle Hill pamphlet 248)*, 1983, p 13.

2.22 Thomas R Kelly, *A testament of devotion*, 1941, pp 38-39; 1949 edn, pp 33-34.

2.23 Harold Loukes, *Quaker findings*, 1967, p 40.

2.24 William Littleboy, *The meaning and practice of prayer*, 1937, pp 7-9; repr from *The Friend*, vol 95 (1937), p 202, of an address found among William Littleboy's papers.

2.25 'More like marriage' in Louie Horne, *A shining-place: poems*, 1987, p 6.

2.26 Diana Lampen, *Facing death*, 1979, pp 34-35.

2.27 'Anna', in *An exercise of the spirit: Quakers and prayer*, comp Leila Ward, 1984, p 20.

2.28 Elisabeth Holmgaard, *'Be still and know that I am God': thoughts on prayer*, 1984, p 17.

2.29 Thomas F Green, *Preparation for growth (Swarthmore lecture)*, 1952, p 31; 1989 edn, p 18.

2.30 Caroline E Stephen, *Quaker strongholds*, 1890, pp 67-68; 1923 edn, pp 55-56.

2.31 T Edmund Harvey, *Along the road of prayer*, 1929, p 26.

2.32 Douglas Steere, *Prayer and worship*, 1938, p 17.

2.33 Jack Dobbs, *The desert and the marketplace*, 1984, p 6; first given as a talk to Devon & Cornwall GM, 1982; the reference is to Isaiah 35:7.

2.34 William Littleboy, *The meaning and practice of prayer*, 1937, p 10 (see note to 2.24).

2.35 George Fox, *A collection of...epistles*, 1698, epistle 149, 'To Friends, to know one another in the Light' (1657), p 115.

2.36 Thomas R Kelly, *The eternal promise*, 1966, p 34; 1988 edn, pp 44-45. The passage is translated from Thomas Kelly, *Das Ewige in seiner Gegenwärtigkeit und zeitlichen Führung (Richard L Cary Vorlesung)*, 1938, pp 25-26.

2.37 Unpublished writing by John Punshon, 1987.

2.38 Adapted by 1994 Revision Committee from 'Some thoughts from the weekend gathering on fundamental elements of Quakerism' in *Young Quaker*, vol 32 no 2 (Feb 1986), p 6.

2.39 Caroline E Stephen, *Light arising*, 1908, pp 68-69.

2.40 Thomas R Kelly, *The gathered meeting*, 1940; repr in Thomas R Kelly, *The eternal promise*, 1966, p 79; 1988 edn, p 94.

2.41 Letter of Alexander Parker to Friends, 14 xi 1659 [January 1660], printed in

Thomas Salthouse & Alexander Parker, *A manifestation of divine love...*, 1660, pp 15-17; repr in Abram Rawlinson Barclay, ed, *Letters, &c, of early friends*, 1841, pp 365-366.

2.42 Advices II, ¶1, 1964.

2.43 Epistle of YM 1765, repr in *Epistles from the Yearly Meeting of Friends held in London...from 1681 to 1857*, 1858, vol 1, p 338.

2.44 Minute of Berks & Oxon Quarterly Meeting Ministry & Extension Committee, 20 iii 1948; the extract is taken direct from the manuscript minute book.

2.45 Minute of Berks & Oxon QM Ministry & Extension Committee, 3 v 1947; the extract is taken direct from the manuscript minute book.

2.46 Drafted by 1959 and amended by 1994 Revision Committee.

2.47 Thomas R Bodine, 'Does punctuality matter?', *The Friend*, vol 138 (1980), p 277.

2.48 Isaac Penington, *Letters*, ed John Barclay, 1828, pp 5-6; 3rd edn, 1844, pp 6-7 (letter III, to Bridget Atley, undated).

2.49 Thomas F Green, *Preparation for growth (Swarthmore lecture)*, 1952, pp 29-30; 1989 edn, pp 24-25.

2.50 Unpublished letter from Anne Hosking in response to an inquiring parent.

2.51 [Dorothy Marshall], in *What do you do in meeting for worship?: twenty-seven responses by members and attenders of Newcastle upon Tyne...meeting*, 1989, p 1; first published 1987.

2.52 John William Graham, *The faith of a Quaker*, 1920, p 245.

2.53 John Edward Southall, *The power of stillness*, [c1900]; this passage is part of the pamphlet often separately repr under the title *Silence*.

2.54 Tayeko Yamanouchi, *Ways of worship*, 1980; written as a background paper for the 1979 Triennial Meeting of Friends World Committee for Consultation and printed in *Friends world news*, no 113 (1979/1980), p 13.

2.55 Advices II, ¶2, 1964.

2.56 Margaret Hope Bacon, *Mothers of feminism*, 1986, p 32. The quotation is from 'The life of Jane Hoskens' in

Friends' library, Philadelphia, vol 1, 1837, p 463.

2.57 John Woolman, *The journal and major essays*, ed Phillips P Moulton, 1971, p 31.

2.58 'A Friend' [Elisabeth Salisbury], 'On first rising to minister', *Quaker monthly*, vol 47 (1968), p 98.

2.59 Samuel Bownas, *A description of the qualifications necessary to a gospel minster*, 1750, p 107; 1989 edn, pp 98-99.

2.60 Adapted by 1994 Revision Committee from 'Some thoughts from the weekend gathering on fundamental elements of Quakerism' in *Young Quaker*, vol 32 no 2 (Feb 1986), p 6.

2.61 *An account of the gospel labours of...John Churchman*, 1780, p 32, probably referring to early 1734.

2.62 Caroline E Stephen, *Quaker strongholds*, 1890, pp 55-56; 1923 edn, p 46.

2.63 Adapted by 1994 Revision Committee from 'Some thoughts from the weekend gathering on fundamental elements of Quakerism' in *Young Quaker*, vol 32 (1986) no 2, p 6.

2.64 L Violet Holdsworth, *Silent worship, the way of wonder (Swarthmore lecture)*, 1919, pp 77-78.

2.65 Robert Hewison, 'In the life', *The Friend*, vol 123 (1965), p 547.

2.66 Marrianne McMullen, 'Lessons in ministry', *Friendly woman*, vol 8 no 1 (Winter 1987), p 4.

2.67 Drafted by 1967 and amended by 1994 Revision Committee.

2.68 Ormerod Greenwood, 'Tripping', *The Friend*, vol 138 (1980), p 962.

2.69 A Neave Brayshaw, *The Quakers, their story and message*, 1921, p 103; 1953 edn, p 275.

2.70 Douglas Steere, *On speaking out of the silence (Pendle Hill pamphlet 182)*, 1972, p 11.

2.71 Drafted by 1925 and amended by 1959 Revision Committee.

2.72 William Penn, preface (1694) to George Fox, *Journal*, ed J L Nickalls, 1952, pp xliii-xliv. Penn's preface was also issued as *A brief account of the rise and progress...of the Quakers*, 1694.

2.73 George Fox, *Something concerning silent meetings*, [1657], repr in *Gospel truth demonstrated*, 1706, p 103.

2.74 George Gorman, *The amazing fact of Quaker worship (Swarthmore lecture)*, 1973, p 141.

2.75 Jean Brown, *Held by a thread (Sunderland P Gardner lecture)*, 1984, p 16.

2.76 Anne Hosking, 'A child's gift of worship', *Friends quarterly*, vol 23 (1983-1985), pp 226-227.

2.77 Jack Dobbs, *The desert and the market place*, 1984, p 2 and see note to 2.33.

2.78 Joan Mary Fry, 'Thoughts of a British Friend', *Friends world news*, no 23 (Spring 1947), p 9.

2.79 Jo Farrow, 'On keeping a journal', *Gifts and discoveries: phase 1*, 1986, unit 1, background paper 2, pp 1-2.

2.80 Kathy Tweet, in Kathy Tweet & Jean Brown, 'A place to stand', *Journal of Woodbrooke College*, no 2 (Winter 1992/3), pp 9-10.

2.81 Damaris Parker-Rhodes, *The way out is the way in*, 1985, pp 122-123.

2.82 Alec Davison, 'Meetings for learning', *Friends quarterly*, vol 23 (1983-1985), p 102.

2.83 London Yearly Meeting 1905, *Letter to isolated members*; the second and fourth sentences were drafted by the 1911 Revision Committee. The extract as printed is considerably abridged and omissions are not indicated in the text. The document is not printed in *London YM Proc*, but for reference to the concern see *London YM Proc*, 1905, pp 30, 71.

2.84 David W Robson, *Amateur Christians*, 1971, p 21.

2.85 John Punshon, *Encounter with silence: reflections from the Quaker tradition*, 1987, p 95.

2.86 Query 8, 1964.

2.87 Edward Burrough, 'A testimony concerning the beginning of the work of the Lord' (1662), printed in Abram Rawlinson Barclay, ed, *Letters, &c, of early Friends*, 1841, p 305. The passage is considerably abridged and omissions are not indicated in the text.

2.88 London Yearly Meeting, *To Lima with love: the response...to the World Council of Churches document*

'Baptism, eucharist and ministry', 1987, as approved by London Yearly Meeting 1986, p 3.

2.89 Epistle of London YM, 1984, *London YM Proc*, 1984, p 267.

2.90 John Punshon, *Encounter with silence: reflections from the Quaker tradition*, 1987, p 98.

2.91 Minute 14 of London Yearly Meeting 1936, *London YM Proc*, 1936, p 300.

2.92 Paul Anderson, 'An experience of transforming love', in World Gathering of Young Friends, Greensboro, North Carolina, 1985, *Let our lives speak: visioning a future for Friends*, 1986, pp 62, 64.

GENERAL COUNSEL ON CHURCH AFFAIRS

3.08 Query 7, 1928.

3.22 ¶1 Quotation from 1 Cor 12: 4 - 7 (Bible, New Revised Standard Version, 1989).

3.30 George Fox, *A collection of...epistles*, 1698, epistle 162 (1658), p 124.

MONTHLY MEETINGS AND THEIR CONSTITUENT MEETINGS

4.17 The quotation is from §21 of the report of 28 January 1978 from the Minute 24 Committee to Meeting for Sufferings, received by London Yearly Meeting 1978, and printed in *London YM Proc*, 1978, p 151.

4.25 Testimony of Hertford MM concerning Hannah Brown, in Yearly Meeting manuscript 'Testimonies concerning ministers deceased' vol 3 (1774 - 1791), p 155.

YEARLY MEETING

6.01 ¶2 Quotation from manuscript diary of Joseph Rowntree (LSF manuscript vol S 128, p 36).

¶3 Quotation from Caroline Fox, *Memories of old friends*, ed H N Pym, 3rd edn, 1882, vol 1, p 293.

¶4 First quotation from 'A Quakers' meeting' by Charles Lamb in *Essays of Elia*. Second quotation from *YM Proc*, 1896, p 36.

¶6 First quotation from *Extracts from the minutes and advices of the Yearly*

Meeting of Friends held in London, 1783, p 226. Second quotation from Daniel Pickard, *An expostulation on behalf of the truth against departures in doctrine, practice and discipline*, 1864, p 120.

¶7 Quotation from chart showing use of time at London Yearly Meeting 1902. The accompanying memorandum 'Yearly Meeting procedure' is signed by John Wilhelm Rowntree and Edward Worsdell, and dated July 10th, 1902 (LSF tract vol O/119-122).

¶8 Minute 19 of London Yearly Meeting 1905 includes the response in full; printed in *London YM Proc*, 1905, pp 11-12.

6.02 Epistle of ministering Friends, Christmas 1668, repr in *Epistles from the Yearly Meeting of Friends held in London...from 1681 to 1857*, 1858, vol 1, p xiv.

6.03 Epistle of YM 1718, repr in *Epistles from the Yearly Meeting of Friends held in London...*, 1858, vol 1, pp 147-148.

6.05 Roger Wilson, *Authority, leadership and concern (Swarthmore lecture)*, 1949, p 36.

6.06 Report of Meeting for Sufferings Committee on Right Holding of Yearly Meeting, 1960, *London YM Proc*, 1961, p 49.

6.07 Testimony of Mid Somerset MM concerning John Morland, *London YM Proc*, 1935, p 237.

6.08 Rosa Hobhouse, *Mary Hughes: her life for the dispossessed*, 1949, pp 96 - 97, quoting Ann Cumming.

MEETING FOR SUFFERINGS

7.01 ¶2 First three quotations from 'A memorandum of those generall things discoursed & assented unto by the late meeting about sufferings the 18th of the 8 month [October] 1675', bound into Meeting for Sufferings manuscript minutes, vol 1 (1675-1680). Final quotation from YM manuscript minutes vol 3 (1683-1684), p 23.

¶5 Quotation from Anna L Littleboy, 'The Meeting for Sufferings', *Friends quarterly examiner*, vol 61 (1927), p 324.

¶7 Quotation from 1964 report of Right Holding of Yearly Meeting Committee, accepted by London Yearly Meeting 1965, and printed in *London YM Proc*, 1965, p 15.

¶8 Quotations from minute 10 of London Special Yearly Meeting 1965, printed in *London Special YM Minutes*, 1965, p 4; and from the first report of the Constitution Review Committee, printed in *London YM Proc*, 1972, p 25.

¶9 *Rules of discipline of…Yearly Meeting*, held in London, 1834, p 107.

7.09 Adapted from minute 3 of Meeting for Sufferings held 5 November 1994, and approved in amended form by Britain Yearly Meeting 1998 (minute 10), to take account of the establishment in 1997 of the Management Meeting. Printed here with minor changes.

BELONGING TO A QUAKER MEETING

10.01 Isaac Penington, *Letters*, ed John Barclay, 1828, p 139; 3rd edn, 1844, p 138 (Letter LII, to Friends in Amersham, dated Aylesbury, 4 iii [May] 1667).

10.02 London Yearly Meeting, *To Lima with love: the response…to the World Council of Churches document 'Baptism, eucharist and ministry'*, 1987, as approved by London Yearly Meeting 1986, p 8.

10.04 William Charles Braithwaite, 'The widening of Quaker fellowship', *Friends quarterly examiner* vol 39 (1905), p 535, repr in Anna Ll B Thomas & Elizabeth B Emmott, *William Charles Braithwaite…memoir and papers*, 1931, p 118.

10.05 London Yearly Meeting, *To Lima with love*, 1987, pp 12-13.

10.06 Drafted by 1959 Revision Committee.

10.07 'The problem of a free ministry' (written 1899), in John Wilhelm Rowntree, *Essays and addresses*, 1905, pp 130, 133-134. The passage is considerably abridged and omissions are not indicated in the text.

10.08 William G Sewell, *Brentford & Isleworth PM newsletter*, 1977.

10.09 Written by William Fraser for the 1994 Revision Committee, 1989.

10.10 Peggy McGeoghegan, 'Can you tell me?', *Quaker monthly*, vol 55 (1976), p 223.

10.11 June Ellis, 'Nurturing relationships in the local meeting', *QSRE journal*, vol 8 (1986), no 3, pp 23-24.

10.12 Ruth Fawell, 'The later years – III: the last loss', *The Friend*, vol 125 (1967), pp 1121-1122.

10.13 Epistle of Black, white, Asian and mixed-heritage Friends, meeting at Charney Manor, 1991, in QSRE, *Worship without prejudice?: an information pack on race relations within the Religious Society of Friends*, 1992. The passage is considerably abridged and omissions are not indicated in the text.

10.14 Text by Dwyfor Meeting/Cyfarfod Dwyfor submitted to Yearly Meeting 1994.

10.15 'Young people and the Society of Friends: thoughts from the Hulme Hall conference', *Young Quaker*, vol 31 (1985), no 10, p 6.

10.16 Text by Nick Putz submitted to Yearly Meeting 1994.

10.17 Drafted by 1925 Revision Committee.

10.18 Olive Tyson, 'One man's part', *The Friend*, vol 124 (1966), p 460.

10.19 Parker J Palmer, *A place called community* (Pendle Hill pamphlet 212), 1977, p 20.

10.20 George Gorman, 'Religion and life', *Quaker monthly*, vol 61 (1982), p 64.

10.21 Drafted by 1994 Revision Committee.

10.22 Joan Fitch, *The present tense: 'Talking to our time'. A discussion paper for Quakers*, 1980, p 38.

10.23 Text by John Miles submitted to Yearly Meeting 1994.

10.24 Kenneth C Barnes, *Integrity in the arts*, 1984, p 52.

10.25 Written by a group of Young Friends, 1986, and printed with amendments in *Young Quaker*, vol 32 (1986), no 4, pp 1-2.

10.26 William Littleboy, *The appeal of Quakerism to the non-mystic*, [1916], pp 4; 1964 edn, p 5.

10.27 Isaac Penington, *Letters*, ed John Barclay, 1828, pp 68-69; 3rd edn,

1844, pp 55-56 (letter XXI: postscript to epistle to Friends of Truth in and about the Chalfonts, dated Aylesbury prison, 26 xi 1666 [January 1667]).

10.28 Beth Allen, 'The cost of discipleship', *Friends quarterly,* vol 23 (1983-1985), p 306.

10.29 From the manuscript translation of Pierre Ceresole's application for membership to the Friends Service Council (FSC Foreign Membership files 6/237: letter of 9 ix 1936, pp 8-9).

10.30 Text by Dorothy Havergal Shaw submitted to Yearly Meeting 1994.

10.31 Text by some members of North Northumberland Meeting submitted to Yearly Meeting 1994.

10.32 Ranjit M Chetsingh, 'Listening to God and each other', in *No time but this present: studies preparatory to the fourth World Conference of Friends 1967,* 1967, pp 110-111.

10.33 Donald Court, *A scientific age and a declining church: what has a Friend to say?,* 1965, pp 10-12, repr from *The Friend,* vol 123 (1965), p 1143. The extract as printed is considerably abridged and omissions are not indicated in the text.

10.34 Unpublished writing by Jai Penna, 1989.

MEMBERSHIP

11.01 ¶1 Quotation from 'Francis Howgill's testimony concerning...Edward Burrough', 1663, in Edward Burrough, *The memorable works of a son of thunder,* 1672, prelim leaf e3. The extract as printed is considerably abridged and omissions are not indicated in the text. For a longer extract see 19.08.

11.18 Edgar G Dunstan, *Quakers and the religious quest (Swarthmore lecture),* 1956, p 68. The phrase 'humble learner in the school of Christ' appeared in *Church government,* 1931, III.16.

11.48 Quotation in ¶1 from Rufus M Jones' introduction to William Charles Braithwaite, *The second period of Quakerism,* 1919, p xxvii; quotation in ¶3 from Phil 3: 12-14 (Revised Version), changed by Rufus Jones from singular to plural.

CARING FOR ONE ANOTHER

12.02 London Yearly Meeting, *To Lima with love,* 1987, p 12.

12.03 London Yearly Meeting, *To Lima with love,* 1987, p 13.

12.04 *New life from old roots: the organisation of the Society of Friends. Documents in advance for [London] Special Yearly Meeting...1965,* 1965, §18.

12.05 William Dewsbury, 'This is the word of the living God to his church...', 1653, in *The faithful testimony of that antient servant of the Lord... William Dewsbery, in his books, epistles and writings,* [1689], p 1.

12.08 Testimony of Reading MM concerning Beatrice Saxon Snell, *London YM Proc,* 1983, p 130.

12.17 George Fox, *A collection of...epistles,* 1698, epistle 264 (1669), p 284.

12.18 Epistle of YM 1851, repr in *Epistles from the Yearly Meeting of Friends in London...from 1681 to 1857,* 1858, vol 2, pp 360-361.

12.19 Epistle of YM 1871, *YM Proc,* 1871, p 33.

VARIETIES OF RELIGIOUS SERVICE

13.03 Barry & Jill Wilsher, quoted in appendix 3(b) of Meeting for Sufferings, *The nature and variety of concern: the report of a working party,* 1986, p 22; 1992 edn, p 24.

13.04 George Murphy, quoted in appendix 3(a) of Meeting for Sufferings, *The nature and variety of concern: the report of a working party,* 1986, p 18; 1992 edn, p 20.

13.07 Roger Wilson, *Authority, leadership and concern (Swarthmore lecture),* 1949, p 12.

13.10 William Charles Braithwaite, *Spiritual guidance in the experience of the Society of Friends (Swarthmore lecture),* 1909, p 101.

13.20 Drafted by 1925 Revision Committee.

13.24 John Woolman, *The journal and major essays,* ed Phillips P Moulton, 1971, p 229 (appendix F).

13.25 Text by Arthur & Ursula Windsor submitted to Yearly Meeting 1994.

13.26 Minute 92/7 (part) of London Yearly Meeting Quaker World Relations Committee, February 1992.

13.30 Text by Richard Schardt submitted to Yearly Meeting 1994; for a longer extract from the Woolman passage, see 27.02.

13.31 Text by Ingrid Williams submitted to Yearly Meeting 1994.

13.32 'A message to Friends' from the QHS Conference on Wardenship, Manchester, June 1981.

FINANCE

14.01 Beryl Hibbs, foreword to London Yearly Meeting, *Financing the Society's central work: report of working party*, 1985, p[ii]. The foreword was not printed with the report in *London YM Proc*, 1986.

QUAKER MARRIAGE

16.01 George Fox, *A collection of...epistles*, 1698, epistle 264 (1669), p 281.

16.02 ¶1 Thomas Ellwood, *History of the life*, 1714, p 257; ed G C Crump, 1900, p 160 (entry for 1669).

QUAKER FUNERALS & MEMORIAL MEETINGS

17.01 Hardshaw East MM Elders & Overseers, 'A supplement to *Friends and the practical aspects of death*', 1986.

17.02 Drafted by 1925 Revision Committee.

17.03 Minute of Berks & Oxon QM Ministry & Extension Committee, 29 xi 1951. The extract is taken direct from the manuscript minute book.

17.04 Document issued by Warwickshire North MM Ministry Committee, 1912, and printed in *London YM Proc*, 1912, pp 80-81.

17.05 Warwickshire MM Elders, *Burials and cremations*, 1960, p 8.

17.06 Diana Lampen, *Facing death*, 1979, pp 22, 27.

17.16 George Gorman, *The amazing fact of Quaker worship (Swarthmore lecture)*, 1973, p 144.

FAITHFUL LIVES

18.01 Testimony of Westminster & Longford MM concerning Joseph Bevan Braithwaite, *London YM Proc*, 1906, pp 215-216.

18.02 Testimony of George Fox concerning Elizabeth Hooton, dated 17 ix [November] 1690, LSF manuscript Portfolio 16/74.

18.03 'Testimony of Upperside [of Buckinghamshire] Women's MM concerning him', in Thomas Ellwood, *History of the life*, 1714, prelim leaf b 2; ed C G Crump, 1900, p xlii.

18.04 Testimony of Carlisle MM concerning Christopher Story, *A collection of testimonies concerning several ministers of the gospel*, 1760, p 3.

18.05 Testimony of Brighouse MM concerning Joshua Barber, *A collection of testimonies concerning several ministers of the gospel*, 1760, pp 69-70.

18.06 Testimony of Shropshire MM concerning Abiah Darby, YM manuscript 'Testimonies concerning ministers deceased', vol 4 (1792-1812), p 73.

18.07 Testimony of Buckinghamshire QM concerning William Coles, YM manuscript 'Testimonies concerning ministers deceased', vol 5 (1813-1830), p 49.

18.08 *Memoir of the life of Elizabeth Fry...edited by two of her daughters [Katherine Fry & Rachel Cresswell]*, 1847, vol 2, pp 522-523.

18.09 Testimony of Darlington MM concerning Hannah Chapman Backhouse, *Testimonies concerning deceased ministers...1851*, 1851, pp 15-16.

18.10 *Memorial of the Monthly Meeting of Dublin concerning Joseph Bewley, an elder*, 1852, pp 6-7.

18.11 Joshua Rowntree, *Social service: its place in the Society of Friends (Swarthmore lecture)*, 1913, pp 78-79.

18.12 Testimony of Warwickshire North MM concerning John Henry Barlow, *London YM Proc*, 1925, pp 168-171.

18.13 Foreword by Howard Spring to Rosa Hobhouse, *Mary Hughes: her life for the dispossessed*, 1949, pp 4-7.

18.14 Testimony of Ratcliff & Barking MM concerning Mary Ann Stokeley, *London YM Proc*, 1955, p 161.

18.15 Testimony of Warwickshire MM concerning Joseph Edward Southall, *London YM Proc*, 1946, p 194.

18.16 Testimony of Sutton Preparative Meeting concerning Jessie Ritch, in *Jessie Alice Stuart Ritch: a memoir*, 1953, p 8.

18.17 Testimony of Hertford & Hitchin MM concerning Lucy Elizabeth Harris, *London YM Proc*, 1963, pp 58 - 60.

18.18 Testimony of Hardshaw East MM concerning Annie Morris, *London YM Proc*, 1981, pp 197 - 8.

18.19 Pleasaunce Holtom, 'Katie's prayer', *Quaker monthly*, vol 60 (1981), p 82.

18.20 Drafted by J Ormerod Greenwood for the 1959 Revision Committee.

OPENINGS

19.01 George Fox, *Journal*, ed J L Nickalls, 1952, pp 2 - 3 (entry for 1643).

19.02 *ibid*, p 11 (entry for 1647).

19.03 *ibid*, p 19 (entry for 1647).

19.04 *ibid*, p 33 (entry for 1648).

19.05 *The discovery of the great enmity of the serpent*, 1655, pp 12 - 15; repr in William Dewsbury, *The faithful testimony of that antient servant of the Lord...William Dewsbery, in his books, epistles and writings*, 1689, pp 44 - 47. The passage is considerably abridged, omissions are not indicated in the text, and the order has been slightly rearranged.

19.06 George Fox, *Journal*, ed J L Nickalls, 1952, pp 103 - 104.

19.07 'The testimony of Margaret Fox concerning her late husband', in George Fox, *Journal*, 1694, p ii; bicent edn, 1891, vol 2, pp 512 - 514; not in Nickalls edn.

19.08 'Francis Howgill's testimony concerning...Edward Burrough', 1663, in Edward Burrough, *The memorable works of a son of thunder*, 1672, prelim leaf e3. The extract as printed is considerably abridged and omissions are not indicated in the text.

19.09 'The examination of James Nayler...at Appleby', January 1652 [1653], in James Nayler, *A collection of sundry books, epistles and papers*, 1716, pp 12 - 13.

19.10 *A book of some of the sufferings...of Myles Halhead*, 1690, p 8.

19.11 'To all the dearly beloved people of God', 1659, in James Nayler, *A collection of sundry books, epistles and papers*, 1716, p xxviii.

19.12 'His last testimony', 1660, in James Nayler, *A collection of sundry books, epistles and papers*, 1716, p 696.

19.13 Mary Penington, *Experiences in the life of Mary Penington*, ed Norman Penney, 1911, repr 1992, pp 44 - 45. A number of manuscript sources in LSF, notably Penington MSS vol 4 and Row MSS vol 6, form the basis for the published text.

19.14 'An account of his spiritual travail' (1667), quoted in 'The testimony of Thomas Ellwood', in Isaac Penington, *Works*, 1681, prelim leaves c3, c4; 1761 edn, vol 1, pp xxxvii-xxxix; 1784 edn, vol 1, pp xliv-xlvii. The extract as printed is abridged and omissions are not indicated in the text.

19.15 Thomas Ellwood, *History of the life*, 1714, pp 21 - 25; ed C G Crump, 1900, pp 14 - 16. Entry for 1659, abridged; omissions are not indicated in the text.

19.16 *ibid*, pp 33 - 34; ed C G Crump, 1900, pp 23 - 24 (entry for 1659).

19.17 Joseph Besse, *A collection of the sufferings of the people called Quakers*, 1753, vol 2, pp 201 - 202.

19.18 *ibid*, vol 2, pp 206 - 207. George Fox, *Journal*, ed J L Nickalls, 1952, p 48 (entry for 1649), p 107 (entry for 1652), p 237 (entry for 1656).

19.19 *First publishers of truth*, ed Norman Penney, 1907, pp 244 - 245.

19.20 Edward Burrough, 'The epistle to the reader' in George Fox, *The great mystery of the great whore unfolded*, 1659, prelim leaves b1-b2.

19.21 Robert Barclay, *Apology for the true Christian divinity*, prop 11, sect 7, 1678 London edn, p 240; 1886 Glasgow edn, p 255.

19.22 *No more but my love: letters of George Fox 1624 - 91*, ed Cecil Sharman, 1980, p 65. For the full text, see George Fox, *A collection of...epistles*, 1698, epistle 171, 'An epistle general to them who are of the royal priesthood' (c1659), pp 129-131.

19.23 Robert Barclay, *Apology for the true Christian divinity*, prop 10, sect 24, 1678 London edn, p 214; 1886 Glasgow edn, pp 228-229.

19.24 George Fox, *Journal*, ed J L Nickalls, 1952, p 40 (entry for 1649). On women's meetings, see George Fox, *A collection of...epistles*, 1698, epistle 320, 'An encouragement to all the faithful women's-meetings in the world' (1676), p 388.

19.25 Elizabeth Bathurst, *The sayings of women...in several places of the Scriptures*, 1683, pp 13, 23.

19.26 George Fox, *Journal*, ed J L Nickalls, 1952, p 163 (entry for 1653).

19.27 Letter from Mary Fisher to Thomas Killam, Thomas Aldam & John Killam, in LSF Caton MSS vol 1, p 164, printed in Mabel R Brailsford, *Quaker women, 1650 - 1690*, 1915, p 130.

19.28 'Some fruits of solitude', 1693, maxims 519, 507, William Penn, *A collection of the works*, 1726, vol 1, p 842; *Select works*, 1782, vol 5, pp 164-165, 163.

19.29 George Fox, *Journal*, 1694, p 385; bicent edn, 1891, vol 2, pp 199-200; Nickalls edn, 1952, p 665.

19.30 Isaac Penington, *Letters*, ed John Barclay, 1828, p 40; 3rd edn, 1844, p 41 (Letter XVII: to the friend of Francis Fines, undated).

19.31 George Fox, *A collection of...epistles*, 1698, epistle 249, 'A general epistle to Friends' (1667), p 244.

19.32 George Fox, *Journal*, ed J L Nickalls, 1952, p 263 (entry for 1656). The full text is in George Fox, *Journal*, 1694, pp 212*-214*; bicent edn, 1891, vol 1, pp 315-317.

19.33 ¶1 William Dewsbury, *The faithful testimony of that antient servant of the Lord...in his books, epistles and writings*, 1689, prelim unnumbered page.
¶2 *First publishers of truth*, ed Norman Penney, 1907, p 199.

19.34 *Extracts from the minutes and advices of the Yearly Meeting of Friends held in London*, 1783, p 125. The extract is taken from the written advices of Yearly Meeting 1675 (see manuscript

Yearly Meeting minutes vol 1 (1672-1693), p 17).

19.35 Joseph Besse, *A collection of the sufferings of the people called Quakers*, 1753, vol 1, p 66.

19.36 'This is a sweet salutation to God's elect church in England and Ireland', dated Malta, 11th month 1661 [January 1662], in *This is a short relation of some of the cruel sufferings...of Katharine Evans and Sarah Chevers*, 1662, p 68.

19.37 Joseph Besse, *A collection of the sufferings of the people called Quakers*, 1753, vol 1, p 314; cf George Fox, *Journal*, ed J L Nickalls, 1952, p 485 (entry for 1665).

19.38 ¶1 Joseph Besse, *A collection of the sufferings of the people called Quakers*, 1753, vol 1, p 312.
¶2 Margaret Fox, *A brief collection of remarkable passages relating to... Margaret Fell*, 1710, p 8.

19.39 *First publishers of truth*, ed Norman Penney, 1907, pp 250-251.

19.40 Thomas Ellwood, *History of the life*, 1714, pp 82-84; ed C G Crump, 1900, pp 51-54 (entry for 1659), abridged.

19.41 *God's mighty power magnified, as manifested and revealed in...Joan Vokins*, 1691, p 104.

19.42 Thomas Chalkley, *A collection of the works...to which is prefixed a journal of his life*, 1751, pp 1-2 (entry for 1684).

19.43 Isaac Penington, *Letters*, ed John Barclay, 1828, pp 213-214; 3rd edn, 1844, pp 174-175 (Letter LXIV: to Bridget Atley, dated 1665).

19.44 From manuscript Portfolio 25/66 in LSF. The passage is considerably abridged and omissions are not indicated in the text.

19.45 *The discovery of the great enmity of the serpent*, 1655, pp 12-15; repr in William Dewsbury, *The faithful testimony of that antient servant of the Lord..., in his books, epistles and writings*, 1689, pp 44-47. The passage is considerably abridged and omissions are not indicated in the text; the order has been slightly rearranged.

19.46 'A declaration and an information from us, the people of God called Quakers, to the...king and both houses of Parliament' (1660), in Margaret Fox, *A brief collection of remarkable passages relating to...Margaret Fell*, 1710, pp 208-210.

19.47 Samuel M Janney, *Life of William Penn*, 1852, p 166; 6th edn, 1882, p 175.

19.48 William Penn's preface to George Fox, *Journal*, 1694, prelim leaf F1; bicent edn, 1891, vol 1, p xxxvii; issued also as *A brief account of the rise and progress...of the Quakers*, 1694; not in Nickalls edn.

19.49 George Fox, *Journal*, ed J L Nickalls, 1952, p 525 (entry under 1668).

19.50 George Fox, *A collection of...epistles*, 1698, epistle 291, 'To all the women's meetings, that are believers in the truth' (1672), p 323.

19.51 George Fox, *Journal*, ed J L Nickalls, 1952, p 373 (entry for 1660).

19.52 George Fox, *Journal*, ed Norman Penney, 1911, vol 2, pp 31-32; not in Nickalls edn.

19.53 Joseph Besse, *A collection of the sufferings of the people called Quakers*, 1753, vol 1, p 381.

19.54 Manuscript letter from Rebecca Travers to George Fox, 17.vi [August 16]76 (LSF Gibson MSS 2/11).

19.55 London Women's Quarterly Meeting to women Friends in the country, 4. xi 1674 [January 1675?], printed with some variations in Abram Rawlinson Barclay, ed, *Letters, &c, of early Friends*, 1841, pp 344-345.

19.56 *A testimony for the Lord and his truth, given forth by the women Friends at their Yearly Meeting at York*. Dated 28.iv [June] 1688 (some later edns are misdated 1668).

19.57 Transcript by Beatrice Saxon Snell (in LSF) of Wiltshire QM minute book, 1678-1708 (manuscript original at Wiltshire Record Office, Trowbridge), p 3.

19.58 William Penn's preface to George Fox, *Journal*, 1694, prelim leaf G2; bicent edn, 1891, vol 1, p xli-xlii; issued also as *A brief account of the rise and progress...of the Quakers*, 1694, but not in Nickalls edn.

19.59 William Penn's preface to George Fox, *Journal*, 1694, prelim leaves L3-L4; bicent edn, 1891, vol 1, pp lvi-lviii; not in Nickalls edn.

19.60 Samuel Bownas, *Life and travels*, 1756, pp 4-5, 7 (entry for 1696).

19.61 Margaret Fox, *A brief collection of remarkable passages relating to... Margaret Fell*, 1710, p 47.

LIVING FAITHFULLY TODAY

20.01 Inazo Nitobe, *Selection from Inazo Nitobe's writings*, 1936, p 159.

20.02 Job Scott, *Journal*, New York, 1797, p 8; 1843 London edn, p 7.

20.03 John Greenleaf Whittier, 'The brewing of soma', first published in *The Atlantic monthly*, vol 29 (1872), p 473; repr in the numerous edns of his collected works.

20.04 Joseph John Armistead, *Ten years near the Arctic circle*, 1913, p 176.

20.05 Jo Vellacott, 'Women, peace and power', in Pam McAllister, ed, *Reweaving the web of life: feminism and nonviolence*, 1982, p 34.

20.06 Letter from Philip Rack, *The Friend*, vol 137 (1979), p 863.

20.07 Susan Lawrence, 'Living adventurously', *The Friend*, vol 142 (1984), p 1013.

20.08 Mary F Smith, 'The place of prayer in life' in Gerald K Hibbert, ed, *Studies in Quaker thought and practice*, part 2, 2nd edn, 1936, pp 25-26. The extract is not printed in the 1st edn.

20.09 Donald Court, *Leading a double life*, 1970, pp 16-17. From an address to a gathering of elders at London Yearly Meeting 1970, first printed as 'Coping with our double lives' in *The Friend*, vol 128 (1970), pp 1109-1110.

20.10 John Woolman, *The journal and major essays*, ed Phillips P Moulton, 1971, p 160 (entry for 1770).

20.11 'Advice to his children', 1699, ch 2, §27, William Penn, *A collection of the works*, 1726, vol 1, p 899; *Select works*, 1782, vol 5, p 448.

20.12 Anne Hosking, in Leila Ward, comp, *An exercise of the spirit: Quakers and prayer*, 1984, p 3.

20.13 Joan Fitch, *The present tense: 'Talking to our time'. A discussion paper for Quakers*, 1980, pp 32-33.

20.14 Letter from Margaret Glover, *The Friend*, vol 147 (1989), p 830.

20.15 Gerald Littleboy, 'Service: an interpretation for Quakers', 1945, *London YM Proc*, 1946, p 52.

20.16 Lorna M Marsden, 'The Quaker faith as evocation', an address at Canterbury, 14 June 1986, repr in *The prepared heart: an anthology of the writings of Lorna M Marsden*, 1988, p 98.

20.17 Chris Lawson, 'Quaker testimonies and development education' in QPS Committee on Sharing World Resources, *Quaker approaches to development*, 1987, p 57; 2nd edn, 1988, p 55.

20.18 John Punshon, *Encounter with silence: reflections from the Quaker tradition*, 1987, pp 44-45.

20.19 Epistle of London YM 1909, *London YM Proc*, 1909, p 167.

20.20 Harvey Gillman, *A light that is shining: an introduction to the Quakers*, 1988, p 5; 2nd edn, 1997, p 12.

20.21 'And in the day when my God lift my feet out of the pit, was this given forth' in James Nayler, *To the life of God in all*, 1659, p 7, repr in James Nayler, *A collection of sundry books, epistles and papers*, 1716, p xlix.

20.22 William Charles Braithwaite, *The second period of Quakerism*, 1919, pp 552-553. Luke Cock's Weeping Cross sermon at York as printed here is slightly modified after comparison with various manuscripts in LSF.

20.23 George Fox, *A collection of...epistles*, 1698, epistle 227 (1663), p 99.

20.24 *Questions & counsel*, §4, 1988.

20.25 Industry and the Social Order Conference, 1958, *Preparatory document no 5, Christian responsibility and material possessions*, [1958], p 5.

20.26 Kathleen Lonsdale, 'Explanation, experience and experiment', a talk given on BBC radio in 1967, printed in *Quakers talk to sixth formers*, 1970, pp 39-40, and repr in *The Christian life – lived experimentally: an anthology of the writings of Kathleen Lonsdale*, selected by James Hough, 1976, pp 17-18.

20.27 North Carolina YM (Conservative), *Faith & practice*, 1983, p 7.

20.28 Epistle of YM 1691, repr in *Epistles from the Yearly Meeting of Friends held in London...from 1681 to 1857*, 1858, vol 1, p 55. The passage is considerably abridged and omissions are not indicated in the text.

20.29 William Penn, *No cross, no crown*, modern English edn, rev and ed by Ronald Selleck, 1981, pp 84-85; not in 1st edn, 1669, but in 2nd edn, 1682, part 1, ch 11, §9; repr in William Penn, *A collection of the works*, 1726, vol 1, p 334; *Select works*, 1782, vol 2, p 135.

20.30 'An epistle to Friends', dated Swarthmore, 4th month [June], 1698, printed in Margaret Fox, *A brief collection of remarkable passages relating to...Margaret Fell*, 1710, p 535.

20.31 From manuscript Portfolio 25/66 in LSF. The passage is considerably abridged and omissions are not indicated in the text.

20.32 'A plea for the poor', ch 2, John Woolman, *The journal and major essays*, ed Phillips P Moulton, 1971, pp 239-240.

20.33 *ibid*, p 240.

20.34 Michael Lee, 'Inflation and personal responsibilities', in Jim Platts & David Eversley, eds, *Public resources and private lives*, 1976, p 220.

20.35 L Hugh Doncaster, 'Simplicity', in Jim Platts & David Eversley, eds, *Public resources and private lives*, 1976, pp 233-234.

20.36 Thomas R Kelly, *A testament of devotion*, 1941 edn, p 110; 1979 edn, p 101.

20.37 Minutes of Hardshaw MM, 17 ix [Nov] 1691, deposited in Manchester Central Library.

20.38 Epistle of YM 1751, repr in *Epistles from the Yearly Meeting of Friends held in London...from 1681 to 1857*, 1858, vol 1, p 273. Quotation from I Thess 5: 22.

20.39 T. Edmund Harvey, *Moderation or abstinence*, 1931, pp 16-17.

20.40 Drafted by 1994 Revision Committee.

20.41 Baltimore YM, *Faith & practice*, 1988, pp 17-18.

20.42 George Fox, *A collection of...epistles*, 1698, epistle 10 (1652), p 11.

20.43 Query 15, 1964.

20.44 Kenneth C Barnes, *The future of the Society of Friends*, 1972, pp 26-27.

20.45 QPS, 'Integrity and truthfulness in Quaker work', background document for guidance of QPS workers, unpublished, 1992.

20.46 John Woolman, *The journal and major essays*, ed Phillips P Moulton, 1971, p 51 (entry for 1756).

20.47 'A plea for the poor', ch 6, John Woolman, *The journal and major essays*, ed Phillips P Moulton, 1971, pp 247-248.

20.48 Drafted by 1967 Revision Committee.

20.49 George Fox, *Journal*, ed J L Nickalls, 1952, p 463 (entry for 1664).

20.50 North Carolina YM (Conservative), *Faith & practice*, 1983, pp 7-8. The extract as printed is abridged and omissions are not indicated in the text.

20.51 Drafted by 1967 and amended by 1994 Revision Committee.

20.52 Drafted by 1994 Revision Committee.

20.53 Drafted by 1994 Revision Committee.

20.54 Drafted by 1959 and amended by 1994 Revision Committee.

20.55 'A plea for the poor', ch 7, John Woolman, *The journal and major essays*, ed Phillips P Moulton, 1971, p 249.

20.56 Drafted by 1925 and amended by 1959 and 1994 Revision Committees. This extract and 20.59 are based on a paper prepared by the Committee on Social Questions and issued by Yearly Meeting 1910 as 'The stewardship of wealth' (see *London YM Proc*, 1910, pp 158-160).

20.57 Part of minute 9 of Young Friends Central Committee, January 1980, *London YM Proc*, 1980, p 9.

20.58 Epistle of YM 1858, *YM Proc*, 1858, pp 25-26.

20.59 Drafted by 1925 and amended by 1959 and 1994 Revision Committees.

20.60 Drafted by 1925 and slightly amended by 1959 Revision Committee: based on an extract of the 1911 Revision

Committee and part of the YM epistle of 1872 (see *YM Proc*, 1872, p 28).

20.61 Drafted by 1959 and amended by 1994 Revision Committee.

20.62 Baltimore YM, *Faith & practice*, 1988, p 18.

20.63 Shipley N Brayshaw, *Unemployment and plenty (Swarthmore lecture)*, 1933, p 45.

20.64 Drafted by 1959 Revision Committee.

20.65 Drafted by 1967 and amended by 1994 Revision Committee.

20.66 Drafted by 1782 and amended by 1911, 1959 and 1994 Revision Committees.

20.67 George Fox, *A collection of...epistles*, 1698, epistle 131 (1656), p 102.

20.68 Sue Norris, 'The meeting never stops', *The Friend*, vol 141 (1983), p 171.

20.69 Kathleen Lonsdale, *Is peace possible?*, 1957, p 120, repr in *The Christian life – lived experimentally: an anthology of the writings of Kathleen Lonsdale*, selected by James Hough, 1976, p 43.

20.70 Epistle of YM 1692, repr in *Epistles from the Yearly Meeting of Friends held in London...from 1681 to 1857*, 1858, vol 1, p 65.

20.71 Mary Lou Leavitt, 'Conflict resolution', *Gifts and discoveries: phase 2A*, 1988, unit 2, background paper 3, pp 1-3. The passage is taken from an address to Ireland Yearly Meeting 1986, and as printed is abridged; omissions are not indicated in the text.

20.72 Drafted by 1833 Revision Committee.

20.73 Drafted by 1833 Revision Committee.

20.74 Drafted by 1994 Revision Committee.

20.75 Alison Sharman [Leonard], 'Women in search of truth', *The Friend*, vol 144 (1986), p 1392.

PERSONAL JOURNEY

21.01 Rufus Jones, *Finding the trail of life*, 1926, pp 21-22. The extract is an amplification of a passage from his *A boy's religion from memory*, 1903, p 16.

21.02 Elizabeth Fox Howard, *Mainstream, a record of many years*, 1943, p 1.

21.03 William Penn's preface to George Fox, *Journal*, 1694, prelim leaf L2; bicent edn, 1891, vol 1, p lxvi; issued also as

A brief account of the rise and progress...of the Quakers, 1694; not in Nickalls edn.

21.04 Report of Young Friends Committee to London Yearly Meeting 1926, *London YM Proc*, 1926, pp 98-99.

21.05 Text by Roger Davies submitted to Yearly Meeting 1994.

21.06 Epistle of Junior Yearly Meeting 1991, *London YM Proc*, 1991, pp 206-207.

21.07 Kenneth C Barnes, 'What is wholeness?', *The Friend*, vol 143 (1985), p 1454.

21.08 Letter from Anna Bidder, *The Friend*, vol 136 (1978), p 903. Some changes have been made in the text.

21.09 *Memoir of the life of Elizabeth Fry... edited by two of her daughters [Katherine Fry & Rachel Cresswell]*, 2nd edn, 1848, vol 2, pp 509 (entry for 1844). The extract does not appear in the 1st edn of the *Memoir*, but is in the *Annual monitor for 1846*, pp 129-130.

21.10 Lorna M Marsden, ' "The arrows of the Almighty" ', *The Friend*, vol 141 (1983), p 1334, repr in *The prepared heart: an anthology of the writings of Lorna M Marsden*, 1988, p 41.

21.11 Jack H Wallis, *Jung and the Quaker way*, 1988, p 24.

21.12 Edward Grubb, *Flowers of the inner life*, 1933, p 3.

21.13 Phyllis Richards, '"That they also may be one" ', *The Friend*, vol 106 (1948), p 229.

21.14 June Ellis, unpublished introduction to a session of London Yearly Meeting 1986.

21.15 Margaret S Gibbins, 'Encounter through worship-sharing', in Charles W Cooper, ed, *Break the new ground: seven essays by contemporary Quakers*, 1969, p 109.

21.16 Alice Wiser, speech to the International Forum, United Nations End of the Decade of Women Conference, Nairobi, Kenya, July 1985.

21.17 William Penn, *No cross, no crown*, 2nd edn, 1682, part 1, ch 5 §12; repr in William Penn, *A collection of the works*, 1726, vol 1, p 296; *Select works*, 1782, vol 2, p 53; not in 1669 edn.

21.18 *Questions & counsel*, §3, 1988.

21.19 Dorothy Nimmo, 'The Society of Friends inside out', *Quaker monthly*, vol 58 (1979), pp 159-160.

21.20 Edward H Milligan, 'Membership and pastoral care', *Friends quarterly*, vol 5 (1951), p 156. The final sentence is taken from some of the last words of Friedrich von Hügel, as quoted in Gwendolen Greene, ed, *Letters from baron von Hügel to a niece*, 1928, pp xliii, xlv.

21.21 Horace B Pointing, *The Society of Friends*, 1946, p 20.

21.22 Caroline C Graveson, *Religion and culture (Swarthmore lecture)*, 1937, pp 37-40.

21.23 Phyllis Richards, 'What do ye to excess?', *The Friend*, vol 107 (1948), p 306.

21.24 Bella Bown, written about 1980.

21.25 Gerald Priestland, abridged version of address to Friends Home Service Committee, 20 Nov 1976, printed in the Open Letter Movement, *A conversation between Friends*, no 5 [1977], p 35.

21.26 *Memoir of the late Hannah Kilham*, ed Sarah Biller, 1837, p 386.

21.27 Ralph Hetherington, *The sense of glory: a psychological study of peak-experiences (Swarthmore lecture)*, 1975, p 1.

21.28 Caroline C Graveson, *Religion and culture (Swarthmore lecture)*, 1937, pp 24-25.

21.29 Robin Tanner, 'Life is art', the second part of his address to a symposium at Bath 'Towards a Quaker view of the arts', printed in *The Friend*, vol 124 (1966), p 285.

21.30 Letter from Elizabeth Fry to Joseph John Gurney, 27.ii.1833, printed in *Journal of Friends Historical Society*, vol 34 (1937), p 25.

21.31 Text by John Sheldon submitted to Yearly Meeting 1994; the quotations are from J Ormerod Greenwood, *Signs of life: art and religious experience (Swarthmore lecture)*, 1978, pp 13-14, 17.

21.32 Horace B Pointing, *Art, religion and the common life*, 1944, pp 29, 45.

21.33 Waldo Williams, 'Mewn dau gae' in *Dail pren: cerddi*, 1956, pp 26-27. The translation is from *Welsh verse: translations by Tony Conran*, Seren, [1986], pp 289-290.

21.34 George Gorman, *The amazing fact of Quaker worship (Swarthmore lecture)*, 1973, pp 31-32.

21.35 Howard H Brinton, *Creative worship (Swarthmore lecture)*, 1931, p 73.

21.36 From an unpublished lecture, 1963, printed in Robin Tanner, *What I believe: lectures and other writings*, 1989, p 3.

21.37 Text by Graham Clarke submitted to Yearly Meeting 1994.

21.38 Text by Jo Farrow submitted to Yearly Meeting 1994.

21.39 Written by Jennifer Fishpool, 1991, for 1994 Revision Committee.

21.40 Clive Sansom, *The shaping spirit (James Backhouse lecture)*, 1965, p 16.

21.41 Walter Rose, *The village carpenter*, 1938, pp 43-44, 46, 135-136.

21.42 Howard H Brinton, *Creative worship (Swarthmore lecture)*, 1931, p 13.

21.43 Clifford Haigh, 'Magnificent opportunities', *The Friend*, vol 120 (1962), p 1058.

21.44 William Littleboy, *The day of our visitation (Swarthmore lecture)*, 1917, p 55.

21.45 Evelyn Sturge, *The glory of growing old*, 1950 edn, pp[7-8].

21.46 Epistle of London Yearly Meeting 1923, *London YM Proc*, 1923, p 355.

21.47 Katharine Moore, 'Old age', *The Friend*, vol 146 (1988), p 758.

21.48 Logan Pearsall Smith, ed, *A religious rebel: the letters of H W Smith*, 1949, pp 156-157.

21.49 George Fox, *Journal*, ed J L Nickalls, 1952, pp 759-760 (entry for 1691).

21.50 Testimony from the National Half-year's Meeting, Dublin, concerning Abigail Watson, 1753, *A collection of testimonies concerning several ministers of the gospel*, 1760, pp 272-273.

21.51 Job Scott, *Journal*, New York, 1797, pp 358-360; 1843 London edn, pp 357-359.

21.52 Anne Hosking, ' "And this I knew experimentally" ', *Quaker monthly*, vol 59 (1980), pp 174-175.

21.53 Ruth Fawell, 'A future life (to a seven-year-old)', *The Friend*, vol 134 (1976), p 792.

21.54 William Littleboy, *Our beloved dead*, [1918], p 11; 1948 edn, p 10.

21.55 Bob Lindsay, 'Death and afterlife', *Dundee Quaker*, July 1989, p 3.

21.56 Last letter of Joan Mary Fry to her friends. This letter is not printed and the extract is taken from the copy in LSF. Quotation from George Fox, *A collection of...epistles*, 1698, p 553, epistle 412 (1687), p 553.

21.57 Jenifer Faulkner, 'Out of the depths', *The Friend*, vol 140 (1982), pp 805-806, abbreviated with the author's consent.

21.58 'Walter Martin writing during his illness', *The Friend*, vol 147 (1989), p 523.

21.59 Joan Fitch, *Handicap and bereavement*, 1988, pp 4-5.

21.60 Jonathan Griffith, 'Feelings of earlier days', *The Friend*, vol 135 (1977), p 1174.

21.61 *A passing traveller: the life of Bernard Brett (1935-1982) in his own words*, 1987, p 21.

21.62 Thomas Story, *Journal*, 1747, pp 463-464 (entry for 1714).

21.63 Hilary Pimm, 'A young girl in 1944', *Quaker monthly*, vol 62 (1983), pp 21-22.

21.64 John Woolman, *The journal and major essays*, ed Phillips P Moulton, 1971, p 185 (entry for 26th 8th month 1772).

21.65 James Nayler, *A collection of sundry books, epistles and papers*, 1716, pp lv-lvi, dated 1659.

21.66 S Jocelyn Burnell, *Broken for life (Swarthmore lecture)*, 1989, p 47.

21.67 Rosalind M Baker, 'Release', *The Friend*, vol 144 (1986), p 1196.

21.68 Iain Law, 'Living with AIDS', *The Friend*, vol 149 (1991), p 1498; the order of sentences has been rearranged.

21.69 Fortunato Castillo, 'Sadness as a sacrament', *The Friend*, vol 136 (1978), p 664.

21.70 Damaris Parker-Rhodes, *The way out is the way in*, 1985, p 165.

21.71 Text by Joolz Saunders submitted to Yearly Meeting 1994.

21.72 Jim Pym, *What kind of God, what kind of healing?*, 1990, p 6.

21.73 Jack Dobbs, *The desert and the marketplace*, 1984, p 14; and see note to 2.33.

CLOSE RELATIONSHIPS

22.01 'Some fruits of solitude', 1693, maxim 548, William Penn, *A collection of the works*, 1726, vol 1, p 843; *Select works*, 1782, vol 5, p 166.

22.02 Drafted by 1994 Revision Committee.

22.03 Sandra Cronk, *Peace be with you*, [1983], p 16.

22.04 Elizabeth Seale Carnall, 'Towards a new advice on personal relationships, including marriage', in South East Scotland MM Peace & Social Responsibility Committee, *A monthly meeting looks at love, friendship and the sexes*, 1981, p 8.

22.05 Damaris Parker-Rhodes, *Truth: a path and not a possession (Swarthmore lecture)*, 1977, p 64.

22.06 Christopher Holdsworth, *Steps in a large room: a Quaker explores the monastic tradition (Swarthmore lecture)*, 1985, p 65.

22.07 John Punshon, *Encounter with silence*, 1987, p 38.

22.08 George Gorman, 'Faith and fellowship in the light of experience', *Friends quarterly*, vol 22 (1980-1982), p 547.

22.09 Douglas Steere, *Where words come from (Swarthmore lecture)*, 1955, p 1.

22.10 John Macmurray, 'Ye are my Friends', [1942], p 3.

22.11 Drafted by 1994 Revision Committee.

22.12 Elizabeth Seale Carnall, 'Towards a new advice on personal relationships, including marriage', in South East Scotland MM Peace & Social Responsibility Committee, *A monthly meeting looks at love, friendship and the sexes*, 1981, p 8.

22.13 *Towards a Quaker view of sex*, by a group of Friends, 1963, pp 38-39.

22.14 Text by Bill Edgar submitted to Yearly Meeting 1994.

22.15 *Towards a Quaker view of sex*, by a group of Friends, 1963, p 36.

22.16 Minute 9 of Wandsworth Preparative Meeting, 12 March 1989; the extract is taken direct from the manuscript minute book.

22.17 Gordon Macphail, 'AIDS, sin and the Society of Friends', *Friends quarterly*, vol 26 (1990-1991), p 129. The order of some sentences has been changed.

22.18 *Towards a Quaker view of sex*, by a group of Friends, 1963, p 45.

22.19 Minute 48 of London Yearly Meeting, *London YM Proc*, 1994, p 238.

22.20 Query 10, 1964.

22.21 Drafted by 1994 Revision Committee.

22.22 *A journal of the life of...William Caton*, 1689, p 8; cf A R Barclay, ed, *Journals of...William Caton and John Burnyeat*, 1839, pp 9-10 (entry for 1652).

22.23 Testimony of Hardshaw East MM concerning Amy Lewis, *London YM Proc*, 1952, p 168.

22.24 Drafted by 1959 Revision Committee.

22.25 Ruth Fawell, *Courage to grow*, 1987, p 15.

22.26 Written by Margaret McNeill for the 1994 Revision Committee, 1990.

22.27 Rachel Rowlands, 'Space and freedom in a community', *The Friend*, vol 147 (1989), p 955.

22.28 Letter from Margaret Glover, *The Friend*, vol 146 (1988), p 671.

22.29 Gordon Macphail, 'The pastoral care of gay Friends', *The Friend*, vol 146 (1988), p 1371.

22.30 Caroline E Stephen, *Light arising*, 1908, pp 130-131.

22.31 Written by Jennifer Johnson for the 1994 Revision Committee, 1990.

22.32 Written by 'Some Westminster Friends' for the 1994 Revision Committee, 1990.

22.33 Drafted by 1994 Revision Committee.

22.34 Elise Boulding, *One small plot of heaven: reflections on family life by a Quaker sociologist*, 1989, pp 2-3.

22.35 'Some fruits of solitude', 1693, maxims 79, 100, 101, 103, 81, 97, 99; William Penn, *A collection of the works*, 1726, vol 1, pp 825-826; *Select works*, 1782, vol 5, pp 129-132.

22.36 Job Scott, *Journal*, New York, 1797, pp 74-75; 1843 London edn, pp 69-70: letter to his future wife Eunice Anthony, 22 January 1780.

22.37 Ruth I Midgley, *Quakerism and family life*, 1950, pp 5-6.

22.38 Elizabeth Watson, 'Each of us inevitable': keynote address to the midwinter gathering of Friends Committee for Gay Concerns, 20 February 1977, New York, in Robert Leuze, ed, *Each of us inevitable*.

Friends for Lesbian and Gay Concerns: some keynote addresses...1977- 1989, 1989, p2.

22.39 Unpublished writing by William G Sewell, 1982.

22.40 Testimony of Worcestershire & Shropshire MM concerning Jessie Gadsden, *London YM Proc*, 1991, p139.

22.41 Harold Loukes, *Christians and sex: a Quaker comment*, 1962, pp26-27.

22.42 Donald A Green, 'The transforming power of the love of God' in Mary Green, ed, *A part of my heart left here: renewal messages of Donald A Green*, 1986, pp15-16.

22.43 Drafted by 1959 Revision Committee.

22.44 Text by Don Grimsditch & Doris Mitchell-Grimsditch submitted to Yearly Meeting 1994.

22.45 Minute 3 of Meeting for Sufferings, 4 July 1987, printed in *The Friend*, vol145 (1987), p880.

22.46 The first two paragraphs are taken from Alison Davis, 'Let the revolution begin?', *Quaker monthly*, vol73 (1994), pp144-145; omissions are not indicated in the text. The final paragraph was jointly written by Alison Davis & Mark Hughes.

22.47 Drafted by 1994 Revision Committee.

22.48 Drafted by 1959 Revision Committee.

22.49 *Towards a Quaker view of sex*, by a group of Friends, revised edn, 1964, p24. This passage does not appear in the 1st edn.

22.50 S Jocelyn Burnell, *Broken for life (Swarthmore lecture)*, 1989, p40.

22.51 Elizabeth Seale Carnall, 'Towards a new advice on personal relationships, including marriage', in South East Scotland MM Peace & Social Responsibility Committee, *A monthly meeting looks at love, friendship and the sexes*, 1981, p8.

22.52 Peter Wallis, 'Briefly', *The Friend*, vol145 (1987), p786.

22.53 [Loraine Brown], 'The family', in QSRE, *Human relationships and sexuality: a study pack*, 1985.

22.54 Text by Anne Hosking submitted to Yearly Meeting 1994.

22.55 Written anonymously, 1990, for the 1994 Revision Committee.

22.56 Text by Jane Heydecker submitted to Yearly Meeting 1994.

22.57 Text by Pauline Condon submitted to Yearly Meeting 1994.

22.58 Text submitted anonymously to Yearly Meeting 1994.

22.59 Text submitted anonymously to Yearly Meeting 1994.

22.60 Drafted by 1959 Revision Committee.

22.61 Damaris Parker-Rhodes, *The way out is the way in*, 1985, p96.

22.62 Dorothy Steere, *On listening to God and to each other*, 1984, pp3-4.

22.63 Elizabeth Watson, 'Parents and children in the Quaker home', *Quaker monthly*, vol59 (1980), p70; repr from *The Canadian Friend*, vol75, no5 (Sept-Oct 1979), pp14-15.

22.64 Juliet Batten, in *Relative experience: a contemporary anthology of Quaker family life*, collected and edited by Keith Redfern with Sue Collins, 1994, pp60-62.

22.65 Douglas & Jenny Butterfield, 'Family feeling', *The Friend*, vol144 (1986), p809.

22.66 [Rosalind Priestman], 'Personal relationships', QSRE, *Human relationships and sexuality: a study pack*, 1985.

22.67 [Caroline Jones], in *Relative experience: a contemporary anthology of Quaker family life*, collected and edited by Keith Redfern with Sue Collins, 1994, pp63-66; omissions are not indicated in the text.

22.68 Hugh Pyper, *A sense of adventure*, 1986, p17.

22.69 Arthur Hardy, 'Helping parents to understand', *The Friend*, vol147 (1989), p19.

22.70 Kenneth C Barnes, *Discipline in the Quaker home*, 1960, p23.

22.71 Anne Hosking, 'A child's gift of worship', *Friends quarterly*, vol23 (1983-1985), p228.

22.72 Unpublished writing by William G Sewell, 1982.

22.73 Drafted by 1994 Revision Committee.

22.74 [Rosalind Priestman], 'Personal relationships', in QSRE, *Human relationships and sexuality: a study pack*, 1985; printed here with minor changes.

22.75 'Chris', 'Marriage breakdown in the Society', *The Friend*, vol 144 (1986), pp 773-774.

22.76 Harold Loukes, *Christians and sex: a Quaker comment*, 1962, pp 27-28.

22.77 Maria Bruce, report of a conversation, c1980.

22.78 'Janet' [Jennifer Morris], in Anne Hosking & Alison Sharman, eds, *Quakers in the eighties: what it's like to be a Friend*, 1980, p 15.

22.79 New England YM Committee on Ministry & Counsel (Family Life Subcommittee), *Living with oneself and others: working papers on aspects of family life*, 1985, p 42.

22.80 Ruth Fawell, *Courage to grow*, 1987, p 81.

22.81 Written by Margery Still for the 1994 Revision Committee, 1990.

22.82 Robert Tod, 'Where is your sadness?', *The Friend*, vol 147 (1989), p 266.

22.83 Sheila Bovell, ' "I wish it would always be Wednesday" ', *The Friend*, vol 146 (1988), p 1013.

22.84 Rufus Jones, *The luminous trail*, 1947, pp 163-164.

22.85 'A father' [Peter Tatton-Brown], 'The thread is not broken', *The Friend*, vol 147 (1989), p 13.

22.86 Joan Fitch, *Handicap and bereavement*, 1988, p 16.

22.87 Zoe White, *A Quaker theology of pastoral care: the art of the everyday (Pendle Hill pamphlet 281)*, 1988, p 9.

22.88 Text by Vivien Whitaker submitted to Yearly Meeting 1994.

22.89 Diana Lampen, *Facing death*, 1979, pp 9-10, 17. The order of some sentences has been changed.

22.90 Margaret Torrie, *Begin again: a book for women alone*, 1975 edn, p 146.

22.91 Unpublished writing by William G Sewell, 1982.

22.92 Drafted by 1994 Revision Committee.

22.93 Caroline E Stephen, *Light arising*, 1908, pp 164-165.

22.94 'In memoriam' (1905), in John Wilhelm Rowntree, *Essays and addresses*, 1905, pp 417-418.

22.95 'Some fruits of solitude', 1693, maxims 489, 490, 498-503, 505, and 'More fruits', 1693, maxims 127-134; William Penn, *A collection of the works*, 1726, vol 1, pp 841, 850-851; *Select works*, 1782, vol 5, pp 162-163, 183.

SOCIAL RESPONSIBILITY

23.01 Advices IV, ¶4, 1964.

23.02 *No cross, no crown*, 2nd edn, 1682, part 1, ch 5 §12; William Penn, *A collection of the works*, 1726, vol 1, p 296; *Select works*, 1782, vol 2, p 53.

23.03 H G Wood, 'The nature of Christian responsibility for the industrial and social order', *Friends quarterly*, vol 13 (1959-1961), pp 19-20; quotation from Horace Bushnell.

23.04 Eva I Pinthus, 'Faith and politics hand in hand?', *The Friend*, vol 145 (1987), p 483.

23.05 William Charles Braithwaite, *The second period of Quakerism*, 1919, p 596.

23.06 Lucy F Morland, *The new social outlook (Swarthmore lecture)*, 1919, p 45.

23.07 Testimony of Marsden MM concerning John Bright, YM Proc, 1889, Appendix C, p xii.

23.08 Roger Wilson, 'Silver and gold have I none', in Jim Platts & David Eversley, eds, *Public resources and private lives*, 1976, pp 225-226.

23.09 Michael Sorensen, *Working on self-respect*, 1986, p 55.

23.10 Gordon Matthews, 'Mixing prayer and politics', *The Friend*, vol 147 (1989), p 717.

23.11 'To the present distracted and broken nation', 1659, Edward Burrough, *The memorable works of a son of thunder*, 1672, p 604.

23.12 Harvey Gillman, *A light that is shining: an introduction to the Quakers*, 1988, pp 48-49; 2nd edn, 1997, p 56.

23.13 William Charles Braithwaite, *The second period of Quakerism*, 1919, pp 596-597.

23.14 'A plea for the poor', 1763, ch 3 and ch 13 , John Woolman, *The journal and major essays*, ed Phillips P Moulton, 1971, pp 241, 262.

23.15 Pierre Ceresole, *Vivre sa vérité: carnets de route*, 2nd edn, 1950, pp 194, 196; translated by Edward Dommen for the 1994 Revision Committee.

23.16 'Foundations of a true social order', approved by London Yearly Meeting 1918, and printed in *London YM Proc*, 1918, pp 80 - 81. The quotations in the preamble are from John Woolman, 'A plea for the poor', ch 10, in *The journal and major essays*, ed Phillips P Moulton, 1971, p 255.

23.17 Joseph Rowntree, from an essay 'Pauperism in England and Wales', 1865, quoted in Anne Vernon, *A Quaker business man: the life of Joseph Rowntree, 1836 - 1925*, 1958, p 64.

23.18 Joseph Rowntree, memorandum to the Rowntree trustees, 1904, quoted in Anne Vernon, *A Quaker business man: the life of Joseph Rowntree, 1836-1925*, 1958, p 64.

23.19 Query 20, 1964.

23.20 Letter from Richard Allen, *The Friend*, vol 142 (1984), pp 765 - 766.

23.21 Minute 30 of London Yearly Meeting 1987, *London YM Proc*, 1987, p 225.

23.22 Martin Wyatt, 'Responding to poverty', *Gifts and discoveries: phase 2A*, 1988, unit 4, background paper 3, p 4.

23.23 Richard Hilken, 'First steps towards a housing testimony', *Friends quarterly*, vol 27 (1992-1993), p 160, with additions by the author, 1993.

23.24 *Extracts from the minutes and advices of the Yearly Meeting of Friends held in London*, 1783, p 227. Minute of Yearly Meeting 1727 (see manuscript minutes, vol 6, pp 457 - 458). The minute reaffirms the answer given by the YM correspondents to Friends of Pennsylvania and the Jerseys, 17 vi [August] 1713, and to Friends of Pennsylvania, 3 viii [October] 1715.

23.25 Epistle of YM 1772, repr in *Epistles from the Yearly Meeting of Friends held in London...from 1681 to 1857*, 1858, vol 2, p 10.

23.26 Yearly Meeting, *An address to the inhabitants of Europe on the iniquities of the slave trade*, 1822 , pp 8, 10.

23.27 Minute 27 of London YM, 1958, *London YM Proc*, 1958, p 238.

23.28 Reginald Sorensen, *An analysis of slavery*, 1966, pp 6 - 7.

23.29 James Challis & David Elliman in association with the Anti-Slavery Society, *Child workers today*, 1979, pp 1, 3, 170.

23.30 Introduction to London Yearly Meeting session 'The contagion of torture', *London YM Proc*, 1974, p 49.

23.31 Statement adopted by FWCC at its 13th triennial, Hamilton, Ontario, Canada, 1976.

23.32 Ursula Franklin, *Perspectives on Friends' testimonies in today's world (Sunderland P Gardner lecture)*, 1979, pp 3 - 4.

23.33 Unpublished writing by Meg Maslin, 1990.

23.34 Testimony of Purley & Sutton MM concerning Dorothy Fell Kenworthy Case, 1979, *London YM Proc*, 1979, p 167.

23.35 Epistle from London Junior YM, 1988, *London YM Proc*, 1988, p 259.

23.36 *Statement of intent on racism, made by Meeting for Sufferings on behalf of London Yearly Meeting*, 1988; the wording differs slightly from that in *London YM Proc*, 1988, pp 57 - 58.

23.37 Jonathan Griffith, 'The meaning of severe disability'; paper delivered at a QSRE conference 'Attitudes to disability', Birmingham, 14 November 1981, duplicated typescript.

23.38 Carol Gardiner, 'Thinking about Yearly Meeting', *Quaker monthly*, vol 68 (1989) pp 169-170, with minor amendments by the author.

23.39 Lucretia Mott, speaking at the Women's Rights Meeting, West Chester, Pennsylvania, in 1852, quoted in Margaret Hope Bacon, *Lucretia Mott speaking: extracts from the sermons and speeches (Pendle Hill pamphlet 234)*, 1980, p 14.

23.40 Epistle of the First International Theological Conference of Quaker Women held at Woodbrooke, 1990, *[Conference proceedings]* 1990, p 4.

23.41 Lucretia Mott, 'Memoranda on herself' (undated, after 1840) quoted in Margaret Hope Bacon, *Lucretia Mott speaking: extracts from the sermons and speeches (Pendle Hill pamphlet 234)*, 1980, pp 7, 8.

23.42 Pauline Leader, 'A sexist view' in QHS & Woodbrooke College, *Freeing each other: a Quaker study pack on sexism*, 1986, sheet B 28.

23.43 Elizabeth Bathurst, *The sayings of women...in several places of the Scriptures*, 1683, p 23.

23.44 Quaker Women's Group, *Bringing the invisible into the light (Swarthmore lecture)*, 1986, p 4; and Quaker Women's Group advice and query in QHS & Woodbrooke College, *Freeing each other: a Quaker study pack on sexism*, 1986, p D51, quoting *Quaker Women's Group newsletter*, no 10 (January 1982), f 8.

23.45 Tessa Fairweather, 'Glad to be in Leeds', *Young Quaker*, vol 39 (1993), no 4, p 12.

23.46 Letter from Susan Rooke-Matthews, *The Friend*, vol 151 (1993), p 953.

23.47 Grigor McClelland, *And a new earth (Swarthmore lecture)*, 1976, p 83.

23.48 Parker J Palmer, *A place called community (Pendle Hill pamphlet 212)*, 1977, p 27.

23.49 Martin Wyatt, 'Faith in the people', *QSRE journal*, vol 8 (1986), no 3, pp 21-22.

23.50 Jonathan Dale, 'Who is my neighbour?', *QSRE journal*, vol 10 (1988), no 3, pp 20-21. The extract as printed is amended by the author.

23.51 Testimony of Hertford & Hitchin MM concerning Stephen Hobhouse, 1961, *London YM Proc*, 1962, pp 70-71.

23.52 Deborah Haines, 'Living in harmony with Heaven on earth' in John L Bond, ed, *Friends search for wholeness*, 1978, p 139.

23.53 David Eversley, 'Conclusion' in Jim Platts & David Eversley, eds, *Public resources and private lives*, 1976, pp 244-245.

23.54 Jim Platts, 'Towards wholeness' in Jim Platts & David Eversley, eds, *Public resources and private lives*, 1976, pp 192-193.

23.55 Rachel Jackson, 'Small business: big rewards', *QSRE journal*, vol 12 (1990), no 1, p 20.

23.56 Jane Stokes, 'Work from a family perspective', in QSRE, *Life and work: some Quakers look at work and its place in our lives*, 1992, pp 20-21.

23.57 Scott Bader Commonwealth Limited, preamble to revised Articles of Association, 23 March 1963.

23.58 Testimony of Hereford & Radnor MM concerning Arthur Basil Reynolds, 1961, *London YM Proc*, 1961, p 185.

23.59 Testimony of Kingston MM concerning Percy Cleave, 1958, *London YM Proc*, 1959, pp 197-198.

23.60 Testimony of Southampton & Portsmouth MM concerning Joan Frances Layton, 1990, *London YM Proc*, 1991, pp 151-152.

23.61 Epistle of London YM 1911, *London YM Proc*, 1911, p 166-167.

23.62 Edward W Fox, *Quakers and modern industry: a dialogue about human relations*, 1969, p 25.

23.63 Helen Edwards, 'Balancing family and work', *The Friend*, vol 150 (1992), pp 435-436.

23.64 Unpublished writing by Jane Stokes, 1992.

23.65 Grigor McClelland, *And a new earth (Swarthmore lecture)*, 1976, pp 72-73.

23.66 Gerald Littleboy, 'Service: an interpretation for Quakers', *London YM Proc*, 1946, p 52. (Quotation from *Christian practice*, 1925, §6, p 166, drafted by 1925 Revision Committee.)

23.67 George Clarke, *People, technology and unemployment*, 1973, p 1.

23.68 John Bellers, *An essay towards the improvement of physick*, 1714, p 37; repr in George Clarke, ed, *John Bellers: his life, times and writings*, 1987, p 204.

23.69 Shipley N Brayshaw, *Unemployment and plenty (Swarthmore lecture)*, 1933, p 101.

23.70 Minute 19 of London Yearly Meeting 1978, *London YM Proc*, 1978, pp 311-312.

23.71 George Fox, *Journal*, ed J L Nickalls, 1952, p 520 (entry for 1668).

23.72 Epistle of Bristol Yearly Meeting 1695, quoted in A Neave Brayshaw, *The Quakers, their story and message*, 2nd edn, 1927, p 182, 1953 edn, p 211; not in 1st edn.

23.73 Janet Scott, in Elizabeth R Perkins, ed, *Affirmation, communication and co-operation: papers from the QSRE conference on education, July 1988*, 1988, pp 73-74. The order of some sentences has been changed.

23.74 Friends Schools Joint Council, *Quakers and their schools*, 1980, p 6. The Isaac

Penington quotation is from *An examination of the grounds and causes which are said to induce the Court of Boston, in New England, to make that order or law of banishment upon pain of death against the Quakers*, 1659, p 84; repr in Isaac Penington, *Works*, 1681, part 1, p 240; 1761 edn, vol 1, p 321; 1784 edn, vol 1, p 444

23.75 Barbara Windle, in Elizabeth R Perkins, ed, *Affirmation, communication and co-operation*, 1988, p 108.

23.76 D June Ellis, 'Are we being educated?'. Presidential address to the Guild of Friends in Education, 1981, duplicated typescript, p 2.

23.77 Sarah Worster, in Elizabeth R Perkins, ed, *Affirmation, communication and co-operation*, 1988, pp 86-87.

23.78 Barbara Windle, in Elizabeth R Perkins, ed, *Affirmation, communication and co-operation*, 1988, pp 107, 106-107.

23.79 Caroline C Graveson, *Religion and culture (Swarthmore lecture)*, 1937, pp 21-22.

23.80 William Fraser, *Einige Aufgaben und Möglichkeiten der Erziehung (Richard L Cary Vorlesung)*, 1973, pp 13-14; translation by William Fraser.

23.81 'On schools' [probably 1758], John Woolman, *The journal and essays*, ed A M Gummere, 1922, p 392; not in John Woolman, *The journal and major essays*, ed Phillips P Moulton, 1971.

23.82 Written by John Guest, 1987, for the 1994 Revision Committee.

23.83 From a paper read at the meeting of Friends Educational Society, 1841, and printed in FES, *Five papers on the past proceedings and experience of the Society of Friends in connexion with ...education*, 1843, pp 96-97. The passage is from a document written by one of the proprietors of a school for girls in York, founded in 1784.

23.84 Eva I Pinthus, *Peace education*, [1983], p 2, based on the introduction to a session of London Yearly Meeting 1982.

23.85 Janet Gilbraith, 'Hope and imagination', in QSRE, *Learners all: Quaker experiences in education*, 1986, pp 62-63.

23.86 *A just and righteous plea presented unto the king of England*, 1661, p 24,
repr in Edward Burrough, *The memorable works of a son of thunder*, 1672, p 786 (misnumbered 778).

23.87 William Robertson, *Life and times of John Bright*, 1892, vol 2 p 266 (speech in the House of Commons, 17 July 1882); see *Hansard*, 3rd series, vol 272, col 722 ff.

23.88 T Edmund Harvey, 'The individual and the state', in Friends World Conference 1937, *Official report*, p 36.

23.89 Statement presented to London Yearly Meeting 1915, by young men of enlistment age, printed in *London YM Proc*, 1915, p 193.

23.90 Statement issued by Meeting for Sufferings, 7 xii 1917, and printed in *London YM Proc*, 1918, p 9.

23.91 Epistle of London YM 1990, *London YM Proc*, 1990, p 235.

23.92 Minute 157 of Adjourned London Yearly Meeting, 1st month 1916, *London YM Proc*, 1916, pp 241-242.

23.93 'The Society of Friends and military conscription', adopted by Meeting for Sufferings, 6 iv 1945, *London YM Proc*, 1945, pp 34-35.

23.94 Drafted by 1911 and amended by 1925, 1959 and 1994 Revision Committees.

23.95 Harold Loukes, *The discovery of Quakerism*, 1960, p 118.

23.96 Select Committee on Capital Punishment, *Report*, 1930, §283; letter from John Bright to Martin H Bovee, Wisconsin, 3 January 1868.

23.97 'Statement on the death penalty' contained in minute 39 of London Yearly Meeting, *London YM Proc*, 1956, p 241.

23.98 Elizabeth Fry, *Observations on the visiting of female prisoners*, 1827, pp 21-22.

23.99 *Memoir of the life of Elizabeth Fry... edited by two of her daughters [Katherine Fry & Rachel Cresswell]*, 1847, vol 2, p 182; reprinted in Mrs Francis Cresswell [Rachel Cresswell], *A memoir of Elizabeth Fry: by her daughter...abridged from the larger memoir*, 1868, pp 183-184; quoted in John Lampen, *Mending hurts (Swarthmore lecture)*, 1987, p 24. The passage, by Priscilla Buxton (later Johnston), relates to 1834.

23.100 Charles Tylor, ed, *Memoirs of Elizabeth Dudley*, 1861, pp 72-73, (entry for 1818).

23.101 John Lampen, *Mending hurts (Swarthmore lecture)*, 1987, pp 71, 73.

23.102 Six Quakers, 'A testimony against punishment', *Friends quarterly*, vol 23 (1983-1985), p 472; repr from *The Friend*, vol 141 (1983), p 1425, with minor alteration. The passage was originally drafted in 1981 by the Friends who wrote *Six Quakers look at crime and punishment*, 1979.

23.103 John Lampen, *Mending hurts (Swarthmore lecture)*, 1987, pp 49, 53, 55, 57, 61, 63.

OUR PEACE TESTIMONY

24.01 George Fox, *Journal*, ed J L Nickalls, 1952, p 65 (entry for 1651).

24.02 Robert Barclay, *Apology for the true Christian divinity*, prop 15, sect 13; 1678 London edn, pp 382-383; 1886 Glasgow edn, pp 401-402.

24.03 'Some fruits of solitude', 1693, maxims 537, 540, 543-546; William Penn, *A collection of the works*, 1726, vol 1, p 843; *Select works*, 1782, vol 5, p 166.

24.04 *A declaration from the harmless and innocent people of God called Quakers, against all plotters and fighters in the world*, 1660, pp 1-3. The extract as printed is considerably abridged and omissions are not indicated in the text.

24.05 Epistle of YM 1744, repr in *Epistles from the Yearly Meeting of Friends held in London...from 1681 to 1857*, 1858, vol 1, p 247.

24.06 Epistles of YM 1804, 1805, repr in *Epistles from the Yearly Meeting of Friends held in London...from 1681 to 1857*, 1858, vol 2, pp 123-124, 129

24.07 'Christianity and war: an address by the Religious Society of Friends', adopted by London YM, 1900, *London YM Proc*, 1900, pp 65-66.

24.08 Minute 13 of London Yearly Meeting 1915, *London YM Proc*, 1915, pp 9-10.

24.09 'To all men everywhere' issued by London Yearly Meeting 1943, *London YM Proc*, 1943, pp 236-237.

24.10 Statement issued by Aotearoa/New Zealand Yearly Meeting 1987, printed in *London YM Proc*, 1987, pp 210-211. The extract as printed is abridged and omissions are not indicated in the text.

24.11 Minute 23 (part) of London Yearly Meeting, *London YM Proc*, 1993, p 227.

24.12 Wolf Mendl, *Prophets and reconcilers (Swarthmore lecture)*, 1974, p 16.

24.13 Hubert Fox, ed, *Marion Fox, Quaker: a selection of her letters*, 1951, pp 33-34 (note made in 1914).

24.14 Part of an unpublished letter from Eric Baker to Josiah Knight, 20 viii 1941.

24.15 Kathleen Lonsdale, *I believe... (Arthur Stanley Eddington memorial lecture)*, 1964, pp 54-55; repr in *The Christian life – lived experimentally: an anthology of the writings of Kathleen Lonsdale*, selected by James Hough, 1976, p 10.

24.16 Susumu Ishitani, 'How I became a Quaker', *Friends world news*, no 32, 1989/1, pp 16-17, slightly altered by the author.

24.17 John Woolman, *The journal and major essays*, ed Phillips P Moulton, 1971, p 75 (entry for 1755).

24.18 Arthur & Ursula Windsor in QPS, *My conscience, my tax: personal accounts of Quakers who resisted paying taxes for war*, 1992, p 30.

24.19 Letter from Peter Eccles, clerk of Meeting for Sufferings, to the Inspector of Taxes, dated 24 December 1991, *London YM Proc*, 1992, pp 44-45.

24.20 Joan Hewitt in QPS, *My conscience, my tax: personal accounts of Quakers who resisted paying taxes for war*, 1992, p 51.

24.21 Isaac Penington, *Somewhat spoken to a weighty question, concerning the magistrate's protection of the innocent*, 1661, p 8, 4; repr in *Works*, 1681, p 323; 1761 edn, vol 1, p 448.

24.22 Wolf Mendl, *Prophets and reconcilers (Swarthmore lecture)*, 1974, p 10.

24.23 Statement by Corder Catchpool, printed in *The Friend*, vol 58 new series (1918), p 242.

24.24 Roger Wilson, *Authority, leadership and concern (Swarthmore lecture)*, 1949, pp 9-10.

24.25 Kenneth C Barnes, 'The sterility of perfectionism', *The Friend*, vol 145 (1987), p 1382.

24.26 Kathleen Lonsdale, *Removing the causes of war (Swarthmore lecture)*, 1953, pp 68 - 69.

24.27 Statement by Helen Steven in Dumbarton Sheriff Court, printed in *Quakers in Scotland*, 1989, pp 40 - 41.

24.28 Unidentified contributor to Quaker Women's Group, *Bringing the invisible into the light (Swarthmore lecture)*, 1986, pp 94 - 95.

24.29 *Life of William Allen*, 1846, vol 1, p 148.

24.30 Roger Wilson, *Authority, leadership and concern (Swarthmore lecture)*, 1949, pp 15, 18 - 19.

24.31 John S Hoyland, *Digging for a new England*, 1936, pp 221 - 223.

24.32 Sydney Bailey, 'Our vocation of reconciliation', *Friends quarterly*, vol 22 (1980 - 1982), p 244.

24.33 Kathleen Lonsdale, *Removing the causes of war (Swarthmore lecture)*, 1953, pp 67 - 68; repr in *The Christian life – lived experimentally: an anthology of the writings of Kathleen Lonsdale*, selected by James Hough, 1976, p 53.

24.34 Margarethe Lachmund, 'The attitude of Christians in the tensions between east and west', *Friends quarterly*, vol 12 (1958), pp 154 - 159; repr as *Christians in a divided world*, 1959, pp 6 - 12. The extract as printed is considerably abridged and omissions are not indicated in the text.

24.35 Adam Curle, *True justice: Quaker peace makers and peace making (Swarthmore lecture)*, 1981, pp 91, 1.

24.36 Sydney Bailey, 'Non-official mediation in disputes: reflections on Quaker experience' in Royal Institute of International Affairs, *International affairs*, vol 61 (1985), p 208.

24.37 Sue Williams, 'In praise of harmlessness', *The Friend*, vol 146 (1988), pp 1367, 1368.

24.38 Written 1991 by Sue Bowers for 1994 Revision Committee.

24.39 William Rotch, *Memorandum written in the 80th year of his age*, 1916, pp 3 - 5.

24.40 All Friends Conference, 1920, *Report of Commission II*, p 66.

24.41 'An appeal to all men and women', adopted by Meeting for Sufferings, 6 v 1955, *London YM Proc*, 1956, p 4.

24.42 Nicholas A Sims, 'Quaker approaches to disarmament – what have we learned?', *Friends quarterly*, vol 23 (1983 - 1985), pp 545 - 546.

24.43 J Duncan Wood, *Building the institutions of peace (Swarthmore lecture)*, 1962, pp 84 - 85.

24.44 *An essay towards the present and future peace of Europe*, 1693, sect 4; repr in William Penn, *A collection of the works*, 1726, vol 2, p 841; not repr in *Select works*, 1782.

24.45 Drafted by 1925 Revision Committee; preamble drafted by 1959 Revision Committee.

24.46 Konrad Braun, *Justice and the law of love (Swarthmore lecture)*, 1950, p 46.

24.47 *Our vision of Europe: a statement* by the Quaker Council for European Affairs, 1987.

24.48 Preface by Stuart Morton to QPS Sharing World Resources Committee, *Sharing world resources: which ways forward?*, 1988, p 2.

24.49 Minute 17 of London Yearly Meeting 1986, *London YM Proc*, 1986 p 320.

24.50 Epistle from London Yearly Meeting 1937, *London YM Proc*, 1937, p 305.

24.51 Minute 18 of London Yearly Meeting 1968, *London YM Proc*, 1968, p 225.

24.52 This statement for the press, to be opened only after his death, was left by S Douglas Smith, and printed in *The Friend*, vol 139 (1981), p 1442.

24.53 J Duncan Wood, *Building the institutions of peace (Swarthmore lecture)*, 1962, pp 90 - 91.

24.54 Sue Bowers & Tom Leimdorfer, in Elizabeth R Perkins, ed, *Affirmation, communication and co-operation: papers from the QSRE conference on education*, July 1988, 1988, pp 37 - 38; revised by the authors, 1990.

24.55 Mary Lou Leavitt, *Star wars – SDI: the spiritual challenge*, 1987, pp [6 - 8].

24.56 Letter to L Violet Holdsworth, July 1937, quoted in Elizabeth Gray Vining, *Friend of life: the biography of Rufus M Jones*, 1958 edn, p 269; 1959 edn, p 272.

24.57 Sydney Bailey, *Peace is a process (Swarthmore lecture)*, 1993, p 173.

24.58 J Duncan Wood, *Building the institutions of peace (Swarthmore lecture)*, 1962, pp 95-96.

24.59 Mothers for Peace, *Bridge builders for peace*, 1983, p 2.

24.60 Wolf Mendl, *Prophets and reconcilers (Swarthmore lecture)*, 1974, pp 101-102.

UNITY OF CREATION

25.01 'Conversations on the true harmony of mankind', manuscript, 1772, printed in John Woolman, *The journal and essays*, ed A M Gummere, 1922, p 462; not in John Woolman, *The journal and major essays*, ed Phillips P Moulton, 1971.

25.02 Minute 25 of London Yearly Meeting 1988, *London YM Proc*, 1988, p 262.

25.03 Damaris Parker-Rhodes, 'A kind of resurrection', *Quaker monthly*, vol 61 (1982), p 86.

25.04 Text by Audrey Urry submitted to Yearly Meeting 1994.

25.05 John Woolman, *The journal and major essays*, ed Phillips P Moulton, 1971, p 28.

25.06 [Vera Haley], 'We should extend our compassion to animals', in *Five and twenty Quakers: Winchmore Hill tercentenary 1988*, 1988, p 35; revised by the author.

25.07 Minute of Norfolk Cambs & Hunts QM, 20 vii 1957; the extract is taken from the official minute book.

25.08 Pamela Umbima, letter in *The Friend*, vol 150 (1992) pp 963-964.

25.09 Richard J Foster, 'The discipline of simplicity – installment 3', *Quaker life*, vol 20 no 7 (July 1979), pp 14-16. The passage is considerably abridged and omissions are not indicated in the text.

25.10 Epistle of London Yearly Meeting 1989, *London YM Proc*, 1989, p 304.

25.11 Ruth Tod, writing adapted 1990, for the 1994 Revision Committee.

25.12 Minute 16, '...When did we see you hungry?', of London Yearly Meeting 1975, *London YM Proc*, 1975, p 231.

25.13 *No cross, no crown*, modern English edn rev and ed by Ronald Selleck, 1981, pp 84-85; in 2nd edn, 1682, part 1, ch 18, §10; in William Penn, *A collection of the works*, 1726, vol 1, p 372; *Select works*, 1782, vol 2, pp 217-218.

25.14 Keith Helmuth, 'Economics as a religious responsibility', *BeFriending creation (Newsletter of Friends Committee on Unity with Nature of North America)*, vol 3 no 7 (March 1990), p 4.

25.15 Rex Ambler, 'Befriending the earth: a theological challenge', *Friends quarterly*, vol 26 (1990-1991), p 17.

REFLECTIONS

26.01 Advices I, ¶1, 1964.

26.02 George Fox, *Journal*, ed J L Nickalls, 1952, p 25 (entry for 1643).

26.03 George Fox, *Journal*, ed J L Nickalls, 1952, p 27 (entry probably for 1648).

26.04 Caroline Fox, *Memories of old friends*, ed H N Pym, 3rd edn, 1882, vol 1, p xxii (entry for 1841).

26.05 *Reality and radiance: selected autobiographical works of Emilia Fogelklou*, introduced and translated by Howard T Lutz, 1985, pp 82-83.

26.06 Rufus Jones, 'The death of John Wilhelm Rowntree', *American Friend*, vol 12 (1905), p 176, repr in John Wilhelm Rowntree, *Essays and addresses*, 1905, pp 433-434.

26.07 Hilda Clark, *War and its aftermath: letters*, ed E M Pye, [1957], pp 6-7.

26.08 Howard E Collier, *The Quaker meeting: a personal experience and method described and analysed*, 1943, p 5.

26.09 G M Ll Davies, *Joseph Rowntree Gillett: a memoir*, 1942, p 35.

26.10 Francis H Knight, 'The faith of a sceptic', *The wayfarer*, vol 24 (1945), pp 110-111.

26.11 John Macmurray, 'What makes an experience religious?' a talk given on BBC radio in 1967, repr in *Quakers talk to sixth formers*, 1970, p 58.

26.12 Geoffrey Hubbard, *Quaker by convincement*, 1974, p 117-118.

26.13 Roy Farrant, 'Christ's fool', *The Friend*, vol 132 (1974), p 1357.

26.14 Walter Martin, 'On being physically disabled', *The Friend*, vol 142 (1984), p 1261.

26.15 Epistle of London Yearly Meeting 1928, *London YM Proc*, 1928, p 330.

26.16 Arthur S Eddington, *Science and the unseen world (Swarthmore lecture)*, 1929, p 53.

26.17 Ole Olden, letter in *The Friend*, vol 113 (1955), p 1026.

26.18 Ruth Fawell, *Courage to grow*, 1987, p 9.

26.19 Janet Scott, *What canst thou say? (Swarthmore lecture)*, 1980, pp 71-72.

26.20 Jean West, 'Reason and mystery', *Friends quarterly*, vol 25 (1988-1989), pp 40-41.

26.21 John W Harvey, *The salt and the leaven (Swarthmore lecture)*, 1947, p 76.

26.22 Kenneth C Barnes, *The creative imagination (Swarthmore lecture)*, 1960, p 78.

26.23 From one of six talks given on BBC radio in May 1962 by Kathleen Lonsdale, printed in *The Friend*, vol 120 (1962); repr separately as *A scientist tries to answer some of her own questions about religion*, 1962, p 6, and repr in *The Christian life – lived experimentally: an anthology of the writings of Kathleen Lonsdale*, selected by James Hough, 1976, p 31.

26.24 Written for the 1994 Revision Committee by eleven Quaker scientists, convened in Cambridge by Anna M Bidder, 1989.

26.25 Unpublished introduction to London Yearly Meeting session 'The kingdom in our midst' by S Jocelyn Burnell, 1976.

26.26 Pierre Ceresole, *Vivre sa vérité: carnets de route*, 2nd edn, 1950, pp 178-179; translated by J Ormerod Greenwood for the 1994 Revision Committee.

26.27 Tony Brown, 'Knock, knock, who's there?', *The Friend*, vol 142 (1984), pp 165-166.

26.28 Christopher Holdsworth, *Steps in a large room: a Quaker explores the monastic tradition (Swarthmore lecture)*, 1985, p 10.

26.29 Jo Farrow, 'Spirituality and self-awareness', *Friends quarterly*, vol 23 (1983-1985), pp 317-318.

26.30 Isaac Penington, *Some of the mysteries of God's kingdom glanced at*, 1663, p 9; repr in *Works*, 1681, pt 1, p 420; 1761 edn, vol 1, p 602.

26.31 Harvey Gillman, *A minority of one (Swarthmore lecture)*, 1988, pp 81-82.

26.32 Rufus Jones, 'Where the beyond breaks through', *The Friend*, vol 60 new series (1920), p 26.

26.33 John Lampen, *Twenty questions about Jesus*, 1985, p 91.

26.34 Katharine Moore, *She for God*, 1978, p 209-210.

26.35 Rose Ketterer, 'G-d/ess' web', *Friendly woman*, vol 8 (1987), no 1, p 11.

26.36 Text by Jo Farrow submitted to Yearly Meeting 1994.

26.37 Bernard Canter, 'Look everywhere', editorial in *The Friend*, vol 120 (1962), p 770.

26.38 Donald Court, *A scientific age and a declining church: what has a Friend to say?*, 1965, p 8, repr from *The Friend*, vol 123 (1965), p 1142.

26.39 Charles Carter, *On having a sense of all conditions (Swarthmore lecture)*, 1971, p 25.

26.40 *Memoir of the life of Elizabeth Fry... edited by two of her daughters [Katherine Fry & Rachel Cresswell]*, 1847, vol 1, p 41 (entry for 1798).

26.41 Frederick Parker-Rhodes, *The Friend*, vol 135 (1977), p 636.

26.42 George Fox, *Journal*, ed J L Nickalls, 1952, p 33; 1694 edn, p 22; bicent edn, 1891, vol 1, pp 34-35 (entry for 1648).

26.43 L Hugh Doncaster, *The Quaker message: a personal affirmation (James Backhouse lecture: Pendle Hill pamphlet 181)*, 1972, pp 6-7. Omissions are not indicated in the text.

26.44 William Penn's preface to George Fox, *Journal*, 1694, prelim leaf M2; bicent edn, 1891, vol 1, pp lx-lxi; not in 1952 Nickalls edn.

26.45 Job Scott, *Works*, Philadelphia, 1831, vol 1, p 520: 'Some openings of truth', believed to have been written shortly before Job Scott sailed for Europe in December 1792.

26.46 Yorkshire QM's memorandum on the book of discipline, section 3, 'The divinity and humanity of Christ', *London YM Proc*, 1919, pp 182-183.

26.47 *For peace and truth: from the note-books of Pierre Ceresole*, trans and ed John W Harvey and Christina Yates, 1954, p 82. The passage is dated as

1920 in Pierre Ceresole, *Vivre sa vérité: carnets de route*, 2nd edn, 1950, pp 143.

26.48 T Edmund Harvey, *Workaday saints*, 1949, p 124.

26.49 'Man's relation to God: III. What has Jesus to say to the individual?' (1904), John Wilhelm Rowntree, *Essays and addresses*, 1905, pp 361-362.

26.50 Janet Scott, *What canst thou say? (Swarthmore lecture)*, 1980, pp 60-61.

26.51 Lorna M Marsden, letter in *The Friend*, vol 143 (1985), p 923.

26.52 L Hugh Doncaster, *God in every man (Swarthmore lecture)*, 1963, p 74-75.

26.53 Paul Oestreicher, quoted in Gerald Priestland, *Priestland's progress: one man's search for Christianity now*, 1981, p 43.

26.54 Ruth Fawell, *Courage to grow*, 1987, pp 114-115.

26.55 Hugh Pyper, *A sense of adventure*, 1986, p 9.

26.56 S Jocelyn Burnell, *Broken for life (Swarthmore lecture)*, 1989, pp 51-52.

26.57 J Ormerod Greenwood, 'Letter from a Friend', *Quaker monthly*, vol 52 (1973), pp 179-180.

26.58 Damaris Parker-Rhodes, *The way out is the way in*, 1985, pp 54-55.

26.59 Rosamund Robertson, *Growing Friends: worship, prayer and spiritual experience with children*, 1990, pp 8-9.

26.60 Richard Rowntree, 'The particular mission of Friends - 1', *The Friend*, vol 145 (1987), p 998.

26.61 John Woolman, 'Considerations on keeping negroes, part second', 1762, in John Woolman, *The journal and major essays*, ed Phillips P Moulton, 1971, p 236.

26.62 Thomas R Kelly, 'The children of the light', publ as introduction to the Wider Quaker Fellowship annual report, 1941; repr in Richard M Kelly, *Thomas Kelly: a biography*, 1966, p 125.

26.63 Epistle of YM 1879, *YM Proc*, 1879, p 39. The scriptural quotations are from - I John 2:2; Rev 22:17; Ps 89:15.

26.64 Waldo Williams, from 'Paham yr wyf yn Grynwr', a talk given on BBC Radio in July 1956, and printed in *Seren Gomer*, 25 June 1971, p 8. Omissions are not indicated in the texts.

26.65 L Hugh Doncaster, *The Quaker message: a personal affirmation (James Backhouse lecture: Pendle Hill pamphlet 181)*, 1972, p 6.

26.66 London Yearly Meeting, *To Lima with love*, 1987, p 7.

26.67 H G Wood, *Theology and prayer*, 1951, p 9. An address given to elders at London Yearly Meeting 1951 and repr from *Friends quarterly*, vol 5 (1951).

26.68 Ellen S Bosanquet, *The inward light*, 1927, p 6.

26.69 Edgar B Castle, *Approach to Quakerism*, 1961, pp 48-49.

26.70 Isaac Penington, *Some directions to the panting soul*, 1671, p 5; repr in Isaac Penington, *Works*, 1681, pt 1, p 347; 1761 edn, vol 1, p 486; 1784 edn, vol 2, p 241.

26.71 *A lamentation for the scattered tribes*, 1656, repr in Francis Howgill, *The dawnings of the gospel day*, 1676, p 46.

26.72 Thomas R Kelly, *A testament of devotion*, 1941, pp 18-19; 1979 edn, p 17. From a lecture delivered January 1938, except the last sentence, which is from a letter to Rufus Jones, April 1938.

26.73 George Gorman, *The amazing fact of Quaker worship (Swarthmore lecture)*, 1973, p 71.

26.74 Stephen Allott, 'Meanings', *The Friend*, vol 139 (1981), p 630.

26.75 'How shall we think of God?' anonymously written and dated 1970, in Edward Cell, ed, *Daily readings from Quaker spirituality*, Springfield, Illinois, Templegate Press ©, 1987, p 94.

26.76 Pam Lunn, 'Love and politics', *Friends quarterly*, vol 26 (1990-1991), p 51.

26.77 Letter from Beatrice Saxon Snell, *The Friend*, vol 119 (1961), pp 60-61.

26.78 William Penn, *A key opening a way to every common understanding*, 1692; repr in William Penn, *A collection of the works*, 1726, vol 2, p 781; *Select works*, 1782, vol 5, pp 9-10.

UNITY AND DIVERSITY

27.01 'Some fruits of solitude', 1693, maxim 519; repr in William Penn, *A collection of the works*, 1726, vol 1, p 842; *Select works*, 1782, vol 5, pp 164-165.

27.02 *The journal and major essays of John Woolman*, ed Phillips P Moulton, 1971, pp 127-128 (journal entry for 12 vi 1763).

27.03 John Lampen, *Twenty questions about Jesus*, 1985, p 86.

27.04 Text by Alastair Heron, Ralph Hetherington & Joseph Pickvance submitted to Yearly Meeting 1994, based on talks given by them to a special interest group at Yearly Meeting 1993.

27.05 Robert Barclay, *Apology for the true Christian divinity*, prop 10, sect 2; 1678 London edn, pp 181-182; 1886 Glasgow edn, pp 194-195.

27.06 Caroline Fox, *Memories of old friends*, ed H N Pym, 4th edn, 1882, vol 2, p 52 (entry for 1846).

27.07 H G Wood, *Henry T Hodgkin: a memoir*, 1937, pp 275-277. Letter of H T Hodgkin to Ronald Hodgkin, 1933.

27.08 John Punshon, *Encounter with silence: reflections from the Quaker tradition*, 1987, p 52.

27.09 Yukio Irie, 'Comment from Japan', in Edwin B Bronner, ed, *Sharing our Quaker faith*, 1959, p 123.

27.10 Swami Tripurananda [Jonathan Carter], 'In spirit and in truth', 1979, repr in Swami Tripurananda, Anne Bancroft & rabbi Jeffery Newman, *Three spiritual journeys*, 1984, pp 7-8, and edited in consultation with the author.

27.11 Marjorie Sykes, 'Friends and world religions' (written 1957), in Edwin B Bronner, ed, *Sharing our Quaker faith*, 1959, pp 104-105. Some minor amendments have been made.

27.12 Thomas Story, *Discourse at Horslydown*, 1737, title-page.

27.13 *An examination of the grounds and causes which are said to induce the Court of Boston, in New England, to make that order or law of banishment upon pain of death against the Quakers*, 1659, pp 83-84; repr in Isaac Penington, *Works*, 1681, part 1, pp 240; 1761 edn, vol 1, pp 320-321; 1784 edn, vol 1, pp 443-444.

27.14 London Yearly Meeting, *To Lima with love*, 1987, p 14.

27.15 William Charles Braithwaite, *The second period of Quakerism*, 1919, p 641.

27.16 William G Sewell, 'The out-reaching service of our Society', *Friends world news*, no 21 (1946), p 4.

27.17 World Conference of Friends, 1952, *Friends face their fourth century [official report]*, 1952, p 54 (report of group on 'Friends and the ecumenical movement').

27.18 Gerald Priestland, *Who needs the church? (Barclay lecture)*, 1983, pp 7-8.

27.19 John Punshon, *Encounter with silence: reflections from the Quaker tradition*, 1987, p 128.

27.20 Rex Ambler, *Creeds and the search for unity: a Quaker view*, 1989, p 9.

27.21 'Man's relation to God: III. What has Jesus to say to the individual?' (1904), in John Wilhelm Rowntree, *Essays and addresses*, 1905, p 349.

27.22 Isaac Penington, *The life of a Christian*, 1653, first page, unnumbered; not repr in his *Works*.

27.23 *The true basis of Christian unity*, prepared by London Yearly Meeting's Commission on Faith & Order and presented to London Yearly Meeting 1917, printed in *London YM Proc*, 1917, pp 158-159. The document was prepared as a result of a statement *Towards Christian unity*, issued in 1916 by a group of Anglicans and Free Churchmen and considered by Friends unsatisfactory because it implied that unity was to be sought along a line of agreement in doctrine and practice without sufficiently emphasising 'the essential basis of Christian experience and the Christian spirit and way of life'. The calling of the World Conference on Faith & Order at Lausanne in 1927 led to a revision of the statement as *The basis of Christian unity*, and a further revision under this title was issued in 1937.

27.24 Arthur S Eddington, *Science and the unseen world (Swarthmore lecture)*, 1929, pp 55-56.

27.25 John Punshon, 'Uncertain trumpets', *The Friend*, vol 136 (1978), p 278.

27.26 Janet Scott, *What canst thou say? (Swarthmore lecture)*, 1980, pp 4-5.

27.27 John Barclay, ed, *Letters of Isaac Penington*, 1828, pp 39-40; 3rd edn, 1844, pp 39-40 (Letter XVI, recipient's name not given, undated).

27.28 Robert Barclay, *Apology for the true Christian divinity*, prop 3, sect 2; 1678 London edn, p 38; 1886 Glasgow edn, p 46.

27.29 T Edmund Harvey, *Workaday saints*, 1949, pp 124-125.

27.30 George Boobyer, *Friends and the Bible*, [1988], pp 3-4.

27.31 Henry J Cadbury, *A Quaker approach to the Bible (Ward lecture)*, 1953, pp 14-15.

27.32 Elsa Cedergren, 'Freedom and integrity', *Friends quarterly*, vol 22 (1980-1982), p 523; repr in Hans Eirik Aarek [et al], eds, *Quakerism: a way of life. In homage to Sigrid Helliesen Lund on her 90th birthday*, 1982, p 101. The article was based on a talk to Swedish Friends, Stockholm, 23 September 1979, printed as 'Frihet och förankring', in *Kväkartidskrift*, vol 7 (1980), no 3, p 4.

27.33 Joan Fitch, *The present tense: 'Talking to our time'. A discussion paper for Quakers*, 1980, pp 29, 30.

27.34 London Yearly Meeting, *To Lima with love*, 1987, p 7.

27.35 *ibid*, pp 11-12. Omissions are not indicated in the text.

27.36 Harvey Gillman, *A light that is shining: an introduction to the Quakers*, 1988, pp 14-15; in 2nd edn, 1997, pp 22-23, the text differs slightly.

27.37 'The basis of the Quaker faith' (1902), in John Wilhelm Rowntree, *Essays and addresses*, 1905, p 100.

27.38 London Yearly Meeting, *To Lima with love*, 1987, p 7.

27.39 Gerald K Hibbert, *Quaker fundamentals*, 1941, pp 7-8.

27.40 London Yearly Meeting, *To Lima with love*, 1987, p 8.

27.41 *ibid*, p 10.

27.42 Text by Janet Scott submitted to Yearly Meeting 1994.

27.43 A Barratt Brown, *Wayside sacraments*, 1932, pp 9, 10.

27.44 Damaris Parker-Rhodes, *The way out is the way in*, 1985, pp 159, 161, 177.

SHARING THE QUAKER EXPERIENCE

28.01 Henry T Hodgkin, *Friends beyond seas*, 1916, pp 224-225.

28.02 William Penn, 'A tender visitation' (1677), printed in William Penn, *A collection of the works*, 1726, vol 1, p 219; *Select works*, 1782, vol 3, pp 360-361. The original text was printed in Dutch, as part of *Het Christenrijk ten Oordeel gedagvaart*, 1678.

28.03 George Fox, *Journal*, ed J L Nickalls, 1952, p 34; 1694 edn, p 22; bicent edn, 1891, vol 1, pp 35-36 (entry for 1648).

28.04 'An address to her children', dated 1832, but written at several different periods, *A selection from the letters of the late Sarah Grubb (formerly Sarah Lynes)*, 1848, pp 2-4, 8-9.

28.05 *Memoir of the late Hannah Kilham*, ed Sarah Biller, 1837, p 119.

28.06 George B Jeffery, *Christ yesterday and today (Swarthmore lecture)*, 1934, p 47.

28.07 Edgar G Dunstan, *Quakers and the religious quest (Swarthmore lecture)*, 1956, p 61.

28.08 Harold Loukes, 'God speaking through us', in Maurice A Creasey & Harold Loukes, *The next 50 years*, 1956, p 58.

28.09 Written by Edrey Allott for QHS outreach conference, 1990.

28.10 From a letter, amended for the 1994 Revision Committee, by Harvey Gillman, 1993.

28.11 Drafted by 1925 Revision Committee.

28.12 Val Ferguson, *Carrying the Quaker message today: address at FWCC annual meeting, 1987*, 1988, p 13.

28.13 Quaker Tapestry panel B2. For a full-colour reproduction of the completed panel see Quaker Tapestry at Kendal, *Pictorial guide to the Quaker Tapestry in colour*, 1998, revising *The Quaker Tapestry guide*, 1989, from which the cartoon is taken.

LEADINGS

29.01 Gordon Matthews, 'With a smile into the dark', *The Friend*, vol 145 (1987), p 353. The quotation is from Thomas Kelly, *Testament of devotion*.

29.02 Minute 7 of Meeting for Sufferings, March 1992.

29.03 Pat Saunders, 'Dare we hope?: a Quaker response to environmental degradation', QPS Committee on

Sharing World Resources, *Quaker approaches to development*, 1987, p 97; 2nd edn, 1988, p 95.

29.04 Text by Ralph Rowarth submitted to Yearly Meeting 1994.

29.05 Text by Amber Carroll & Grace Jantzen submitted to Yearly Meeting 1994.

29.06 Helen Steven, 'Two years in a lifetime', QPS Committee on Sharing World Resources, *Quaker approaches to development*, 1987, p 24; 2nd edn, 1988, p 24.

29.07 Adam Curle, 'Excerpts from a talk by Adam Curle at a colloquium on Quaker international affairs held by AFSC at Philadelphia, January 1992', unpublished typescript.

29.08 Diana Lampen, 'Faith in action', in *Faith in action: encounters with Friends. Report from the fifth World Conference, 1991,* 1992, p 71.

29.09 Jo Vallentine, 'Peace, justice and the integrity of creation...moving away from weapons and toward women's wisdom' in *Faith in action: encounters with Friends. Report from the fifth World Conference, 1991,* 1992, p 213.

29.10 Minute 27, 'Taxation for war purposes', of London Yearly Meeting 1987, *London YM Proc*, 1987, p 224.

29.11 Conference on 'The secret state' convened by Warwickshire Monthly Meeting, 1989.

29.12 Cecil R Evans, 'Speaking truth to power', QPS Committee on Sharing World Resources, *Quaker approaches to development*, 1987, p 36; 2nd edn, 1988, p 36.

29.13 Epistle of London Yearly Meeting 1987, *London YM Proc*, 1987, p 229.

29.14 London Yearly Meeting Committee on Christian Relationships, 'Response to reports of working parties on ecumenical instruments', approved by Meeting for Sufferings, July 1988, and printed in *London YM Proc*, 1989, pp 102-103.

29.15 Epistle of Black, white, Asian and mixed-heritage Friends, meeting at Charney Manor, 1991, in QSRE, *Worship without prejudice?: an information pack on race relations within the Religious Society of Friends,* 1992. The passage is considerably abridged and omissions are not indicated in the text.

29.16 Val Ferguson in *Faith in action: encounters with Friends. Report from the fifth World Conference, 1991,* 1992, p 183.

29.17 Epistle of World Gathering of Young Friends, Greensboro, North Carolina, 1985, in *London YM Proc*, 1986, pp 226-227.

29.18 Grace Blindell, 'The challenge of creation spirituality', *The Friend*, vol 150 (1992), p 1524.

29.19 William Dewsbury, 'A general epistle' (1675) in *The faithful testimony of...William Dewsbury,* [1689], p 338.

Indexes

These three indexes are intended to cover the need of most readers to find a passage in the text quickly.

The first index (below) is of authors and of bodies responsible for extracts, including yearly meetings, conferences, committees and monthly meetings. Dates of birth are not given for living authors; the dates given against responsible bodies are those of minutes, statements, testimonies and so on. This index also includes the names of Friends who were the subjects of testimonies and other memorials.

The second index (page 657) is of subjects (excluding individuals). In this index extracts in Welsh (but not those in English) have been indexed by both Welsh and English terms.

The third (page 669) is an index of keywords in often-used phrases.

Index of authors, names and titles

( ) indicate dates
T indicates a testimony or similar to the Friend named

Subject index

Figures in bold type indicate that the entire chapter is relevant.

caring for others: 18.03, 18.06, 18.08, 18.10-11, 18.13, 18.19, 19.53, 23.08, 23.34, 23.64-65, 23.74, 23.78, 29.02

caring in the meeting: *see* meetings local, pastoral care; *see also* home

censorship: 23.90

changes of address, notifying: 4.36, 11.27

changing oneself: 19.48, 20.18, 25.12, 29.08

Channel Isles: 6.01, 6.09, 16.24

chaplains: *see* prison chaplains, college chaplains

Charities Acts: 15.01, 15.12

charity: 23.17-18

Charity Commission(ers): 14.19, 14.26, 15.01, 15.04-06, 15.10, 15.12

Charney Manor: 8.07

child labour: 23.29; *see also* slavery

Child Poverty Action Group: 23.20

children: 1.02.19, 1.02.25, 1.03.19, 1.03.25, 10.10, 12.01, 22.33, 22.60, 25.03; in care of PM: 4.38.c; death: 22.83-86; education: 23.71-85; elders' & overseers' responsibilities: 12.12.i, 12.13.e-f; keeping the meeting: 19.35; in meeting: 2.50, 2.74-76; ministry of: 10.09, 19.26; monthly meeting committee: 4.03; nurturing: 10.10, 22.63; & parents: 22.51-53, 22.60-72; passing on Quaker heritage to: 2.75, 10.10, 21.04, 22.71; religious education: 22.71, 23.81, 23.83; separation & divorce: 1.02.25, 1.03.25, 10.23, 22.73; spiritual experience: 2.76, 21.01-02, 26.28; welcoming to meeting: 10.09; *see also* membership, monthly meetings, parents & children, young people

Children of the Light: 4.25, 11.01, 18.20

Christ: 2.92, 19.02, 19.18, 19.23, 19.29, 20.18-19, 20.49, 24.02, 24.28, 26.51, 27.11, 27.40; disciple of: 18.09, 19.39, 23.19, 23.51; equality in: 19.25, 19.50, 23.43-44; followers: 4.25, 20.19, 24.09; friendship: 22.10; kingdom: 19.45, 24.04; life: 20.19, 21.22; light: 11.48, 19.04, 19.07, 19.15, 19.20, 19.25 (preamble), 24.12, 26.42-60, 27.04; living: 2.10, 27.08; love: 12.19, 22.03, ch 24 (intro); power: 19.58, ch 24 (intro); presence: 2.10, 2.67, 17.03, ch 19 (intro); righteousness: 19.29-31; school: 11.18, 27.13; seed: 20.23; spirit: 1.01, 1.02.2, 1.03.2, 1.02.31, 1.03.31, 19.23, 19.60, 23.92, ch 24 (intro), 24.04, 24.13, 24.18-19, 26.15, 26.25; truth: 2.87; universal light: 11.48, 19.25 (intro), 26.43; words 19.07; *see also* Jesus, Light, Spirit, Truth

Christian: 23.02, 23.08; basis of Quakerism: 11.48; becoming a: 19.21; community: 3.03,

3.22, 3.29, 4.38.k, l, 12.04, 13.01; conduct: 6.03, 20.60, 23.97; heritage: 1.02.4, 1.03.4, 10.10; life: 19.33 (preamble), 20.24-26, 21.21, 21.44, 23.07, 23.13, 23.16, 23.88, 24.61-62, 24.43, 24.52, 26.04; marriage: 22.41; morality: 22.15; perspective: 11.01, ch 24 (intro); true: 19.31, 26.78, and not: 19.01, 20.39; *see also* language, Quakerism

Christian church – Friends and: 1.02.6, 1.03.6, 27.12-20; BYM as part of: 9.01, 9.08-14, 11.14; *and see* ecumenical relations

Christian faith and practice: p13-p14, 11.48, 18.20

Christianity: 1.02.2, 1.03. 2, 11.14, 18.07, 22.13, 23.73, 23.90, 24.31, 24.40, 26.20-21, 26.51

Christmas: 27.42

Church government: 11.48, 12.08

church government: p15, 1.02.15, 1.03.15, 9.16, 9.20, 10.21, 11.21

Churches Together in England (CTE): 9.09, 9.12

Churches Together in Wales: *see Cristnogion Ymlaen Tuag at Undeb*

citizenship: 1.02.34, 1.03.34, 20.59, 23.01, 23.36, 23.53. 23.88, 23.90, 23.93, 23.102, ch 24 (intro) 24.46, 24.48; *see also* responsibilities

class, social: 10.13, 18.10, 23.03, 23.16, 23.41, 23.44, 24.31, 24.45

clearness: 1.02.27, 1.03.27; for marriage: 12.22, 16.05, 16.19 *see also* meetings for clearness

clerks and clerkship: 3.01, 3.12, 3.24.i; assistant: 3.12, 3.24.i; co-clerks: 3.03, 3.12, 3.24.i; discerning unity: 3.07, 3.15-16; duties and responsibilities: 3.13-20; exercise of authority: 3.18; minute-making: 3.6-7, 3.11, 3.14-15; preparations: 3.13; servant of meeting: 3.13; signing minutes: 3.15; upholding: 3.07-11; *see also* Meeting for Sufferings, MMs, PMs, Yearly Meeting

college chaplains: 13.54-56

commitment – celebration of: 22.44-46; faithful: p15, p17; financial: 1.02.20, 1.03.20, 11.01; in marriage: 1.02.23, 1.03.23, 16.02; in relationships: 22.33, 22.45-46; *see also* **ch 10**, marriage, membership

Committee for Christian & Interfaith Relations: *see* Quaker Committee for Christian & Interfaith Relations

committees: 3.01, 20.36, 21.22; of BYM **ch 8**; *and see* diagram 8.04; *and see individual entries*; *see also* BYM, Meeting for Sufferings

communication: 10.25, 12.20

Communication & Fundraising Department: *see* Quaker Communications

dress: *see* plainness
drink: *see* alcohol
drugs: 1.02.40, 1.03.40, 20.40-41, 22.81, 25.03
duty: *see* responsibilities
dying: *see* death

Easter: 27.42
economic affairs: *see* social justice, work
ecumenical relationships: 1.02.6, 1.03.6, 2.46,
9.01, 9.08-20, 27.01-20; *see also* interfaith
contacts
education: 23.71-85; peace: 23.84-85, 24.54;
purposes: 23.78-80; QSRE and: 8.10;
religious: 4.38.c, 8.07, 12.12.h, 22.71, 23.72-
74, 23.81, 23.83, 28.05; *see also* schools,
study, teaching
elderly, care of: 12.13.p; homes: 12.13.p, 22.26;
see also growing old, old age
elders & eldership: 2.71, 3.19, 12.05-12;
appointed by MM: 4.03, 4.07.d, 12.05-09;
children and young people: 12.12.i; co-
operation with overseers: 12.14-16; duties
12.12; 'eldering': 12.17; encourage religious
education: 12.12.h; enquirers and attenders:
12.12.j; funerals: 17.08, 17.10; history:
12.05; meetings for clearness: 12.24, 16.21.b;
nurture of ministry: 2.71, 12.12.c, 12.12.l,
and of spiritual life: 12.11-12, 12.18;
resolving conflict: 10.21, 12.12.h;
responsibilities for church affairs: 12.12.e, for
special occasions: 12.12.f, 16.31, 17.09, for
worship: 10.12, 12.05, 12.11, 12.12.b
employers: 23.56-57, 23.61; Friends as: 4.39,
8.21, 13.34-39
enquirers: 1.05, 4.38.h; 8.07, 12.12.j; 12.13.d;
see also attenders
environment: 1.02.42, 1.03.42, 20.32, ch 25,
29.03, 29.06; *see also* creation, exploitation,
sharing world resources
epistles from BYM: 6.19; from other YMs:
6.04.c, 6.21
equality: 2.75, 19.25; 19.33 (preamble), 19.39-
40, 20.18, 20.32, 22.38, 23.08, 23.32, 23.36,
23.73; gender: 19.25, 19.31, 19.50, 23.42-44,
29.16; *see also* simplicity
ethical investment: 14.14, 14.24, 15.07, 20.56-57
Ethical Investment Research Service (EIRIS): 15.07
Europe: 8.05, 24.44, 24.47; QCEA and: 9.07
Europe & Middle East Section (EMES) of
FWCC: 8.17, 9.04-05
executors: 20.65; *see also* wills
exploitation of earth's resources: 23.40, 23.64,
24.47, 25.01-2, 25.07, 25.10-15
extension work: *see* outreach

facilitators, helping meetings with problems: 10.21
faith: p13, p15, 9.08-09, 10.02, 10.10, 19.22,
20.08, 21.01, 23.01-10, 26.13-14, 26.26,
26.35, 26.39, 26.65, 27.19, 29.16; Friends &
other: 27.01-11; multifaith community:
1.02.6, 1.02.16, 1.03.6, 1.03.16, 23.73,
29.14; *see also* ecumenical relationships,
interfaith contacts
family: 22.51-72, 23.63-64; ending of
relationships: 22.73-79; *see also* parents &
children
finance: 1.02.20, 1.03.20, ch 14, **ch 15**; accounts
and accounting: 4.38.e, 14.20-23; auditing:
14.22, 20.64; committees: 4.03, 7.01;
indemnification: 14.25; investments: 14.14,
15.01-03, 15.07, 20.56-57, 25.11; legislation:
14.23, 14.26; overseers advise: 12.13.m, n;
public scrutiny: 14.19; stewardship: 14.18-
19; support for concerns: 13.12.b, 13.13;
travelling in the ministry: 13.18; *see also*
funds, income, legacies
Finance Committee: *see* Quaker Finance &
Property
financial arrangements in divorce: 22.73
financial responsibility for Quaker work: 4.35.e,
ch14
forgiveness: 1.02.32, 1.03.32, 11.48, 19.12,
22.74-75, 24.03, 26.33, 26.49, 26.51; *see
also* reconciliation, repentance
Friends Ambulance Unit (FAU): 24.12, 24.23
Friends Book Centre: *see* Quaker Bookshop
Friends House, London: 8.03, 8.09, 8.21, 8.25,
14.12
Friends Trusts Limited: 14.10, 15.01-03, 15.10-11
Friends World Committee for Consultation
(FWCC): p16, 8.17, 9.03-06, 13.13, 24.49;
minute on torture: 23.31; moving abroad:
11.27; service abroad under concern: 13.13;
travel: 13.23
Friends, world family: p16, 1.02.16, 1.03.16,
9.01-07, 29.16-17; visiting: 13.20-31
friendship: 1.02.7, 1.02.21-22, 1.02.26, 1.03.7,
1.03.21-22, 1.03.26, 2.81-82, 12.13.j, 22.02-
10; within meetings: 3.10, 10.33, 12.13.c;
see also relationships
funds: 14.11; stewardship: 4.07.l, 14.18-26,
20.55, 20.64; *see also* finance
funerals: **ch 17**; guidance on conduct: 12.12.f,
17.15, 22.92; *see also* bereavement, burials,
death, grief, prayer, suffering

gair: 2.05
gambling: 1.02.39, 1.03.39, 20.61-63
gender: *see* equality, sexism, women

668

Index of well-loved phrases

arranged alphabetically by key words

answering that of God (G Fox): 19.32

And oh, how sweet and pleasant it is to the truly spiritual eye to see several sorts of **believers** (I Penington): 27.13

Caring matters most (E Milligan, quoting F von Hügel): 21.20

They were **changed** men themselves before they went about to change others (W Penn): 19.48

Christ as fully human and fully divine (Yorkshire QM): 26.46

There is one, even **Christ** Jesus, that can speak to thy condition (G Fox): 19.02

It is not opinion, or speculation, or notions of what is true ... that ... makes a man a true believer or a true **Christian** (W Penn): 26.78

Now I am **clear**, I am fully clear (G Fox): 21.49

And this is the **comfort** of the good, that the grave cannot hold them (W Penn): 22.95

I should have a sense of all **conditions** (G Fox): 19.03

every **country** my country, and every man my brother (D Wheeler): 2.04

Death is but crossing the world (W Penn): 22.95

Death is not an end, but a beginning (Wm Littleboy): 21.54

we do utterly **deny** ... all outward wars, and strife, and fightings with outward weapons, for any end ... and this is our testimony to the whole world (Declaration to Charles II): 24.04

The poor without employment are like rough **diamonds**, their worth is unknown (J Bellers): 23.68

Are there not **different** states, different degrees, different growths, different places? (I Penington): 10.27

The truest **end** of life, is to know the life that never ends (W Penn): 22.95

know one another in that which is **eternal** (G Fox): 2.35

the **evil** weakening in me and the good raised up (R Barclay): 19.21

And this I knew **experimentally** (G Fox): 19.02

She [Mary Dyer] did hang as a **flag** for others to take example by: 19.18

Why **gad** you abroad? (F Howgill) : 26.71

that of **God** in every one (G Fox): 19.32

give **God** the glory; I'll have none (W Dewsbury): 19.33

True **godliness** don't turn men out of the world (W Penn): 23.02

The **humble**, meek, merciful, just, pious, and devout souls are everywhere of one religion (W Penn): 19.28

Gross **impiety** it is that a nation's pride should be maintained in the face of its poor (W Penn): 20.29

to **impoverish** the earth now to support outward greatness appears to be an injury to the succeeding age (J Woolman): 25.01

all Friends take heed of **jars** and strife (G Fox): 20.67

Keep your meetings in the power of God (G Fox): 3.30

humble **learners** in the school of Christ (E Dunstan): 11.18

Our life is love, and peace, and tenderness
(I Penington): 10.01

Live up to the light thou hast, and more will be
granted thee (quoted in C Fox): 26.04

Dear Lord and Father of mankind
(J G Whittier): 20.03

Love is the hardest lesson in Christianity; but, for
that reason, it should be most our care to
learn it (W Penn): 22.01

Love was the first motion (J Woolman): 27.02

A touch of love doth this in measure; perfect love
doth this in fullness (I Penington): 26.30

Never marry but for love; but see that thou
lovest what is lovely (W Penn): 22.35

we marry none; it is the Lord's work (G Fox):
16.01

Think it possible that you may be mistaken
(A&Q): 1.02.17, 1.03.17

The Kingdom of Heaven did gather us and catch
us all, as in a net (F Howgill): 19.08

All things were new, and all the creation gave
another smell (G Fox): 26.03

for the Lord is at work in this thick night of
darkness (G Fox): 20.23

an ocean of darkness and death, but an infinite
ocean of light and love, which flowed over the
ocean of darkness: (G Fox): 19.03

Are you open to new light, from whatever source
(A&Q): 1.02.7, 1.03.7

I have been in Paradise these several days
(M Dyer): 19.18

Be patterns, be examples (G Fox): 19.32

the Lord let me see atop of the hill in what places
he had a great people to be gathered (G Fox):
19.06

We came to know a place to stand in and what
to wait in (F Howgill): 19.08

and try whether the seeds of war have
nourishment in these our possessions
(J Woolman): 23.16 (intro)

So will you be possessors as well as professors of
the truth (W Penn): 19.59

the power of the Lord will work through all
(G Fox): 3.30

The place of prayer is a precious habitation
(J Woolman): 20.10

The priesthood of all believers (LYM): 27.35

There is a principle which is pure, placed in the
human mind (J Woolman): 26.61

The Society of Friends might be thought of as a
prism through which the Divine Light passes
(drafted by 1959 Revision Committee):
18.20

I ... joyfully entered prisons as palaces
(W Dewsbury): 19.33

Although I am out of the king's protection, I am
not out of the protection of the Almighty God
(M Fell): 19.38

Mind that which is pure in you to guide you to
God (E B Castle, quoting G Fox): 26.69

quiet processes and small circles (R Jones): 24.56

these things we do not lay upon you as a rule or
form to walk by (Balby elders): 1.01

the whole of life is sacramental (A B Brown):
27.43

what canst thou say? (quoted in M Fell): 19.07

Oh, no, it is not the scriptures (G Fox): 19.24

I have met with the Seed (I Penington): 19.14

when I came into the silent assemblies of God's
people (R Barclay): 19.21

but we must be all in one dress and one colour:
this is a silly poor Gospel (M Fox): 20.31

Sing and rejoice, ye Children of the Day and of the Light (G Fox): 20.23

what thou speakest is it inwardly from God? (G Fox): 19.07

The intent of all speaking is to bring into the life (G Fox): 2.73

That spirit of Christ by which we are guided, is not changeable (Declaration to Charles II): 24.04

There is a spirit which I feel that delights to do no evil (J Nayler): 19.12

stand fast in that liberty wherewith Christ hath made us free (M Fox): 19.44

Be still and cool in thy own mind and spirit (G Fox): 2.18

We are all thieves (M Fox): 19.07

True silence ... is to the spirit what sleep is to the body, nourishment and refreshment (W Penn): 20.11

trust in the Lord, and he will carry thee through all (Job Scott): 21.51

All Truth is a shadow except the last (I Penington): 27.22

Has Truth been advancing among you? (quoted by T Kelly): 26.72

though they be called Turks, the seed of them is near unto God (M Fisher): 19.27

turn all the treasures we possess into the channel of universal love (J Woolman): 23.14

turn in thy mind to the light, and wait upon God (A Parker): 2.41

For this is the true ground of love and unity, not that such a man walks and does just as I do, but because I feel the same Spirit and life in him (I Penington): 27.13

The unity of Christians never did nor ever will or can stand in uniformity of thought and opinion, but in Christian love only (T Story): 27.12

essential unity of the work undertaken in the name of the Yearly Meeting (Constitution Review Committee, 1972): 7.01

I lived in the virtue of that life and power that took away the occasion of all wars (G Fox): 24.01

Therefore, dear Friends, wait in the Light, that the Word of the Lord may dwell plentifully in you (W Dewsbury): 29.19

walk cheerfully over the world (G Fox): 19.32

watch every one to feel and know his own place and service in the body, and to be sensible of the gifts, places, and services of others (I Penington): 10.27

we are all to watch over one another for good (LYM 1851): 12.18

wear it [sword] as long as thou canst (G Fox to W Penn, quoted in S Janney): 19.47

And the end of words is to bring men to the knowledge of things beyond what words can utter (I Penington): 27.27

That which is morally wrong cannot be politically right (LYM 1822): 23.26